connect™

W9-BKC-424

Student Quick Tips

Use this Student Quick Tips guide for a quick and easy start with McGraw-Hill Connect. You'll get valuable tips on registering, doing assignments, and accessing resources, as well as information about the support center hours.

Getting Started

TIP: To get started in Connect, you will need the following:

• Your instructor's Connect Web Address

    Sample of Connect Web Address:

    http://www.mcgrawhillconnect.com/class/instructorname_section_name

• Connect Access Code

TIP: If you do not have an access code or have not yet secured your tuition funds, you can click "Free Trial" during registration. This trial will provide temporary Connect access (typically three weeks) and will remind you to purchase online access before the end of your trial.

Registration and Sign In

1. Go to the Connect Web Address provided by your instructor
2. Click on **Register Now**
3. Enter your email address

TIP: If you already have a McGraw-Hill account, you will be asked for your password and will not be required to create a new account.

4. Enter a registration code or choose **Buy Online** to purchase access online

5. Follow the on-screen directions

TIP: Please choose your Security Question and Answer carefully. We will ask you for this information if you forget your password.

6. When registration is complete, click on **Go to Connect Now**

7. You are now ready to use **Connect**

Trouble Logging In?

* Ensure you are using the same email address you used during registration

* If you have forgotten your password, click on the "Forgot Password?" link at your Instructor's Connect Course Web Address

* When logged into Connect, you can update your account information (e.g. email address, password, and security question/answer) by clicking on the *"My Account"* link located at the top-right corner

Home (Assignments)

TIP: If you are unable to begin an assignment, verify the following:

* The assignment is available (start and due dates)

* That you have not exceeded the maximum number of attempts

* That you have not achieved a score of 100%

* If your assignment contains questions that require manual grading, you will not be able to begin your next attempt until your instructor has graded those questions

TIP: Based on the assignment policy settings established by your Instructor, you may encounter the following limitations when working on your assignment(s):

- Ability to Print Assignment

- Timed assignments – once you begin a "*timed assignment*," the timer will not stop by design

TIP: "*Save & Exit*" vs. "*Submit*" button

- If you are unable to complete your assignment in one sitting, utilize the "*Save & Exit*" button to save your work and complete it at a later time

- Once you have completed your assignment, utilize the "*Submit*" button in order for your assignment to be graded

Library

TIP: The *Library* section of your Connect account provides shortcuts to various resources.

- If you purchased ConnectPlus, you will see an *eBook* link, which can also be accessed from the section information widget of the *Home* tab

- *Recorded Lectures* can be accessed if your instructor is using *Tegrity Campus* to capture lectures. You may also access recorded lectures when taking an assignment by clicking on the projector icon in the navigation bar

- Many McGraw-Hill textbooks offer additional resources such as narrated slides and additional problems, which are accessible through the *Student Resources* link

McGraw Hill

Reports

TIP: Once you submit your assignment, you can view your available results in the *Reports* tab.

• If you see a dash (-) as your score, your instructor has either delayed or restricted your ability to see the assignment feedback

• Your instructor has the ability to limit the amount of information (e.g. questions, answers, scores) you can view for each submitted assignment

Need More Help?

CONTACT US ONLINE

Visit us at:

www.mcgrawhillconnect.com/support

Browse our support materials including tutorial videos and our searchable Connect knowledge base. If you cannot find an answer to your question, click on "Contact Us" button to send us an email.

GIVE US A CALL

Call us at:

1-800-331-5094

Our live support is available:

Mon-Thurs:	9 am – 12 pm ET
Friday:	9 am – 7 pm ET
Sunday:	7 pm – 12 pm ET

 Connect Learn Succeed

FIN 300

University at Albany

Selected Material from

FUNDAMENTALS OF CORPORATE FINANCE
Standard Edition-9e

Stephen Ross
Massachusetts Institute of Technology

Randolph Westerfield
University of Southern California

Bradford Jordan
University of Kentucky-Lexington

Boston   Burr Ridge, IL   Dubuque, IA   New York   San Francisco   St. Louis
Bangkok   Bogotá   Caracas   Lisbon   London   Madrid
Mexico City   Milan   New Delhi   Seoul   Singapore   Sydney   Taipei   Toronto

The McGraw·Hill Companies

FIN 300
University at Albany

Copyright © 2010 by The McGraw-Hill Companies, Inc. All rights reserved. Printed in the United States of America. Except as permitted under the United States Copyright Act of 1976, no part of this publication may be reproduced or distributed in any form or by any means, or stored in a data base retrieval system, without prior written permission of the publisher.

This book is a McGraw-Hill Learning Solutions textbook and contains select material from *Fundamentals of Corporate Finance*, Ninth Edition by Stephen A. Ross, Randolph W. Westerfield and Bradford D. Jordan. Copyright © 2010, 2008, 2006, 2003, 2000, 1998, 1995, 1993, 1991 by The McGraw-Hill Companies, Inc. Reprinted with permission of the publisher. Many custom published texts are modified versions or adaptations of our best-selling textbooks. Some adaptations are printed in black and white to keep prices at a minimum, while others are in color

2 3 4 5 6 7 8 9 0 BRP BRP 13 12 11

ISBN-13: 978-0-07-754662-5
ISBN-10: 0-07-754662-8
Part of:
ISBN-13: 978-0-07-754860-5
ISBN-10: 0-07-754860-4

Learning Solutions Representative: Nicole Schmitt
Production Editor: Jennifer Pickel
Printer/Binder: BR Printers

To our families and friends with love and gratitude.

S.A.R. R.W.W. B.D.J.

STEPHEN A. ROSS

Sloan School of Management, Franco Modigliani Professor of Finance and Economics, Massachusetts Institute of Technology

Stephen A. Ross is the Franco Modigliani Professor of Finance and Economics at the Sloan School of Management, Massachusetts Institute of Technology. One of the most widely published authors in finance and economics, Professor Ross is recognized for his work in developing the Arbitrage Pricing Theory and his substantial contributions to the discipline through his research in signaling, agency theory, option pricing, and the theory of the term structure of interest rates, among other topics. A past president of the American Finance Association, he currently serves as an associate editor of several academic and practitioner journals. He is a trustee of CalTech.

RANDOLPH W. WESTERFIELD

Marshall School of Business, University of Southern California

Randolph W. Westerfield is Dean Emeritus of the University of Southern California's Marshall School of Business and is the Charles B. Thornton Professor of Finance.

He came to USC from the Wharton School, University of Pennsylvania, where he was the chairman of the finance department and a member of the finance faculty for 20 years. He is a member of several public company boards of directors including Health Management Associates, Inc., and the Nicholas Applegate growth fund. His areas of expertise include corporate financial policy, investment management, and stock market price behavior.

BRADFORD D. JORDAN

Gatton College of Business and Economics, University of Kentucky

Bradford D. Jordan is Professor of Finance and holder of the Richard W. and Janis H. Furst Endowed Chair in Finance at the University of Kentucky. He has a long-standing interest in both applied and theoretical issues in corporate finance and has extensive experience teaching all levels of corporate finance and financial management policy. Professor Jordan has published numerous articles on issues such as cost of capital, capital structure, and the behavior of security prices. He is a past president of the Southern Finance Association, and he is coauthor of *Fundamentals of Investments: Valuation and Management,* 5e, a leading investments text, also published by McGraw-Hill/Irwin.

When the three of us decided to write a book, we were united by one strongly held principle: Corporate finance should be developed in terms of a few integrated, powerful ideas. We believed that the subject was all too often presented as a collection of loosely related topics, unified primarily by virtue of being bound together in one book, and we thought there must be a better way.

One thing we knew for certain was that we didn't want to write a "me-too" book. So, with a lot of help, we took a hard look at what was truly important and useful. In doing so, we were led to eliminate topics of dubious relevance, downplay purely theoretical issues, and minimize the use of extensive and elaborate calculations to illustrate points that are either intuitively obvious or of limited practical use.

As a result of this process, three basic themes became our central focus in writing *Fundamentals of Corporate Finance*:

AN EMPHASIS ON INTUITION

We always try to separate and explain the principles at work on a common sense, intuitive level before launching into any specifics. The underlying ideas are discussed first in very general terms and then by way of examples that illustrate in more concrete terms how a financial manager might proceed in a given situation.

A UNIFIED VALUATION APPROACH

We treat net present value (NPV) as the basic concept underlying corporate finance. Many texts stop well short of consistently integrating this important principle. The most basic and important notion, that NPV represents the excess of market value over cost, often is lost in an overly mechanical approach that emphasizes computation at the expense of comprehension. In contrast, every subject we cover is firmly rooted in valuation, and care is taken throughout to explain how particular decisions have valuation effects.

A MANAGERIAL FOCUS

Students shouldn't lose sight of the fact that financial management concerns management. We emphasize the role of the financial manager as decision maker, and we stress the need for managerial input and judgment. We consciously avoid "black box" approaches to finance, and, where appropriate, the approximate, pragmatic nature of financial analysis is made explicit, possible pitfalls are described, and limitations are discussed.

In retrospect, looking back to our 1991 first edition IPO, we had the same hopes and fears as any entrepreneurs. How would we be received in the market? At the time, we had no idea that just 18 years later, we would be working on a ninth edition. We certainly never dreamed that in those years we would work with friends and colleagues from around the world to create country-specific Australian, Canadian, and South African editions, an International edition, Chinese, French, Polish, Portuguese, Thai, Russian, Korean, and Spanish language editions, and an entirely separate book, *Essentials of Corporate Finance,* now in its sixth edition.

Today, as we prepare to once more enter the market, our goal is to stick with the basic principles that have brought us this far. However, based on the enormous amount of feedback we have received from you and your colleagues, we have made this edition and its package even *more flexible* than previous editions. We offer flexibility in coverage, by continuing to offer two editions, and flexibility in pedagogy, by providing a wide variety of features in the book to help students to learn about corporate finance. We also provide flexibility in package options by offering the most extensive collection of teaching, learning, and technology aids of any corporate finance text. Whether you use only the textbook, or the book in conjunction with our other products, we believe you will find a combination with this edition that will meet your current as well as your changing course needs.

Stephen A. Ross
Randolph W. Westerfield
Bradford D. Jordan

Coverage

This book was designed and developed explicitly for a first course in business or corporate finance, for both finance majors and non-majors alike. In terms of background or prerequisites, the book is nearly self-contained, assuming some familiarity with basic algebra and accounting concepts, while still reviewing important accounting principles very early on. The organization of this text has been developed to give instructors the flexibility they need. Two important changes have been made to the ninth edition chapter organization, one of which is the exciting addition of a behavioral finance chapter in the Alternate Edition. Also, the chapter on options and corporate finance, Chapter 14 in the eighth edition, has been moved to the Alternate Edition.

The following grid presents, for each chapter, some of the most significant features as well as a few selected chapter highlights of the ninth edition of *Fundamentals*. Of course, in every chapter, opening vignettes, boxed features, in-chapter illustrated examples using real companies, and end-of-chapter material have been thoroughly updated as well.

Chapters	Selected Topics of Interest	Benefits to You
PART 1 Overview of Corporate Finance		
Chapter 1 Introduction to Corporate Finance	Sarbanes–Oxley.	
	Goal of the firm and agency problems.	Stresses value creation as the most fundamental aspect of management and describes agency issues that can arise.
	Ethics, financial management, and executive compensation.	Brings in real-world issues concerning conflicts of interest and current controversies surrounding ethical conduct and management pay.
Chapter 2 Financial Statements, Taxes, and Cash Flow	*Minicase:* Cash Flows and Financial Statements at Sunset Boards, Inc.	Reinforces key cash flow concepts in a small-business setting.
	Cash flow vs. earnings.	Clearly defines cash flow and spells out the differences between cash flow and earnings.
	Market values vs. book values.	Emphasizes the relevance of market values over book values.
PART 2 Financial Statements and Long-Term Financial Planning		
Chapter 3 Working with Financial Statements	*Ratios:* PEG, price-to-sales, and Tobin's Q.	
	Expanded Du Pont analysis.	Expands the basic Du Pont equation to better explore the interrelationships between operating and financial performance.
	Du Pont analysis for real companies using data from S&P *Market Insight*.	Analysis shows students how to get and use real-world data, thereby applying key chapter ideas.
	Ratio and financial statement analysis using smaller firm data.	Uses firm data from *RMA* to show students how to actually get and evaluate financial statements benchmarks.
	Understanding financial statements.	Thorough coverage of standardized financial statements and key ratios.

Chapters	Selected Topics of Interest	Benefits to You
Chapter 4 Long-Term Financial Planning and Growth	Expanded discussion on sustainable growth calculations. *Minicase:* Planning for Growth at S&S Air.	Illustrates the importance of financial planning in a small firm.
	Explanation of alternative formulas for sustainable and internal growth rates.	Explanation of growth rate formulas clears up a common misunderstanding about these formulas and the circumstances under which alternative formulas are correct.
	Thorough coverage of sustainable growth as a planning tool.	Provides a vehicle for examining the interrelationships between operations, financing, and growth.
	Long-range financial planning.	Covers percentage of sales approach to creating *pro forma* statements.

PART 3   Valuation of Future Cash Flows

Chapters	Selected Topics of Interest	Benefits to You
Chapter 5 Introduction to Valuation: The Time Value of Money	First of two chapters on time value of money.	Relatively short chapter introduces just the basic ideas on time value of money to get students started on this traditionally difficult topic.
Chapter 6 Discounted Cash Flow Valuation	Growing annuities and perpetuities. Second of two chapters on time value of money. *New minicase:* The MBA Decision.	Covers more advanced time value topics with numerous examples, calculator tips, and Excel spreadsheet exhibits. Contains many real-world examples.
Chapter 7 Interest Rates and Bond Valuation	Inflation and present values.	
	"Clean" vs. "dirty" bond prices and accrued interest.	Clears up the pricing of bonds between coupon payment dates and also bond market quoting conventions.
	NASD's new TRACE system and transparency in the corporate bond market.	Up-to-date discussion of new developments in fixed income with regard to price, volume, and transactions reporting.
	"Make-whole" call provisions. *Minicase:* Financing S&S Air's Expansion Plans with a Bond Issue.	Up-to-date discussion of a relatively new type of call provision that has become very common.
	Bond valuation.	Complete coverage of bond valuation and bond features.
	Interest rates.	Discusses real versus nominal rates and the determinants of the term structure.
Chapter 8 Stock Valuation	*Minicase:* Stock Valuation at Ragan, Inc.	Examines the debt issuance process for a small firm.
	Stock valuation.	Thorough coverage of constant and non-constant growth models.
	NYSE and NASDAQ Market Operations.	Up-to-date description of major stock market operations.

Coverage *(continued)*

Chapters	Selected Topics of Interest	Benefits to You
PART 4 Capital Budgeting		
Chapter 9 Net Present Value and Other Investment Criteria	Modified internal rate of return (MIRR) *New case:* Bullock Gold Mining. First of three chapters on capital budgeting.	Relatively short chapter introduces key ideas on an intuitive level to help students with this traditionally difficult topic.
	NPV, IRR, payback, discounted payback, and accounting rate of return.	Consistent, balanced examination of advantages and disadvantages of various criteria.
Chapter 10 Making Capital Investment Decisions	Project cash flow.	Thorough coverage of project cash flows and the relevant numbers for a project analysis.
	Alternative cash flow definitions.	Emphasizes the equivalence of various formulas, thereby removing common misunderstandings.
	Special cases of DCF analysis.	Considers important applications of chapter tools.
Chapter 11 Project Analysis and Evaluation	*Minicase:* Conch Republic Electronics.	Analyzes capital budgeting issues and complexities.
	Sources of value.	Stresses the need to understand the economic basis for value creation in a project.
	Scenario and sensitivity "what-if" analyses.	Illustrates how to actually apply and interpret these tools in a project analysis.
	Break-even analysis.	Covers cash, accounting, and financial break-even levels.
PART 5 Risk and Return		
Chapter 12 Some Lessons from Capital Market History	*Minicase:* A Job at S&S Air.	
	Expanded discussion of geometric vs. arithmetic returns.	Discusses calculation and interpretation of geometric returns. Clarifies common misconceptions regarding appropriate use of arithmetic vs. geometric average returns.
	Capital market history.	Extensive coverage of historical returns, volatilities, and risk premiums.
	Market efficiency.	Efficient markets hypothesis discussed along with common misconceptions.
	New! The equity risk premium.	New section discusses the equity premium puzzle and latest international evidence.
Chapter 13 Return, Risk, and the Security Market Line	*Minicase:* The Beta for Colgate-Palmolive.	
	Diversification, systematic and unsystematic risk.	Illustrates basics of risk and return in a straightforward fashion.
	Beta and the security market line.	Develops the security market line with an intuitive approach that bypasses much of the usual portfolio theory and statistics.

Chapters	Selected Topics of Interest	Benefits to You
PART 6 Cost of Capital and Long-Term Financial Policy		
Chapter 14 Cost of Capital	Internal equity and flotation costs.	
	Geometric vs. arithmetic growth rates.	Both approaches are used in practice. Clears up issues surrounding growth rate estimates.
	Cost of capital estimation.	Contains a complete, Web-based illustration of cost of capital for a real company.
Chapter 15 Raising Capital	*Minicase:* S&S Air Goes Public.	
	Dutch auction IPOs.	Explains uniform price auctions using recent Google IPO as an example.
	IPO "quiet periods."	Explains the SEC's quiet period rules.
	Rights vs. warrants.	Clarifies the option-like nature of rights prior to their expiration dates.
	IPO valuation.	Extensive, up-to-date discussion of IPOs, including the 1999–2000 period.
Chapter 16 Financial Leverage and Capital Structure Policy	The pecking-order theory of capital structure.	
	Minicase: Stephenson Real Estate Recapitalization.	
	Basics of financial leverage.	Illustrates effect of leverage on risk and return.
	Optimal capital structure.	Describes the basic trade-offs leading to an optimal capital structure.
	Financial distress and bankruptcy.	Briefly surveys the bankruptcy process.
Chapter 17 Dividends and Dividend Policy	*Minicase:* Electronic Timing, Inc.	Analyzes cost of capital estimation for a non-public firm.
	Very recent survey evidence on dividend policy.	New survey results show the most important (and least important) factors considered by financial managers in setting dividend policy.
	Effect of new tax laws.	Discusses implications of new, lower dividend, and capital gains rates.
	Dividends and dividend policy.	Describes dividend payments and the factors favoring higher and lower payout policies.
	New! Optimal payout policy.	Extensive discussion of the latest research and survey evidence on dividend policy, including life-cycle theory.
	Stock repurchases.	Thorough coverage of buybacks as an alternative to cash dividends.

Coverage *(continued)*

Chapters	Selected Topics of Interest	Benefits to You
PART 7 Short-Term Financial Planning and Management		
Chapter 18 Short-Term Finance and Planning	Operating and cash cycles.	Stresses the importance of cash flow timing.
	Short-term financial planning.	Illustrates creation of cash budgets and potential need for financing.
Chapter 19 Cash and Liquidity Management	Check Clearing Act of the 21st Century.	
	Minicase: Cash Management at Webb Corporation.	
	Float management.	Thorough coverage of float management and potential ethical issues.
	Cash collection and disbursement.	Examination of systems used by firms to handle cash inflows and outflows.
Chapter 20 Credit and Inventory Management	*Minicase:* Credit Policy at Howlett Industries.	Evaluates working capital issues for a small firm.
	Credit management	Analysis of credit policy and implementation.
	Inventory management	Brief overview of important inventory concepts.
PART 8 Topics in Corporate Finance		
Chapter 21 International Corporate Finance	*Minicase:* S&S Air Goes International.	
	Foreign exchange.	Covers essentials of exchange rates and their determination.
	International capital budgeting.	Shows how to adapt basic DCF approach to handle exchange rates.
	Exchange rate and political risk.	Discusses hedging and issues surrounding sovereign risk.

To meet the varied needs of its intended audience, *Fundamentals of Corporate Finance* is rich in valuable learning tools and support.

CHAPTER-OPENING VIGNETTES

Vignettes drawn from real-world events introduce students to the chapter concepts. For examples, see Chapter 4, page 87; Chapter 5, page 119.

LEARNING OBJECTIVES

After studying this chapter, you should understand:

LO1 How to determine the relevant cash flows for a proposed project.

LO2 How to determine if a project is acceptable.

LO3 How to set a bid price for a project.

LO4 How to evaluate the equivalent annual cost of a project.

PART 4 — Capital Budgeting

10 MAKING CAPITAL INVESTMENT DECISIONS

IS THERE GREEN IN GREEN? General Electric (GE) thinks so. Through its "Ecomagination" program, the company planned to double research and development spending on green products, from $700 million in 2004 to $1.5 billion in 2010. With products such as a hybrid railroad locomotive (described as a 200-ton, 6,000-horsepower "Prius on rails"), GE's green initiative seems to be paying off. Revenue from green products was $14 billion in 2007, with a target of $25 billion in 2010. The company's internal commitment to reduced energy consumption saved it more than $100 million from 2004 to 2007, and the company was on target to reduce its water consumption by 20 percent by 2012, another considerable cost savings.

As you no doubt recognize from your study of the previous chapter, GE's decision to develop and market green technology represents a capital budgeting decision. In this chapter, we further investigate such decisions, how they are made, and how to look at them objectively.

This chapter follows up on our previous one by delving more deeply into capital budgeting. We have two main tasks. First, recall that in the last chapter, we saw that cash flow estimates are the critical input into a net present value analysis, but we didn't say much about where these cash flows come from; so we will now examine this question in some detail. Our second goal is to learn how to critically examine NPV estimates, and, in particular, how to evaluate the sensitivity of NPV estimates to assumptions made about the uncertain future.

Master the ability to solve problems in this chapter by using a spreadsheet. Access Excel Master on the student Web site www.mhhe.com/rwj.

So far, we've covered various parts of the capital budgeting decision. Our task in this chapter is to start bringing these pieces together. In particular, we will show you how to "spread the numbers" for a proposed investment or project and, based on those numbers, make an initial assessment about whether the project should be undertaken.

In the discussion that follows, we focus on the process of setting up a discounted cash flow analysis. From the last chapter, we know that the projected future cash flows are the key element in such an evaluation. Accordingly, we emphasize working with financial and accounting information to come up with these figures.

In evaluating a proposed investment, we pay special attention to deciding what information is relevant to the decision at hand and what information is not. As we will see, it is easy to overlook important pieces of the capital budgeting puzzle.

CHAPTER LEARNING OBJECTIVES

New to this edition, this feature maps out the topics and learning goals in every chapter. Each end-of-chapter problem and test bank question is linked to a learning objective, to help you organize your assessment of knowledge and comprehension.

PEDAGOGICAL USE OF COLOR

This learning tool continues to be an important feature of *Fundamentals of Corporate Finance*. In almost every chapter, color plays an extensive, nonschematic, and largely self-evident role. A guide to the functional use of color is on the endsheets of the text.

FIGURE 9.8

NPV Profiles for Mutually Exclusive Investments

IN THEIR OWN WORDS BOXES

This series of boxes are the popular articles updated from previous editions written by a distinguished scholar or practitioner on key topics in the text. Boxes include essays by Merton Miller on capital structure, Fischer Black on dividends, and Roger Ibbotson on capital market history. A complete list of "In Their Own Words" boxes appears on page xli.

IN THEIR OWN WORDS ...

Jeremy J. Siegel on Stocks for the Long Run

The most fascinating characteristic about the data on real financial market returns that I collected is the stability of the long-run real equity returns. The compound annual (geometric) real return on U.S. stocks averaged 6.8% per year from 1802 through 2007 and this return had remained remarkably stable over long-term periods. From 1802 through 1871, the real return averaged 7.0%, from 1871, when the Cowles Foundation data became available, through 1925, the real return on stocks averaged 6.6% per year, and since 1925, which the well-known Ibbotson data cover, the real return has averaged 6.7%. Despite the fact that the price level has increased over ten times since the end of the Second World War, real stock returns have still averaged 6.8%.

The long run stability of real returns on stocks is strongly indicative of *mean reversion of equity return*. Mean reversion means that stock returns can be very volatile in the short run, but show a remarkable stability in the long run. When my research was first published, there was much skepticism of the mean reversion properties of equity market returns, but now this concept is widely accepted for stocks. If mean reversion prevails, portfolios geared for the long-term should have a greater share of equities than short-term portfolios. This conclusion has long been the "conventional" wisdom on investing, but it does not follow if stock returns follow a random walk, a concept widely accepted by academics in the 1970s and 1980s.

When my data first appeared, there was also much discussion of "survivorship bias," the fact that the U.S. stock returns are unusually good because the U.S. was the most successful capitalist country. But three British researchers, Elroy Dimson, Paul Marsh, and Michael Staunton, surveyed stock returns in 16 countries since the beginning of the 20th century and wrote up their results in a book entitled *Triumph of the Optimists*. The authors concluded that U.S. stock returns do not give a distorted picture of the superiority of stocks over bonds worldwide.

Jeremy J. Siegel is the Russell E. Palmer Professor of Finance at The Wharton School of the University of Pennsylvania and author of Stocks for the Long Run and The Future Investors. His research covers macroeconomics and monetary policy, financial market returns, and long-term economic trends.

WORK THE WEB

Bond quotes have become more available with the rise of the Internet. One site where you can find current bond prices is cxa.marketwatch.com/finra/MarketData/Default.aspx. We went to the Web site and searched for bonds issued by Chevron. Here is a look at part of what we found for one of the bonds:

CVX.GP / CUSIP: 881685BD2   Search for Bond Trade Activity   Add to Watchlist

Last: **$108.500**   Yield: **5.934%**

Security Category:	Corporate
Issue Description:	GTD DEB
Issuer Name:	TEXACO CAP INC
Coupon Rate:	7.500%
Coupon Type:	Fixed
Maturity Date:	03/01/2043

Price | Yield

Price ▦   5/7/2008

$120
$115
$110
$105
$100
$95

Aug/07   Oct/07   Jan/08   May/08

5 day 3 mo 6 mo **1 year**

Composite Trade Information

Last Sale		**Daily Trade Summary**	
Date	05/07/2008	High Price / Equivalent Yield	$108.500 / 6.57100%
Price	$108.500	Low Price / Equivalent Yield	$105.750 / 5.93400%
Yield	5.934%	Net Change (Price)	$1.000

The bond has a coupon rate of 7.50 percent and matures on March 1, 2043. The last sale on this bond was at a price of 108.50 percent of par, which gives a yield to maturity of about 5.93 percent. Not only does the site provide the most recent price and yield information, but it also provides more important information about the bond, such as the credit rating, coupon date, call date, and call price. We'll leave it up to you to have a look at the page and the rest of the information available there.

Questions

1. Go to this Web site and find the bond shown above. When was this bond issued? What was the size of the bond issue? What were the yield to maturity and price when the bond was issued?
2. When you search for Chevron bonds (CVX), you will find bonds for several companies listed. Why do you think Chevron has bonds issued with different corporate names?

ENHANCED! WORK THE WEB BOXES

These boxes show students how to research financial issues using the Web and then how to use the information they find to make business decisions. **New** to this edition, now all of the Work the Web boxes also include interactive follow-up questions and exercises.

REAL-WORLD EXAMPLES

Actual events are integrated throughout the text, tying chapter concepts to real life through illustration and reinforcing the relevance of the material. Some examples tie into the chapter opening vignette for added reinforcement. See Example 5.10 on page 133.

SPREADSHEET STRATEGIES

This feature introduces students to Excel and shows them how to set up spreadsheets in order to analyze common financial problems—a vital part of every business student's education.

SPREADSHEET STRATEGIES

How to Calculate Present Values with Multiple Future Cash Flows Using a Spreadsheet

Just as we did in our previous chapter, we can set up a basic spreadsheet to calculate the present values of the individual cash flows as follows. Notice that we have simply calculated the present values one at a time and added them up:

	A	B	C	D	E
1					
2		Using a spreadsheet to value multiple future cash flows			
3					
4	What is the present value of $200 in one year, $400 the next year, $600 the next year, and				
5	$800 the last year if the discount rate is 12 percent?				
6					
7	Rate:	.12			
8					
9	Year	Cash flows	Present values	Formula used	
10	1	$200	$178.57	=PV($B$7,A10,0,−B10)	
11	2	$400	$318.88	=PV($B$7,A11,0,−B11)	
12	3	$600	$427.07	=PV($B$7,A12,0,−B12)	
13	4	$800	$508.41	=PV($B$7,A13,0,−B13)	
14					
15		Total PV:	$1,432.93	=SUM(C10:C13)	
16					
17	Notice the negative signs inserted in the PV formulas. These just make the present values have				
18	positive signs. Also, the discount rate in cell B7 is entered as $B$7 (an "absolute" reference)				
19	because it is used over and over. We could have just entered ".12" instead, but our approach is more				
20	flexible.				
21					
22					

CALCULATOR HINTS

Brief calculator tutorials appear in selected chapters to help students learn or brush up on their financial calculator skills. These complement the Spreadsheet Strategies.

CALCULATOR HINTS

Annuity Present Values

To find annuity present values with a financial calculator, we need to use the **PMT** key (you were probably wondering what it was for). Compared to finding the present value of a single amount, there are two important differences. First, we enter the annuity cash flow using the **PMT** key. Second, we don't enter anything for the future value, **FV**. So, for example, the problem we have been examining is a three-year, $500 annuity. If the discount rate is 10 percent, we need to do the following (after clearing out the calculator!):

Enter		3	10	500		
		N	**I/Y**	**PMT**	**PV**	**FV**
Solve for					−1,243.43	

As usual, we get a negative sign on the PV.

CONCEPT BUILDING

Chapter sections are intentionally kept short to promote a step-by-step, building block approach to learning. Each section is then followed by a series of short concept questions that highlight the key ideas just presented. Students use these questions to make sure they can identify and understand the most important concepts as they read.

Concept Questions

3.3a What are the five groups of ratios? Give two or three examples of each kind.

3.3b Given the total debt ratio, what other two ratios can be computed? Explain how.

3.3c Turnover ratios all have one of two figures as the numerator. What are these two figures? What do these ratios measure? How do you interpret the results?

3.3d Profitability ratios all have the same figure in the numerator. What is it? What do these ratios measure? How do you interpret the results?

SUMMARY TABLES

These tables succinctly restate key principles, results, and equations. They appear whenever it is useful to emphasize and summarize a group of related concepts. For examples, see Chapter 6, page 161.

EXAMPLE 9.4   Calculating the IRR

A project has a total up-front cost of $435.44. The cash flows are $100 in the first year, $200 in the second year, and $300 in the third year. What's the IRR? If we require an 18 percent return, should we take this investment?

We'll describe the NPV profile and find the IRR by calculating some NPVs at different discount rates. You should check our answers for practice. Beginning with 0 percent, we have:

Discount Rate	NPV
0%	$164.56
5%	100.36
10%	46.15
15%	.00
20%	− 39.61

The NPV is zero at 15 percent, so 15 percent is the IRR. If we require an 18 percent return, then we should not take the investment. The reason is that the NPV is negative at 18 percent (verify that it is −$24.47). The IRR rule tells us the same thing in this case. We shouldn't take this investment because its 15 percent return is below our required 18 percent return.

LABELED EXAMPLES

Separate numbered and titled examples are extensively integrated into the chapters. These examples provide detailed applications and illustrations of the text material in a step-by-step format. Each example is completely self-contained so students don't have to search for additional information. Based on our classroom testing, these examples are among the most useful learning aids because they provide both detail and explanation.

KEY TERMS

Key Terms are printed in bold type and defined within the text the first time they appear. They also appear in the margins with definitions for easy location and identification by the student. See Chapter 7, page 203 for an example.

EXPLANATORY WEB LINKS

These Web links are provided in the margins of the text. They are specifically selected to accompany text material and provide students and instructors with a quick way to check for additional information using the Internet.

If you go to the Web site and click on a particular bond, you will get a lot of information about the bond, including the credit rating, the call schedule, original issue information, and trade information.

The Federal Reserve Bank of St. Louis maintains dozens of online files containing macroeconomic data as well as rates on U.S. Treasury issues. Go to www.stls.frb.org/fred/files.

As we mentioned before, the U.S. Treasury market is the largest securities market in the world. As with bond markets in general, it is an OTC market, so there is limited transparency. However, unlike the situation with bond markets in general, trading in Treasury issues, particularly recently issued ones, is very heavy. Each day, representative prices for outstanding Treasury issues are reported.

Figure 7.4 shows a portion of the daily Treasury note and bond listings from the Web site wsj.com. The entry that begins "2021 Nov 15" is highlighted. This information tells us that the bond will mature in November of 2021. The next column is the coupon rate, which is 8.000 percent for this bond. Treasury bonds all make semiannual payments and have a face value of $1,000, so this bond will pay $40 per six months until it matures.

KEY EQUATIONS

Called out in the text, key equations are identified by an equation number. The list in Appendix B shows the key equations by chapter, providing students with a convenient reference.

Based on our examples, we can now write the general expression for the value of a bond. If a bond has (1) a face value of F paid at maturity, (2) a coupon of C paid per period, (3) t periods to maturity, and (4) a yield of r per period, its value is:

$$\text{Bond value} = C \times [1 - 1/(1 + r)^t]/r \quad + \quad F/(1 + r)^t$$

$$\text{Bond value} = \begin{array}{c} \text{Present value} \\ \text{of the coupons} \end{array} + \begin{array}{c} \text{Present value} \\ \text{of the face amount} \end{array}$$

[7.1]

HIGHLIGHTED CONCEPTS

Throughout the text, important ideas are pulled out and presented in a highlighted box—signaling to students that this material is particularly relevant and critical for their understanding. For examples, see Chapter 7, page 218; Chapter 9, page 265.

CHAPTER SUMMARY AND CONCLUSIONS

Every chapter ends with a concise, but thorough, summary of the important ideas—helping students review the key points and providing closure to the chapter.

5.1 **Calculating Future Values** Assume you deposit $10,000 today in an account that pays 6 percent interest. How much will you have in five years?

5.2 **Calculating Present Values** Suppose you have just celebrated your 19th birthday. A rich uncle has set up a trust fund for you that will pay you $150,000 when you turn 30. If the relevant discount rate is 9 percent, how much is this fund worth today?

5.3 **Calculating Rates of Return** You've been offered an investment that will double your money in 10 years. What rate of return are you being offered? Check your answer using the Rule of 72.

5.4 **Calculating the Number of Periods** You've been offered an investment that will pay you 9 percent per year. If you invest $15,000, how long until you have $30,000? How long until you have $45,000?

ANSWERS TO CHAPTER REVIEW AND SELF-TEST PROBLEMS

5.1 We need to calculate the future value of $10,000 at 6 percent for five years. The future value factor is:

$$1.06^5 = 1.3382$$

The future value is thus $10,000 \times 1.3382 = \$13,382.26$.

5.2 We need the present value of $150,000 to be paid in 11 years at 9 percent. The discount factor is:

$$1/1.09^{11} = 1/2.5804 = .3875$$

The present value is thus about $58,130.

CHAPTER REVIEW AND SELF-TEST PROBLEMS

Appearing after the Summary and Conclusion, each chapter includes a Chapter Review and Self-Test Problem section. These questions and answers allow students to test their abilities in solving key problems related to the chapter content and provide instant reinforcement.

CONCEPTS REVIEW AND CRITICAL THINKING QUESTIONS

This successful end-of-chapter section facilitates your students' knowledge of key principles, as well as intuitive understanding of the chapter concepts. A number of the questions relate to the chapter-opening vignette—reinforcing student critical-thinking skills and the learning of chapter material.

CONCEPTS REVIEW AND CRITICAL THINKING QUESTIONS

1. **Present Value** [LO2] The basic present value equation has four parts. What are they?

2. **Compounding** [LO1, 2] What is compounding? What is discounting?

3. **Compounding and Period** [LO1] As you increase the length of time involved, what happens to future values? What happens to present values?

4. **Compounding and Interest Rates** [LO1] What happens to a future value if you increase the rate r? What happens to a present value?

5. **Ethical Considerations** [LO2] Take a look back at Example 5.7. Is it deceptive advertising? Is it unethical to advertise a future value like this without a disclaimer?

   To answer the next five questions, refer to the TMCC security we discussed to open the chapter.

END-OF-CHAPTER QUESTIONS AND PROBLEMS

Students learn better when they have plenty of opportunity to practice; therefore, *FCF*, 9e provides extensive end-of-chapter questions and problems. The end-of-chapter support greatly exceeds typical introductory textbooks. The questions and problems are segregated into three learning levels: Basic, Intermediate, and Challenge. Answers to selected end-of-chapter material appear in Appendix C. Also, all problems are available in McGraw-Hill's Homework Manager—see page xxiv for details.

---

112   PART 2   Financial Statements and Long-Term Financial Planning

QUESTIONS AND PROBLEMS HM™

BASIC
(Questions 1–15)

1. **Pro Forma Statements** [LO1] Consider the following simplified financial statements for the Phillips Corporation (assuming no income taxes):

Income Statement		Balance Sheet			
Sales	$23,000	Assets	$15,800	Debt	$ 5,200
Costs	16,700			Equity	10,600
Net income	$ 6,300	Total	$15,800	Total	$15,800

Phillips has predicted a sales increase of 15 percent. It has predicted that every item on the balance sheet will increase by 15 percent as well. Create the pro forma statements and reconcile them. What is the plug variable here?

2. **Pro Forma Statements and EFN** [LO1, 2] In the previous question, assume Phillips pays out half of net income in the form of a cash dividend. Costs and assets vary with sales, but debt and equity do not. Prepare the pro forma statements and determine the external financing needed.

END-OF-CHAPTER CASES

Located at the end of the book's chapters, these minicases focus on real-life company situations that embody important corporate finance topics. Each case presents a new scenario, data, and a dilemma. Several questions at the end of each case require students to analyze and focus on all of the material they learned from each chapter.

MINICASE

Financing S&S Air's Expansion Plans with a Bond Issue

Mark Sexton and Todd Story, the owners of S&S Air, have decided to expand their operations. They instructed their newly hired financial analyst, Chris Guthrie, to enlist an underwriter to help sell $35 million in new 10-year bonds to finance construction. Chris has entered into discussions with Kim McKenzie, an underwriter from the firm of Raines and Warren, about which bond features S&S Air should consider and what coupon rate the issue will likely have.

Although Chris is aware of the bond features, he is uncertain about the costs and benefits of some features, so he isn't sure how each feature would affect the coupon rate of the bond issue. You are Kim's assistant, and she has asked you to prepare a memo to Chris describing the effect of each of the following bond features on the coupon rate of the bond. She would also like you to list any advantages or disadvantages of each feature:

QUESTIONS

1. The security of the bond—that is, whether the bond has collateral.

2. The seniority of the bond.

3. The presence of a sinking fund.

4. A call provision with specified call dates and call prices.

5. A deferred call accompanying the call provision.

6. A make-whole call provision.

7. Any positive covenants. Also, discuss several possible positive covenants S&S Air might consider.

8. Any negative covenants. Also, discuss several possible negative covenants S&S Air might consider.

9. A conversion feature (note that S&S Air is not a publicly traded company).

10. A floating-rate coupon.

WEB EXERCISES (ONLINE ONLY)

For instructors interested in integrating even more online resources and problems into their course, these Web activities show students how to learn from the vast amount of financial resources available on the Internet. In the 9th edition of *Fundamentals*, these Web exercises are available to students and instructors on the Online Learning Center.

Comprehensive Teaching and Learning Package

This edition of *Fundamentals* has several options in terms of the textbook, instructor supplements, student supplements, and multimedia products. Mix and match to create a package that is perfect for your course!

TEXTBOOK

As with the previous editions, we are offering two versions of this text. Choose the length and topics suitable for your course.

- Standard Edition (21 Chapters)
- Alternate Edition (27 Chapters)

Instructor's CD-ROM

Keep all the supplements in one place! This CD contains all the necessary supplements—Instructor's Manual, Solutions, Test Bank, Computerized Test Bank, and PowerPoint—all in one useful product in an electronic format.

- **Instructor's Manual (IM)**

  Prepared by Steve Dolvin, Butler University

  A great place to find new lecture ideas! The annotated outline for each chapter includes lecture tips, real-world tips, ethics notes, suggested PowerPoint slides, and, when appropriate, a video synopsis.

- **Solutions Manual (SM)**

  Prepared by Joseph Smolira, Belmont University

  The *Fundamentals* Solutions Manual provides detailed solutions to the extensive end-of-chapter material, including concept review questions, quantitative problems, and cases.

- **Test Bank**

  Prepared by Kay Johnson, Penn State University—Erie

  Over 100 questions and problems per chapter! Each chapter is divided into **FIVE** parts. *Part I* contains questions that test the understanding of the key terms in the book. *Part II* includes questions patterned after the learning objectives, concept questions, chapter-opening vignettes, boxes, and highlighted phrases. *Part III* contains multiple-choice problems patterned after the end-of-chapter questions, in basic, intermediate, and challenge levels. *Part IV* provides essay questions to test problem-solving skills and more advanced understanding of concepts. *Part V* is a **new** section that picks up questions directly from the end-of-chapter material and converts them into parallel test bank questions. For your reference, each TB question in this part is linked with its corresponding question in the EOC.

- **Computerized Test Bank (Windows)**

  Create your own tests in a snap! These additional questions are found in a computerized test bank utilizing McGraw-Hill's EZ Test testing software to quickly create customized exams. This user-friendly program allows instructors to sort questions by format; edit existing questions or add new ones; and scramble questions for multiple versions of the same test.

- **PowerPoint Presentations**

  Prepared by Steve Dolvin, Butler University

  The PowerPoint slides for the ninth edition have been revised to include a wealth of instructor material, including lecture tips, real world examples, and international notes. Each presentation now also includes slides dedicated entirely to ethics notes that relate to the chapter topics. In addition, the PPTs provide exhibits and examples both from the book and from outside sources. Applicable slides have Web links that take you directly to specific Internet sites, or a spreadsheet link to show an example in Excel. Go to the Notes Page function for more tips and information while presenting the slides to your class.

Customize our content for your course! If you already have PowerPoint installed on your PC, you have the ability to add, delete, edit, print, or rearrange the complete presentation to focus on your course needs.

Videos (DVD Format)
Current set of videos on hot topics! McGraw-Hill/Irwin produced a series of finance videos that are 10-minute case studies on topics such as Financial Markets, Careers, Rightsizing, Capital Budgeting, EVA (Economic Value Added), Mergers and Acquisitions, and International Finance.

ONLINE SUPPORT

Online learning center at www.mhhe.com/rwj
The Online Learning Center (OLC) contains FREE access to additional Web-based study and teaching aids created for this text, such as:

Student Support
A great resource for those seeking additional practice, students can access self-grading quizzes, Excel template problems, electronic flashcards, and the brand new program, Excel Master, designed by Brad Jordan and Joe Smolira.

- **Premium Content Access**

    iPod Content—The library isn't the only place to study! Students lead active and mobile lives. Harness the power of one of the most popular technology tools today and study on the go. Our innovative approach allows you to download Narrated PowerPoints and quizzes right into your iPod or other MP3 player device.

    Narrated PowerPoint Slides—*Created by Kent Ragan, Missouri State University.* The narrated PowerPoints provide real-world examples accompanied by step by step instructions and explanations for solving problems presented in the chapter. The Concept Checks from the text are also integrated into the slides to reinforce the key topics in the chapter. Designed specifically to appeal to the different learning methods of students, the slides provide a visual and audio explanation of topics and problems. Click on the slide and listen to the accompanying narration! You can view this slides via computer or download them onto your video iPod.

Teaching Support
Along with having access to all of the same material your students can view on the book's OLC, you also have password protected access to the Instructor's Manual, solutions to end-of-chapter problems and cases, Instructor's PowerPoint, Excel Template Solutions, Video clips and Video projects and questions.

WebCT and Blackboard course cartridges allow instructors to manage their course and administer examinations online. Increase ease, organization, and efficiency and ask your representative for more details about course cartridges today!

McGraw-Hill Investments Trader
Students receive free access to this Web-based portfolio simulation with a hypothetical $100,000 brokerage account to buy and sell stocks and mutual funds. Students can use the real data found at this site in conjunction with the chapters on investments. They can

also compete against students around the United States. This site is powered by Stock-Trak, the leading provider of investment simulation services to the academic community.

McGraw-Hill's Homework Manager and Homework Manager Plus™

Are you looking for a way to spend less time grading and to have more flexibility with the problems you assign as homework and tests? McGraw-Hill's Homework Manager is an exciting new package option developed for this text! Homework Manager is a Web-based tool for instructors and students for delivering, answering, and grading end-of-chapter problems and tests, and providing a limitless supply of self-graded practice for students.

All of the book's end-of-chapter Questions and Problems are loaded into Homework Manager, and instructors can choose to assign the exact problems as stated in the book, or algorithmic versions of them so each student has a unique set of variables for the problems. You create the assignments and control parameters such as do you want your students to receive hints, is this a graded assignment or practice, etc. The test bank is also available in Homework Manager, giving you the ability to use those questions for online tests. Both the problems and the tests are automatically graded and the results are stored in a private grade book, which is created when you set up your class. Detailed results let you see at a glance how each student does on an assignment or an individual problem—you can even see how many tries it took them to solve it. If you order this special package, students will receive a Homework Manager User's Guide and an access code packaged with their text.

There is also an enhanced version of McGraw-Hill's Homework Manager through the Homework Manager Plus package option. If you order the text packaged with Homework Manager Plus, your students will receive Homework Manager as described above, but with an integrated online text included. When students are in Homework Manager and need more help to solve a problem, there will be a link that takes them to the section of the text online that explains the concept they are struggling with. All of McGraw-Hill's media assets, such as videos, narrated lectures, and additional online quizzing, are also integrated at the appropriate places of the online text to provide students with a full learning experience. If you order this special package, students will receive the Homework Manager Plus card packaged with their text, which gives them access to all of these products.

McGraw-Hill's Homework Manager is powered by Brownstone.

AVAILABLE FOR PURCHASE & PACKAGING

Student Problem Manual ISBN 0077246225

Prepared by Thomas Eyssell, University of Missouri–St. Louis

Need additional reinforcement of the concepts? This valuable resource provides students with additional problems for practice. Each chapter begins with Concepts for Review, followed by Chapter Highlights. These re-emphasize the key terms and concepts in the chapter. A short Concept Test, averaging 10 questions and answers, appears next. Each chapter concludes with additional problems for the student to review. Answers to these problems appear at the end of the Student Problem Manual.

BusinessWeek

Your students can subscribe to 15 weeks of *BusinessWeek* for a special price of $8.25 in addition to the price of the text. Students will receive a pass-code card shrink-wrapped with their new text. The card directs students to a Web site where they enter the code and then gain access to *BusinessWeek's* registration page to enter address info and set up their print and online subscription.

FinGame Online 5.0

By LeRoy Brooks, John Carroll University
(ISBN 10: 0077219880/ISBN 13: 9780077219888)
Just $15.00 when packaged with this text. In this comprehensive simulation game, students control a hypothetical company over numerous periods of operation. The game is now tied to the text by exercises found on the Online Learning Center. As students make major financial and operating decisions for their company, they will develop and enhance their skills in financial management and financial accounting statement analysis.

Financial Analysis with an Electronic Calculator, Sixth Edition

By Mark A. White, University of Virginia, McIntire School of Commerce
(ISBN 10: 0073217093/ISBN 13: 9780073217093)
The information and procedures in this supplementary text enable students to master the use of financial calculators and develop a working knowledge of financial mathematics and problem solving. Complete instructions are included for solving all major problem types on three popular models: HP 10B and 12C, TI BA II Plus, and TI-84. Hands-on problems with detailed solutions allow students to practice the skills outlined in the text and obtain instant reinforcement. *Financial Analysis with an Electronic Calculator* is a self-contained supplement to the introductory financial management course.

Assurance of Learning Ready

Assurance of learning is an important element of many accreditation standards. *Fundamentals of Corporate Finance,* 9e, is designed specifically to support your assurance of learning initiatives.

Each chapter in the book begins with a list of numbered learning objectives that appear throughout the chapter, as well as in the end-of-chapter problems and exercises. Every test bank question is also linked to one of these objectives, in addition to level of difficulty, topic area, Bloom's Taxonomy level, and AACSB skill area. *EZ Test,* McGraw-Hill's easy-to-use test bank software, can search the test bank by these and other categories, providing an engine for targeted Assurance of Learning analysis and assessment.

AACSB Statement

The McGraw-Hill Companies is a proud corporate member of AACSB International. Understanding the importance and value of AACSB accreditation, the ninth edition of *Fundamentals of Corporate Finance* has sought to recognize the curricula guidelines detailed in the AACSB standards for business accreditation by connecting selected questions in the test bank to the general knowledge and skill guidelines found in the AACSB standards.

The statements contained in the test bank are provided only as a guide for the users of this text. The AACSB leaves content coverage and assessment within the purview of individual schools, the mission of the school, and the faculty. While *Fundamentals of Corporate Finance* and the teaching package make no claim of any specific AACSB qualification or evaluation, we have, within the test bank, labeled selected questions according to the six general knowledge and skills areas.

Acknowledgments

To borrow a phrase, writing an introductory finance textbook is easy—all you do is sit down at a word processor and open a vein. We never would have completed this book without the incredible amount of help and support we received from literally hundreds of our colleagues, students, editors, family members, and friends. We would like to thank, without implicating, all of you.

Clearly, our greatest debt is to our many colleagues (and their students) who, like us, wanted to try an alternative to what they were using and made the decision to change. Needless to say, without this support, we would not be publishing a ninth edition!

A great many of our colleagues read the drafts of our first and subsequent editions. The fact that this book has so little in common with our earliest drafts, along with the many changes and improvements we have made over the years, is a reflection of the value we placed on the many comments and suggestions that we received. To the following reviewers, then, we are grateful for their many contributions:

Ibrahim Affeneh
Sung C. Bae
Robert Benecke
Gary Benesh
Scott Besley
Sanjai Bhaghat
Elizabeth Booth
Denis Boudreaux
William Brent
Ray Brooks
Charles C. Brown
Mary Chaffin
Fan Chen
Raju Chenna
Barbara J. Childs
Charles M. Cox
Natalya Delcoure
Michael Dorigan
David A. Dumpe
Michael Dunn
Alan Eastman
Adrian C. Edwards
Steve Engel
Angelo V. Esposito
Cheri Etling
Thomas H. Eyssell
Michael Ferguson
Deborah Ann Ford
Jim Forjan
Micah Frankel
Jennifer R. Frazier

Deborah M. Giarusso
Devra Golbe
A. Steven Graham
Darryl E. J. Gurley
Wendy D. Habegger
David Harraway
John M. Harris, Jr.
R. Stevenson Hawkey
Delvin D. Hawley
Robert C. Higgins
Karen Hogan
Steve Isberg
James Jackson
Pankaj Jain
James M. Johnson
Randy Jorgensen
Jarl G. Kallberg
Terry Keasler
David N. Ketcher
Jim Keys
Kee Kim
Robert Kleinman
David Kuipers
Morris A. Lamberson
Qin Lan
Adam Y. C. Lei
George Lentz
John Lightstone
Jason Lin
Robert Lutz
Pawan Madhogarhia

Timothy Manuel
David G. Martin
Dubos J. Masson
John McDougald
Bob McElreath
Gordon Melms
Richard R. Mendenhall
Wayne Mikkelson
Lalatendu Misra
Karlyn Mitchell
Sunil Mohanty
Scott Moore
Frederick H. Mull
Michael J. Murray
Randy Nelson
Bulent Parker
Megan Partch
Samuel Penkar
Pamela P. Peterson
Robert Phillips
George A. Racette
Charu G. Raheja
Narendar V. Rao
Russ Ray
Ron Reiber
Thomas Rietz
Jay R. Ritter
Ricardo J. Rodriguez
Kenneth Roskelley
Gary Sanger
Travis Sapp

Martha A. Schary

Robert Schwebach

Roger Severns

Dilip K. Shome

Neil W. Sicherman

Timothy Smaby

Michael F. Spivey

Vic Stanton

Charlene Sullivan

George S. Swales, Jr.

Philip Swensen

Philip Swicegood

John G. Thatcher

Harry Thiewes

A. Frank Thompson

Joseph Trefzger

Michael R. Vetsuypens

Joe Walker

Jun Wang

James Washam

Alan Weatherford

Marsha Weber

Jill Wetmore

Mark White

Annie Wong

David J. Wright

Steve B. Wyatt

Tung-Hsiao Yang

Morris Yarmish

Michael Young

Mei Zhang

J. Kenton Zumwalt

Tom Zwirlein

Reviews from the following instructors helped us to shape our development plan for the ninth edition of *Fundamentals of Corporate Finance*.

Mike Anderson
University of Massachusetts, Dartmouth

Vigdis Boasson
Central Michigan University

Jim Boyd
Louisiana State University

Lawrence Byerly
Thomas More College

Steve Byers
Idaho State University

Steve Caples
McNeese State University

Asim Celik
University of Nevada, Reno

Christina Cella
Indiana University, Bloomington

Karen Hallows
George Mason University

Dina Layish
Binghamton University

Chun Lee
Loyola Marymount University

Scott Lowe
James Madison University

Bahlous Mejda
University of Alabama-Huntsville

Belinda Mucklow
University of Wisconsin, Madison

Barry Mulholland
University of Wisconsin, Oshkosh

Odom Oris
University of Texas, Tyler

Keith Osher
Boston University

Greg Pierce
Penn State University

Robert Puelz
Southern Methodist University

Stu Rosenstein
East Carolina University

Ivan Roten
Appalachian State University

Michael Sher
Metropolitan State University

Ahmad Sohrabian
California State Polytechnic University

Charlene Sullivan
Purdue University

Lee Swartz
University of Southern California

Brian Tarrant
Central Michigan University

Rhonda Tenkku
University of Missouri

George Turk
Florida State University

Elike Uchenna
Alabama A&M University

Gwendolyn Webb
Bernard M. Baruch College

Colbrin Wright
Central Michigan University

Several of our most respected colleagues contributed original essays for this edition, which are entitled "In Their Own Words," and appear in selected chapters. To these individuals we extend a special thanks:

Edward I. Altman
New York University

Fischer Black

Robert C. Higgins
University of Washington

Roger Ibbotson
Yale University, Ibbotson Associates

Erik Lie
University of Iowa

Robert C. Merton
Harvard University

Merton H. Miller

Jay R. Ritter
University of Florida

Richard Roll
*University of
California
at Los Angeles*

Jeremy Siegel
University of Pennsylvania

Hersh Shefrin
Santa Clara University

Bennett Stewart
Stern Stewart & Co.

Samuel C. Weaver
Lehigh University

We are lucky to have had skilled and experienced instructors developing the supplement material for this edition. Thank you to Steve Dolvin, Butler University, for his work thoroughly revising and updating the Instructor's Manual and the PowerPoint Presentations and for organizing and distributing the wealth of annotated instructor notes from the book into these teaching materials. We greatly appreciate the contributions of Joe Smolira, Belmont University, who worked closely with us to develop the Solutions Manual and to create Excel Templates for many of the end of chapter problems. Thank you also to Kay Johnson, Penn State University, Erie, for her thorough updating, revising, and tagging of every problem in the test bank. Thanks to Kent Ragan, Missouri State University, for expertly developing and extending the Student Narrated PowerPoint slides for the ninth edition. We owe a special thank you to Thomas Eyssell of the University of Missouri for his exceptional work on the Student Problem Manual.

The following University of Kentucky students did outstanding work on this edition of *Fundamentals:* Laura Coogan, Tony Cox, and Steve Hailey. To them fell the unenviable task of technical proofreading, and in particular, careful checking of each calculation throughout the text and Instructor's Manual.

Finally, in every phase of this project, we have been privileged to have had the complete and unwavering support of a great organization, McGraw-Hill/Irwin. We especially thank the McGraw-Hill/Irwin sales group. The suggestions they provide, their professionalism in assisting potential adopters, and the service they provide to current users have been a major factor in our success.

We are deeply grateful to the select group of professionals who served as our development team on this edition: Michele Janicek, Executive Editor; Elizabeth Hughes, Development Editor; Ashley Smith, Marketing Manager; Christine Vaughan, Lead Project Manager; Pam Verros, Designer; and Brian Nacik, Media Producer. Others at McGraw-Hill/Irwin, too numerous to list here, have improved the book in countless ways.

Throughout the development of this edition, we have taken great care to discover and eliminate errors. Our goal is to provide the best textbook available on the subject. To ensure that future editions are error-free, we gladly offer $10 per arithmetic error to the first individual reporting it as a modest token of our appreciation. More than this, we would like to hear from instructors and students alike. Please write and tell us how to make this a better text. Forward your comments to: Dr. Brad Jordan, c/o Editorial—Finance, McGraw-Hill/Irwin, 1333 Burr Ridge Parkway, Burr Ridge, IL 60527 or visit us online at www.mhhe.com/rwj.

Stephen A. Ross
Randolph W. Westerfield
Bradford D. Jordan

Brief Contents

Contents

PART 3   Valuation of Future Cash Flows

CHAPTER 5

INTRODUCTION TO VALUATION: THE TIME VALUE
OF MONEY   *119*

PART 4 Capital Budgeting

PART 5   Risk and Return

In Their Own Words Boxes

LEARNING OBJECTIVES

After studying this chapter, you should understand:

LO1 The basic types of financial management decisions and the role of the financial manager.
LO2 The goal of financial management.
LO3 The financial implications of the different forms of business organization.
LO4 The conflicts of interest that can arise between managers and owners.

INTRODUCTION TO CORPORATE FINANCE

1

COMPENSATION OF CORPORATE EXECUTIVES in the United States continues to be a hot button issue. It is widely viewed that CEO pay has grown to exorbitant levels (at least in some cases). In response, in April 2007, the U.S. House of Representatives passed the "Say on Pay" bill. The bill requires corporations to allow a nonbinding shareholder vote on executive pay. (Note that because the bill applies to corporations, it does not give voters a "say on pay" for U.S. Representatives.)

Specifically, the measure allows shareholders to approve or disapprove a company's executive compensation plans. Because the bill is nonbinding,

it does not permit shareholders to veto a compensation package and does not place limits on executive pay. Some companies had actually already begun initiatives to allow shareholders a say on pay before Congress got involved. On May 5, 2008, Aflac, the insurance company with the well-known "spokesduck," held the first shareholder vote on executive pay in the U.S.

Understanding how a corporation sets executive pay, and the role of shareholders in that process, takes us into issues involving the corporate form of organization, corporate goals, and corporate control, all of which we cover in this chapter.

Master the ability to solve problems in this chapter by using a spreadsheet. Access Excel Master on the student Web site www.mhhe.com/rwj.

To begin our study of modern corporate finance and financial management, we need to address two central issues. First, what is corporate finance and what is the role of the financial manager in the corporation? Second, what is the goal of financial management? To describe the financial management environment, we consider the corporate form of organization and discuss some conflicts that can arise within the corporation. We also take a brief look at financial markets in the United States.

1.1 Corporate Finance and the Financial Manager

In this section, we discuss where the financial manager fits in the corporation. We start by defining *corporate finance* and the financial manager's job.

WHAT IS CORPORATE FINANCE?

Imagine that you were to start your own business. No matter what type you started, you would have to answer the following three questions in some form or another:

1. What long-term investments should you take on? That is, what lines of business will you be in and what sorts of buildings, machinery, and equipment will you need?
2. Where will you get the long-term financing to pay for your investment? Will you bring in other owners or will you borrow the money?
3. How will you manage your everyday financial activities such as collecting from customers and paying suppliers?

These are not the only questions by any means, but they are among the most important. Corporate finance, broadly speaking, is the study of ways to answer these three questions. Accordingly, we'll be looking at each of them in the chapters ahead.

THE FINANCIAL MANAGER

Check out the companion Web site for this text at www.mhhe.com/rwj.

A striking feature of large corporations is that the owners (the stockholders) are usually not directly involved in making business decisions, particularly on a day-to-day basis. Instead, the corporation employs managers to represent the owners' interests and make decisions on their behalf. In a large corporation, the financial manager would be in charge of answering the three questions we raised in the preceding section.

For current issues facing CFOs, see www.cfo.com.

The financial management function is usually associated with a top officer of the firm, such as a vice president of finance or some other chief financial officer (CFO). Figure 1.1 is a simplified organizational chart that highlights the finance activity in a large firm. As shown, the vice president of finance coordinates the activities of the treasurer and the controller. The controller's office handles cost and financial accounting, tax payments, and management information systems. The treasurer's office is responsible for managing the firm's cash and credit, its financial planning, and its capital expenditures. These treasury activities are all related to the three general questions raised earlier, and the chapters ahead deal primarily with these issues. Our study thus bears mostly on activities usually associated with the treasurer's office.

FINANCIAL MANAGEMENT DECISIONS

As the preceding discussion suggests, the financial manager must be concerned with three basic types of questions. We consider these in greater detail next.

Capital Budgeting   The first question concerns the firm's long-term investments. The process of planning and managing a firm's long-term investments is called **capital budgeting**. In capital budgeting, the financial manager tries to identify investment opportunities that are worth more to the firm than they cost to acquire. Loosely speaking, this means that the value of the cash flow generated by an asset exceeds the cost of that asset.

The types of investment opportunities that would typically be considered depend in part on the nature of the firm's business. For example, for a large retailer such as Wal-Mart, deciding whether to open another store would be an important capital budgeting decision.

capital budgeting
The process of planning and managing a firm's long-term investments.

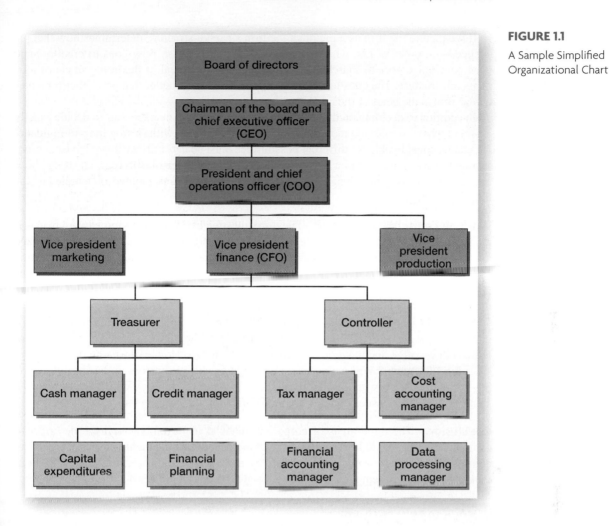

FIGURE 1.1

A Sample Simplified
Organizational Chart

Similarly, for a software company such as Oracle or Microsoft, the decision to develop and market a new spreadsheet program would be a major capital budgeting decision. Some decisions, such as what type of computer system to purchase, might not depend so much on a particular line of business.

Regardless of the specific nature of an opportunity under consideration, financial managers must be concerned not only with how much cash they expect to receive, but also with when they expect to receive it and how likely they are to receive it. Evaluating the *size, timing,* and *risk* of future cash flows is the essence of capital budgeting. In fact, as we will see in the chapters ahead, whenever we evaluate a business decision, the size, timing, and risk of the cash flows will be by far the most important things we will consider.

Capital Structure The second question for the financial manager concerns ways in which the firm obtains and manages the long-term financing it needs to support its long-term investments. A firm's **capital structure** (or financial structure) is the specific mixture of long-term debt and equity the firm uses to finance its operations. The financial manager has two concerns in this area. First, how much should the firm borrow? That is, what mixture of debt and equity is best? The mixture chosen will affect both the risk and the value of the firm. Second, what are the least expensive sources of funds for the firm?

capital structure
The mixture of debt and equity maintained by a firm.

If we picture the firm as a pie, then the firm's capital structure determines how that pie is sliced—in other words, what percentage of the firm's cash flow goes to creditors and what percentage goes to shareholders. Firms have a great deal of flexibility in choosing a financial structure. The question of whether one structure is better than any other for a particular firm is the heart of the capital structure issue.

In addition to deciding on the financing mix, the financial manager has to decide exactly how and where to raise the money. The expenses associated with raising long-term financing can be considerable, so different possibilities must be carefully evaluated. Also, corporations borrow money from a variety of lenders in a number of different, and sometimes exotic, ways. Choosing among lenders and among loan types is another job handled by the financial manager.

working capital
A firm's short-term assets and liabilities.

Working Capital Management   The third question concerns **working capital** management. The term *working capital* refers to a firm's short-term assets, such as inventory, and its short-term liabilities, such as money owed to suppliers. Managing the firm's working capital is a day-to-day activity that ensures that the firm has sufficient resources to continue its operations and avoid costly interruptions. This involves a number of activities related to the firm's receipt and disbursement of cash.

Some questions about working capital that must be answered are the following: (1) How much cash and inventory should we keep on hand? (2) Should we sell on credit? If so, what terms will we offer, and to whom will we extend them? (3) How will we obtain any needed short-term financing? Will we purchase on credit or will we borrow in the short term and pay cash? If we borrow in the short term, how and where should we do it? These are just a small sample of the issues that arise in managing a firm's working capital.

Conclusion   The three areas of corporate financial management we have described—capital budgeting, capital structure, and working capital management—are very broad categories. Each includes a rich variety of topics, and we have indicated only a few questions that arise in the different areas. The chapters ahead contain greater detail.

Concept Questions

1.1a What is the capital budgeting decision?

1.1b What do you call the specific mixture of long-term debt and equity that a firm chooses to use?

1.1c Into what category of financial management does cash management fall?

1.2 Forms of Business Organization

Large firms in the United States, such as Ford and Microsoft, are almost all organized as corporations. We examine the three different legal forms of business organization—sole proprietorship, partnership, and corporation—to see why this is so. Each form has distinct advantages and disadvantages for the life of the business, the ability of the business to raise cash, and taxes. A key observation is that as a firm grows, the advantages of the corporate form may come to outweigh the disadvantages.

SOLE PROPRIETORSHIP

sole proprietorship
A business owned by a single individual.

A **sole proprietorship** is a business owned by one person. This is the simplest type of business to start and is the least regulated form of organization. Depending on where you live, you might be able to start a proprietorship by doing little more than getting a business license and opening your doors. For this reason, there are more proprietorships than any other type of business, and many businesses that later become large corporations start out as small proprietorships.

The owner of a sole proprietorship keeps all the profits. That's the good news. The bad news is that the owner has *unlimited liability* for business debts. This means that creditors can look beyond business assets to the proprietor's personal assets for payment. Similarly, there is no distinction between personal and business income, so all business income is taxed as personal income.

The life of a sole proprietorship is limited to the owner's life span, and the amount of equity that can be raised is limited to the amount of the proprietor's personal wealth. This limitation often means that the business is unable to exploit new opportunities because of insufficient capital. Ownership of a sole proprietorship may be difficult to transfer because this transfer requires the sale of the entire business to a new owner.

For more information about forms of business organization, see the "Small Business" section at www.nolo.com.

PARTNERSHIP

A **partnership** is similar to a proprietorship except that there are two or more owners (partners). In a *general partnership,* all the partners share in gains or losses, and all have unlimited liability for *all* partnership debts, not just some particular share. The way partnership gains (and losses) are divided is described in the *partnership agreement.* This agreement can be an informal oral agreement, such as "let's start a lawn mowing business," or a lengthy, formal written document.

partnership
A business formed by two or more individuals or entities.

In a *limited partnership,* one or more *general partners* will run the business and have unlimited liability, but there will be one or more *limited partners* who will not actively participate in the business. A limited partner's liability for business debts is limited to the amount that partner contributes to the partnership. This form of organization is common in real estate ventures, for example.

The advantages and disadvantages of a partnership are basically the same as those of a proprietorship. Partnerships based on a relatively informal agreement are easy and inexpensive to form. General partners have unlimited liability for partnership debts, and the partnership terminates when a general partner wishes to sell out or dies. All income is taxed as personal income to the partners, and the amount of equity that can be raised is limited to the partners' combined wealth. Ownership of a general partnership is not easily transferred because a transfer requires that a new partnership be formed. A limited partner's interest can be sold without dissolving the partnership, but finding a buyer may be difficult.

Because a partner in a general partnership can be held responsible for all partnership debts, having a written agreement is very important. Failure to spell out the rights and duties of the partners frequently leads to misunderstandings later on. Also, if you are a limited partner, you must not become deeply involved in business decisions unless you are willing to assume the obligations of a general partner. The reason is that if things go badly, you may be deemed to be a general partner even though you say you are a limited partner.

Based on our discussion, the primary disadvantages of sole proprietorships and partnerships as forms of business organization are (1) unlimited liability for business debts on the part of the owners, (2) limited life of the business, and (3) difficulty of transferring ownership. These three disadvantages add up to a single, central problem: the ability of such businesses to grow can be seriously limited by an inability to raise cash for investment.

CORPORATION

The **corporation** is the most important form (in terms of size) of business organization in the United States. A corporation is a legal "person" separate and distinct from its owners,

corporation
A business created as a distinct legal entity composed of one or more individuals or entities.

and it has many of the rights, duties, and privileges of an actual person. Corporations can borrow money and own property, can sue and be sued, and can enter into contracts. A corporation can even be a general partner or a limited partner in a partnership, and a corporation can own stock in another corporation.

Not surprisingly, starting a corporation is somewhat more complicated than starting the other forms of business organization. Forming a corporation involves preparing *articles of incorporation* (or a charter) and a set of *bylaws*. The articles of incorporation must contain a number of things, including the corporation's name, its intended life (which can be forever), its business purpose, and the number of shares that can be issued. This information must normally be supplied to the state in which the firm will be incorporated. For most legal purposes, the corporation is a "resident" of that state.

The bylaws are rules describing how the corporation regulates its existence. For example, the bylaws describe how directors are elected. These bylaws may be a simple statement of a few rules and procedures, or they may be quite extensive for a large corporation. The bylaws may be amended or extended from time to time by the stockholders.

In a large corporation, the stockholders and the managers are usually separate groups. The stockholders elect the board of directors, who then select the managers. Managers are charged with running the corporation's affairs in the stockholders' interests. In principle, stockholders control the corporation because they elect the directors.

As a result of the separation of ownership and management, the corporate form has several advantages. Ownership (represented by shares of stock) can be readily transferred, and the life of the corporation is therefore not limited. The corporation borrows money in its own name. As a result, the stockholders in a corporation have limited liability for corporate debts. The most they can lose is what they have invested.

The relative ease of transferring ownership, the limited liability for business debts, and the unlimited life of the business are why the corporate form is superior for raising cash. If a corporation needs new equity, for example, it can sell new shares of stock and attract new investors. Apple is an example. Apple was a pioneer in the personal computer business. As demand for its products exploded, Apple had to convert to the corporate form of organization to raise the capital needed to fund growth and new product development. The number of owners can be huge; larger corporations have many thousands or even millions of stockholders. For example, in 2008, General Electric Corporation (better known as GE) had about 4 million stockholders and about 10 billion shares outstanding. In such cases, ownership can change continuously without affecting the continuity of the business.

The corporate form has a significant disadvantage. Because a corporation is a legal person, it must pay taxes. Moreover, money paid out to stockholders in the form of dividends is taxed again as income to those stockholders. This is *double taxation,* meaning that corporate profits are taxed twice: at the corporate level when they are earned and again at the personal level when they are paid out.[1]

Today, all 50 states have enacted laws allowing for the creation of a relatively new form of business organization, the limited liability company (LLC). The goal of this entity is to operate and be taxed like a partnership but retain limited liability for owners, so an LLC is essentially a hybrid of partnership and corporation. Although states have differing definitions for LLCs, the more important scorekeeper is the Internal Revenue Service (IRS). The IRS will consider an LLC a corporation, thereby subjecting it to double taxation, unless it meets certain specific criteria. In essence, an LLC cannot be too corporationlike, or it will be treated as one by the IRS. LLCs have become common. For example, Goldman, Sachs and Co., one of Wall Street's last remaining partnerships, decided to convert from a private

How hard is it to form an LLC? Visit www.llc.com *to find out.*

---

[1]An S corporation is a special type of small corporation that is essentially taxed like a partnership and thus avoids double taxation. In 2008, the maximum number of shareholders in an S corporation was 100.

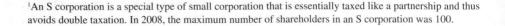

TABLE 1.1   International Corporations

Company	Country of Origin	Type of Company	
		In Original Language	Translated
Bayerische Motorenwerke (BMW) AG	Germany	Aktiengesellschaft	Corporation
Dornier GmBH	Germany	Gesellschaft mit Beschraenkter Haftung	Limited liability company
Rolls-Royce PLC	United Kingdom	Public limited company	Public limited company
Shell UK Ltd.	United Kingdom	Limited	Corporation
Unilever NV	Netherlands	Naamloze Vennootschap	Joint stock company
Fiat SpA	Italy	Societa per Azioni	Joint stock company
Volvo AB	Sweden	Aktiebolag	Joint stock company
Peugeot SA	France	Société Anonyme	Joint stock company

partnership to an LLC (It later "went public," becoming a publicly held corporation). Large accounting firms and law firms by the score have converted to LLCs.

As the discussion in this section illustrates, the need of large businesses for outside investors and creditors is such that the corporate form will generally be the best for such firms. We focus on corporations in the chapters ahead because of the importance of the corporate form in the U.S. and world economies. Also, a few important financial management issues, such as dividend policy, are unique to corporations. However, businesses of all types and sizes need financial management, so the majority of the subjects we discuss bear on any form of business.

A CORPORATION BY ANOTHER NAME . . .

The corporate form of organization has many variations around the world. The exact laws and regulations differ from country to country, of course, but the essential features of public ownership and limited liability remain. These firms are often called *joint stock companies, public limited companies,* or *limited liability companies,* depending on the specific nature of the firm and the country of origin.

Table 1.1 gives the names of a few well-known international corporations, their countries of origin, and a translation of the abbreviation that follows the company name.

Concept Questions

1.2a What are the three forms of business organization?
1.2b What are the primary advantages and disadvantages of sole proprietorships and partnerships?
1.2c What is the difference between a general and a limited partnership?
1.2d Why is the corporate form superior when it comes to raising cash?

The Goal of Financial Management   1.3

Assuming that we restrict ourselves to for-profit businesses, the goal of financial management is to make money or add value for the owners. This goal is a little vague, of course, so we examine some different ways of formulating it to come up with a more precise definition. Such a definition is important because it leads to an objective basis for making and evaluating financial decisions.

POSSIBLE GOALS

If we were to consider possible financial goals, we might come up with some ideas like the following:

Survive.

Avoid financial distress and bankruptcy.

Beat the competition.

Maximize sales or market share.

Minimize costs.

Maximize profits.

Maintain steady earnings growth.

These are only a few of the goals we could list. Furthermore, each of these possibilities presents problems as a goal for the financial manager.

For example, it's easy to increase market share or unit sales: All we have to do is lower our prices or relax our credit terms. Similarly, we can always cut costs simply by doing away with things such as research and development. We can avoid bankruptcy by never borrowing any money or never taking any risks, and so on. It's not clear that any of these actions are in the stockholders' best interests.

Profit maximization would probably be the most commonly cited goal, but even this is not a precise objective. Do we mean profits this year? If so, we should note that actions such as deferring maintenance, letting inventories run down, and taking other short-run cost-cutting measures will tend to increase profits now, but these activities aren't necessarily desirable.

The goal of maximizing profits may refer to some sort of "long-run" or "average" profits, but it's still unclear exactly what this means. First, do we mean something like accounting net income or earnings per share? As we will see in more detail in the next chapter, these accounting numbers may have little to do with what is good or bad for the firm. Second, what do we mean by the long run? As a famous economist once remarked, in the long run, we're all dead! More to the point, this goal doesn't tell us what the appropriate trade-off is between current and future profits.

The goals we've listed here are all different, but they tend to fall into two classes. The first of these relates to profitability. The goals involving sales, market share, and cost control all relate, at least potentially, to different ways of earning or increasing profits. The goals in the second group, involving bankruptcy avoidance, stability, and safety, relate in some way to controlling risk. Unfortunately, these two types of goals are somewhat contradictory. The pursuit of profit normally involves some element of risk, so it isn't really possible to maximize both safety and profit. What we need, therefore, is a goal that encompasses both factors.

THE GOAL OF FINANCIAL MANAGEMENT

The financial manager in a corporation makes decisions for the stockholders of the firm. Given this, instead of listing possible goals for the financial manager, we really need to answer a more fundamental question: From the stockholders' point of view, what is a good financial management decision?

If we assume that stockholders buy stock because they seek to gain financially, then the answer is obvious: Good decisions increase the value of the stock, and poor decisions decrease the value of the stock.

Given our observations, it follows that the financial manager acts in the shareholders' best interests by making decisions that increase the value of the stock. The appropriate goal for the financial manager can thus be stated quite easily:

> **The goal of financial management is to maximize the current value per share of the existing stock.**

The goal of maximizing the value of the stock avoids the problems associated with the different goals we listed earlier. There is no ambiguity in the criterion, and there is no short-run versus long-run issue. We explicitly mean that our goal is to maximize the *current* stock value.

If this goal seems a little strong or one-dimensional to you, keep in mind that the stockholders in a firm are residual owners. By this we mean that they are entitled to only what is left after employees, suppliers, and creditors (and anyone else with a legitimate claim) are paid their due. If any of these groups go unpaid, the stockholders get nothing. So, if the stockholders are winning in the sense that the leftover, residual portion is growing, it must be true that everyone else is winning also.

Because the goal of financial management is to maximize the value of the stock, we need to learn how to identify investments and financing arrangements that favorably impact the value of the stock. This is precisely what we will be studying. In fact, we could have defined *corporate finance* as the study of the relationship between business decisions and the value of the stock in the business.

A MORE GENERAL GOAL

Given our goal as stated in the preceding section (maximize the value of the stock), an obvious question comes up: What is the appropriate goal when the firm has no traded stock? Corporations are certainly not the only type of business; and the stock in many corporations rarely changes hands, so it's difficult to say what the value per share is at any given time.

As long as we are dealing with for-profit businesses, only a slight modification is needed. The total value of the stock in a corporation is simply equal to the value of the owners' equity. Therefore, a more general way of stating our goal is as follows: Maximize the market value of the existing owners' equity.

With this in mind, it doesn't matter whether the business is a proprietorship, a partnership, or a corporation. For each of these, good financial decisions increase the market value of the owners' equity and poor financial decisions decrease it. In fact, although we focus on corporations in the chapters ahead, the principles we develop apply to all forms of business. Many of them even apply to the not-for-profit sector.

Finally, our goal does not imply that the financial manager should take illegal or unethical actions in the hope of increasing the value of the equity in the firm. What we mean is that the financial manager best serves the owners of the business by identifying goods and services that add value to the firm because they are desired and valued in the free marketplace.

SARBANES–OXLEY

In response to corporate scandals at companies such as Enron, WorldCom, Tyco, and Adelphia, Congress enacted the Sarbanes–Oxley Act in 2002. The act, better known as "Sarbox," is intended to protect investors from corporate abuses. For example, one section of Sarbox prohibits personal loans from a company to its officers, such as the ones that were received by WorldCom CEO Bernie Ebbers.

One of the key sections of Sarbox took effect on November 15, 2004. Section 404 requires, among other things, that each company's annual report must have an assessment of the company's internal control structure and financial reporting. The auditor must then evaluate and attest to management's assessment of these issues.

Sarbox contains other key requirements. For example, the officers of the corporation must review and sign the annual reports. They must explicitly declare that the annual report does not contain any false statements or material omissions; that the financial statements fairly represent the financial results; and that they are responsible for all internal controls. Finally, the annual report must list any deficiencies in internal controls. In essence, Sarbox makes company management responsible for the accuracy of the company's financial statements.

Because of its extensive reporting requirements, compliance with Sarbox can be very costly, which has led to some unintended results. Since its implementation, hundreds of public firms have chosen to "go dark," meaning that their shares are no longer traded on the major stock exchanges, in which case Sarbox does not apply. Most of these companies stated that their reason was to avoid the cost of compliance. Ironically, in such cases, the law had the effect of eliminating public disclosure instead of improving it.

Sarbox has also probably affected the number of companies choosing to go public in the United States. Instead, many U.S.-based companies have chosen to go public on the London Stock Exchange's Alternative Investment Market (AIM). The cost savings can be enormous, especially for small companies. For example, Pronotex Technologies, a fuel cell developer based in Southborough, Massachusetts, estimated that it costs about $1 million per year in compliance costs and mailings to stockholders to be listed on the AIM. In contrast, the annual cost to be listed on the NASDAQ would be about $3 million, with a large part of the increase due to Sarbox compliance costs.

For more about Sarbanes–Oxley, visit www.sarbanes-oxley.com.

Concept Questions

1.3a What is the goal of financial management?

1.3b What are some shortcomings of the goal of profit maximization?

1.3c Can you give a definition of *corporate finance?*

1.4 The Agency Problem and Control of the Corporation

We've seen that the financial manager acts in the best interests of the stockholders by taking actions that increase the value of the stock. However, we've also seen that in large corporations ownership can be spread over a huge number of stockholders. This dispersion of ownership arguably means that management effectively controls the firm. In this case, will management necessarily act in the best interests of the stockholders? Put another way, might not management pursue its own goals at the stockholders' expense? In the following pages, we briefly consider some of the arguments relating to this question.

AGENCY RELATIONSHIPS

The relationship between stockholders and management is called an *agency relationship*. Such a relationship exists whenever someone (the principal) hires another (the agent) to represent his or her interests. For example, you might hire someone (an agent) to sell a car you own while you are away at school. In all such relationships, there is a possibility of conflict of interest between the principal and the agent. Such a conflict is called an **agency problem**.

agency problem
The possibility of conflict of interest between the stockholders and management of a firm.

Suppose you hire someone to sell your car and agree to pay that person a flat fee when he or she sells the car. The agent's incentive in this case is to make the sale, not necessarily to get you the best price. If you offer a commission of, say, 10 percent of the sales price instead of a flat fee, then this problem might not exist. This example illustrates that the way in which an agent is compensated is one factor that affects agency problems.

MANAGEMENT GOALS

To see how management and stockholder interests might differ, imagine that the firm is considering a new investment. The new investment is expected to favorably impact the share value, but it is also a relatively risky venture. The owners of the firm will wish to take the investment (because the stock value will rise), but management may not because there is the possibility that things will turn out badly and management jobs will be lost. If management does not take the investment, then the stockholders may lose a valuable opportunity. This is one example of an agency cost.

More generally, the term *agency costs* refers to the costs of the conflict of interest between stockholders and management. These costs can be indirect or direct. An indirect agency cost is a lost opportunity, such as the one we have just described.

Direct agency costs come in two forms. The first type is a corporate expenditure that benefits management but costs the stockholders. Perhaps the purchase of a luxurious and unneeded corporate jet would fall under this heading. The second type of direct agency cost is an expense that arises from the need to monitor management actions. Paying outside auditors to assess the accuracy of financial statement information could be one example.

It is sometimes argued that, left to themselves, managers would tend to maximize the amount of resources over which they have control or, more generally, corporate power or wealth. This goal could lead to an overemphasis on corporate size or growth. For example, cases in which management is accused of overpaying to buy up another company just to increase the size of the business or to demonstrate corporate power are not uncommon. Obviously, if overpayment does take place, such a purchase does not benefit the stockholders of the purchasing company.

Our discussion indicates that management may tend to overemphasize organizational survival to protect job security. Also, management may dislike outside interference, so independence and corporate self-sufficiency may be important goals.

DO MANAGERS ACT IN THE STOCKHOLDERS' INTERESTS?

Whether managers will, in fact, act in the best interests of stockholders depends on two factors. First, how closely are management goals aligned with stockholder goals? This question relates, at least in part, to the way managers are compensated. Second, can managers be replaced if they do not pursue stockholder goals? This issue relates to control of the firm. As we will discuss, there are a number of reasons to think that even in the largest firms, management has a significant incentive to act in the interests of stockholders.

Managerial Compensation Management will frequently have a significant economic incentive to increase share value for two reasons. First, managerial compensation, particularly at the top, is usually tied to financial performance in general and often to share value in particular. For example, managers are frequently given the option to buy stock at a bargain price. The more the stock is worth, the more valuable is this option. In fact, options are often used to motivate employees of all types, not just top managers. For example, in 2007, Google announced that it was issuing new stock options to all of its 16,000 employees, thereby giving its workforce a significant stake in its stock price and better aligning employee and shareholder interests. Many other corporations, large and small, have adopted similar policies.

The second incentive managers have relates to job prospects. Better performers within the firm will tend to get promoted. More generally, managers who are successful in pursuing stockholder goals will be in greater demand in the labor market and thus command higher salaries.

In fact, managers who are successful in pursuing stockholder goals can reap enormous rewards. For example, the best-paid executive in 2007 was Lawrence Ellison, the CEO of Oracle. According to *Forbes* magazine, he made about $193 million. By way of comparison, Ellison made less than J.K. Rowling ($300 million) and Oprah Winfrey ($275 million), and

Business ethics are considered at www.business-ethics.com.

way more than Tiger Woods ($115 million). Over the period 2003–2007, Apple CEO Steve Jobs was the highest-paid executive, earning about $661 million. Information about executive compensation, along with lots of other information, can be easily found on the Web for almost any public company. Our nearby *Work the Web* box shows you how to get started.

Control of the Firm   Control of the firm ultimately rests with stockholders. They elect the board of directors, who in turn hire and fire managers. The fact that stockholders control the corporation was made abundantly clear by Steven Jobs's experience at Apple. Even though he was a founder of the corporation and was largely responsible for its most successful products, there came a time when shareholders, through their elected directors, decided that Apple would be better off without him, so out he went. Of course, he was later rehired and helped turn Apple around with great new products such as the iPod and iPhone.

An important mechanism by which unhappy stockholders can act to replace existing management is called a *proxy fight.* A proxy is the authority to vote someone else's stock. A proxy fight develops when a group solicits proxies in order to replace the existing board and thereby replace existing managers. For example, in early 2002, the proposed merger between Hewlett-Packard (HP) and Compaq triggered one of the most widely followed, bitterly contested, and expensive proxy fights in history, with an estimated price tag of well over $100 million. One group of shareholders, which included Walter B. Hewlett (a board member and heir to a cofounder of HP), opposed the merger and launched a proxy fight for control of HP. Another group, led by HP CEO Carly Fiorina, supported the merger. In a very close vote, Ms. Fiorina prevailed, the merger went through, and Mr. Hewlett resigned from the board.

Another way that managers can be replaced is by takeover. Firms that are poorly managed are more attractive as acquisitions than well-managed firms because a greater profit potential exists. Thus, avoiding a takeover by another firm gives management another incentive to act in the stockholders' interests. For example, in the spring of 2008, Web portal Yahoo! was battling a $42 billion unsolicited takeover bid from software giant Microsoft. Yahoo!'s management argued that the bid significantly undervalued the company, even though it was 62 percent higher than the then current stock price. In an effort to thwart Microsoft's takeover attempt, Yahoo! entered into an advertising agreement with Internet search engine rival Google, and it began discussions with other companies such as AOL about a possible merger.

Conclusion   The available theory and evidence are consistent with the view that stockholders control the firm and that stockholder wealth maximization is the relevant goal of the corporation. Even so, there will undoubtedly be times when management goals are pursued at the expense of the stockholders, at least temporarily.

STAKEHOLDERS

Our discussion thus far implies that management and stockholders are the only parties with an interest in the firm's decisions. This is an oversimplification, of course. Employees, customers, suppliers, and even the government all have a financial interest in the firm.

stakeholder
Someone other than a stockholder or creditor who potentially has a claim on the cash flows of the firm.

Taken together, these various groups are called **stakeholders** in the firm. In general, a stakeholder is someone other than a stockholder or creditor who potentially has a claim on the cash flows of the firm. Such groups will also attempt to exert control over the firm, perhaps to the detriment of the owners.

Concept Questions

1.4a What is an agency relationship?

1.4b What are agency problems and how do they come about? What are agency costs?

1.4c What incentives do managers in large corporations have to maximize share value?

WORK THE WEB

The Web is a great place to learn more about individual companies, and there are a slew of sites available to help you. Try pointing your Web browser to finance.yahoo.com. Once you get there, you should see something like this on the page:

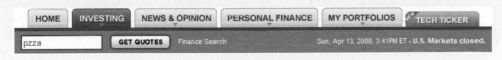

To look up a company, you must know its "ticker symbol" (or just ticker for short), which is a unique one- to four-letter identifier. You can click on the "Symbol Lookup" link and type in the company's name to find the ticker. For example, we typed in "PZZA," which is the ticker for pizza maker Papa John's. Here is a portion of what we got:

PAPA JOHN'S INTL (NasdaqGS: PZZA)
After Hours: 24.76 ↑ .31 (1.25%) on 04/11/08

Last Trade:	**24.45**	Day's Range:	24.44 - 25.43
Trade Time:	**Apr 11**	52wk Range:	20.57 - 34.86
Change:	↓ .80 (3.17%)	Volume:	162,132
Prev Close:	25.25	Avg Vol (3m):	374,356
Open:	24.98	Market Cap:	705.31M
Bid:	22.15 x 1000	P/E (ttm):	22.41
Ask:	N/A	EPS (ttm):	1.09
1y Target Est:	33.00	Div & Yield:	N/A (N/A)

There's a lot of information here and many links for you to explore, so have at it. By the end of the term, we hope it all makes sense to you!

Questions

1. Go to finance.yahoo.com and find the current stock prices for Southwest Airlines (LUV), Harley-Davidson (HOG), and Starwood Hotels & Resorts (HOT).
2. Get a quote for American Express (AXP) and follow the "Key Statistics" link. What information is available on this link? What do mrq, ttm, yoy, and lfy mean?

Financial Markets and the Corporation   1.5

We've seen that the primary advantages of the corporate form of organization are that ownership can be transferred more quickly and easily than with other forms and that money can be raised more readily. Both of these advantages are significantly enhanced by the existence of financial markets, and financial markets play an extremely important role in corporate finance.

CASH FLOWS TO AND FROM THE FIRM

The interplay between the corporation and the financial markets is illustrated in Figure 1.2. The arrows in Figure 1.2 trace the passage of cash from the financial markets to the firm and from the firm back to the financial markets.

Suppose we start with the firm selling shares of stock and borrowing money to raise cash. Cash flows to the firm from the financial markets (A). The firm invests the cash in current and fixed assets (B). These assets generate cash (C), some of which goes to pay corporate taxes (D). After taxes are paid, some of this cash flow is reinvested in the firm (E). The rest goes back to the financial markets as cash paid to creditors and shareholders (F).

A financial market, like any market, is just a way of bringing buyers and sellers together. In financial markets, it is debt and equity securities that are bought and sold. Financial markets differ in detail, however. The most important differences concern the types of securities that are traded, how trading is conducted, and who the buyers and sellers are. Some of these differences are discussed next.

PRIMARY VERSUS SECONDARY MARKETS

Financial markets function as both primary and secondary markets for debt and equity securities. The term *primary market* refers to the original sale of securities by governments and corporations. The *secondary markets* are those in which these securities are bought and sold after the original sale. Equities are, of course, issued solely by corporations. Debt securities are issued by both governments and corporations. In the discussion that follows, we focus on corporate securities only.

Primary Markets   In a primary market transaction, the corporation is the seller, and the transaction raises money for the corporation. Corporations engage in two types of primary

FIGURE 1.2

Cash Flows between the Firm and the Financial Markets

A. Firm issues securities to raise cash.
B. Firm invests in assets.
C. Firm's operations generate cash flow.
D. Cash is paid to government as taxes. Other stakeholders may receive cash.
E. Reinvested cash flows are plowed back into firm.
F. Cash is paid out to investors in the form of interest and dividends.

market transactions: public offerings and private placements. A public offering, as the name suggests, involves selling securities to the general public, whereas a private placement is a negotiated sale involving a specific buyer.

By law, public offerings of debt and equity must be registered with the Securities and Exchange Commission (SEC). Registration requires the firm to disclose a great deal of information before selling any securities. The accounting, legal, and selling costs of public offerings can be considerable.

To learn more about the SEC, visit www.sec.gov.

Partly to avoid the various regulatory requirements and the expense of public offerings, debt and equity are often sold privately to large financial institutions such as life insurance companies or mutual funds. Such private placements do not have to be registered with the SEC and do not require the involvement of underwriters (investment banks that specialize in selling securities to the public).

Secondary Markets   A secondary market transaction involves one owner or creditor selling to another. Therefore, the secondary markets provide the means for transferring ownership of corporate securities. Although a corporation is directly involved only in a primary market transaction (when it sells securities to raise cash), the secondary markets are still critical to large corporations. The reason is that investors are much more willing to purchase securities in a primary market transaction when they know that those securities can later be resold if desired.

Dealer versus Auction Markets   There are two kinds of secondary markets: *auction* markets and *dealer* markets. Generally speaking, dealers buy and sell for themselves, at their own risk. A car dealer, for example, buys and sells automobiles. In contrast, brokers and agents match buyers and sellers, but they do not actually own the commodity that is bought or sold. A real estate agent, for example, does not normally buy and sell houses.

Dealer markets in stocks and long-term debt are called *over-the-counter* (OTC) markets. Most trading in debt securities takes place over the counter. The expression *over the counter* refers to days of old when securities were literally bought and sold at counters in offices around the country. Today, a significant fraction of the market for stocks and almost all of the market for long-term debt have no central location; the many dealers are connected electronically.

Auction markets differ from dealer markets in two ways. First, an auction market or exchange has a physical location (like Wall Street). Second, in a dealer market, most of the buying and selling is done by the dealer. The primary purpose of an auction market, on the other hand, is to match those who wish to sell with those who wish to buy. Dealers play a limited role.

Trading in Corporate Securities   The equity shares of most of the large firms in the United States trade in organized auction markets. The largest such market is the New York Stock Exchange (NYSE), which accounts for more than 85 percent of all the shares traded in auction markets. Other auction exchanges include the American Stock Exchange (AMEX) and regional exchanges such as the Pacific Stock Exchange.

In addition to the stock exchanges, there is a large OTC market for stocks. In 1971, the National Association of Securities Dealers (NASD) made available to dealers and brokers an electronic quotation system called NASDAQ (which originally stood for NASD Automated Quotation system and is pronounced "naz-dak"). There are roughly two times as many companies on NASDAQ as there are on the NYSE, but they tend to be much smaller and trade less actively. There are exceptions, of course. Both Microsoft and Intel trade OTC, for example. Nonetheless, the total value of NASDAQ stocks is much less than the total value of NYSE stocks.

To learn more about the exchanges, visit www.nyse.com and www.nasdaq.com.

Visit us at www.mhhe.com/rwj

There are many large and important financial markets outside the United States, of course, and U.S. corporations are increasingly looking to these markets to raise cash. The Tokyo Stock Exchange and the London Stock Exchange (TSE and LSE, respectively) are two well-known examples. The fact that OTC markets have no physical location means that national borders do not present a great barrier, and there is now a huge international OTC debt market. Because of globalization, financial markets have reached the point where trading in many investments never stops; it just travels around the world.

Listing   Stocks that trade on an organized exchange are said to be *listed* on that exchange. To be listed, firms must meet certain minimum criteria concerning, for example, asset size and number of shareholders. These criteria differ from one exchange to another.

The NYSE has the most stringent requirements of the exchanges in the United States. For example, to be listed on the NYSE, a company is expected to have a market value for its publicly held shares of at least $100 million. There are additional minimums on earnings, assets, and number of shares outstanding.

Concept Questions

1.5a What is a dealer market? How do dealer and auction markets differ?

1.5b What does *OTC* stand for? What is the large OTC market for stocks called?

1.5c What is the largest auction market in the United States?

1.6 Summary and Conclusions

This chapter introduced you to some of the basic ideas in corporate finance:

1. Corporate finance has three main areas of concern:
   a. Capital budgeting: What long-term investments should the firm take?
   b. Capital structure: Where will the firm get the long-term financing to pay for its investments? In other words, what mixture of debt and equity should the firm use to fund operations?
   c. Working capital management: How should the firm manage its everyday financial activities?

2. The goal of financial management in a for-profit business is to make decisions that increase the value of the stock or, more generally, increase the market value of the equity.

3. The corporate form of organization is superior to other forms when it comes to raising money and transferring ownership interests, but it has the significant disadvantage of double taxation.

4. There is the possibility of conflicts between stockholders and management in a large corporation. We called these conflicts *agency problems* and discussed how they might be controlled and reduced.

5. The advantages of the corporate form are enhanced by the existence of financial markets. Financial markets function as both primary and secondary markets for corporate securities and can be organized as either dealer or auction markets.

Of the topics we've discussed thus far, the most important is the goal of financial management: maximizing the value of the stock. Throughout the text, we will be analyzing many different financial decisions, but we will always ask the same question: How does the decision under consideration affect the value of the stock?

CONCEPTS REVIEW AND CRITICAL THINKING QUESTIONS

1. **The Financial Management Decision Process** [LO1] What are the three types of financial management decisions? For each type of decision, give an example of a business transaction that would be relevant.

2. **Sole Proprietorships and Partnerships** [LO3] What are the four primary disadvantages of the sole proprietorship and partnership forms of business organization? What benefits are there to these types of business organization as opposed to the corporate form?

3. **Corporations** [LO3] What is the primary disadvantage of the corporate form of organization? Name at least two advantages of corporate organization.

4. **Sarbanes–Oxley** [LO4] In response to the Sarbanes–Oxley Act, many small firms in the United States have opted to "go dark" and delist their stock. Why might a company choose this route? What are the costs of "going dark"?

5. **Corporate Finance Organization** [LO4] In a large corporation, what are the two distinct groups that report to the chief financial officer? Which group is the focus of corporate finance?

6. **Goal of Financial Management** [LO2] What goal should always motivate the actions of a firm's financial manager?

7. **Agency Problems** [LO4] Who owns a corporation? Describe the process whereby the owners control the firm's management. What is the main reason that an agency relationship exists in the corporate form of organization? In this context, what kinds of problems can arise?

8. **Primary versus Secondary Markets** [LO3] You've probably noticed coverage in the financial press of an initial public offering (IPO) of a company's securities. Is an IPO a primary market transaction or a secondary market transaction?

9. **Auction versus Dealer Markets** [LO3] What does it mean when we say the New York Stock Exchange is an auction market? How are auction markets different from dealer markets? What kind of market is NASDAQ?

10. **Not-for-Profit Firm Goals** [LO2] Suppose you were the financial manager of a not-for-profit business (a not-for-profit hospital, perhaps). What kinds of goals do you think would be appropriate?

11. **Goal of the Firm** [LO2] Evaluate the following statement: Managers should not focus on the current stock value because doing so will lead to an overemphasis on short-term profits at the expense of long-term profits.

12. **Ethics and Firm Goals** [LO2] Can our goal of maximizing the value of the stock conflict with other goals, such as avoiding unethical or illegal behavior? In particular, do you think subjects like customer and employee safety, the environment, and the general good of society fit in this framework, or are they essentially ignored? Think of some specific scenarios to illustrate your answer.

13. **International Firm Goal** [LO2] Would our goal of maximizing the value of the stock be different if we were thinking about financial management in a foreign country? Why or why not?

14.   **Agency Problems** [LO4] Suppose you own stock in a company. The current price per share is $25. Another company has just announced that it wants to buy your company and will pay $35 per share to acquire all the outstanding stock. Your company's management immediately begins fighting off this hostile bid. Is management acting in the shareholders' best interests? Why or why not?

15.   **Agency Problems and Corporate Ownership** [LO4] Corporate ownership varies around the world. Historically individuals have owned the majority of shares in public corporations in the United States. In Germany and Japan, however, banks, other large financial institutions, and other companies own most of the stock in public corporations. Do you think agency problems are likely to be more or less severe in Germany and Japan than in the United States? Why? In recent years, large financial institutions such as mutual funds and pension funds have been becoming the dominant owners of stock in the United States, and these institutions are becoming more active in corporate affairs. What are the implications of this trend for agency problems and corporate control?

16.   **Executive Compensation** [LO3] Critics have charged that compensation to top managers in the United States is simply too high and should be cut back. For example, focusing on large corporations, Ray Irani of Occidental Petroleum has been one of the best-compensated CEOs in the United States, earning about $54.4 million in 2007 alone and $550 million over the 2003–2007 period. Are such amounts excessive? In answering, it might be helpful to recognize that superstar athletes such as Tiger Woods, top entertainers such as Tom Hanks and Oprah Winfrey, and many others at the top of their respective fields earn at least as much, if not a great deal more.

MINICASE

The McGee Cake Company

In early 2003, Doc and Lyn McGee formed the McGee Cake Company. The company produced a full line of cakes, and its specialties included chess cake, lemon pound cake, and double-iced, double-chocolate cake. The couple formed the company as an outside interest, and both continued to work at their current jobs. Doc did all the baking, and Lyn handled the marketing and distribution. With good product quality and a sound marketing plan, the company grew rapidly. In early 2008, the company was featured in a widely distributed entrepreneurial magazine. Later that year, the company was featured in *Gourmet Desserts,* a leading specialty food magazine. After the article appeared in *Gourmet Desserts,* sales exploded, and the company began receiving orders from all over the world.

Because of the increased sales, Doc left his other job, followed shortly by Lyn. The company hired additional workers to meet demand. Unfortunately, the fast growth experienced by the company led to cash flow and capacity problems. The company is currently producing as many cakes as possible with the assets it owns, but demand for its cakes is still growing. Further, the company has been approached by a national supermarket chain with a proposal to put four of its cakes in all of the chain's stores, and a national restaurant chain has contacted the company about selling McGee cakes in its restaurants. The restaurant would sell the cakes without a brand name.

Doc and Lyn have operated the company as a sole proprietorship. They have approached you to help manage and direct the company's growth. Specifically, they have asked you to answer the following questions.

QUESTIONS

1.   What are the advantages and disadvantages of changing the company organization from a sole proprietorship to an LLC?

2.   What are the advantages and disadvantages of changing the company organization from a sole proprietorship to a corporation?

3.   Ultimately, what action would you recommend the company undertake? Why?

LEARNING OBJECTIVES

After studying this chapter, you should understand:

LO1 The difference between accounting value (or "book" value) and market value.

LO2 The difference between accounting income and cash flow.

LO3 The difference between average and marginal tax rates.

LO4 How to determine a firm's cash flow from its financial statements.

FINANCIAL STATEMENTS, TAXES, AND CASH FLOW

2

A WRITE-OFF BY A COMPANY frequently means that the value of the company's assets has declined. In November 2007, for example, General Motors (GM) announced that it would take a write-off of about $39 billion, meaning that it was reducing net income for the third quarter of the year by that amount. GM took the charge because of deferred tax credits that the company was not going to be able to use. What made GM's write-off so unusual is that the total value of the company's stock at the time was slightly less than $20 billion. In other words, the write-off was about twice the value of the company's stock!

GM's write-off was a big one, but not a record. Possibly the largest write-offs in history were done by the media company Time Warner, which took a charge of $45.5 billion in the fourth quarter of 2002. This enormous write-off followed an earlier, even larger charge of $54 billion.

So did stockholders in General Motors lose $39 billion because of the loss of the tax credits? The answer is probably not. Understanding why ultimately leads us to the main subject of this chapter: that all-important substance known as *cash flow*.

> Master the ability to solve problems in this chapter by using a spreadsheet. Access Excel Master on the student Web site www.mhhe.com/rwj.

In this chapter, we examine financial statements, taxes, and cash flow. Our emphasis is not on preparing financial statements. Instead, we recognize that financial statements are frequently a key source of information for financial decisions, so our goal is to briefly examine such statements and point out some of their more relevant features. We pay special attention to some of the practical details of cash flow.

As you read, pay particular attention to two important differences: (1) the difference between accounting value and market value and (2) the difference between accounting income and cash flow. These distinctions will be important throughout the book.

2.1 The Balance Sheet

balance sheet
Financial statement showing a firm's accounting value on a particular date.

The **balance sheet** is a snapshot of the firm. It is a convenient means of organizing and summarizing what a firm owns (its assets), what a firm owes (its liabilities), and the difference between the two (the firm's equity) at a given point in time. Figure 2.1 illustrates how the balance sheet is constructed. As shown, the left side lists the assets of the firm, and the right side lists the liabilities and equity.

ASSETS: THE LEFT SIDE

Assets are classified as either *current* or *fixed*. A fixed asset is one that has a relatively long life. Fixed assets can be either *tangible,* such as a truck or a computer, or *intangible,* such as a trademark or patent. A current asset has a life of less than one year. This means that the asset will convert to cash within 12 months. For example, inventory would normally be purchased and sold within a year and is thus classified as a current asset. Obviously, cash itself is a current asset. Accounts receivable (money owed to the firm by its customers) are also current assets.

Three excellent sites for company financial information are finance.yahoo.com, finance.google.com, *and* money.cnn.com.

LIABILITIES AND OWNERS' EQUITY: THE RIGHT SIDE

The firm's liabilities are the first thing listed on the right side of the balance sheet. These are classified as either *current* or *long-term*. Current liabilities, like current assets, have a life of less than one year (meaning they must be paid within the year) and are listed before long-term liabilities. Accounts payable (money the firm owes to its suppliers) are one example of a current liability.

A debt that is not due in the coming year is classified as a long-term liability. A loan that the firm will pay off in five years is one such long-term debt. Firms borrow in the long term from a variety of sources. We will tend to use the terms *bond* and *bondholders* generically to refer to long-term debt and long-term creditors, respectively.

Finally, by definition, the difference between the total value of the assets (current and fixed) and the total value of the liabilities (current and long-term) is the *shareholders' equity,* also called *common equity* or *owners' equity*. This feature of the balance sheet is intended to reflect the fact that, if the firm were to sell all its assets and use the money to pay off its debts, then whatever residual value remained would belong to the shareholders. So, the balance sheet "balances" because the value of the left side always equals the value

FIGURE 2.1

The Balance Sheet. Left Side: Total Value of Assets. Right Side: Total Value of Liabilities and Shareholders' Equity.

of the right side. That is, the value of the firm's assets is equal to the sum of its liabilities and shareholders' equity:[1]

Assets = Liabilities + Shareholders' equity   [2.1]

This is the *balance sheet identity*, or equation, and it always holds because shareholders' equity is defined as the difference between assets and liabilities.

NET WORKING CAPITAL

As shown in Figure 2.1, the difference between a firm's current assets and its current liabilities is called **net working capital**. Net working capital is positive when current assets exceed current liabilities. Based on the definitions of current assets and current liabilities, this means the cash that will become available over the next 12 months exceeds the cash that must be paid over the same period. For this reason, net working capital is usually positive in a healthy firm.

net working capital
Current assets less current liabilities.

Building the Balance Sheet	**EXAMPLE 2.1**

A firm has current assets of $100, net fixed assets of $500, short-term debt of $70, and long-term debt of $200. What does the balance sheet look like? What is shareholders' equity? What is net working capital?

In this case, total assets are $100 + 500 = $600 and total liabilities are $70 + 200 = $270, so shareholders' equity is the difference: $600 − 270 = $330. The balance sheet would look like this:

Assets		Liabilities and Shareholders' Equity	
Current assets	$100	Current liabilities	$ 70
Net fixed assets	500	Long-term debt	200
		Shareholders' equity	330
Total assets	$600	Total liabilities and shareholders' equity	$600

Net working capital is the difference between current assets and current liabilities, or $100 − 70 = $30.

Table 2.1 shows simplified balance sheets for the fictitious U.S. Corporation. The assets on the balance sheet are listed in order of the length of time it takes for them to convert to cash in the normal course of business. Similarly, the liabilities are listed in the order in which they would normally be paid.

The structure of the assets for a particular firm reflects the line of business the firm is in and also managerial decisions about how much cash and inventory to have and about credit policy, fixed asset acquisition, and so on.

The liabilities side of the balance sheet primarily reflects managerial decisions about capital structure and the use of short-term debt. For example, in 2009, total long-term debt for U.S. was $454 and total equity was $640 + 1,629 = $2,269, so total long-term financing was $454 + 2,269 = $2,723. (Note that, throughout, all figures are in millions of dollars.) Of this amount, $454/2,723 = 16.67% was long-term debt. This percentage reflects capital structure decisions made in the past by the management of U.S.

Disney has a good investor relations site at disney.go.com.

---

[1]The terms *owners' equity, shareholders' equity,* and *stockholders' equity* are used interchangeably to refer to the equity in a corporation. The term *net worth* is also used. Variations exist in addition to these.

TABLE 2.1
Balance Sheets

U.S. CORPORATION 2008 and 2009 Balance Sheets ($ in millions)					
Assets			**Liabilities and Owner's Equity**		
	2008	**2009**		**2008**	**2009**
Current assets			Current liabilities		
Cash	$ 104	$ 160	Accounts payable	$ 232	$ 266
Accounts receivable	455	688	Notes payable	196	123
Inventory	553	555	Total	$ 428	$ 389
Total	$1,112	$1,403			
Fixed assets					
Net plant and equipment	$1,644	$1,709	Long-term debt	$ 408	$ 454
			Owners' equity		
			Common stock and paid-in surplus	600	640
			Retained earnings	1,320	1,629
			Total	$1,920	$2,269
Total assets	$2,756	$3,112	Total liabilities and owners' equity	$2,756	$3,112

There are three particularly important things to keep in mind when examining a balance sheet: liquidity, debt versus equity, and market value versus book value.

LIQUIDITY

Liquidity refers to the speed and ease with which an asset can be converted to cash. Gold is a relatively liquid asset; a custom manufacturing facility is not. Liquidity actually has two dimensions: ease of conversion versus loss of value. Any asset can be converted to cash quickly if we cut the price enough. A highly liquid asset is therefore one that can be quickly sold without significant loss of value. An illiquid asset is one that cannot be quickly converted to cash without a substantial price reduction.

Assets are normally listed on the balance sheet in order of decreasing liquidity, meaning that the most liquid assets are listed first. Current assets are relatively liquid and include cash and assets we expect to convert to cash over the next 12 months. Accounts receivable, for example, represent amounts not yet collected from customers on sales already made. Naturally, we hope these will convert to cash in the near future. Inventory is probably the least liquid of the current assets, at least for many businesses.

Annual and quarterly financial statements (and lots more) for most public U.S. corporations can be found in the EDGAR database at www.sec.gov.

Fixed assets are, for the most part, relatively illiquid. These consist of tangible things such as buildings and equipment that don't convert to cash at all in normal business activity (they are, of course, used in the business to generate cash). Intangible assets, such as a trademark, have no physical existence but can be very valuable. Like tangible fixed assets, they won't ordinarily convert to cash and are generally considered illiquid.

Liquidity is valuable. The more liquid a business is, the less likely it is to experience financial distress (that is, difficulty in paying debts or buying needed assets). Unfortunately, liquid assets are generally less profitable to hold. For example, cash holdings are the most liquid of all investments, but they sometimes earn no return at all—they just sit there. There is therefore a trade-off between the advantages of liquidity and forgone potential profits.

DEBT VERSUS EQUITY

To the extent that a firm borrows money, it usually gives first claim to the firm's cash flow to creditors. Equity holders are entitled to only the residual value, the portion left after creditors are paid. The value of this residual portion is the sharcholders' equity in the firm, which is just the value of the firm's assets less the value of the firm's liabilities:

Sharcholders' equity = Assets − Liabilities

This is true in an accounting sense because shareholders' equity is defined as this residual portion. More important, it is true in an economic sense: If the firm sells its assets and pays its debts, whatever cash is left belongs to the shareholders.

The use of debt in a firm's capital structure is called *financial leverage*. The more debt a firm has (as a percentage of assets), the greater is its degree of financial leverage. As we discuss in later chapters, debt acts like a lever in the sense that using it can greatly magnify both gains and losses. So, financial leverage increases the potential reward to shareholders, but it also increases the potential for financial distress and business failure.

MARKET VALUE VERSUS BOOK VALUE

The values shown on the balance sheet for the firm's assets are *book values* and generally are not what the assets are actually worth. Under **Generally Accepted Accounting Principles (GAAP)**, audited financial statements in the United States generally show assets at *historical cost.* In other words, assets are "carried on the books" at what the firm paid for them, no matter how long ago they were purchased or how much they are worth today.

For current assets, market value and book value might be somewhat similar because current assets are bought and converted into cash over a relatively short span of time. In other circumstances, the two values might differ quite a bit. Moreover, for fixed assets, it would be purely a coincidence if the actual market value of an asset (what the asset could be sold for) were equal to its book value. For example, a railroad might own enormous tracts of land purchased a century or more ago. What the railroad paid for that land could be hundreds or thousands of times less than what the land is worth today. The balance sheet would nonetheless show the historical cost.

The difference between market value and book value is important for understanding the impact of reported gains and losses. For example, to open the chapter, we discussed the huge charges against earnings taken by GM. What actually happened is that these charges were the result of accounting rule changes that led to reductions in the book value of certain types of assets. However, a change in accounting rules all by itself has no effect on what the assets in question are really worth. Instead, the market value of an asset depends on things like its riskiness and cash flows, neither of which have anything to do with accounting.

The balance sheet is potentially useful to many different parties. A supplier might look at the size of accounts payable to see how promptly the firm pays its bills. A potential creditor would examine the liquidity and degree of financial leverage. Managers within the firm can track things like the amount of cash and the amount of inventory the firm keeps on hand. Uses such as these are discussed in more detail in Chapter 3.

Managers and investors will frequently be interested in knowing the value of the firm. This information is not on the balance sheet. The fact that balance sheet assets are listed at cost means that there is no necessary connection between the total assets shown and the value of the firm. Indeed, many of the most valuable assets a firm might have—good management, a good reputation, talented employees—don't appear on the balance sheet at all.

Similarly, the shareholders' equity figure on the balance sheet and the true value of the stock need not be related. For example, in early 2008, the book value of IBM's equity was

Generally Accepted Accounting Principles (GAAP)
The common set of standards and procedures by which audited financial statements are prepared.

The home page for the Financial Accounting Standards Board (FASB) is www.fasb.org.

about $28 billion, while the market value was $164 billion. At the same time, Google's book value was $23 billion, while the market value was $136 billion.

For financial managers, then, the accounting value of the stock is not an especially important concern; it is the market value that matters. Henceforth, whenever we speak of the value of an asset or the value of the firm, we will normally mean its *market value*. So, for example, when we say the goal of the financial manager is to increase the value of the stock, we mean the market value of the stock.

| EXAMPLE 2.2 | Market Value versus Book Value |

The Klingon Corporation has net fixed assets with a book value of $700 and an appraised market value of about $1,000. Net working capital is $400 on the books, but approximately $600 would be realized if all the current accounts were liquidated. Klingon has $500 in long-term debt, both book value and market value. What is the book value of the equity? What is the market value?

We can construct two simplified balance sheets, one in accounting (book value) terms and one in economic (market value) terms:

KLINGON CORPORATION Balance Sheets Market Value versus Book Value					
Assets			**Liabilities and Shareholders' Equity**		
	Book	**Market**		**Book**	**Market**
Net working capital	$ 400	$ 600	Long-term debt	$ 500	$ 500
Net fixed assets	700	1,000	Shareholders' equity	600	1,100
	$1,100	$1,600		$1,100	$1,600

In this example, shareholders' equity is actually worth almost twice as much as what is shown on the books. The distinction between book and market values is important precisely because book values can be so different from true economic value.

Concept Questions

2.1a What is the balance sheet identity?

2.1b What is liquidity? Why is it important?

2.1c What do we mean by *financial leverage*?

2.1d Explain the difference between accounting value and market value. Which is more important to the financial manager? Why?

2.2 The Income Statement

income statement
Financial statement summarizing a firm's performance over a period of time.

The **income statement** measures performance over some period of time, usually a quarter or a year. The income statement equation is:

$$\text{Revenues} - \text{Expenses} = \text{Income} \qquad [2.2]$$

If you think of the balance sheet as a snapshot, then you can think of the income statement as a video recording covering the period between before and after pictures. Table 2.2 gives a simplified income statement for U.S. Corporation.

TABLE 2.2

Income Statement

U.S. CORPORATION 2000 Income Statement ($ in millions)		
Net sales		$1,509
Cost of goods sold		750
Depreciation		65
Earnings before Interest and taxes		$ 694
Interest paid		70
Taxable income		$ 624
Taxes (34%)		212
Net income		$ 412
Dividends	$103	
Addition to retained earnings	309	

The first thing reported on an income statement would usually be revenue and expenses from the firm's principal operations. Subsequent parts include, among other things, financing expenses such as interest paid. Taxes paid are reported separately. The last item is *net income* (the so-called bottom line). Net income is often expressed on a per-share basis and called *earnings per share (EPS)*.

As indicated, U.S. paid cash dividends of $103. The difference between net income and cash dividends, $309, is the addition to retained earnings for the year. This amount is added to the cumulative retained earnings account on the balance sheet. If you look back at the two balance sheets for U.S. Corporation, you'll see that retained earnings did go up by this amount: $1,320 + 309 = $1,629.

Calculating Earnings and Dividends per Share	**EXAMPLE 2.3**

Suppose U.S. had 200 million shares outstanding at the end of 2009. Based on the income statement in Table 2.2, what was EPS? What were dividends per share?

From the income statement, we see that U.S. had a net income of $412 million for the year. Total dividends were $103 million. Because 200 million shares were outstanding, we can calculate earnings per share, or EPS, and dividends per share as follows:

Earnings per share = Net income/Total shares outstanding
= $412/200 = $2.06 per share
Dividends per share = Total dividends/Total shares outstanding
= $103/200 = $.515 per share

When looking at an income statement, the financial manager needs to keep three things in mind: GAAP, cash versus noncash items, and time and costs.

GAAP AND THE INCOME STATEMENT

An income statement prepared using GAAP will show revenue when it accrues. This is not necessarily when the cash comes in. The general rule (the *recognition* or *realization principle*) is to recognize revenue when the earnings process is virtually complete and the value of an exchange of goods or services is known or can be reliably determined. In practice, this principle usually means that revenue is recognized at the time of sale, which need not be the same as the time of collection.

Expenses shown on the income statement are based on the *matching principle*. The basic idea here is to first determine revenues as described previously and then match those revenues with the costs associated with producing them. So, if we manufacture a product and then sell it on credit, the revenue is realized at the time of sale. The production and other costs associated with the sale of that product will likewise be recognized at that time. Once again, the actual cash outflows may have occurred at some different time.

As a result of the way revenues and expenses are realized, the figures shown on the income statement may not be at all representative of the actual cash inflows and outflows that occurred during a particular period.

NONCASH ITEMS

noncash items
Expenses charged against revenues that do not directly affect cash flow, such as depreciation.

A primary reason that accounting income differs from cash flow is that an income statement contains **noncash items**. The most important of these is *depreciation*. Suppose a firm purchases an asset for $5,000 and pays in cash. Obviously, the firm has a $5,000 cash outflow at the time of purchase. However, instead of deducting the $5,000 as an expense, an accountant might depreciate the asset over a five-year period.

If the depreciation is straight-line and the asset is written down to zero over that period, then $5,000/5 = $1,000 will be deducted each year as an expense.[2] The important thing to recognize is that this $1,000 deduction isn't cash—it's an accounting number. The actual cash outflow occurred when the asset was purchased.

The depreciation deduction is simply another application of the matching principle in accounting. The revenues associated with an asset would generally occur over some length of time. So, the accountant seeks to match the expense of purchasing the asset with the benefits produced from owning it.

As we will see, for the financial manager, the actual timing of cash inflows and outflows is critical in coming up with a reasonable estimate of market value, so we need to learn how to separate the cash flows from the noncash accounting entries. In reality, the difference between cash flow and accounting income can be pretty dramatic. For example, consider the case of insurance company Conseco. For its 2007 fiscal year, Conseco reported a net loss of $194 million. Sounds bad; but Conseco also reported a *positive* cash flow of $703 million, a difference of about $897 million! The reason is that the company took several large deductions to reflect a decrease in the value of certain assets. These deductions were purely an accounting adjustment and had nothing to do with the cash flow the company generated for the year.

TIME AND COSTS

It is often useful to think of the future as having two distinct parts: the short run and the long run. These are not precise time periods. The distinction has to do with whether costs are fixed or variable. In the long run, all business costs are variable. Given sufficient time, assets can be sold, debts can be paid, and so on.

If our time horizon is relatively short, however, some costs are effectively fixed—they must be paid no matter what (property taxes, for example). Other costs such as wages to laborers and payments to suppliers are still variable. As a result, even in the short run, the firm can vary its output level by varying expenditures in these areas.

The distinction between fixed and variable costs is important, at times, to the financial manager, but the way costs are reported on the income statement is not a good guide to

---

[2]By *straight-line*, we mean that the depreciation deduction is the same every year. By *written down to zero*, we mean that the asset is assumed to have no value at the end of five years. Depreciation is discussed in more detail in Chapter 10.

WORK THE WEB

The U.S. Securities and Exchange Commission (SEC) requires that most public companies file regular reports, including annual and quarterly financial statements. The SEC has a public site named EDGAR that makes these free reports available at www.sec.gov. We went to "Search for Company Filings," "Companies & Other Filers," and entered "Sun Microsystems":

Enter your search information:

Company name: [sun microsystems]

or <u>CIK</u> or Ticker Symbol: [   ] *(Central Index Key)*
(Tickers for 10000 largest publicly traded companies)

or File Number: [   ]

or <u>State/Country</u>: [   ] *(two-letter abbreviation)*

and/or <u>SIC</u>: [   ]

and Ownership Forms 3, 4, and 5?   ⊙ Include   ○ Exclude   ○ Only

[**Find Companies**]

Here is partial view of what we got:

SUN MICROSYSTEMS, INC. (0000709519)

SIC: 3571 - Electronic Computers
State location: CA | State of Inc.: DE | Fiscal Year End: 0630
formerly: SUN MICROSYSTEMS INC (filings through 2005-02-14)

Business Address	Mailing Address
4150 NETWORK CIRCLE	4150 NETWORK CIRCLE
SANTA CLARA CA 95054	SANTA CLARA CA 95054
6509601300	

To limit filing results, enter form type or date (as 2002/05/23).

Form Type [   ]
Prior to [   ]
Ownership? ○ Include ○ Exclude ○ Only
[40 Entries ▾]   [Retrieve Selected Filings]
[Retrieve All Filings]

Key to Descriptions

[Paper] Paper filings are available by film number.
[Cover] Filing contains an SEC-released cover letter or correspondence.

Items 1 - 40

Form	Formats		Description	Filing Date	File/Film No
4	[html][text]	9 KB	Statement of changes in beneficial ownership of securities Acc-no: 0001181431 00 013879	2008-02-26	
4	[html][text]	12 KB	Statement of changes in beneficial ownership of securities Acc-no: 0001181431-08-013878	2008-02-26	
SC 13G/A	[html][text]	19 KB	[Amend]Statement of acquisition of beneficial ownership by individuals Acc-no: 0000888002-08-000559 (34 Act)	2008-02-14	005-39044 08608276
SC 13G	[html][text]	64 KB	Statement of acquisition of beneficial ownership by individuals Acc-no: 0001104659-08-010142 (34 Act)	2008-02-14	005-39044 08606904
10-Q/A	[html][text]	24 KB	[Amend]Quarterly report [Sections 13 or 15(d)] Acc-no: 0001193125-08-025866 (34 Act)	2008-02-11	000-15086 08594220
10 Q	[html][text]	1 MB	Quarterly report [Sections 13 or 15(d)] Acc-no: 0001193125-08-020649 (34 Act)	2008-02-06	000-15086 08578267
8-K	[html][text]	642 KB	Current report, items 2.02 and 9.01 Acc-no: 0001193125-08-011450 (34 Act)	2008 01 24	000-15086 08547712
8-K	[html][text]	21 KB	Current report, items 2.02 and 9.01 Acc-no: 0001193125-08-007221 (34 Act)	2008-01-16	000-15086 08532665
SC TO-I/A	[html][text]	40 KB	[Amend]Tender offer statement by Issuer Acc-no: 0001104659-07-089640 (34 Act)	2007-12-18	005-39044 071313987
4	[html][text]	25 KB	Statement of changes in beneficial ownership of securities Acc-no: 0001181431-07-074103	2007-12-07	

The two reports we look at the most are the 10-K, which is the annual report filed with the SEC, and the 10-Q. The 10-K includes the list of officers and their salaries, financial statements for the previous fiscal year, and an explanation by the company of the financial results. The 10-Q is a smaller report that includes the financial statements for the quarter.

Questions

1. *As you can imagine, electronic filing of documents with the SEC has not been around for very long. Go to www.sec.gov and find the filings for General Electric. What is the date of the oldest 10-K available on the website for General Electric? Look up the 10-K forms for IBM and Apple to see if the year of the first electronic filing is the same for these companies.*
2. *Go to www.sec.gov and find out when the following forms are used: Form DEF 14A, Form 8-K, and Form 6-K.*

which costs are which. The reason is that, in practice, accountants tend to classify costs as either product costs or period costs.

Product costs include such things as raw materials, direct labor expense, and manufacturing overhead. These are reported on the income statement as costs of goods sold, but they include both fixed and variable costs. Similarly, *period costs* are incurred during a particular time period and might be reported as selling, general, and administrative expenses. Once again, some of these period costs may be fixed and others may be variable. The company president's salary, for example, is a period cost and is probably fixed, at least in the short run.

The balance sheets and income statement we have been using thus far are hypothetical. Our nearby *Work the Web* box shows how to find actual balance sheets and income statements online for almost any company.

Concept Questions

2.2a What is the income statement equation?

2.2b What are the three things to keep in mind when looking at an income statement?

2.2c Why is accounting income not the same as cash flow? Give two reasons.

2.3 Taxes

Taxes can be one of the largest cash outflows a firm experiences. For example, for the fiscal year 2007, ExxonMobil's earnings before taxes were about $71.88 billion. Its tax bill, including all taxes paid worldwide, was a whopping $29.86 billion, or about 41 percent of its pretax earnings. Also for fiscal year 2007, Wal-Mart had a taxable income of $6.88 billion, and the company paid $2.14 billion in taxes, an average tax rate of 31 percent.

The size of a company's tax bill is determined by the tax code, an often amended set of rules. In this section, we examine corporate tax rates and how taxes are calculated. If the various rules of taxation seem a little bizarre or convoluted to you, keep in mind that the tax code is the result of political, not economic, forces. As a result, there is no reason why it has to make economic sense.

CORPORATE TAX RATES

Corporate tax rates in effect for 2009 are shown in Table 2.3. A peculiar feature of taxation instituted by the Tax Reform Act of 1986 and expanded in the 1993 Omnibus Budget Reconciliation Act is that corporate tax rates are not strictly increasing. As shown, corporate tax rates rise from 15 percent to 39 percent, but they drop back to 34 percent on income over $335,000. They then rise to 38 percent and subsequently fall to 35 percent.

Taxable Income		Tax Rate
$ 0 – 50,000		15%
50,001 – 75,000		25
75,001 – 100,000		34
100,001 – 335,000		39
335,001 10,000,000		34
10,000,001 – 15,000,000		35
15,000,001 – 18,333,333		38
18,333,334+		35

TABLE 2.3

Corporate Tax Rates

According to the originators of the current tax rules, there are only four corporate rates: 15 percent, 25 percent, 34 percent, and 35 percent. The 38 and 39 percent brackets arise because of "surcharges" applied on top of the 34 and 35 percent rates. A tax is a tax is a tax, however, so there are really six corporate tax brackets, as we have shown.

AVERAGE VERSUS MARGINAL TAX RATES

In making financial decisions, it is frequently important to distinguish between average and marginal tax rates. Your **average tax rate** is your tax bill divided by your taxable income— in other words, the percentage of your income that goes to pay taxes. Your **marginal tax rate** is the rate of the extra tax you would pay if you earned one more dollar. The percentage tax rates shown in Table 2.3 are all marginal rates. Put another way, the tax rates in Table 2.3 apply to the part of income in the indicated range only, not all income.

The difference between average and marginal tax rates can best be illustrated with a simple example. Suppose our corporation has a taxable income of $200,000. What is the tax bill? Using Table 2.3, we can figure our tax bill:

average tax rate
Total taxes paid divided by total taxable income.

marginal tax rate
Amount of tax payable on the next dollar earned.

```
.15($  50,000)          = $  7,500
.25($  75,000    50,000)  –    6,250
.34($100,000 – 75,000) =      8,500
.39($200,000 – 100,000) =    39,000
                            $61,250
```

Our total tax is thus $61,250.

In our example, what is the average tax rate? We had a taxable income of $200,000 and a tax bill of $61,250, so the average tax rate is $61,250/200,000 = 30.625%. What is the marginal tax rate? If we made one more dollar, the tax on that dollar would be 39 cents, so our marginal rate is 39 percent.

The IRS has a great Web site! (www.irs.gov)

Deep in the Heart of Taxes   **EXAMPLE 2.4**

Algernon, Inc., has a taxable income of $85,000. What is its tax bill? What is its average tax rate? Its marginal tax rate?

From Table 2.3, we see that the tax rate applied to the first $50,000 is 15 percent; the rate applied to the next $25,000 is 25 percent; and the rate applied after that up to $100,000 is 34 percent. So Algernon must pay .15 × $50,000 + .25 × 25,000 + .34 × (85,000 – 75,000) = $17,150. The average tax rate is thus $17,150/85,000 = 20.18%. The marginal rate is 34 percent because Algernon's taxes would rise by 34 cents if it had another dollar in taxable income.

TABLE 2.4

Corporate Taxes and
Tax Rates

(1) Taxable Income	(2) Marginal Tax Rate	(3) Total Tax	(3)/(1) Average Tax Rate
$ 45,000	15%	$ 6,750	15.00%
70,000	25	12,500	17.86
95,000	34	20,550	21.63
250,000	39	80,750	32.30
1,000,000	34	340,000	34.00
17,500,000	38	6,100,000	34.86
50,000,000	35	17,500,000	35.00
100,000,000	35	35,000,000	35.00

Table 2.4 summarizes some different taxable incomes, marginal tax rates, and average tax rates for corporations. Notice how the average and marginal tax rates come together at 35 percent.

With a *flat-rate* tax, there is only one tax rate, so the rate is the same for all income levels. With such a tax, the marginal tax rate is always the same as the average tax rate. As it stands now, corporate taxation in the United States is based on a modified flat-rate tax, which becomes a true flat rate for the highest incomes.

In looking at Table 2.4, notice that the more a corporation makes, the greater is the percentage of taxable income paid in taxes. Put another way, under current tax law, the average tax rate never goes down, even though the marginal tax rate does. As illustrated, for corporations, average tax rates begin at 15 percent and rise to a maximum of 35 percent.

Normally the marginal tax rate is relevant for financial decision making. The reason is that any new cash flows will be taxed at that marginal rate. Because financial decisions usually involve new cash flows or changes in existing ones, this rate will tell us the marginal effect of a decision on our tax bill.

There is one last thing to notice about the tax code as it affects corporations. It's easy to verify that the corporate tax bill is just a flat 35 percent of taxable income if our taxable income is more than $18.33 million. Also, for the many midsize corporations with taxable incomes in the range of $335,000 to $10,000,000, the tax rate is a flat 34 percent. Because we will normally be talking about large corporations, you can assume that the average and marginal tax rates are 35 percent unless we explicitly say otherwise.

Before moving on, we should note that the tax rates we have discussed in this section relate to federal taxes only. Overall tax rates can be higher if state, local, and any other taxes are considered.

Concept Questions

2.3a What is the difference between a marginal and an average tax rate?

2.3b Do the wealthiest corporations receive a tax break in terms of a lower tax rate? Explain.

2.4 Cash Flow

At this point, we are ready to discuss perhaps one of the most important pieces of financial information that can be gleaned from financial statements: cash flow. By *cash flow,* we simply mean the difference between the number of dollars that came in and the number that went out. For example, if you were the owner of a business, you might be very interested in how much cash you actually took out of your business in a given year. How to determine this amount is one of the things we discuss next.

No standard financial statement presents this information in the way that we wish. We will therefore discuss how to calculate cash flow for U.S. Corporation and point out how the result differs from that of standard financial statement calculations. There is a standard financial accounting statement called the *statement of cash flows,* but it is concerned with a somewhat different issue that should not be confused with what is discussed in this section. The accounting statement of cash flows is discussed in Chapter 3.

From the balance sheet identity, we know that the value of a firm's assets is equal to the value of its liabilities plus the value of its equity. Similarly, the cash flow from the firm's assets must equal the sum of the cash flow to creditors and the cash flow to stockholders (or owners):

Cash flow from assets = Cash flow to creditors + Cash flow to stockholders   **[2.3]**

This is the *cash flow identity.* It says that the cash flow from the firm's assets is equal to the cash flow paid to suppliers of capital to the firm. What it reflects is the fact that a firm generates cash through its various activities, and that cash is either used to pay creditors or paid out to the owners of the firm. We discuss the various things that make up these cash flows next.

CASH FLOW FROM ASSETS

Cash flow from assets involves three components: operating cash flow, capital spending, and change in net working capital. **Operating cash flow** refers to the cash flow that results from the firm's day-to-day activities of producing and selling. Expenses associated with the firm's financing of its assets are not included because they are not operating expenses.

As we discussed in Chapter 1, some portion of the firm's cash flow is reinvested in the firm. *Capital spending* refers to the net spending on fixed assets (purchases of fixed assets less sales of fixed assets). Finally, *change in net working capital* is measured as the net change in current assets relative to current liabilities for the period being examined and represents the amount spent on net working capital. The three components of cash flow are examined in more detail next.

cash flow from assets
The total of cash flow to creditors and cash flow to stockholders, consisting of the following: operating cash flow, capital spending, and change in net working capital.

operating cash flow
Cash generated from a firm's normal business activities.

Operating Cash Flow   To calculate operating cash flow (OCF), we want to calculate revenues minus costs, but we don't want to include depreciation because it's not a cash outflow, and we don't want to include interest because it's a financing expense. We do want to include taxes because taxes are (unfortunately) paid in cash.

If we look at U.S. Corporation's income statement (Table 2.2), we see that earnings before interest and taxes (EBIT) are $694. This is almost what we want because it doesn't include interest paid. We need to make two adjustments. First, recall that depreciation is a noncash expense. To get cash flow, we first add back the $65 in depreciation because it wasn't a cash deduction. The other adjustment is to subtract the $212 in taxes because these were paid in cash. The result is operating cash flow:

U.S. CORPORATION 2009 Operating Cash Flow	
Earnings before interest and taxes	$694
+ Depreciation	65
− Taxes	212
Operating cash flow	$547

U.S. Corporation thus had a 2009 operating cash flow of $547.

Operating cash flow is an important number because it tells us, on a very basic level, whether a firm's cash inflows from its business operations are sufficient to cover its everyday cash outflows. For this reason, a negative operating cash flow is often a sign of trouble.

There is an unpleasant possibility of confusion when we speak of operating cash flow. In accounting practice, operating cash flow is often defined as net income plus depreciation. For U.S. Corporation, this would amount to $412 + 65 = $477.

The accounting definition of operating cash flow differs from ours in one important way: Interest is deducted when net income is computed. Notice that the difference between the $547 operating cash flow we calculated and this $477 is $70, the amount of interest paid for the year. This definition of cash flow thus considers interest paid to be an operating expense. Our definition treats it properly as a financing expense. If there were no interest expense, the two definitions would be the same.

To finish our calculation of cash flow from assets for U.S. Corporation, we need to consider how much of the $547 operating cash flow was reinvested in the firm. We consider spending on fixed assets first.

Capital Spending   Net capital spending is just money spent on fixed assets less money received from the sale of fixed assets. At the end of 2008, net fixed assets for U.S. Corporation (Table 2.1) were $1,644. During the year, U.S. wrote off (depreciated) $65 worth of fixed assets on the income statement. So, if the firm didn't purchase any new fixed assets, net fixed assets would have been $1,644 − 65 = $1,579 at year's end. The 2009 balance sheet shows $1,709 in net fixed assets, so U.S. must have spent a total of $1,709 − 1,579 = $130 on fixed assets during the year:

Ending net fixed assets	$1,709
− Beginning net fixed assets	1,644
+ Depreciation	65
Net capital spending	$ 130

This $130 is the net capital spending for 2009.

Could net capital spending be negative? The answer is yes. This would happen if the firm sold off more assets than it purchased. The *net* here refers to purchases of fixed assets net of any sales of fixed assets. You will often see capital spending called CAPEX, which is an acronym for capital expenditures. It usually means the same thing.

Change in Net Working Capital   In addition to investing in fixed assets, a firm will also invest in current assets. For example, going back to the balance sheets in Table 2.1, we see that at the end of 2009, U.S. had current assets of $1,403. At the end of 2008, current assets were $1,112; so, during the year, U.S. invested $1,403 − 1,112 = $291 in current assets.

As the firm changes its investment in current assets, its current liabilities will usually change as well. To determine the change in net working capital, the easiest approach is just to take the difference between the beginning and ending net working capital (NWC) figures. Net working capital at the end of 2009 was $1,403 − 389 = $1,014. Similarly, at the end of 2008, net working capital was $1,112 − 428 = $684. Given these figures, we have the following:

Ending NWC	$1,014
− Beginning NWC	684
Change in NWC	$ 330

Net working capital thus increased by $330. Put another way, U.S. Corporation had a net investment of $330 in NWC for the year. This change in NWC is often referred to as the "addition to" NWC.

Conclusion   Given the figures we've come up with, we're ready to calculate cash flow from assets. The total cash flow from assets is given by operating cash flow less the amounts invested in fixed assets and net working capital. So, for U.S., we have:

U.S. CORPORATION 2009 Cash Flow from Assets	
Operating cash flow	$547
− Net capital spending	130
− Change in NWC	000
Cash flow from assets	$ 87

From the cash flow identity given earlier, we know that this $87 cash flow from assets equals the sum of the firm's cash flow to creditors and its cash flow to stockholders. We consider these next.

It wouldn't be at all unusual for a growing corporation to have a negative cash flow. As we see next, a negative cash flow means that the firm raised more money by borrowing and selling stock than it paid out to creditors and stockholders during the year.

A Note about "Free" Cash Flow   Cash flow from assets sometimes goes by a different name, **free cash flow**. Of course, there is no such thing as "free" cash (we wish!). Instead the name refers to cash that the firm is free to distribute to creditors and stockholders because it is not needed for working capital or fixed asset investments. We will stick with "cash flow from assets" as our label for this important concept because, in practice, there is some variation in exactly how free cash flow is computed; different users calculate it in different ways. Nonetheless, whenever you hear the phrase "free cash flow," you should understand that what is being discussed is cash flow from assets or something quite similar.

free cash flow
Another name for cash flow from assets.

CASH FLOW TO CREDITORS AND STOCKHOLDERS

The cash flows to creditors and stockholders represent the net payments to creditors and owners during the year. Their calculation is similar to that of cash flow from assets. **Cash flow to creditors** is interest paid less net new borrowing; **cash flow to stockholders** is dividends paid less net new equity raised.

cash flow to creditors
A firm's interest payments to creditors less net new borrowings.

cash flow to stockholders
Dividends paid out by a firm less net new equity raised.

Cash Flow to Creditors   Looking at the income statement in Table 2.2, we see that U.S. paid $70 in interest to creditors. From the balance sheets in Table 2.1, we see that long-term debt rose by $454 − 408 = $46. So U.S. Corporation paid out $70 in interest, but it borrowed an additional $46. Thus, net cash flow to creditors is:

U.S. CORPORATION 2009 Cash Flow to Creditors	
Interest paid	$70
− Net new borrowing	46
Cash flow to creditors	$24

Cash flow to creditors is sometimes called cash *flow to bondholders;* we will use these terms interchangeably.

Cash Flow to Stockholders   From the income statement, we see that dividends paid to stockholders amounted to $103. To get net new equity raised, we need to look at the

TABLE 2.5

Cash Flow Summary

I.   The cash flow identity

Cash flow from assets = Cash flow to creditors (bondholders)
+ Cash flow to stockholders (owners)

II. Cash flow from assets

Cash flow from assets = Operating cash flow
− Net capital spending
− Change in net working capital (NWC)

where:

Operating cash flow = Earnings before interest and taxes (EBIT)
+ Depreciation − Taxes
Net capital spending = Ending net fixed assets − Beginning net fixed assets
+ Depreciation
Change in NWC = Ending NWC − Beginning NWC

III. Cash flow to creditors (bondholders)

Cash flow to creditors = Interest paid − Net new borrowing

IV. Cash flow to stockholders (owners)

Cash flow to stockholders = Dividends paid − Net new equity raised

common stock and paid-in surplus account. This account tells us how much stock the company has sold. During the year, this account rose by $40, so $40 in net new equity was raised. Given this, we have the following:

U.S. CORPORATION 2009 Cash Flow to Stockholders	
Dividends paid	$103
− Net new equity raised	40
Cash flow to stockholders	$ 63

The cash flow to stockholders for 2009 was thus $63.

The last thing we need to do is to verify that the cash flow identity holds to be sure we didn't make any mistakes. From the previous section, we know that cash flow from assets is $87. Cash flow to creditors and stockholders is $24 + 63 = $87, so everything checks out. Table 2.5 contains a summary of the various cash flow calculations for future reference.

As our discussion indicates, it is essential that a firm keep an eye on its cash flow. The following serves as an excellent reminder of why doing so is a good idea, unless the firm's owners wish to end up in the "Po'" house:

QUOTH THE BANKER, "WATCH CASH FLOW"

Once upon a midnight dreary as I pondered weak and weary
Over many a quaint and curious volume of accounting lore,
Seeking gimmicks (without scruple) to squeeze through
    some new tax loophole,
Suddenly I heard a knock upon my door,
    Only this, and nothing more.

Then I felt a queasy tingling and I heard the cash a-jingling
As a fearsome banker entered whom I'd often seen before.
His face was money-green and in his eyes there could be seen
Dollar-signs that seemed to glitter as he reckoned up the score.
    "Cash flow," the banker said, and nothing more.

I had always thought it fine to show a jet black bottom line.
But the banker sounded a resounding, "No.
Your receivables are high, mounting upward toward the sky;

Write-offs loom. What matters is cash flow."
   He repeated, "Watch cash flow."

Then I tried to tell the story of our lovely inventory
Which, though large, is full of most delightful stuff.
But the banker saw its growth, and with a mighty oath
He waved his arms and shouted, "Stop! Enough!
   Pay the interest, and don't give me any guff!"

Next I looked for noncash items which could add ad infinitum
To replace the ever-outward flow of cash,
But to keep my statement black I'd held depreciation back,
And my banker said that I'd done something rash.
   He quivered, and his teeth began to gnash.

When I asked him for a loan, he responded, with a groan,
That the interest rate would be just prime plus eight,
And to guarantee my purity he'd insist on some security—
All my assets plus the scalp upon my pate.
   Only this, a standard rate.

Though my bottom line is black, I am flat upon my back,
My cash flows out and customers pay slow.
The growth of my receivables is almost unbelievable:
The result is certain—unremitting woe!
And I hear the banker utter an ominous low mutter,
   "Watch cash flow."

Herbert S. Bailey Jr.

Source: Reprinted from the January 13, 1975, issue of *Publishers Weekly*, published by R. R. Bowker, a Xerox company. Copyright © 1975 by the Xerox Corporation.

To which we can only add, "Amen."

AN EXAMPLE: CASH FLOWS FOR DOLE COLA

This extended example covers the various cash flow calculations discussed in the chapter. It also illustrates a few variations that may arise.

Operating Cash Flow   During the year, Dole Cola, Inc., had sales and cost of goods sold of $600 and $300, respectively. Depreciation was $150 and interest paid was $30. Taxes were calculated at a straight 34 percent. Dividends were $30. (All figures are in millions of dollars.) What was operating cash flow for Dole? Why is this different from net income?

   The easiest thing to do here is to create an income statement. We can then pick up the numbers we need. Dole Cola's income statement is given here:

DOLE COLA 2009 Income Statement		
Net sales		$600
Cost of goods sold		300
Depreciation		150
Earnings before interest and taxes		$150
Interest paid		30
Taxable income		$120
Taxes		41
Net income		$ 79
Dividends	$30	
Addition to retained earnings	49	

Net income for Dole was thus $79. We now have all the numbers we need. Referring back to the U.S. Corporation example and Table 2.5, we have this:

DOLE COLA 2009 Operating Cash Flow	
Earnings before interest and taxes	$150
+ Depreciation	150
− Taxes	41
Operating cash flow	$259

As this example illustrates, operating cash flow is not the same as net income because depreciation and interest are subtracted out when net income is calculated. If you recall our earlier discussion, we don't subtract these out in computing operating cash flow because depreciation is not a cash expense and interest paid is a financing expense, not an operating expense.

Net Capital Spending   Suppose beginning net fixed assets were $500 and ending net fixed assets were $750. What was the net capital spending for the year?

From the income statement for Dole, we know that depreciation for the year was $150. Net fixed assets rose by $250. Dole thus spent $250 along with an additional $150, for a total of $400.

Change in NWC and Cash Flow from Assets   Suppose Dole Cola started the year with $2,130 in current assets and $1,620 in current liabilities, and the corresponding ending figures were $2,260 and $1,710. What was the change in NWC during the year? What was cash flow from assets? How does this compare to net income?

Net working capital started out as $2,130 − 1,620 = $510 and ended up at $2,260 − 1,710 = $550. The addition to NWC was thus $550 − 510 = $40. Putting together all the information for Dole, we have the following:

DOLE COLA 2009 Cash Flow from Assets	
Operating cash flow	$259
− Net capital spending	400
− Change in NWC	40
Cash flow from assets	−$181

Dole had a cash flow from assets of −$181. Net income was positive at $79. Is the fact that cash flow from assets was negative a cause for alarm? Not necessarily. The cash flow here is negative primarily because of a large investment in fixed assets. If these are good investments, the resulting negative cash flow is not a worry.

Cash Flow to Stockholders and Creditors   We saw that Dole Cola had cash flow from assets of −$181. The fact that this is negative means that Dole raised more money in the form of new debt and equity than it paid out for the year. For example, suppose we know that Dole didn't sell any new equity for the year. What was cash flow to stockholders? To creditors?

Because it didn't raise any new equity, Dole's cash flow to stockholders is just equal to the cash dividend paid:

DOLE COLA	
2009 Cash Flow to Stockholders	
Dividends paid	$30
− Net new equity raised	0
Cash flow to stockholders	$30

Now, from the cash flow identity, we know that the total cash paid to creditors and stockholders was −$181. Cash flow to stockholders is $30, so cash flow to creditors must be equal to −$181 − 30 = −$211:

Cash flow to creditors + Cash flow to stockholders = −$181
Cash flow to creditors + $30   = −$181
Cash flow to creditors   = −$211

Because we know that cash flow to creditors is −$211 and interest paid is $30 (from the income statement), we can now determine net new borrowing. Dole must have borrowed $241 during the year to help finance the fixed asset expansion:

DOLE COLA	
2009 Cash Flow to Creditors	
Interest paid	$ 30
− Net new borrowing	− 241
Cash flow to creditors	−$211

Concept Questions

2.4a What is the cash flow identity? Explain what it says.

2.4b What are the components of operating cash flow?

2.4c Why is interest paid not a component of operating cash flow?

Summary and Conclusions   2.5

This chapter has introduced some of the basics of financial statements, taxes, and cash flow:

1. The book values on an accounting balance sheet can be very different from market values. The goal of financial management is to maximize the market value of the stock, not its book value.

2. Net income as it is computed on the income statement is not cash flow. A primary reason is that depreciation, a noncash expense, is deducted when net income is computed.

3. Marginal and average tax rates can be different, and it is the marginal tax rate that is relevant for most financial decisions.

4. The marginal tax rate paid by the corporations with the largest incomes is 35 percent.

5. There is a cash flow identity much like the balance sheet identity. It says that cash flow from assets equals cash flow to creditors and stockholders.

The calculation of cash flow from financial statements isn't difficult. Care must be taken in handling noncash expenses, such as depreciation, and not to confuse operating costs with financing costs. Most of all, it is important not to confuse book values with market values, or accounting income with cash flow.

Visit us at www.mhhe.com/rwj

Visit us at www.mhhe.com/rwj

CHAPTER REVIEW AND SELF-TEST PROBLEM

2.1   Cash Flow for Mara Corporation   This problem will give you some practice working with financial statements and figuring cash flow. Based on the following information for Mara Corporation, prepare an income statement for 2009 and balance sheets for 2008 and 2009. Next, following our U.S. Corporation examples in the chapter, calculate cash flow from assets, cash flow to creditors, and cash flow to stockholders for Mara for 2009. Use a 35 percent tax rate throughout. You can check your answers against ours, found in the following section.

	2008	2009
Sales	$4,203	$4,507
Cost of goods sold	2,422	2,633
Depreciation	785	952
Interest	180	196
Dividends	225	250
Current assets	2,205	2,429
Net fixed assets	7,344	7,650
Current liabilities	1,003	1,255
Long-term debt	3,106	2,085

ANSWER TO CHAPTER REVIEW AND SELF-TEST PROBLEM

2.1   In preparing the balance sheets, remember that shareholders' equity is the residual. With this in mind, Mara's balance sheets are as follows:

MARA CORPORATION
2008 and 2009 Balance Sheets

	2008	2009		2008	2009
Current assets	$2,205	$ 2,429	Current liabilities	$1,003	$ 1,255
Net fixed assets	7,344	7,650	Long-term debt	3,106	2,085
			Equity	5,440	6,739
Total assets	$9,549	$10,079	Total liabilities and shareholders' equity	$9,549	$10,079

The income statement is straightforward:

MARA CORPORATION
2009 Income Statement

Sales	$4,507
Cost of goods sold	2,633
Depreciation	952
Earnings before interest and taxes	$ 922
Interest paid	196
Taxable income	$ 726
Taxes (35%)	254
Net income	$ 472
Dividends	$250
Addition to retained earnings	222

Notice that we've used an average 35 percent tax rate. Also notice that the addition to retained earnings is just net income less cash dividends.

We can now pick up the figures we need to get operating cash flow:

MARA CORPORATION 2009 Operating Cash Flow	
Earnings before interest and taxes	$ 922
+ Depreciation	952
− Taxes	254
Operating cash flow	$1,620

Next, we get the net capital spending for the year by looking at the change in fixed assets, remembering to account for depreciation:

Ending net fixed assets	$7,650
− Beginning net fixed assets	7,344
+ Depreciation	952
Net capital spending	$1,258

After calculating beginning and ending NWC, we take the difference to get the change in NWC:

Ending NWC	$1,174
− Beginning NWC	1,202
Change in NWC	−$ 28

We now combine operating cash flow, net capital spending, and the change in net working capital to get the total cash flow from assets:

MARA CORPORATION 2009 Cash Flow from Assets	
Operating cash flow	$1,620
− Net capital spending	1,258
− Change in NWC	−28
Cash flow from assets	$ 390

To get cash flow to creditors, notice that long-term borrowing decreased by $1,021 during the year and that interest paid was $196:

MARA CORPORATION 2009 Cash Flow to Creditors	
Interest paid	$ 196
− Net new borrowing	−1,021
Cash flow to creditors	$ 1,217

Visit us at www.mhhe.com/rwj

Finally, dividends paid were $250. To get net new equity raised, we have to do some extra calculating. Total equity was up by $6,739 − 5,440 = $1,299. Of this increase, $222 was from additions to retained earnings, so $1,077 in new equity was raised during the year. Cash flow to stockholders was thus:

MARA CORPORATION 2009 Cash Flow to Stockholders	
Dividends paid	$ 250
− Net new equity raised	1,077
Cash flow to stockholders	−$ 827

As a check, notice that cash flow from assets ($390) equals cash flow to creditors plus cash flow to stockholders ($1,217 − 827 = $390).

CONCEPTS REVIEW AND CRITICAL THINKING QUESTIONS

1. **Liquidity** [LO1] What does liquidity measure? Explain the trade-off a firm faces between high liquidity and low liquidity levels.
2. **Accounting and Cash Flows** [LO2] Why might the revenue and cost figures shown on a standard income statement not be representative of the actual cash inflows and outflows that occurred during a period?
3. **Book Values versus Market Values** [LO1] In preparing a balance sheet, why do you think standard accounting practice focuses on historical cost rather than market value?
4. **Operating Cash Flow** [LO4] In comparing accounting net income and operating cash flow, name two items you typically find in net income that are not in operating cash flow. Explain what each is and why it is excluded in operating cash flow.
5. **Book Values versus Market Values** [LO1] Under standard accounting rules, it is possible for a company's liabilities to exceed its assets. When this occurs, the owners' equity is negative. Can this happen with market values? Why or why not?
6. **Cash Flow from Assets** [LO4] Suppose a company's cash flow from assets is negative for a particular period. Is this necessarily a good sign or a bad sign?
7. **Operating Cash Flow** [LO4] Suppose a company's operating cash flow has been negative for several years running. Is this necessarily a good sign or a bad sign?
8. **Net Working Capital and Capital Spending** [LO4] Could a company's change in NWC be negative in a given year? (*Hint:* Yes.) Explain how this might come about. What about net capital spending?
9. **Cash Flow to Stockholders and Creditors** [LO4] Could a company's cash flow to stockholders be negative in a given year? (*Hint:* Yes.) Explain how this might come about. What about cash flow to creditors?
10. **Firm Values** [LO1] Referring back to the General Motors example used at the beginning of the chapter, note that we suggested that General Motors' stockholders probably didn't suffer as a result of the reported loss. What do you think was the basis for our conclusion?

Visit us at www.mhhe.com/rwj

11. **Enterprise Value** [LO1] A firm's *enterprise value* is equal to the market value of its debt and equity, less the firm's holdings of cash and cash equivalents. This figure is particularly relevant to potential purchasers of the firm. Why?

12. **Earnings Management** [LO2] Companies often try to keep accounting earnings growing at a relatively steady pace, thereby avoiding large swings in earnings from period to period. They also try to meet earnings targets. To do so, they use a variety of tactics. The simplest way is to control the timing of accounting revenues and costs, which all firms can do to at least some extent. For example, if earnings are looking too low this quarter, then some accounting costs can be deferred until next quarter. This practice is called earnings management. It is common, and it raises a lot of questions. Why do firms do it? Why are firms even allowed to do it under GAAP? Is it ethical? What are the implications for cash flow and shareholder wealth?

HM™

QUESTIONS AND PROBLEMS

1. **Building a Balance Sheet** [LO1] Penguin Pucks, Inc., has current assets of $5,100, net fixed assets of $23,800, current liabilities of $4,300, and long-term debt of $7,400. What is the value of the shareholders' equity account for this firm? How much is net working capital?

BASIC
(Questions 1–13)

2. **Building an Income Statement** [LO1] Papa Roach Exterminators, Inc., has sales of $586,000, costs of $247,000, depreciation expense of $43,000, interest expense of $32,000, and a tax rate of 35 percent. What is the net income for this firm?

3. **Dividends and Retained Earnings** [LO1] Suppose the firm in Problem 2 paid out $73,000 in cash dividends. What is the addition to retained earnings?

4. **Per-Share Earnings and Dividends** [LO1] Suppose the firm in Problem 3 had 85,000 shares of common stock outstanding. What is the earnings per share, or EPS, figure? What is the dividends per share figure?

5. **Market Values and Book Values** [LO1] Klingon Widgets, Inc., purchased new cloaking machinery three years ago for $7 million. The machinery can be sold to the Romulans today for $4.9 million. Klingon's current balance sheet shows net fixed assets of $3.7 million, current liabilities of $1.1 million, and net working capital of $380,000. If all the current assets were liquidated today, the company would receive $1.6 million cash. What is the book value of Klingon's assets today? What is the market value?

6. **Calculating Taxes** [LO3] The Renata Co. had $236,000 in 2009 taxable income. Using the rates from Table 2.3 in the chapter, calculate the company's 2009 income taxes.

7. **Tax Rates** [LO3] In Problem 6, what is the average tax rate? What is the marginal tax rate?

8. **Calculating OCF** [LO4] So Long, Inc., has sales of $27,500, costs of $13,280, depreciation expense of $2,300, and interest expense of $1,105. If the tax rate is 35 percent, what is the operating cash flow, or OCF?

9. **Calculating Net Capital Spending** [LO4] Earnhardt Driving School's 2008 balance sheet showed net fixed assets of $3.4 million, and the 2009 balance sheet showed net fixed assets of $4.2 million. The company's 2009 income statement showed a depreciation expense of $385,000. What was net capital spending for 2009?

Visit us at www.mhhe.com/rwj

10. **Calculating Additions to NWC [LO4]** The 2008 balance sheet of Saddle Creek, Inc., showed current assets of $2,100 and current liabilities of $1,380. The 2009 balance sheet showed current assets of $2,250 and current liabilities of $1,710. What was the company's 2009 change in net working capital, or NWC?

11. **Cash Flow to Creditors [LO4]** The 2008 balance sheet of Maria's Tennis Shop, Inc., showed long-term debt of $2.6 million, and the 2009 balance sheet showed long-term debt of $2.9 million. The 2009 income statement showed an interest expense of $170,000. What was the firm's cash flow to creditors during 2009?

12. **Cash Flow to Stockholders [LO4]** The 2008 balance sheet of Maria's Tennis Shop, Inc., showed $740,000 in the common stock account and $5.2 million in the additional paid-in surplus account. The 2009 balance sheet showed $815,000 and $5.5 million in the same two accounts, respectively. If the company paid out $490,000 in cash dividends during 2009, what was the cash flow to stockholders for the year?

13. **Calculating Total Cash Flows [LO4]** Given the information for Maria's Tennis Shop, Inc., in Problems 11 and 12, suppose you also know that the firm's net capital spending for 2009 was $940,000, and that the firm reduced its net working capital investment by $85,000. What was the firm's 2009 operating cash flow, or OCF?

INTERMEDIATE
(Questions 14–22)

14. **Calculating Total Cash Flows [LO4]** Jetson Spacecraft Corp. shows the following information on its 2009 income statement: sales = $196,000; costs = $104,000; other expenses = $6,800; depreciation expense = $9,100; interest expense = $14,800; taxes = $21,455; dividends = $10,400. In addition, you're told that the firm issued $5,700 in new equity during 2009 and redeemed $7,300 in outstanding long-term debt.
    a. What is the 2009 operating cash flow?
    b. What is the 2009 cash flow to creditors?
    c. What is the 2009 cash flow to stockholders?
    d. If net fixed assets increased by $27,000 during the year, what was the addition to NWC?

15. **Using Income Statements [LO1]** Given the following information for Rosato Pizza Co., calculate the depreciation expense: sales = $41,000; costs = $19,500; addition to retained earnings = $5,100; dividends paid = $1,500; interest expense = $4,500; tax rate = 35 percent.

16. **Preparing a Balance Sheet [LO1]** Prepare a 2009 balance sheet for Bertinelli Corp. based on the following information: cash = $195,000; patents and copyrights = $780,000; accounts payable = $405,000; accounts receivable = $137,000; tangible net fixed assets = $2,800,000; inventory = $264,000; notes payable = $160,000; accumulated retained earnings = $1,934,000; long-term debt = $1,195,300.

17. **Residual Claims [LO1]** Dimeback, Inc., is obligated to pay its creditors $7,300 during the year.
    a. What is the market value of the shareholders' equity if assets have a market value of $8,400?
    b. What if assets equal $6,700?

18. **Marginal versus Average Tax Rates** [LO3] (Refer to Table 2.3.) Corporation Growth has $88,000 in taxable income, and Corporation Income has $8,800,000 in taxable income.

    a. What is the tax bill for each firm?

    b. Suppose both firms have identified a new project that will increase taxable income by $10,000. How much in additional taxes will each firm pay? Why is this amount the same?

19. **Net Income and OCF** [LO2] During 2009, Raines Umbrella Corp. had sales of $730,000. Cost of goods sold, administrative and selling expenses, and depreciation expenses were $580,000, $105,000, and $135,000, respectively. In addition, the company had an interest expense of $75,000 and a tax rate of 35 percent. (Ignore any tax loss carryback or carryforward provisions.)

    a. What is Raines's net income for 2009?

    b. What is its operating cash flow?

    c. Explain your results in (a) and (b).

20. **Accounting Values versus Cash Flows** [LO4] In Problem 19, suppose Raines Umbrella Corp. paid out $25,000 in cash dividends. Is this possible? If spending on net fixed assets and net working capital was zero, and if no new stock was issued during the year, what do you know about the firm's long-term debt account?

21. **Calculating Cash Flows** [LO2] Dahlia Industries had the following operating results for 2009: sales = $22,800; cost of goods sold = $16,050; depreciation expense = $4,050; interest expense = $1,830; dividends paid − $1,300. At the beginning of the year, net fixed assets were $13,650, current assets were $4,800, and current liabilities were $2,700. At the end of the year, net fixed assets were $16,800, current assets were $5,930, and current liabilities were $3,150. The tax rate for 2009 was 34 percent.

    a. What is net income for 2009?

    b. What is the operating cash flow for 2009?

    c. What is the cash flow from assets for 2009? Is this possible? Explain.

    d. If no new debt was issued during the year, what is the cash flow to creditors? What is the cash flow to stockholders? Explain and interpret the positive and negative signs of your answers in (a) through (d).

22. **Calculating Cash Flows** [LO4] Consider the following abbreviated financial statements for Parrothead Enterprises:

PARROTHEAD ENTERPRISES 2008 and 2009 Partial Balance Sheets					
Assets			**Liabilities and Owners' Equity**		
	2008	2009		2008	2009
Current assets	$ 653	$ 707	Current liabilities	$ 261	$ 293
Net fixed assets	2,691	3,240	Long-term debt	1,422	1,512

PARROTHEAD ENTERPRISES 2009 Income Statement	
Sales	$8,280
Costs	3,861
Depreciation	738
Interest paid	211

    a. What is owners' equity for 2008 and 2009?

    b. What is the change in net working capital for 2009?

    c. In 2009, Parrothead Enterprises purchased $1,350 in new fixed assets. How much in fixed assets did Parrothead Enterprises sell? What is the cash flow from assets for the year? (The tax rate is 35 percent.)

Visit us at www.mhhe.com/rwj

Visit us at www.mhhe.com/rwj

d. During 2009, Parrothead Enterprises raised $270 in new long-term debt. How much long-term debt must Parrothead Enterprises have paid off during the year? What is the cash flow to creditors?

CHALLENGE
(Questions 23–26)

23. Net Fixed Assets and Depreciation [LO4] On the balance sheet, the net fixed assets (NFA) account is equal to the gross fixed assets (FA) account (which records the acquisition cost of fixed assets) minus the accumulated depreciation (AD) account (which records the total depreciation taken by the firm against its fixed assets). Using the fact that NFA = FA − AD, show that the expression given in the chapter for net capital spending, $NFA_{end} - NFA_{beg} + D$ (where D is the depreciation expense during the year), is equivalent to $FA_{end} - FA_{beg}$.

24. Tax Rates [LO3] Refer to the corporate marginal tax rate information in Table 2.3.

a. Why do you think the marginal tax rate jumps up from 34 percent to 39 percent at a taxable income of $100,001, and then falls back to a 34 percent marginal rate at a taxable income of $335,001?

b. Compute the average tax rate for a corporation with exactly $335,001 in taxable income. Does this confirm your explanation in part (a)? What is the average tax rate for a corporation with exactly $18,333,334? Is the same thing happening here?

c. The 39 percent and 38 percent tax rates both represent what is called a tax "bubble." Suppose the government wanted to lower the upper threshold of the 39 percent marginal tax bracket from $335,000 to $200,000. What would the new 39 percent bubble rate have to be?

Use the following information for Taco Swell, Inc., for Problems 25 and 26 (assume the tax rate is 34 percent):

	2008	2009
Sales	$ 7,233	$ 8,085
Depreciation	1,038	1,085
Cost of goods sold	2,487	2,942
Other expenses	591	515
Interest	485	579
Cash	3,792	4,041
Accounts receivable	5,021	5,892
Short-term notes payable	732	717
Long-term debt	12,700	15,435
Net fixed assets	31,805	33,921
Accounts payable	3,984	4,025
Inventory	8,927	9,555
Dividends	882	1,011

25. Financial Statements [LO1] Draw up an income statement and balance sheet for this company for 2008 and 2009.

26. Calculating Cash Flow [LO4] For 2009, calculate the cash flow from assets, cash flow to creditors, and cash flow to stockholders.

Cash Flows and Financial Statements at Sunset Boards, Inc.

Sunset Boards is a small company that manufactures and sells surfboards in Malibu. Tad Marks, the founder of the company, is in charge of the design and sale of the surfboards, but his background is in surfing, not business. As a result, the company's financial records are not well maintained.

The initial investment in Sunset Boards was provided by Tad and his friends and family. Because the initial investment was relatively small, and the company has made surfboards only for its own store, the investors haven't required detailed financial statements from Tad. But thanks to word of mouth among professional surfers, sales have picked up recently, and Tad is considering a major expansion. His plans include opening another surfboard store in Hawaii, as well as supplying his "sticks" (surfer lingo for boards) to other sellers.

Tad's expansion plans require a significant investment, which he plans to finance with a combination of additional funds from outsiders plus some money borrowed from banks. Naturally, the new investors and creditors require more organized and detailed financial statements than Tad has previously prepared. At the urging of his investors, Tad has hired financial analyst Christina Wolfe to evaluate the performance of the company over the past year.

After rooting through old bank statements, sales receipts, tax returns, and other records, Christina has assembled the following information:

Sunset Boards currently pays out 50 percent of net income as dividends to Tad and the other original investors, and has a 20 percent tax rate. You are Christina's assistant, and she has asked you to prepare the following:

1. An income statement for 2008 and 2009.
2. A balance sheet for 2008 and 2009.
3. Operating cash flow for each year.
4. Cash flow from assets for 2009.
5. Cash flow to creditors for 2009.
6. Cash flow to stockholders for 2009.

QUESTIONS

1. How would you describe Sunset Boards' cash flows for 2009? Write a brief discussion.

2. In light of your discussion in the previous question, what do you think about Tad's expansion plans?

	2008	2009
Cost of goods sold	$126,038	$159,143
Cash	18,187	27,478
Depreciation	35,581	40,217
Interest expense	7,735	8,866
Selling and administrative	24,787	32,352
Accounts payable	32,143	36,404
Net fixed assets	156,975	191,250
Sales	247,259	301,392
Accounts receivable	12,887	16,717
Notes payable	14,651	15,997
Long-term debt	79,235	91,195
Inventory	27,119	37,216
New equity	0	15,600

After studying this chapter, you should understand:

LO1 How to standardize financial statements for comparison purposes.

LO2 How to compute and, more importantly, interpret some common ratios.

LO3 The determinants of a firm's profitability.

LO4 Some of the problems and pitfalls in financial statement analysis.

3

WORKING WITH FINANCIAL STATEMENTS

THE PRICE OF A SHARE OF COMMON STOCK in hotel company Marriott International, Inc. closed at about $36 on April 3, 2008. At that price, Marriott had a price–earnings (PE) ratio of 21. That is, investors were willing to pay $21 for every dollar in income earned by Marriott. At the same time, investors were willing to pay $67, $32, and $12 for each dollar earned by Amazon.com, Apple, and Bank of America, respectively. At the other extreme were XM Satellite Radio and Sirius Satellite Radio, both relative newcomers to the stock market. Each had negative earnings for the previous year, yet XM was priced at about $12 per share and Sirius at about $3 per share.

Because they had negative earnings, their PE ratios would have been negative, so they were not reported. At the time, the typical stock in the S&P 500 Index of large company stocks was trading at a PE of about 19, or about 19 times earnings, as they say on Wall Street.

Price-to-earnings comparisons are examples of the use of financial ratios. As we will see in this chapter, there are a wide variety of financial ratios, all designed to summarize specific aspects of a firm's financial position. In addition to discussing how to analyze financial statements and compute financial ratios, we will have quite a bit to say about who uses this information and why.

Master the ability to solve problems in this chapter by using a spreadsheet. Access Excel Master on the student Web site www.mhhe.com/rwj.

In Chapter 2, we discussed some of the essential concepts of financial statements and cash flow. Part 2, this chapter and the next, continues where our earlier discussion left off. Our goal here is to expand your understanding of the uses (and abuses) of financial statement information.

Financial statement information will crop up in various places in the remainder of our book. Part 2 is not essential for understanding this material, but it will help give you an overall perspective on the role of financial statement information in corporate finance.

A good working knowledge of financial statements is desirable simply because such statements, and numbers derived from those statements, are the primary means of communicating financial information both within the firm and outside the firm. In short, much of the language of corporate finance is rooted in the ideas we discuss in this chapter.

Furthermore, as we will see, there are many different ways of using financial statement information and many different types of users. This diversity reflects the fact that financial statement information plays an important part in many types of decisions.

In the best of all worlds, the financial manager has full market value information about all of the firm's assets. This will rarely (if ever) happen. So, the reason we rely on accounting figures for much of our financial information is that we are almost always unable to obtain all (or even part) of the market information we want. The only meaningful yardstick for evaluating business decisions is whether they create economic value (see Chapter 1).

However, in many important situations, it will not be possible to make this judgment directly because we can't see the market value effects of decisions.

We recognize that accounting numbers are often just pale reflections of economic reality, but they are frequently the best available information. For privately held corporations, not-for-profit businesses, and smaller firms, for example, very little direct market value information exists at all. The accountant's reporting function is crucial in these circumstances.

Clearly, one important goal of the accountant is to report financial information to the user in a form useful for decision making. Ironically, the information frequently does not come to the user in such a form. In other words, financial statements don't come with a user's guide. This chapter and the next are first steps in filling this gap.

Cash Flow and Financial Statements: A Closer Look

3.1

At the most fundamental level, firms do two different things: They generate cash and they spend it. Cash is generated by selling a product, an asset, or a security. Selling a security involves either borrowing or selling an equity interest (shares of stock) in the firm. Cash is spent in paying for materials and labor to produce a product and in purchasing assets. Payments to creditors and owners also require the spending of cash.

In Chapter 2, we saw that the cash activities of a firm could be summarized by a simple identity:

Cash flow from assets = Cash flow to creditors + Cash flow to owners

This cash flow identity summarizes the total cash result of all transactions a firm engages in during the year. In this section, we return to the subject of cash flow by taking a closer look at the cash events during the year that lead to these total figures.

SOURCES AND USES OF CASH

Activities that bring in cash are called **sources of cash**. Activities that involve spending cash are called **uses** (or applications) **of cash**. What we need to do is to trace the changes in the firm's balance sheet to see how the firm obtained and spent its cash during some period.

To get started, consider the balance sheets for the Prufrock Corporation in Table 3.1. Notice that we have calculated the change in each of the items on the balance sheets.

Looking over the balance sheets for Prufrock, we see that quite a few things changed during the year. For example, Prufrock increased its net fixed assets by $149 and its inventory by $29. (Note that, throughout, all figures are in millions of dollars.) Where did the money come from? To answer this and related questions, we need to first identify those changes that used up cash (uses) and those that brought cash in (sources).

A little common sense is useful here. A firm uses cash by either buying assets or making payments. So, loosely speaking, an increase in an asset account means the firm, on a net basis, bought some assets—a use of cash. If an asset account went down, then on a net basis, the firm sold some assets. This would be a net source. Similarly, if a liability account goes down, then the firm has made a net payment—a use of cash.

Given this reasoning, there is a simple, albeit mechanical, definition you may find useful. An increase in a left-side (asset) account or a decrease in a right-side (liability or equity) account is a use of cash. Likewise, a decrease in an asset account or an increase in a liability (or equity) account is a source of cash.

sources of cash
A firm's activities that generate cash.

uses of cash
A firm's activities in which cash is spent. Also called *applications of cash*.

Company financial information can be found in many places on the Web, including www.financials.com, finance.yahoo.com, finance.google.com, *and* moneycentral.msn.com.

TABLE 3.1

PRUFROCK CORPORATION 2008 and 2009 Balance Sheets ($ in millions)			
	2008	**2009**	**Change**
Assets			
Current assets			
Cash	$ 84	$ 98	+$ 14
Accounts receivable	165	188	+ 23
Inventory	393	422	+ 29
Total	$ 642	$ 708	+$ 66
Fixed assets			
Net plant and equipment	$2,731	$2,880	+$149
Total assets	$3,373	$3,588	+$215
Liabilities and Owners' Equity			
Current liabilities			
Accounts payable	$ 312	$ 344	+$ 32
Notes payable	231	196	− 35
Total	$ 543	$ 540	−$ 3
Long-term debt	$ 531	$ 457	−$ 74
Owners' equity			
Common stock and paid-in surplus	$ 500	$ 550	+$ 50
Retained earnings	1,799	2,041	+ 242
Total	$2,299	$2,591	+$292
Total liabilities and owners' equity	$3,373	$3,588	+$215

Looking again at Prufrock, we see that inventory rose by $29. This is a net use because Prufrock effectively paid out $29 to increase inventories. Accounts payable rose by $32. This is a source of cash because Prufrock effectively has borrowed an additional $32 payable by the end of the year. Notes payable, on the other hand, went down by $35, so Prufrock effectively paid off $35 worth of short-term debt—a use of cash.

Based on our discussion, we can summarize the sources and uses of cash from the balance sheet as follows:

Sources of cash:	
Increase in accounts payable	$ 32
Increase in common stock	50
Increase in retained earnings	242
Total sources	$324
Uses of cash:	
Increase in accounts receivable	$ 23
Increase in inventory	29
Decrease in notes payable	35
Decrease in long-term debt	74
Net fixed asset acquisitions	149
Total uses	$310
Net addition to cash	$ 14

The net addition to cash is just the difference between sources and uses, and our $14 result here agrees with the $14 change shown on the balance sheet.

TABLE 3.2

PRUFROCK CORPORATION 2009 Income Statement ($ in millions)		
Sales		$2,311
Cost of goods sold		1,344
Depreciation		276
Earnings before interest and taxes		$ 691
Interest paid		141
Taxable income		$ 550
Taxes (34%)		187
Net income		$ 363
Dividends	$121	
Addition to retained earnings	242	

This simple statement tells us much of what happened during the year, but it doesn't tell the whole story. For example, the increase in retained earnings is net income (a source of funds) less dividends (a use of funds). It would be more enlightening to have these reported separately so we could see the breakdown. Also, we have considered only net fixed asset acquisitions. Total or gross spending would be more interesting to know.

To further trace the flow of cash through the firm during the year, we need an income statement. For Prufrock, the results for the year are shown in Table 3.2.

Notice here that the $242 addition to retained earnings we calculated from the balance sheet is just the difference between the net income of $363 and the dividends of $121.

THE STATEMENT OF CASH FLOWS

There is some flexibility in summarizing the sources and uses of cash in the form of a financial statement. However it is presented, the result is called the **statement of cash flows**.

We present a particular format for this statement in Table 3.3. The basic idea is to group all the changes into three categories: operating activities, financing activities, and investment activities. The exact form differs in detail from one preparer to the next.

Don't be surprised if you come across different arrangements. The types of information presented will be similar; the exact order can differ. The key thing to remember in this case is that we started out with $84 in cash and ended up with $98, for a net increase of $14. We're just trying to see what events led to this change.

Going back to Chapter 2, we note that there is a slight conceptual problem here. Interest paid should really go under financing activities, but unfortunately that's not the way the accounting is handled. The reason, you may recall, is that interest is deducted as an expense when net income is computed. Also, notice that the net purchase of fixed assets was $149. Because Prufrock wrote off $276 worth of assets (the depreciation), it must have actually spent a total of $149 + 276 = $425 on fixed assets.

Once we have this statement, it might seem appropriate to express the change in cash on a per-share basis, much as we did for net income. Ironically, despite the interest we might have in some measure of cash flow per share, standard accounting practice expressly prohibits reporting this information. The reason is that accountants feel that cash flow (or some component of cash flow) is not an alternative to accounting income, so only earnings per share are to be reported.

As shown in Table 3.4, it is sometimes useful to present the same information a bit differently. We will call this the "sources and uses of cash" statement. There is no such

statement of cash flows
A firm's financial statement that summarizes its sources and uses of cash over a specified period.

TABLE 3.3

PRUFROCK CORPORATION 2009 Statement of Cash Flows ($ in millions)	
Cash, beginning of year	$ 84
Operating activity	
Net income	$363
Plus:	
Depreciation	276
Increase in accounts payable	32
Less:	
Increase in accounts receivable	− 23
Increase in inventory	− 29
Net cash from operating activity	$619
Investment activity	
Fixed asset acquisitions	−$425
Net cash from investment activity	−$425
Financing activity	
Decrease in notes payable	−$ 35
Decrease in long-term debt	− 74
Dividends paid	− 121
Increase in common stock	50
Net cash from financing activity	−$180
Net increase in cash	$ 14
Cash, end of year	$ 98

TABLE 3.4

PRUFROCK CORPORATION 2009 Sources and Uses of Cash ($ in millions)	
Cash, beginning of year	$ 84
Sources of cash	
Operations:	
Net income	$363
Depreciation	276
	$639
Working capital:	
Increase in accounts payable	$ 32
Long-term financing:	
Increase in common stock	50
Total sources of cash	$721
Uses of cash	
Working capital:	
Increase in accounts receivable	$ 23
Increase in inventory	29
Decrease in notes payable	35
Long-term financing:	
Decrease in long-term debt	74
Fixed asset acquisitions	425
Dividends paid	121
Total uses of cash	$707
Net addition to cash	$ 14
Cash, end of year	$ 98

statement in financial accounting, but this arrangement resembles one used many years ago. As we will discuss, this form can come in handy, but we emphasize again that it is not the way this information is normally presented.

Now that we have the various cash pieces in place, we can get a good idea of what happened during the year. Prufrock's major cash outlays were fixed asset acquisitions and cash dividends. It paid for these activities primarily with cash generated from operations.

Prufrock also retired some long-term debt and increased current assets. Finally, current liabilities were not greatly changed, and a relatively small amount of new equity was sold. Altogether, this short sketch captures Prufrock's major sources and uses of cash for the year.

Concept Questions

3.1a What is a source of cash? Give three examples.

3.1b What is a use, or application, of cash? Give three examples.

Standardized Financial Statements

3.2

The next thing we might want to do with Prufrock's financial statements is compare them to those of other similar companies. We would immediately have a problem, however. It's almost impossible to directly compare the financial statements for two companies because of differences in size.

For example, Ford and GM are serious rivals in the auto market, but GM is much larger (in terms of market share), so it is difficult to compare them directly. For that matter, it's difficult even to compare financial statements from different points in time for the same company if the company's size has changed. The size problem is compounded if we try to compare GM and, say, Toyota. If Toyota's financial statements are denominated in yen, then we have size *and* currency differences.

To start making comparisons, one obvious thing we might try to do is to somehow standardize the financial statements. One common and useful way of doing this is to work with percentages instead of total dollars. In this section, we describe two different ways of standardizing financial statements along these lines.

COMMON-SIZE STATEMENTS

To get started, a useful way of standardizing financial statements is to express each item on the balance sheet as a percentage of assets and to express each item on the income statement as a percentage of sales. The resulting financial statements are called **common-size statements**. We consider these next.

common-size statement
A standardized financial statement presenting all items in percentage terms. Balance sheet items are shown as a percentage of assets and income statement items as a percentage of sales.

Common-Size Balance Sheets   One way, though not the only way, to construct a common-size balance sheet is to express each item as a percentage of total assets. Prufrock's 2008 and 2009 common-size balance sheets are shown in Table 3.5.

Notice that some of the totals don't check exactly because of rounding. Also notice that the total change has to be zero because the beginning and ending numbers must add up to 100 percent.

In this form, financial statements are relatively easy to read and compare. For example, just looking at the two balance sheets for Prufrock, we see that current assets were 19.7 percent of total assets in 2009, up from 19.1 percent in 2008. Current liabilities declined

TABLE 3.5

PRUFROCK CORPORATION Common-Size Balance Sheets 2008 and 2009			
	2008	**2009**	**Change**
Assets			
Current assets			
Cash	2.5%	2.7%	+ .2%
Accounts receivable	4.9	5.2	+ .3
Inventory	11.7	11.8	+ .1
Total	19.1	19.7	+ .6
Fixed assets			
Net plant and equipment	80.9	80.3	− .6
Total assets	100.0%	100.0%	.0
Liabilities and Owners' Equity			
Current liabilities			
Accounts payable	9.2%	9.6%	+ .4%
Notes payable	6.8	5.5	−1.3
Total	16.0	15.1	− .9
Long-term debt	15.7	12.7	−3.0
Owners' equity			
Common stock and paid-in surplus	14.8	15.3	+ .5
Retained earnings	53.3	56.9	+3.6
Total	68.1	72.2	+4.1
Total liabilities and owners' equity	100.0%	100.0%	.0

from 16.0 percent to 15.1 percent of total liabilities and equity over that same time. Similarly, total equity rose from 68.1 percent of total liabilities and equity to 72.2 percent.

Overall, Prufrock's liquidity, as measured by current assets compared to current liabilities, increased over the year. Simultaneously, Prufrock's indebtedness diminished as a percentage of total assets. We might be tempted to conclude that the balance sheet has grown "stronger." We will say more about this later.

Common-Size Income Statements   A useful way of standardizing the income statement is to express each item as a percentage of total sales, as illustrated for Prufrock in Table 3.6.

This income statement tells us what happens to each dollar in sales. For Prufrock, interest expense eats up $.061 out of every sales dollar and taxes take another $.081. When all is said and done, $.157 of each dollar flows through to the bottom line (net income), and that amount is split into $.105 retained in the business and $.052 paid out in dividends.

These percentages are useful in comparisons. For example, a relevant figure is the cost percentage. For Prufrock, $.582 of each $1 in sales goes to pay for goods sold. It would be interesting to compute the same percentage for Prufrock's main competitors to see how Prufrock stacks up in terms of cost control.

TABLE 3.6

PRUFROCK CORPORATION Common-Size Income Statement 2009		
Sales		100.0%
Cost of goods sold		58.2
Depreciation		11.9
Earnings before interest and taxes		29.9
Interest paid		6.1
Taxable income		23.8
Taxes (34%)		8.1
Net income		15.7%
Dividends	5.2%	
Addition to retained earnings	10.5	

Common-Size Statements of Cash Flows   Although we have not presented it here, it is also possible and useful to prepare a common-size statement of cash flows. Unfortunately, with the current statement of cash flows, there is no obvious denominator such as total assets or total sales. However, if the information is arranged in a way similar to that in Table 3.4, then each item can be expressed as a percentage of total sources (or total uses). The results can then be interpreted as the percentage of total sources of cash supplied or as the percentage of total uses of cash for a particular item.

COMMON–BASE YEAR FINANCIAL STATEMENTS: TREND ANALYSIS

Imagine we were given balance sheets for the last 10 years for some company and we were trying to investigate trends in the firm's pattern of operations. Does the firm use more or less debt? Has the firm grown more or less liquid? A useful way of standardizing financial statements in this case is to choose a base year and then express each item relative to the base amount. We will call the resulting statements **common–base year statements**.

For example, from 2008 to 2009, Prufrock's inventory rose from $393 to $422. If we pick 2008 as our base year, then we would set inventory equal to 1.00 for that year. For the next year, we would calculate inventory relative to the base year as $422/393 = 1.07$. In this case, we could say inventory grew by about 7 percent during the year. If we had multiple years, we would just divide the inventory figure for each one by $393. The resulting series is easy to plot, and it is then easy to compare companies. Table 3.7 summarizes these calculations for the asset side of the balance sheet.

common–base year statement
A standardized financial statement presenting all items relative to a certain base year amount.

COMBINED COMMON-SIZE AND BASE YEAR ANALYSIS

The trend analysis we have been discussing can be combined with the common-size analysis discussed earlier. The reason for doing this is that as total assets grow, most of the other accounts must grow as well. By first forming the common-size statements, we eliminate the effect of this overall growth.

For example, looking at Table 3.7, we see that Prufrock's accounts receivable were $165, or 4.9 percent of total assets, in 2008. In 2009, they had risen to $188, which was 5.2 percent of total assets. If we do our analysis in terms of dollars, then the 2009 figure would be $188/165 = 1.14$, representing a 14 percent increase in receivables. However, if we work with the common-size statements, then the 2009 figure would be 5.2%/4.9% = 1.06. This tells us accounts receivable, as a percentage of total assets, grew by 6 percent. Roughly speaking, what we see is that of the 14 percent total increase, about 8 percent (= 14% 6%) is attributable simply to growth in total assets.

TABLE 3.7

PRUFROCK CORPORATION Summary of Standardized Balance Sheets (Asset Side Only)						
	Assets ($ in millions)		Common-Size Assets		Common–Base Year Assets	Combined Common-Size and Base Year Assets
	2008	2009	2008	2009	2009	2009
Current assets						
Cash	$ 84	$ 98	2.5%	2.7%	1.17	1.08
Accounts receivable	165	188	4.9	5.2	1.14	1.06
Inventory	393	422	11.7	11.8	1.07	1.01
Total current assets	$ 642	$ 708	19.1	19.7	1.10	1.03
Fixed assets						
Net plant and equipment	$2,731	$2,880	80.9	80.3	1.05	.99
Total assets	$3,373	$3,588	100.0%	100.0%	1.06	1.00

NOTE: The common-size numbers are calculated by dividing each item by total assets for that year. For example, the 2008 common-size cash amount is $84/3,373 = 2.5%. The common–base year numbers are calculated by dividing each 2009 item by the base year (2008) dollar amount. The common-base cash is thus $98/84 = 1.17, representing a 17 percent increase. The combined common-size and base year figures are calculated by dividing each common-size amount by the base year (2008) common-size amount. The cash figure is therefore 2.7%/2.5% = 1.08, representing an 8 percent increase in cash holdings as a percentage of total assets. Columns may not total precisely due to rounding.

Concept Questions

3.2a Why is it often necessary to standardize financial statements?

3.2b Name two types of standardized statements and describe how each is formed.

3.3 Ratio Analysis

financial ratios
Relationships determined from a firm's financial information and used for comparison purposes.

Another way of avoiding the problems involved in comparing companies of different sizes is to calculate and compare **financial ratios**. Such ratios are ways of comparing and investigating the relationships between different pieces of financial information. Using ratios eliminates the size problem because the size effectively divides out. We're then left with percentages, multiples, or time periods.

There is a problem in discussing financial ratios. Because a ratio is simply one number divided by another, and because there are so many accounting numbers out there, we could examine a huge number of possible ratios. Everybody has a favorite. We will restrict ourselves to a representative sampling.

In this section, we only want to introduce you to some commonly used financial ratios. These are not necessarily the ones we think are the best. In fact, some of them may strike you as illogical or not as useful as some alternatives. If they do, don't be concerned. As a financial analyst, you can always decide how to compute your own ratios.

What you do need to worry about is the fact that different people and different sources seldom compute these ratios in exactly the same way, and this leads to much confusion. The specific definitions we use here may or may not be the same as ones you have seen or will see elsewhere. If you are ever using ratios as a tool for analysis, you should be careful to document how you calculate each one; and if you are comparing your numbers to numbers from another source, be sure you know how those numbers are computed.

We will defer much of our discussion of how ratios are used and some problems that come up with using them until later in the chapter. For now, for each of the ratios we discuss, we consider several questions:

1. How is it computed?
2. What is it intended to measure, and why might we be interested?
3. What is the unit of measurement?
4. What might a high or low value tell us? How might such values be misleading?
5. How could this measure be improved?

Financial ratios are traditionally grouped into the following categories:

1. Short-term solvency, or liquidity, ratios.
2. Long-term solvency, or financial leverage, ratios.
3. Asset management, or turnover, ratios.
4. Profitability ratios.
5. Market value ratios.

We will consider each of these in turn. In calculating these numbers for Prufrock, we will use the ending balance sheet (2009) figures unless we say otherwise. Also notice that the various ratios are color keyed to indicate which numbers come from the income statement and which come from the balance sheet.

SHORT-TERM SOLVENCY, OR LIQUIDITY, MEASURES

As the name suggests, short-term solvency ratios as a group are intended to provide information about a firm's liquidity, and these ratios are sometimes called *liquidity measures*. The primary concern is the firm's ability to pay its bills over the short run without undue stress. Consequently, these ratios focus on current assets and current liabilities.

For obvious reasons, liquidity ratios are particularly interesting to short-term creditors. Because financial managers work constantly with banks and other short-term lenders, an understanding of these ratios is essential.

One advantage of looking at current assets and liabilities is that their book values and market values are likely to be similar. Often (though not always), these assets and liabilities just don't live long enough for the two to get seriously out of step. On the other hand, like any type of near-cash, current assets and liabilities can and do change fairly rapidly, so today's amounts may not be a reliable guide to the future.

Go to www.reuters.com *to examine comparative ratios for a huge number of companies.*

Current Ratio   One of the best known and most widely used ratios is the *current ratio*. As you might guess, the current ratio is defined as follows:

$$\text{Current ratio} = \frac{\text{Current assets}}{\text{Current liabilities}} \qquad \text{[3.1]}$$

Here is Prufrock's 2009 current ratio:

$$\text{Current ratio} = \frac{\$708}{\$540} = 1.31 \text{ times}$$

Because current assets and liabilities are, in principle, converted to cash over the following 12 months, the current ratio is a measure of short-term liquidity. The unit of measurement is either dollars or times. So, we could say Prufrock has $1.31 in current assets for every $1 in current liabilities, or we could say Prufrock has its current liabilities covered 1.31 times over.

To a creditor—particularly a short-term creditor such as a supplier—the higher the current ratio, the better. To the firm, a high current ratio indicates liquidity, but it also may indicate an inefficient use of cash and other short-term assets. Absent some extraordinary circumstances, we would expect to see a current ratio of at least 1 because a current ratio of less than 1 would mean that net working capital (current assets less current liabilities) is negative. This would be unusual in a healthy firm, at least for most types of businesses.

The current ratio, like any ratio, is affected by various types of transactions. For example, suppose the firm borrows over the long term to raise money. The short-run effect would be an increase in cash from the issue proceeds and an increase in long-term debt. Current liabilities would not be affected, so the current ratio would rise.

Finally, note that an apparently low current ratio may not be a bad sign for a company with a large reserve of untapped borrowing power.

EXAMPLE 3.1	Current Events

Suppose a firm pays off some of its suppliers and short-term creditors. What happens to the current ratio? Suppose a firm buys some inventory. What happens in this case? What happens if a firm sells some merchandise?

The first case is a trick question. What happens is that the current ratio moves away from 1. If it is greater than 1 (the usual case), it will get bigger; but if it is less than 1, it will get smaller. To see this, suppose the firm has $4 in current assets and $2 in current liabilities for a current ratio of 2. If we use $1 in cash to reduce current liabilities, then the new current ratio is ($4 − 1)/($2 − 1) = 3. If we reverse the original situation to $2 in current assets and $4 in current liabilities, then the change will cause the current ratio to fall to 1/3 from 1/2.

The second case is not quite as tricky. Nothing happens to the current ratio because cash goes down while inventory goes up—total current assets are unaffected.

In the third case, the current ratio will usually rise because inventory is normally shown at cost and the sale will normally be at something greater than cost (the difference is the markup). The increase in either cash or receivables is therefore greater than the decrease in inventory. This increases current assets, and the current ratio rises.

The Quick (or Acid-Test) Ratio   Inventory is often the least liquid current asset. It's also the one for which the book values are least reliable as measures of market value because the quality of the inventory isn't considered. Some of the inventory may later turn out to be damaged, obsolete, or lost.

More to the point, relatively large inventories are often a sign of short-term trouble. The firm may have overestimated sales and overbought or overproduced as a result. In this case, the firm may have a substantial portion of its liquidity tied up in slow-moving inventory.

To further evaluate liquidity, the *quick,* or *acid-test, ratio* is computed just like the current ratio, except inventory is omitted:

$$\text{Quick ratio} = \frac{\text{Current assets} - \text{Inventory}}{\text{Current liabilities}} \qquad [3.2]$$

Notice that using cash to buy inventory does not affect the current ratio, but it reduces the quick ratio. Again, the idea is that inventory is relatively illiquid compared to cash.

For Prufrock, this ratio for 2009 was:

$$\text{Quick ratio} = \frac{\$708 - 422}{\$540} = .53 \text{ times}$$

The quick ratio here tells a somewhat different story than the current ratio because inventory accounts for more than half of Prufrock's current assets. To exaggerate the point, if this inventory consisted of, say, unsold nuclear power plants, then this would be a cause for concern.

To give an example of current versus quick ratios, based on recent financial statements, Wal-Mart and Manpower Inc. had current ratios of .81 and 1.60, respectively. However, Manpower carries no inventory to speak of, whereas Wal-Mart's current assets are virtually all inventory. As a result, Wal-Mart's quick ratio was only .21, whereas Manpower's was 1.60, the same as its current ratio.

Other Liquidity Ratios We briefly mention three other measures of liquidity. A very short-term creditor might be interested in the *cash ratio:*

$$\text{Cash ratio} = \frac{\text{Cash}}{\text{Current liabilities}} \qquad [3.3]$$

You can verify that for 2009 this works out to be .18 times for Prufrock.

Because net working capital, or NWC, is frequently viewed as the amount of short-term liquidity a firm has, we can consider the ratio of *NWC to total assets:*

$$\text{Net working capital to total assets} = \frac{\text{Net working capital}}{\text{Total assets}} \qquad [3.4]$$

A relatively low value might indicate relatively low levels of liquidity. Here, this ratio works out to be ($708 − 540)/$3,588 = 4.7%.

Finally, imagine that Prufrock was facing a strike and cash inflows began to dry up. How long could the business keep running? One answer is given by the *interval measure:*

$$\text{Interval measure} = \frac{\text{Current assets}}{\text{Average daily operating costs}} \qquad [3.5]$$

Total costs for the year, excluding depreciation and interest, were $1,344. The average daily cost was $1,344/365 = $3.68 per day.[1] The interval measure is thus $708/$3.68 = 192 days. Based on this, Prufrock could hang on for six months or so.[2]

The interval measure (or something similar) is also useful for newly founded or start-up companies that often have little in the way of revenues. For such companies, the interval measure indicates how long the company can operate until it needs another round of financing. The average daily operating cost for start-up companies is often called the burn rate, meaning the rate at which cash is burned in the race to become profitable.

LONG-TERM SOLVENCY MEASURES

Long-term solvency ratios are intended to address the firm's long-term ability to meet its obligations, or, more generally, its financial leverage. These are sometimes called *financial leverage ratios* or just *leverage ratios*. We consider three commonly used measures and some variations.

Total Debt Ratio The *total debt ratio* takes into account all debts of all maturities to all creditors. It can be defined in several ways, the easiest of which is this:

$$\text{Total debt ratio} = \frac{\text{Total assets} - \text{Total equity}}{\text{Total assets}} \qquad [3.6]$$

$$= \frac{\$3,588 - 2,591}{\$3,588} = .28 \text{ times}$$

The online Women's Business Center has more information about financial statements, ratios, and small business topics (www.onlinewbc.gov).

---

[1]For many of these ratios that involve average daily amounts, a 360-day year is often used in practice. This so-called banker's year has exactly four quarters of 90 days each and was computationally convenient in the days before pocket calculators. We'll use 365 days.

[2]Sometimes depreciation and/or interest is included in calculating average daily costs. Depreciation isn't a cash expense, so its inclusion doesn't make a lot of sense. Interest is a financing cost, so we excluded it by definition (we looked at only operating costs). We could, of course, define a different ratio that included interest expense.

In this case, an analyst might say that Prufrock uses 28 percent debt.[3] Whether this is high or low or whether it even makes any difference depends on whether capital structure matters, a subject we discuss in Part 6.

Prufrock has $.28 in debt for every $1 in assets. Therefore, there is $.72 in equity ($1 − .28) for every $.28 in debt. With this in mind, we can define two useful variations on the total debt ratio—the *debt–equity ratio* and the *equity multiplier:*

$$\text{Debt–equity ratio} = \text{Total debt/Total equity}$$
$$= \$.28/\$.72 = .39 \text{ times} \tag{3.7}$$

$$\text{Equity multiplier} = \text{Total assets/Total equity}$$
$$= \$1/\$.72 = 1.39 \text{ times} \tag{3.8}$$

The fact that the equity multiplier is 1 plus the debt–equity ratio is not a coincidence:

$$\text{Equity multiplier} = \text{Total assets/Total equity} = \$1/\$.72 = 1.39$$
$$= (\text{Total equity} + \text{Total debt})/\text{Total equity}$$
$$= 1 + \text{Debt–equity ratio} = 1.39 \text{ times}$$

The thing to notice here is that given any one of these three ratios, you can immediately calculate the other two; so, they all say exactly the same thing.

Ratios used to analyze technology firms can be found at www.chalfin.com under the "Publications" link.

A Brief Digression: Total Capitalization versus Total Assets   Frequently, financial analysts are more concerned with a firm's long-term debt than its short-term debt because the short-term debt will constantly be changing. Also, a firm's accounts payable may reflect trade practice more than debt management policy. For these reasons, the *long-term debt ratio* is often calculated as follows:

$$\text{Long-term debt ratio} = \frac{\text{Long-term debt}}{\text{Long-term debt} + \text{Total equity}}$$
$$= \frac{\$457}{\$457 + 2{,}591} = \frac{\$457}{\$3{,}048} = .15 \text{ times} \tag{3.9}$$

The $3,048 in total long-term debt and equity is sometimes called the firm's *total capitalization,* and the financial manager will frequently focus on this quantity rather than on total assets.

To complicate matters, different people (and different books) mean different things by the term *debt ratio.* Some mean a ratio of total debt, and some mean a ratio of long-term debt only, and, unfortunately, a substantial number are simply vague about which one they mean.

This is a source of confusion, so we choose to give two separate names to the two measures. The same problem comes up in discussing the debt–equity ratio. Financial analysts frequently calculate this ratio using only long-term debt.

Times Interest Earned   Another common measure of long-term solvency is the *times interest earned* (TIE) *ratio.* Once again, there are several possible (and common) definitions, but we'll stick with the most traditional:

$$\text{Times interest earned ratio} = \frac{\text{EBIT}}{\text{Interest}}$$
$$= \frac{\$691}{\$141} = 4.9 \text{ times} \tag{3.10}$$

---

[3]Total equity here includes preferred stock (discussed in Chapter 8 and elsewhere), if there is any. An equivalent numerator in this ratio would be Current liabilities + Long-term debt.

As the name suggests, this ratio measures how well a company has its interest obligations covered, and it is often called the *interest coverage ratio*. For Prufrock, the interest bill is covered 4.9 times over.

Cash Coverage   A problem with the TIE ratio is that it is based on EBIT, which is not really a measure of cash available to pay interest. The reason is that depreciation, a noncash expense, has been deducted out. Because interest is definitely a cash outflow (to creditors), one way to define the *cash coverage ratio* is this:

$$\text{Cash coverage ratio} = \frac{\text{EBIT} + \text{Depreciation}}{\text{Interest}}$$

$$= \frac{\$691 + 276}{\$141} = \frac{\$967}{\$141} = 6.9 \text{ times}$$

[3.11]

The numerator here, EBIT plus depreciation, is often abbreviated EBITD (earnings before interest, taxes, and depreciation—say "ebbit-dee"). It is a basic measure of the firm's ability to generate cash from operations, and it is frequently used as a measure of cash flow available to meet financial obligations.

A common variation on EBITD is earnings before interest, taxes, depreciation, and amortization (EBITDA—say "ebbit-dah"). Here *amortization* refers to a noncash deduction similar conceptually to depreciation, except it applies to an intangible asset (such as a patent) rather than a tangible asset (such as machine). Note that the word *amortization* here does not refer to the repayment of debt, a subject we discuss in a later chapter.

ASSET MANAGEMENT, OR TURNOVER, MEASURES

We next turn our attention to the efficiency with which Prufrock uses its assets. The measures in this section are sometimes called *asset utilization ratios*. The specific ratios we discuss can all be interpreted as measures of turnover. What they are intended to describe is how efficiently or intensively a firm uses its assets to generate sales. We first look at two important current assets: inventory and receivables.

Inventory Turnover and Days' Sales in Inventory   During the year, Prufrock had a cost of goods sold of $1,344. Inventory at the end of the year was $422. With these numbers, *inventory turnover* can be calculated as follows:

$$\text{Inventory turnover} = \frac{\text{Cost of goods sold}}{\text{Inventory}}$$

$$= \frac{\$1,344}{\$422} = 3.2 \text{ times}$$

[3.12]

In a sense, Prufrock sold off or turned over the entire inventory 3.2 times.[4] As long as we are not running out of stock and thereby forgoing sales, the higher this ratio is, the more efficiently we are managing inventory.

If we know we turned our inventory over 3.2 times during the year, we can immediately figure out how long it took us to turn it over on average. The result is the average *days' sales in inventory:*

$$\text{Days' sales in inventory} = \frac{365 \text{ days}}{\text{Inventory turnover}}$$

$$= \frac{365 \text{ days}}{3.2} = 114 \text{ days}$$

[3.13]

---

[4]Notice that we used cost of goods sold in the top of this ratio. For some purposes, it might be more useful to use sales instead of costs. For example, if we wanted to know the amount of sales generated per dollar of inventory, we could just replace the cost of goods sold with sales.

This tells us that, roughly speaking, inventory sits 114 days on average before it is sold. Alternatively, assuming we have used the most recent inventory and cost figures, it will take about 114 days to work off our current inventory.

For example, in February 2008, General Motors had a 153-day supply of its Chevrolet Silverado, more than the 60-day supply considered normal. This figure means that at the then-current rate of sales, it would have taken General Motors 153 days to deplete the available supply, or, equivalently, that General Motors had 153 days of Silverado sales in inventory. General Motors also had a 152-day supply of the GMC Sierra and a 164-day supply of the GMC Yukon. While these figures look very high (and they are), they also show why you should not look at any ratio in isolation. The reason that General Motors had such a large inventory was an expected strike at supplier American Axle & Manufacturing Holdings. General Motors wanted the excess inventory because it would be unable to produce any of these SUVs without the critical parts supplied by American Axle. By the end of March 2008, General Motors had temporarily closed two plants and had over 17,000 workers idled because of the strike at its supplier.

It might make more sense to use the average inventory in calculating turnover. Inventory turnover would then be $1,344/[($393 + 422)/2] = 3.3$ times.[5] It depends on the purpose of the calculation. If we are interested in how long it will take us to sell our current inventory, then using the ending figure (as we did initially) is probably better.

In many of the ratios we discuss in this chapter, average figures could just as well be used. Again, it depends on whether we are worried about the past, in which case averages are appropriate, or the future, in which case ending figures might be better. Also, using ending figures is common in reporting industry averages; so, for comparison purposes, ending figures should be used in such cases. In any event, using ending figures is definitely less work, so we'll continue to use them.

Receivables Turnover and Days' Sales in Receivables   Our inventory measures give some indication of how fast we can sell product. We now look at how fast we collect on those sales. The *receivables turnover* is defined much like inventory turnover:

$$\text{Receivables turnover} = \frac{\text{Sales}}{\text{Accounts receivable}}$$

$$= \frac{\$2,311}{\$188} = 12.3 \text{ times} \qquad \text{[3.14]}$$

Loosely speaking, Prufrock collected its outstanding credit accounts and reloaned the money 12.3 times during the year.[6]

This ratio makes more sense if we convert it to days, so here is the *days' sales in receivables:*

$$\text{Days' sales in receivables} = \frac{365 \text{ days}}{\text{Receivables turnover}}$$

$$= \frac{365}{12.3} = 30 \text{ days} \qquad \text{[3.15]}$$

Therefore, on average, Prufrock collects on its credit sales in 30 days. For obvious reasons, this ratio is frequently called the *average collection period* (ACP).

Note that if we are using the most recent figures, we could also say that we have 30 days' worth of sales currently uncollected. We will learn more about this subject when we study credit policy in a later chapter.

---

[5]Notice that we calculated the average as (Beginning value + Ending value)/2.

[6]Here we have implicitly assumed that all sales are credit sales. If they were not, we would simply use total credit sales in these calculations, not total sales.

| Payables Turnover | EXAMPLE 3.2 |

Here is a variation on the receivables collection period. How long, on average, does it take for Prufrock Corporation to pay its bills? To answer, we need to calculate the accounts payable turnover rate using cost of goods sold. We will assume that Prufrock purchases everything on credit.

The cost of goods sold is $1,344, and accounts payable are $344. The turnover is therefore $1,344/$344 = 3.9 times. So, payables turned over about every 365/3.9 = 94 days. On average, then, Prufrock takes 94 days to pay. As a potential creditor, we might take note of this fact.

Asset Turnover Ratios   Moving away from specific accounts like inventory or receivables, we can consider several "big picture" ratios. For example, *NWC turnover* is:

$$\text{NWC turnover} = \frac{\text{Sales}}{\text{NWC}}$$

$$= \frac{\$2,311}{\$708 - 540} = 13.8 \text{ times}$$ [3.16]

This ratio measures how much "work" we get out of our working capital. Once again, assuming we aren't missing out on sales, a high value is preferred. (Why?)

Similarly, *fixed asset turnover* is:

$$\text{Fixed asset turnover} = \frac{\text{Sales}}{\text{Net fixed assets}}$$

$$= \frac{\$2,311}{\$2,880} = .80 \text{ times}$$ [3.17]

With this ratio, it probably makes more sense to say that for every dollar in fixed assets, Prufrock generated $.80 in sales.

Our final asset management ratio, the *total asset turnover,* comes up quite a bit. We will see it later in this chapter and in the next chapter. As the name suggests, the total asset turnover is:

$$\text{Total asset turnover} = \frac{\text{Sales}}{\text{Total assets}}$$

$$= \frac{\$2,311}{\$3,588} = .64 \text{ times}$$ [3.18]

In other words, for every dollar in assets, Prufrock generated $.64 in sales.

To give an example of fixed and total asset turnover, based on recent financial statements, Southwest Airlines had a total asset turnover of .59, compared to .82 for IBM. However, the much higher investment in fixed assets in an airline is reflected in Southwest's fixed asset turnover of .80, compared to IBM's 1.46.

| More Turnover | EXAMPLE 3.3 |

Suppose you find that a particular company generates $.40 in sales for every dollar in total assets. How often does this company turn over its total assets?

The total asset turnover here is .40 times per year. It takes 1/.40 = 2.5 years to turn total assets over completely.

PROFITABILITY MEASURES

The three measures we discuss in this section are probably the best known and most widely used of all financial ratios. In one form or another, they are intended to measure how efficiently a firm uses its assets and manages its operations. The focus in this group is on the bottom line, net income.

Profit Margin   Companies pay a great deal of attention to their *profit margins:*

$$\text{Profit margin} = \frac{\text{Net income}}{\text{Sales}}$$

$$= \frac{\$363}{\$2,311} = 15.7\%$$

[3.19]

This tells us that Prufrock, in an accounting sense, generates a little less than 16 cents in profit for every dollar in sales.

All other things being equal, a relatively high profit margin is obviously desirable. This situation corresponds to low expense ratios relative to sales. However, we hasten to add that other things are often not equal.

For example, lowering our sales price will usually increase unit volume but will normally cause profit margins to shrink. Total profit (or, more important, operating cash flow) may go up or down; so the fact that margins are smaller isn't necessarily bad. After all, isn't it possible that, as the saying goes, "Our prices are so low that we lose money on everything we sell, but we make it up in volume"?[7]

Return on Assets   *Return on assets* (ROA) is a measure of profit per dollar of assets. It can be defined several ways, but the most common is this:

$$\text{Return on assets} = \frac{\text{Net income}}{\text{Total assets}}$$

$$= \frac{\$363}{\$3,588} = 10.12\%$$

[3.20]

Return on Equity   *Return on equity* (ROE) is a measure of how the stockholders fared during the year. Because benefiting shareholders is our goal, ROE is, in an accounting sense, the true bottom-line measure of performance. ROE is usually measured as follows:

$$\text{Return on equity} = \frac{\text{Net income}}{\text{Total equity}}$$

$$= \frac{\$363}{\$2,591} = 14\%$$

[3.21]

For every dollar in equity, therefore, Prufrock generated 14 cents in profit; but again this is correct only in accounting terms.

Because ROA and ROE are such commonly cited numbers, we stress that it is important to remember they are accounting rates of return. For this reason, these measures should properly be called *return on book assets* and *return on book equity*. In fact, ROE is sometimes called *return on net worth*. Whatever it's called, it would be inappropriate to compare the result to, for example, an interest rate observed in the financial markets. We will have more to say about accounting rates of return in later chapters.

The fact that ROE exceeds ROA reflects Prufrock's use of financial leverage. We will examine the relationship between these two measures in more detail next.

EXAMPLE 3.4   **ROE and ROA**

Because ROE and ROA are usually intended to measure performance over a prior period, it makes a certain amount of sense to base them on average equity and average assets, respectively. For Prufrock, how would you calculate these?

continued

---
[7]No, it's not.

We first need to calculate average assets and average equity:

Average assets = ($3,373 + 3,588)/2 = $3,481
Average equity = ($2,299 + 2,591)/2 = $2,445

With these averages, we can recalculate ROA and ROE as follows:

$$ROA = \frac{\$363}{\$3,481} = 10.43\%$$

$$ROE = \frac{\$363}{\$2,445} = 14.85\%$$

These are slightly higher than our previous calculations because assets and equity grew during the year, with the result that the average is below the ending value.

MARKET VALUE MEASURES

Our final group of measures is based, in part, on information not necessarily contained in financial statements—the market price per share of stock. Obviously, these measures can be calculated directly only for publicly traded companies.

We assume that Prufrock has 33 million shares outstanding and the stock sold for $88 per share at the end of the year. If we recall that Prufrock's net income was $363 million, we can calculate its earnings per share:

$$EPS = \frac{\text{Net income}}{\text{Shares outstanding}} = \frac{\$363}{33} = \$11$$

Price–Earnings Ratio   The first of our market value measures, the *price–earnings* (PE) *ratio* (or multiple), is defined here:

$$PE \text{ ratio} = \frac{\text{Price per share}}{\text{Earnings per share}}$$

$$= \frac{\$88}{\$11} = 8 \text{ times}$$

[3.22]

In the vernacular, we would say that Prufrock shares sell for eight times earnings, or we might say that Prufrock shares have or "carry" a PE multiple of 8.

PE ratios vary substantially across companies, but, in 2009, a typical large company in the United States had a PE in the 15–20 range. This is on the high side by historical standards, but not dramatically so. A low point for PEs was about 5 in 1974. PEs also vary across countries. For example, Japanese PEs have historically been much higher than those of their U.S. counterparts.

Because the PE ratio measures how much investors are willing to pay per dollar of current earnings, higher PEs are often taken to mean the firm has significant prospects for future growth. Of course, if a firm had no or almost no earnings, its PE would probably be quite large; so, as always, care is needed in interpreting this ratio.

Sometimes analysts divide PE ratios by expected future earnings growth rates (after multiplying the growth rate by 100). The result is the PEG ratio. Suppose Prufrock's anticipated growth rate in EPS was 6 percent. Its PEG ratio would then be 8/6 = 1.33. The idea behind the PEG ratio is that whether a PE ratio is high or low depends on expected future growth. High PEG ratios suggest that the PE is too high relative to growth, and vice versa.

Price–Sales Ratio   In some cases, companies will have negative earnings for extended periods, so their PE ratios are not very meaningful. A good example is a recent start-up. Such companies usually do have some revenues, so analysts will often look at the *price–sales ratio:*

Price–sales ratio = Price per share/Sales per share

In Prufrock's case, sales were \$2,311, so here is the price–sales ratio:

Price–sales ratio = \$88/(\$2,311/33) = \$88/\$70 = 1.26

As with PE ratios, whether a particular price–sales ratio is high or low depends on the industry involved.

Market-to-Book Ratio   A second commonly quoted market value measure is the *market-to-book ratio:*

$$\text{Market-to-book ratio} = \frac{\text{Market value per share}}{\text{Book value per share}}$$ [3.23]

$$= \frac{\$88}{(\$2,591/33)} = \frac{\$88}{\$78.5} = 1.12 \text{ times}$$

Notice that book value per share is total equity (not just common stock) divided by the number of shares outstanding.

Because book value per share is an accounting number, it reflects historical costs. In a loose sense, the market-to-book ratio therefore compares the market value of the firm's investments to their cost. A value less than 1 could mean that the firm has not been successful overall in creating value for its stockholders.

Market-to-book ratios in recent years appear high relative to past values. For example, for the 30 blue-chip companies that make up the widely followed Dow-Jones Industrial Average, the historical norm is about 1.7; however, the market-to-book ratio for this group has recently been twice this size.

Another ratio, called *Tobin's Q ratio,* is much like the market-to-book ratio. Tobin's Q is the market value of the firm's assets divided by their replacement cost:

Tobin's Q = Market value of firm's assets/Replacement cost of firm's assets
        = Market value of firm's debt and equity/Replacement cost of firm's assets

Notice that we used two equivalent numerators here: the market value of the firm's assets and the market value of its debt and equity.

Conceptually, the Q ratio is superior to the market-to-book ratio because it focuses on what the firm is worth today relative to what it would cost to replace it today. Firms with high Q ratios tend to be those with attractive investment opportunities or significant competitive advantages (or both). In contrast, the market-to-book ratio focuses on historical costs, which are less relevant.

As a practical matter, however, Q ratios are difficult to calculate with accuracy because estimating the replacement cost of a firm's assets is not an easy task. Also, market values for a firm's debt are often unobservable. Book values can be used instead in such cases, but accuracy may suffer.

CONCLUSION

This completes our definitions of some common ratios. We could tell you about more of them, but these are enough for now. We'll go on to discuss some ways of using these ratios instead of just how to calculate them. Table 3.8 summarizes the ratios we've discussed.

Concept Questions

3.3a What are the five groups of ratios? Give two or three examples of each kind.

3.3b Given the total debt ratio, what other two ratios can be computed? Explain how.

3.3c Turnover ratios all have one of two figures as the numerator. What are these two figures? What do these ratios measure? How do you interpret the results?

3.3d Profitability ratios all have the same figure in the numerator. What is it? What do these ratios measure? How do you interpret the results?

TABLE 3.8 Common Financial Ratios

I. Short-term solvency, or liquidity, ratios	II. Long-term solvency, or financial leverage, ratios
Current ratio $= \dfrac{\text{Current assets}}{\text{Current liabilities}}$	Total debt ratio $= \dfrac{\text{Total assets} - \text{Total equity}}{\text{Total assets}}$
Quick ratio $= \dfrac{\text{Current assets} - \text{Inventory}}{\text{Current liabilities}}$	Debt–equity ratio = Total debt/Total equity
Cash ratio $= \dfrac{\text{Cash}}{\text{Current liabilities}}$	Equity multiplier = Total assets/Total equity
Net working capital to total assets $= \dfrac{\text{Net working capital}}{\text{Total assets}}$	Long-term debt ratio $= \dfrac{\text{Long-term debt}}{\text{Long-term debt} + \text{Total equity}}$
Interval measure $= \dfrac{\text{Current assets}}{\text{Average daily operating costs}}$	Times interest earned ratio $= \dfrac{\text{EBIT}}{\text{Interest}}$
	Cash coverage ratio $= \dfrac{\text{EBIT} + \text{Depreciation}}{\text{Interest}}$
III. Asset management, or turnover, ratios	**IV. Profitability ratios**
Inventory turnover $= \dfrac{\text{Cost of goods sold}}{\text{Inventory}}$	Profit margin $= \dfrac{\text{Net income}}{\text{Sales}}$
Days' sales in inventory $= \dfrac{365 \text{ days}}{\text{Inventory turnover}}$	Return on assets (ROA) $= \dfrac{\text{Net income}}{\text{Total assets}}$
Receivables turnover $= \dfrac{\text{Sales}}{\text{Accounts receivable}}$	Return on equity (ROE) $= \dfrac{\text{Net income}}{\text{Total equity}}$
Days' sales in receivables $= \dfrac{365 \text{ days}}{\text{Receivables turnover}}$	ROE $= \dfrac{\text{Net income}}{\text{Sales}} \times \dfrac{\text{Sales}}{\text{Assets}} \times \dfrac{\text{Assets}}{\text{Equity}}$
NWC turnover $= \dfrac{\text{Sales}}{\text{NWC}}$	**V. Market value ratios**
Fixed asset turnover $= \dfrac{\text{Sales}}{\text{Net fixed assets}}$	Price–earnings ratio $= \dfrac{\text{Price per share}}{\text{Earnings per share}}$
Total asset turnover $= \dfrac{\text{Sales}}{\text{Total assets}}$	PEG ratio $= \dfrac{\text{Price–earnings ratio}}{\text{Earnings growth rate (\%)}}$
	Price–sales ratio $= \dfrac{\text{Price per share}}{\text{Sales per share}}$
	Market-to-book-ratio $= \dfrac{\text{Market value per share}}{\text{Book value per share}}$
	Tobin's Q Ratio $= \dfrac{\text{Market value of assets}}{\text{Replacement cost of assets}}$

The Du Pont Identity

3.4

As we mentioned in discussing ROA and ROE, the difference between these two profitability measures is a reflection of the use of debt financing, or financial leverage. We illustrate the relationship between these measures in this section by investigating a famous way of decomposing ROE into its component parts.

A CLOSER LOOK AT ROE

To begin, let's recall the definition of ROE:

$$\text{Return on equity} = \frac{\text{Net income}}{\text{Total equity}}$$

If we were so inclined, we could multiply this ratio by Assets/Assets without changing anything:

$$\text{Return on equity} = \frac{\text{Net income}}{\text{Total equity}} = \frac{\text{Net income}}{\text{Total equity}} \times \frac{\text{Assets}}{\text{Assets}}$$

$$= \frac{\text{Net income}}{\text{Assets}} \times \frac{\text{Assets}}{\text{Total equity}}$$

Notice that we have expressed the ROE as the product of two other ratios—ROA and the equity multiplier:

$$\text{ROE} = \text{ROA} \times \text{Equity multiplier} = \text{ROA} \times (1 + \text{Debt–equity ratio})$$

Looking back at Prufrock, for example, we see that the debt–equity ratio was .39 and ROA was 10.12 percent. Our work here implies that Prufrock's ROE, as we previously calculated, is this:

$$\text{ROE} = 10.12\% \times 1.39 = 14\%$$

The difference between ROE and ROA can be substantial, particularly for certain businesses. For example, in 2008, Bank of America has an ROA of only .53 percent, which is fairly typical for a large bank. However, banks tend to borrow a lot of money and, as a result, have relatively large equity multipliers. For Bank of America, ROE is about 5.75 percent, implying an equity multiplier of 10.85.

We can further decompose ROE by multiplying the top and bottom by total sales:

$$\text{ROE} = \frac{\text{Sales}}{\text{Sales}} \times \frac{\text{Net income}}{\text{Assets}} \times \frac{\text{Assets}}{\text{Total equity}}$$

If we rearrange things a bit, ROE looks like this:

$$\text{ROE} = \underbrace{\frac{\text{Net income}}{\text{Sales}} \times \frac{\text{Sales}}{\text{Assets}}}_{\text{Return on assets}} \times \frac{\text{Assets}}{\text{Total equity}} \qquad \text{[3.24]}$$

$$= \text{Profit margin} \times \text{Total asset turnover} \times \text{Equity multiplier}$$

What we have now done is to partition ROA into its two component parts, profit margin and total asset turnover. The last expression of the preceding equation is called the **Du Pont identity**, after the Du Pont Corporation, which popularized its use.

We can check this relationship for Prufrock by noting that the profit margin was 15.7 percent and the total asset turnover was .64:

$$\text{ROE} = \text{Profit margin} \times \text{Total asset turnover} \times \text{Equity multiplier}$$
$$= 15.7\% \qquad \times .64 \qquad\qquad \times 1.39$$
$$= 14\%$$

Du Pont identity
Popular expression breaking ROE into three parts: operating efficiency, asset use efficiency, and financial leverage.

This 14 percent ROE is exactly what we had before.

The Du Pont identity tells us that ROE is affected by three things:

1. Operating efficiency (as measured by profit margin).
2. Asset use efficiency (as measured by total asset turnover).
3. Financial leverage (as measured by the equity multiplier).

Weakness in either operating or asset use efficiency (or both) will show up in a diminished return on assets, which will translate into a lower ROE.

Considering the Du Pont identity, it appears that the ROE could be leveraged up by increasing the amount of debt in the firm. However, notice that increasing debt also increases interest expense, which reduces profit margins, which acts to reduce ROE. So, ROE could go up or down, depending. More important, the use of debt financing has a number of other effects, and as we discuss at some length in Part 6, the amount of leverage a firm uses is governed by its capital structure policy.

The decomposition of ROE we've discussed in this section is a convenient way of systematically approaching financial statement analysis. If ROE is unsatisfactory by some measure, then the Du Pont identity tells you where to start looking for the reasons.

General Motors provides a good example of how Du Pont analysis can be very useful and also illustrates why care must be taken in interpreting ROE values. In 1989, GM had an ROE of 12.1 percent. By 1993, its ROE had improved to 44.1 percent, a dramatic improvement. On closer inspection, however, we find that over the same period GM's profit margin had declined from 3.4 to 1.8 percent, and ROA had declined from 2.4 to 1.3 percent. The decline in ROA was moderated only slightly by an increase in total asset turnover from .71 to .73 over the period.

Given this information, how is it possible for GM's ROE to have climbed so sharply? From our understanding of the Du Pont identity, it must be the case that GM's equity multiplier increased substantially. In fact, what happened was that GM's book equity value was almost wiped out overnight in 1992 by changes in the accounting treatment of pension liabilities. If a company's equity value declines sharply, its equity multiplier rises. In GM's case, the multiplier went from 4.95 in 1989 to 33.62 in 1993. In sum, the dramatic "improvement" in GM's ROE was almost entirely due to an accounting change that affected the equity multiplier and doesn't really represent an improvement in financial performance at all.

AN EXPANDED DU PONT ANALYSIS

So far, we've seen how the Du Pont equation lets us break down ROE into its basic three components: profit margin, total asset turnover, and financial leverage. We now extend this analysis to take a closer look at how key parts of a firm's operations feed into ROE. To get going, we went to the *S&P Market Insight* Web page (www.mhhe.com/edumarketinsight) and pulled abbreviated financial statements for science and technology giant Du Pont. What we found is summarized in Table 3.9.

Using the information in Table 3.9, Figure 3.1 shows how we can construct an expanded Du Pont analysis for Du Pont and present that analysis in chart form. The advantage of the extended Du Pont chart is that it lets us examine several ratios at once, thereby getting a better overall picture of a company's performance and also allowing us to determine possible items to improve.

Looking at the left side of our Du Pont chart in Figure 3.1, we see items related to profitability. As always, profit margin is calculated as net income divided by sales. But as our

TABLE 3.9

FINANCIAL STATEMENTS FOR DU PONT 12 months ending December 31, 2007 (All numbers are in millions)				
Income Statement		**Balance Sheet**		
Sales	$30,454	Current assets		Current liabilities	
CoGS	20,318	Cash	$ 1,436	Accounts payable	$ 2,723
Gross profit	$10,136	Accounts receivable	5,683	Notes payable	1,346
SG&A expense	4,547	Inventory	6,041	Other	4,472
Depreciation	1,371	Total	$13,160	Total	$ 8,541
EBIT	$ 4,218				
Interest	482	Fixed assets	$20,971	Total long-term debt	$14,454
EBT	$ 3,736				
Taxes	748			Total equity	$11,136
Net income	$ 2,988	Total assets	$34,131	Total liabilities and equity	$34,131

FIGURE 3.1   Extended Du Pont Chart for Du Pont

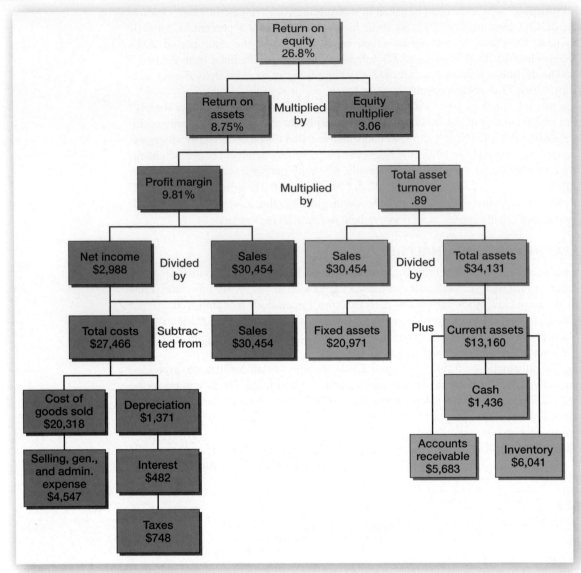

chart emphasizes, net income depends on sales and a variety of costs, such as cost of goods sold (CoGS) and selling, general, and administrative expenses (SG&A expense). Du Pont can increase its ROE by increasing sales and also by reducing one or more of these costs. In other words, if we want to improve profitability, our chart clearly shows us the areas on which we should focus.

Turning to the right side of Figure 3.1, we have an analysis of the key factors underlying total asset turnover. Thus, for example, we see that reducing inventory holdings through more efficient management reduces current assets, which reduces total assets, which then improves total asset turnover.

Concept Questions

3.4a Return on assets, or ROA, can be expressed as the product of two ratios. Which two?

3.4b Return on equity, or ROE, can be expressed as the product of three ratios. Which three?

Using Financial Statement Information   **3.5**

Our last task in this chapter is to discuss in more detail some practical aspects of financial statement analysis. In particular, we will look at reasons for analyzing financial statements, how to get benchmark information, and some problems that come up in the process.

WHY EVALUATE FINANCIAL STATEMENTS?

As we have discussed, the primary reason for looking at accounting information is that we don't have, and can't reasonably expect to get, market value information. We stress that whenever we have market information, we will use it instead of accounting data. Also, if there is a conflict between accounting and market data, market data should be given precedence.

Financial statement analysis is essentially an application of "management by exception." In many cases, such analysis will boil down to comparing ratios for one business with average or representative ratios. Those ratios that seem to differ the most from the averages are tagged for further study.

Internal Uses   Financial statement information has a variety of uses within a firm. Among the most important of these is performance evaluation. For example, managers are frequently evaluated and compensated on the basis of accounting measures of performance such as profit margin and return on equity. Also, firms with multiple divisions frequently compare the performance of those divisions using financial statement information.

Another important internal use we will explore in the next chapter is planning for the future. As we will see, historical financial statement information is useful for generating projections about the future and for checking the realism of assumptions made in those projections.

External Uses   Financial statements are useful to parties outside the firm, including short-term and long-term creditors and potential investors. For example, we would find such information quite useful in deciding whether to grant credit to a new customer.

We would also use this information to evaluate suppliers, and suppliers would review our statements before deciding to extend credit to us. Large customers use this information to decide if we are likely to be around in the future. Credit-rating agencies rely on financial statements in assessing a firm's overall creditworthiness. The common theme here is that financial statements are a prime source of information about a firm's financial health.

We would also find such information useful in evaluating our main competitors. We might be thinking of launching a new product. A prime concern would be whether the competition would jump in shortly thereafter. In this case, we would be interested in learning about our competitors' financial strength to see if they could afford the necessary development.

Finally, we might be thinking of acquiring another firm. Financial statement information would be essential in identifying potential targets and deciding what to offer.

CHOOSING A BENCHMARK

Given that we want to evaluate a division or a firm based on its financial statements, a basic problem immediately comes up. How do we choose a benchmark, or a standard of comparison? We describe some ways of getting started in this section.

Time Trend Analysis   One standard we could use is history. Suppose we found that the current ratio for a particular firm is 2.4 based on the most recent financial statement information. Looking back over the last 10 years, we might find that this ratio had declined fairly steadily over that period.

Based on this, we might wonder if the liquidity position of the firm has deteriorated. It could be, of course, that the firm has made changes that allow it to more efficiently use its current assets, the nature of the firm's business has changed, or business practices have changed. If we investigate, we might find any of these possible explanations behind the decline. This is an example of what we mean by management by exception—a deteriorating time trend may not be bad, but it does merit investigation.

Peer Group Analysis   The second means of establishing a benchmark is to identify firms similar in the sense that they compete in the same markets, have similar assets, and operate in similar ways. In other words, we need to identify a *peer group*. There are obvious problems with doing this because no two companies are identical. Ultimately the choice of which companies to use as a basis for comparison is subjective.

One common way of identifying potential peers is based on **Standard Industrial Classification (SIC) codes.** These are four-digit codes established by the U.S. government for statistical reporting. Firms with the same SIC code are frequently assumed to be similar.

The first digit in a SIC code establishes the general type of business. For example, firms engaged in finance, insurance, and real estate have SIC codes beginning with 6. Each additional digit narrows down the industry. So, companies with SIC codes beginning with 60 are mostly banks and banklike businesses; those with codes beginning with 602 are mostly commercial banks; and SIC code 6025 is assigned to national banks that are members of the Federal Reserve system. Table 3.10 lists selected two-digit codes (the first two digits of the four-digit SIC codes) and the industries they represent.

SIC codes are far from perfect. For example, suppose you were examining financial statements for Wal-Mart, the largest retailer in the United States. The relevant two-digit SIC code is 53, General Merchandise Stores. In a quick scan of the nearest financial database, you would find about 20 large, publicly owned corporations with a similar SIC code, but you might not be comfortable with some of them. Target would seem to be a reasonable peer, but Neiman Marcus also carries the same industry code. Are Wal-Mart and Neiman Marcus really comparable?

As this example illustrates, it is probably not appropriate to blindly use SIC code–based averages. Instead, analysts often identify a set of primary competitors and then compute a set of averages based on just this group. Also, we may be more concerned with a group of the top firms in an industry, not the average firm. Such a group is called an *aspirant group* because we aspire to be like its members. In this case, a financial statement analysis reveals how far we have to go.

Beginning in 1997, a new industry classification system was initiated. Specifically, the North American Industry Classification System (NAICS, pronounced "nakes") is intended to replace the older SIC codes, and it will eventually. Currently, however, SIC codes are still widely used.

With these caveats about SIC codes in mind, we can now take a look at a specific industry. Suppose we are in the retail hardware business. Table 3.11 contains some condensed

Standard Industrial Classification (SIC) code

A U.S. government code used to classify a firm by its type of business operations.

Learn more about NAICS at www.naics.com.

Agriculture, Forestry, and Fishing	Wholesale Trade
01 Agriculture production—crops	50 Wholesale trade—durable goods
08 Forestry	51 Wholesale trade—nondurable goods
09 Fishing, hunting, and trapping	
Mining	**Retail Trade**
10 Metal mining	54 Food stores
12 Bituminous coal and lignite mining	55 Automobile dealers and gas stations
13 Oil and gas extraction	58 Eating and drinking places
Construction	**Finance, Insurance, and Real Estate**
15 Building construction	60 Banking
16 Construction other than building	63 Insurance
17 Construction—special trade contractors	65 Real estate
Manufacturing	**Services**
28 Chemicals and allied products	78 Motion pictures
29 Petroleum refining and related industries	80 Health services
35 Machinery, except electrical	82 Educational services
37 Transportation equipment	
Transportation, Communication, Electric, Gas, and Sanitary Service	
40 Railroad transportation	
45 Transportation by air	
49 Electric, gas, and sanitary services	

TABLE 3.10

Selected Two-Digit SIC Codes

common-size financial statements for this industry from the Risk Management Association (RMA, formerly known as Robert Morris Associates), one of many sources of such information. Table 3.12 contains selected ratios from the same source.

There is a large amount of information here, most of which is self-explanatory. On the right in Table 3.11, we have current information reported for different groups based on sales. Within each sales group, common-size information is reported. For example, firms with sales in the $10 million to $25 million range have cash and equivalents equal to 7 percent of total assets. There are 38 companies in this group, out of 326 in all.

On the left, we have three years' worth of summary historical information for the entire group. For example, operating profit fell from 3.0 percent of sales to 2.5 percent over that time.

Table 3.12 contains some selected ratios, again reported by sales groups on the right and time period on the left. To see how we might use this information, suppose our firm has a current ratio of 2. Based on these ratios, is this value unusual?

Looking at the current ratio for the overall group for the most recent year (third column from the left in Table 3.12), we see that three numbers are reported. The one in the middle, 2.5, is the median, meaning that half of the 326 firms had current ratios that were lower and half had bigger current ratios. The other two numbers are the upper and lower quartiles. So, 25 percent of the firms had a current ratio larger than 3.9 and 25 percent had a current ratio smaller than 1.6. Our value of 2 falls comfortably within these bounds, so it doesn't appear too unusual. This comparison illustrates how knowledge of the range of ratios is important

TABLE 3.11 Selected Financial Statement Information

Retail—Hardware Stores SIC# 5072, 5251 (NAICS 444130)									
COMPARATIVE HISTORICAL DATA				**CURRENT DATA SORTED BY SALES**					
			Type of Statement						
21	12	10	Unqualified		4			2	4
51	51	50	Reviewed	1	10	8	13	13	5
94	81	94	Compiled	6	44	21	15	7	1
60	77	77	Tax Returns	17	33	15	7	3	2
81	86	95	Other	11	24	21	12	13	14
4/1/04– 3/31/05 **ALL** 307	4/1/05– 3/31/06 **ALL** 307	4/1/06– 3/31/07 **ALL** 326	**NUMBER OF STATEMENTS**	62 (4/1–9/30/06)		264 (10/1/06–3/31/07)			
				0-1MM 35	**1-3MM** 115	**3-5MM** 65	**5-10MM** 47	**10-25MM** 38	**25MM & OVER** 26
			Assets						
6.1%	6.1%	6.0%	Cash & Equivalents	4.6%	6.5%	5.6%	6.7%	7.0%	4.7%
14.6	14.6	12.6	Trade Receivables (net)	7.4	9.9	14.0	15.2	17.6	16.7
50.0	51.3	52.2	Inventory	59.2	53.7	52.6	47.9	49.4	47.4
1.4	2.4	2.0	All Other Current	.9	2.7	1.8	2.3	1.1	1.9
72.2	74.4	72.9	Total Current	72.1	72.7	74.0	72.1	75.2	70.8
16.6	14.3	16.1	Fixed Assets (net)	14.9	16.4	14.0	15.7	16.4	22.6
2.3	2.6	2.0	Intangibles (net)	4.8	1.8	1.1	2.7	1.3	1.3
8.9	8.7	8.9	All Other Non-Current	8.2	9.1	10.9	9.6	7.2	5.4
100.0	100.0	100.0	Total	100.0	100.0	100.0	100.0	100.0	100.0
			Liabilities						
10.4	11.7	9.9	Notes Payable-Short Term	15.7	9.4	7.2	9.9	9.6	11.2
3.5	3.3	3.2	Cur. Mat.-L.T.D.	3.7	2.7	4.7	3.6	2.5	1.0
14.7	15.2	13.7	Trade Payables	14.7	11.2	14.4	15.1	14.6	17.4
.2	.2	.2	Income Taxes Payable	.0	.2	.2	.2	.1	.3
6.9	7.3	6.9	All Other Current	5.1	6.9	6.1	7.6	9.1	7.4
35.7	37.7	33.8	Total Current	39.2	30.3	32.7	36.4	35.9	37.4
21.3	19.5	20.3	Long-Term Debt	35.5	24.6	18.5	11.7	13.9	9.9
.2	.2	.1	Deferred Taxes	.0	.0	.1	.1	.2	.4
4.9	7.4	7.6	All Other Non-Current	11.4	8.3	10.1	4.8	2.6	5.3
37.9	35.3	38.2	Net Worth	13.8	36.7	38.6	47.0	47.4	47.0
100.0	100.0	100.0	Total Liabilities & Net Worth	100.0	100.0	100.0	100.0	100.0	100.0
			Income Data						
100.0	100.0	100.0	Net Sales	100.0	100.0	100.0	100.0	100.0	100.0
35.6	36.0	36.7	Gross Profit	38.3	37.9	37.3	35.5	33.9	34.4
32.6	34.1	34.2	Operating Expenses	38.9	35.1	34.4	32.9	30.2	31.7
3.0	2.0	2.5	Operating Profit	−.6	2.8	2.8	2.6	3.6	2.7
.2	−.1	.2	All Other Expenses (net)	1.2	.3	.1	−.2	.0	.2
2.7	2.1	2.3	Profit Before Taxes	−1.8	2.5	2.7	2.8	3.6	2.5

M = $ thousand; MM = $ million.

Interpretation of Statement Studies Figures: RMA cautions that the studies be regarded only as a general guideline and not as an absolute industry norm. This is due to limited samples within categories, the categorization of companies by their primary Standard Industrial Classification (SIC) number only, and different methods of operations by companies within the same industry. For these reasons, RMA recommends that the figures be used only as general guidelines in addition to other methods of financial analysis.

© 2007 by RMA. All rights reserved. No part of this table may be reproduced or utilized in any form or by any means, electronic or mechanical, including photocopying, recording, or by any information storage and retrieval system, without permission in writing from RMA.

TABLE 3.12 Selected Ratios

Retail—Hardware Stores SIC# 5072, 5251 (NAICS 444130)									
COMPARATIVE HISTORICAL DATA				**CURRENT DATA SORTED BY SALES**					
			Type of Statement						
21	12	10	Unqualified		4			2	4
51	51	50	Reviewed	1	10	8	13	13	5
94	81	94	Compiled	6	44	21	15	7	1
60	77	77	Tax Returns	17	33	15	7	3	2
81	86	95	Other	11	24	21	12	13	14
4/1/04–3/31/05 ALL 307	4/1/05–3/31/06 ALL 307	4/1/06–3/31/07 ALL 326	**NUMBER OF STATEMENTS**	62 (4/1–9/30/06)		264 (10/1/06–3/31/07)			
				0-1MM 35	1-3MM 115	3-5MM 65	5-10MM 47	10-25MM 38	25MM & OVER 26
			Ratios						
3.5	3.5	3.9	Current	4.3	4.6	4.1	3.2	3.6	2.9
2.3	2.1	2.3		2.9	2.0	2.6	2.1	2.4	1.7
1.5	1.5	1.6		1.8	1.7	1.0	1.6	1.4	1.3
1.1	1.0	1.1	Quick	.6	1.4	1.4	1.0	1.3	1.2
.6	.5	.5		.3	.5	.5	.6	.7	.4
.3	.2	.2		.1	.2	.2	.3	.3	.2
6 58.1	7 55.3	7 50.5	Sales/Receivables	5 69.3	8 48.6	8 45.7	9 42.5	8 46.5	7 55.6
15 24.0	14 26.3	13 28.6		11 34.2	13 28.6	12 30.7	17 21.5	19 19.5	14 26.9
31 11.6	31 11.8	25 14.6		16 22.7	20 17.9	26 14.3	24 15.0	37 10.0	45 8.1
76 4.8	79 4.6	92 4.0	Cost of Sales/Inventory	154 2.4	115 3.2	94 3.9	75 4.9	59 6.2	77 4.8
116 3.1	121 3.0	136 2.7		209 1.7	152 2.4	125 2.9	98 3.7	108 3.4	97 3.8
161 2.3	178 2.0	187 2.0		323 1.1	191 1.9	168 2.2	167 2.2	180 2.0	147 2.5
18 20.7	17 21.6	15 24.5	Cost of Sales/Payables	11 31.8	13 27.2	17 21.1	19 19.0	15 24.9	21 17.6
28 13.0	27 13.3	27 13.7		28 13.2	25 14.7	27 13.5	27 13.4	24 15.3	33 11.0
42 8.8	46 8.1	43 8.6		56 6.6	38 9.7	47 7.8	39 9.3	39 9.4	64 6.8
4.4	4.1	3.9	Sales/Working Capital	2.7	3.6	4.1	4.2	4.8	5.1
6.8	6.6	5.5		4.4	5.0	6.2	6.8	6.1	8.7
12.6	12.1	9.7		10.5	7.1	10.1	12.2	11.6	19.1
9.1	8.5	7.2	EBIT/Interest	3.0	5.5	9.3	8.2	10.5	17.5
(285) 3.7	(282) 3.1	(304) 3.0		(33) 1.5	(104) 2.6	(62) 4.8	(45) 3.4	(34) 4.7	4.5
1.4	1.3	1.3		−.4	1.2	1.3	1.3	1.6	1.0
5.1	3.8	2.9	Net Profit + Depr., Dep., Amort./Cur. Mat. L/T/D		2.0	2.8	3.4	10.0	
(63) 2.0	(56) 1.6	(63) 1.5			(14) 1.3	(14) 1.5	(14) 2.0	(10) 1.7	
.7	.6	.8			.8	.5	.7	.8	
.1	.1	.1	Fixed/Worth	.1	.1	.1	.1	.1	.2
.4	.4	.3		1.4	.3	.3	.4	.3	.5
1.1	.9	1.0		−1.1	1.3	.8	.7	.7	.9
.7	.8	.7	Debt/Worth	1.8	.7	.7	.5	.4	.6
1.7	1.7	1.5		4.4	1.5	1.4	1.6	1.2	1.1
4.6	4.5	3.8		−5.9	4.9	3.8	2.9	2.3	1.8
30.2	29.7	32.3	% Profit Before Taxes/ Tangible Net Worth	22.3	33.9	41.3	30.5	36.9	30.5
(274) 13.6	(269) 13.5	(287) 12.3		(21) 6.8	(98) 13.7	(59) 13.1	10.0	(36) 12.3	11.9
4.2	3.7	4.3		−2.2	5.6	4.5	2.5	4.7	3.5

(continued)

TABLE 3.12   (continued)

4/1/04–3/31/05 ALL 307	4/1/05–3/31/06 ALL 307	4/1/06–3/31/07 ALL 326	NUMBER OF STATEMENTS	62 (4/1–9/30/06)		264 (10/1/06–3/31/07)			
				0-1MM 35	1-3MM 115	3-5MM 65	5-10MM 47	10-25MM 38	25MM & OVER 26
11.2 5.2 1.0	10.5 5.3 .7	11.1 4.8 1.0	% Profit Before Taxes/Total Assets	6.3 2.4 -5.2	11.9 4.8 .9	12.3 5.2 1.2	11.0 4.7 1.4	13.6 7.1 3.1	13.3 6.4 .5
49.9 21.1 9.8	59.6 22.9 10.7	52.0 20.3 9.8	Sales/Net Fixed Assets	40.5 13.9 8.4	59.4 21.1 9.0	60.1 23.7 12.5	46.1 18.5 9.8	57.0 20.2 10.2	37.9 14.2 7.8
3.2 2.5 1.9	3.1 2.5 1.9	2.8 2.4 1.7	Sales/Total Assets	2.3 1.6 1.2	2.7 2.2 1.6	3.1 2.5 2.0	3.2 2.5 2.0	3.3 2.5 2.3	3.0 2.6 1.9
(249) .7 1.2 2.0	(262) .5 1.0 1.9	(274) .7 1.2 2.0	% Depr., Dep., Amort./Sales	(26) .6 2.0 3.4	(94) .6 1.3 2.7	(63) .7 1.3 1.7	(43) .5 1.1 2.0	(33) .7 1.0 1.4	(25) .8 1.0 1.9
(164) 1.7 3.5 6.2	(187) 2.0 3.4 5.7	(193) 1.8 3.2 5.3	% Officers', Directors', Owners' Comp/Sales	(23) 3.0 4.5 8.2	(69) 2.2 3.7 5.7	(44) 2.1 3.2 5.1	(31) 1.3 3.0 4.8	(19) 1.3 1.8 2.7	
5346164M 2015818M	5361226M 1926895M	4969626M 1977145M	Net Sales ($) Total Assets ($)	24032M 16500M	215140M 109029M	247741M 106265M	336160M 157126M	620293M 251225M	3526260M 1337000M

M = $ thousand; MM = $ million.

© 2007 by RMA. All rights reserved. No part of this table may be reproduced or utilized in any form or by any means, electronic or mechanical, including photocopying, recording, or by any information storage and retrieval system, without permission in writing from RMA.

in addition to knowledge of the average. Notice how stable the current ratio has been for the last three years.

EXAMPLE 3.5   **More Ratios**

Take a look at the most recent numbers reported for Sales/Receivables and EBIT/Interest in Table 3.12. What are the overall median values? What are these ratios?

If you look back at our discussion, you will see that these are the receivables turnover and the times interest earned, or TIE, ratios. The median value for receivables turnover for the entire group is 28.6 times. So, the days in receivables would be 365/28.6 = 13, which is the bold-faced number reported. The median for the TIE is 3.0 times. The number in parentheses indicates that the calculation is meaningful for, and therefore based on, only 304 of the 326 companies. In this case, the reason is that only 304 companies paid any significant amount of interest.

There are many sources of ratio information in addition to the one we examine here. Our nearby *Work the Web* box shows how to get this information for just about any company, along with some useful benchmarking information. Be sure to look it over and then benchmark your favorite company.

PROBLEMS WITH FINANCIAL STATEMENT ANALYSIS

We close our chapter on financial statements by discussing some additional problems that can arise in using financial statements. In one way or another, the basic problem with financial statement analysis is that there is no underlying theory to help us identify which quantities to look at and to guide us in establishing benchmarks.

As we discuss in other chapters, there are many cases in which financial theory and economic logic provide guidance in making judgments about value and risk. Little such help exists with financial statements. This is why we can't say which ratios matter the most and what a high or low value might be.

One particularly severe problem is that many firms are conglomerates, owning more or less unrelated lines of business. The consolidated financial statements for such firms don't fit any neat industry category. Going back to department stores, for example, Sears has had an SIC code of 6710 (Holding Offices) because of its diverse financial and retailing operations. More generally, the kind of peer group analysis we have been describing works best when the firms are strictly in the same line of business, the industry is competitive, and there is only one way of operating.

Another problem that is becoming increasingly common is that major competitors and natural peer group members in an industry may be scattered around the globe. The automobile industry is an obvious example. The problem here is that financial statements from outside the

WORK THE WEB

As we discussed in this chapter, ratios are an important tool for examining a company's performance. Gathering the necessary financial statements to calculate ratios can be tedious and time-consuming. Fortunately many sites on the Web provide this information for free. One of the best is www.reuters.com. We went there, entered a ticker symbol ("AZO" for AutoZone), and selected the "Ratios" link. Here is an abbreviated look at the results:

AutoZone Inc AZO (NYSE)

Sector: Services **Industry:** Retail (Specialty) ▸ View **AZO** on other exchanges

As of 2:27 PM EST	Price Change	Percent Change
$117.07 USD	▾.71	▾.60%

FINANCIAL STRENGTH

	Company	Industry	Sector	S&P 500
Quick Ratio (MRQ)	.12	.89	.68	1.16
Current Ratio (MRQ)	1.01	1.76	1.07	1.64
LT Debt to Equity (MRQ)	7.42	.63	.93	.59
Total Debt to Equity (MRQ)	7.42	.68	1.13	.78
Interest Coverage (TTM)	8.84	20.88	8.80	14.00

Most of the information is self-explanatory. Interest Coverage ratio is the same as the Times Interest Earned ratio discussed in the text. The abbreviation MRQ refers to results from the most recent quarterly financial statements, and TTM refers to results covering the previous ("trailing") 12 months. This site also provides a comparison to the industry, business sector, and S&P 500 averages for the ratios. Other ratios available on the site have five-year averages calculated. Have a look!

Questions

1. Go to www.reuters.com and find the major ratio categories listed on this website. How do the categories differ from the categories listed in the textbook?

2. On www.reuters.com, the profitability ratios and management effectiveness ratios have the 5-year average ratios presented. How do these ratios for the current year for Microsoft compare to its 5-year average? How does Microsoft compare to the industry for these ratios?

United States do not necessarily conform at all to GAAP. The existence of different standards and procedures makes it difficult to compare financial statements across national borders.

Even companies that are clearly in the same line of business may not be comparable. For example, electric utilities engaged primarily in power generation are all classified in the same group (SIC 4911). This group is often thought to be relatively homogeneous. However, most utilities operate as regulated monopolies, so they don't compete much with each other, at least not historically. Many have stockholders, and many are organized as cooperatives with no stockholders. There are several different ways of generating power, ranging from hydroelectric to nuclear, so the operating activities of these utilities can differ quite a bit. Finally, profitability is strongly affected by regulatory environment, so utilities in different locations can be similar but show different profits.

Several other general problems frequently crop up. First, different firms use different accounting procedures—for inventory, for example. This makes it difficult to compare statements. Second, different firms end their fiscal years at different times. For firms in seasonal businesses (such as a retailer with a large Christmas season), this can lead to difficulties in comparing balance sheets because of fluctuations in accounts during the year. Finally, for any particular firm, unusual or transient events, such as a one-time profit from an asset sale, may affect financial performance. In comparing firms, such events can give misleading signals.

Concept Questions

3.5a What are some uses for financial statement analysis?

3.5b Why do we say that financial statement analysis is management by exception?

3.5c What are SIC codes and how might they be useful?

3.5d What are some problems that can come up with financial statement analysis?

3.6 Summary and Conclusions

This chapter has discussed aspects of financial statement analysis:

1. *Sources and uses of cash:* We discussed how to identify the ways in which businesses obtain and use cash, and we described how to trace the flow of cash through a business over the course of the year. We briefly looked at the statement of cash flows.

2. *Standardized financial statements:* We explained that differences in size make it difficult to compare financial statements, and we discussed how to form common-size and common–base period statements to make comparisons easier.

3. *Ratio analysis:* Evaluating ratios of accounting numbers is another way of comparing financial statement information. We therefore defined and discussed a number of the most commonly reported and used financial ratios. We also discussed the famous Du Pont identity as a way of analyzing financial performance.

4. *Using financial statements:* We described how to establish benchmarks for comparison and discussed some types of information that are available. We then examined potential problems that can arise.

After you have studied this chapter, we hope that you have some perspective on the uses and abuses of financial statements. You should also find that your vocabulary of business and financial terms has grown substantially.

3.1   **Sources and Uses of Cash** Consider the following balance sheets for the Philippe Corporation. Calculate the changes in the various accounts and, where applicable, identify the change as a source or use of cash. What were the major sources and uses of cash? Did the company become more or less liquid during the year? What happened to cash during the year?

PHILIPPE CORPORATION 2008 and 2009 Balance Sheets ($ in millions)		
	2008	**2009**
Assets		
Current assets		
Cash	$ 210	$ 215
Accounts receivable	355	310
Inventory	507	328
Total	$1,072	$ 853
Fixed assets		
Net plant and equipment	$6,085	$6,527
Total assets	$7,157	$7,380
Liabilities and Owners' Equity		
Current liabilities		
Accounts payable	$ 207	$ 298
Notes payable	1,715	1,427
Total	$1,922	$1,725
Long-term debt	$1,987	$2,308
Owners' equity		
Common stock and paid-in surplus	$1,000	$1,000
Retained earnings	2,248	2,347
Total	$3,248	$3,347
Total liabilities and owners' equity	$7,157	$7,380

3.2   **Common-Size Statements** Here is the most recent income statement for Philippe. Prepare a common-size income statement based on this information. How do you interpret the standardized net income? What percentage of sales goes to cost of goods sold?

PHILIPPE CORPORATION 2009 Income Statement ($ in millions)	
Sales	$4,053
Cost of goods sold	2,780
Depreciation	550
Earnings before interest and taxes	$ 723
Interest paid	502
Taxable income	$ 221
Taxes (34%)	75
Net income	$ 146
Dividends	$47
Addition to retained earnings	99

3.3   Financial Ratios Based on the balance sheets and income statement in the previous two problems, calculate the following ratios for 2009:

Current ratio _____

Quick ratio _____

Cash ratio _____

Inventory turnover _____

Receivables turnover _____

Days' sales in inventory _____

Days' sales in receivables _____

Total debt ratio _____

Long-term debt ratio _____

Times interest earned ratio _____

Cash coverage ratio _____

3.4   ROE and the Du Pont Identity Calculate the 2009 ROE for the Philippe Corporation and then break down your answer into its component parts using the Du Pont identity.

ANSWERS TO CHAPTER REVIEW AND SELF-TEST PROBLEMS

3.1   We've filled in the answers in the following table. Remember, increases in assets and decreases in liabilities indicate that we spent some cash. Decreases in assets and increases in liabilities are ways of getting cash.

Philippe used its cash primarily to purchase fixed assets and to pay off short-term debt. The major sources of cash to do this were additional long-term borrowing, reductions in current assets, and additions to retained earnings.

PHILIPPE CORPORATION 2008 and 2009 Balance Sheets ($ in millions)				
	2008	2009	Change	Source or Use of Cash
Assets				
Current assets				
Cash	$ 210	$ 215	+$ 5	
Accounts receivable	355	310	− 45	Source
Inventory	507	328	− 179	Source
Total	$1,072	$ 853	−$219	
Fixed assets				
Net plant and equipment	$6,085	$6,527	+$442	Use
Total assets	$7,157	$7,380	+$223	
Liabilities and Owners' Equity				
Current liabilities				
Accounts payable	$ 207	$ 298	+$ 91	Source
Notes payable	1,715	1,427	− 288	Use
Total	$1,922	$1,725	−$197	
Long-term debt	$1,987	$2,308	+$321	Source
Owners' equity				
Common stock and paid-in surplus	$1,000	$1,000	+$ 0	—
Retained earnings	2,248	2,347	+ 99	Source
Total	$3,248	$3,347	+$ 99	
Total liabilities and owners' equity	$7,157	$7,380	+$223	

Visit us at www.mhhe.com/rwj

The current ratio went from $1,072/1,922 = .56 to $853/1,725 = .49, so the firm's liquidity appears to have declined somewhat. Overall, however, the amount of cash on hand increased by $5.

3.2 We've calculated the common-size income statement here. Remember that we simply divide each item by total sales.

PHILIPPE CORPORATION 2009 Common-Size Income Statement		
Sales		100.0%
Cost of goods sold		68.6
Depreciation		13.6
Earnings before interest and taxes		17.8
Interest paid		12.3
Taxable income		5.5
Taxes (34%)		1.9
Net income		3.6%
Dividends	1.2%	
Addition to retained earnings	2.4%	

Net income is 3.6 percent of sales. Because this is the percentage of each sales dollar that makes its way to the bottom line, the standardized net income is the firm's profit margin. Cost of goods sold is 68.6 percent of sales.

3.3 We've calculated the following ratios based on the ending figures. If you don't remember a definition, refer back to Table 3.8.

Current ratio	$853/$1,725	= .49 times
Quick ratio	$525/$1,725	= .30 times
Cash ratio	$215/$1,725	= .12 times
Inventory turnover	$2,780/$328	= 8.48 times
Receivables turnover	$4,053/$310	= 13.07 times
Days' sales in inventory	365/8.48	= 43.06 days
Days' sales in receivables	365/13.07	= 27.92 days
Total debt ratio	$4,033/$7,380	= 54.6%
Long-term debt ratio	$2,308/$5,655	= 40.8%
Times interest earned ratio	$723/$502	= 1.44 times
Cash coverage ratio	$1,273/$502	= 2.54 times

3.4 The return on equity is the ratio of net income to total equity. For Philippe, this is $146/$3,347 = 4.4%, which is not outstanding.

Given the Du Pont identity, ROE can be written as follows:

ROE = Profit margin × Total asset turnover × Equity multiplier
= $146/$4,053 × $4,053/$7,380 × $7,380/$3,347
= 3.6% × .549 × 2.20
= 4.4%

Notice that return on assets, ROA, is 3.6% × .549 = 1.98%.

Visit us at www.mhhe.com/rwj

CONCEPTS REVIEW AND CRITICAL THINKING QUESTIONS

1. **Current Ratio** [LO2] What effect would the following actions have on a firm's current ratio? Assume that net working capital is positive.

   a. Inventory is purchased.
   b. A supplier is paid.
   c. A short-term bank loan is repaid.
   d. A long-term debt is paid off early.
   e. A customer pays off a credit account.
   f. Inventory is sold at cost.
   g. Inventory is sold for a profit.

2. **Current Ratio and Quick Ratio** [LO2] In recent years, Dixie Co. has greatly increased its current ratio. At the same time, the quick ratio has fallen. What has happened? Has the liquidity of the company improved?

3. **Current Ratio** [LO2] Explain what it means for a firm to have a current ratio equal to .50. Would the firm be better off if the current ratio were 1.50? What if it were 15.0? Explain your answers.

4. **Financial Ratios** [LO2] Fully explain the kind of information the following financial ratios provide about a firm:

   a. Quick ratio.
   b. Cash ratio.
   c. Total asset turnover.
   d. Equity multiplier.
   e. Long-term debt ratio.
   f. Times interest earned ratio.
   g. Profit margin.
   h. Return on assets.
   i. Return on equity.
   j. Price–earnings ratio.

5. **Standardized Financial Statements** [LO1] What types of information do common-size financial statements reveal about the firm? What is the best use for these common-size statements? What purpose do common–base year statements have? When would you use them?

6. **Peer Group Analysis** [LO2] Explain what peer group analysis is. As a financial manager, how could you use the results of peer group analysis to evaluate the performance of your firm? How is a peer group different from an aspirant group?

7. **Du Pont Identity** [LO3] Why is the Du Pont identity a valuable tool for analyzing the performance of a firm? Discuss the types of information it reveals compared to ROE considered by itself.

8. **Industry-Specific Ratios** [LO2] Specialized ratios are sometimes used in specific industries. For example, the so-called book-to-bill ratio is closely watched for semiconductor manufacturers. A ratio of .93 indicates that for every $100 worth of chips shipped over some period, only $93 worth of new orders were received. In January 2008, the semiconductor equipment industry's book-to-bill ratio was .89, compared to .85 during the month of December 2007. The book-to-bill ratio reached a recent low of .79 during September 2007. The three-month average of worldwide bookings in January 2008 was $1.12 billion, a decrease of 3 percent from December 2007, while the three-month average of billings was $1.27 billion, a 7 percent decrease from December 2007. What is this ratio intended to measure? Why do you think it is so closely followed?

9. **Industry-Specific Ratios** [LO2] So-called same-store sales are a very important measure for companies as diverse as McDonald's and Sears. As the name suggests, examining same-store sales means comparing revenues from the same stores or restaurants at two different points in time. Why might companies focus on same-store sales rather than total sales?

10. **Industry-Specific Ratios** [LO2] There are many ways of using standardized financial information beyond those discussed in this chapter. The usual goal is to put firms on an equal footing for comparison purposes. For example, for auto manufacturers, it is common to express sales, costs, and profits on a per-car basis. For each of the following industries, give an example of an actual company and discuss one or more potentially useful means of standardizing financial information:

    a. Public utilities.   **d.** Online services.

    b. Large retailers.   **e.** Hospitals.

    c. Airlines.   **f.** College textbook publishers.

11. **Statement of Cash Flows** [LO4] In recent years, several manufacturing companies have reported the cash flow from the sale of Treasury securities in the cash from operations section of the statement of cash flows. What is the problem with this practice? Is there any situation in which this practice would be acceptable?

12. **Statement of Cash Flows** [LO4] Suppose a company lengthens the time it takes to pay suppliers. How would this affect the statement of cash flows? How sustainable is the change in cash flows from this practice?

HM™

QUESTIONS AND PROBLEMS

1. **Calculating Liquidity Ratios** [LO2] SDJ, Inc., has net working capital of $1,370, current liabilities of $3,720, and inventory of $1,950. What is the current ratio? What is the quick ratio?

BASIC
(Questions 1–17)

2. **Calculating Profitability Ratios** [LO2] Wakers, Inc., has sales of $29 million, total assets of $17.5 million, and total debt of $6.3 million. If the profit margin is 8 percent, what is net income? What is ROA? What is ROE?

3. **Calculating the Average Collection Period** [LO2] Ortiz Lumber Yard has a current accounts receivable balance of $431,287. Credit sales for the year just ended were $3,943,709. What is the receivables turnover? The days' sales in receivables? How long did it take on average for credit customers to pay off their accounts during the past year?

4. **Calculating Inventory Turnover** [LO2] The Blue Moon Corporation has ending inventory of $407,534, and cost of goods sold for the year just ended was $4,105,612. What is the inventory turnover? The days' sales in inventory? How long on average did a unit of inventory sit on the shelf before it was sold?

5. **Calculating Leverage Ratios** [LO2] Crystal Lake, Inc., has a total debt ratio of .63. What is its debt–equity ratio? What is its equity multiplier?

6. **Calculating Market Value Ratios** [LO2] Bach Corp. had additions to retained earnings for the year just ended of $430,000. The firm paid out $175,000 in cash dividends, and it has ending total equity of $5.3 million. If the company currently has 210,000 shares of common stock outstanding, what are earnings per share? Dividends per share? Book value per share? If the stock currently sells for $63 per share, what is the market-to-book ratio? The price–earnings ratio? If the company had sales of $4.5 million, what is the price–sales ratio?

7. **Du Pont Identity** [LO4] If Roten Rooters, Inc., has an equity multiplier of 2.80, total asset turnover of 1.15, and a profit margin of 5.5 percent, what is its ROE?

8. **Du Pont Identity** [LO4] Braam Fire Prevention Corp. has a profit margin of 6.80 percent, total asset turnover of 1.95, and ROE of 18.27 percent. What is this firm's debt–equity ratio?

9. **Sources and Uses of Cash** [LO4] Based only on the following information for Bennington Corp., did cash go up or down? By how much? Classify each event as a source or use of cash.

Decrease in inventory	$375
Decrease in accounts payable	190
Increase in notes payable	210
Increase in accounts receivable	105

10. **Calculating Average Payables Period** [LO2] Tortoise, Inc., had a cost of goods sold of $28,834. At the end of the year, the accounts payable balance was $6,105. How long on average did it take the company to pay off its suppliers during the year? What might a large value for this ratio imply?

11. **Cash Flow and Capital Spending** [LO4] For the year just ended, Ypsilanti Yak Yogurt shows an increase in its net fixed assets account of $835. The company took $148 in depreciation expense for the year. How much did the company spend on new fixed assets? Is this a source or use of cash?

12. **Equity Multiplier and Return on Equity** [LO3] Organic Chicken Company has a debt–equity ratio of .65. Return on assets is 8.5 percent, and total equity is $540,000. What is the equity multiplier? Return on equity? Net income?

Just Dew It Corporation reports the following balance sheet information for 2008 and 2009. Use this information to work Problems 13 through 17.

JUST DEW IT CORPORATION 2008 and 2009 Balance Sheets					
Assets			**Liabilities and Owners' Equity**		
	2008	**2009**		**2008**	**2009**
Current assets			Current liabilities		
Cash	$ 8,436	$ 10,157	Accounts payable	$ 43,050	$ 46,821
Accounts receivable	21,530	23,406	Notes payable	18,384	17,382
Inventory	38,760	42,650	Total	$ 61,434	$ 64,203
Total	$ 68,726	$ 76,213			
			Long-term debt	$ 25,000	$ 32,000
			Owners' equity		
			Common stock and paid-in surplus	$ 40,000	$ 40,000
			Retained earnings	168,998	188,316
Net plant and equipment	$226,706	$248,306	Total	$208,998	$228,316
			Total liabilities and owners' equity		
Total assets	$295,432	$324,519	owners' equity	$295,432	$324,519

13. **Preparing Standardized Financial Statements** [LO1] Prepare the 2008 and 2009 common-size balance sheets for Just Dew It.

14. **Preparing Standardized Financial Statements** [LO1] Prepare the 2009 common–base year balance sheet for Just Dew It.

15. **Preparing Standardized Financial Statements** [LO1] Prepare the 2009 combined common-size, common–base year balance sheet for Just Dew It.

16. **Sources and Uses of Cash** [LO4] For each account on this company's balance sheet, show the change in the account during 2009 and note whether this change was a source or use of cash. Do your numbers add up and make sense? Explain your answer for total assets as compared to your answer for total liabilities and owners' equity.

17. **Calculating Financial Ratios** [LO2] Based on the balance sheets given for Just Dew It, calculate the following financial ratios for each year:

    a. Current ratio.

    b. Quick ratio.

    c. Cash ratio.

    d. NWC to total assets ratio.

    e. Debt–equity ratio and equity multiplier.

    f. Total debt ratio and long-term debt ratio.

18. **Using the Du Pont Identity** [LO3] Y3K, Inc., has sales of $5,276, total assets of $3,105, and a debt–equity ratio of 1.40. If its return on equity is 15 percent, what is its net income?

INTERMEDIATE
(Questions 18–30)

19. **Days' Sales in Receivables** [LO2] A company has net income of $218,000, a profit margin of 8.70 percent, and an accounts receivable balance of $132,850. Assuming 70 percent of sales are on credit, what is the company's days' sales in receivables?

20. **Ratios and Fixed Assets** [LO2] The Ashwood Company has a long-term debt ratio of .45 and a current ratio of 1.25. Current liabilities are $875, sales are $5,780, profit margin is 9.5 percent, and ROE is 18.5 percent. What is the amount of the firm's net fixed assets?

21. **Profit Margin** [LO4] In response to complaints about high prices, a grocery chain runs the following advertising campaign: "If you pay your child $3 to go buy $50 worth of groceries, then your child makes twice as much on the trip as we do." You've collected the following information from the grocery chain's financial statements:

(millions)	
Sales	$750
Net income	22.5
Total assets	420
Total debt	280

Evaluate the grocery chain's claim. What is the basis for the statement? Is this claim misleading? Why or why not?

22. **Return on Equity** [LO2] Firm A and firm B have debt–total asset ratios of 35% and 30% and returns on total assets of 12% and 11%, respectively. Which firm has a greater return on equity?

23. **Calculating the Cash Coverage Ratio** [LO2] Sherwood Inc.'s net income for the most recent year was $13,168. The tax rate was 34 percent. The firm paid $3,605 in total interest expense and deducted $2,382 in depreciation expense. What was the cash coverage ratio for the year?

24. **Cost of Goods Sold** [LO2] Holliman Corp. has current liabilities of $365,000, a quick ratio of .85, inventory turnover of 5.8, and a current ratio of 1.4. What is the cost of goods sold for the company?

25. **Ratios and Foreign Companies** [LO2] Prince Albert Canning PLC had a net loss of £13,482 on sales of £138,793 (both in thousands of pounds). What was the company's profit margin? Does the fact that these figures are quoted in a foreign currency make any difference? Why? In dollars, sales were $274,213,000. What was the net loss in dollars?

Some recent financial statements for Smolira Golf Corp. follow. Use this information to work Problems 26 through 30.

SMOLIRA GOLF 2008 and 2009 Balance Sheets					
Assets			**Liabilities and Owners' Equity**		
	2008	**2009**		**2008**	**2009**
Current assets			Current liabilities		
Cash	$21,860	$ 22,050	Accounts payable	$ 19,320	$ 22,850
Accounts receivable	11,316	13,850	Notes payable	10,000	9,000
Inventory	23,084	24,650	Other	9,643	11,385
Total	$56,260	$ 60,550	Total	$ 38,963	$ 43,235
			Long-term debt	$ 75,000	$ 85,000
			Owners' equity		
			Common stock and paid-in surplus	$ 25,000	$ 25,000
Fixed assets			Accumulated retained earnings	151,365	167,840
Net plant and equipment	234,068	260,525	Total	$176,365	$192,840
Total assets	$290,328	$321,075	Total liabilities and owners' equity	$290,328	$321,075

SMOLIRA GOLF, Inc. 2009 Income Statement		
Sales		$305,830
Cost of goods sold		210,935
Depreciation		26,850
Earnings before interest and taxes		$ 68,045
Interest paid		11,930
Taxable income		$ 56,115
Taxes (35%)		19,640
Net income		$ 36,475
Dividends	$20,000	
Retained earnings	16,475	

26. **Calculating Financial Ratios [LO2]** Find the following financial ratios for Smolira Golf Corp. (use year-end figures rather than average values where appropriate):

    Short-term solvency ratios:

    a. Current ratio   _____

    b. Quick ratio   _____

    c. Cash ratio   _____

    Asset utilization ratios:

    d. Total asset turnover   _____

    e. Inventory turnover   _____

    f. Receivables turnover   _____

Long-term solvency ratios:

g. Total debt ratio   _____

h. Debt–equity ratio   _____

i. Equity multiplier   _____

j. Times interest earned ratio _____

k. Cash coverage ratio   _____

Profitability ratios:

l. Profit margin   _____

m. Return on assets   _____

n. Return on equity   _____

27. **Du Pont Identity [LO3]** Construct the Du Pont identity for Smolira Golf Corp.

28. **Statement of Cash Flows [LO4]** Prepare the 2009 statement of cash flows for Smolira Golf Corp.

29. **Market Value Ratios [LO2]** Smolira Golf Corp. has 25,000 shares of common stock outstanding, and the market price for a share of stock at the end of 2009 was $43. What is the price–earnings ratio? What are the dividends per share? What is the market-to-book ratio at the end of 2009? If the company's growth rate is 9 percent, what is the PEG ratio?

30. **Tobin's Q [LO2]** What is Tobin's Q for Smolira Golf? What assumptions are you making about the book value of debt and the market value of debt? What about the book value of assets and the market value of assets? Are these assumptions realistic? Why or why not?

MINICASE

Ratio Analysis at S&S Air, Inc.

Chris Guthrie was recently hired by S&S Air, Inc., to assist the company with its financial planning and to evaluate the company's performance. Chris graduated from college five years ago with a finance degree. He has been employed in the finance department of a *Fortune* 500 company since then.

S&S Air was founded 10 years ago by friends Mark Sexton and Todd Story. The company has manufactured and sold light airplanes over this period, and the company's products have received high reviews for safety and reliability. The company has a niche market in that it sells primarily to individuals who own and fly their own airplanes. The company has two models; the Birdie, which sells for $53,000, and the Eagle, which sells for $78,000.

Although the company manufactures aircraft, its operations are different from commercial aircraft companies. S&S Air builds aircraft to order. By using prefabricated parts, the company can complete the manufacture of an airplane in only five weeks. The company also receives a deposit on each order, as well as another partial payment before the order is complete. In contrast, a commercial airplane may take one

and one-half to two years to manufacture once the order is placed.

Mark and Todd have provided the following financial statements. Chris has gathered the industry ratios for the light airplane manufacturing industry.

S&S AIR, INC. 2009 Income Statement	
Sales	$30,499,420
Cost of goods sold	22,224,580
Other expenses	3,067,500
Depreciation	1,366,680
EBIT	$ 3,040,660
Interest	478,240
Taxable income	$ 2,562,420
Taxes (40%)	1,024,968
Net income	$ 1,537,452

Dividends	$560,000	
Add to retained earnings	977,452	

Visit us at www.mhhe.com/rwj

Visit us at www.mhhe.com/rwj

S&S AIR, INC.			
2006 Balance Sheet			
Assets		**Liabilities and Equity**	
Current assets		Current liabilities	
Cash	$ 441,000	Accounts payable	$ 889,000
Accounts receivable	708,400	Notes payable	2,030,000
Inventory	1,037,120	Total current liabilities	$ 2,919,000
Total current assets	$ 2,186,520		
		Long-term debt	$ 5,320,000
Fixed assets			
		Shareholder equity	
Net plant and equipment	$16,122,400	Common stock	$ 350,000
		Retained earnings	9,719,920
		Total equity	$10,069,920
Total assets	$18,308,920	Total liabilities and equity	$18,308,920

Light Airplane Industry Ratios			
	Lower Quartile	Median	Upper Quartile
Current ratio	.50	1.43	1.89
Quick ratio	.21	.38	.62
Cash ratio	.08	.21	.39
Total asset turnover	.68	.85	1.38
Inventory turnover	4.89	6.15	10.89
Receivables turnover	6.27	9.82	14.11
Total debt ratio	.44	.52	.61
Debt–equity ratio	.79	1.08	1.56
Equity multiplier	1.79	2.08	2.56
Times interest earned	5.18	8.06	9.83
Cash coverage ratio	5.84	8.43	10.27
Profit margin	4.05%	6.98%	9.87%
Return on assets	6.05%	10.53%	13.21%
Return on equity	9.93%	16.54%	26.15%

QUESTIONS

1. Using the financial statements provided for S&S Air, calculate each of the ratios listed in the table for the light aircraft industry.

2. Mark and Todd agree that a ratio analysis can provide a measure of the company's performance. They have chosen Boeing as an aspirant company. Would you choose Boeing as an aspirant company? Why or why not? There are other aircraft manufacturers S&S Air could use as aspirant companies. Discuss whether it is appropriate to use any of the following companies: Bombardier, Embraer, Cirrus Design Corporation, and Cessna Aircraft Company.

3. Compare the performance of S&S Air to the industry. For each ratio, comment on why it might be viewed as positive or negative relative to the industry. Suppose you create an inventory ratio calculated as inventory divided by current liabilities. How do you think S&S Air's ratio would compare to the industry average?

LEARNING OBJECTIVES

After studying this chapter, you should understand:

LO1 How to determine the future value of an investment made today.

LO2 How to determine the present value of cash to be received at a future date.

LO3 How to find the return on an investment.

LO4 How long it takes for an investment to reach a desired value.

INTRODUCTION TO VALUATION: THE TIME VALUE OF MONEY

5

TOYOTA MOTOR CREDIT CORPORATION (TMCC), a subsidiary of Toyota Motor, offered some securities for sale to the public on March 28, 2008. Under the terms of the deal, TMCC promised to repay the owner of one of these securities $100,000 on March 28, 2038, but investors would receive nothing until then. Investors paid TMCC $24,099 for each of these securities; so they gave up $24,099 on March 28, 2008, for the promise of a $100,000 payment 30 years later. Such a security, for which you pay some amount today in exchange for a promised lump sum to be received at a future date, is about the simplest possible type. Is giving up $24,099 in exchange for $100,000 in 30 years a good deal? On the plus side, you get back about $4 for every $1 you put up. That probably sounds good; but on the down side, you have to wait 30 years to get it. What you need to know is how to analyze this trade-off; this chapter gives you the tools you need.

> Master the ability to solve problems in this chapter by using a spreadsheet. Access Excel Master on the student Web site www.mhhe.com/rwj.

One of the basic problems faced by the financial manager is how to determine the value today of cash flows expected in the future. For example, the jackpot in a PowerBall™ lottery drawing was $110 million. Does this mean the winning ticket was worth $110 million? The answer is no because the jackpot was actually going to pay out over a 20-year period at a rate of $5.5 million per year. How much was the ticket worth then? The answer depends on the time value of money, the subject of this chapter.

In the most general sense, the phrase *time value of money* refers to the fact that a dollar in hand today is worth more than a dollar promised at some time in the future. On a practical level, one reason for this is that you could earn interest while you waited; so a dollar today would grow to more than a dollar later. The trade-off between money now and money later thus depends on, among other things, the rate you can earn by investing. Our goal in this chapter is to explicitly evaluate this trade-off between dollars today and dollars at some future time.

A thorough understanding of the material in this chapter is critical to understanding material in subsequent chapters, so you should study it with particular care. We will present a number of examples in this chapter. In many problems, your answer may differ from ours slightly. This can happen because of rounding and is not a cause for concern.

5.1 Future Value and Compounding

future value (FV)
The amount an investment is worth after one or more periods.

The first thing we will study is future value. **Future value (FV)** refers to the amount of money an investment will grow to over some period of time at some given interest rate. Put another way, future value is the cash value of an investment at some time in the future. We start out by considering the simplest case: a single-period investment.

INVESTING FOR A SINGLE PERIOD

Suppose you invest $100 in a savings account that pays 10 percent interest per year. How much will you have in one year? You will have $110. This $110 is equal to your original *principal* of $100 plus $10 in interest that you earn. We say that $110 is the future value of $100 invested for one year at 10 percent, and we simply mean that $100 today is worth $110 in one year, given that 10 percent is the interest rate.

In general, if you invest for one period at an interest rate of r, your investment will grow to $(1 + r)$ per dollar invested. In our example, r is 10 percent, so your investment grows to $1 + .10 = 1.1$ dollars per dollar invested. You invested $100 in this case, so you ended up with $100 \times 1.10 = \$110$.

INVESTING FOR MORE THAN ONE PERIOD

Going back to our $100 investment, what will you have after two years, assuming the interest rate doesn't change? If you leave the entire $110 in the bank, you will earn $110 \times .10 = \$11$ in interest during the second year, so you will have a total of $110 + 11 = \$121$. This $121 is the future value of $100 in two years at 10 percent. Another way of looking at it is that one year from now you are effectively investing $110 at 10 percent for a year. This is a single-period problem, so you'll end up with $1.10 for every dollar invested, or $110 \times 1.1 = \$121$ total.

This $121 has four parts. The first part is the $100 original principal. The second part is the $10 in interest you earned in the first year, and the third part is another $10 you earn in the second year, for a total of $120. The last $1 you end up with (the fourth part) is interest you earn in the second year on the interest paid in the first year: $10 \times .10 = \$1$.

compounding
The process of accumulating interest on an investment over time to earn more interest.

This process of leaving your money and any accumulated interest in an investment for more than one period, thereby *reinvesting* the interest, is called **compounding**. Compounding the interest means earning **interest on interest**, so we call the result **compound interest**. With **simple interest**, the interest is not reinvested, so interest is earned each period only on the original principal.

interest on interest
Interest earned on the reinvestment of previous interest payments.

EXAMPLE 5.1   **Interest on Interest**

Suppose you locate a two-year investment that pays 14 percent per year. If you invest $325, how much will you have at the end of the two years? How much of this is simple interest? How much is compound interest?

At the end of the first year, you will have $325 \times (1 + .14) = \$370.50$. If you reinvest this entire amount and thereby compound the interest, you will have $370.50 \times 1.14 = \$422.37$ at the end of the second year. The total interest you earn is thus $422.37 - 325 = \$97.37$. Your $325 original principal earns $325 \times .14 = \$45.50$ in interest each year, for a two-year total of $91 in simple interest. The remaining $97.37 - 91 = \$6.37$ results from compounding. You can check this by noting that the interest earned in the first year is $45.50. The interest on interest earned in the second year thus amounts to $45.50 \times .14 = \$6.37$, as we calculated.

We now take a closer look at how we calculated the $121 future value. We multiplied $110 by 1.1 to get $121. The $110, however, was $100 also multiplied by 1.1. In other words:

$$\$121 = \$110 \times 1.1$$
$$= (\$100 \times 1.1) \times 1.1$$
$$= \$100 \times (1.1 \times 1.1)$$
$$= \$100 \times 1.1^2$$
$$= \$100 \times 1.21$$

compound interest
Interest earned on both the initial principal and the interest reinvested from prior periods.

simple interest
Interest earned only on the original principal amount invested.

At the risk of belaboring the obvious, let's ask: How much would our $100 grow to after three years? Once again, in two years, we'll be investing $121 for one period at 10 percent. We'll end up with $1.10 for every dollar we invest, or $121 × 1.1 = $133.10 total. This $133.10 is thus:

$$\$133.10 = \$121 \times 1.1$$
$$= (\$110 \times 1.1) \times 1.1$$
$$= (\$100 \times 1.1) \times 1.1 \times 1.1$$
$$= \$100 \times (1.1 \times 1.1 \times 1.1)$$
$$= \$100 \times 1.1^3$$
$$= \$100 \times 1.331$$

 For a discussion of time value concepts (and lots more) see www.financeprofessor.com.

You're probably noticing a pattern to these calculations, so we can now go ahead and state the general result. As our examples suggest, the future value of $1 invested for t periods at a rate of r per period is this:

$$\text{Future value} = \$1 \times (1 + r)^t \qquad \text{[5.1]}$$

The expression $(1 + r)^t$ is sometimes called the *future value interest factor* (or just *future value factor*) for $1 invested at r percent for t periods and can be abbreviated as FVIF(r, t).

In our example, what would your $100 be worth after five years? We can first compute the relevant future value factor as follows:

$$(1 + r)^t = (1 + .10)^5 = 1.1^5 = 1.6105$$

Your $100 will thus grow to:

$$\$100 \times 1.6105 = \$161.05$$

The growth of your $100 each year is illustrated in Table 5.1. As shown, the interest earned in each year is equal to the beginning amount multiplied by the interest rate of 10 percent.

Year	Beginning Amount	Simple Interest	Compound Interest	Total Interest Earned	Ending Amount
1	$100.00	$10	$ .00	$10.00	$110.00
2	110.00	10	1.00	11.00	121.00
3	121.00	10	2.10	12.10	133.10
4	133.10	10	3.31	13.31	146.41
5	146.41	10	4.64	14.64	161.05
		Total $50 simple interest	Total $11.05 compound interest	Total $61.05 interest	

TABLE 5.1

Future Value of $100 at 10 percent

FIGURE 5.1

Future Value, Simple
Interest, and Compound
Interest

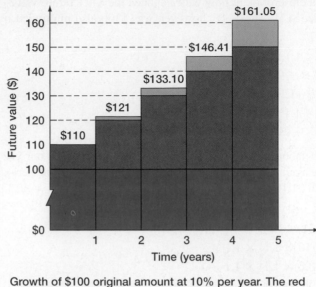

Growth of $100 original amount at 10% per year. The red
shaded area shows the simple interest. The green shaded
area represents the portion of the total that results from
compounding of interest.

In Table 5.1, notice the total interest you earn is $61.05. Over the five-year span of this
investment, the simple interest is $100 × .10 = $10 per year, so you accumulate $50 this
way. The other $11.05 is from compounding.

Figure 5.1 illustrates the growth of the compound interest in Table 5.1. Notice how the
simple interest is constant each year, but the amount of compound interest you earn gets
bigger every year. The amount of the compound interest keeps increasing because more
and more interest builds up and there is thus more to compound.

Future values depend critically on the assumed interest rate, particularly for long-lived
investments. Figure 5.2 illustrates this relationship by plotting the growth of $1 for differ-
ent rates and lengths of time. Notice the future value of $1 after 10 years is about $6.20 at
a 20 percent rate, but it is only about $2.60 at 10 percent. In this case, doubling the interest
rate more than doubles the future value.

To solve future value problems, we need to come up with the relevant future value factors. There are several different ways of doing this. In our example, we could have multiplied 1.1 by itself five times. This would work just fine, but it would get to be very tedious
for, say, a 30-year investment.

Fortunately, there are several easier ways to get future value factors. Most calculators
have a key labeled "y^x." You can usually just enter 1.1, press this key, enter 5, and press the
"=" key to get the answer. This is an easy way to calculate future value factors because it's
quick and accurate.

Alternatively, you can use a table that contains future value factors for some common
interest rates and time periods. Table 5.2 contains some of these factors. Table A.1 in the
appendix at the end of the book contains a much larger set. To use the table, find the column
that corresponds to 10 percent. Then look down the rows until you come to five periods.
You should find the factor that we calculated, 1.6105.

Tables such as 5.2 are not as common as they once were because they predate inexpensive calculators and are available only for a relatively small number of rates. Interest rates

*A brief intro-
duction to key financial
concepts is available at*
www.teachmefinance.com.

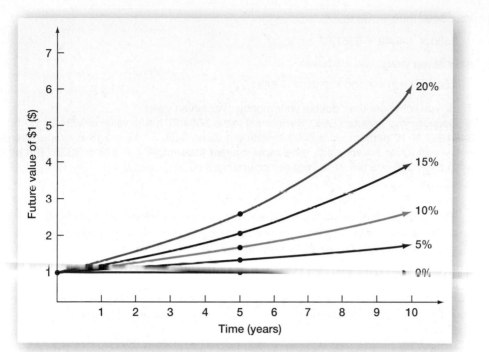

FIGURE 5.2

Future Value of $1 for Different Periods and Rates

TABLE 5.2

Future Value Interest Factors

Number of Periods	Interest Rate			
	5%	**10%**	**15%**	**20%**
1	1.0500	1.1000	1.1500	1.2000
2	1.1025	1.2100	1.3225	1.4400
3	1.1576	1.3310	1.5209	1.7280
4	1.2155	1.4641	1.7400	2.0736
5	1.2763	1.6105	2.0114	2.4883

are often quoted to three or four decimal places, so the tables needed to deal with these accurately would be quite large. As a result, the real world has moved away from using them. We will emphasize the use of a calculator in this chapter.

These tables still serve a useful purpose. To make sure you are doing the calculations correctly, pick a factor from the table and then calculate it yourself to see that you get the same answer. There are plenty of numbers to choose from.

Compound Interest

EXAMPLE 5.2

You've located an investment that pays 12 percent per year. That rate sounds good to you, so you invest $400. How much will you have in three years? How much will you have in seven years? At the end of seven years, how much interest will you have earned? How much of that interest results from compounding?

Based on our discussion, we can calculate the future value factor for 12 percent and three years as follows:

$$(1 + r)^t = 1.12^3 = 1.4049$$

(continued)

Your $400 thus grows to:

$400 × 1.4049 = $561.97

After seven years, you will have:

$400 × 1.12^7 = $400 × 2.2107 = $884.27

Thus, you will more than double your money over seven years.

Because you invested $400, the interest in the $884.27 future value is $884.27 − 400 = $484.27. At 12 percent, your $400 investment earns $400 × .12 = $48 in simple interest every year. Over seven years, the simple interest thus totals 7 × $48 = $336. The other $484.27 − 336 = $148.27 is from compounding.

The effect of compounding is not great over short time periods, but it really starts to add up as the horizon grows. To take an extreme case, suppose one of your more frugal ancestors had invested $5 for you at a 6 percent interest rate 200 years ago. How much would you have today? The future value factor is a substantial $1.06^{200} = 115{,}125.90$ (you won't find this one in a table), so you would have $5 × 115,125.90 = $575,629.52 today. Notice that the simple interest is just $5 × .06 = $.30 per year. After 200 years, this amounts to $60. The rest is from reinvesting. Such is the power of compound interest!

EXAMPLE 5.3   **How Much for That Island?**

To further illustrate the effect of compounding for long horizons, consider the case of Peter Minuit and the American Indians. In 1626, Minuit bought all of Manhattan Island for about $24 in goods and trinkets. This sounds cheap, but the Indians may have gotten the better end of the deal. To see why, suppose the Indians had sold the goods and invested the $24 at 10 percent. How much would it be worth today?

About 383 years have passed since the transaction. At 10 percent, $24 will grow by quite a bit over that time. How much? The future value factor is roughly:

$$(1 + r)^t = 1.1^{383} \approx 7{,}100{,}000{,}000{,}000{,}000$$

That is, 7.1 followed by 14 zeroes. The future value is thus on the order of $24 × 7.1 = $170 *quadrillion* (give or take a few hundreds of trillions).

Well, $170 quadrillion is a lot of money. How much? If you had it, you could buy the United States. All of it. Cash. With money left over to buy Canada, Mexico, and the rest of the world, for that matter.

This example is something of an exaggeration, of course. In 1626, it would not have been easy to locate an investment that would pay 10 percent every year without fail for the next 383 years.

CALCULATOR HINTS

Using a Financial Calculator

Although there are the various ways of calculating future values we have described so far, many of you will decide that a financial calculator is the way to go. If you are planning on using one, you should read this extended hint; otherwise, skip it.

A financial calculator is simply an ordinary calculator with a few extra features. In particular, it knows some of the most commonly used financial formulas, so it can directly compute things like future values.

(*continued*)

Financial calculators have the advantage that they handle a lot of the computation, but that is really all. In other words, you still have to understand the problem; the calculator just does some of the arithmetic. In fact, there is an old joke (somewhat modified) that goes like this: Anyone can make a mistake on a time value of money problem, but to really screw one up takes a financial calculator! We therefore have two goals for this section. First, we'll discuss how to compute future values. After that, we'll show you how to avoid the most common mistakes people make when they start using financial calculators.

How to Calculate Future Values with a Financial Calculator

Examining a typical financial calculator, you will find five keys of particular interest. They usually look like this:

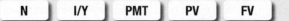

For now, we need to focus on four of these. The keys labeled **PV** and **FV** are just what you would guess: present value and future value. The key labeled **N** refers to the number of periods, which is what we have been calling *t*. Finally, **I/Y** stands for the interest rate, which we have called *r*.[1]

If we have the financial calculator set up right (see our next section), then calculating a future value is very simple. Take a look back at our question involving the future value of $100 at 10 percent for five years. We have seen that the answer is $161.05. The exact keystrokes will differ depending on what type of calculator you use, but here is basically all you do:

1. Enter −100. Press the **PV** key. (The negative sign is explained in the next section.)
2. Enter 10. Press the **I/Y** key. (Notice that we entered 10, not .10; see the next section.)
3. Enter 5. Press the **N** key.

Now we have entered all of the relevant information. To solve for the future value, we need to ask the calculator what the FV is. Depending on your calculator, either you press the button labeled "CPT" (for compute) and then press **FV**, or you just press **FV**. Either way, you should get 161.05. If you don't (and you probably won't if this is the first time you have used a financial calculator!), we will offer some help in our next section.

Before we explain the kinds of problems you are likely to run into, we want to establish a standard format for showing you how to use a financial calculator. Using the example we just looked at, in the future, we will illustrate such problems like this:

Enter

Solve for   161.05

Here is an important tip: Appendix D (which can be found on our Web site) contains more detailed instructions for the most common types of financial calculators. See if yours is included; if it is, follow the instructions there if you need help. Of course, if all else fails, you can read the manual that came with the calculator.

How to Get the Wrong Answer Using a Financial Calculator

There are a couple of common (and frustrating) problems that cause a lot of trouble with financial calculators. In this section, we provide some important *dos* and *don'ts*. If you just can't seem to get a problem to work out, you should refer back to this section.

There are two categories we examine: three things you need to do only once and three things you need to do every time you work a problem. The things you need to do just once deal with the following calculator settings:

1. *Make sure your calculator is set to display a large number of decimal places*. Most financial calculators display only two decimal places; this causes problems because we frequently work with numbers—like interest rates—that are very small.

(continued)

---

2. *Make sure your calculator is set to assume only one payment per period or per year.* Most financial calculators assume monthly payments (12 per year) unless you say otherwise.

3. *Make sure your calculator is in "end" mode.* This is usually the default, but you can accidently change to "begin" mode.

If you don't know how to set these three things, see Appendix D on our Web site or your calculator's operating manual. There are also three things you need to do *every time you work a problem*:

1. *Before you start, completely clear out the calculator.* This is very important. Failure to do this is the number one reason for wrong answers; you simply must get in the habit of clearing the calculator every time you start a problem. How you do this depends on the calculator (see Appendix D on our Web site), but you must do more than just clear the display. For example, on a Texas Instruments BA II Plus you must press `2nd` then `CLR TVM` for *clear time value of money*. There is a similar command on your calculator. Learn it!

   Note that turning the calculator off and back on won't do it. Most financial calculators remember everything you enter, even after you turn them off. In other words, they remember all your mistakes unless you explicitly clear them out. Also, if you are in the middle of a problem and make a mistake, *clear it out and start over*. Better to be safe than sorry.

2. *Put a negative sign on cash outflows.* Most financial calculators require you to put a negative sign on cash outflows and a positive sign on cash inflows. As a practical matter, this usually just means that you should enter the present value amount with a negative sign (because normally the present value represents the amount you give up today in exchange for cash inflows later). By the same token, when you solve for a present value, you shouldn't be surprised to see a negative sign.

3. *Enter the rate correctly.* Financial calculators assume that rates are quoted in percent, so if the rate is .08 (or 8 percent), you should enter 8, not .08.

If you follow these guidelines (especially the one about clearing out the calculator), you should have no problem using a financial calculator to work almost all of the problems in this and the next few chapters. We'll provide some additional examples and guidance where appropriate.

A NOTE ABOUT COMPOUND GROWTH

If you are considering depositing money in an interest-bearing account, then the interest rate on that account is just the rate at which your money grows, assuming you don't remove any of it. If that rate is 10 percent, then each year you simply have 10 percent more money than you had the year before. In this case, the interest rate is just an example of a compound growth rate.

The way we calculated future values is actually quite general and lets you answer some other types of questions related to growth. For example, your company currently has 10,000 employees. You've estimated that the number of employees grows by 3 percent per year. How many employees will there be in five years? Here, we start with 10,000 people instead of dollars, and we don't think of the growth rate as an interest rate, but the calculation is exactly the same:

$$10,000 \times 1.03^5 = 10,000 \times 1.1593 = 11,593 \text{ employees}$$

There will be about 1,593 net new hires over the coming five years.

To give another example, according to Value Line (a leading supplier of business information for investors), Wal-Mart's 2007 sales were about $374 billion. Suppose sales are projected to increase at a rate of 15 percent per year. What will Wal-Mart's sales be in the year 2012 if this is correct? Verify for yourself that the answer is about $752 billion—just over twice as large.

Dividend Growth	**EXAMPLE 5.4**

The TICO Corporation currently pays a cash dividend of $5 per share. You believe the dividend will be increased by 4 percent each year indefinitely. How big will the dividend be in eight years?

Here we have a cash dividend growing because it is being increased by management; but once again the calculation is the same:

Future value = $5 × 1.04^8 = $5 × 1.3686 = $6.84

The dividend will grow by $1.84 over that period. Dividend growth is a subject we will return to in a later chapter.

Concept Questions

5.1a What do we mean by the future value of an investment?

5.1b What does it mean to compound interest? How does compound interest differ from simple interest?

5.1c In general, what is the future value of $1 invested at r per period for t periods?

Present Value and Discounting

5.2

When we discuss future value, we are thinking of questions like: What will my $2,000 investment grow to if it earns a 6.5 percent return every year for the next six years? The answer to this question is what we call the future value of $2,000 invested at 6.5 percent for six years (verify that the answer is about $2,918).

Another type of question that comes up even more often in financial management is obviously related to future value. Suppose you need to have $10,000 in 10 years, and you can earn 6.5 percent on your money. How much do you have to invest today to reach your goal? You can verify that the answer is $5,327.26. How do we know this? Read on.

THE SINGLE-PERIOD CASE

We've seen that the future value of $1 invested for one year at 10 percent is $1.10. We now ask a slightly different question: How much do we have to invest today at 10 percent to get $1 in one year? In other words, we know the future value here is $1, but what is the **present value (PV)**? The answer isn't too hard to figure out. Whatever we invest today will be 1.1 times bigger at the end of the year. Because we need $1 at the end of the year:

Present value × 1.1 = $1

Or solving for the present value:

Present value = $1/1.1 = $.909

In this case, the present value is the answer to the following question: What amount, invested today, will grow to $1 in one year if the interest rate is 10 percent? Present value is thus just the reverse of future value. Instead of compounding the money forward into the future, we **discount** it back to the present.

present value (PV)
The current value of future cash flows discounted at the appropriate discount rate.

discount
Calculate the present value of some future amount.

EXAMPLE 5.5	Single-Period PV

Suppose you need $400 to buy textbooks next year. You can earn 7 percent on your money. How much do you have to put up today?

We need to know the PV of $400 in one year at 7 percent. Proceeding as in the previous example:

Present value × 1.07 = $400

We can now solve for the present value:

Present value = $400 × (1/1.07) = $373.83

Thus, $373.83 is the present value. Again, this just means that investing this amount for one year at 7 percent will give you a future value of $400.

From our examples, the present value of $1 to be received in one period is generally given as follows:

$$PV = \$1 \times [1/(1 + r)] = \$1/(1 + r)$$

We next examine how to get the present value of an amount to be paid in two or more periods into the future.

PRESENT VALUES FOR MULTIPLE PERIODS

Suppose you need to have $1,000 in two years. If you can earn 7 percent, how much do you have to invest to make sure you have the $1,000 when you need it? In other words, what is the present value of $1,000 in two years if the relevant rate is 7 percent?

Based on your knowledge of future values, you know the amount invested must grow to $1,000 over the two years. In other words, it must be the case that:

$$\$1,000 = PV \times 1.07 \times 1.07$$
$$= PV \times 1.07^2$$
$$= PV \times 1.1449$$

Given this, we can solve for the present value:

Present value = $1,000/1.1449 = $873.44

Therefore, $873.44 is the amount you must invest to achieve your goal.

EXAMPLE 5.6	Saving Up

You would like to buy a new automobile. You have $50,000 or so, but the car costs $68,500. If you can earn 9 percent, how much do you have to invest today to buy the car in two years? Do you have enough? Assume the price will stay the same.

What we need to know is the present value of $68,500 to be paid in two years, assuming a 9 percent rate. Based on our discussion, this is:

$$PV = \$68,500/1.09^2 = \$68,500/1.1881 = \$57,655.08$$

You're still about $7,655 short, even if you're willing to wait two years.

	Interest Rate			
Number of Periods	**5%**	**10%**	**15%**	**20%**
1	.9524	.9091	.8696	.8333
2	.9070	.8264	.7561	.6944
3	.8638	.7513	.6575	.5787
4	.8227	.6830	.5718	.4823
5	.7835	.6209	.4972	.4019

TABLE 5.3

Present Value Interest Factors

As you have probably recognized by now, calculating present values is quite similar to calculating future values, and the general result looks much the same. The present value of $1 to be received t periods into the future at a discount rate of r is:

$$PV = \$1 \times [1/(1 + r)^t] = \$1/(1 + r)^t \qquad [5.2]$$

The quantity in brackets, $1/(1 + r)^t$, goes by several different names. Because it's used to discount a future cash flow, it is often called a *discount factor*. With this name, it is not surprising that the rate used in the calculation is often called the **discount rate**. We will tend to call it this in talking about present values. The quantity in brackets is also called the *present value interest factor* (or just *present value factor*) for $1 at r percent for t periods and is sometimes abbreviated as PVIF(r, t). Finally, calculating the present value of a future cash flow to determine its worth today is commonly called **discounted cash flow (DCF) valuation**.

To illustrate, suppose you need $1,000 in three years. You can earn 15 percent on your money. How much do you have to invest today? To find out, we have to determine the present value of $1,000 in three years at 15 percent. We do this by discounting $1,000 back three periods at 15 percent. With these numbers, the discount factor is:

$$1/(1 + .15)^3 = 1/1.5209 = .6575$$

The amount you must invest is thus:

$$\$1,000 \times .6575 = \$657.50$$

We say that $657.50 is the present or discounted value of $1,000 to be received in three years at 15 percent.

There are tables for present value factors just as there are tables for future value factors, and you use them in the same way (if you use them at all). Table 5.3 contains a small set. A much larger set can be found in Table A.2 in the book's appendix.

In Table 5.3, the discount factor we just calculated (.6575) can be found by looking down the column labeled "15%" until you come to the third row.

discount rate
The rate used to calculate the present value of future cash flows.

discounted cash flow (DCF) valuation
Calculating the present value of a future cash flow to determine its value today.

CALCULATOR HINTS

You solve present value problems on a financial calculator just as you do future value problems. For the example we just examined (the present value of $1,000 to be received in three years at 15 percent), you would do the following:

Enter	3	15			1,000
	N	I/Y	PMT	PV	FV
Solve for				−657.50	

Notice that the answer has a negative sign; as we discussed earlier, that's because it represents an outflow today in exchange for the $1,000 inflow later.

| EXAMPLE 5.7 | **Deceptive Advertising?** |

Businesses sometimes advertise that you should "Come try our product. If you do, we'll give you $100 just for coming by!" If you read the fine print, what you find out is that they will give you a savings certificate that will pay you $100 in 25 years or so. If the going interest rate on such certificates is 10 percent per year, how much are they really giving you today?

What you're actually getting is the present value of $100 to be paid in 25 years. If the discount rate is 10 percent per year, then the discount factor is:

$$1/1.1^{25} = 1/10.8347 = .0923$$

This tells you that a dollar in 25 years is worth a little more than nine cents today, assuming a 10 percent discount rate. Given this, the promotion is actually paying you about .0923 × $100 = $9.23. Maybe this is enough to draw customers, but it's not $100.

As the length of time until payment grows, present values decline. As Example 5.7 illustrates, present values tend to become small as the time horizon grows. If you look out far enough, they will always approach zero. Also, for a given length of time, the higher the discount rate is, the lower is the present value. Put another way, present values and discount rates are inversely related. Increasing the discount rate decreases the PV and vice versa.

The relationship between time, discount rates, and present values is illustrated in Figure 5.3. Notice that by the time we get to 10 years, the present values are all substantially smaller than the future amounts.

FIGURE 5.3

Present Value of $1 for Different Periods and Rates

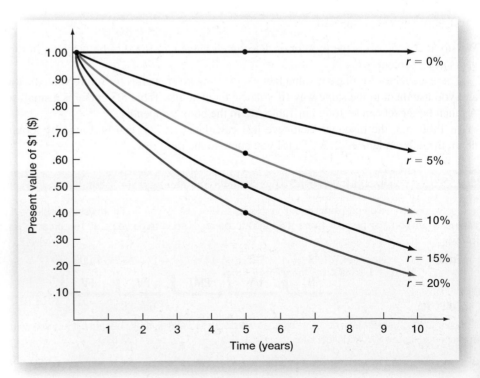

Concept Questions

5.2a What do we mean by the present value of an investment?

5.2b The process of discounting a future amount back to the present is the opposite of doing what?

5.2c What do we mean by discounted cash flow, or DCF, valuation?

5.2d In general, what is the present value of $1 to be received in t periods, assuming a discount rate of r per period?

More about Present and Future Values   5.3

If you look back at the expressions we came up with for present and future values, you will see a simple relationship between the two. We explore this relationship and some related issues in this section.

PRESENT VERSUS FUTURE VALUE

What we called the present value factor is just the reciprocal of (that is, 1 divided by) the future value factor:

Future value factor $= (1 + r)^t$

Present value factor $= 1/(1 + r)^t$

In fact, the easy way to calculate a present value factor on many calculators is to first calculate the future value factor and then press the "$1/x$" key to flip it over.

If we let FV_t stand for the future value after t periods, then the relationship between future value and present value can be written simply as one of the following:

$$PV \times (1 + r)^t = FV_t$$
$$PV = FV_t/(1 + r)^t = FV_t \times [1/(1 + r)^t]$$

[5.3]

This last result we will call the *basic present value equation*. We will use it throughout the text. A number of variations come up, but this simple equation underlies many of the most important ideas in corporate finance.

Evaluating Investments	**EXAMPLE 5.8**

To give you an idea of how we will be using present and future values, consider the following simple investment. Your company proposes to buy an asset for $335. This investment is very safe. You would sell off the asset in three years for $400. You know you could invest the $335 elsewhere at 10 percent with very little risk. What do you think of the proposed investment?

This is not a good investment. Why not? Because you can invest the $335 elsewhere at 10 percent. If you do, after three years it will grow to:

$335 $\times (1 + r)^t$ = $335 $\times 1.1^3$

    = $335 $\times 1.331$

    = $445.89

(continued)

Because the proposed investment pays out only $400, it is not as good as other alternatives we have. Another way of seeing the same thing is to notice that the present value of $400 in three years at 10 percent is:

$$\$400 \times [1/(1 + r)^t] = \$400/1.1^3 = \$400/1.331 = \$300.53$$

This tells us that we have to invest only about $300 to get $400 in three years, not $335. We will return to this type of analysis later on.

DETERMINING THE DISCOUNT RATE

We frequently need to determine what discount rate is implicit in an investment. We can do this by looking at the basic present value equation:

$$PV = FV_t /(1 + r)^t$$

There are only four parts to this equation: the present value (PV), the future value (FV_t), the discount rate (r), and the life of the investment (t). Given any three of these, we can always find the fourth.

For a downloadable, Windows-based financial calculator, go to www.calculator.org.

EXAMPLE 5.9	**Finding *r* for a Single-Period Investment**

You are considering a one-year investment. If you put up $1,250, you will get back $1,350. What rate is this investment paying?

First, in this single-period case, the answer is fairly obvious. You are getting a total of $100 in addition to your $1,250. The implicit rate on this investment is thus $100/1,250 = 8 percent.

More formally, from the basic present value equation, the present value (the amount you must put up today) is $1,250. The future value (what the present value grows to) is $1,350. The time involved is one period, so we have:

$$\$1,250 = \$1,350 /(1 + r)^1$$
$$1 + r = \$1,350 /1,250 = 1.08$$
$$r = 8\%$$

In this simple case, of course, there was no need to go through this calculation. But as we describe next, it gets a little harder with more than one period.

To illustrate what happens with multiple periods, let's say we are offered an investment that costs us $100 and will double our money in eight years. To compare this to other investments, we would like to know what discount rate is implicit in these numbers. This discount rate is called the *rate of return,* or sometimes just the *return,* on the investment. In this case, we have a present value of $100, a future value of $200 (double our money), and an eight-year life. To calculate the return, we can write the basic present value equation as:

$$PV = FV_t /(1 + r)^t$$
$$\$100 = \$200/(1 + r)^8$$

It could also be written as:

$$(1 + r)^8 = \$200/100 = 2$$

We now need to solve for r. There are three ways we could do it:

1. Use a financial calculator.
2. Solve the equation for $1 + r$ by taking the eighth root of both sides. Because this is the same thing as raising both sides to the power of ⅛ or .125, this is actually easy to do with the "y^x" key on a calculator. Just enter 2, then press "y^x," enter .125, and press the "=" key. The eighth root should be about 1.09, which implies that r is 9 percent.
3. Use a future value table. The future value factor after eight years is equal to 2. If you look across the row corresponding to eight periods in Table A.1, you will see that a future value factor of 2 corresponds to the 9 percent column, again implying that the return here is 9 percent.

Actually, in this particular example, there is a useful "back of the envelope" means of solving for r—the Rule of 72. For reasonable rates of return, the time it takes to double your money is given approximately by $72/r\%$. In our example, this means that $72/r\% = 8$ years, implying that r is 9 percent, as we calculated. This rule is fairly accurate for discount rates in the 5 percent to 20 percent range.

Baseball Collectibles as Investments   EXAMPLE 5.10

In April 2008, the last baseball hit for a home run by Barry Bonds was auctioned off for about $376,000. The price of the ball was considered a bargain, in part because potential buyers were unsure if Bonds would play again. "Experts" on such collectibles often argue that collectibles such as this will double in value over a 10-year period.

So would the ball have been a good investment? By the Rule of 72, you already know the experts were predicting that the ball would double in value in 10 years; so the return predicted would be about $72/10 = 7.2$ percent per year, which is only so-so.

At one time at least, a rule of thumb in the rarefied world of fine art collecting was "your money back in 5 years, double your money in 10 years." Given this, let's see how an investment stacked up. In 1998, the Alberto Giacometti bronze statue *Homme Qui Marche III* sold for $2,972,500. Five years later, the statue was sold again, walking out the door at a price of $4,039,500. How did the seller do?

The rule of thumb has us doubling our money in 10 years; so, from the Rule of 72, we have that 7.2 percent per year was the norm. The statue was resold in almost exactly five years. The present value is $2,972,500, and the future value is $4,039,500. We need to solve for the unknown rate, r, as follows:

Why does the Rule of 72 work? See www.moneychimp.com.

$$\$2,972,500 = \$4,039,500/(1 + r)^5$$

$$(1 + r)^5 = 1.3590$$

Solving for r, we find the seller earned about 6.33 percent per year—less than the 7.2 percent rule of thumb. At least the seller made his money back.

What about other collectibles? To a philatelist (a stamp collector to you and us), one of the most prized stamps is the 1918 24-cent inverted Jenny C3a. The stamp is a collectible because it has a picture of an upside-down biplane. One of these stamps sold at auction for $825,000 in 2007. At what rate did its value grow? Verify for yourself that the answer is about 18.42 percent, assuming an 89-year period.

Of course not all collectibles perform as well. In 2008, an 1851 octagonal $50 gold coin minted in San Francisco sold for $189,750. Assuming that 157 years had passed, see if you agree that this collectible gained about 5.39 percent per year.

Perhaps the most desired coin for numismatists (coin collectors) is the 1933 $20 gold double eagle. Outside of the U.S. Mint and the Smithsonian, only one of these coins is in circulation. In 2002, the coin sold at auction for $7,590,020. See if you agree that this collectible gained about 20.5 percent per year.

A slightly more extreme example involves money bequeathed by Benjamin Franklin, who died on April 17, 1790. In his will, he gave 1,000 pounds sterling to Massachusetts and the city of Boston. He gave a like amount to Pennsylvania and the city of Philadelphia. The money had been paid to Franklin when he held political office, but he believed that politicians should not be paid for their service (it appears that this view is not widely shared by modern politicians).

Franklin originally specified that the money should be paid out 100 years after his death and used to train young people. Later, however, after some legal wrangling, it was agreed that the money would be paid out in 1990, 200 years after Franklin's death. By that time, the Pennsylvania bequest had grown to about $2 million; the Massachusetts bequest had grown to $4.5 million. The money was used to fund the Franklin Institutes in Boston and Philadelphia. Assuming that 1,000 pounds sterling was equivalent to $1,000, what rate of return did the two states earn? (The dollar did not become the official U.S. currency until 1792.)

For Pennsylvania, the future value is $2 million and the present value is $1,000. There are 200 years involved, so we need to solve for r in the following:

$$\$1,000 = \$2 \text{ million}/(1 + r)^{200}$$

$$(1 + r)^{200} = 2,000$$

Solving for r, we see that the Pennsylvania money grew at about 3.87 percent per year. The Massachusetts money did better; verify that the rate of return in this case was 4.3 percent. Small differences in returns can add up!

CALCULATOR HINTS

We can illustrate how to calculate unknown rates using a financial calculator with these numbers. For Pennsylvania, you would do the following:

Enter	200			−1,000	2,000,000
	N	I/Y	PMT	PV	FV
Solve for		3.87			

As in our previous examples, notice the minus sign on the present value, representing Franklin's outlay made many years ago. What do you change to work the problem for Massachusetts?

EXAMPLE 5.11 | **Saving for College**

You estimate that you will need about $80,000 to send your child to college in eight years. You have about $35,000 now. If you can earn 20 percent per year, will you make it? At what rate will you just reach your goal?

(continued)

If you can earn 20 percent, the future value of your $35,000 in eight years will be:

$$FV = \$35,000 \times 1.20^8 = \$35,000 \times 4.2998 = \$150,493.59$$

So, you will make it easily. The minimum rate is the unknown r in the following:

$$FV = \$35,000 \times (1 + r)^8 = \$80,000$$
$$(1 + r)^8 = \$80,000/35,000 = 2.2857$$

Therefore, the future value factor is 2.2857. Looking at the row in Table A.1 that corresponds to eight periods, we see that our future value factor is roughly halfway between the ones shown for 10 percent (2.1436) and 12 percent (2.4760), so you will just reach your goal if you earn approximately 11 percent. To get the exact answer, we could use a financial calculator or we could solve for r:

$$(1 + r)^8 = \$80,000/35,000 = 2.2857$$
$$1 + r = 2.2857^{(1/8)} = 2.2857^{.125} = 1.1089$$
$$r = 10.89\%$$

Only 18,262.5 Days to Retirement

EXAMPLE 5.12

You would like to retire in 50 years as a millionaire. If you have $10,000 today, what rate of return do you need to earn to achieve your goal?

The future value is $1,000,000. The present value is $10,000, and there are 50 years until payment. We need to calculate the unknown discount rate in the following:

$$\$10,000 = \$1,000,000/(1 + r)^{50}$$
$$(1 + r)^{50} = 100$$

The future value factor is thus 100. You can verify that the implicit rate is about 9.65 percent.

Not taking the time value of money into account when computing growth rates or rates of return often leads to some misleading numbers in the real world. For example, the most loved (and hated) team in baseball, the New York Yankees, had the highest payroll during the 1988 season, about $19 million. In 2008, the Yankees again had the highest payroll, a staggering $210 million: an increase of 1,005 percent! If history is any guide, we can get a rough idea of the future growth in baseball payrolls. See if you don't agree that this represents an annual increase of 12.8 percent, a substantial growth rate, but much less than the gaudy 1,005 percent.

How about classic maps? A few years ago, the first map of America, printed in Rome in 1507, was valued at about $135,000, 69 percent more than the $80,000 it was worth 10 years earlier. Your return on investment if you were the proud owner of the map over those 10 years? Verify that it's about 5.4 percent per year—far worse than the 69 percent reported increase in price.

Whether with maps or baseball payrolls, it's easy to be misled when returns are quoted without considering the time value of money. However, it's not just the uninitiated who are guilty of this slight form of deception. The title of a feature article in a leading business magazine predicted the Dow Jones Industrial Average would soar to a 70 percent gain over the coming five years. Do you think it meant a 70 percent return per year on your money? Think again!

How much do you need at retirement? Check out the "Money in Your 20s" link at www.about.com.

FINDING THE NUMBER OF PERIODS

Suppose we are interested in purchasing an asset that costs $50,000. We currently have $25,000. If we can earn 12 percent on this $25,000, how long until we have the $50,000? Finding the answer involves solving for the last variable in the basic present value equation, the number of periods. You already know how to get an approximate answer to this particular problem. Notice that we need to double our money. From the Rule of 72, this will take about $72/12 = 6$ years at 12 percent.

To come up with the exact answer, we can again manipulate the basic present value equation. The present value is $25,000, and the future value is $50,000. With a 12 percent discount rate, the basic equation takes one of the following forms:

$$\$25,000 = \$50,000/1.12^t$$
$$\$50,000/25,000 = 1.12^t = 2$$

We thus have a future value factor of 2 for a 12 percent rate. We now need to solve for t. If you look down the column in Table A.1 that corresponds to 12 percent, you will see that a future value factor of 1.9738 occurs at six periods. It will thus take about six years, as we calculated. To get the exact answer, we have to explicitly solve for t (or use a financial calculator). If you do this, you will see that the answer is 6.1163 years, so our approximation was quite close in this case.

CALCULATOR HINTS

If you use a financial calculator, here are the relevant entries:

Enter		12		−25,000	50,000
	N	**I/Y**	**PMT**	**PV**	**FV**
Solve for	6.1163				

EXAMPLE 5.13   **Waiting for Godot**

You've been saving up to buy the Godot Company. The total cost will be $10 million. You currently have about $2.3 million. If you can earn 5 percent on your money, how long will you have to wait? At 16 percent, how long must you wait?

At 5 percent, you'll have to wait a long time. From the basic present value equation:

$$\$2.3 \text{ million} = \$10 \text{ million}/1.05^t$$
$$1.05^t = 4.35$$
$$t = 30 \text{ years}$$

At 16 percent, things are a little better. Verify for yourself that it will take about 10 years.

Learn more about using Excel for time value and other calculations at www.studyfinance.com.

U.S. EE Savings Bonds are a familiar investment for many. You purchase them for half of their $100 face value. In other words, you pay $50 today and get $100 at some point in the future when the bond "matures." You receive no interest in between, and the interest rate is adjusted every six months, so the length of time until your $50 grows to $100

SPREADSHEET STRATEGIES

Using a Spreadsheet for Time Value of Money Calculations

More and more, businesspeople from many different areas (not just finance and accounting) rely on spreadsheets to do all the different types of calculations that come up in the real world. As a result, in this section, we will show you how to use a spreadsheet to handle the various time value of money problems we presented in this chapter. We will use Microsoft Excel™, but the commands are similar for other types of software. We assume you are already familiar with basic spreadsheet operations.

As we have seen, you can solve for any one of the following four potential unknowns: future value, present value, the discount rate, or the number of periods. With a spreadsheet, there is a separate formula for each. In Excel, these are shown in a nearby box.

In these formulas, pv and fv are present and future value, nper is the number of periods, and rate is the discount, or interest, rate.

Two things are a little tricky here. First, unlike a financial calculator, the spreadsheet requires that the rate be entered as a decimal. Second, as with most financial calculators, you have to put a negative sign on either the present value or the future value to solve for the rate or

To Find	Enter This Formula
Future value	= FV (rate,nper,pmt,pv)
Present value	= PV (rate,nper,pmt,fv)
Discount rate	= RATE (nper,pmt,pv,fv)
Number of periods	= NPER (rate,pmt,pv,fv)

the number of periods. For the same reason, if you solve for a present value, the answer will have a negative sign unless you input a negative future value. The same is true when you compute a future value.

To illustrate how you might use these formulas, we will go back to an example in the chapter. If you invest $25,000 at 12 percent per year, how long until you have $50,000? You might set up a spreadsheet like this:

	A	B	C	D	E	F	G	H
1								
2		Using a spreadsheet for time value of money calculations						
3								
4	If we invest $25,000 at 12 percent, how long until we have $50,000? We need to solve							
5	for the unknown number of periods, so we use the formula NPER(rate, pmt, pv, fv).							
6								
7	Present value (pv):	$25,000						
8	Future value (fv):	$50,000						
9	Rate (rate):	.12						
10								
11	Periods:	6.1162554						
12								
13	The formula entered in cell B11 is =NPER(B9,0,-B7,B8); notice that pmt is zero and that pv							
14	has a negative sign on it. Also notice that rate is entered as a decimal, not a percentage.							

depends on future interest rates. However, at worst, the bonds are guaranteed to be worth $100 at the end of 17 years, so this is the longest you would ever have to wait. If you do have to wait the full 17 years, what rate do you earn?

Because this investment is doubling in value in 17 years, the Rule of 72 tells you the answer right away: 72/17 = 4.24%. Remember, this is the minimum guaranteed return, so you might do better. This example finishes our introduction to basic time value concepts. Table 5.4 summarizes present and future value calculations for future reference. As our nearby *Work the Web* box shows, online calculators are widely available to handle these calculations; but it is still important to know what is really going on.

WORK THE WEB

How important is the time value of money? A recent search on one Web search engine returned over 259 million hits! Although you must understand the calculations behind the time value of money, the advent of financial calculators and spreadsheets has eliminated the need for tedious calculations. In fact, many Web sites offer time value of money calculators. The following is one example from www.investopedia.com. You have $10,000 today and will invest it at 11.5 percent for 35 years. How much will it be worth at that time? With the Investopedia calculator, you simply enter the values and hit Calculate. The results look like this:

Interest Rate Per Time Period:	11.5	%
Number of Time Periods:	35	
Present Value:	10000	
	Calculate	
Future Value:	**$451,461.12**	

Who said time value of money calculations are hard?

Questions

1. *Use the present value calculator on this Web site to answer the following: Suppose you want to have $140,000 in 25 years. If you can earn a 10 percent return, how much do you have to invest today?*
2. *Use the future value calculator on this Web site to answer the following question: Suppose you have $8,000 today that you plan to save for your retirement in 40 years. If you earn a return of 10.8 percent per year, how much will this account be worth when you are ready to retire?*

TABLE 5.4

Summary of Time Value Calculations

I.	**Symbols:**
	PV = Present value, what future cash flows are worth today
	FV_t = Future value, what cash flows are worth in the future
	r = Interest rate, rate of return, or discount rate per period—typically, but not always, one year
	t = Number of periods—typically, but not always, the number of years
	C = Cash amount
II.	**Future Value of C Invested at r Percent for t Periods:**
	$FV_t = C \times (1 + r)^t$
	The term $(1 + r)^t$ is called the *future value factor*.
III.	**Present Value of C to Be Received in t Periods at r Percent per Period:**
	$PV = C/(1 + r)^t$
	The term $1/(1 + r)^t$ is called the *present value factor*.
IV.	**The Basic Present Value Equation Giving the Relationship between Present and Future Value:**
	$PV = FV_t/(1 + r)^t$

Concept Questions

5.3a What is the basic present value equation?

5.3b What is the Rule of 72?

Summary and Conclusions

This chapter has introduced you to the basic principles of present value and discounted cash flow valuation. In it, we explained a number of things about the time value of money, including these:

1. For a given rate of return, we can determine the value at some point in the future of an investment made today by calculating the future value of that investment.
2. We can determine the current worth of a future cash flow or series of cash flows for a given rate of return by calculating the present value of the cash flow(s) involved.
3. The relationship between present value (PV) and future value (FV) for a given rate r and time t is given by the basic present value equation:

    $$PV = FV_t/(1 + r)^t$$

    As we have shown, it is possible to find any one of the four components (PV, FV, r, or t) given the other three.

The principles developed in this chapter will figure prominently in the chapters to come. The reason for this is that most investments, whether they involve real assets or financial assets, can be analyzed using the discounted cash flow (DCF) approach. As a result, the DCF approach is broadly applicable and widely used in practice. Before going on, therefore, you might want to do some of the problems that follow.

Visit us at www.mhhe.com/rwj

CHAPTER REVIEW AND SELF-TEST PROBLEMS

5.1   Calculating Future Values Assume you deposit $10,000 today in an account that pays 6 percent interest. How much will you have in five years?

5.2   Calculating Present Values Suppose you have just celebrated your 19th birthday. A rich uncle has set up a trust fund for you that will pay you $150,000 when you turn 30. If the relevant discount rate is 9 percent, how much is this fund worth today?

5.3   Calculating Rates of Return You've been offered an investment that will double your money in 10 years. What rate of return are you being offered? Check your answer using the Rule of 72.

5.4   Calculating the Number of Periods You've been offered an investment that will pay you 9 percent per year. If you invest $15,000, how long until you have $30,000? How long until you have $45,000?

ANSWERS TO CHAPTER REVIEW AND SELF-TEST PROBLEMS

5.1   We need to calculate the future value of $10,000 at 6 percent for five years. The future value factor is:

$$1.06^5 = 1.3382$$

The future value is thus $10,000 × 1.3382 = $13,382.26.

5.2   We need the present value of $150,000 to be paid in 11 years at 9 percent. The discount factor is:

$$1/1.09^{11} = 1/2.5804 = .3875$$

The present value is thus about $58,130.

5.3   Suppose you invest $1,000. You will have $2,000 in 10 years with this investment. So, $1,000 is the amount you have today, or the present value, and $2,000 is the amount you will have in 10 years, or the future value. From the basic present value equation, we have:

$$\$2,000 = \$1,000 \times (1 + r)^{10}$$
$$2 = (1 + r)^{10}$$

From here, we need to solve for r, the unknown rate. As shown in the chapter, there are several different ways to do this. We will take the 10th root of 2 (by raising 2 to the power of $1/10$):

$$2^{(1/10)} = 1 + r$$
$$1.0718 = 1 + r$$
$$r = 7.18\%$$

Using the Rule of 72, we have $72/t = r\%$, or $72/10 = 7.2\%$, so, our answer looks good (remember that the Rule of 72 is only an approximation).

5.4   The basic equation is this:

$$\$30,000 = \$15,000 \times (1 + .09)^t$$
$$2 = (1 + .09)^t$$

If we solve for t, we find that $t = 8.04$ years. Using the Rule of 72, we get $72/9 = 8$ years, so once again our answer looks good. To get $45,000, verify for yourself that you will have to wait 12.75 years.

CONCEPTS REVIEW AND CRITICAL THINKING QUESTIONS

1.   **Present Value** [LO2]   The basic present value equation has four parts. What are they?

2.   **Compounding** [LO1, 2]   What is compounding? What is discounting?

3.   **Compounding and Period** [LO1]   As you increase the length of time involved, what happens to future values? What happens to present values?

4.   **Compounding and Interest Rates** [LO1]   What happens to a future value if you increase the rate r? What happens to a present value?

5.   **Ethical Considerations** [LO2]   Take a look back at Example 5.7. Is it deceptive advertising? Is it unethical to advertise a future value like this without a disclaimer?

To answer the next five questions, refer to the TMCC security we discussed to open the chapter.

6.   **Time Value of Money** [LO2]   Why would TMCC be willing to accept such a small amount today ($24,099) in exchange for a promise to repay about four times that amount ($100,000) in the future?

7.   **Call Provisions** [LO2]   TMCC has the right to buy back the securities on the anniversary date at a price established when the securities were issued (this feature is a term of this particular deal). What impact does this feature have on the desirability of this security as an investment?

8.   **Time Value of Money** [LO2]   Would you be willing to pay $24,099 today in exchange for $100,000 in 30 years? What would be the key considerations in answering yes or no? Would your answer depend on who is making the promise to repay?

9.   **Investment Comparison** [LO2]   Suppose that when TMCC offered the security for $24,099 the U.S. Treasury had offered an essentially identical security. Do you think it would have had a higher or lower price? Why?

Visit us at www.mhhe.com/rwj

10. **Length of Investment** [LO2] The TMCC security is bought and sold on the New York Stock Exchange. If you looked at the price today, do you think the price would exceed the $24,099 original price? Why? If you looked in the year 2019, do you think the price would be higher or lower than today's price? Why?

HM™

QUESTIONS AND PROBLEMS

1. **Simple Interest versus Compound Interest** [LO1] First City Bank pays 8 percent simple interest on its savings account balances, whereas Second City Bank pays 8 percent interest compounded annually. If you made a $5,000 deposit in each bank, how much more money would you earn from your Second City Bank account at the end of 10 years?

BASIC
(Questions 1–15)

2. **Calculating Future Values** [LO1] For each of the following, compute the future value:

Present Value	Years	Interest Rate	Future Value
$ 2,250	11	10%	
8,752	7	8	
76,355	14	17	
183,796	8	7	

3. **Calculating Present Values** [LO2] For each of the following, compute the present value:

Present Value	Years	Interest Rate	Future Value
	6	7%	$ 15,451
	7	13	51,557
	23	14	886,073
	18	9	550,164

4. **Calculating Interest Rates** [LO3] Solve for the unknown interest rate in each of the following:

Present Value	Years	Interest Rate	Future Value
$ 240	2		$ 297
360	10		1,080
39,000	15		185,382
38,261	30		531,618

5. **Calculating the Number of Periods** [LO4] Solve for the unknown number of years in each of the following:

Present Value	Years	Interest Rate	Future Value
$ 560		9%	$ 1,284
810		10	4,341
18,400		17	364,518
21,500		15	173,439

6. **Calculating Interest Rates** [LO3] Assume the total cost of a college education will be $290,000 when your child enters college in 18 years. You presently have $55,000 to invest. What annual rate of interest must you earn on your investment to cover the cost of your child's college education?

Visit us at www.mhhe.com/rwj

7. **Calculating the Number of Periods** [LO4] At 7 percent interest, how long does it take to double your money? To quadruple it?

8. **Calculating Interest Rates** [LO3] In January 2007, the average house price in the United States was $314,600. In January 2000, the average price was $200,300. What was the annual increase in selling price?

9. **Calculating the Number of Periods** [LO4] You're trying to save to buy a new $170,000 Ferrari. You have $40,000 today that can be invested at your bank. The bank pays 5.3 percent annual interest on its accounts. How long will it be before you have enough to buy the car?

10. **Calculating Present Values** [LO2] Imprudential, Inc. has an unfunded pension liability of $650 million that must be paid in 20 years. To assess the value of the firm's stock, financial analysts want to discount this liability back to the present. If the relevant discount rate is 7.4 percent, what is the present value of this liability?

11. **Calculating Present Values** [LO2] You have just received notification that you have won the $1 million first prize in the Centennial Lottery. However, the prize will be awarded on your 100th birthday (assuming you're around to collect), 80 years from now. What is the present value of your windfall if the appropriate discount rate is 10 percent?

12. **Calculating Future Values** [LO1] Your coin collection contains fifty 1952 silver dollars. If your grandparents purchased them for their face value when they were new, how much will your collection be worth when you retire in 2057, assuming they appreciate at a 4.5 percent annual rate?

13. **Calculating Interest Rates and Future Values** [LO1, 3] In 1895, the first U.S. Open Golf Championship was held. The winner's prize money was $150. In 2007, the winner's check was $1,260,000. What was the percentage increase per year in the winner's check over this period? If the winner's prize increases at the same rate, what will it be in 2040?

14. **Calculating Interest Rates** [LO3] In 2008, a gold Morgan dollar minted in 1895 sold for $43,125. For this to have been true, what rate of return did this coin return for the lucky numismatist?

15. **Calculating Rates of Return** [LO3] Although appealing to more refined tastes, art as a collectible has not always performed so profitably. During 2003, Sotheby's sold the Edgar Degas bronze sculpture *Petite Danseuse de Quatorze Ans* at auction for a price of $10,311,500. Unfortunately for the previous owner, he had purchased it in 1999 at a price of $12,377,500. What was his annual rate of return on this sculpture?

INTERMEDIATE
(Questions 16–20)

16. **Calculating Rates of Return** [LO3] Referring to the TMCC security we discussed at the very beginning of the chapter:

   a. Based on the $24,099 price, what rate was TMCC paying to borrow money?

   b. Suppose that, on March 28, 2020, this security's price is $38,260. If an investor had purchased it for $24,099 at the offering and sold it on this day, what annual rate of return would she have earned?

   c. If an investor had purchased the security at market on March 28, 2020, and held it until it matured, what annual rate of return would she have earned?

17. **Calculating Present Values** [LO2] Suppose you are still committed to owning a $170,000 Ferrari (see Problem 9). If you believe your mutual fund can achieve a 12 percent annual rate of return and you want to buy the car in 9 years on the day you turn 30, how much must you invest today?

18. **Calculating Future Values [LO1]** You have just made your first $4,000 contribution to your retirement account. Assuming you earn an 11 percent rate of return and make no additional contributions, what will your account be worth when you retire in 45 years? What if you wait 10 years before contributing? (Does this suggest an investment strategy?)

19. **Calculating Future Values [LO1]** You are scheduled to receive $20,000 in two years. When you receive it, you will invest it for six more years at 8.4 percent per year. How much will you have in eight years?

20. **Calculating the Number of Periods [LO4]** You expect to receive $10,000 at graduation in two years. You plan on investing it at 11 percent until you have $75,000. How long will you wait from now?

Visit us at www.mhhe.com/rwj

6

DISCOUNTED CASH FLOW VALUATION

LEARNING OBJECTIVES

After studying this chapter, you should understand:

LO1 How to determine the future and present value of investments with multiple cash flows.

LO2 How loan payments are calculated and how to find the interest rate on a loan.

LO3 How loans are amortized or paid off.

LO4 How interest rates are quoted (and misquoted).

THE SIGNING OF BIG-NAME ATHLETES is often accompanied by great fanfare, but the numbers are often misleading. For example, in 2007, catcher Jorge Posada reached a deal with the New York Yankees, signing a contract with a reported value of $52.4 million. Not bad, especially for someone who makes a living using the "tools of ignorance" (jock jargon for a catcher's equipment). Another example is the contract signed by quarterback Tony Romo of the Dallas Cowboys, which had a stated value of about $67.5 million.

It looks like Jorge and Tony did pretty well, but then there was Jorge's teammate Alex Rodriguez, or A-Rod as he is known to fans, who signed for a stated value of $275 million. This amount was actually payable over several years and consisted of $2 million immediately, along with $28 million in the first year plus $245 million in future salary to be paid in the years 2009 through 2017. Jorge's and Tony's payments were similarly spread over time. Because all three contracts called for payments that are made at future dates, we must consider the time value of money, which means none of these players received the quoted amounts. How much did they really get? This chapter gives you the "tools of knowledge" to answer this question.

Master the ability to solve problems in this chapter by using a spreadsheet. Access Excel Master on the student Web site www.mhhe.com/rwj.

In our previous chapter, we covered the basics of discounted cash flow valuation. However, so far, we have dealt with only single cash flows. In reality, most investments have multiple cash flows. For example, if Target is thinking of opening a new department store, there will be a large cash outlay in the beginning and then cash inflows for many years. In this chapter, we begin to explore how to value such investments.

When you finish this chapter, you should have some very practical skills. For example, you will know how to calculate your own car payments or student loan payments. You will also be able to determine how long it will take to pay off a credit card if you make the minimum payment each month (a practice we do not recommend). We will show you how to compare interest rates to determine which are the highest and which are the lowest, and we will also show you how interest rates can be quoted in different—and at times deceptive—ways.

FIGURE 6.1

Drawing and Using a Time Line

Future and Present Values of Multiple Cash Flows

6.1

Thus far, we have restricted our attention to either the future value of a lump sum present amount or the present value of some single future cash flow. In this section, we begin to study ways to value multiple cash flows. We start with future value.

FUTURE VALUE WITH MULTIPLE CASH FLOWS

Suppose you deposit $100 today in an account paying 8 percent. In one year, you will deposit another $100. How much will you have in two years? This particular problem is relatively easy. At the end of the first year, you will have $108 plus the second $100 you deposit, for a total of $208. You leave this $208 on deposit at 8 percent for another year. At the end of this second year, it is worth:

$208 × 1.08 = $224.64

Figure 6.1 is a *time line* that illustrates the process of calculating the future value of these two $100 deposits. Figures such as this are useful for solving complicated problems. Almost anytime you are having trouble with a present or future value problem, drawing a time line will help you see what is happening.

In the first part of Figure 6.1, we show the cash flows on the time line. The most important thing is that we write them down where they actually occur. Here, the first cash flow occurs today, which we label as time 0. We therefore put $100 at time 0 on the time line. The second $100 cash flow occurs one year from today, so we write it down at the point labeled as time 1. In the second part of Figure 6.1, we calculate the future values one period at a time to come up with the final $224.64.

Saving Up Revisited	EXAMPLE 6.1

You think you will be able to deposit $4,000 at the end of each of the next three years in a bank account paying 8 percent interest. You currently have $7,000 in the account. How much will you have in three years? In four years?

At the end of the first year, you will have:

$7,000 × 1.08 + 4,000 = $11,560

(continued)

At the end of the second year, you will have:

$11,560 × 1.08 + 4,000 = $16,484.80

Repeating this for the third year gives:

$16,484.80 × 1.08 + 4,000 = $21,803.58

Therefore, you will have $21,803.58 in three years. If you leave this on deposit for one more year (and don't add to it), at the end of the fourth year, you'll have:

$21,803.58 × 1.08 = $23,547.87

When we calculated the future value of the two $100 deposits, we simply calculated the balance as of the beginning of each year and then rolled that amount forward to the next year. We could have done it another, quicker way. The first $100 is on deposit for two years at 8 percent, so its future value is:

$100 × 1.08² = $100 × 1.1664 = $116.64

The second $100 is on deposit for one year at 8 percent, and its future value is thus:

$100 × 1.08 = $108

The total future value, as we previously calculated, is equal to the sum of these two future values:

$116.64 + 108 = $224.64

Based on this example, there are two ways to calculate future values for multiple cash flows: (1) Compound the accumulated balance forward one year at a time or (2) calculate the future value of each cash flow first and then add them up. Both give the same answer, so you can do it either way.

To illustrate the two different ways of calculating future values, consider the future value of $2,000 invested at the end of each of the next five years. The current balance is zero, and the rate is 10 percent. We first draw a time line, as shown in Figure 6.2.

On the time line, notice that nothing happens until the end of the first year, when we make the first $2,000 investment. This first $2,000 earns interest for the next four (not five) years. Also notice that the last $2,000 is invested at the end of the fifth year, so it earns no interest at all.

Figure 6.3 illustrates the calculations involved if we compound the investment one period at a time. As illustrated, the future value is $12,210.20.

FIGURE 6.2

Time Line for $2,000 per Year for Five Years

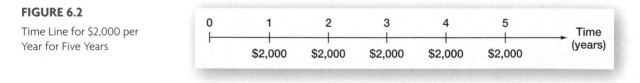

FIGURE 6.3   Future Value Calculated by Compounding Forward One Period at a Time

FIGURE 6.4   Future Value Calculated by Compounding Each Cash Flow Separately

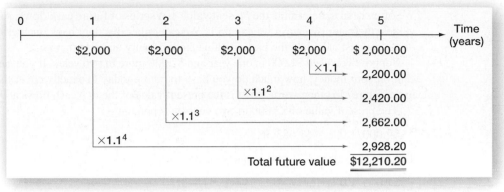

Figure 6.4 goes through the same calculations, but the second technique is used. Naturally, the answer is the same.

Saving Up Once Again

EXAMPLE 6.2

If you deposit $100 in one year, $200 in two years, and $300 in three years, how much will you have in three years? How much of this is interest? How much will you have in five years if you don't add additional amounts? Assume a 7 percent interest rate throughout.

We will calculate the future value of each amount in three years. Notice that the $100 earns interest for two years, and the $200 earns interest for one year. The final $300 earns no interest. The future values are thus:

$$\begin{array}{ll}
\$100 \times 1.07^2 & = \$114.49 \\
\$200 \times 1.07 & = 214.00 \\
+\$300 & = 300.00 \\
\hline
\text{Total future value} & = \$628.49
\end{array}$$

The total future value is thus $628.49. The total interest is:

$$\$628.49 - (100 + 200 + 300) - \$28.49$$

How much will you have in five years? We know that you will have $628.49 in three years. If you leave that in for two more years, it will grow to:

$$\$628.49 \times 1.07^2 = \$628.49 \times 1.1449 = \$719.56$$

Notice that we could have calculated the future value of each amount separately. Once again, be careful about the lengths of time. As we previously calculated, the first $100 earns interest for only four years, the second deposit earns three years' interest, and the last earns two years' interest:

$$\begin{array}{lll}
\$100 \times 1.07^4 = \$100 \times 1.3108 & = & \$131.08 \\
\$200 \times 1.07^3 = \$200 \times 1.2250 & = & 245.01 \\
+\$300 \times 1.07^2 = \$300 \times 1.1449 & = & 343.47 \\
\hline
\text{Total future value} & = & \$719.56
\end{array}$$

PRESENT VALUE WITH MULTIPLE CASH FLOWS

We often need to determine the present value of a series of future cash flows. As with future values, there are two ways we can do it. We can either discount back one period at a time, or we can just calculate the present values individually and add them up.

Suppose you need $1,000 in one year and $2,000 more in two years. If you can earn 9 percent on your money, how much do you have to put up today to exactly cover these amounts in the future? In other words, what is the present value of the two cash flows at 9 percent?

The present value of $2,000 in two years at 9 percent is:

$$\$2,000/1.09^2 = \$1,683.36$$

The present value of $1,000 in one year is:

$$\$1,000/1.09 = \$917.43$$

Therefore, the total present value is:

$$\$1,683.36 + 917.43 = \$2,600.79$$

To see why $2,600.79 is the right answer, we can check to see that after the $2,000 is paid out in two years, there is no money left. If we invest $2,600.79 for one year at 9 percent, we will have:

$$\$2,600.79 \times 1.09 = \$2,834.86$$

We take out $1,000, leaving $1,834.86. This amount earns 9 percent for another year, leaving us with:

$$\$1,834.86 \times 1.09 = \$2,000$$

This is just as we planned. As this example illustrates, the present value of a series of future cash flows is simply the amount you would need today to exactly duplicate those future cash flows (for a given discount rate).

An alternative way of calculating present values for multiple future cash flows is to discount back to the present, one period at a time. To illustrate, suppose we had an investment that was going to pay $1,000 at the end of every year for the next five years. To find the present value, we could discount each $1,000 back to the present separately and then add them up. Figure 6.5 illustrates this approach for a 6 percent discount rate; as shown, the answer is $4,212.37 (ignoring a small rounding error).

FIGURE 6.5

Present Value Calculated by Discounting Each Cash Flow Separately

FIGURE 6.6   Present Value Calculated by Discounting Back One Period at a Time

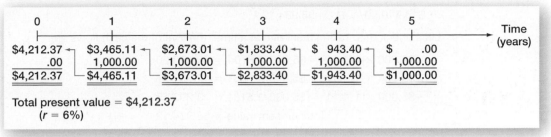

Alternatively, we could discount the last cash flow back one period and add it to the next-to-the-last cash flow:

$$(\$1,000/1.06) + 1,000 = \$943.40 + 1,000 = \$1,943.40$$

We could then discount this amount back one period and add it to the year 3 cash flow:

$$(\$1,943.40/1.06) + 1,000 = \$1,833.40 + 1,000 = \$2,833.40$$

This process could be repeated as necessary. Figure 6.6 illustrates this appoach and the remaining calculations.

How Much Is It Worth?   EXAMPLE 6.3

You are offered an investment that will pay you $200 in one year, $400 the next year, $600 the next year, and $800 at the end of the fourth year. You can earn 12 percent on very similar investments. What is the most you should pay for this one?

We need to calculate the present value of these cash flows at 12 percent. Taking them one at a time gives:

$$
\begin{aligned}
\$200 \times 1/1.12^1 &= \$200/1.1200 = \$\ \ 178.57 \\
\$400 \times 1/1.12^2 &= \$400/1.2544 = \ \ \ \ 318.88 \\
\$600 \times 1/1.12^3 &= \$600/1.4049 = \ \ \ \ 427.07 \\
+\$800 \times 1/1.12^4 &= \$800/1.5735 = \ \ \underline{\ \ \ \ 508.41} \\
\text{Total present value} &= \underline{\underline{\$1,432.93}}
\end{aligned}
$$

If you can earn 12 percent on your money, then you can duplicate this investment's cash flows for $1,432.93, so this is the most you should be willing to pay.

How Much Is It Worth? Part 2   EXAMPLE 6.4

You are offered an investment that will make three $5,000 payments. The first payment will occur four years from today. The second will occur in five years, and the third will follow in six years. If you can earn 11 percent, what is the most this investment is worth today? What is the future value of the cash flows?

We will answer the questions in reverse order to illustrate a point. The future value of the cash flows in six years is:

$$(\$5,000 \times 1.11^2) + (5,000 \times 1.11) + 5,000 = \$6,160.50 + 5,550 + 5,000$$
$$= \$16,710.50$$

(continued)

The present value must be:

$16,710.50/1.11^6 = $8,934.12

Let's check this. Taking them one at a time, the PVs of the cash flows are:

$$\$5,000 \times 1/1.11^6 = \$5,000/1.8704 = \$2,673.20$$
$$\$5,000 \times 1/1.11^5 = \$5,000/1.6851 = 2,967.26$$
$$+\$5,000 \times 1/1.11^4 = \$5,000/1.5181 = \underline{3,293.65}$$
$$\text{Total present value} = \underline{\$8,934.12}$$

This is as we previously calculated. The point we want to make is that we can calculate present and future values in any order and convert between them using whatever way seems most convenient. The answers will always be the same as long as we stick with the same discount rate and are careful to keep track of the right number of periods.

CALCULATOR HINTS

How to Calculate Present Values with Multiple Future Cash Flows Using a Financial Calculator

To calculate the present value of multiple cash flows with a financial calculator, we will simply discount the individual cash flows one at a time using the same technique we used in our previous chapter, so this is not really new. However, we can show you a shortcut. We will use the numbers in Example 6.3 to illustrate.

To begin, of course we first remember to clear out the calculator! Next, from Example 6.3, the first cash flow is $200 to be received in one year and the discount rate is 12 percent, so we do the following:

Enter   1   12   200

Solve for   −178.57

Now, you can write down this answer to save it, but that's inefficient. All calculators have a memory where you can store numbers. Why not just save it there? Doing so cuts way down on mistakes because you don't have to write down and/or rekey numbers, and it's much faster.

Next we value the second cash flow. We need to change N to 2 and FV to 400. As long as we haven't changed anything else, we don't have to reenter I/Y or clear out the calculator, so we have:

Enter   2   400

Solve for   −318.88

You save this number by adding it to the one you saved in our first calculation, and so on for the remaining two calculations.

As we will see in a later chapter, some financial calculators will let you enter all of the future cash flows at once, but we'll discuss that subject when we get to it.

SPREADSHEET STRATEGIES

How to Calculate Present Values with Multiple Future Cash Flows Using a Spreadsheet

Just as we did in our previous chapter, we can set up a basic spreadsheet to calculate the present values of the individual cash flows as follows. Notice that we have simply calculated the present values one at a time and added them up:

	A	B	C	D	E
1					
2		Using a spreadsheet to value multiple future cash flows			
3					
4	What is the present value of $200 in one year, $400 the next year, $600 the next year, and				
5	$800 the last year if the discount rate is 12 percent?				
6					
7	Rate:	12			
8					
9	Year	Cash flows	Present values	Formula used	
10	1	$200	$178.57	=PV($B$7,A10,0,−B10)	
11	2	$400	$318.88	=PV($B$7,A11,0,−B11)	
12	3	$600	$427.07	=PV($B$7,A12,0,−B12)	
13	4	$800	$508.41	=PV($B$7,A13,0,−B13)	
14					
15		Total PV:	**$1,432.93**	=SUM(C10:C13)	
16					
17	Notice the negative signs inserted in the PV formulas. These just make the present values have				
18	positive signs. Also, the discount rate in cell B7 is entered as $B$7 (an "absolute" reference)				
19	because it is used over and over. We could have just entered ".12" instead, but our approach is more				
20	flexible.				
21					
22					

A NOTE ABOUT CASH FLOW TIMING

In working present and future value problems, cash flow timing is critically important. In almost all such calculations, it is implicitly assumed that the cash flows occur at the *end* of each period. In fact, all the formulas we have discussed, all the numbers in a standard present value or future value table, and (very important) all the preset (or default) settings on a financial calculator assume that cash flows occur at the end of each period. Unless you are explicitly told otherwise, you should always assume that this is what is meant.

As a quick illustration of this point, suppose you are told that a three-year investment has a first-year cash flow of $100, a second-year cash flow of $200, and a third-year cash flow of $300. You are asked to draw a time line. Without further information, you should always assume that the time line looks like this:

On our time line, notice how the first cash flow occurs at the end of the first period, the second at the end of the second period, and the third at the end of the third period.

We will close this section by answering the question we posed at the beginning of the chapter concerning baseball player Alex Rodriguez's contract. Recall that the contract called for $2 million immediately and $28 million in 2008. The remaining $245 million was to be paid as $33 million in 2009, $33 million in 2010, $32 million in 2011, $30 million in 2012, $32 million in 2013, $25 million in 2014, $21 million in 2015, and $20 million in 2016 and 2017. If 12 percent is the appropriate interest rate, what kind of deal did the Yankees' infielder field?

To answer, we can calculate the present value by discounting each year's salary back to the present as follows (notice we assume that all the payments are made at year-end):

$$
\begin{array}{lll}
\text{Year 0 (2007):} & \$\ 2{,}000{,}000 & = \$\ 2{,}000{,}000.00 \\
\text{Year 1 (2008):} & \$28{,}000{,}000 \times 1/1.12^1 & = \$25{,}000{,}000.00 \\
\text{Year 2 (2009):} & \$33{,}000{,}000 \times 1/1.12^2 & = \$26{,}307{,}397.96 \\
\text{Year 3 (2010):} & \$33{,}000{,}000 \times 1/1.12^3 & = \$23{,}488{,}748.18 \\
& \quad\cdot \\
& \quad\cdot \\
\text{Year 10 (2017):} & \$20{,}000{,}000 \times 1/1.12^{10} & = \$\ 6{,}439{,}464.73
\end{array}
$$

If you fill in the missing rows and then add (do it for practice), you will see that A-Rod's contract had a present value of about $163 million, or about 60 percent of the stated $275 million value.

Concept Questions

6.1a Describe how to calculate the future value of a series of cash flows.

6.1b Describe how to calculate the present value of a series of cash flows.

6.1c Unless we are explicitly told otherwise, what do we always assume about the timing of cash flows in present and future value problems?

6.2 Valuing Level Cash Flows: Annuities and Perpetuities

We will frequently encounter situations in which we have multiple cash flows that are all the same amount. For example, a common type of loan repayment plan calls for the borrower to repay the loan by making a series of equal payments over some length of time. Almost all consumer loans (such as car loans) and home mortgages feature equal payments, usually made each month.

annuity
A level stream of cash flows for a fixed period of time.

More generally, a series of constant or level cash flows that occur at the end of each period for some fixed number of periods is called an ordinary **annuity**; more correctly, the cash flows are said to be in *ordinary annuity form*. Annuities appear frequently in financial arrangements, and there are some useful shortcuts for determining their values. We consider these next.

PRESENT VALUE FOR ANNUITY CASH FLOWS

Suppose we were examining an asset that promised to pay $500 at the end of each of the next three years. The cash flows from this asset are in the form of a three-year, $500 annuity. If we wanted to earn 10 percent on our money, how much would we offer for this annuity?

From the previous section, we know that we can discount each of these $500 payments back to the present at 10 percent to determine the total present value:

$$
\begin{aligned}
\text{Present value} &= (\$500/1.1^1) + (500/1.1^2) + (500/1.1^3) \\
&= (\$500/1.1) + (500/1.21) + (500/1.331) \\
&= \$454.55 + 413.22 + 375.66 \\
&= \$1,243.43
\end{aligned}
$$

This approach works just fine. However, we will often encounter situations in which the number of cash flows is quite large. For example, a typical home mortgage calls for monthly payments over 30 years, for a total of 360 payments. If we were trying to determine the present value of those payments, it would be useful to have a shortcut.

Because the cash flows of an annuity are all the same, we can come up with a handy variation on the basic present value equation. The present value of an annuity of C dollars per period for t periods when the rate of return or interest rate is r is given by:

$$
\begin{aligned}
\text{Annuity present value} &= C \times \left(\frac{1 - \text{Present value factor}}{r} \right) \\
&= C \times \left\{ \frac{1 - [1/(1 + r)^t]}{r} \right\}
\end{aligned}
$$
[6.1]

The term in parentheses on the first line is sometimes called the *present value interest factor for annuities* and abbreviated PVIFA(r, t).

The expression for the annuity present value may look a little complicated, but it isn't difficult to use. Notice that the term in square brackets on the second line, $1/(1 + r)^t$, is the same present value factor we've been calculating. In our example from the beginning of this section, the interest rate is 10 percent and there are three years involved. The usual present value factor is thus:

$$
\text{Present value factor} = 1/1.1^3 = 1/1.331 = .751315
$$

To calculate the annuity present value factor, we just plug this in:

$$
\begin{aligned}
\text{Annuity present value factor} &= (1 - \text{Present value factor})/r \\
&= (1 - .751315)/.10 \\
&= .248685/.10 = 2.48685
\end{aligned}
$$

Just as we calculated before, the present value of our $500 annuity is then:

$$
\text{Annuity present value} = \$500 \times 2.48685 = \$1,243.43
$$

How Much Can You Afford?	EXAMPLE 6.5

After carefully going over your budget, you have determined you can afford to pay $632 per month toward a new sports car. You call up your local bank and find out that the going rate is 1 percent per month for 48 months. How much can you borrow?

To determine how much you can borrow, we need to calculate the present value of $632 per month for 48 months at 1 percent per month. The loan payments are in ordinary annuity

(continued)

form, so the annuity present value factor is:

$$\text{Annuity PV factor} = (1 - \text{Present value factor})/r$$
$$= [1 - (1/1.01^{48})]/.01$$
$$= (1 - .6203)/.01 = 37.9740$$

With this factor, we can calculate the present value of the 48 payments of $632 each as:

$$\text{Present value} = \$632 \times 37.9740 = \$24,000$$

Therefore, $24,000 is what you can afford to borrow and repay.

Annuity Tables   Just as there are tables for ordinary present value factors, there are tables for annuity factors as well. Table 6.1 contains a few such factors; Table A.3 in the appendix to the book contains a larger set. To find the annuity present value factor we calculated just before Example 6.5, look for the row corresponding to three periods and then find the column for 10 percent. The number you see at that intersection should be 2.4869 (rounded to four decimal places), as we calculated. Once again, try calculating a few of these factors yourself and compare your answers to the ones in the table to make sure you know how to do it. If you are using a financial calculator, just enter $1 as the payment and calculate the present value; the result should be the annuity present value factor.

TABLE 6.1

Annuity Present Value
Interest Factors

Number of Periods	Interest Rate			
	5%	**10%**	**15%**	**20%**
1	.9524	.9091	.8696	.8333
2	1.8594	1.7355	1.6257	1.5278
3	2.7232	2.4869	2.2832	2.1065
4	3.5460	3.1699	2.8550	2.5887
5	4.3295	3.7908	3.3522	2.9906

CALCULATOR HINTS

Annuity Present Values

To find annuity present values with a financial calculator, we need to use the PMT key (you were probably wondering what it was for). Compared to finding the present value of a single amount, there are two important differences. First, we enter the annuity cash flow using the PMT key. Second, we don't enter anything for the future value, FV. So, for example, the problem we have been examining is a three-year, $500 annuity. If the discount rate is 10 percent, we need to do the following (after clearing out the calculator!):

Enter   3   10   500

| N | I/Y | PMT | PV | FV |

Solve for   −1,243.43

As usual, we get a negative sign on the PV.

SPREADSHEET STRATEGIES

Annuity Present Values

Using a spreadsheet to find annuity present values goes like this:

	A	B	C	D	E	F	G
1							
2		Using a spreadsheet to find annuity present values					
3							
4	What is the present value of $500 per year for 3 years if the discount rate is 10 percent?						
5	We need to solve for the unknown present value, so we use the formula PV(rate, nper, pmt, fv).						
6							
7	Payment amount per period:	$500					
8	Number of payments:	3					
9	Discount rate:	.1					
10							
11	Annuity present value:	$1,243.43					
12							
13	The formula entered in cell B11 is =PV(B9,B8,-B7,0); notice that fv is zero and that						
14	pmt has a negative sign on it. Also notice that rate is entered as a decimal, not a percentage.						
15							
16							
17							

Finding the Payment Suppose you wish to start up a new business that specializes in the latest of health food trends, frozen yak milk. To produce and market your product, the Yak-kee Doodle Dandy, you need to borrow $100,000. Because it strikes you as unlikely that this particular fad will be long-lived, you propose to pay off the loan quickly by making five equal annual payments. If the interest rate is 18 percent, what will the payment be?

In this case, we know the present value is $100,000. The interest rate is 18 percent, and there are five years. The payments are all equal, so we need to find the relevant annuity factor and solve for the unknown cash flow:

$$\text{Annuity present value} = \$100,000 = C \times [(1 - \text{Present value factor})/r]$$
$$= C \times \{[1 - (1/1.18^5)]/.18\}$$
$$= C \times [(1 - .4371)/.18]$$
$$= C \times 3.1272$$
$$C = \$100,000/3.1272 = \$31,978$$

Therefore, you'll make five payments of just under $32,000 each.

CALCULATOR HINTS

Annuity Payments

Finding annuity payments is easy with a financial calculator. In our yak example, the PV is $100,000, the interest rate is 18 percent, and there are five years. We find the payment as follows:

Enter	5	18		100,000	
	N	I/Y	PMT	PV	FV
Solve for			−31,978		

Here, we get a negative sign on the payment because the payment is an outflow for us.

SPREADSHEET STRATEGIES

Annuity Payments

Using a spreadsheet to work the same problem goes like this:

	A	B	C	D	E	F	G
1							
2	**Using a spreadsheet to find annuity payments**						
3							
4	What is the annuity payment if the present value is $100,000, the interest rate is 18 percent, and						
5	there are 5 periods? We need to solve for the unknown payment in an annuity, so we use the						
6	formula PMT(rate, nper, pv, fv).						
7							
8	Annuity present value:	$100,000					
9	Number of payments:	5					
10	Discount rate:	.18					
11							
12	Annuity payment:	$31,977.78					
13							
14	The formula entered in cell B12 is =PMT(B10, B9, -B8,0); notice that fv is zero and that the payment						
15	has a negative sign because it is an outflow to us.						
16							

EXAMPLE 6.6	**Finding the Number of Payments**

You ran a little short on your spring break vacation, so you put $1,000 on your credit card. You can afford only the minimum payment of $20 per month. The interest rate on the credit card is 1.5 percent per month. How long will you need to pay off the $1,000?

   What we have here is an annuity of $20 per month at 1.5 percent per month for some unknown length of time. The present value is $1,000 (the amount you owe today). We need to do a little algebra (or use a financial calculator):

$$\$1,000 = \$20 \times [(1 - \text{Present value factor})/.015]$$
$$(\$1,000/20) \times .015 = 1 - \text{Present value factor}$$
$$\text{Present value factor} = .25 = 1/(1 + r)^t$$
$$1.015^t = 1/.25 = 4$$

At this point, the problem boils down to asking, How long does it take for your money to quadruple at 1.5 percent per month? Based on our previous chapter, the answer is about 93 months:

$$1.015^{93} = 3.99 \approx 4$$

It will take you about 93/12 = 7.75 years to pay off the $1,000 at this rate. If you use a financial calculator for problems like this, you should be aware that some automatically round up to the next whole period.

CALCULATOR HINTS

Finding the Number of Payments

To solve this one on a financial calculator, do the following:

Enter		1.5	−20	1,000	
	N	I/Y	PMT	PV	FV
Solve for	93.11				

Notice that we put a negative sign on the payment you must make, and we have solved for the number of months. You still have to divide by 12 to get our answer. Also, some financial calculators won't report a fractional value for N; they automatically (without telling you) round up to the next whole period (not to the nearest value). With a spreadsheet, use the function =NPER(rate,pmt,pv,fv); be sure to put in a zero for fv and to enter −20 as the payment.

Finding the Rate The last question we might want to ask concerns the interest rate implicit in an annuity. For example, an insurance company offers to pay you $1,000 per year for 10 years if you will pay $6,710 up front. What rate is implicit in this 10-year annuity?

In this case, we know the present value ($6,710), we know the cash flows ($1,000 per year), and we know the life of the investment (10 years). What we don't know is the discount rate:

$$\$6{,}710 = \$1{,}000 \times [(1 - \text{Present value factor})/r]$$
$$\$6{,}710/1{,}000 = 6.71 = \{1 - [1/(1 + r)^{10}]\}/r$$

So, the annuity factor for 10 periods is equal to 6.71, and we need to solve this equation for the unknown value of r. Unfortunately, this is mathematically impossible to do directly. The only way to do it is to use a table or trial and error to find a value for r.

If you look across the row corresponding to 10 periods in Table A.3, you will see a factor of 6.7101 for 8 percent, so we see right away that the insurance company is offering just about 8 percent. Alternatively, we could just start trying different values until we got very close to the answer. Using this trial-and-error approach can be a little tedious, but fortunately machines are good at that sort of thing.[1]

To illustrate how to find the answer by trial and error, suppose a relative of yours wants to borrow $3,000. She offers to repay you $1,000 every year for four years. What interest rate are you being offered?

The cash flows here have the form of a four-year, $1,000 annuity. The present value is $3,000. We need to find the discount rate, r. Our goal in doing so is primarily to give you a feel for the relationship between annuity values and discount rates.

We need to start somewhere, and 10 percent is probably as good a place as any to begin. At 10 percent, the annuity factor is:

Annuity present value factor = $[1 - (1/1.10^4)]/.10 = 3.1699$

---

[1]Financial calculators rely on trial and error to find the answer. That's why they sometimes appear to be "thinking" before coming up with the answer. Actually, it is possible to directly solve for r if there are fewer than five periods, but it's usually not worth the trouble.

The present value of the cash flows at 10 percent is thus:

Present value = $1,000 × 3.1699 = $3,169.90

You can see that we're already in the right ballpark.

Is 10 percent too high or too low? Recall that present values and discount rates move in opposite directions: Increasing the discount rate lowers the PV and vice versa. Our present value here is too high, so the discount rate is too low. If we try 12 percent, we're almost there:

Present value = $1,000 × \{[1 − (1/1.12^4)]/.12\} = $3,037.35

We are still a little low on the discount rate (because the PV is a little high), so we'll try 13 percent:

Present value = $1,000 × \{[1 − (1/1.13^4)]/.13\} = $2,974.47

This is less than $3,000, so we now know that the answer is between 12 percent and 13 percent, and it looks to be about 12.5 percent. For practice, work at it for a while longer and see if you find that the answer is about 12.59 percent.

To illustrate a situation in which finding the unknown rate can be useful, let us consider that the Tri-State Megabucks lottery in Maine, Vermont, and New Hampshire offers you a choice of how to take your winnings (most lotteries do this). In a recent drawing, participants were offered the option of receiving a lump sum payment of $250,000 or an annuity of $500,000 to be received in equal installments over a 25-year period. (At the time, the lump sum payment was always half the annuity option.) Which option was better?

To answer, suppose you were to compare $250,000 today to an annuity of $500,000/25 = $20,000 per year for 25 years. At what rate do these have the same value? This is the same type of problem we've been looking at; we need to find the unknown rate, r, for a present value of $250,000, a $20,000 payment, and a 25-year period. If you grind through the calculations (or get a little machine assistance), you should find that the unknown rate is about 6.24 percent. You should take the annuity option if that rate is attractive relative to other investments available to you. Notice that we have ignored taxes in this example, and taxes can significantly affect our conclusion. Be sure to consult your tax adviser anytime you win the lottery.

CALCULATOR HINTS

Finding the Rate

Alternatively, you could use a financial calculator to do the following:

Enter	4		1,000	−3,000	
	N	I/Y	PMT	PV	FV
Solve for		12.59			

Notice that we put a negative sign on the present value (why?). With a spreadsheet, use the function =RATE(nper,pmt,pv,fv); be sure to put in a zero for fv and to enter 1,000 as the payment and −3,000 as the pv.

FUTURE VALUE FOR ANNUITIES

On occasion, it's also handy to know a shortcut for calculating the future value of an annuity. As you might guess, there are future value factors for annuities as well as present value factors. In general, here is the future value factor for an annuity:

$$\text{Annuity FV factor} = (\text{Future value factor} - 1)/r$$
$$= [(1 + r)^t - 1]/r \qquad\qquad \textbf{[6.2]}$$

To see how we use annuity future value factors, suppose you plan to contribute $2,000 every year to a retirement account paying 8 percent. If you retire in 30 years, how much will you have?

The number of years here, t, is 30, and the interest rate, r, is 8 percent; so we can calculate the annuity future value factor as:

$$\text{Annuity FV factor} = (\text{Future value factor} - 1)/r$$
$$= (1.08^{30} - 1)/.08$$
$$= (10.0627 - 1)/.08$$
$$= 113.2832$$

The future value of this 30-year, $2,000 annuity is thus:

$$\text{Annuity future value} = \$2,000 \times 113.28$$
$$= \$226,566$$

CALCULATOR HINTS

Future Values of Annuities

Of course, you could solve this problem using a financial calculator by doing the following:

Enter	30	8	−2,000		
	N	I/Y	PMT	PV	FV
Solve for					226,566

Notice that we put a negative sign on the payment (why?). With a spreadsheet, use the function =FV(rate,nper, pmt,pv); be sure to put in a zero for pv and to enter −2,000 as the payment.

Sometimes we need to find the unknown rate, r, in the context of an annuity future value. For example, if you had invested $100 per month in stocks over the 25-year period ended December 1978, your investment would have grown to $76,374. This period had the *worst* stretch of stock returns of any 25-year period between 1925 and 2005. How bad was it?

Here we have the cash flows ($100 per month), the *future* value ($76,374), and the time period (25 years, or 300 months). We need to find the implicit rate, r:

$$\$76,374 = \$100 \times [(\text{Future value factor} - 1)/r]$$
$$763.74 = [(1 + r)^{300} - 1]/r$$

Because this is the worst period, let's try 1 percent:

$$\text{Annuity future value factor} = (1.01^{300} - 1)/.01 = 1,878.85$$

We see that 1 percent is too high. From here, it's trial and error. See if you agree that r is about .55 percent per month. As you will see later in the chapter, this works out to be about 6.8 percent per year.

A NOTE ABOUT ANNUITIES DUE

So far we have only discussed ordinary annuities. These are the most important, but there is a fairly common variation. Remember that with an ordinary annuity, the cash flows occur at the end of each period. When you take out a loan with monthly payments, for example, the first loan payment normally occurs one month after you get the loan. However, when you lease an apartment, the first lease payment is usually due immediately. The second payment is due at the beginning of the second month, and so on. A lease is an example of an **annuity due**. An annuity due is an annuity for which the cash flows occur at the beginning of each period. Almost any type of arrangement in which we have to prepay the same amount each period is an annuity due.

> **annuity due**
> An annuity for which the cash flows occur at the beginning of the period.

There are several different ways to calculate the value of an annuity due. With a financial calculator, you simply switch it into "due" or "beginning" mode. Remember to switch it back when you are done! Another way to calculate the present value of an annuity due can be illustrated with a time line. Suppose an annuity due has five payments of $400 each, and the relevant discount rate is 10 percent. The time line looks like this:

Notice how the cash flows here are the same as those for a *four*-year ordinary annuity, except that there is an extra $400 at Time 0. For practice, check to see that the value of a four-year ordinary annuity at 10 percent is $1,267.95. If we add on the extra $400, we get $1,667.95, which is the present value of this annuity due.

Time value applications abound on the Web. See, for example, www.collegeboard.com, and personal.fidelity.com.

There is an even easier way to calculate the present or future value of an annuity due. If we assume cash flows occur at the end of each period when they really occur at the beginning, then we discount each one by one period too many. We could fix this by simply multiplying our answer by $(1 + r)$, where r is the discount rate. In fact, the relationship between the value of an annuity due and an ordinary annuity is just this:

$$\text{Annuity due value} = \text{Ordinary annuity value} \times (1 + r) \qquad \text{[6.3]}$$

This works for both present and future values, so calculating the value of an annuity due involves two steps: (1) Calculate the present or future value as though it were an ordinary annuity, and (2) multiply your answer by $(1 + r)$.

PERPETUITIES

We've seen that a series of level cash flows can be valued by treating those cash flows as an annuity. An important special case of an annuity arises when the level stream of cash flows continues forever. Such an asset is called a **perpetuity** because the cash flows are perpetual. Perpetuities are also called **consols**, particularly in Canada and the United Kingdom. See Example 6.7 for an important example of a perpetuity.

> **perpetuity**
> An annuity in which the cash flows continue forever.
>
> **consol**
> A type of perpetuity.

Because a perpetuity has an infinite number of cash flows, we obviously can't compute its value by discounting each one. Fortunately, valuing a perpetuity turns out to be the easiest possible case. The present value of a perpetuity is simply:

$$\text{PV for a perpetuity} = C/r \qquad \text{[6.4]}$$

For example, an investment offers a perpetual cash flow of $500 every year. The return you require on such an investment is 8 percent. What is the value of this investment? The value of this perpetuity is:

$$\text{Perpetuity PV} = C/r = \$500/.08 = \$6,250$$

TABLE 6.2

Summary of Annuity and Perpetuity Calculations

I.　Symbols:

PV = Present value, what future cash flows are worth today

FV_t = Future value, what cash flows are worth in the future

r = Interest rate, rate of return, or discount rate per period—typically, but not always, one year

t = Number of periods—typically, but not always, the number of years

C = Cash amount

II.　Future Value of C per Period for t Periods at r Percent per Period:

$FV_t = C \times \{[(1 + r)^t - 1]/r\}$

A series of identical cash flows is called an *annuity*, and the term $[(1 + r)^t - 1]/r$ is called the *annuity future value factor.*

III.　Present Value of C per Period for t Periods at r Percent per Period:

$PV = C \times \{1 - [1/(1 + r)^t]\}/r$

The term $\{1 - [1/(1 + r)^t]\}/r$ is called the *annuity present value factor.*

IV.　Present Value of a Perpetuity of C per Period:

$PV = C/r$

A *perpetuity* has the same cash flow every year forever.

For future reference, Table 6.2 contains a summary of the annuity and perpetuity basic calculations we described. By now, you probably think that you'll just use online calculators to handle annuity problems. Before you do, see our nearby *Work the Web* box!

Preferred Stock　　　　　　　　　　　　　**EXAMPLE 6.7**

Preferred stock (or preference stock) is an important example of a perpetuity. When a corporation sells preferred stock, the buyer is promised a fixed cash dividend every period (usually every quarter) forever. This dividend must be paid before any dividend can be paid to regular stockholders—hence the term *preferred.*

Suppose the Fellini Co. wants to sell preferred stock at $100 per share. A similar issue of preferred stock already outstanding has a price of $40 per share and offers a dividend of $1 every quarter. What dividend will Fellini have to offer if the preferred stock is going to sell?

The issue that is already out has a present value of $40 and a cash flow of $1 every quarter forever. Because this is a perpetuity:

Present value = $40 = $1 × (1/r)

r = 2.5%

To be competitive, the new Fellini issue will also have to offer 2.5 percent *per quarter;* so if the present value is to be $100, the dividend must be such that:

Present value = $100 = C × (1/.025)

C = $2.50 (per quarter)

GROWING ANNUITIES AND PERPETUITIES

Annuities commonly have payments that grow over time. Suppose, for example, that we are looking at a lottery payout over a 20-year period. The first payment, made one year from now, will be $200,000. Every year thereafter, the payment will grow by 5 percent, so the payment in the second year will be $200,000 \times 1.05 = $210,000$. The payment in the third year will be $210,000 \times 1.05 = $220,500$, and so on. What's the present value if the appropriate discount rate is 11 percent?

If we use the symbol g to represent the growth rate, we can calculate the value of a growing annuity using a modified version of our regular annuity formula:

$$\text{Growing annuity present value} = C \times \left[\frac{1 - \left(\frac{1 + g}{1 + r}\right)^t}{r - g} \right] \qquad [6.5]$$

Plugging in the numbers from our lottery example (and letting $g = .05$), we get:

$$PV = \$200,000 \times \left[\frac{1 - \left(\frac{1 + .05}{1 + .11}\right)^{20}}{.11 - .05} \right] = \$200,000 \times 11.18169 = \$2,236,337.06$$

WORK THE WEB

As we discussed in the previous chapter, many Web sites have financial calculators. One of these sites is MoneyChimp, which is located at www.moneychimp.com. Suppose you are lucky enough to have $1,500,000. You think you will be able to earn a 10 percent return. How much can you withdraw each year for the next 30 years? Here is what MoneyChimp says:

Inputs		
Starting Principal:	$	1,500,000.00
Growth Rate:		10 %
Years to Pay Out:		30
	Calculate	
Results		
Annual Payout Amount:	$	144,653.52

According to the MoneyChimp calculator, the answer is $144,653.52. How important is it to understand what you are doing? Calculate this one for yourself, and you should get $159,118.87. Which one is right? You are, of course! What's going on is that MoneyChimp assumes (but does not tell you) that the annuity is in the form of an annuity due, not an ordinary annuity. Recall that with an annuity due, the payments occur at the beginning of the period rather than the end of the period. The moral of the story is clear: *caveat calculator*.

Questions

1. Go to the calculator at www.moneychimp.com and find out how much the Web site says you could withdraw each year if you have $2,500,000, earn an 8 percent interest rate, and make annual withdrawals for 35 years. How much more are the withdrawals if they are in the form of an ordinary annuity?

2. Suppose you have $500,000 and want to make withdrawals each month for the next 10 years. The first withdrawal is today and the appropriate interest rate is 9 percent compounded monthly. Using this Web site, how much are your withdrawals?

There is also a formula for the present value of a growing perpetuity:

$$\text{Growing perpetuity present value} = C \times \left[\frac{1}{r-g}\right] = \frac{C}{r-g} \qquad \text{[6.6]}$$

In our lottery example, now suppose the payments continue forever. In this case, the present value is:

$$PV = \$200,000 \times \frac{1}{.11-.05} = \$200,000 \times 16.6667 = \$3,333,333.33$$

The notion of a growing perpetuity may seem a little odd because the payments get bigger every period forever; but, as we will see in a later chapter, growing perpetuities play a key role in our analysis of stock prices.

Before we go on, there is one important note about our formulas for growing annuities and perpetuities. In both cases, the cash flow in the formula, C, is the cash flow that is going to occur exactly one period from today.

Concept Questions

6.2a In general, what is the present value of an annuity of C dollars per period at a discount rate of r per period? The future value?

6.2b In general, what is the present value of a perpetuity?

Comparing Rates: The Effect of Compounding

6.3

The next issue we need to discuss has to do with the way interest rates are quoted. This subject causes a fair amount of confusion because rates are quoted in many different ways. Sometimes the way a rate is quoted is the result of tradition, and sometimes it's the result of legislation. Unfortunately, at times, rates are quoted in deliberately deceptive ways to mislead borrowers and investors. We will discuss these topics in this section.

EFFECTIVE ANNUAL RATES AND COMPOUNDING

If a rate is quoted as 10 percent compounded semiannually, this means the investment actually pays 5 percent every six months. A natural question then arises: Is 5 percent every six months the same thing as 10 percent per year? It's easy to see that it is not. If you invest $1 at 10 percent per year, you will have $1.10 at the end of the year. If you invest at 5 percent every six months, then you'll have the future value of $1 at 5 percent for two periods:

$$\$1 \times 1.05^2 = \$1.1025$$

This is $.0025 more. The reason is simple: Your account was credited with $1 × .05 = 5 cents in interest after six months. In the following six months, you earned 5 percent on that nickel, for an extra 5 × .05 = .25 cents.

As our example illustrates, 10 percent compounded semiannually is actually equivalent to 10.25 percent per year. Put another way, we would be indifferent between

10 percent compounded semiannually and 10.25 percent compounded annually. Anytime we have compounding during the year, we need to be concerned about what the rate really is.

In our example, the 10 percent is called a **stated**, or **quoted, interest rate**. Other names are used as well. The 10.25 percent, which is actually the rate you will earn, is called the **effective annual rate (EAR)**. To compare different investments or interest rates, we will always need to convert to effective rates. Some general procedures for doing this are discussed next.

stated interest rate
The interest rate expressed in terms of the interest payment made each period. Also known as the *quoted interest rate.*

effective annual rate (EAR)
The interest rate expressed as if it were compounded once per year.

CALCULATING AND COMPARING EFFECTIVE ANNUAL RATES

To see why it is important to work only with effective rates, suppose you've shopped around and come up with the following three rates:

Bank A: 15 percent compounded daily

Bank B: 15.5 percent compounded quarterly

Bank C: 16 percent compounded annually

Which of these is the best if you are thinking of opening a savings account? Which of these is best if they represent loan rates?

To begin, Bank C is offering 16 percent per year. Because there is no compounding during the year, this is the effective rate. Bank B is actually paying $.155/4 = .03875$ or 3.875 percent per quarter. At this rate, an investment of $1 for four quarters would grow to:

$$\$1 \times 1.03875^4 = \$1.1642$$

The EAR, therefore, is 16.42 percent. For a saver, this is much better than the 16 percent rate Bank C is offering; for a borrower, it's worse.

Bank A is compounding every day. This may seem a little extreme, but it is common to calculate interest daily. In this case, the daily interest rate is actually:

$$.15/365 = .000411$$

This is .0411 percent per day. At this rate, an investment of $1 for 365 periods would grow to:

$$\$1 \times 1.000411^{365} = \$1.1618$$

The EAR is 16.18 percent. This is not as good as Bank B's 16.42 percent for a saver, and not as good as Bank C's 16 percent for a borrower.

This example illustrates two things. First, the highest quoted rate is not necessarily the best. Second, compounding during the year can lead to a significant difference between the quoted rate and the effective rate. Remember that the effective rate is what you actually get or what you pay.

If you look at our examples, you see that we computed the EARs in three steps. We first divided the quoted rate by the number of times that the interest is compounded. We then added 1 to the result and raised it to the power of the number of times the interest is compounded. Finally, we subtracted the 1. If we let m be the number of times the interest is compounded during the year, these steps can be summarized simply as:

$$\text{EAR} = [1 + (\text{Quoted rate}/m)]^m - 1 \qquad \text{[6.7]}$$

For example, suppose you are offered 12 percent compounded monthly. In this case, the interest is compounded 12 times a year; so m is 12. You can calculate the effective rate as:

$$EAR = [1 + (\text{Quoted rate}/m)]^m - 1$$
$$= [1 + (.12/12)]^{12} - 1$$
$$= 1.01^{12} - 1$$
$$= 1.126825 - 1$$
$$= 12.6825\%$$

What's the EAR?

EXAMPLE 6.8

A bank is offering 12 percent compounded quarterly. If you put $100 in an account, how much will you have at the end of one year? What's the EAR? How much will you have at the end of two years?

The bank is effectively offering 12%/4 = 3% every quarter. If you invest $100 for four periods at 3 percent per period, the future value is:

Future value = $100 × 1.03^4
               = $100 × 1.1255
               = $112.55

The EAR is 12.55 percent: $100 × (1 + .1255) = $112.55.

We can determine what you would have at the end of two years in two different ways. One way is to recognize that two years is the same as eight quarters. At 3 percent per quarter, after eight quarters, you would have:

$100 × 1.03^8 = $100 × 1.2668 = $126.68

Alternatively, we could determine the value after two years by using an EAR of 12.55 percent; so after two years you would have:

$100 × 1.1255^2 = $100 × 1.2688 = $126.68

Thus, the two calculations produce the same answer. This illustrates an important point. Anytime we do a present or future value calculation, the rate we use must be an actual or effective rate. In this case, the actual rate is 3 percent per quarter. The effective annual rate is 12.55 percent. It doesn't matter which one we use once we know the EAR.

Quoting a Rate

EXAMPLE 6.9

Now that you know how to convert a quoted rate to an EAR, consider going the other way. As a lender, you know you want to actually earn 18 percent on a particular loan. You want to quote a rate that features monthly compounding. What rate do you quote?

In this case, we know the EAR is 18 percent, and we know this is the result of monthly compounding. Let q stand for the quoted rate. We thus have:

$$EAR = [1 + (\text{Quoted rate}/m)]^m - 1$$
$$.18 = [1 + (q/12)]^{12} - 1$$
$$1.18 = [1 + (q/12)]^{12}$$

(continued)

We need to solve this equation for the quoted rate. This calculation is the same as the ones we did to find an unknown interest rate in Chapter 5:

$$1.18^{(1/12)} = 1 + (q/12)$$
$$1.18^{.08333} - 1 + (q/12)$$
$$1.0139 = 1 + (q/12)$$
$$q = .0139 \times 12$$
$$= 16.68\%$$

Therefore, the rate you would quote is 16.68 percent, compounded monthly.

EARs AND APRs

annual percentage
rate (APR)
The interest rate charged
per period multiplied by the
number of periods per year.

Sometimes it's not altogether clear whether a rate is an effective annual rate. A case in point concerns what is called the **annual percentage rate (APR)** on a loan. Truth-in-lending laws in the United States require that lenders disclose an APR on virtually all consumer loans. This rate must be displayed on a loan document in a prominent and unambiguous way.

Given that an APR must be calculated and displayed, an obvious question arises: Is an APR an effective annual rate? Put another way, if a bank quotes a car loan at 12 percent APR, is the consumer actually paying 12 percent interest? Surprisingly, the answer is no. There is some confusion over this point, which we discuss next.

The confusion over APRs arises because lenders are required by law to compute the APR in a particular way. By law, the APR is simply equal to the interest rate per period multiplied by the number of periods in a year. For example, if a bank is charging 1.2 percent per month on car loans, then the APR that must be reported is $1.2\% \times 12 = 14.4\%$. So, an APR is in fact a quoted, or stated, rate in the sense we've been discussing. For example, an APR of 12 percent on a loan calling for monthly payments is really 1 percent per month. The EAR on such a loan is thus:

$$EAR = [1 + (APR/12)]^{12} - 1$$
$$= 1.01^{12} - 1 = 12.6825\%$$

| EXAMPLE 6.10 | **What Rate Are You Paying?** |

Depending on the issuer, a typical credit card agreement quotes an interest rate of 18 percent APR. Monthly payments are required. What is the actual interest rate you pay on such a credit card?

Based on our discussion, an APR of 18 percent with monthly payments is really $.18/12 = .015$ or 1.5 percent per month. The EAR is thus:

$$EAR = [1 + (.18/12)]^{12} - 1$$
$$= 1.015^{12} - 1$$
$$= 1.1956 - 1$$
$$= 19.56\%$$

This is the rate you actually pay.

It is somewhat ironic that truth-in-lending laws sometimes require lenders to be *un*truthful about the actual rate on a loan. There are also truth-in-saving laws that require banks and other borrowers to quote an "annual percentage yield," or APY, on things like savings accounts. To make things a little confusing, an APY is an EAR. As a result, by law, the rates quoted to borrowers (APRs) and those quoted to savers (APYs) are not computed the same way.

There can be a huge difference between the APR and EAR when interest rates are large. For example, consider "payday loans." Payday loans are short-term loans made to consumers, often for less than two weeks, and are offered by companies such as AmeriCash Advance and National Payday. The loans work like this: You write a check today that is postdated (the date on the check is in the future) and give it to the company. They give you some cash. When the check date arrives, you either go to the store and pay the cash amount of the check, or the company cashes it (or else automatically renews the loan).

For example, in one particular state, AmeriCash Advance allows you to write a check for $120 dated 15 days in the future, for which they give you $100 today. So what are the APR and EAR of this arrangement? First, we need to find the interest rate, which we can find by the FV equation as follows:

$$FV = PV \times (1 + r)^1$$
$$\$120 = \$100 \times (1 + r)^1$$
$$1.2 = (1 + r)$$
$$r = .20 \text{ or } 20\%$$

That doesn't seem too bad until you remember this is the interest rate for *15 days!* The APR of the loan is:

$$APR = .20 \times 365/15$$
$$APR = 4.8667 \text{ or } 486.67\%$$

And the EAR for this loan is:

$$EAR = (1 + \text{Quoted rate}/m)^m - 1$$
$$EAR = (1 + .20)^{365/15} - 1$$
$$EAR = 83.4780 \text{ or } 8,347.80\%$$

Now that's an interest rate! Just to see what a difference a day (or three) makes, AmeriCash will also allow you to write a postdated check for the same amount, but will give you 18 days to repay. Check for yourself that the APR of this arrangement is 405.56 percent and the EAR is 3,932.92 percent. Still not a loan we would like to take out!

TAKING IT TO THE LIMIT: A NOTE ABOUT CONTINUOUS COMPOUNDING

If you made a deposit in a savings account, how often could your money be compounded during the year? If you think about it, there isn't really any upper limit. We've seen that daily compounding, for example, isn't a problem. There is no reason to stop here, however. We could compound every hour or minute or second. How high would the EAR get in this case? Table 6.3 illustrates the EARs that result as 10 percent is compounded at shorter and shorter intervals. Notice that the EARs do keep getting larger, but the differences get very small.

As the numbers in Table 6.3 seem to suggest, there is an upper limit to the EAR. If we let q stand for the quoted rate, then, as the number of times the interest is compounded gets extremely large, the EAR approaches:

$$EAR = e^q - 1 \hspace{4cm} [6.8]$$

TABLE 6.3

Compounding Frequency and Effective Annual Rates

Compounding Period	Number of Times Compounded	Effective Annual Rate
Year	1	10.00000%
Quarter	4	10.38129
Month	12	10.47131
Week	52	10.50648
Day	365	10.51558
Hour	8,760	10.51703
Minute	525,600	10.51709

where e is the number 2.71828 (look for a key labeled "e^x" on your calculator). For example, with our 10 percent rate, the highest possible EAR is:

$$
\begin{aligned}
\text{EAR} &= e^q - 1 \\
&= 2.71828^{.10} - 1 \\
&= 1.1051709 - 1 \\
&= 10.51709\%
\end{aligned}
$$

In this case, we say that the money is continuously, or instantaneously, compounded. Interest is being credited the instant it is earned, so the amount of interest grows continuously.

EXAMPLE 6.11   **What's the Law?**

At one time, commercial banks and savings and loan associations (S&Ls) were restricted in the interest rates they could offer on savings accounts. Under what was known as Regulation Q, S&Ls were allowed to pay at most 5.5 percent, and banks were not allowed to pay more than 5.25 percent (the idea was to give the S&Ls a competitive advantage; it didn't work). The law did not say how often these rates could be compounded, however. Under Regulation Q, then, what were the maximum allowed interest rates?

The maximum allowed rates occurred with continuous, or instantaneous, compounding. For the commercial banks, 5.25 percent compounded continuously would be:

$$
\begin{aligned}
\text{EAR} &= e^{.0525} - 1 \\
&= 2.71828^{.0525} - 1 \\
&= 1.0539026 - 1 \\
&= 5.39026\%
\end{aligned}
$$

This is what banks could actually pay. Check for yourself to see that S&Ls could effectively pay 5.65406 percent.

Concept Questions

6.3a If an interest rate is given as 12 percent compounded daily, what do we call this rate?

6.3b What is an APR? What is an EAR? Are they the same thing?

6.3c In general, what is the relationship between a stated interest rate and an effective interest rate? Which is more relevant for financial decisions?

6.3d What does continuous compounding mean?

Loan Types and Loan Amortization   6.4

Whenever a lender extends a loan, some provision will be made for repayment of the principal (the original loan amount). A loan might be repaid in equal installments, for example, or it might be repaid in a single lump sum. Because the way that the principal and interest are paid is up to the parties involved, there are actually an unlimited number of possibilities.

In this section, we describe a few forms of repayment that come up quite often, and more complicated forms can usually be built up from these. The three basic types of loans are pure discount loans, interest-only loans, and amortized loans. Working with these loans is a very straightforward application of the present value principles that we have already developed.

PURE DISCOUNT LOANS

The *pure discount loan* is the simplest form of loan. With such a loan, the borrower receives money today and repays a single lump sum at some time in the future. A one-year, 10 percent pure discount loan, for example, would require the borrower to repay $1.10 in one year for every dollar borrowed today.

Because a pure discount loan is so simple, we already know how to value one. Suppose a borrower was able to repay $25,000 in five years. If we, acting as the lender, wanted a 12 percent interest rate on the loan, how much would we be willing to lend? Put another way, what value would we assign today to that $25,000 to be repaid in five years? Based on our work in Chapter 5, we know the answer is just the present value of $25,000 at 12 percent for five years:

$$\text{Present value} = \$25,000/1.12^5$$
$$= \$25,000/1.7623$$
$$= \$14,186$$

Pure discount loans are common when the loan term is short—say a year or less. In recent years, they have become increasingly common for much longer periods.

Treasury Bills   **EXAMPLE 6.12**

When the U.S. government borrows money on a short-term basis (a year or less), it does so by selling what are called *Treasury bills,* or *T-bills* for short. A T-bill is a promise by the government to repay a fixed amount at some time in the future—for example, 3 months or 12 months.

Treasury bills are pure discount loans. If a T-bill promises to repay $10,000 in 12 months, and the market interest rate is 7 percent, how much will the bill sell for in the market?

Because the going rate is 7 percent, the T-bill will sell for the present value of $10,000 to be repaid in one year at 7 percent:

Present value = $10,000/1.07 = $9,345.79

INTEREST-ONLY LOANS

A second type of loan repayment plan calls for the borrower to pay interest each period and to repay the entire principal (the original loan amount) at some point in the future. Loans with such a repayment plan are called *interest-only loans*. Notice that if there is just one period, a pure discount loan and an interest-only loan are the same thing.

For example, with a three-year, 10 percent, interest-only loan of $1,000, the borrower would pay $1,000 × .10 = $100 in interest at the end of the first and second years. At the end of the third year, the borrower would return the $1,000 along with another $100 in interest for that year. Similarly, a 50-year interest-only loan would call for the borrower to pay interest every year for the next 50 years and then repay the principal. In the extreme, the borrower pays the interest every period forever and never repays any principal. As we discussed earlier in the chapter, the result is a perpetuity.

Most corporate bonds have the general form of an interest-only loan. Because we will be considering bonds in some detail in the next chapter, we will defer further discussion of them for now.

AMORTIZED LOANS

With a pure discount or interest-only loan, the principal is repaid all at once. An alternative is an *amortized loan,* with which the lender may require the borrower to repay parts of the loan amount over time. The process of providing for a loan to be paid off by making regular principal reductions is called *amortizing* the loan.

A simple way of amortizing a loan is to have the borrower pay the interest each period plus some fixed amount. This approach is common with medium-term business loans. For example, suppose a business takes out a $5,000, five-year loan at 9 percent. The loan agreement calls for the borrower to pay the interest on the loan balance each year and to reduce the loan balance each year by $1,000. Because the loan amount declines by $1,000 each year, it is fully paid in five years.

In the case we are considering, notice that the total payment will decline each year. The reason is that the loan balance goes down, resulting in a lower interest charge each year, whereas the $1,000 principal reduction is constant. For example, the interest in the first year will be $5,000 × .09 = $450. The total payment will be $1,000 + 450 = $1,450. In the second year, the loan balance is $4,000, so the interest is $4,000 × .09 = $360, and the total payment is $1,360. We can calculate the total payment in each of the remaining years by preparing a simple *amortization schedule* as follows:

Year	Beginning Balance	Total Payment	Interest Paid	Principal Paid	Ending Balance
1	$5,000	$1,450	$ 450	$1,000	$4,000
2	4,000	1,360	360	1,000	3,000
3	3,000	1,270	270	1,000	2,000
4	2,000	1,180	180	1,000	1,000
5	1,000	1,090	90	1,000	0
Totals		$6,350	$1,350	$5,000	

Notice that in each year, the interest paid is given by the beginning balance multiplied by the interest rate. Also notice that the beginning balance is given by the ending balance from the previous year.

Probably the most common way of amortizing a loan is to have the borrower make a single, fixed payment every period. Almost all consumer loans (such as car loans) and mortgages work this way. For example, suppose our five-year, 9 percent, $5,000 loan was amortized this way. How would the amortization schedule look?

We first need to determine the payment. From our discussion earlier in the chapter, we know that this loan's cash flows are in the form of an ordinary annuity. In this case, we can solve for the payment as follows:

$$\$5,000 = C \times \{[1 - (1/1.09^5)]/.09\}$$
$$= C \times [(1 - .6499)/.09]$$

This gives us:

$$C = \$5,000/3.8897$$
$$= \$1,285.46$$

The borrower will therefore make five equal payments of $1,285.46. Will this pay off the loan? We will check by filling in an amortization schedule.

In our previous example, we knew the principal reduction each year. We then calculated the interest owed to get the total payment. In this example, we know the total payment. We will thus calculate the interest and then subtract it from the total payment to calculate the principal portion in each payment.

In the first year, the interest is $450, as we calculated before. Because the total payment is $1,285.46, the principal paid in the first year must be:

Principal paid = $1,285.46 − 450 = $835.46

The ending loan balance is thus:

Ending balance = $5,000 − 835.46 = $4,164.54

The interest in the second year is $4,164.54 × .09 = $374.81, and the loan balance declines by $1,285.46 − 374.81 = $910.65. We can summarize all of the relevant calculations in the following schedule:

Year	Beginning Balance	Total Payment	Interest Paid	Principal Paid	Ending Balance
1	$5,000.00	$1,285.46	$ 450.00	$ 835.46	$4,164.54
2	4,164.54	1,285.46	374.81	910.65	3,253.88
3	3,253.88	1,285.46	292.85	992.61	2,261.27
4	2,261.27	1,285.46	203.51	1,081.95	1,179.32
5	1,179.32	1,285.46	106.14	1,179.32	0.00
Totals		$6,427.30	$1,427.31	$5,000.00	

Because the loan balance declines to zero, the five equal payments do pay off the loan. Notice that the interest paid declines each period. This isn't surprising because the loan balance is going down. Given that the total payment is fixed, the principal paid must be rising each period.

If you compare the two loan amortizations in this section, you will see that the total interest is greater for the equal total payment case: $1,427.31 versus $1,350. The reason for this is that the loan is repaid more slowly early on, so the interest is somewhat higher. This doesn't mean that one loan is better than the other; it simply means that one is effectively paid off faster than the other. For example, the principal reduction in the first year is $835.46 in the equal total payment case as compared to $1,000 in the first case. Many Web sites offer loan amortization schedules. See our nearby *Work the Web* box for an example.

WORK THE WEB

Preparing an amortization table is one of the more tedious time value of money applications. Using a spreadsheet makes it relatively easy, but there are also Web sites available that will prepare an amortization schedule very quickly and simply. One such site is www.bankrate.com. This site has a mortgage calculator for home loans, but the same calculations apply to most other types of loans such as car loans and student loans. Suppose you graduate with a student loan of $25,000 and will repay the loan over the next 10 years at 6.8 percent. What are your monthly payments? Using the calculator we get:

Try this example yourself and click the "Show/Recalculate Amortization Table" button. You will find that your first payment will consist of $146.03 in principal and $141.67 in interest. Over the life of the loan you will pay a total of $9,524.10 in interest.

Questions

1. Suppose you take out a 30-year mortgage for $250,000 at an interest rate of 6.8 percent. Use this Web site to construct an amortization table for the loan. What are the interest payment and principal amounts in the 110th payment? How much in total interest will you pay over the life of the loan?
2. You take out a 30-year mortgage for $275,000 at an interest rate of 7.3 percent. How much will you pay in interest over the life of this loan? Now assume you pay an extra $100 per month on this loan. How much is your total interest now? How much sooner will the mortgage be paid off?

We will close this chapter with an example that may be of particular relevance. Federal Stafford loans are an important source of financing for many college students, helping to cover the cost of tuition, books, new cars, condominiums, and many other things. Sometimes students do not seem to fully realize that Stafford loans have a serious drawback: They must be repaid in monthly installments, usually beginning six months after the student leaves school.

Some Stafford loans are subsidized, meaning that the interest does not begin to accrue until repayment begins (this is a good thing). If you are a dependent undergraduate student under this particular option, the total debt you can run up is, at most, $23,000. The maximum interest rate in 2008–2009 is 6.0 percent, or $6.0/12 = .50$ percent per month. Under the "standard repayment plan," the loans are amortized over 10 years (subject to a minimum payment of $50).

Suppose you max out borrowing under this program and also get stuck paying the maximum interest rate. Beginning six months after you graduate (or otherwise depart the ivory tower), what will your monthly payment be? How much will you owe after making payments for four years?

Given our earlier discussions, see if you don't agree that your monthly payment assuming a $23,000 total loan is $255.35 per month. Also, as explained in Example 6.13, after making payments for four years, you still owe the present value of the remaining payments. There are 120 payments in all. After you make 48 of them (the first four years), you have 72 to go. By now, it should be easy for you to verify that the present value of $255.35 per month for 72 months at .50 percent per month is about $15,400, so you still have a long way to go.

<table>
<tr><td>**Partial Amortization, or "Bite the Bullet"**</td><td>**EXAMPLE 6.13**</td></tr>
</table>

A common arrangement in real estate lending might call for a 5-year loan with, say, a 15-year amortization. What this means is that the borrower makes a payment every month of a fixed amount based on a 15-year amortization. However, after 60 months, the borrower makes a single, much larger payment called a "balloon" or "bullet" to pay off the loan. Because the monthly payments don't fully pay off the loan, the loan is said to be partially amortized.

Suppose we have a $100,000 commercial mortgage with a 12 percent APR and a 20-year (240-month) amortization. Further suppose the mortgage has a five-year balloon. What will the monthly payment be? How big will the balloon payment be?

The monthly payment can be calculated based on an ordinary annuity with a present value of $100,000. There are 240 payments, and the interest rate is 1 percent per month. The payment is:

$$\$100,000 = C \times [(1 - 1/1.01^{240})/.01]$$
$$= C \times 90.8194$$
$$C = \$1,101.09$$

Now, there is an easy way and a hard way to determine the balloon payment. The hard way is to actually amortize the loan for 60 months to see what the balance is at that time. The easy way is to recognize that after 60 months, we have a $240 - 60 = 180$-month loan. The payment is still $1,101.09 per month, and the interest rate is still 1 percent per month. The loan balance is thus the present value of the remaining payments:

$$\text{Loan balance} = \$1,101.09 \times [(1 - 1/1.01^{180})/.01]$$
$$= \$1,101.09 \times 83.3217$$
$$= \$91,744.69$$

The balloon payment is a substantial $91,744. Why is it so large? To get an idea, consider the first payment on the mortgage. The interest in the first month is $100,000 \times .01 = $1,000. Your payment is $1,101.09, so the loan balance declines by only $101.09. Because the loan balance declines so slowly, the cumulative "pay down" over five years is not great.

SPREADSHEET STRATEGIES

Loan Amortization Using a Spreadsheet

Loan amortization is a common spreadsheet application. To illustrate, we will set up the problem that we examined earlier: a five-year, $5,000, 9 percent loan with constant payments. Our spreadsheet looks like this:

	A	B	C	D	E	F	G	H
1								
2				Using a spreadsheet to amortize a loan				
3								
4			Loan amount:	$5,000				
5			Interest rate:	.09				
6			Loan term:	5				
7			Loan payment:	$1,285.46				
8				Note: Payment is calculated using PMT(rate,nper,-pv,fv).				
9		Amortization table:						
10								
11		Year	Beginning	Total	Interest	Principal	Ending	
12			Balance	Payment	Paid	Paid	Balance	
13		1	$5,000.00	$1,285.46	$450.00	$835.46	$4,164.54	
14		2	4,164.54	1,285.46	374.81	910.65	3,253.88	
15		3	3,253.88	1,285.46	292.85	992.61	2,261.27	
16		4	2,261.27	1,285.46	203.51	1,081.95	1,179.32	
17		5	1,179.32	1,285.46	106.14	1,179.32	.00	
18		Totals		6,427.31	1,427.31	5,000.00		
19								
20		Formulas in the amortization table:						
21								
22		Year	Beginning	Total	Interest	Principal	Ending	
23			Balance	Payment	Paid	Paid	Balance	
24		1	=+D4	=$D$7	=+$D$5*C13	=+D13-E13	=+C13-F13	
25		2	=+G13	=$D$7	=+$D$5*C14	=+D14-E14	=+C14-F14	
26		3	=+G14	=$D$7	=+$D$5*C15	=+D15-E15	=+C15-F15	
27		4	=+G15	=$D$7	=+$D$5*C16	=+D16-E16	=+C16-F16	
28		5	=+G16	=$D$7	=+$D$5*C17	=+D17-E17	=+C17-F17	
29								
30		Note: Totals in the amortization table are calculated using the SUM formula.						
31								

Of course, it is possible to rack up much larger debts. According to the Association of American Medical Colleges, medical students who borrowed to attend medical school and graduated in 2007 had an average student loan balance of $140,000. Ouch! How long will it take the average student to pay off her medical school loans?

Let's say she makes a monthly payment of $1,000, and the loan has an interest rate of 7 percent per year, or .5833 percent per month. See if you agree that it will take 292 months, or just over 24 years, to pay off the loan. Maybe MD really stands for "mucho debt"!

Concept Questions

6.4a What is a pure discount loan? An interest-only loan?

6.4b What does it mean to amortize a loan?

6.4c What is a balloon payment? How do you determine its value?

Summary and Conclusions   6.5

This chapter rounded out your understanding of fundamental concepts related to the time value of money and discounted cash flow valuation. Several important topics were covered:

1. There are two ways of calculating present and future values when there are multiple cash flows. Both approaches are straightforward extensions of our earlier analysis of single cash flows.

2. A series of constant cash flows that arrive or are paid at the end of each period is called an ordinary annuity, and we described some useful shortcuts for determining the present and future values of annuities.

3. Interest rates can be quoted in a variety of ways. For financial decisions, it is important that any rates being compared be first converted to effective rates. The relationship between a quoted rate, such as an annual percentage rate (APR), and an effective annual rate (EAR) is given by:

$$EAR = [1 + (Quoted\ rate/m)]^m - 1$$

   where m is the number of times during the year the money is compounded or, equivalently, the number of payments during the year.

4. Many loans are annuities. The process of providing for a loan to be paid off gradually is called amortizing the loan, and we discussed how amortization schedules are prepared and interpreted.

The principles developed in this chapter will figure prominently in the chapters to come. The reason for this is that most investments, whether they involve real assets or financial assets, can be analyzed using the discounted cash flow (DCF) approach. As a result, the DCF approach is broadly applicable and widely used in practice. For example, the next two chapters show how to value bonds and stocks using an extension of the techniques presented in this chapter. Before going on, therefore, you might want to do some of the problems that follow.

CHAPTER REVIEW AND SELF-TEST PROBLEMS

6.1 Present Values with Multiple Cash Flows A first-round draft choice quarterback has been signed to a three-year, $25 million contract. The details provide for an immediate cash bonus of $2 million. The player is to receive $5 million in salary at the end of the first year, $8 million the next, and $10 million at the end of the last year. Assuming a 15 percent discount rate, is this package worth $25 million? If not, how much is it worth?

6.2 Future Value with Multiple Cash Flows You plan to make a series of deposits in an individual retirement account. You will deposit $1,000 today, $2,000 in two years, and $2,000 in five years. If you withdraw $1,500 in three years and $1,000 in seven years, assuming no withdrawal penalties, how much will you have after eight years if the interest rate is 7 percent? What is the present value of these cash flows?

6.3 Annuity Present Value You are looking into an investment that will pay you $12,000 per year for the next 10 years. If you require a 15 percent return, what is the most you would pay for this investment?

6.4   APR versus EAR   The going rate on student loans is quoted as 8 percent APR. The terms of the loans call for monthly payments. What is the effective annual rate (EAR) on such a student loan?

6.5   It's the Principal That Matters   Suppose you borrow $10,000. You are going to repay the loan by making equal annual payments for five years. The interest rate on the loan is 14 percent per year. Prepare an amortization schedule for the loan. How much interest will you pay over the life of the loan?

6.6   Just a Little Bit Each Month   You've recently finished your MBA at the Darnit School. Naturally, you must purchase a new BMW immediately. The car costs about $21,000. The bank quotes an interest rate of 15 percent APR for a 72-month loan with a 10 percent down payment. You plan on trading the car in for a new one in two years. What will your monthly payment be? What is the effective interest rate on the loan? What will the loan balance be when you trade the car in?

ANSWERS TO CHAPTER REVIEW AND SELF-TEST PROBLEMS

6.1   Obviously, the package is not worth $25 million because the payments are spread out over three years. The bonus is paid today, so it's worth $2 million. The present values for the three subsequent salary payments are:

$$(\$5/1.15) + (8/1.15^2) + (10/1.15^3) = (\$5/1.15) + (8/1.32) + (10/1.52)$$
$$= \$16.9721 \text{ million}$$

The package is worth a total of $18.9721 million.

6.2   We will calculate the future values for each of the cash flows separately and then add them up. Notice that we treat the withdrawals as negative cash flows:

$$\$1,000 \times 1.07^8 = \quad \$1,000 \times 1.7812 = \$\ 1,718.19$$
$$\$2,000 \times 1.07^6 = \quad \$2,000 \times 1.5007 = \quad 3,001.46$$
$$-\$1,500 \times 1.07^5 = -\$1,500 \times 1.4026 = -2,103.83$$
$$\$2,000 \times 1.07^3 = \quad \$2,000 \times 1.2250 = \quad 2,450.09$$
$$-\$1,000 \times 1.07^1 = -\$1,000 \times 1.0700 = \underline{-1,070.00}$$
$$\text{Total future value} \qquad\qquad\qquad = \$\ \underline{3,995.91}$$

This value includes a small rounding error.

To calculate the present value, we could discount each cash flow back to the present or we could discount back a single year at a time. However, because we already know that the future value in eight years is $3,995.91, the easy way to get the PV is just to discount this amount back eight years:

$$\text{Present value} = \$3,995.91/1.07^8$$
$$= \$3,995.91/1.7182$$
$$= \$2,325.64$$

We again ignore a small rounding error. For practice, you can verify that this is what you get if you discount each cash flow back separately.

6.3   The most you would be willing to pay is the present value of $12,000 per year for 10 years at a 15 percent discount rate. The cash flows here are in ordinary annuity form, so the relevant present value factor is:

$$\text{Annuity present value factor} = (1 - \text{Present value factor})/r$$
$$= [1 - (1/1.15^{10})]/.15$$
$$= (1 - .2472)/.15$$
$$= 5.0188$$

The present value of the 10 cash flows is thus:

$$\text{Present value} = \$12,000 \times 5.0188$$
$$= \$60,225$$

This is the most you would pay.

6.4   A rate of 8 percent APR with monthly payments is actually $8\%/12 = .67\%$ per month. The EAR is thus:

$$\text{EAR} = [1 + (.08/12)]^{12} - 1 = 8.30\%$$

6.5   We first need to calculate the annual payment. With a present value of $10,000, an interest rate of 14 percent, and a term of five years, the payment can be determined from:

$$\$10,000 = \text{Payment} \times \{[1 - (1/1.14^5)]/.14\}$$
$$= \text{Payment} \times 3.4331$$

Therefore, the payment is $10,000/3.4331 = $2,912.84 (actually, it's $2,912.8355; this will create some small rounding errors in the following schedule). We can now prepare the amortization schedule as follows:

Year	Beginning Balance	Total Payment	Interest Paid	Principal Paid	Ending Balance
1	$10,000.00	$ 2,912.84	$1,400.00	$ 1,512.84	$8,487.16
2	8,487.16	2,912.84	1,188.20	1,724.63	6,762.53
3	6,762.53	2,912.84	946.75	1,066.08	4,796.45
4	4,796.45	2,912.84	671.50	2,241.33	2,555.12
5	2,555.12	2,912.84	357.72	2,555.12	0.00
Totals		$14,564.17	$4,564.17	$10,000.00	

6.6   The cash flows on the car loan are in annuity form, so we need to find only the payment. The interest rate is $15\%/12 = 1.25\%$ per month, and there are 72 months. The first thing we need is the annuity factor for 72 periods at 1.25 percent per period:

$$\text{Annuity present value factor} = (1 - \text{Present value factor})/r$$
$$= [1 - (1/1.0125^{72})]/.0125$$
$$= [1 - (1/2.4459)]/.0125$$
$$= (1 - .4088)/.0125$$
$$= 47.2925$$

The present value is the amount we finance. With a 10 percent down payment, we will be borrowing 90 percent of $21,000, or $18,900. To find the payment, we need to solve for C:

$$\$18,900 = C \times \text{Annuity present value factor}$$
$$= C \times 47.2925$$

Visit us at www.mhhe.com/rwj

Rearranging things a bit, we have:

$$C = \$18,900 \times (1/47.2925)$$
$$= \$18,900 \times .02115$$
$$= \$399.64$$

Your payment is just under \$400 per month.

The actual interest rate on this loan is 1.25 percent per month. Based on our work in the chapter, we can calculate the effective annual rate as:

$$EAR = (1.0125)^{12} - 1 = 16.08\%$$

The effective rate is about one point higher than the quoted rate.

To determine the loan balance in two years, we could amortize the loan to see what the balance is at that time. This would be fairly tedious to do by hand. Using the information already determined in this problem, we can instead simply calculate the present value of the remaining payments. After two years, we have made 24 payments, so there are $72 - 24 = 48$ payments left. What is the present value of 48 monthly payments of \$399.64 at 1.25 percent per month? The relevant annuity factor is:

$$\text{Annuity present value factor} = (1 - \text{Present value factor})/r$$
$$= [1 - (1/1.0125^{48})]/.0125$$
$$= [1 - (1/1.8154)]/.0125$$
$$= (1 - .5509)/.0125$$
$$= 35.9315$$

The present value is thus:

$$\text{Present value} = \$399.64 \times 35.9315 = \$14,359.66$$

You will owe about \$14,360 on the loan in two years.

CONCEPTS REVIEW AND CRITICAL THINKING QUESTIONS

1. **Annuity Factors** [LO1] There are four pieces to an annuity present value. What are they?

2. **Annuity Period** [LO1] As you increase the length of time involved, what happens to the present value of an annuity? What happens to the future value?

3. **Interest Rates** [LO1] What happens to the future value of an annuity if you increase the rate r? What happens to the present value?

4. **Present Value** [LO1] What do you think about the Tri-State Megabucks lottery discussed in the chapter advertising a \$500,000 prize when the lump sum option is \$250,000? Is it deceptive advertising?

5. **Present Value** [LO1] If you were an athlete negotiating a contract, would you want a big signing bonus payable immediately and smaller payments in the future, or vice versa? How about looking at it from the team's perspective?

6. **Present Value** [LO1] Suppose two athletes sign 10-year contracts for \$80 million. In one case, we're told that the \$80 million will be paid in 10 equal installments. In the other case, we're told that the \$80 million will be paid in 10 installments, but the installments will increase by 5 percent per year. Who got the better deal?

Visit us at www.mhhe.com/rwj

7. **APR and EAR** [LO4] Should lending laws be changed to require lenders to report EARs instead of APRs? Why or why not?

8. **Time Value** [LO1] On subsidized Stafford loans, a common source of financial aid for college students, interest does not begin to accrue until repayment begins. Who receives a bigger subsidy, a freshman or a senior? Explain. In words, how would you go about valuing the subsidy on a subsidized Stafford loan?

9. **Time Value** [LO1] Eligibility for a subsidized Stafford loan is based on current financial need. However, both subsidized and unsubsidized Stafford loans are repaid out of future income. Given this, do you see a possible objection to having two types?

10. **Time Value** [LO1] A viatical settlement is a lump sum of money given to a terminally ill individual in exchange for his life insurance policy. When the insured person dies, the purchaser receives the payout from the life insurance policy. What factors determine the value of the viatical settlement? Do you think such settlements are ethical? Why or why not?

QUESTIONS AND PROBLEMS

1. **Present Value and Multiple Cash Flows** [LO1] Seaborn Co. has identified an investment project with the following cash flows. If the discount rate is 10 percent, what is the present value of these cash flows? What is the present value at 18 percent? At 24 percent?

BASIC
(Questions 1–28)

Year	Cash Flow
1	$ 950
2	1,040
3	1,130
4	1,075

2. **Present Value and Multiple Cash Flows** [LO1] Investment X offers to pay you $6,000 per year for nine years, whereas Investment Y offers to pay you $8,000 per year for six years. Which of these cash flow streams has the higher present value if the discount rate is 5 percent? If the discount rate is 15 percent?

3. **Future Value and Multiple Cash Flows** [LO1] Paradise, Inc., has identified an investment project with the following cash flows. If the discount rate is 8 percent, what is the future value of these cash flows in year 4? What is the future value at a discount rate of 11 percent? At 24 percent?

Year	Cash Flow
1	$ 940
2	1,090
3	1,340
4	1,405

4. **Calculating Annuity Present Value** [LO1] An investment offers $5,300 per year for 15 years, with the first payment occurring one year from now. If the required return is 7 percent, what is the value of the investment? What would the value be if the payments occurred for 40 years? For 75 years? Forever?

5. **Calculating Annuity Cash Flows** [LO1] If you put up $34,000 today in exchange for a 7.65 percent, 15-year annuity, what will the annual cash flow be?

6. Calculating Annuity Values [LO1] Your company will generate $73,000 in annual revenue each year for the next eight years from a new information database. If the appropriate interest rate is 8.5 percent, what is the present value of the savings?

7. Calculating Annuity Values [LO1] If you deposit $4,000 at the end of each of the next 20 years into an account paying 11.2 percent interest, how much money will you have in the account in 20 years? How much will you have if you make deposits for 40 years?

8. Calculating Annuity Values [LO1] You want to have $90,000 in your savings account 10 years from now, and you're prepared to make equal annual deposits into the account at the end of each year. If the account pays 6.8 percent interest, what amount must you deposit each year?

9. Calculating Annuity Values [LO2] Dinero Bank offers you a $50,000, seven-year term loan at 7.5 percent annual interest. What will your annual loan payment be?

10. Calculating Perpetuity Values [LO1] The Maybe Pay Life Insurance Co. is trying to sell you an investment policy that will pay you and your heirs $25,000 per year forever. If the required return on this investment is 7.2 percent, how much will you pay for the policy?

11. Calculating Perpetuity Values [LO1] In the previous problem, suppose a sales associate told you the policy costs $375,000. At what interest rate would this be a fair deal?

12. Calculating EAR [LO4] Find the EAR in each of the following cases:

Stated Rate (APR)	Number of Times Compounded	Effective Rate (EAR)
8%	Quarterly	
16	Monthly	
12	Daily	
15	Infinite	

13. Calculating APR [LO4] Find the APR, or stated rate, in each of the following cases:

Stated Rate (APR)	Number of Times Compounded	Effective Rate (EAR)
	Semiannually	8.6%
	Monthly	19.8
	Weekly	9.4
	Infinite	16.5

14. Calculating EAR [LO4] First National Bank charges 14.2 percent compounded monthly on its business loans. First United Bank charges 14.5 percent compounded semiannually. As a potential borrower, which bank would you go to for a new loan?

15. Calculating APR [LO4] Barcain Credit Corp. wants to earn an effective annual return on its consumer loans of 16 percent per year. The bank uses daily compounding on its loans. What interest rate is the bank required by law to report to potential borrowers? Explain why this rate is misleading to an uninformed borrower.

16. Calculating Future Values [LO1] What is the future value of $2,100 in 17 years assuming an interest rate of 8.4 percent compounded semiannually?

17. **Calculating Future Values** [LO1] Gold Door Credit Bank is offering 9.3 percent compounded daily on its savings accounts. If you deposit $4,500 today, how much will you have in the account in 5 years? In 10 years? In 20 years?

18. **Calculating Present Values** [LO1] An investment will pay you $58,000 in seven years. If the appropriate discount rate is 10 percent compounded daily, what is the present value?

19. **EAR versus APR** [LO4] Big Dom's Pawn Shop charges an interest rate of 30 percent per month on loans to its customers. Like all lenders, Big Dom must report an APR to consumers. What rate should the shop report? What is the effective annual rate?

20. **Calculating Loan Payments** [LO2, 4] You want to buy a new sports coupe for $68,500, and the finance office at the dealership has quoted you a 6.9 percent APR loan for 60 months to buy the car. What will your monthly payments be? What is the effective annual rate on this loan?

21. **Calculating Number of Periods** [LO3] One of your customers is delinquent on his accounts payable balance. You've mutually agreed to a repayment schedule of $500 per month. You will charge 1.3 percent per month interest on the overdue balance. If the current balance is $18,000, how long will it take for the account to be paid off?

22. **Calculating EAR** [LO4] Friendly's Quick Loans, Inc., offers you "three for four or 1 knock on your door." This means you get $3 today and repay $4 when you get your paycheck in one week (or else). What's the effective annual return Friendly's earns on this lending business? If you were brave enough to ask, what APR would Friendly's say you were paying?

23. **Valuing Perpetuities** [LO1] Live Forever Life Insurance Co. is selling a perpetuity contract that pays $1,800 monthly. The contract currently sells for $95,000. What is the monthly return on this investment vehicle? What is the APR? The effective annual return?

24. **Calculating Annuity Future Values** [LO1] You are planning to make monthly deposits of $300 into a retirement account that pays 10 percent interest compounded monthly. If your first deposit will be made one month from now, how large will your retirement account be in 30 years?

25. **Calculating Annuity Future Values** [LO1] In the previous problem, suppose you make $3,600 annual deposits into the same retirement account. How large will your account balance be in 30 years?

26. **Calculating Annuity Present Values** [LO1] Beginning three months from now, you want to be able to withdraw $2,300 each quarter from your bank account to cover college expenses over the next four years. If the account pays .65 percent interest per quarter, how much do you need to have in your bank account today to meet your expense needs over the next four years?

27. **Discounted Cash Flow Analysis** [LO1] If the appropriate discount rate for the following cash flows is 11 percent compounded quarterly, what is the present value of the cash flows?

Year	Cash Flow
1	$ 725
2	980
3	0
4	1,360

Visit us at www.mhhe.com/rwj

28. **Discounted Cash Flow Analysis** [LO1] If the appropriate discount rate for the following cash flows is 8.45 percent per year, what is the present value of the cash flows?

Year	Cash Flow
1	$1,650
2	0
3	4,200
4	2,430

INTERMEDIATE
(Questions 29–56)

29. **Simple Interest versus Compound Interest** [LO4] First Simple Bank pays 7 percent simple interest on its investment accounts. If First Complex Bank pays interest on its accounts compounded annually, what rate should the bank set if it wants to match First Simple Bank over an investment horizon of 10 years?

30. **Calculating EAR** [LO4] You are looking at an investment that has an effective annual rate of 17 percent. What is the effective semiannual return? The effective quarterly return? The effective monthly return?

31. **Calculating Interest Expense** [LO2] You receive a credit card application from Shady Banks Savings and Loan offering an introductory rate of 1.5 percent per year, compounded monthly for the first six months, increasing thereafter to 18 percent compounded monthly. Assuming you transfer the $5,000 balance from your existing credit card and make no subsequent payments, how much interest will you owe at the end of the first year?

32. **Calculating Annuities** [LO1] You are planning to save for retirement over the next 30 years. To do this, you will invest $700 a month in a stock account and $300 a month in a bond account. The return of the stock account is expected to be 11 percent, and the bond account will pay 6 percent. When you retire, you will combine your money into an account with a 9 percent return. How much can you withdraw each month from your account assuming a 25-year withdrawal period?

33. **Calculating Future Values** [LO1] You have an investment that will pay you 1.17 percent per month. How much will you have per dollar invested in one year? In two years?

34. **Calculating Annuity Payments** [LO1] You want to be a millionaire when you retire in 40 years. How much do you have to save each month if you can earn a 12 percent annual return? How much do you have to save if you wait 10 years before you begin your deposits? 20 years?

35. **Calculating Rates of Return** [LO2] Suppose an investment offers to triple your money in 12 months (don't believe it). What rate of return per quarter are you being offered?

36. **Comparing Cash Flow Streams** [LO1] You've just joined the investment banking firm of Dewey, Cheatum, and Howe. They've offered you two different salary arrangements. You can have $95,000 per year for the next two years, or you can have $70,000 per year for the next two years, along with a $45,000 signing bonus today. The bonus is paid immediately, and the salary is paid at the end of each year. If the interest rate is 10 percent compounded monthly, which do you prefer?

37. **Growing Annuity** [LO1] You have just won the lottery and will receive $1,000,000 in one year. You will receive payments for 30 years, which will increase 5 percent per year. If the appropriate discount rate is 8 percent, what is the present value of your winnings?

38. **Growing Annuity** [LO1] Your job pays you only once a year for all the work you did over the previous 12 months. Today, December 31, you just received your salary of $50,000 and you plan to spend all of it. However, you want to start saving for retirement beginning next year. You have decided that one year from today you will begin depositing 5 percent of your annual salary in an account that will earn 11 percent per year. Your salary will increase at 4 percent per year throughout your career. How much money will you have on the date of your retirement 40 years from today?

39. **Present Value and Interest Rates** [LO1] What is the relationship between the value of an annuity and the level of interest rates? Suppose you just bought a 15-year annuity of $9,000 per year at the current interest rate of 10 percent per year. What happens to the value of your investment if interest rates suddenly drop to 5 percent? What if interest rates suddenly rise to 15 percent?

40. **Calculating the Number of Payments** [LO2] You're prepared to make monthly payments of $340, beginning at the end of this month, into an account that pays 6 percent interest compounded monthly. How many payments will you have made when your account balance reaches $20,000?

41. **Calculating Annuity Present Values** [LO2] You want to borrow $73,000 from your local bank to buy a new sailboat. You can afford to make monthly payments of $1,450, but no more. Assuming monthly compounding, what is the highest rate you can afford on a 60-month APR loan?

42. **Calculating Loan Payments** [LO2] You need a 30-year, fixed-rate mortgage to buy a new home for $240,000. Your mortgage bank will lend you the money at a 6.35 percent APR for this 360-month loan. However, you can afford monthly payments of only $1,150, so you offer to pay off any remaining loan balance at the end of the loan in the form of a single balloon payment. How large will this balloon payment have to be for you to keep your monthly payments at $1,150?

43. **Present and Future Values** [LO1] The present value of the following cash flow stream is $6,550 when discounted at 10 percent annually. What is the value of the missing cash flow?

Year	Cash Flow
1	$1,700
2	?
3	2,100
4	2,800

44. **Calculating Present Values** [LO1] You just won the TVM Lottery. You will receive $1 million today plus another 10 annual payments that increase by $500,000 per year. Thus, in one year, you receive $1.5 million. In two years you get $2 million, and so on. If the appropriate interest rate is 9 percent, what is the present value of your winnings?

45. **EAR versus APR** [LO4] You have just purchased a new warehouse. To finance the purchase, you've arranged for a 30-year mortgage loan for 80 percent of the $2,900,000 purchase price. The monthly payment on this loan will be $15,000. What is the APR on this loan? The EAR?

46. Present Value and Break-Even Interest [LO1] Consider a firm with a contract to sell an asset for $165,000 four years from now. The asset costs $94,000 to produce today. Given a relevant discount rate on this asset of 13 percent per year, will the firm make a profit on this asset? At what rate does the firm just break even?

47. Present Value and Multiple Cash Flows [LO1] What is the present value of $4,000 per year, at a discount rate of 10 percent, if the first payment is received 8 years from now and the last payment is received 25 years from now?

48. Variable Interest Rates [LO1] A 15-year annuity pays $1,500 per month, and payments are made at the end of each month. If the interest rate is 11 percent compounded monthly for the first seven years, and 7 percent compounded monthly thereafter, what is the present value of the annuity?

49. Comparing Cash Flow Streams [LO1] You have your choice of two investment accounts. Investment A is a 15-year annuity that features end-of-month $1,200 payments and has an interest rate of 8.5 percent compounded monthly. Investment B is an 8 percent continuously compounded lump sum investment, also good for 15 years. How much money would you need to invest in B today for it to be worth as much as investment A 15 years from now?

50. Calculating Present Value of a Perpetuity [LO1] Given an interest rate of 6.2 percent per year, what is the value at date $t = 7$ of a perpetual stream of $3,500 payments that begins at date $t = 15$?

51. Calculating EAR [LO4] A local finance company quotes a 16 percent interest rate on one-year loans. So, if you borrow $25,000, the interest for the year will be $4,000. Because you must repay a total of $29,000 in one year, the finance company requires you to pay $29,000/12, or $2,416.67, per month over the next 12 months. Is this a 16 percent loan? What rate would legally have to be quoted? What is the effective annual rate?

52. Calculating Present Values [LO1] A 5-year annuity of ten $7,000 semiannual payments will begin 8 years from now, with the first payment coming 8.5 years from now. If the discount rate is 10 percent compounded monthly, what is the value of this annuity five years from now? What is the value three years from now? What is the current value of the annuity?

53. Calculating Annuities Due [LO1] Suppose you are going to receive $10,000 per year for five years. The appropriate interest rate is 11 percent.

a. What is the present value of the payments if they are in the form of an ordinary annuity? What is the present value if the payments are an annuity due?

b. Suppose you plan to invest the payments for five years. What is the future value if the payments are an ordinary annuity? What if the payments are an annuity due?

c. Which has the highest present value, the ordinary annuity or annuity due? Which has the highest future value? Will this always be true?

54. Calculating Annuities Due [LO1] You want to buy a new sports car from Muscle Motors for $68,000. The contract is in the form of a 60-month annuity due at an 7.85 percent APR. What will your monthly payment be?

55. Amortization with Equal Payments [LO3] Prepare an amortization schedule for a five-year loan of $42,000. The interest rate is 8 percent per year, and the loan calls for equal annual payments. How much interest is paid in the third year? How much total interest is paid over the life of the loan?

56. **Amortization with Equal Principal Payments [LO3]** Rework Problem 55 assuming that the loan agreement calls for a principal reduction of $8,400 every year instead of equal annual payments.

57. **Calculating Annuity Values [LO1]** Bilbo Baggins wants to save money to meet three objectives. First, he would like to be able to retire 30 years from now with retirement income of $20,000 per month for 25 years, with the first payment received 30 years and 1 month from now. Second, he would like to purchase a cabin in Rivendell in 10 years at an estimated cost of $380,000. Third, after he passes on at the end of the 25 years of withdrawals, he would like to leave an inheritance of $900,000 to his nephew Frodo. He can afford to save $2,500 per month for the next 10 years. If he can earn a 10 percent EAR before he retires and a 7 percent EAR after he retires, how much will he have to save each month in years 11 through 30?

CHALLENGE
(Questions 57–78)

58. **Calculating Annuity Values [LO1]** After deciding to buy a new car, you can either lease the car or purchase it on a three-year loan. The car you wish to buy costs $32,000. The dealer has a special leasing arrangement where you pay $99 today and $450 per month for the next three years. If you purchase the car, you will pay it off in monthly payments over the next three years at a 7 percent APR. You believe you will be able to sell the car for $23,000 in three years. Should you buy or lease the car? What break-even resale price in three years would make you indifferent between buying and leasing?

59. **Calculating Annuity Values [LO1]** An All-Pro defensive lineman is in contract negotiations. The team has offered the following salary structure:

Time	Salary
0	$7,000,000
1	$4,500,000
2	$5,000,000
3	$6,000,000
4	$6,800,000
5	$7,900,000
6	$8,800,000

All salaries are to be paid in lump sums. The player has asked you as his agent to renegotiate the terms. He wants a $9 million signing bonus payable today and a contract value increase of $1,400,000. He also wants an equal salary paid every three months, with the first paycheck three months from now. If the interest rate is 5.5 percent compounded daily, what is the amount of his quarterly check? Assume 365 days in a year.

60. **Discount Interest Loans [LO4]** This question illustrates what is known as *discount interest.* Imagine you are discussing a loan with a somewhat unscrupulous lender. You want to borrow $25,000 for one year. The interest rate is 15 percent. You and the lender agree that the interest on the loan will be .15 × $25,000 = $3,750. So the lender deducts this interest amount from the loan up front and gives you $21,250. In this case, we say that the discount is $3,750. What's wrong here?

61. **Calculating Annuity Values [LO1]** You are serving on a jury. A plaintiff is suing the city for injuries sustained after a freak street sweeper accident. In the trial, doctors testified that it will be five years before the plaintiff is able to return to

work. The jury has already decided in favor of the plaintiff. You are the foreperson of the jury and propose that the jury give the plaintiff an award to cover the following: (a) The present value of two years' back pay. The plaintiff's annual salary for the last two years would have been $47,000 and $50,000, respectively. (b) The present value of five years' future salary. You assume the salary will be $55,000 per year. (c) $100,000 for pain and suffering. (d) $20,000 for court costs. Assume that the salary payments are equal amounts paid at the end of each month. If the interest rate you choose is an 8 percent EAR, what is the size of the settlement? If you were the plaintiff, would you like to see a higher or lower interest rate?

62. **Calculating EAR with Points** [LO4] You are looking at a one-year loan of $10,000. The interest rate is quoted as 8 percent plus three points. A *point* on a loan is simply 1 percent (one percentage point) of the loan amount. Quotes similar to this one are common with home mortgages. The interest rate quotation in this example requires the borrower to pay three points to the lender up front and repay the loan later with 8 percent interest. What rate would you actually be paying here?

63. **Calculating EAR with Points** [LO4] The interest rate on a one-year loan is quoted as 11 percent plus two points (see the previous problem). What is the EAR? Is your answer affected by the loan amount?

64. **EAR versus APR** [LO4] Two banks in the area offer 30-year, $240,000 mortgages at 6.8 percent and charge a $2,300 loan application fee. However, the application fee charged by Insecurity Bank and Trust is refundable if the loan application is denied, whereas that charged by I.M. Greedy and Sons Mortgage Bank is not. The current disclosure law requires that any fees that will be refunded if the applicant is rejected be included in calculating the APR, but this is not required with nonrefundable fees (presumably because refundable fees are part of the loan rather than a fee). What are the EARs on these two loans? What are the APRs?

65. **Calculating EAR with Add-On Interest** [LO4] This problem illustrates a deceptive way of quoting interest rates called *add-on interest*. Imagine that you see an advertisement for Crazy Judy's Stereo City that reads something like this: "$1,000 Instant Credit! 14% Simple Interest! Three Years to Pay! Low, Low Monthly Payments!" You're not exactly sure what all this means and somebody has spilled ink over the APR on the loan contract, so you ask the manager for clarification.

Judy explains that if you borrow $1,000 for three years at 14 percent interest, in three years you will owe:

$$\$1,000 \times 1.14^3 = \$1,000 \times 1.41854 = \$1,481.54$$

Now, Judy recognizes that coming up with $1,481.54 all at once might be a strain, so she lets you make "low, low monthly payments" of $1,481.54/36 = $41.15 per month, even though this is extra bookkeeping work for her.

Is this a 14 percent loan? Why or why not? What is the APR on this loan? What is the EAR? Why do you think this is called add-on interest?

66. **Calculating Annuity Payments** [LO1] This is a classic retirement problem. A time line will help in solving it. Your friend is celebrating her 35th birthday today and wants to start saving for her anticipated retirement at age 65. She wants to be able to withdraw $105,000 from her savings account on each birthday for 20 years following her retirement; the first withdrawal will be on her 66th birthday. Your

Visit us at www.mhhe.com/rwj

friend intends to invest her money in the local credit union, which offers 7 percent interest per year. She wants to make equal annual payments on each birthday into the account established at the credit union for her retirement fund.

a. If she starts making these deposits on her 36th birthday and continues to make deposits until she is 65 (the last deposit will be on her 65th birthday), what amount must she deposit annually to be able to make the desired withdrawals at retirement?

b. Suppose your friend has just inherited a large sum of money. Rather than making equal annual payments, she has decided to make one lump sum payment on her 35th birthday to cover her retirement needs. What amount does she have to deposit?

c. Suppose your friend's employer will contribute $1,500 to the account every year as part of the company's profit-sharing plan. In addition, your friend expects a $150,000 distribution from a family trust fund on her 55th birthday, which she will also put into the retirement account. What amount must she deposit annually now to be able to make the desired withdrawals at retirement?

67. **Calculating the Number of Periods [LO2]** Your Christmas ski vacation was great, but it unfortunately ran a bit over budget. All is not lost: You just received an offer in the mail to transfer your $10,000 balance from your current credit card, which charges an annual rate of 19.8 percent, to a new credit card charging a rate of 6.2 percent. How much faster could you pay the loan off by making your planned monthly payments of $200 with the new card? What if there was a 2 percent fee charged on any balances transferred?

68. **Future Value and Multiple Cash Flows [LO1]** An insurance company is offering a new policy to its customers. Typically, the policy is bought by a parent or grandparent for a child at the child's birth. The details of the policy are as follows: The purchaser (say, the parent) makes the following six payments to the insurance company:

First birthday:	$ 900
Second birthday:	$ 900
Third birthday:	$1,000
Fourth birthday:	$1,000
Fifth birthday:	$1,100
Sixth birthday:	$1,100

After the child's sixth birthday, no more payments are made. When the child reaches age 65, he or she receives $500,000. If the relevant interest rate is 12 percent for the first six years and 8 percent for all subsequent years, is the policy worth buying?

69. **Calculating a Balloon Payment [LO2]** You have just arranged for a $750,000 mortgage to finance the purchase of a large tract of land. The mortgage has an 8.1 percent APR, and it calls for monthly payments over the next 30 years. However, the loan has an eight-year balloon payment, meaning that the loan must be paid off then. How big will the balloon payment be?

70. **Calculating Interest Rates [LO4]** A financial planning service offers a college savings program. The plan calls for you to make six annual payments of $9,000 each, with the first payment occurring today, your child's 12th birthday. Beginning on your child's 18th birthday, the plan will provide $20,000 per year for four years. What return is this investment offering?

71. **Break-Even Investment Returns [LO4]** Your financial planner offers you two different investment plans. Plan X is a $20,000 annual perpetuity. Plan Y is a 20-year, $28,000 annual annuity. Both plans will make their first payment one year from today. At what discount rate would you be indifferent between these two plans?

72. **Perpetual Cash Flows [LO1]** What is the value of an investment that pays $15,000 every *other* year forever, if the first payment occurs one year from today and the discount rate is 10 percent compounded daily? What is the value today if the first payment occurs four years from today?

73. **Ordinary Annuities and Annuities Due [LO1]** As discussed in the text, an annuity due is identical to an ordinary annuity except that the periodic payments occur at the beginning of each period and not at the end of the period. Show that the relationship between the value of an ordinary annuity and the value of an otherwise equivalent annuity due is:

Annuity due value = Ordinary annuity value $\times (1 + r)$

Show this for both present and future values.

74. **Calculating Growing Annuities [LO1]** You have 40 years left until retirement and want to retire with $2 million. Your salary is paid annually, and you will receive $40,000 at the end of the current year. Your salary will increase at 3 percent per year, and you can earn an 11 percent return on the money you invest. If you save a constant percentage of your salary, what percentage of your salary must you save each year?

75. **Calculating EAR [LO4]** A check-cashing store is in the business of making personal loans to walk-up customers. The store makes only one-week loans at 7 percent interest per week.

 a. What APR must the store report to its customers? What EAR are customers actually paying?

 b. Now suppose the store makes one-week loans at 7 percent discount interest per week (see Problem 60). What's the APR now? The EAR?

 c. The check-cashing store also makes one-month add-on interest loans at 7 percent discount interest per week. Thus if you borrow $100 for one month (four weeks), the interest will be ($100 $\times$ 1.07^4) − 100 = $31.08. Because this is discount interest, your net loan proceeds today will be $68.92. You must then repay the store $100 at the end of the month. To help you out, though, the store lets you pay off this $100 in installments of $25 per week. What is the APR of this loan? What is the EAR?

76. **Present Value of a Growing Perpetuity [LO1]** What is the equation for the present value of a growing perpetuity with a payment of *C* one period from today if the payments grow by *C* each period?

77. **Rule of 72 [LO4]** Earlier, we discussed the Rule of 72, a useful approximation for many interest rates and periods for the time it takes a lump sum to double in value. For a 10 percent interest rate, show that the "Rule of 73" is slightly better. For what rate is the Rule of 72 exact? (*Hint:* Use the Solver function in Excel.)

78. **Rule of 69.3 [LO4]** A corollary to the Rule of 72 is the Rule of 69.3. The Rule of 69.3 is exactly correct except for rounding when interest rates are compounded continuously. Prove the Rule of 69.3 for continuously compounded interest.

The MBA Decision

Ben Bates graduated from college six years ago with a finance undergraduate degree. Although he is satisfied with his current job, his goal is to become an investment banker. He feels that an MBA degree would allow him to achieve this goal. After examining schools, he has narrowed his choice to either Wilton University or Mount Perry College. Although internships are encouraged by both schools, to get class credit for the internship, no salary can be paid. Other than internships, neither school will allow its students to work while enrolled in its MBA program.

Ben currently works at the money management firm of Dewey and Louis. His annual salary at the firm is $55,000 per year, and his salary is expected to increase at 3 percent per year until retirement. He is currently 28 years old and expects to work for 38 more years. His current job includes a fully paid health insurance plan, and his current average tax rate is 26 percent. Ben has a savings account with enough money to cover the entire cost of his MBA program.

The Ritter College of Business at Wilton University is one of the top MBA programs in the country. The MBA degree requires two years of full-time enrollment at the university. The annual tuition is $63,000, payable at the beginning of each school year. Books and other supplies are estimated to cost $2,500 per year. Ben expects that after graduation from Wilton, he will receive a job offer for about $98,000 per year, with a $15,000 signing bonus. The salary at this job will increase at 4 percent per year. Because of the higher salary, his average income tax rate will increase to 31 percent.

The Bradley School of Business at Mount Perry College began its MBA program 16 years ago. The Bradley School is smaller and less well known than the Ritter College. Bradley offers an accelerated one-year program, with a tuition cost of $80,000 to be paid upon matriculation. Books and other supplies for the program are expected to cost $3,500. Ben thinks that he will receive an offer of $81,000 per year upon graduation, with a $10,000 signing bonus. The salary at this job will increase at 3.5 percent per year. His average tax rate at this level of income will be 29 percent.

Both schools offer a health insurance plan that will cost $3,000 per year, payable at the beginning of the year. Ben also estimates that room and board expenses will cost $20,000 per year at both schools. The appropriate discount rate is 6.5 percent.

QUESTIONS

1. How does Ben's age affect his decision to get an MBA?

2. What other, perhaps nonquantifiable, factors affect Ben's decision to get an MBA?

3. Assuming all salaries are paid at the end of each year, what is the best option for Ben from a strictly financial standpoint?

4. Ben believes that the appropriate analysis is to calculate the future value of each option. How would you evaluate this statement?

5. What initial salary would Ben need to receive to make him indifferent between attending Wilton University and staying in his current position?

6. Suppose, instead of being able to pay cash for his MBA, Ben must borrow the money. The current borrowing rate is 5.4 percent. How would this affect his decision?

Visit us at www.mhhe.com/rwj

INTEREST RATES AND BOND VALUATION

LEARNING OBJECTIVES

After studying this chapter, you should understand:

LO1 Important bond features and types of bonds.

LO2 Bond values and yields and why they fluctuate.

LO3 Bond ratings and what they mean.

LO4 The impact of inflation on interest rates.

LO5 The term structure of interest rates and the determinants of bond yields.

PART 3 Valuation of Future Cash Flows

IN ITS MOST BASIC FORM, a bond is a pretty simple thing. You lend a company some money, say $1,000. The company pays you interest regularly, and it repays the original loan amount of $1,000 at some point in the future. But bonds also can have complex features, and in 2008, a type of bond known as *a mortgage-backed security,* or *MBS,* was causing havoc in the global financial system.

An MBS, as the name suggests, is a bond that is backed by a pool of home mortgages. The bondholders receive payments derived from payments on the underlying mortgages, and these payments can be divided up in various ways to create different classes of bonds. Defaults on the underlying mortgages lead to losses to MBS bondholders, particularly those in the riskier classes, and as the U.S. housing crunch hit in 2007–2008, defaults increased sharply. Losses to investors were still piling up in mid-2008, so the total damage wasn't known, but estimates ranged from $250 billion to $500 billion or more, colossal sums by any measure.

Master the ability to solve problems in this chapter by using a spreadsheet. Access Excel Master on the student Web site www.mhhe.com/rwj.

Our goal in this chapter is to introduce you to bonds. We begin by showing how the techniques we developed in Chapters 5 and 6 can be applied to bond valuation. From there, we go on to discuss bond features and how bonds are bought and sold. One important thing we learn is that bond values depend, in large part, on interest rates. We therefore close the chapter with an examination of interest rates and their behavior.

Bonds and Bond Valuation   7.1

When a corporation or government wishes to borrow money from the public on a long-term basis, it usually does so by issuing or selling debt securities that are generically called *bonds*. In this section, we describe the various features of corporate bonds and some of the terminology associated with bonds. We then discuss the cash flows associated with a bond and how bonds can be valued using our discounted cash flow procedure.

BOND FEATURES AND PRICES

As we mentioned in our previous chapter, a bond is normally an interest-only loan, meaning that the borrower will pay the interest every period, but none of the principal will be repaid until the end of the loan. For example, suppose the Beck Corporation wants to borrow $1,000 for 30 years. The interest rate on similar debt issued by similar corporations is 12 percent. Beck will thus pay .12 × $1,000 = $120 in interest every year for 30 years. At the end of 30 years, Beck will repay the $1,000. As this example suggests, a bond is a fairly simple financing arrangement. There is, however, a rich jargon associated with bonds, so we will use this example to define some of the more important terms.

In our example, the $120 regular interest payments that Beck promises to make are called the bond's **coupons**. Because the coupon is constant and paid every year, the type of bond we are describing is sometimes called a *level coupon bond*. The amount that will be repaid at the end of the loan is called the bond's **face value**, or **par value**. As in our example, this par value is usually $1,000 for corporate bonds, and a bond that sells for its par value is called a *par value bond*. Government bonds frequently have much larger face, or par, values. Finally, the annual coupon divided by the face value is called the **coupon rate** on the bond; in this case, because $120/1,000 = 12%, the bond has a 12 percent coupon rate.

The number of years until the face value is paid is called the bond's time to **maturity**. A corporate bond will frequently have a maturity of 30 years when it is originally issued, but this varies. Once the bond has been issued, the number of years to maturity declines as time goes by.

BOND VALUES AND YIELDS

As time passes, interest rates change in the marketplace. The cash flows from a bond, however, stay the same. As a result, the value of the bond will fluctuate. When interest rates rise, the present value of the bond's remaining cash flows declines, and the bond is worth less. When interest rates fall, the bond is worth more.

To determine the value of a bond at a particular point in time, we need to know the number of periods remaining until maturity, the face value, the coupon, and the market interest rate for bonds with similar features. This interest rate required in the market on a bond is called the bond's **yield to maturity (YTM)**. This rate is sometimes called the bond's *yield* for short. Given all this information, we can calculate the present value of the cash flows as an estimate of the bond's current market value.

For example, suppose the Xanth (pronounced "zanth") Co. were to issue a bond with 10 years to maturity. The Xanth bond has an annual coupon of $80. Similar bonds have a yield to maturity of 8 percent. Based on our preceding discussion, the Xanth bond will pay $80 per year for the next 10 years in coupon interest. In 10 years, Xanth will pay $1,000 to the owner of the bond. The cash flows from the bond are shown in Figure 7.1. What would this bond sell for?

As illustrated in Figure 7.1, the Xanth bond's cash flows have an annuity component (the coupons) and a lump sum (the face value paid at maturity). We thus estimate the

coupon
The stated interest payment made on a bond.

face value
The principal amount of a bond that is repaid at the end of the term. Also called *par value*.

coupon rate
The annual coupon divided by the face value of a bond.

maturity
The specified date on which the principal amount of a bond is paid.

yield to maturity (YTM)
The rate required in the market on a bond.

FIGURE 7.1   Cash Flows for Xanth Co. Bond

Cash flows

Year	0	1	2	3	4	5	6	7	8	9	10
Coupon		$80	$80	$80	$80	$80	$80	$80	$80	$80	$ 80
Face value											1,000
		$80	$80	$80	$80	$80	$80	$80	$80	$80	$1,080

As shown, the Xanth bond has an annual coupon of $80 and a face, or par, value of $1,000 paid at maturity in 10 years.

market value of the bond by calculating the present value of these two components separately and adding the results together. First, at the going rate of 8 percent, the present value of the $1,000 paid in 10 years is:

Present value $= \$1,000/1.08^{10} = \$1,000/2.1589 = \$463.19$

Second, the bond offers $80 per year for 10 years; the present value of this annuity stream is:

Annuity present value $= \$80 \times (1 - 1/1.08^{10})/.08$
$= \$80 \times (1 - 1/2.1589)/.08$
$= \$80 \times 6.7101$
$= \$536.81$

We can now add the values for the two parts together to get the bond's value:

Total bond value $= \$463.19 + 536.81 = \$1,000$

This bond sells for exactly its face value. This is not a coincidence. The going interest rate in the market is 8 percent. Considered as an interest-only loan, what interest rate does this bond have? With an $80 coupon, this bond pays exactly 8 percent interest only when it sells for $1,000.

To illustrate what happens as interest rates change, suppose a year has gone by. The Xanth bond now has nine years to maturity. If the interest rate in the market has risen to 10 percent, what will the bond be worth? To find out, we repeat the present value calculations with 9 years instead of 10, and a 10 percent yield instead of an 8 percent yield. First, the present value of the $1,000 paid in nine years at 10 percent is:

Present value $= \$1,000/1.10^9 = \$1,000/2.3579 = \$424.10$

Second, the bond now offers $80 per year for nine years; the present value of this annuity stream at 10 percent is:

Annuity present value $= \$80 \times (1 - 1/1.10^9)/.10$
$= \$80 \times (1 - 1/2.3579)/.10$
$= \$80 \times 5.7590$
$= \$460.72$

We can now add the values for the two parts together to get the bond's value:

Total bond value $= \$424.10 + 460.72 = \$884.82$

Therefore, the bond should sell for about $885. In the vernacular, we say that this bond, with its 8 percent coupon, is priced to yield 10 percent at $885.

The Xanth Co. bond now sells for less than its $1,000 face value. Why? The market interest rate is 10 percent. Considered as an interest-only loan of $1,000, this bond pays only 8 percent, its coupon rate. Because this bond pays less than the going rate, investors are willing to lend only something less than the $1,000 promised repayment. Because the bond sells for less than face value, it is said to be a *discount bond*.

A good bond site to visit is bonds.yahoo. com, *which has loads of useful information.*

The only way to get the interest rate up to 10 percent is to lower the price to less than $1,000 so that the purchaser, in effect, has a built-in gain. For the Xanth bond, the price of $885 is $115 less than the face value, so an investor who purchased and kept the bond would get $80 per year and would have a $115 gain at maturity as well. This gain compensates the lender for the below-market coupon rate.

Another way to see why the bond is discounted by $115 is to note that the $80 coupon is $20 below the coupon on a newly issued par value bond, based on current market conditions. The bond would be worth $1,000 only if it had a coupon of $100 per year. In a sense, an investor who buys and keeps the bond gives up $20 per year for nine years. At 10 percent, this annuity stream is worth:

$$\text{Annuity present value} = \$20 \times (1 - 1/1.10^9)/.10$$
$$= \$20 \times 5.7590$$
$$= \$115.18$$

This is just the amount of the discount.

What would the Xanth bond sell for if interest rates had dropped by 2 percent instead of rising by 2 percent? As you might guess, the bond would sell for more than $1,000. Such a bond is said to sell at a *premium* and is called a *premium bond*.

Online bond calculators are available at personal.fidelity.com; *interest rate information is available at* money.cnn.com/markets/ bondcenter *and* www.bankrate.com.

This case is just the opposite of that of a discount bond. The Xanth bond now has a coupon rate of 8 percent when the market rate is only 6 percent. Investors are willing to pay a premium to get this extra coupon amount. In this case, the relevant discount rate is 6 percent, and there are nine years remaining. The present value of the $1,000 face amount is:

$$\text{Present value} = \$1,000/1.06^9 = \$1,000/1.6895 = \$591.89$$

The present value of the coupon stream is:

$$\text{Annuity present value} = \$80 \times (1 - 1/1.06^9)/.06$$
$$= \$80 \times (1 - 1/1.6895)/.06$$
$$= \$80 \times 6.8017$$
$$= \$544.14$$

We can now add the values for the two parts together to get the bond's value:

$$\text{Total bond value} = \$591.89 + 544.14 = \$1,136.03$$

Total bond value is therefore about $136 in excess of par value. Once again, we can verify this amount by noting that the coupon is now $20 too high, based on current market conditions. The present value of $20 per year for nine years at 6 percent is:

$$\text{Annuity present value} = \$20 \times (1 - 1/1.06^9)/.06$$
$$= \$20 \times 6.8017$$
$$= \$136.03$$

This is just as we calculated.

Based on our examples, we can now write the general expression for the value of a bond. If a bond has (1) a face value of F paid at maturity, (2) a coupon of C paid per period, (3) t periods to maturity, and (4) a yield of r per period, its value is:

$$\text{Bond value} = C \times [1 - 1/(1 + r)^t]/r \;+\; F/(1 + r)^t$$

$$\text{Bond value} = \begin{array}{c}\text{Present value}\\ \text{of the coupons}\end{array} + \begin{array}{c}\text{Present value}\\ \text{of the face amount}\end{array}$$

[7.1]

EXAMPLE 7.1   **Semiannual Coupons**

In practice, bonds issued in the United States usually make coupon payments twice a year. So, if an ordinary bond has a coupon rate of 14 percent, then the owner will get a total of $140 per year, but this $140 will come in two payments of $70 each. Suppose we are examining such a bond. The yield to maturity is quoted at 16 percent.

Bond yields are quoted like APRs; the quoted rate is equal to the actual rate per period multiplied by the number of periods. In this case, with a 16 percent quoted yield and semi-annual payments, the true yield is 8 percent per six months. The bond matures in seven years. What is the bond's price? What is the effective annual yield on this bond?

Based on our discussion, we know the bond will sell at a discount because it has a coupon rate of 7 percent every six months when the market requires 8 percent every six months. So, if our answer exceeds $1,000, we know we have made a mistake.

To get the exact price, we first calculate the present value of the bond's face value of $1,000 paid in seven years. This seven-year period has 14 periods of six months each. At 8 percent per period, the value is:

$$\text{Present value} = \$1,000/1.08^{14} = \$1,000/2.9372 = \$340.46$$

The coupons can be viewed as a 14-period annuity of $70 per period. At an 8 percent discount rate, the present value of such an annuity is:

$$
\begin{aligned}
\text{Annuity present value} &= \$70 \times (1 - 1/1.08^{14})/.08\\
&= \$70 \times (1 - .3405)/.08\\
&= \$70 \times 8.2442\\
&= \$577.10
\end{aligned}
$$

The total present value gives us what the bond should sell for:

$$\text{Total present value} = \$340.46 + 577.10 = \$917.56$$

To calculate the effective yield on this bond, note that 8 percent every six months is equivalent to:

$$\text{Effective annual rate} = (1 + .08)^2 - 1 = 16.64\%$$

The effective yield, therefore, is 16.64 percent.

Visit investorguide.com *to learn more about bonds.*

As we have illustrated in this section, bond prices and interest rates always move in opposite directions. When interest rates rise, a bond's value, like any other present value, will decline. Similarly, when interest rates fall, bond values rise. Even if we are considering a bond that is riskless in the sense that the borrower is certain to make all the payments, there is still risk in owning a bond. We discuss this next.

INTEREST RATE RISK

The risk that arises for bond owners from fluctuating interest rates is called *interest rate risk*. How much interest rate risk a bond has depends on how sensitive its price is to interest rate changes. This sensitivity directly depends on two things: the time to maturity and the coupon rate. As we will see momentarily, you should keep the following in mind when looking at a bond:

1. All other things being equal, the longer the time to maturity, the greater the interest rate risk.

2. All other things being equal, the lower the coupon rate, the greater the interest rate risk.

We illustrate the first of these two points in Figure 7.2. As shown, we compute and plot prices under different interest rate scenarios for 10 percent coupon bonds with maturities of 1 year and 30 years. Notice how the slope of the line connecting the prices is much steeper for the 30-year maturity than it is for the 1-year maturity. This steepness tells us that a relatively small change in interest rates will lead to a substantial change in the bond's value. In comparison, the one-year bond's price is relatively insensitive to interest rate changes.

Intuitively, we can see that longer-term bonds have greater interest rate sensitivity because a large portion of a bond's value comes from the $1,000 face amount. The present value of this amount isn't greatly affected by a small change in interest rates if the amount is to be received in one year. Even a small change in the interest rate, however, once it is

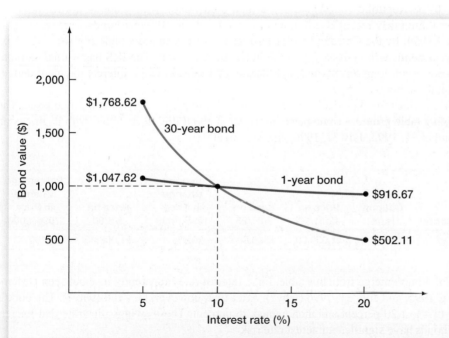

FIGURE 7.2

Interest Rate Risk and Time to Maturity

Value of a Bond with a 10 Percent Coupon Rate for Different Interest Rates and Maturities

	Time to Maturity	
Interest Rate	1 Year	30 Years
5%	$1,047.62	$1,768.62
10	1,000.00	1,000.00
15	956.52	671.70
20	916.67	502.11

compounded for 30 years, can have a significant effect on the present value. As a result, the present value of the face amount will be much more volatile with a longer-term bond.

The other thing to know about interest rate risk is that, like most things in finance and economics, it increases at a decreasing rate. In other words, if we compared a 10-year bond to a 1-year bond, we would see that the 10-year bond has much greater interest rate risk. However, if you were to compare a 20-year bond to a 30-year bond, you would find that the 30-year bond has somewhat greater interest rate risk because it has a longer maturity, but the difference in the risk would be fairly small.

The reason that bonds with lower coupons have greater interest rate risk is essentially the same. As we discussed earlier, the value of a bond depends on the present value of its coupons and the present value of the face amount. If two bonds with different coupon rates have the same maturity, then the value of the one with the lower coupon is proportionately more dependent on the face amount to be received at maturity. As a result, all other things being equal, its value will fluctuate more as interest rates change. Put another way, the bond with the higher coupon has a larger cash flow early in its life, so its value is less sensitive to changes in the discount rate.

Bonds are rarely issued with maturities longer than 30 years. However, low interest rates in recent years have led to the issuance of much longer-term issues. In the 1990s, Walt Disney issued "Sleeping Beauty" bonds with a 100-year maturity. Similarly, BellSouth (now known as AT&T), Coca-Cola, and Dutch banking giant ABN AMRO all issued bonds with 100-year maturities. These companies evidently wanted to lock in the historical low interest rates for a *long* time. The current record holder for corporations looks to be Republic National Bank, which sold bonds with 1,000 years to maturity. Before these fairly recent issues, it appears the last time 100-year bonds were issued was in May 1954, by the Chicago and Eastern Railroad. If you are wondering when the next 100-year bonds will be issued, you might have a long wait. The IRS has warned companies about such long-term issues and threatened to disallow the interest payment deduction on these bonds.

We can illustrate the effect of interest rate risk using the 100-year BellSouth issue. The following table provides some basic information about this issue, along with its prices on December 31, 1995, July 31, 1996, and May 6, 2008:

Maturity	Coupon Rate	Price on 12/31/95	Price on 7/31/96	Percentage Change in Price 1995–1996	Price on 5/6/08	Percentage Change in Price 1996–2008
2095	7.00%	$1,000.00	$800.00	−20.0%	$1,008.40	+26 %

Several things emerge from this table. First, interest rates apparently rose between December 31, 1995, and July 31, 1996 (why?). After that, however, they fell (why?). The bond's price first lost 20 percent and then gained 26 percent. These swings illustrate that longer-term bonds have significant interest rate risk.

FINDING THE YIELD TO MATURITY: MORE TRIAL AND ERROR

Frequently, we will know a bond's price, coupon rate, and maturity date, but not its yield to maturity. For example, suppose we are interested in a six-year, 8 percent coupon bond. A broker quotes a price of $955.14. What is the yield on this bond?

We've seen that the price of a bond can be written as the sum of its annuity and lump sum components. Knowing that there is an $80 coupon for six years and a $1,000 face value, we can say that the price is:

$$\$955.14 = \$80 \times [1 - 1/(1 + r)^6]/r + 1{,}000/(1 + r)^6$$

where r is the unknown discount rate, or yield to maturity. We have one equation here and one unknown, but we cannot solve it for r explicitly. The only way to find the answer is to use trial and error.

This problem is essentially identical to the one we examined in the last chapter when we tried to find the unknown interest rate on an annuity. However, finding the rate (or yield) on a bond is even more complicated because of the $1,000 face amount.

We can speed up the trial-and-error process by using what we know about bond prices and yields. In this case, the bond has an $80 coupon and is selling at a discount. We thus know that the yield is greater than 8 percent. If we compute the price at 10 percent:

$$\text{Bond value} = \$80 \times (1 - 1/1.10^6)/.10 + 1{,}000/1.10^6$$
$$= \$80 \times 4.3553 + 1{,}000/1.7716$$
$$= \$912.89$$

At 10 percent, the value we calculate is lower than the actual price, so 10 percent is too high. The true yield must be somewhere between 8 and 10 percent. At this point, it's "plug and chug" to find the answer. You would probably want to try 9 percent next. If you did, you would see that this is in fact the bond's yield to maturity.

A bond's yield to maturity should not be confused with its **current yield**, which is simply a bond's annual coupon divided by its price. In the example we just worked, the bond's annual coupon was $80, and its price was $955.14. Given these numbers, we see that the current yield is $80/955.14 = 8.38$ percent, which is less than the yield to maturity of 9 percent. The reason the current yield is too low is that it considers only the coupon portion of your return; it doesn't consider the built-in gain from the price discount. For a premium bond, the reverse is true, meaning that current yield would be higher because it ignores the built-in loss.

Our discussion of bond valuation is summarized in Table 7.1.

Current market rates are available at www.bankrate.com.

current yield
A bond's annual coupon divided by its price.

I.	**Finding the Value of a Bond**
	Bond value = $C \times [1 - 1/(1 + r)^t]/r + F/(1 + r)^t$
	where
	$\quad C$ = Coupon paid each period
	$\quad r$ = Rate per period
	$\quad t$ = Number of periods
	$\quad F$ = Bond's face value
II.	**Finding the Yield on a Bond**
	Given a bond value, coupon, time to maturity, and face value, it is possible to find the implicit discount rate, or yield to maturity, by trial and error only. To do this, try different discount rates until the calculated bond value equals the given value (or let a financial calculator do it for you). Remember that increasing the rate *decreases* the bond value.

TABLE 7.1

Summary of Bond Valuation

| **EXAMPLE 7.2** | **Current Events** |

A bond has a quoted price of $1,080.42. It has a face value of $1,000, a semiannual coupon of $30, and a maturity of five years. What is its current yield? What is its yield to maturity? Which is bigger? Why?

Notice that this bond makes semiannual payments of $30, so the annual payment is $60. The current yield is thus $60/1,080.42 = 5.55 percent. To calculate the yield to maturity, refer back to Example 7.1. In this case, the bond pays $30 every six months and has 10 six-month periods until maturity. So, we need to find r as follows:

$$\$1,080.42 = \$30 \times [1 - 1/(1 + r)^{10}]/r + 1,000/(1 + r)^{10}$$

After some trial and error, we find that r is equal to 2.1 percent. But, the tricky part is that this 2.1 percent is the yield *per six months*. We have to double it to get the yield to maturity, so the yield to maturity is 4.2 percent, which is less than the current yield. The reason is that the current yield ignores the built-in loss of the premium between now and maturity.

| **EXAMPLE 7.3** | **Bond Yields** |

You're looking at two bonds identical in every way except for their coupons and, of course, their prices. Both have 12 years to maturity. The first bond has a 10 percent annual coupon rate and sells for $935.08. The second has a 12 percent annual coupon rate. What do you think it would sell for?

Because the two bonds are similar, they will be priced to yield about the same rate. We first need to calculate the yield on the 10 percent coupon bond. Proceeding as before, we know that the yield must be greater than 10 percent because the bond is selling at a discount. The bond has a fairly long maturity of 12 years. We've seen that long-term bond prices are relatively sensitive to interest rate changes, so the yield is probably close to 10 percent. A little trial and error reveals that the yield is actually 11 percent:

Bond value = $100 × (1 − 1/1.11^{12})/.11 + 1,000/1.11^{12}
= $100 × 6.4924 + 1,000/3.4985
= $649.24 + 285.84
= $935.08

With an 11 percent yield, the second bond will sell at a premium because of its $120 coupon. Its value is:

Bond value = $120 × (1 − 1/1.11^{12})/.11 + 1,000/1.11^{12}
= $120 × 6.4924 + 1,000/3.4985
= $779.08 + 285.84
= $1,064.92

CALCULATOR HINTS

How to Calculate Bond Prices and Yields Using a Financial Calculator

Many financial calculators have fairly sophisticated built-in bond valuation routines. However, these vary quite a lot in implementation, and not all financial calculators have them. As a result, we will illustrate a simple way to handle bond problems that will work on just about any financial calculator.

(continued)

To begin, of course, we first remember to clear out the calculator! Next, for Example 7.3, we have two bonds to consider, both with 12 years to maturity. The first one sells for $935.08 and has a 10 percent annual coupon rate. To find its yield, we can do the following:

Enter	12		100	−935.08	1,000
	N	**I/Y**	**PMT**	**PV**	**FV**
Solve for		11			

Notice that here we have entered both a future value of $1,000, representing the bond's face value, and a payment of 10 percent of $1,000, or $100, per year, representing the bond's annual coupon. Also, notice that we have a negative sign on the bond's price, which we have entered as the present value.

For the second bond, we now know that the relevant yield is 11 percent. It has a 12 percent annual coupon and 12 years to maturity, so what's the price? To answer, we just enter the relevant values and solve for the present value of the bond's cash flows:

Enter	12	11	120		1,000
	N	**I/Y**	**PMT**	**PV**	**FV**
Solve for				−1,064.92	

There is an important detail that comes up here. Suppose we have a bond with a price of $902.29, 10 years to maturity, and a coupon rate of 6 percent. As we mentioned earlier, most bonds actually make semiannual payments. Assuming that this is the case for the bond here, what's the bond's yield? To answer, we need to enter the relevant numbers like this:

Enter	20		30	−902.29	1,000
	N	**I/Y**	**PMT**	**PV**	**FV**
Solve for		3.7			

Notice that we entered $30 as the payment because the bond actually makes payments of $30 every six months. Similarly, we entered 20 for N because there are actually 20 six-month periods. When we solve for the yield, we get 3.7 percent. The tricky thing to remember is that this is the yield *per six months,* so we have to double it to get the right answer: $2 \times 3.7 = 7.4$ percent, which would be the bond's reported yield.

SPREADSHEET STRATEGIES

How to Calculate Bond Prices and Yields Using a Spreadsheet

Most spreadsheets have fairly elaborate routines available for calculating bond values and yields; many of these routines involve details we have not discussed. However, setting up a simple spreadsheet to calculate prices or

(continued)

yields is straightforward, as our next two spreadsheets show:

	A	B	C	D	E	F	G	H
1								
2	**Using a spreadsheet to calculate bond values**							
3								
4	Suppose we have a bond with 22 years to maturity, a coupon rate of 8 percent, and a yield to							
5	maturity of 9 percent. If the bond makes semiannual payments, what is its price today?							
6								
7	Settlement date:	1/1/00						
8	Maturity date:	1/1/22						
9	Annual coupon rate:	.08						
10	Yield to maturity:	.09						
11	Face value (% of par):	100						
12	Coupons per year:	2						
13	Bond price (% of par):	**90.49**						
14								
15	The formula entered in cell B13 is =PRICE(B7,B8,B9,B10,B11,B12); notice that face value and bond							
16	price are given as a percentage of face value.							

	A	B	C	D	E	F	G	H
1								
2	**Using a spreadsheet to calculate bond yields**							
3								
4	Suppose we have a bond with 22 years to maturity, a coupon rate of 8 percent, and a price of							
5	$960.17. If the bond makes semiannual payments, what is its yield to maturity?							
6								
7	Settlement date:	1/1/00						
8	Maturity date:	1/1/22						
9	Annual coupon rate:	.08						
10	Bond price (% of par):	96.017						
11	Face value (% of par):	100						
12	Coupons per year:	2						
13	Yield to maturity:	**.084**						
14								
15	The formula entered in cell B13 is =YIELD(B7,B8,B9,B10,B11,B12); notice that face value and bond							
16	price are entered as a percentage of face value.							
17								

In our spreadsheets, notice that we had to enter two dates: a settlement date and a maturity date. The settlement date is just the date you actually pay for the bond, and the maturity date is the day the bond actually matures. In most of our problems, we don't explicitly have these dates, so we have to make them up. For example, because our bond has 22 years to maturity, we just picked 1/1/2000 (January 1, 2000) as the settlement date and 1/1/2022 (January 1, 2022) as the maturity date. Any two dates would do as long as they are exactly 22 years apart, but these are particularly easy to work with. Finally, notice that we had to enter the coupon rate and yield to maturity in annual terms and then explicitly provide the number of coupon payments per year.

Concept Questions

7.1a What are the cash flows associated with a bond?

7.1b What is the general expression for the value of a bond?

7.1c Is it true that the only risk associated with owning a bond is that the issuer will not make all the payments? Explain.

More about Bond Features   **7.2**

In this section, we continue our discussion of corporate debt by describing in some detail the basic terms and features that make up a typical long-term corporate bond. We discuss additional issues associated with long-term debt in subsequent sections.

Securities issued by corporations may be classified roughly as *equity securities* and *debt securities*. At the crudest level, a debt represents something that must be repaid; it is the result of borrowing money. When corporations borrow, they generally promise to make regularly scheduled interest payments and to repay the original amount borrowed (that is, the principal). The person or firm making the loan is called the *creditor* or *lender*. The corporation borrowing the money is called the *debtor* or *borrower*.

From a financial point of view, the main differences between debt and equity are the following:

1. Debt is not an ownership interest in the firm. Creditors generally do not have voting power.
2. The corporation's payment of interest on debt is considered a cost of doing business and is fully tax deductible. Dividends paid to stockholders are *not* tax deductible.
3. Unpaid debt is a liability of the firm. If it is not paid, the creditors can legally claim the assets of the firm. This action can result in liquidation or reorganization, two of the possible consequences of bankruptcy. Thus, one of the costs of issuing debt is the possibility of financial failure. This possibility does not arise when equity is issued.

Information on bond investing can be found at www.investinginbonds.com.

IS IT DEBT OR EQUITY?

Sometimes it is not clear if a particular security is debt or equity. For example, suppose a corporation issues a perpetual bond with interest payable solely from corporate income if and only if earned. Whether this is really a debt is hard to say and is primarily a legal and semantic issue. Courts and taxing authorities would have the final say.

Corporations are adept at creating exotic, hybrid securities that have many features of equity but are treated as debt. Obviously, the distinction between debt and equity is important for tax purposes. So, one reason that corporations try to create a debt security that is really equity is to obtain the tax benefits of debt and the bankruptcy benefits of equity.

As a general rule, equity represents an ownership interest, and it is a residual claim. This means that equity holders are paid after debt holders. As a result of this, the risks and benefits associated with owning debt and equity are different. To give just one example, note that the maximum reward for owning a debt security is ultimately fixed by the amount of the loan, whereas there is no upper limit to the potential reward from owning an equity interest.

LONG-TERM DEBT: THE BASICS

Ultimately, all long-term debt securities are promises made by the issuing firm to pay principal when due and to make timely interest payments on the unpaid balance. Beyond this, a number of features distinguish these securities from one another. We discuss some of these features next.

The maturity of a long-term debt instrument is the length of time the debt remains out-standing with some unpaid balance. Debt securities can be *short-term* (with maturities of one year or less) or *long-term* (with maturities of more than one year).[1] Short-term debt is sometimes referred to as *unfunded debt.*[2]

Debt securities are typically called *notes, debentures,* or *bonds.* Strictly speaking, a bond is a secured debt. However, in common usage, the word *bond* refers to all kinds of secured and unsecured debt. We will therefore continue to use the term generically to refer to long-term debt. Also, usually the only difference between a note and a bond is the origi-nal maturity. Issues with an original maturity of 10 years or less are often called notes. Longer-term issues are called bonds.

The two major forms of long-term debt are public issue and privately placed. We con-centrate on public-issue bonds. Most of what we say about them holds true for private-issue, long-term debt as well. The main difference between public-issue and privately placed debt is that the latter is directly placed with a lender and not offered to the public. Because this is a private transaction, the specific terms are up to the parties involved.

There are many other dimensions to long-term debt, including such things as security, call features, sinking funds, ratings, and protective covenants. The following table illus-trates these features for a bond issued by drug maker Bristol-Myers Squibb. If some of these terms are unfamiliar, have no fear. We will discuss them all presently.

Information about individual bonds can be found at www.finra.org/marketdata and www.bondresources.com.

Features of a Bristol-Myers Squibb Bond		
Term		**Explanation**
Amount of issue	$1 billion	The company issued $1 billion worth of bonds.
Date of issue	05/01/2008	The bonds were sold on 05/01/2008.
Maturity	05/01/2038	The bonds mature on 05/01/2038.
Face value	$1,000	The denomination of the bonds is $1,000.
Annual coupon	6.125	Each bondholder will receive $61.25 per bond per year (6.125% of face value).
Offer price	99.375	The offer price will be 99.375% of the $1,000 face value, or $993.75, per bond.
Coupon payment dates	5/01, 11/01	Coupons of $61.25/2 = $30.625 will be paid on these dates.
Security	None	The bonds are not secured by specific assets.
Sinking fund	None	The bonds have no sinking fund.
Call provision	At any time	The bonds do not have a deferred call.
Call price	Treasury rate plus .30%	The bonds have a "make whole" call price.
Rating	Moody's A2 S&P A	The bonds have a relatively high credit rating (but not the best possible rating).

Many of these features will be detailed in the bond indenture, so we discuss this first.

---

[1] There is no universally agreed-upon distinction between short-term and long-term debt. In addition, people often refer to *intermediate-term debt,* which has a maturity of more than 1 year and less than 3 to 5, or even 10, years.

[2] The word *funding* is part of the jargon of finance. It generally refers to the long term. Thus, a firm planning to "fund" its debt requirements may be replacing short-term debt with long-term debt.

THE INDENTURE

The **indenture** is the written agreement between the corporation (the borrower) and its creditors. It is sometimes referred to as the *deed of trust*.[3] Usually, a trustee (a bank, perhaps) is appointed by the corporation to represent the bondholders. The trust company must (1) make sure the terms of the indenture are obeyed, (2) manage the sinking fund (described in the following pages), and (3) represent the bondholders in default—that is, if the company defaults on its payments to them.

The bond indenture is a legal document. It can run several hundred pages and generally makes for tedious reading. It is an important document, however, because it generally includes the following provisions:

1. The basic terms of the bonds.
2. The total amount of bonds issued.
3. A description of property used as security.
4. The repayment arrangements.
5. The call provisions.
6. Details of the protective covenants.

We discuss these features next.

Terms of a Bond   Corporate bonds usually have a face value (that is, a denomination) of $1,000. This *principal value* is stated on the bond certificate. So, if a corporation wanted to borrow $1 million, 1,000 bonds would have to be sold. The par value (that is, initial accounting value) of a bond is almost always the same as the face value, and the terms are used interchangeably in practice.

Corporate bonds are usually in **registered form**. For example, the indenture might read as follows:

> **Interest is payable semiannually on July 1 and January 1 of each year to the person in whose name the bond is registered at the close of business on June 15 or December 15, respectively.**

This means that the company has a registrar who will record the ownership of each bond and record any changes in ownership. The company will pay the interest and principal by check mailed directly to the address of the owner of record. A corporate bond may be registered and have attached "coupons." To obtain an interest payment, the owner must separate a coupon from the bond certificate and send it to the company registrar (the paying agent).

Alternatively, the bond could be in **bearer form**. This means that the certificate is the basic evidence of ownership, and the corporation will "pay the bearer." Ownership is not otherwise recorded, and, as with a registered bond with attached coupons, the holder of the bond certificate detaches the coupons and sends them to the company to receive payment.

There are two drawbacks to bearer bonds. First, they are difficult to recover if they are lost or stolen. Second, because the company does not know who owns its bonds, it cannot notify bondholders of important events. Bearer bonds were once the dominant type, but they are now much less common (in the United States) than registered bonds.

indenture
The written agreement between the corporation and the lender detailing the terms of the debt issue.

registered form
The form of bond issue in which the registrar of the company records ownership of each bond; payment is made directly to the owner of record.

bearer form
The form of bond issue in which the bond is issued without record of the owner's name; payment is made to whomever holds the bond.

---

[3] The words *loan agreement* or *loan contract* are usually used for privately placed debt and term loans.

Security   Debt securities are classified according to the collateral and mortgages used to protect the bondholder.

Collateral is a general term that frequently means securities (for example, bonds and stocks) that are pledged as security for payment of debt. For example, collateral trust bonds often involve a pledge of common stock held by the corporation. However, the term *collateral* is commonly used to refer to any asset pledged on a debt.

Mortgage securities are secured by a mortgage on the real property of the borrower. The property involved is usually real estate—for example, land or buildings. The legal document that describes the mortgage is called a *mortgage trust indenture* or *trust deed.*

Sometimes mortgages are on specific property, such as a railroad car. More often, blanket mortgages are used. A *blanket mortgage* pledges all the real property owned by the company.[4]

Bonds frequently represent unsecured obligations of the company. A **debenture** is an unsecured bond, for which no specific pledge of property is made. The term **note** is generally used for such instruments if the maturity of the unsecured bond is less than 10 or so years when the bond is originally issued. Debenture holders have a claim only on property not otherwise pledged—in other words, the property that remains after mortgages and collateral trusts are taken into account. The Bristol-Myers Squibb bonds in the table are an example of such an issue.

The terminology that we use here and elsewhere in this chapter is standard in the United States. Outside the United States, these same terms can have different meanings. For example, bonds issued by the British government ("gilts") are called treasury "stock." Also, in the United Kingdom, a debenture is a *secured* obligation.

At the current time, public bonds issued in the United States by industrial and financial companies are typically debentures. However, most utility and railroad bonds are secured by a pledge of assets.

Seniority   In general terms, *seniority* indicates preference in position over other lenders, and debts are sometimes labeled as *senior* or *junior* to indicate seniority. Some debt is *subordinated,* as in, for example, a subordinated debenture.

In the event of default, holders of subordinated debt must give preference to other specified creditors. Usually, this means that the subordinated lenders will be paid off only after the specified creditors have been compensated. However, debt cannot be subordinated to equity.

Repayment   Bonds can be repaid at maturity, at which time the bondholder will receive the stated, or face, value of the bond; or they may be repaid in part or in entirety before maturity. Early repayment in some form is more typical and is often handled through a sinking fund.

A **sinking fund** is an account managed by the bond trustee for the purpose of repaying the bonds. The company makes annual payments to the trustee, who then uses the funds to retire a portion of the debt. The trustee does this by either buying up some of the bonds in the market or calling in a fraction of the outstanding bonds. This second option is discussed in the next section.

There are many different kinds of sinking fund arrangements, and the details would be spelled out in the indenture. For example:

1. Some sinking funds start about 10 years after the initial issuance.
2. Some sinking funds establish equal payments over the life of the bond.

debenture
An unsecured debt, usually with a maturity of 10 years or more.

note
An unsecured debt, usually with a maturity under 10 years.

The Securities Industry and Financial Markets Association (SIFMA) Web site is www.sifma.org.

sinking fund
An account managed by the bond trustee for early bond redemption.

---

[4]Real property includes land and things "affixed thereto." It does not include cash or inventories.

3. Some high-quality bond issues establish payments to the sinking fund that are not sufficient to redeem the entire issue. As a consequence, there is the possibility of a large "balloon payment" at maturity.

The Call Provision   A **call provision** allows the company to repurchase or "call" part or all of the bond issue at stated prices over a specific period. Corporate bonds are usually callable.

Generally, the call price is above the bond's stated value (that is, the par value). The difference between the call price and the stated value is the **call premium**. The amount of the call premium may become smaller over time. One arrangement is to initially set the call premium equal to the annual coupon payment and then make it decline to zero as the call date moves closer to the time of maturity.

Call provisions are often not operative during the first part of a bond's life. This makes the call provision less of a worry for bondholders in the bond's early years. For example, a company might be prohibited from calling its bonds for the first 10 years. This is a **deferred call provision**. During this period of prohibition, the bond is said to be **call protected**.

In recent few years, a new type of call provision, a "make-whole" call, has become widespread in the corporate bond market. With such a feature, bondholders receive approximately what the bonds are worth if they are called. Because bondholders don't suffer a loss in the event of a call, they are "made whole."

To determine the make-whole call price, we calculate the present value of the remaining interest and principal payments at a rate specified in the indenture. For example, looking at our Bristol-Myers Squibb issue, we see that the discount rate is "Treasury rate plus .30%." What this means is that we determine the discount rate by first finding a U.S. Treasury issue with the same maturity. We calculate the yield to maturity on the Treasury issue and then add on .30 percent to get the discount rate we use.

Notice that with a make-whole call provision, the call price is higher when interest rates are lower and vice versa (why?). Also notice that, as is common with a make-whole call, the Bristol-Myers Squibb issue does not have a deferred call feature. Why might investors not be too concerned about the absence of this feature?

Protective Covenants   A **protective covenant** is that part of the indenture or loan agreement that limits certain actions a company might otherwise wish to take during the term of the loan. Protective covenants can be classified into two types: negative covenants and positive (or affirmative) covenants.

A *negative covenant* is a "thou shalt not" type of covenant. It limits or prohibits actions the company might take. Here are some typical examples:

1. The firm must limit the amount of dividends it pays according to some formula.
2. The firm cannot pledge any assets to other lenders.
3. The firm cannot merge with another firm.
4. The firm cannot sell or lease any major assets without approval by the lender.
5. The firm cannot issue additional long-term debt.

A *positive covenant* is a "thou shalt" type of covenant. It specifies an action the company agrees to take or a condition the company must abide by. Here are some examples:

1. The company must maintain its working capital at or above some specified minimum level.
2. The company must periodically furnish audited financial statements to the lender.
3. The firm must maintain any collateral or security in good condition.

call provision
An agreement giving the corporation the option to repurchase a bond at a specified price prior to maturity.

call premium
The amount by which the call price exceeds the par value of a bond.

deferred call provision
A call provision prohibiting the company from redeeming a bond prior to a certain date.

call-protected bond
A bond that, during a certain period, cannot be redeemed by the issuer.

protective covenant
A part of the indenture limiting certain actions that might be taken during the term of the loan, usually to protect the lender's interest.

 Want detailed information about the amount and terms of the debt issued by a particular firm? Check out its latest financial statements by searching SEC filings at www.sec.gov.

This is only a partial list of covenants; a particular indenture may feature many different ones.

Concept Questions

7.2a What are the distinguishing features of debt compared to equity?

7.2b What is the indenture? What are protective covenants? Give some examples.

7.2c What is a sinking fund?

7.3 Bond Ratings

Firms frequently pay to have their debt rated. The two leading bond-rating firms are Moody's and Standard & Poor's (S&P). The debt ratings are an assessment of the creditworthiness of the corporate issuer. The definitions of creditworthiness used by Moody's and S&P are based on how likely the firm is to default and the protection creditors have in the event of a default.

It is important to recognize that bond ratings are concerned *only* with the possibility of default. Earlier, we discussed interest rate risk, which we defined as the risk of a change in the value of a bond resulting from a change in interest rates. Bond ratings do not address this issue. As a result, the price of a highly rated bond can still be quite volatile.

Bond ratings are constructed from information supplied by the corporation. The rating classes and some information concerning them are shown in the following table:

	Investment-Quality Bond Ratings				Low-Quality, Speculative, and/or "Junk" Bond Ratings					
	High Grade		Medium Grade		Low Grade		Very Low Grade			
Standard & Poor's	AAA	AA	A	BBB	BB	B	CCC	CC	C	D
Moody's	Aaa	Aa	A	Baa	Ba	B	Caa	Ca	C	

Moody's	S&P	
Aaa	AAA	Debt rated Aaa and AAA has the highest rating. Capacity to pay interest and principal is extremely strong.
Aa	AA	Debt rated Aa and AA has a very strong capacity to pay interest and repay principal. Together with the highest rating, this group comprises the high-grade bond class.
A	A	Debt rated A has a strong capacity to pay interest and repay principal, although it is somewhat more susceptible to the adverse effects of changes in circumstances and economic conditions than debt in high-rated categories.
Baa	BBB	Debt rated Baa and BBB is regarded as having an adequate capacity to pay interest and repay principal. Whereas it normally exhibits adequate protection parameters, adverse economic conditions or changing circumstances are more likely to lead to a weakened capacity to pay interest and repay principal for debt in this category than in higher-rated categories. These bonds are medium-grade obligations.
Ba; B Caa Ca C	BB; B CCC CC C	Debt rated in these categories is regarded, on balance, as predominantly speculative with respect to capacity to pay interest and repay principal in accordance with the terms of the obligation. BB and Ba indicate the lowest degree of speculation, and Ca, CC, and C the highest degree of speculation. Although such debt is likely to have some quality and protective characteristics, these are outweighed by large uncertainties or major risk exposures to adverse conditions. Issues rated C by Moody's are typically in default.
	D	Debt rated D is in default, and payment of interest and/or repayment of principal is in arrears.

Note: At times, both Moody's and S&P use adjustments (called notches) to these ratings. S&P uses plus and minus signs: A+ is the strongest A rating and A− the weakest. Moody's uses a 1, 2, or 3 designation, with 1 being the highest.

The highest rating a firm's debt can have is AAA or Aaa, and such debt is judged to be the best quality and to have the lowest degree of risk. For example, the 100-year BellSouth issue we discussed earlier was rated AAA. This rating is not awarded very often: As of 2008, only six nonfinancial U.S. companies had AAA ratings. AA or Aa ratings indicate very good quality debt and are much more common.

Want to know what criteria are commonly used to rate corporate and municipal bonds? Go to www.standardandpoors.com, www.moodys.com, or www.fitchinv.com.

A large part of corporate borrowing takes the form of low-grade, or "junk," bonds. If these low-grade corporate bonds are rated at all, they are rated below investment grade by the major rating agencies. Investment-grade bonds are bonds rated at least BBB by S&P or Baa by Moody's.

Rating agencies don't always agree. To illustrate, some bonds are known as "crossover" or "5B" bonds. The reason is that they are rated triple-B (or Baa) by one rating agency and double-B (or Ba) by another, a "split rating." For example, in April 2008, Centerpoint Energy sold an issue of 10-year notes rated BBB− by S&P and Ba1 by Moody's.

A bond's credit rating can change as the issuer's financial strength improves or deteriorates. For example, in May 2008, S&P downgraded cellular company Sprint Nextel's long-term debt from investment grade to junk bond status. Bonds that drop into junk territory like this are called *fallen angels*. Sprint Nextel was downgraded for a lot of reasons, but S&P was concerned about an increased use of financial leverage and increased costs.

Credit ratings are important because defaults really do occur, and when they do, investors can lose heavily. For example, in 2000, AmeriServe Food Distribution, Inc., which supplied restaurants such as Burger King with everything from burgers to giveaway toys, defaulted on $200 million in junk bonds. After the default, the bonds traded at just 18 cents on the dollar, leaving investors with a loss of more than $160 million.

Even worse in AmeriServe's case, the bonds had been issued only four months earlier, thereby making AmeriServe an NCAA champion. Although that might be a good thing for a college basketball team such as the University of Kentucky Wildcats, in the bond market it means "No Coupon At All," and it's not a good thing for investors.

If you're nervous about the level of debt piled up by the U.S. government, don't go to www.publicdebt.treas.gov or to www.brillig.com/debt_clock! Learn all about government bonds at www.ny.frb.org.

Concept Questions

7.3a What does a bond rating say about the risk of fluctuations in a bond's value resulting from interest rate changes?

7.3b What is a junk bond?

Some Different Types of Bonds

7.4

Thus far we have considered only "plain vanilla" corporate bonds. In this section, we briefly look at bonds issued by governments and also at bonds with unusual features.

GOVERNMENT BONDS

The biggest borrower in the world—by a wide margin—is everybody's favorite family member, Uncle Sam. In 2008, the total debt of the U.S. government was $9.4 *trillion,* or about $31,000 per citizen (and growing!). When the government wishes to borrow money for more than one year, it sells what are known as Treasury notes and bonds to the public (in fact, it does so every month). Currently, outstanding Treasury notes and bonds have original maturities ranging from 2 to 30 years.

Most U.S. Treasury issues are just ordinary coupon bonds. Some older issues are callable, and a few have some unusual features. There are two important things to keep in mind, however. First, U.S. Treasury issues, unlike essentially all other bonds, have no default risk because (we hope) the Treasury can always come up with the money to make the payments. Second, Treasury issues are exempt from state income taxes (though not federal income taxes). In other words, the coupons you receive on a Treasury note or bond are taxed only at the federal level.

State and local governments also borrow money by selling notes and bonds. Such issues are called *municipal* notes and bonds, or just "munis." Unlike Treasury issues, munis have varying degrees of default risk, and, in fact, they are rated much like corporate issues. Also, they are almost always callable. The most intriguing thing about munis is that their coupons are exempt from federal income taxes (though not necessarily state income taxes), which makes them very attractive to high-income, high–tax bracket investors.

Because of the enormous tax break they receive, the yields on municipal bonds are much lower than the yields on taxable bonds. For example, in May 2008, long-term Aa-rated corporate bonds were yielding about 5.74 percent. At the same time, long-term Aa munis were yielding about 4.59 percent. Suppose an investor was in a 30 percent tax bracket. All else being the same, would this investor prefer a Aa corporate bond or a Aa municipal bond?

To answer, we need to compare the *aftertax* yields on the two bonds. Ignoring state and local taxes, the muni pays 4.59 percent on both a pretax and an aftertax basis. The corporate issue pays 5.74 percent before taxes, but it pays only $.0574 \times (1 - .30) = .040$, or 4.0 percent, once we account for the 30 percent tax bite. Given this, the muni has a better yield.

Another good bond market site is money.cnn.com.

EXAMPLE 7.4   **Taxable versus Municipal Bonds**

Suppose taxable bonds are currently yielding 8 percent, while at the same time, munis of comparable risk and maturity are yielding 6 percent. Which is more attractive to an investor in a 40 percent bracket? What is the break-even tax rate? How do you interpret this rate?

For an investor in a 40 percent tax bracket, a taxable bond yields $8 \times (1 - .40) = 4.8$ percent after taxes, so the muni is much more attractive. The break-even tax rate is the tax rate at which an investor would be indifferent between a taxable and a nontaxable issue. If we let t^* stand for the break-even tax rate, then we can solve for it as follows:

$$.08 \times (1 - t^*) = .06$$
$$1 - t^* = .06/.08 = .75$$
$$t^* = .25$$

Thus, an investor in a 25 percent tax bracket would make 6 percent after taxes from either bond.

ZERO COUPON BONDS

zero coupon bond
A bond that makes no coupon payments and is thus initially priced at a deep discount.

A bond that pays no coupons at all must be offered at a price that is much lower than its stated value. Such bonds are called **zero coupon bonds**, or just *zeroes*.[5]

Suppose the Eight-Inch Nails (EIN) Company issues a $1,000 face value, five-year zero coupon bond. The initial price is set at $508.35. Even though no interest payments are made on the bond, zero coupon bond calculations use semiannual periods to be consistent with coupon bond calculations. Using semiannual periods, it is straightforward to verify

---

[5]A bond issued with a very low coupon rate (as opposed to a zero coupon rate) is an *original-issue discount (OID) bond*.

Year	Beginning Value	Ending Value	Implicit Interest Expense	Straight-line Interest Expense
1	$508.35	$ 582.01	$ 73.66	$ 98.33
2	582.01	666.34	84.33	98.33
3	666.34	762.90	96.56	98.33
4	762.90	873.44	110.54	98.33
5	873.44	1,000.00	126.56	98.33
Total			$491.65	$491.65

TABLE 7.2

Interest Expense for EIN's Zeroes

that, at this price, the bond yields 14 percent to maturity. The total interest paid over the life of the bond is $1,000 − 508.35 = $491.65.

For tax purposes, the issuer of a zero coupon bond deducts interest every year even though no interest is actually paid. Similarly, the owner must pay taxes on interest accrued every year, even though no interest is actually received.

The way in which the yearly interest on a zero coupon bond is calculated is governed by tax law. Before 1982, corporations could calculate the interest deduction on a straight-line basis. For EIN, the annual interest deduction would have been $491.65/5 = $98.33 per year.

Under current tax law, the implicit interest is determined by amortizing the loan. We do this by first calculating the bond's value at the beginning of each year. For example, after one year, the bond will have four years until maturity, so it will be worth $1,000/1.07^8 = $582.01; the value in two years will be $1,000/1.07^6 = $666.34; and so on. The implicit interest each year is simply the change in the bond's value for the year. The values and interest expenses for the EIN bond are listed in Table 7.2.

Notice that under the old rules, zero coupon bonds were more attractive because the deductions for interest expense were larger in the early years (compare the implicit interest expense with the straight-line expense).

Under current tax law, EIN could deduct $73.66 in interest paid the first year and the owner of the bond would pay taxes on $73.66 in taxable income (even though no interest was actually received). This second tax feature makes taxable zero coupon bonds less attractive to individuals. However, they are still a very attractive investment for tax-exempt investors with long-term dollar-denominated liabilities, such as pension funds, because the future dollar value is known with relative certainty.

Some bonds are zero coupon bonds for only part of their lives. For example, General Motors has a debenture outstanding that matures on March 15, 2036. For the first 20 years of its life, no coupon payments will be made; but, after 20 years, it will begin paying coupons semiannually at a rate of 7.75 percent per year.

FLOATING-RATE BONDS

The conventional bonds we have talked about in this chapter have fixed-dollar obligations because the coupon rates are set as fixed percentages of the par values. Similarly, the principal amounts are set equal to the par values. Under these circumstances, the coupon payments and principal are completely fixed.

With *floating-rate bonds (floaters)*, the coupon payments are adjustable. The adjustments are tied to an interest rate index such as the Treasury bill interest rate or the 30-year Treasury bond rate. The EE Savings Bonds we mentioned in Chapter 5 are a good example of a floater. For EE bonds purchased after May 1, 1997, the interest rate is adjusted every six months. The rate that the bonds earn for a particular six-month period is determined by taking 90 percent of the average yield on ordinary five-year Treasury notes over the previous six months.

The value of a floating-rate bond depends on exactly how the coupon payment adjustments are defined. In most cases, the coupon adjusts with a lag to some base rate. For example, suppose a coupon rate adjustment is made on June 1. The adjustment might be based on the simple average of Treasury bond yields during the previous three months. In addition, the majority of floaters have the following features:

1. The holder has the right to redeem the note at par on the coupon payment date after some specified amount of time. This is called a *put* provision, and it is discussed in the following section.
2. The coupon rate has a floor and a ceiling, meaning that the coupon is subject to a minimum and a maximum. In this case, the coupon rate is said to be "capped," and the upper and lower rates are sometimes called the *collar*.

A particularly interesting type of floating-rate bond is an *inflation-linked* bond. Such bonds have coupons that are adjusted according to the rate of inflation (the principal amount may be adjusted as well). The U.S. Treasury began issuing such bonds in January of 1997. The issues are sometimes called "TIPS," or Treasury Inflation-Protected Securities. Other countries, including Canada, Israel, and Britain, have issued similar securities.

Official information about U.S. inflation-indexed bonds is at www.publicdebt.treas. gov.

OTHER TYPES OF BONDS

Many bonds have unusual or exotic features. So-called catastrophe, or cat, bonds provide an interesting example. In February 2008, the Caitlin Group Limited, a reinsurance company, issued $150 million in cat bonds (reinsurance companies sell insurance to insurance companies). These cat bonds were unique in that they were not based on a specific risk such as an earthquake or hurricane, but rather were triggered if the Caitlin Group lost more than an aggregate amount during any year.

The largest single cat bond issue to date is a series of six bonds sold by Merna Reinsurance in 2007. The six bond issues were to cover various catastrophes the company faced due to its reinsurance of State Farm. The six bonds totaled about $1.2 billion in par value, a large portion of the record $7 billion in cat bonds issued during 2007.

At this point, cat bonds probably seem pretty risky. It therefore might be surprising to learn that since cat bonds were first issued in 1997, only one has not been paid in full. Because of Hurricane Katrina, bondholders in that one issue lost $190 million.

Another possible bond feature is a *warrant*. A warrant gives the buyer of a bond the right to purchase shares of stock in the company at a fixed price. Such a right would be very valuable if the stock price climbed substantially (a later chapter discusses this subject in greater depth). Because of the value of this feature, bonds with warrants are often issued at a very low coupon rate.

As these examples illustrate, bond features are really limited only by the imaginations of the parties involved. Unfortunately, there are far too many variations for us to cover in detail here. We therefore close this discussion by mentioning a few of the more common types.

Income bonds are similar to conventional bonds, except that coupon payments depend on company income. Specifically, coupons are paid to bondholders only if the firm's income is sufficient. This would appear to be an attractive feature, but income bonds are not very common.

A *convertible bond* can be swapped for a fixed number of shares of stock anytime before maturity at the holder's option. Convertibles are relatively common, but the number has been decreasing in recent years.

A *put bond* allows the *holder* to force the issuer to buy back the bond at a stated price. For example, International Paper Co. has bonds outstanding that allow the holder to force International Paper to buy the bonds back at 100 percent of face value if certain "risk" events happen. One such event is a change in credit rating from investment grade to lower than investment grade by Moody's or S&P. The put feature is therefore just the reverse of the call provision.

Edward I. Altman on Junk Bonds and Leveraged Loans

One of the most important developments in corporate finance over the last 30 years has been the reemergence of publicly owned and traded low-rated corporate debt. Originally offered to the public in the early 1900s to help finance some of our emerging growth industries, these high-yield, high-risk bonds virtually disappeared after the rash of bond defaults during the Depression. Recently, however, the junk bond market has been catapulted from being an insignificant element in the corporate fixed-income market to being one of the fastest-growing and most controversial types of financing mechanisms. Technically, high-yield bonds are bonds issued by companies whose rating given by one or more of the major rating agencies, i.e., Fitch, Moody's or Standard & Poors, is below investment grade, e.g., below BBB– by S&P.

The term *junk* emanates from the dominant type of low-rated bond issues outstanding prior to 1977 when the "market" consisted almost exclusively of original-issue investment-grade bonds that fell from their lofty status to a higher-default risk, speculative-grade level. These so called fallen angels amounted to about $8.5 billion in 1977. At the end of 2008, fallen angels comprised about 25 percent of the $1 trillion publicly owned junk bond market. The high-yield bond market in Europe began to grow only recently and reached about €175 billion in 2008.

Beginning in 1977, issuers began to go directly to the public to raise debt capital for growth purposes. Early issuers of junk bonds were energy-related firms, cable TV companies, airlines, and assorted other industrial companies. The emerging growth company rationale coupled with relatively high returns to early investors helped legitimize this sector.

By far the most important and controversial aspect of junk bond financing was its role in the corporate restructuring movement from 1985 to 1989. High-leverage transactions and acquisitions, such as leveraged buyouts (LBOs), which occur when a firm is taken private, and leveraged recapitalizations (debt-for-equity swaps), transformed the face of corporate America, leading to a heated debate as to the economic and social consequences of firms' being transformed with debt-equity ratios of at least 6:1. Similar, but less emotional, comments accompanied a second LBO movement in 2004–2007.

These transactions involved increasingly large companies, and the multibillion dollar takeover became fairly common, finally capped by the huge $25+ billion RJR Nabisco LBO in 1989. LBOs were typically financed with about 60 percent senior bank and insurance company debt, about 25–30 percent subordinated public debt (junk bonds), and 10–15 percent equity. The junk bond segment is sometimes referred to as "mezzanine" financing because it lies between the "balcony" senior debt and the "basement" equity. In the most recent LBO binge, however, more than 30 percent of the financing was equity but the transactions were, on average, much larger than in the late 1980s, with only RJR Nabisco from the earlier vintage still in the "top-10 LBOs."

These restructurings resulted in huge fees to advisors and underwriters and huge premiums to the old shareholders who were bought out, and they continued as long as the market was willing to buy these new debt offerings at what appeared to be a favorable risk-return trade-off. The bottom fell out of the market in the last six months of 1989 due to a number of factors including a marked increase in defaults, government regulation against S&Ls' holding junk bonds, and at least one highly publicized bankruptcy of a highly leveraged financial restructuring—Federated Department Stores.

The default rate rose dramatically to 4 percent in 1989 and then skyrocketed in 1990 and 1991 to 10.1 percent and 10.3 percent, respectively, with about $19 billion of defaults in 1991. By the end of 1990, the pendulum of growth in new junk bond issues and returns to investors swung dramatically downward as prices plummeted and the new-issue market all but dried up. The year 1991 was a pivotal year in that, despite record defaults, bond prices and new issues rebounded strongly as the prospects for the future brightened.

In the early 1990s, the financial market was questioning the very survival of the junk bond market. The answer as to its survival was a resounding "yes," as the amount of new issues soared to record annual levels of $40 billion in 1992, almost $80 billion in 1993, and in 1997 reached an impressive $119 billion. Coupled with plummeting default rates (under 2.0 percent each year in the 1993–97 period) and attractive returns in these years, the risk-return characteristics have been extremely favorable.

The junk bond market in the late 1990s was a quieter one compared to that of the 1980s, but, in terms of growth and returns, it was healthier than ever before. While the low default rates in 1992–98 helped to fuel new investment funds and new issues, the market experienced its ups and downs in subsequent years. Indeed, default rates started to rise in 1999 and accelerated in 2000–2002. The latter year saw defaults reach record levels as the economy slipped into a recession and investors suffered from the excesses of lending in the late 1990s.

(continued)

Since the mid-1990s, a "sister" high-yield debt market has developed in the private leveraged loan market. This low-quality market grew enormously in the United States and Europe in the 2005–2007 period and was at least 30 percent larger than the high-yield bond market in 2008. One of the main reasons for the recent growth and popularity of leveraged loans issued by non-investment grade companies was that the issuing bank could easily sell these loans into structured finance vehicles called collateralized-loan-obligations (CLOs). Usually these private, leveraged loan debt securities have registered lower default rates than high-yield bonds but there were indications that this usual pattern was going to change due to its greater expansion and liberal terms in the years prior to 2008.

The market for leveraged financing rebounded quickly in 2003 and continued to prosper until the credit crisis of 2007–2008. With the "flight-to-quality" caused by the sub-prime mortgage market meltdown in the second-half of 2007 and 2008, returns to investors in high-yield bonds and leveraged loans fell considerably, new issues dried up and default rates increased from the unusually low-risk years that coincided with the leveraged excesses. Despite these highly volatile events and problems with liquidity, we are convinced that high-yield bonds, and its private debt companion, leveraged loans, will continue in the future to be a major source of corporate debt financing and a legitimate asset class for investors.

Edward I. Altman is Max L. Heine Professor of Finance and Director of Credit and Debt Markets Research at the NYU Salomon Center at the Stern School of Business. He is widely recognized as one of the world's leading experts on bankruptcy and credit analysis as well as the high-yield and distressed debt markets.

A given bond may have many unusual features. Two of the most recent exotic bonds are CoCo bonds, which have a coupon payment, and NoNo bonds, which are zero coupon bonds. CoCo and NoNo bonds are contingent convertible, putable, callable, subordinated bonds. The contingent convertible clause is similar to the normal conversion feature, except the contingent feature must be met. For example, a contingent feature may require that the company stock trade at 110 percent of the conversion price for 20 out of the most recent 30 days. Valuing a bond of this sort can be quite complex, and the yield to maturity calculation is often meaningless. For example, in 2008, a NoNo issued by Merrill Lynch was selling at a price of $2,090, with a yield to maturity of negative 122 percent. At the same time, a NoNo issued by Credit Suisse was selling for $1,373.75, which implied a yield to maturity of negative 198 percent!

Concept Questions

7.4a Why might an income bond be attractive to a corporation with volatile cash flows? Can you think of a reason why income bonds are not more popular?

7.4b What do you think would be the effect of a put feature on a bond's coupon? How about a convertibility feature? Why?

7.5 Bond Markets

Bonds are bought and sold in enormous quantities every day. You may be surprised to learn that the trading volume in bonds on a typical day is many, many times larger than the trading volume in stocks (by *trading volume* we simply mean the amount of money that changes hands). Here is a finance trivia question: What is the largest securities market in the world? Most people would guess the New York Stock Exchange. In fact, the largest securities market in the world in terms of trading volume is the U.S. Treasury market.

HOW BONDS ARE BOUGHT AND SOLD

As we mentioned all the way back in Chapter 1, most trading in bonds takes place over the counter, or OTC. Recall that this means there is no particular place where buying and

WORK THE WEB

Bond quotes have become more available with the rise of the Internet. One site where you can find current bond prices is cxa.marketwatch.com/finra/MarketData/Default.aspx. We went to the Web site and searched for bonds issued by Chevron. Here is a look at part of what we found for one of the bonds:

CVX.GP / CUSIP: 881685BD2   Search for Bond Trade Activity   Add to Watchlist

Last: **$108.500**   Yield: **5.934%**

Security Category:	Corporate
Issue Description:	GTD DEB
Issuer Name:	TEXACO CAP INC
Coupon Rate:	7.500%
Coupon Type:	Fixed
Maturity Date:	03/01/2043

Price | Yield

Price ■   5/7/2008

(chart with values $120, $115, $110, $105, $100, $95; x-axis Aug/07, Oct/07, Jan/08, May/08)

5 day 3 mo 6 mo **1 year**

Composite Trade Information

Last Sale

Date	05/07/2008
Price	$108.500
Yield	5.934%

Daily Trade Summary

High Price / Equivalent Yield	$108.500 / 6.57100%
Low Price / Equivalent Yield	$105.750 / 5.93400%
Net Change (Price)	$1.000

The bond has a coupon rate of 7.50 percent and matures on March 1, 2043. The last sale on this bond was at a price of 108.50 percent of par, which gives a yield to maturity of about 5.93 percent. Not only does the site provide the most recent price and yield information, but it also provides more important information about the bond, such as the credit rating, coupon date, call date, and call price. We'll leave it up to you to have a look at the page and the rest of the information available there.

Questions

1. Go to this Web site and find the bond shown above. When was this bond issued? What was the size of the bond issue? What were the yield to maturity and price when the bond was issued?
2. When you search for Chevron bonds (CVX), you will find bonds for several companies listed. Why do you think Chevron has bonds issued with different corporate names?

selling occur. Instead, dealers around the country (and around the world) stand ready to buy and sell. The various dealers are connected electronically.

One reason the bond markets are so big is that the number of bond issues far exceeds the number of stock issues. There are two reasons for this. First, a corporation would typically have only one common stock issue outstanding (there are exceptions to this that we discuss in our next chapter). However, a single large corporation could easily have a dozen or more note and bond issues outstanding. Beyond this, federal, state, and local borrowing is simply enormous. For example, even a small city would usually have a wide variety of notes and bonds outstanding, representing money borrowed to pay for things like roads, sewers, and schools. When you think about how many small cities there are in the United States, you begin to get the picture!

Because the bond market is almost entirely OTC, it has historically had little or no transparency. A financial market is *transparent* if it is possible to easily observe its prices and trading volume. On the New York Stock Exchange, for example, it is possible to see the price and quantity for every single transaction. In contrast, in the bond market, it is often not possible to observe either. Transactions are privately negotiated between parties, and there is little or no centralized reporting of transactions.

Although the total volume of trading in bonds far exceeds that in stocks, only a small fraction of the total bond issues that exist actually trade on a given day. This fact, combined with the lack of transparency in the bond market, means that getting up-to-date prices on individual bonds can be difficult or impossible, particularly for smaller corporate or municipal issues. Instead, a variety of sources of estimated prices exist and are commonly used.

BOND PRICE REPORTING

To learn more about TRACE, visit www.finra.org.

In 2002, transparency in the corporate bond market began to improve dramatically. Under new regulations, corporate bond dealers are now required to report trade information through what is known as the Trade Report and Compliance Engine (TRACE). Our nearby *Work the Web* box shows you how to get TRACE.

TRACE bond quotes are available at www.finra.org/marketdata. As shown in Figure 7.3, the Financial Industry Regulatory Authority (FINRA) provides a daily snapshot from TRACE by reporting the most active issues. The information shown is largely self-explanatory. Notice that the price of the iStar Financial bond dropped more than 1.6 percentage points on this day. What do you think happened to the yield to maturity for this bond? Figure 7.3 focuses on the most active bonds with investment grade ratings, but the most active high-yield and convertible bonds are also available on the Web site.

FIGURE 7.3

Sample TRACE Bond Quotations

Most Active Investment Grade Bonds

Issuer Name	Symbol	Coupon	Maturity	Rating Moody's/S&P/Fitch	High	Low	Last	Change	Yield%
J P MORGAN CHASE & CO	JPM.JPF	6.000%	Jan 2018	Aa2/AA-/AA-	104.361	102.730	103.501	-.023	5.526
MORGAN STANLEY	MS.GGO	6.625%	Apr 2018	Aa3/AA-/AA-	105.266	101.898	104.390	-.388	6.028
SPRINT NEXTEL CORP	S.HM	6.000%	Dec 2016	Baa3/BB/BB+	84.500	83.500	84.000	.000	8.690
ISTAR FINL INC	ISFI.GZ	5.950%	Oct 2013	Baa2/BBB/BBB	89.375	87.750	88.875	-1.625	8.556
WELLS FARGO & CO NEW	WFC.GDT	5.625%	Dec 2017	Aa1/AA+/AA	103.700	102.517	102.562	.294	5.280
NUCOR CORP	NUE.GE	6.400%	Dec 2037	A1/A+/NR	101.060	100.819	100.819	-.360	6.338
UNITED TECHNOLOGIES CORP	UTX.GJ	6.350%	Mar 2011	A2/A/A+	106.957	106.647	106.889	.229	3.730
AT&T INC	T.KG	5.500%	Feb 2018	A2/A/A	102.550	99.500	99.864	.029	5.517
AT&T INC	T.KE	4.950%	Jan 2013	A2/A/A	103.433	101.170	101.706	.294	4.538
GOLDMAN SACHS GROUP INC	GS.YW	6.150%	Apr 2018	Aa3/AA-/AA-	105.677	101.160	104.407	4.657	5.563

If you go to the Web site and click on a particular bond, you will get a lot of information about the bond, including the credit rating, the call schedule, original issue information, and trade information.

As we mentioned before, the U.S. Treasury market is the largest securities market in the world. As with bond markets in general, it is an OTC market, so there is limited transparency. However, unlike the situation with bond markets in general, trading in Treasury issues, particularly recently issued ones, is very heavy. Each day, representative prices for outstanding Treasury issues are reported.

Figure 7.4 shows a portion of the daily Treasury note and bond listings from the Web site wsj.com. The entry that begins "2021 Nov 15" is highlighted. This information tells us that the bond will mature in November of 2021. The next column is the coupon rate, which is 8.000 percent for this bond. Treasury bonds all make semiannual payments and have a face value of $1,000, so this bond will pay $40 per six months until it matures.

The next two pieces of information are the **bid** and **asked prices**. In general, in any OTC or dealer market, the bid price represents what a dealer is willing to pay for a security, and the asked price (or just "ask" price) is what a dealer is willing to take for it. The difference between the two prices is called the **bid–ask spread** (or just "spread"), and it represents the dealer's profit.

For historical reasons, Treasury prices are quoted in 32nds. Thus, the bid price on the 8 percent November 2021 bond, 136:29, actually translates into 136 29/32, or 136.90625 percent of face value. With a $1,000 face value, this price represents $1,369.0625. Because prices are quoted in 32nds, the smallest possible price change is 1/32. This change is called the "tick" size.

The next number quoted is the change in the asked price from the previous day, measured in ticks (in 32nds), so this issue's asked price rose by 5/32 of 1 percent, or .15625 percent, of face value from the previous day. Finally, the last number reported is the yield to maturity, based on the asked price. Notice that this is a premium bond because it sells for more than its face value. Not surprisingly, its yield to maturity (4.36 percent) is less than its coupon rate (8 percent).

The very last ordinary bond listed, the 2038 Feb 15, is often called the "bellwether" bond. This bond's yield is the one that is usually reported in the evening news. So, for example, when you hear that long-term interest rates rose, what is really being said is that the yield on this bond went up (and its price went down).

If you examine the yields on the various issues in Figure 7.4, you will clearly see that they vary by maturity. Why this occurs and what it might mean is one of the things we discuss in our next section.

A NOTE ABOUT BOND PRICE QUOTES

If you buy a bond between coupon payment dates, the price you pay is usually more than the price you are quoted. The reason is that standard convention in the bond market is to quote prices net of "accrued interest," meaning that accrued interest is deducted to arrive at the quoted price. This quoted price is called the **clean price**. The price you actually pay, however, includes the accrued interest. This price is the **dirty price**, also known as the "full" or "invoice" price.

An example is the easiest way to understand these issues. Suppose you buy a bond with a 12 percent annual coupon, payable semiannually. You actually pay $1,080 for this bond, so $1,080 is the dirty, or invoice, price. Further, on the day you buy it, the next coupon is due in four months, so you are between coupon dates. Notice that the next coupon will be $60.

The accrued interest on a bond is calculated by taking the fraction of the coupon period that has passed, in this case two months out of six, and multiplying this fraction by the next

The Federal Reserve Bank of St. Louis maintains dozens of online files containing macroeconomic data as well as rates on U.S. Treasury issues. Go to www.stls.frb.org/fred/files.

bid price
The price a dealer is willing to pay for a security.

asked price
The price a dealer is willing to take for a security.

bid–ask spread
The difference between the bid price and the asked price.

Current and historical Treasury yield information is available at www.publicdebt.treas.gov.

clean price
The price of a bond net of accrued interest; this is the price that is typically quoted.

dirty price
The price of a bond including accrued interest, also known as the *full* or *invoice price*. This is the price the buyer actually pays.

FIGURE 7.4

Sample *Wall Street Journal* U.S. Treasury Note and Bond Prices

SOURCE: wsj.com. Reprinted by permission of *The Wall Street Journal*, via Copyright Clearance Center. © 2008 Dow Jones and Company, Inc., April 29, 2008. All Rights Reserved Worldwide.

Treasury Bonds					
Maturity	**Coupon**	**Bid**	**Asked**	**Chg**	**Asked yield**
2013 Aug 15	12.000	103:00	103:01	−2	1.54
2014 May 15	13.250	111:16	111:17	+1	1.98
2014 Aug 15	12.500	113:02	113:03	+1	2 17
2014 Nov 15	11.750	114:10	114:11	unch.	2.21
2015 Feb 15	11.250	147:10	147:11	+1	3.38
2015 Aug 15	10.625	145:20	145:21	+2	3.48
2015 Nov 15	9.875	141:24	141:25	+1	3.52
2016 Feb 15	9.250	138:10	138:11	+1	3.57
2016 May 15	7.250	124:07	124:08	+2	3.73
2016 Nov 15	7.500	126:26	126:27	+2	3.79
2017 May 15	8.750	136:27	136:28	+2	3.87
2017 Aug 15	8.875	139:07	139:08	+2	3.81
2018 May 15	9.125	142:29	142:30	+4	3.91
2018 Nov 15	9.000	142:04	142:05	+4	4.04
2019 Feb 15	8.875	141:12	141:13	+4	4.09
2019 Aug 15	8.125	135:12	135:13	+4	4.16
2020 Feb 15	8.500	139:15	139:16	+4	4.21
2020 May 15	8.750	142:07	142:08	+4	4.23
2020 Aug 15	8.750	142:18	142:19	+4	4.26
2021 Feb 15	7.875	134:20	134:21	+4	4.32
2021 May 15	8.125	137:19	137:20	+5	4.32
2021 Aug 15	8.125	137:29	137:30	+5	4.34
2021 Nov 15	8.000	136:29	136:30	+5	4.36
2022 Aug 15	7.250	129:27	129:28	+4	4.41
2022 Nov 15	7.625	134:08	134:09	+5	4.40
2023 Feb 15	7.125	129:00	129:00	+4	4.43
2023 Aug 15	6.250	119:23	119:24	+3	4.45
2024 Nov 15	7.500	135:05	135:06	+5	4.47
2025 Feb 15	7.625	136:23	136:24	+4	4.48
2025 Aug 15	6.875	128:01	128:02	+5	4.52
2026 Feb 15	6.000	117:15	117:16	+4	4.55
2026 Aug 15	6.750	127:08	127:09	+4	4.54
2026 Nov 15	6.500	124:11	124:12	+4	4.54
2027 Feb 15	6.625	126:00	126:01	+4	4.55
2027 Aug 15	6.375	123:06	123:07	+4	4.55
2027 Nov 15	6.125	120.07	120:08	+5	4.55
2028 Aug 15	5.500	112:05	112:06	+5	4.57
2028 Nov 15	5.250	108.28	108:29	+4	4.57
2029 Feb 15	5.250	108:28	108:29	+5	4.58
2029 Aug 15	6.125	121:01	121:02	+5	4.56
2030 May 15	6.250	123:16	123:11	+5	4.55
2031 Feb 15	5.375	111:19	111:20	+6	4.55
2036 Feb 15	4.500	99:06	99:07	+5	4.55
2037 Feb 15	4.750	103:05	103:06	+5	4.55
2037 May 15	5.000	107:09	107:10	+5	4.54
2038 Feb 15	4.375	97:01	97:02	+5	4.55

coupon, $60. So, the accrued interest in this example is $2/6 \times \$60 = \$20$. The bond's quoted price (that is, its clean price) would be $\$1,080 - \$20 = \$1,060$.[6]

Concept Questions

7.5a Why do we say bond markets may have little or no transparency?

7.5b In general, what are bid and ask prices?

7.5c What is the difference between a bond's clean price and dirty price?

Inflation and Interest Rates   7.6

So far, we haven't considered the role of inflation in our various discussions of interest rates, yields, and returns. Because this is an important consideration, we consider the impact of inflation next.

REAL VERSUS NOMINAL RATES

In examining interest rates, or any other financial market rates such as discount rates, bond yields, rates of return, and required returns, it is often necessary to distinguish between **real rates** and **nominal rates**. Nominal rates are called "nominal" because they have not been adjusted for inflation. Real rates are rates that have been adjusted for inflation.

To see the effect of inflation, suppose prices are currently rising by 5 percent per year. In other words, the rate of inflation is 5 percent. An investment is available that will be worth $115.50 in one year. It costs $100 today. Notice that with a present value of $100 and a future value in one year of $115.50, this investment has a 15.5 percent rate of return. In calculating this 15.5 percent return, we did not consider the effect of inflation, however, so this is the nominal return.

What is the impact of inflation here? To answer, suppose pizzas cost $5 apiece at the beginning of the year. With $100, we can buy 20 pizzas. Because the inflation rate is 5 percent, pizzas will cost 5 percent more, or $5.25, at the end of the year. If we take the investment, how many pizzas can we buy at the end of the year? Measured in pizzas, what is the rate of return on this investment?

Our $115.50 from the investment will buy us $115.50/5.25 = 22 pizzas. This is up from 20 pizzas, so our pizza rate of return is 10 percent. What this illustrates is that even though the nominal return on our investment is 15.5 percent, our buying power goes up by only 10 percent because of inflation. Put another way, we are really only 10 percent richer. In this case, we say that the real return is 10 percent.

Alternatively, we can say that with 5 percent inflation, each of the $115.50 nominal dollars we get is worth 5 percent less in real terms, so the real dollar value of our investment in a year is:

$115.50/1.05 = $110

What we have done is to *deflate* the $115.50 by 5 percent. Because we give up $100 in current buying power to get the equivalent of $110, our real return is again 10 percent. Because

real rates
Interest rates or rates of return that have been adjusted for inflation.

nominal rates
Interest rates or rates of return that have not been adjusted for inflation.

---

[6]The way accrued interest is calculated actually depends on the type of bond being quoted—for example, Treasury or corporate. The difference has to do with exactly how the fractional coupon period is calculated. In our example here, we implicitly treated the months as having exactly the same length (30 days each, 360 days in a year), which is consistent with the way corporate bonds are quoted. In contrast, for Treasury bonds, actual day counts are used.

we have removed the effect of future inflation here, this $110 is said to be measured in current dollars.

The difference between nominal and real rates is important and bears repeating:

> **The nominal rate on an investment is the percentage change in the number of dollars you have.**
>
> **The real rate on an investment is the percentage change in how much you can buy with your dollars—in other words, the percentage change in your buying power.**

THE FISHER EFFECT

Fisher effect
The relationship between nominal returns, real returns, and inflation.

Our discussion of real and nominal returns illustrates a relationship often called the **Fisher effect** (after the great economist Irving Fisher). Because investors are ultimately concerned with what they can buy with their money, they require compensation for inflation. Let R stand for the nominal rate and r stand for the real rate. The Fisher effect tells us that the relationship between nominal rates, real rates, and inflation can be written as:

$$1 + R = (1 + r) \times (1 + h) \qquad [7.2]$$

where h is the inflation rate.

In the preceding example, the nominal rate was 15.50 percent and the inflation rate was 5 percent. What was the real rate? We can determine it by plugging in these numbers:

$$1 + .1550 = (1 + r) \times (1 + .05)$$
$$1 + r = 1.1550/1.05 = 1.10$$
$$r = 10\%$$

This real rate is the same as we found before. If we take another look at the Fisher effect, we can rearrange things a little as follows:

$$1 + R = (1 + r) \times (1 + h)$$
$$R = r + h + r \times h \qquad [7.3]$$

What this tells us is that the nominal rate has three components. First, there is the real rate on the investment, r. Next, there is the compensation for the decrease in the value of the money originally invested because of inflation, h. The third component represents compensation for the fact that the dollars earned on the investment are also worth less because of the inflation.

This third component is usually small, so it is often dropped. The nominal rate is then approximately equal to the real rate plus the inflation rate:

$$R \approx r + h \qquad [7.4]$$

EXAMPLE 7.5	**The Fisher Effect**

If investors require a 10 percent real rate of return, and the inflation rate is 8 percent, what must be the approximate nominal rate? The exact nominal rate?

The nominal rate is approximately equal to the sum of the real rate and the inflation rate: 10% + 8% = 18%. From the Fisher effect, we have:

$$1 + R = (1 + r) \times (1 + h)$$
$$= 1.10 \times 1.08$$
$$= 1.1880$$

Therefore, the nominal rate will actually be closer to 19 percent.

It is important to note that financial rates, such as interest rates, discount rates, and rates of return, are almost always quoted in nominal terms. To remind you of this, we will henceforth use the symbol R instead of r in most of our discussions about such rates.

INFLATION AND PRESENT VALUES

One question that often comes up is the effect of inflation on present value calculations. The basic principle is simple: Either discount nominal cash flows at a nominal rate or discount real cash flows at a real rate. As long as you are consistent, you will get the same answer.

To illustrate, suppose you want to withdraw money each year for the next three years, and you want each withdrawal to have $25,000 worth of purchasing power as measured in current dollars. If the inflation rate is 4 percent per year, then the withdrawals will simply have to increase by 4 percent each year to compensate. The withdrawals each year will thus be:

$$C_1 = \$25,000(1.04) = \$26,000$$
$$C_2 = \$25,000(1.04)^2 = \$27,040$$
$$C_3 = \$25,000(1.04)^3 = \$28,121.60$$

What is the present value of these cash flows if the appropriate nominal discount rate is 10 percent? This is a standard calculation, and the answer is:

$$PV = \$26,000/1.10 + \$27,040/1.10^2 + \$28,121.60/1.10^3 = \$67,111.65$$

Notice that we discounted the nominal cash flows at a nominal rate.

To calculate the present value using real cash flows, we need the real discount rate. Using the Fisher equation, the real discount rate is:

$$1 + R = (1 + r)(1 + h)$$
$$1 + .10 = (1 + r)(1 + .04)$$
$$r = .0577$$

By design, the real cash flows are an annuity of $25,000 per year. So, the present value in real terms is:

$$PV = \$25,000[1 - (1/1.0577^3)]/.0577 = \$67,111.65$$

Thus, we get exactly the same answer (after allowing for a small rounding error in the real rate). Of course, you could also use the growing annuity equation we discussed in the previous chapter. The withdrawals are increasing at 4 percent per year; so using the growing annuity formula, the present value is:

$$PV = \$26,000 \left[\frac{1 - \left(\frac{1 + .04}{1 + .10} \right)^3}{.10 - .04} \right] = \$26,000\,(2.58122) = \$67,111.65$$

This is exactly the same present value we calculated before.

Concept Questions

7.6a What is the difference between a nominal and a real return? Which is more important to a typical investor?

7.6b What is the Fisher effect?

7.7 Determinants of Bond Yields

We are now in a position to discuss the determinants of a bond's yield. As we will see, the yield on any particular bond reflects a variety of factors, some common to all bonds and some specific to the issue under consideration.

THE TERM STRUCTURE OF INTEREST RATES

At any point in time, short-term and long-term interest rates will generally be different. Sometimes short-term rates are higher, sometimes lower. Figure 7.5 gives us a long-range perspective on this by showing over two centuries of short- and long-term interest rates. As shown, through time, the difference between short- and long-term rates has ranged from essentially zero to up to several percentage points, both positive and negative.

term structure of interest rates
The relationship between nominal interest rates on default-free, pure discount securities and time to maturity; that is, the pure time value of money.

The relationship between short- and long-term interest rates is known as the **term structure of interest rates**. To be a little more precise, the term structure of interest rates tells us what *nominal* interest rates are on *default-free, pure discount* bonds of all maturities. These rates are, in essence, "pure" interest rates because they involve no risk of default and a single, lump sum future payment. In other words, the term structure tells us the pure time value of money for different lengths of time.

When long-term rates are higher than short-term rates, we say that the term structure is upward sloping; when short-term rates are higher, we say it is downward sloping. The term structure can also be "humped." When this occurs, it is usually because rates increase at first, but then begin to decline as we look at longer- and longer-term rates. The most common shape of the term structure, particularly in modern times, is upward sloping; but the degree of steepness has varied quite a bit.

FIGURE 7.5   U.S. Interest Rates: 1800–2007

SOURCE: Jeremy J. Siegel, *Stocks for the Long Run,* 3rd edition, © McGraw-Hill, 2004, updated by the authors.

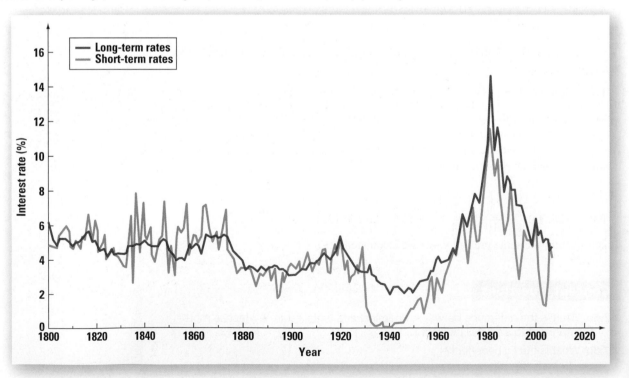

What determines the shape of the term structure? There are three basic components. The first two are the ones we discussed in our previous section: The real rate of interest and the rate of inflation. The real rate of interest is the compensation investors demand for forgoing the use of their money. You can think of it as the pure time value of money after adjusting for the effects of inflation.

The real rate of interest is the basic component underlying every interest rate, regardless of the time to maturity. When the real rate is high, all interest rates will tend to be higher, and vice versa. Thus, the real rate doesn't really determine the shape of the term structure; instead, it mostly influences the overall level of interest rates.

In contrast, the prospect of future inflation strongly influences the shape of the term structure. Investors thinking about lending money for various lengths of time recognize that future inflation erodes the value of the dollars that will be returned. As a result, investors demand compensation for this loss in the form of higher nominal rates. This extra compensation is called the **inflation premium**.

> **inflation premium**
> The portion of a nominal interest rate that represents compensation for expected future inflation.

If investors believe the rate of inflation will be higher in the future, then long-term nominal interest rates will tend to be higher than short-term rates. Thus, an upward-sloping term structure may reflect anticipated increases in inflation. Similarly, a downward-sloping term structure probably reflects the belief that inflation will be falling in the future.

The third, and last, component of the term structure has to do with interest rate risk. As we discussed earlier in the chapter, longer-term bonds have much greater risk of loss resulting from changes in interest rates than do shorter-term bonds. Investors recognize this risk, and they demand extra compensation in the form of higher rates for bearing it. This extra compensation is called the **interest rate risk premium**. The longer is the term to maturity, the greater is the interest rate risk, so the interest rate risk premium increases with maturity. However, as we discussed earlier, interest rate risk increases at a decreasing rate, so the interest rate risk premium does as well.[7]

> **interest rate risk premium**
> The compensation investors demand for bearing interest rate risk.

Putting the pieces together, we see that the term structure reflects the combined effect of the real rate of interest, the inflation premium, and the interest rate risk premium. Figure 7.6 shows how these can interact to produce an upward-sloping term structure (in the top part of Figure 7.6) or a downward-sloping term structure (in the bottom part).

In the top part of Figure 7.6, notice how the rate of inflation is expected to rise gradually. At the same time, the interest rate risk premium increases at a decreasing rate, so the combined effect is to produce a pronounced upward-sloping term structure. In the bottom part of Figure 7.6, the rate of inflation is expected to fall in the future, and the expected decline is enough to offset the interest rate risk premium and produce a downward-sloping term structure. Notice that if the rate of inflation was expected to decline by only a small amount, we could still get an upward-sloping term structure because of the interest rate risk premium.

We assumed in drawing Figure 7.6 that the real rate would remain the same. Actually, expected future real rates could be larger or smaller than the current real rate. Also, for simplicity, we used straight lines to show expected future inflation rates as rising or declining, but they do not necessarily have to look like this. They could, for example, rise and then fall, leading to a humped yield curve.

BOND YIELDS AND THE YIELD CURVE: PUTTING IT ALL TOGETHER

Going back to Figure 7.4, recall that we saw that the yields on Treasury notes and bonds of different maturities are not the same. Each day, in addition to the Treasury prices and yields

---

[7]In days of old, the interest rate risk premium was called a "liquidity" premium. Today, the term *liquidity premium* has an altogether different meaning, which we explore in our next section. Also, the interest rate risk premium is sometimes called a *maturity risk premium*. Our terminology is consistent with the modern view of the term structure.

FIGURE 7.6

The Term Structure of
Interest Rates

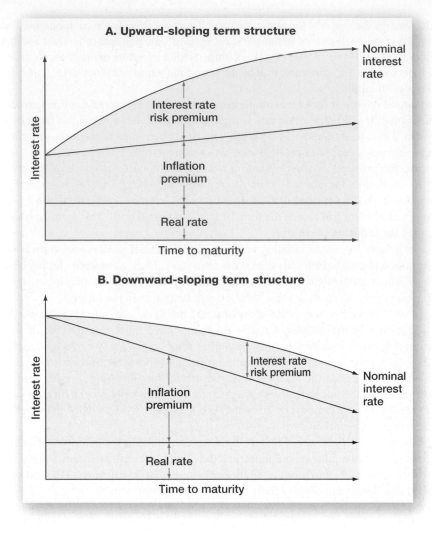

Treasury yield curve
A plot of the yields on
Treasury notes and bonds
relative to maturity.

Online
yield curve information
is available at
www.bloomberg.com/
markets.

default risk premium
The portion of a nominal
interest rate or bond yield
that represents
compensation for the
possibility of default.

shown in Figure 7.4, *The Wall Street Journal* provides a plot of Treasury yields relative to maturity. This plot is called the **Treasury yield curve** (or just the yield curve). Figure 7.7 shows the yield curve as of May 2008.

As you probably now suspect, the shape of the yield curve reflects the term structure of interest rates. In fact, the Treasury yield curve and the term structure of interest rates are almost the same thing. The only difference is that the term structure is based on pure discount bonds, whereas the yield curve is based on coupon bond yields. As a result, Treasury yields depend on the three components that underlie the term structure—the real rate, expected future inflation, and the interest rate risk premium.

Treasury notes and bonds have three important features that we need to remind you of: They are default-free, they are taxable, and they are highly liquid. This is not true of bonds in general, so we need to examine what additional factors come into play when we look at bonds issued by corporations or municipalities.

The first thing to consider is credit risk—that is, the possibility of default. Investors recognize that issuers other than the Treasury may or may not make all the promised payments on a bond, so they demand a higher yield as compensation for this risk. This extra compensation is called the **default risk premium**. Earlier in the chapter, we saw how bonds were

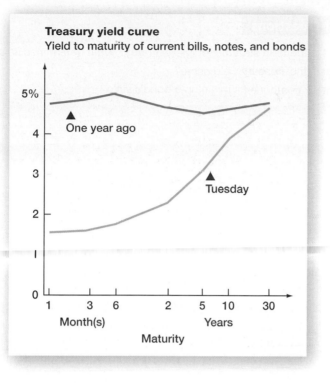

FIGURE 7.7

The Treasury Yield Curve: May, 2008

SOURCE: Reprinted by permission of *The Wall Street Journal,* via Copyright Clearance Center © 2008 by Dow Jones & Company, Inc., 2008. All Rights Reserved Worldwide.

rated based on their credit risk. What you will find if you start looking at bonds of different ratings is that lower-rated bonds have higher yields.

An important thing to recognize about a bond's yield is that it is calculated assuming that all the promised payments will be made. As a result, it is really a promised yield, and it may or may not be what you will earn. In particular, if the issuer defaults, your actual yield will be lower—probably much lower. This fact is particularly important when it comes to junk bonds. Thanks to a clever bit of marketing, such bonds are now commonly called high-yield bonds, which has a much nicer ring to it; but now you recognize that these are really high *promised* yield bonds.

Next, recall that we discussed earlier how municipal bonds are free from most taxes and, as a result, have much lower yields than taxable bonds. Investors demand the extra yield on a taxable bond as compensation for the unfavorable tax treatment. This extra compensation is the **taxability premium**.

Finally, bonds have varying degrees of liquidity. As we discussed earlier, there are an enormous number of bond issues, most of which do not trade regularly. As a result, if you wanted to sell quickly, you would probably not get as good a price as you could otherwise. Investors prefer liquid assets to illiquid ones, so they demand a **liquidity premium** on top of all the other premiums we have discussed. As a result, all else being the same, less liquid bonds will have higher yields than more liquid bonds.

taxability premium
The portion of a nominal interest rate or bond yield that represents compensation for unfavorable tax status.

liquidity premium
The portion of a nominal interest rate or bond yield that represents compensation for lack of liquidity.

CONCLUSION

If we combine all of the things we have discussed regarding bond yields, we find that bond yields represent the combined effect of no fewer than six things. The first is the real rate of interest. On top of the real rate are five premiums representing compensation for (1) expected future inflation, (2) interest rate risk, (3) default risk, (4) taxability, and (5) lack of liquidity. As a result, determining the appropriate yield on a bond requires careful analysis of each of these effects.

Concept Questions

7.7a What is the term structure of interest rates? What determines its shape?

7.7b What is the Treasury yield curve?

7.7c What six components make up a bond's yield?

7.8 Summary and Conclusions

This chapter has explored bonds, bond yields, and interest rates:

1. Determining bond prices and yields is an application of basic discounted cash flow principles.

2. Bond values move in the direction opposite that of interest rates, leading to potential gains or losses for bond investors.

3. Bonds have a variety of features spelled out in a document called the indenture.

4. Bonds are rated based on their default risk. Some bonds, such as Treasury bonds, have no risk of default, whereas so-called junk bonds have substantial default risk.

5. A wide variety of bonds exist, many of which contain exotic or unusual features.

6. Almost all bond trading is OTC, with little or no market transparency in many cases. As a result, bond price and volume information can be difficult to find for some types of bonds.

7. Bond yields and interest rates reflect the effect of six different things: the real interest rate and five premiums that investors demand as compensation for inflation, interest rate risk, default risk, taxability, and lack of liquidity.

In closing, we note that bonds are a vital source of financing to governments and corporations of all types. Bond prices and yields are a rich subject, and our one chapter, necessarily, touches on only the most important concepts and ideas. There is a great deal more we could say, but, instead, we will move on to stocks in our next chapter.

CHAPTER REVIEW AND SELF-TEST PROBLEMS

7.1 Bond Values A Microgates Industries bond has a 10 percent coupon rate and a $1,000 face value. Interest is paid semiannually, and the bond has 20 years to maturity. If investors require a 12 percent yield, what is the bond's value? What is the effective annual yield on the bond?

7.2 Bond Yields A Macrohard Corp. bond carries an 8 percent coupon, paid semiannually. The par value is $1,000, and the bond matures in six years. If the bond currently sells for $911.37, what is its yield to maturity? What is the effective annual yield?

ANSWERS TO CHAPTER REVIEW AND SELF-TEST PROBLEMS

7.1 Because the bond has a 10 percent coupon yield and investors require a 12 percent return, we know that the bond must sell at a discount. Notice that, because the bond pays interest semiannually, the coupons amount to $100/2 = $50 every six months.

The required yield is 12%/2 = 6% every six months. Finally, the bond matures in 20 years, so there are a total of 40 six-month periods.

The bond's value is thus equal to the present value of $50 every six months for the next 40 six-month periods plus the present value of the $1,000 face amount:

$$\text{Bond value} = \$50 \times [(1 - 1/1.06^{40})/.06] + 1,000/1.06^{40}$$
$$= \$50 \times 15.04630 + 1,000/10.2857$$
$$= \$849.54$$

Notice that we discounted the $1,000 back 40 periods at 6 percent per period, rather than 20 years at 12 percent. The reason is that the effective annual yield on the bond is $1.06^2 - 1 = 12.36\%$, not 12 percent. We thus could have used 12.36 percent per year for 20 years when we calculated the present value of the $1,000 face amount, and the answer would have been the same.

7.2 The present value of the bond's cash flows is its current price, $911.37. The coupon is $40 every six months for 12 periods. The face value is $1,000. So the bond's yield is the unknown discount rate in the following:

$$\$911.37 = \$40 \times [1 - 1/(1 + r)^{12}]/r + 1,000/(1 + r)^{12}$$

The bond sells at a discount. Because the coupon rate is 8 percent, the yield must be something in excess of that.

If we were to solve this by trial and error, we might try 12 percent (or 6 percent per six months):

$$\text{Bond value} = \$40 \times (1 - 1/1.06^{12})/.06 + 1,000/1.06^{12}$$
$$= \$832.32$$

This is less than the actual value, so our discount rate is too high. We now know that the yield is somewhere between 8 and 12 percent. With further trial and error (or a little machine assistance), the yield works out to be 10 percent, or 5 percent every six months.

By convention, the bond's yield to maturity would be quoted as $2 \times 5\% = 10\%$. The effective yield is thus $1.05^2 - 1 = 10.25\%$.

CONCEPTS REVIEW AND CRITICAL THINKING QUESTIONS

1. **Treasury Bonds** [LO1] Is it true that a U.S. Treasury security is risk-free?

2. **Interest Rate Risk** [LO2] Which has greater interest rate risk, a 30-year Treasury bond or a 30-year BB corporate bond?

3. **Treasury Pricing** [LO1] With regard to bid and ask prices on a Treasury bond, is it possible for the bid price to be higher? Why or why not?

4. **Yield to Maturity** [LO2] Treasury bid and ask quotes are sometimes given in terms of yields, so there would be a bid yield and an ask yield. Which do you think would be larger? Explain.

5. **Call Provisions** [LO1] A company is contemplating a long-term bond issue. It is debating whether to include a call provision. What are the benefits to the company from including a call provision? What are the costs? How do these answers change for a put provision?

6. **Coupon Rate** [LO1] How does a bond issuer decide on the appropriate coupon rate to set on its bonds? Explain the difference between the coupon rate and the required return on a bond.

7. **Real and Nominal Returns** [LO4] Are there any circumstances under which an investor might be more concerned about the nominal return on an investment than the real return?

8. **Bond Ratings** [LO3] Companies pay rating agencies such as Moody's and S&P to rate their bonds, and the costs can be substantial. However, companies are not required to have their bonds rated; doing so is strictly voluntary. Why do you think they do it?

9. **Bond Ratings** [LO3] U.S. Treasury bonds are not rated. Why? Often, junk bonds are not rated. Why?

10. **Term Structure** [LO5] What is the difference between the term structure of interest rates and the yield curve?

11. **Crossover Bonds** [LO3] Looking back at the crossover bonds we discussed in the chapter, why do you think split ratings such as these occur?

12. **Municipal Bonds** [LO1] Why is it that municipal bonds are not taxed at the federal level, but are taxable across state lines? Why are U.S. Treasury bonds not taxable at the state level? (You may need to dust off the history books for this one.)

13. **Bond Market** [LO1] What are the implications for bond investors of the lack of transparency in the bond market?

14. **Rating Agencies** [LO3] A controversy erupted regarding bond-rating agencies when some agencies began to provide unsolicited bond ratings. Why do you think this is controversial?

15. **Bonds as Equity** [LO1] The 100-year bonds we discussed in the chapter have something in common with junk bonds. Critics charge that, in both cases, the issuers are really selling equity in disguise. What are the issues here? Why would a company want to sell "equity in disguise"?

QUESTIONS AND PROBLEMS

BASIC
(Questions 1–14)

1. **Interpreting Bond Yields** [LO1] Is the yield to maturity on a bond the same thing as the required return? Is YTM the same thing as the coupon rate? Suppose today a 10 percent coupon bond sells at par. Two years from now, the required return on the same bond is 8 percent. What is the coupon rate on the bond then? The YTM?

2. **Interpreting Bond Yields** [LO2] Suppose you buy a 7 percent coupon, 20-year bond today when it's first issued. If interest rates suddenly rise to 15 percent, what happens to the value of your bond? Why?

3. **Bond Prices** [LO2] Staind, Inc., has 7.5 percent coupon bonds on the market that have 10 years left to maturity. The bonds make annual payments. If the YTM on these bonds is 8.75 percent, what is the current bond price?

4. **Bond Yields** [LO2] Ackerman Co. has 9 percent coupon bonds on the market with nine years left to maturity. The bonds make annual payments. If the bond currently sells for $934, what is its YTM?

5. **Coupon Rates** [LO2] Kiss the Sky Enterprises has bonds on the market making annual payments, with 13 years to maturity, and selling for $1,045. At this price, the bonds yield 7.5 percent. What must the coupon rate be on the bonds?

6. **Bond Prices** [LO2] Grohl Co. issued 11-year bonds a year ago at a coupon rate of 6.9 percent. The bonds make semiannual payments. If the YTM on these bonds is 7.4 percent, what is the current bond price?

Visit us at www.mhhe.com/rwj

7. **Bond Yields** [LO2] Ngata Corp. issued 12-year bonds 2 years ago at a coupon rate of 8.4 percent. The bonds make semiannual payments. If these bonds currently sell for 105 percent of par value, what is the YTM?

8. **Coupon Rates** [LO2] Ashes Divide Corporation has bonds on the market with 14.5 years to maturity, a YTM of 6.8 percent, and a current price of $924. The bonds make semiannual payments. What must the coupon rate be on these bonds?

9. **Calculating Real Rates of Return** [LO4] If Treasury bills are currently paying 7 percent and the inflation rate is 3.8 percent, what is the approximate real rate of interest? The exact real rate?

10. **Inflation and Nominal Returns** [LO4] Suppose the real rate is 3 percent and the inflation rate is 4.7 percent. What rate would you expect to see on a Treasury bill?

11. **Nominal and Real Returns** [LO4] An investment offers a 14 percent total return over the coming year. Bill Bernanke thinks the total real return on this investment will be only 9 percent. What does Bill believe the inflation rate will be over the next year?

12. **Nominal versus Real Returns** [LO4] Say you own an asset that had a total return last year of 11.4 percent. If the inflation rate last year was 4.8 percent, what was your real return?

13. **Using Treasury Quotes** [LO2] Locate the Treasury issue in Figure 7.4 maturing in November 2027. Is this a note or a bond? What is its coupon rate? What is its bid price? What was the *previous* day's asked price?

14. **Using Treasury Quotes** [LO2] Locate the Treasury bond in Figure 7.4 maturing in November 2024. Is this a premium or a discount bond? What is its current yield? What is its yield to maturity? What is the bid–ask spread?

15. **Bond Price Movements** [LO2] Bond X is a premium bond making annual payments. The bond pays an 8 percent coupon, has a YTM of 6 percent, and has 13 years to maturity. Bond Y is a discount bond making annual payments. This bond pays a 6 percent coupon, has a YTM of 8 percent, and also has 13 years to maturity. If interest rates remain unchanged, what do you expect the price of these bonds to be one year from now? In three years? In eight years? In 12 years? In 13 years? What's going on here? Illustrate your answers by graphing bond prices versus time to maturity.

INTERMEDIATE
(Questions 15–28)

16. **Interest Rate Risk** [LO2] Both Bond Sam and Bond Dave have 9 percent coupons, make semiannual payments, and are priced at par value. Bond Sam has 3 years to maturity, whereas Bond Dave has 20 years to maturity. If interest rates suddenly rise by 2 percent, what is the percentage change in the price of Bond Sam? Of Bond Dave? If rates were to suddenly fall by 2 percent instead, what would the percentage change in the price of Bond Sam be then? Of Bond Dave? Illustrate your answers by graphing bond prices versus YTM. What does this problem tell you about the interest rate risk of longer-term bonds?

17. **Interest Rate Risk** [LO2] Bond J is a 4 percent coupon bond. Bond K is a 12 percent coupon bond. Both bonds have nine years to maturity, make semiannual payments, and have a YTM of 8 percent. If interest rates suddenly rise by 2 percent, what is the percentage price change of these bonds? What if rates suddenly fall by 2 percent instead? What does this problem tell you about the interest rate risk of lower-coupon bonds?

18. **Bond Yields** [LO2] One More Time Software has 9.2 percent coupon bonds on the market with nine years to maturity. The bonds make semiannual payments and currently sell for 106.8 percent of par. What is the current yield on the bonds? The YTM? The effective annual yield?

Visit us at www.mhhe.com/rwj

19. **Bond Yields [LO2]** Seether Co. wants to issue new 20-year bonds for some much-needed expansion projects. The company currently has 8 percent coupon bonds on the market that sell for $930, make semiannual payments, and mature in 20 years. What coupon rate should the company set on its new bonds if it wants them to sell at par?

20. **Accrued Interest [LO2]** You purchase a bond with an invoice price of $968. The bond has a coupon rate of 7.4 percent, and there are four months to the next semiannual coupon date. What is the clean price of the bond?

21. **Accrued Interest [LO2]** You purchase a bond with a coupon rate of 6.8 percent and a clean price of $1,073. If the next semiannual coupon payment is due in two months, what is the invoice price?

22. **Finding the Bond Maturity [LO2]** River Corp. has 8 percent coupon bonds making annual payments with a YTM of 7.2 percent. The current yield on these bonds is 7.55 percent. How many years do these bonds have left until they mature?

23. **Using Bond Quotes [LO2]** Suppose the following bond quotes for IOU Corporation appear in the financial page of today's newspaper. Assume the bond has a face value of $1,000 and the current date is April 15, 2009. What is the yield to maturity of the bond? What is the current yield?

Company (Ticker)	Coupon	Maturity	Last Price	Last Yield	EST Vol (000s)
IOU (IOU)	7.2	Apr 15, 2023	108.96	??	1,827

24. **Bond Prices versus Yields [LO2]**
    a. What is the relationship between the price of a bond and its YTM?
    b. Explain why some bonds sell at a premium over par value while other bonds sell at a discount. What do you know about the relationship between the coupon rate and the YTM for premium bonds? What about for discount bonds? For bonds selling at par value?
    c. What is the relationship between the current yield and YTM for premium bonds? For discount bonds? For bonds selling at par value?

25. **Interest on Zeroes [LO2]** Tesla Corporation needs to raise funds to finance a plant expansion, and it has decided to issue 25-year zero coupon bonds to raise the money. The required return on the bonds will be 9 percent.
    a. What will these bonds sell for at issuance?
    b. Using the IRS amortization rule, what interest deduction can the company take on these bonds in the first year? In the last year?
    c. Repeat part (b) using the straight-line method for the interest deduction.
    d. Based on your answers in (b) and (c), which interest deduction method would Tesla Corporation prefer? Why?

26. **Zero Coupon Bonds [LO2]** Suppose your company needs to raise $30 million and you want to issue 30-year bonds for this purpose. Assume the required return on your bond issue will be 8 percent, and you're evaluating two issue alternatives: an 8 percent semiannual coupon bond and a zero coupon bond. Your company's tax rate is 35 percent.
    a. How many of the coupon bonds would you need to issue to raise the $30 million? How many of the zeroes would you need to issue?
    b. In 30 years, what will your company's repayment be if you issue the coupon bonds? What if you issue the zeroes?

Visit us at www.mhhe.com/rwj

c. Based on your answers in (a) and (b), why would you ever want to issue the zeroes? To answer, calculate the firm's aftertax cash outflows for the first year under the two different scenarios. Assume the IRS amortization rules apply for the zero coupon bonds.

27. **Finding the Maturity** [LO2] You've just found a 10 percent coupon bond on the market that sells for par value. What is the maturity on this bond?

28. **Real Cash Flows** [LO4] You want to have $1.5 million in real dollars in an account when you retire in 40 years. The nominal return on your investment is 11 percent and the inflation rate is 3.8 percent. What real amount must you deposit each year to achieve your goal?

29. **Components of Bond Returns** [LO2] Bond P is a premium bond with a 12 percent coupon. Bond D is a 6 percent coupon bond currently selling at a discount. Both bonds make annual payments, have a YTM of 9 percent, and have five years to maturity. What is the current yield for bond P? For bond D? If interest rates remain unchanged, what is the expected capital gains yield over the next year for bond P? For bond D? Explain your answers and the interrelationships among the various types of yields.

CHALLENGE
(Questions 29–35)
Z

30. **Holding Period Yield** [LO2] The YTM on a bond is the interest rate you earn on your investment if interest rates don't change. If you actually sell the bond before it matures, your realized return is known as the *holding period yield* (HPY).

a. Suppose that today you buy a 7 percent annual coupon bond for $1,060. The bond has 10 years to maturity. What rate of return do you expect to earn on your investment?

b. Two years from now, the YTM on your bond has declined by 1 percent, and you decide to sell. What price will your bond sell for? What is the HPY on your investment? Compare this yield to the YTM when you first bought the bond. Why are they different?

31. **Valuing Bonds** [LO2] The McKeegan Corporation has two different bonds currently outstanding. Bond M has a face value of $20,000 and matures in 20 years. The bond makes no payments for the first six years, then pays $1,100 every six months over the subsequent eight years, and finally pays $1,400 every six months over the last six years. Bond N also has a face value of $20,000 and a maturity of 20 years; it makes no coupon payments over the life of the bond. If the required return on both these bonds is 7 percent compounded semiannually, what is the current price of bond M? Of bond N?

32. **Valuing the Call Feature** [LO2] Consider the prices in the following three Treasury issues as of May 15, 2007:

6.500	May 13n	106:10	106:12	−13	5.28
8.250	May 13	103:14	103:16	− 3	5.24
12.000	May 13	134:25	134:31	−15	5.32

The bond in the middle is callable in February 2008. What is the implied value of the call feature? (*Hint:* Is there a way to combine the two noncallable issues to create an issue that has the same coupon as the callable bond?)

33. **Treasury Bonds** [LO2] The following Treasury bond quote appeared in *The Wall Street Journal* on May 11, 2004:

9.125	May 09	100:03	100:04	. . .	−2.15

Why would anyone buy this Treasury bond with a negative yield to maturity? How is this possible?

Visit us at www.mhhe.com/rwj

34. **Real Cash Flows [LO4]** When Marilyn Monroe died, ex-husband Joe DiMaggio vowed to place fresh flowers on her grave every Sunday as long as he lived. The week after she died in 1962, a bunch of fresh flowers that the former baseball player thought appropriate for the star cost about $5. Based on actuarial tables, "Joltin' Joe" could expect to live for 30 years after the actress died. Assume that the EAR is 8.4 percent. Also, assume that the price of the flowers will increase at 3.7 percent per year, when expressed as an EAR. Assuming that each year has exactly 52 weeks, what is the present value of this commitment? Joe began purchasing flowers the week after Marilyn died.

35. **Real Cash Flows [LO4]** You are planning to save for retirement over the next 30 years. To save for retirement, you will invest $900 a month in a stock account in real dollars and $450 a month in a bond account in real dollars. The effective annual return of the stock account is expected to be 11 percent, and the bond account will earn 7 percent. When you retire, you will combine your money into an account with a 9 percent effective return. The inflation rate over this period is expected to be 4 percent. How much can you withdraw each month from your account in real terms assuming a 25-year withdrawal period? What is the nominal dollar amount of your last withdrawal?

Visit us at www.mhhe.com/rwj

MINICASE

Financing S&S Air's Expansion Plans with a Bond Issue

Mark Sexton and Todd Story, the owners of S&S Air, have decided to expand their operations. They instructed their newly hired financial analyst, Chris Guthrie, to enlist an underwriter to help sell $35 million in new 10-year bonds to finance construction. Chris has entered into discussions with Kim McKenzie, an underwriter from the firm of Raines and Warren, about which bond features S&S Air should consider and what coupon rate the issue will likely have.

Although Chris is aware of the bond features, he is uncertain about the costs and benefits of some features, so he isn't sure how each feature would affect the coupon rate of the bond issue. You are Kim's assistant, and she has asked you to prepare a memo to Chris describing the effect of each of the following bond features on the coupon rate of the bond. She would also like you to list any advantages or disadvantages of each feature:

QUESTIONS

1. The security of the bond—that is, whether the bond has collateral.

2. The seniority of the bond.

3. The presence of a sinking fund.

4. A call provision with specified call dates and call prices.

5. A deferred call accompanying the call provision.

6. A make-whole call provision.

7. Any positive covenants. Also, discuss several possible positive covenants S&S Air might consider.

8. Any negative covenants. Also, discuss several possible negative covenants S&S Air might consider.

9. A conversion feature (note that S&S Air is not a publicly traded company).

10. A floating-rate coupon.

LEARNING OBJECTIVES

After studying this chapter, you should understand:

LO1 How stock prices depend on future dividends and dividend growth.

LO2 The different ways corporate directors are elected to office.

LO3 How the stock markets work.

STOCK VALUATION

8

WHEN THE STOCK MARKET CLOSED on May 8, 2008, the common stock of McGraw-Hill, publisher of fine quality college textbooks, was going for $40.80 per share. On that same day, stock in Carnival Corp., the cruise line company, closed at $40.46, while stock in Adobe Systems, the software developer, closed at $39.24. Because the stock prices of these three companies were so similar, you might expect that they would be offering similar dividends to their stockholders, but you would be wrong. In fact, Carnival's annual dividend was $2.90 per share, McGraw-Hill's was $.88 per share, and Adobe Systems was paying no dividends at all!

As we will see in this chapter, the dividends currently being paid are one of the primary factors we look at when attempting to value common stocks. However, it is obvious from looking at Adobe that current dividends are not the end of the story. This chapter explores dividends, stock values, and the connection between the two.

Master the ability to solve problems in this chapter by using a spreadsheet. Access Excel Master on the student Web site www.mhhe.com/rwj.

In our previous chapter, we introduced you to bonds and bond valuation. In this chapter, we turn to the other major source of financing for corporations: common and preferred stock. We first describe the cash flows associated with a share of stock and then go on to develop a famous result, the dividend growth model. From there, we move on to examine various important features of common and preferred stock, focusing on shareholder rights. We close the chapter with a discussion of how shares of stock are traded and how stock prices and other important information are reported in the financial press.

8.1 Common Stock Valuation

A share of common stock is more difficult to value in practice than a bond for at least three reasons. First, with common stock, not even the promised cash flows are known in advance. Second, the life of the investment is essentially forever because common stock has no maturity. Third, there is no way to easily observe the rate of return that the market requires. Nonetheless, as we will see, there are cases in which we can come up with the present value of the future cash flows for a share of stock and thus determine its value.

CASH FLOWS

Imagine that you are considering buying a share of stock today. You plan to sell the stock in one year. You somehow know that the stock will be worth $70 at that time. You predict that the stock will also pay a $10 per share dividend at the end of the year. If you require a 25 percent return on your investment, what is the most you would pay for the stock? In other words, what is the present value of the $10 dividend along with the $70 ending value at 25 percent?

If you buy the stock today and sell it at the end of the year, you will have a total of $80 in cash. At 25 percent:

Present value = ($10 + 70)/1.25 = $64

Therefore, $64 is the value you would assign to the stock today.

More generally, let P_0 be the current price of the stock, and assign P_1 to be the price in one period. If D_1 is the cash dividend paid at the end of the period, then:

$$P_0 = (D_1 + P_1)/(1 + R) \qquad \text{[8.1]}$$

where R is the required return in the market on this investment.

Notice that we really haven't said much so far. If we wanted to determine the value of a share of stock today (P_0), we would first have to come up with the value in one year (P_1). This is even harder to do, so we've only made the problem more complicated.

What is the price in one period, P_1? We don't know in general. Instead, suppose we somehow knew the price in two periods, P_2. Given a predicted dividend in two periods, D_2, the stock price in one period would be:

$$P_1 = (D_2 + P_2)/(1 + R)$$

If we were to substitute this expression for P_1 into our expression for P_0, we would have:

$$P_0 = \frac{D_1 + P_1}{1 + R} = \frac{D_1 + \dfrac{D_2 + P_2}{1 + R}}{1 + R}$$

$$= \frac{D_1}{(1 + R)^1} + \frac{D_2}{(1 + R)^2} + \frac{P_2}{(1 + R)^2}$$

Now we need to get a price in two periods. We don't know this either, so we can procrastinate again and write:

$$P_2 = (D_3 + P_3)/(1 + R)$$

If we substitute this back in for P_2, we have:

$$P_0 = \frac{D_1}{(1+R)^1} + \frac{D_2}{(1+R)^2} + \frac{P_2}{(1+R)^2}$$

$$= \frac{D_1}{(1+R)^1} + \frac{D_2}{(1+R)^2} + \frac{\dfrac{D_3 + P_3}{1+R}}{(1+R)^2}$$

$$= \frac{D_1}{(1+R)^1} + \frac{D_2}{(1+R)^2} + \frac{D_3}{(1+R)^3} + \frac{P_3}{(1+R)^3}$$

You should start to notice that we can push the problem of coming up with the stock price off into the future forever. Note that no matter what the stock price is, the present value is essentially zero if we push the sale of the stock far enough away.[1] What we are eventually left with is the result that the current price of the stock can be written as the present value of the dividends beginning in one period and extending out forever.

$$P_0 = \frac{D_1}{(1+R)^1} + \frac{D_2}{(1+R)^2} + \frac{D_3}{(1+R)^3} + \frac{D_4}{(1+R)^4} + \frac{D_5}{(1+R)^5} + \cdots$$

We have illustrated here that the price of the stock today is equal to the present value of all of the future dividends. How many future dividends are there? In principle, there can be an infinite number. This means that we still can't compute a value for the stock because we would have to forecast an infinite number of dividends and then discount them all. In the next section, we consider some special cases in which we can get around this problem.

Growth Stocks	**EXAMPLE 8.1**

You might be wondering about shares of stock in companies such as Yahoo! that currently pay no dividends. Small, growing companies frequently plow back everything and thus pay no dividends. Are such shares worth nothing? It depends. When we say that the value of the stock is equal to the present value of the future dividends, we don't rule out the possibility that some number of those dividends are zero. They just can't *all* be zero.

Imagine a company that has a provision in its corporate charter that prohibits the paying of dividends now or ever. The corporation never borrows any money, never pays out any money to stockholders in any form whatsoever, and never sells any assets. Such a corporation couldn't really exist because the IRS wouldn't like it, and the stockholders could always vote to amend the charter if they wanted to. If it did exist, however, what would the stock be worth?

The stock is worth absolutely nothing. Such a company is a financial "black hole." Money goes in, but nothing valuable ever comes out. Because nobody would ever get any return on this investment, the investment has no value. This example is a little absurd, but it illustrates that when we speak of companies that don't pay dividends, what we really mean is that they are not *currently* paying dividends.

---

[1] The only assumption we make about the stock price is that it is a finite number no matter how far away we push it. It can be extremely large, just not infinitely so. Because no one has ever observed an infinite stock price, this assumption is plausible.

SOME SPECIAL CASES

In a few useful special circumstances, we can come up with a value for the stock. What we have to do is make some simplifying assumptions about the pattern of future dividends. The three cases we consider are the following: (1) The dividend has a zero growth rate, (2) the dividend grows at a constant rate, and (3) the dividend grows at a constant rate after some length of time. We consider each of these separately.

Zero Growth   The case of zero growth is one we've already seen. A share of common stock in a company with a constant dividend is much like a share of preferred stock. From Chapter 6 (Example 6.7), we know that the dividend on a share of preferred stock has zero growth and thus is constant through time. For a zero-growth share of common stock, this implies that:

$$D_1 = D_2 = D_3 = D = \text{constant}$$

So, the value of the stock is:

$$P_0 = \frac{D}{(1 + R)^1} + \frac{D}{(1 + R)^2} + \frac{D}{(1 + R)^3} + \frac{D}{(1 + R)^4} + \frac{D}{(1 + R)^5} + \cdots$$

Because the dividend is always the same, the stock can be viewed as an ordinary perpetuity with a cash flow equal to D every period. The per-share value is thus given by:

$$P_0 = D/R \tag{8.2}$$

where R is the required return.

For example, suppose the Paradise Prototyping Company has a policy of paying a $10 per share dividend every year. If this policy is to be continued indefinitely, what is the value of a share of stock if the required return is 20 percent? The stock in this case amounts to an ordinary perpetuity, so the stock is worth $10/.20 = $50 per share.

Constant Growth   Suppose we know that the dividend for some company always grows at a steady rate. Call this growth rate g. If we let D_0 be the dividend just paid, then the next dividend, D_1, is:

$$D_1 = D_0 \times (1 + g)$$

The dividend in two periods is:

$$D_2 = D_1 \times (1 + g)$$
$$= [D_0 \times (1 + g)] \times (1 + g)$$
$$= D_0 \times (1 + g)^2$$

We could repeat this process to come up with the dividend at any point in the future. In general, from our discussion of compound growth in Chapter 6, we know that the dividend t periods into the future, D_t, is given by:

$$D_t = D_0 \times (1 + g)^t$$

As we have previously seen, an asset with cash flows that grow at a constant rate forever is called a *growing perpetuity*.

The assumption of steady dividend growth might strike you as peculiar. Why would the dividend grow at a constant rate? The reason is that, for many companies, steady growth in dividends is an explicit goal. For example, in 2008, Procter & Gamble, the Cincinnati-based maker of personal care and household products, increased its dividend by 14.3 percent to $1.60 per share; this increase was notable because it was the 52nd in a row. The subject of dividend growth falls under the general heading of dividend policy, so we will defer further discussion of it to a later chapter.

Dividend Growth

EXAMPLE 8.2

The Hedless Corporation has just paid a dividend of $3 per share. The dividend of this company grows at a steady rate of 8 percent per year. Based on this information, what will the dividend be in five years?

Here we have a $3 current amount that grows at 8 percent per year for five years. The future amount is thus:

$3 × 1.08^5 = $3 × 1.4693 = $4.41

The dividend will therefore increase by $1.41 over the coming five years.

If the dividend grows at a steady rate, then we have replaced the problem of forecasting an infinite number of future dividends with the problem of coming up with a single growth rate, a considerable simplification. In this case, if we take D_0 to be the dividend just paid and g to be the constant growth rate, the value of a share of stock can be written as:

$$P_0 = \frac{D_1}{(1 + R)^1} + \frac{D_2}{(1 + R)^2} + \frac{D_3}{(1 + R)^3} + \cdots$$

$$= \frac{D_0(1 + g)^1}{(1 + R)^1} + \frac{D_0(1 + g)^2}{(1 + R)^2} + \frac{D_0(1 + g)^3}{(1 + R)^3} + \cdots$$

As long as the growth rate, g, is less than the discount rate, r, the present value of this series of cash flows can be written simply as:

$$P_0 = \frac{D_0 \times (1 + g)}{R - g} = \frac{D_1}{R - g} \qquad [8.3]$$

This elegant result goes by a lot of different names. We will call it the **dividend growth model**. By any name, it is easy to use. To illustrate, suppose D_0 is $2.30, R is 13 percent, and g is 5 percent. The price per share in this case is:

$$P_0 = D_0 \times (1 + g)/(R - g)$$
$$= \$2.30 \times 1.05/(.13 - .05)$$
$$= \$2.415/.08$$
$$= \$30.19$$

dividend growth model A model that determines the current price of a stock as its dividend next period divided by the discount rate less the dividend growth rate.

We can actually use the dividend growth model to get the stock price at any point in time, not just today. In general, the price of the stock as of time t is:

$$P_t = \frac{D_t \times (1 + g)}{R - g} = \frac{D_{t+1}}{R - g} \qquad [8.4]$$

In our example, suppose we are interested in the price of the stock in five years, P_5. We first need the dividend at time 5, D_5. Because the dividend just paid is $2.30 and the growth rate is 5 percent per year, D_5 is:

$$D_5 = \$2.30 \times 1.05^5 = \$2.30 \times 1.2763 = \$2.935$$

From the dividend growth model, we get the price of the stock in five years:

$$P_5 = \frac{D_5 \times (1 + g)}{R - g} = \frac{\$2.935 \times 1.05}{.13 - .05} = \frac{\$3.0822}{.08} = \$38.53$$

EXAMPLE 8.3 | **Gordon Growth Company**

The next dividend for the Gordon Growth Company will be $4 per share. Investors require a 16 percent return on companies such as Gordon. Gordon's dividend increases by 6 percent every year. Based on the dividend growth model, what is the value of Gordon's stock today? What is the value in four years?

The only tricky thing here is that the next dividend, D_1, is given as $4, so we won't multiply this by $(1 + g)$. With this in mind, the price per share is given by:

$$P_0 = D_1/(R - g)$$
$$= \$4/(.16 - .06)$$
$$= \$4/.10$$
$$= \$40$$

Because we already have the dividend in one year, we know that the dividend in four years is equal to $D_1 \times (1 + g)^3 = \$4 \times 1.06^3 = \$4.764$. The price in four years is therefore:

$$P_4 = D_4 \times (1 + g)/(R - g)$$
$$= \$4.764 \times 1.06/(.16 - .06)$$
$$= \$5.05/.10$$
$$= \$50.50$$

Notice in this example that P_4 is equal to $P_0 \times (1 + g)^4$.

$$P_4 = \$50.50 = \$40 \times 1.06^4 = P_0 \times (1 + g)^4$$

To see why this is so, notice first that:

$$P_4 = D_5/(R - g)$$

However, D_5 is just equal to $D_1 \times (1 + g)^4$, so we can write P_4 as:

$$P_4 = D_1 \times (1 + g)^4/(R - g)$$
$$= [D_1/(R - g)] \times (1 + g)^4$$
$$= P_0 \times (1 + g)^4$$

This last example illustrates that the dividend growth model makes the implicit assumption that the stock price will grow at the same constant rate as the dividend. This really isn't too surprising. What it tells us is that if the cash flows on an investment grow at a constant rate through time, so does the value of that investment.

You might wonder what would happen with the dividend growth model if the growth rate, g, were greater than the discount rate, R. It looks like we would get a negative stock price because $R - g$ would be less than zero. This is not what would happen.

Instead, if the constant growth rate exceeds the discount rate, then the stock price is infinitely large. Why? If the growth rate is bigger than the discount rate, the present value of the dividends keeps getting bigger. Essentially the same is true if the growth rate and the discount rate are equal. In both cases, the simplification that allows us to replace the infinite stream of dividends with the dividend growth model is "illegal," so the answers we get from the dividend growth model are nonsense unless the growth rate is less than the discount rate.

Finally, the expression we came up with for the constant growth case will work for any growing perpetuity, not just dividends on common stock. As we saw in Chapter 6, if C_1 is the next cash flow on a growing perpetuity, then the present value of the cash flows is given by:

Present value $= C_1/(R - g) = C_0(1 + g)/(R - g)$

Notice that this expression looks like the result for an ordinary perpetuity except that we have $R - g$ on the bottom instead of just R.

Nonconstant Growth   The next case we consider is nonconstant growth. The main reason to consider this case is to allow for "supernormal" growth rates over some finite length of time. As we discussed earlier, the growth rate cannot exceed the required return indefinitely, but it certainly could do so for some number of years. To avoid the problem of having to forecast and discount an infinite number of dividends, we will require that the dividends start growing at a constant rate sometime in the future.

For a simple example of nonconstant growth, consider the case of a company that is currently not paying dividends. You predict that, in five years, the company will pay a dividend for the first time. The dividend will be $.50 per share. You expect that this dividend will then grow at a rate of 10 percent per year indefinitely. The required return on companies such as this one is 20 percent. What is the price of the stock today?

To see what the stock is worth today, we first find out what it will be worth once dividends are paid. We can then calculate the present value of that future price to get today's price. The first dividend will be paid in five years, and the dividend will grow steadily from then on. Using the dividend growth model, we can say that the price in four years will be:

$$P_4 = D_4 \times (1 + g)/(R - g)$$
$$= D_5/(R - g)$$
$$= \$.50/(.20 - .10)$$
$$= \$5$$

If the stock will be worth $5 in four years, then we can get the current value by discounting this price back four years at 20 percent:

$$P_0 = \$5/1.20^4 = \$5/2.0736 = \$2.41$$

The stock is therefore worth $2.41 today.

The problem of nonconstant growth is only slightly more complicated if the dividends are not zero for the first several years. For example, suppose you have come up with the following dividend forecasts for the next three years:

Year	Expected Dividend
1	$1.00
2	$2.00
3	$2.50

After the third year, the dividend will grow at a constant rate of 5 percent per year. The required return is 10 percent. What is the value of the stock today?

In dealing with nonconstant growth, a time line can be helpful. Figure 8.1 illustrates one for this problem. The important thing to notice is when constant growth starts. As we've shown, for this problem, constant growth starts at time 3. This means we can use our constant growth model to determine the stock price at time 3, P_3. By far the most common mistake in this situation is to incorrectly identify the start of the constant growth phase and, as a result, calculate the future stock price at the wrong time.

As always, the value of the stock is the present value of all the future dividends. To calculate this present value, we first have to compute the present value of the stock price three years down the road, just as we did before. We then have to add in the present value of the

FIGURE 8.1

Nonconstant Growth

dividends that will be paid between now and then. So, the price in three years is:

$$P_3 = D_3 \times (1 + g)/(R - g)$$
$$= \$2.50 \times 1.05/(.10 - .05)$$
$$= \$52.50$$

We can now calculate the total value of the stock as the present value of the first three dividends plus the present value of the price at time 3, P_3:

$$P_0 = \frac{D_1}{(1 + R)^1} + \frac{D_2}{(1 + R)^2} + \frac{D_3}{(1 + R)^3} + \frac{P_3}{(1 + R)^3}$$
$$= \frac{\$1}{1.10} + \frac{2}{1.10^2} + \frac{2.50}{1.10^3} + \frac{52.50}{1.10^3}$$
$$= \$.91 + 1.65 + 1.88 + 39.44$$
$$= \$43.88$$

The value of the stock today is thus $43.88.

EXAMPLE 8.4 | **Supernormal Growth**

Chain Reaction, Inc., has been growing at a phenomenal rate of 30 percent per year because of its rapid expansion and explosive sales. You believe this growth rate will last for three more years and will then drop to 10 percent per year. If the growth rate then remains at 10 percent indefinitely, what is the total value of the stock? Total dividends just paid were $5 million, and the required return is 20 percent.

Chain Reaction's situation is an example of supernormal growth. It is unlikely that a 30 percent growth rate can be sustained for any extended time. To value the equity in this company, we first need to calculate the total dividends over the supernormal growth period:

Year	Total Dividends (in millions)
1	$5.00 × 1.3 = $ 6.500
2	6.50 × 1.3 = 8.450
3	8.45 × 1.3 = 10.985

The price at time 3 can be calculated as:

$$P_3 = D_3 \times (1 + g)/(R - g)$$

where g is the long-run growth rate. So, we have:

$$P_3 = \$10.985 \times 1.10/(.20 - .10) = \$120.835$$

(continued)

To determine the value today, we need the present value of this amount plus the present value of the total dividends:

$$P_0 = \frac{D_1}{(1 + R)^1} + \frac{D_2}{(1 + R)^2} + \frac{D_3}{(1 + R)^3} + \frac{P_3}{(1 + R)^3}$$

$$= \frac{\$6.50}{1.20} + \frac{8.45}{1.20^2} + \frac{10.985}{1.20^3} + \frac{120.835}{1.20^3}$$

$$= \$5.42 + 5.87 + 6.36 + 69.93$$

$$= \$87.58$$

The total value of the stock today is thus $87.58 million. If there were, for example, 20 million shares, then the stock would be worth $87.58/20 = $4.38 per share.

Two-Stage Growth   The last case we consider is a special case of nonconstant growth: two-stage growth. Here, the idea is that the dividend will grow at a rate of g_1 for t years and then grow at a rate of g_2 thereafter forever. In this case, the value of the stock can be written as:

$$P_0 = \frac{D_1}{R - g_1} \times \left[1 - \left(\frac{1 + g_1}{1 + R} \right)^t \right] + \frac{P_t}{(1 + R)^t} \qquad [8.5]$$

Notice that the first term in our expression is the present value of a growing annuity, which we discussed in Chapter 6. In this first stage, g_1 can be greater than R. The second part is the present value of the stock price once the second stage begins at time t.

We can calculate P_t as follows:

$$P_t = \frac{D_{t+1}}{R - g_2} = \frac{D_0 \times (1 + g_1)^t \times (1 + g_2)}{R - g_2} \qquad [8.6]$$

In this calculation, we need the dividend at time $t + 1$, D_{t+1}, to get the stock price at time t, P_t. Notice that to get it, we grew the current dividend, D_0, at rate g_1 for t periods and then grew it one period at rate g_2. Also, in this second stage, g_2 must be less than R.

Two-Stage Growth	EXAMPLE 8.5

The Highfield Company's dividend is expected to grow at 20 percent for the next five years. After that, the growth is expected to be 4 percent forever. If the required return is 10 percent, what's the value of the stock? The dividend just paid was $2.

There is a fair amount of computation here, but it is mostly just "plug and chug" with a calculator. We can start by calculating the stock price five years from now, P_5:

$$P_5 = \frac{D_6}{R - g_2} = \frac{D_0 \times (1 + g_1)^5 \times (1 + g_2)}{R - g_2}$$

$$= \frac{\$2 \times (1 + .20)^5 \times (1 + .04)}{.10 - .04} = \frac{\$5.18}{.06}$$

$$= \$86.26$$

We then plug into our two-stage growth formula to get the price today:

$$P_0 = \frac{D_1}{R - g_1} \times \left[1 - \left(\frac{1 + g_1}{1 + R} \right)^t \right] + \frac{P_t}{(1 + R)^t}$$

$$= \frac{\$2 \times (1 + .20)}{.10 - .20} \times \left[1 - \left(\frac{1 + .20}{1 + .10} \right)^5 \right] + \frac{\$86.26}{(1 + .10)^5}$$

$$= \$66.64$$

(continued)

Notice that we were given D_0 = \$2 here, so we had to grow it by 20 percent for one period to get D_1. Notice also that g_1 is bigger than R in this problem, but that fact does not cause a problem.

COMPONENTS OF THE REQUIRED RETURN

Thus far, we have taken the required return, or discount rate, R, as given. We will have quite a bit to say about this subject in Chapters 12 and 13. For now, we want to examine the implications of the dividend growth model for this required return. Earlier, we calculated P_0 as:

$$P_0 = D_1/(R - g)$$

If we rearrange this to solve for R, we get:

$$R - g = D_1/P_0$$
$$R = D_1/P_0 + g \qquad\qquad [8.7]$$

This tells us that the total return, R, has two components. The first of these, D_1/P_0, is called the **dividend yield**. Because this is calculated as the expected cash dividend divided by the current price, it is conceptually similar to the current yield on a bond.

dividend yield
A stock's expected cash dividend divided by its current price.

The second part of the total return is the growth rate, g. We know that the dividend growth rate is also the rate at which the stock price grows (see Example 8.3). Thus, this growth rate can be interpreted as the **capital gains yield**—that is, the rate at which the value of the investment grows.[2]

capital gains yield
The dividend growth rate, or the rate at which the value of an investment grows.

To illustrate the components of the required return, suppose we observe a stock selling for \$20 per share. The next dividend will be \$1 per share. You think that the dividend will grow by 10 percent per year more or less indefinitely. What return does this stock offer if this is correct?

The dividend growth model calculates total return as:

$$R = \text{Dividend yield} + \text{Capital gains yield}$$
$$R = \qquad D_1/P_0 \qquad + \qquad g$$

In this case, total return works out to be:

$$R = \$1/20 + 10\%$$
$$= 5\% + 10\%$$
$$= 15\%$$

This stock, therefore, has an expected return of 15 percent.

We can verify this answer by calculating the price in one year, P_1, using 15 percent as the required return. Based on the dividend growth model, this price is:

$$P_1 = D_1 \times (1 + g)/(R - g)$$
$$= \$1 \times 1.10/(.15 - .10)$$
$$= \$1.10/.05$$
$$= \$22$$

---

[2]Here and elsewhere, we use the term *capital gains* a little loosely. For the record, a capital gain (or loss) is, strictly speaking, something defined by the IRS. For our purposes, it would be more accurate (but less common) to use the term *price appreciation* instead of *capital gain*.

Notice that this $22 is $20 × 1.1, so the stock price has grown by 10 percent as it should. If you pay $20 for the stock today, you will get a $1 dividend at the end of the year, and you will have a $22 − 20 = $2 gain. Your dividend yield is thus $1/20 = 5%. Your capital gains yield is $2/20 = 10%, so your total return would be 5% + 10% = 15%.

To get a feel for actual numbers in this context, consider that, according to the 2008 Value Line *Investment Survey,* Procter & Gamble's dividends were expected to grow by 9 percent over the next 5 or so years, compared to a historical growth rate of 10.5 percent over the preceding 5 years and 11 percent over the preceding 10 years. In 2008, the projected dividend for the coming year was given as $1.67. The stock price at that time was about $66 per share. What is the return investors require on P&G? Here, the dividend yield is 2.5 percent and the capital gains yield is 9 percent, giving a total required return of 11.5 percent on P&G stock.

Our discussion of stock valuation is summarized in Table 8.1.

TABLE 8.1

Summary of Stock Valuation

I.   The General Case

In general, the price today of a share of stock, P_0, is the present value of all of its future dividends, $D_1, D_2, D_3, \ldots$:

$$P_0 = \frac{D_1}{(1 + R)^1} + \frac{D_2}{(1 + R)^2} + \frac{D_3}{(1 + R)^3} + \cdots$$

where R is the required return.

II.   Constant Growth Case

If the dividend grows at a steady rate, g, then the price can be written as:

$$P_0 = \frac{D_1}{R - g}$$

This result is called the *dividend growth model.*

III.   Nonconstant Growth

If the dividend grows steadily after t periods, then the price can be written as:

$$P_0 = \frac{D_1}{(1 + R)^1} + \frac{D_2}{(1 + R)^2} + \cdots + \frac{D_t}{(1 + R)^t} + \frac{P_t}{(1 + R)^t}$$

where

$$P_t = \frac{D_t \times (1 + g)}{(R - g)}$$

IV.   Two-Stage Growth

If the dividend grows at rate g_1 for t periods and then grows at rate g_2 thereafter, then the price can be written as:

$$P_0 = \frac{D_1}{R - g_1} \times \left[1 - \left(\frac{1 + g_1}{1 + R}\right)^t\right] + \frac{P_t}{(1 + R)^t}$$

where

$$P_t = \frac{D_{t+1}}{R - g_2} = \frac{D_0 \times (1 + g_1)^t \times (1 + g_2)}{R - g_2}$$

V.   The Required Return

The required return, R, can be written as the sum of two things:

$$R = D_1/P_0 + g$$

where D_1/P_0 is the *dividend yield* and g is the *capital gains yield* (which is the same thing as the growth rate in dividends for the steady growth case).

> **Concept Questions**
>
> **8.1a** What are the relevant cash flows for valuing a share of common stock?
> **8.1b** Does the value of a share of stock depend on how long you expect to keep it?
> **8.1c** What is the value of a share of stock when the dividend grows at a constant rate?

8.2 Some Features of Common and Preferred Stocks

In discussing common stock features, we focus on shareholder rights and dividend payments. For preferred stock, we explain what *preferred* means, and we also debate whether preferred stock is really debt or equity.

COMMON STOCK FEATURES

common stock
Equity without priority for dividends or in bankruptcy.

The term **common stock** means different things to different people, but it is usually applied to stock that has no special preference either in receiving dividends or in bankruptcy.

Shareholder Rights   The conceptual structure of the corporation assumes that shareholders elect directors who, in turn, hire managers to carry out their directives. Shareholders, therefore, control the corporation through the right to elect the directors. Generally, only shareholders have this right.

Directors are elected each year at an annual meeting. Although there are exceptions (discussed next), the general idea is "one share, one vote" (*not* one share*holder,* one vote). Corporate democracy is thus very different from our political democracy. With corporate democracy, the "golden rule" prevails absolutely.[3]

Directors are elected at an annual shareholders' meeting by a vote of the holders of a majority of shares who are present and entitled to vote. However, the exact mechanism for electing directors differs across companies. The most important difference is whether shares must be voted cumulatively or voted straight.

To illustrate the two different voting procedures, imagine that a corporation has two shareholders: Smith with 20 shares and Jones with 80 shares. Both want to be a director. Jones does not want Smith, however. We assume there are a total of four directors to be elected.

cumulative voting
A procedure in which a shareholder may cast all votes for one member of the board of directors.

The effect of **cumulative voting** is to permit minority participation.[4] If cumulative voting is permitted, the total number of votes that each shareholder may cast is determined first. This is usually calculated as the number of shares (owned or controlled) multiplied by the number of directors to be elected.

With cumulative voting, the directors are elected all at once. In our example, this means that the top four vote getters will be the new directors. A shareholder can distribute votes however he or she wishes.

Will Smith get a seat on the board? If we ignore the possibility of a five-way tie, then the answer is yes. Smith will cast $20 \times 4 = 80$ votes, and Jones will cast $80 \times 4 = 320$ votes. If Smith gives all his votes to himself, he is assured of a directorship. The reason is

---

[3]The golden rule: Whosoever has the gold makes the rules.

[4]By *minority participation,* we mean participation by shareholders with relatively small amounts of stock.

that Jones can't divide 320 votes among four candidates in such a way as to give all of them more than 80 votes, so Smith will finish fourth at worst.

In general, if there are N directors up for election, then $1/(N + 1)$ percent of the stock plus one share will guarantee you a seat. In our current example, this is $1/(4 + 1) = 20\%$. So the more seats that are up for election at one time, the easier (and cheaper) it is to win one.

With **straight voting**, the directors are elected one at a time. Each time, Smith can cast 20 votes and Jones can cast 80. As a consequence, Jones will elect all of the candidates. The only way to guarantee a seat is to own 50 percent plus one share. This also guarantees that you will win every seat, so it's really all or nothing.

straight voting
A procedure in which a shareholder may cast all votes for each member of the board of directors.

Buying the Election	**EXAMPLE 8.6**

Stock in JRJ Corporation sells for $20 per share and features cumulative voting. There are 10,000 shares outstanding. If three directors are up for election, how much does it cost to ensure yourself a seat on the board?

The question here is how many shares of stock it will take to get a seat. The answer is 2,501, so the cost is $2,501 \times \$20 = \$50,020$. Why 2,501? Because there is no way the remaining 7,499 votes can be divided among three people to give all of them more than 2,501 votes. For example, suppose two people receive 2,502 votes and the first two seats. A third person can receive at most $10,000 - 2,502 - 2,502 - 2,501 = 2,495$, so the third seat is yours.

As we've illustrated, straight voting can "freeze out" minority shareholders; that is why many states have mandatory cumulative voting. In states where cumulative voting is mandatory, devices have been worked out to minimize its impact.

One such device is to stagger the voting for the board of directors. With staggered elections, only a fraction of the directorships are up for election at a particular time. Thus if only two directors are up for election at any one time, it will take $1/(2 + 1) = 33.33\%$ of the stock plus one share to guarantee a seat.

Overall, staggering has two basic effects:

1. Staggering makes it more difficult for a minority to elect a director when there is cumulative voting because there are fewer directors to be elected at one time.

2. Staggering makes takeover attempts less likely to be successful because it makes it more difficult to vote in a majority of new directors.

We should note that staggering may serve a beneficial purpose. It provides "institutional memory"—that is, continuity on the board of directors. This may be important for corporations with significant long-range plans and projects.

Proxy Voting A **proxy** is the grant of authority by a shareholder to someone else to vote his or her shares. For convenience, much of the voting in large public corporations is actually done by proxy.

As we have seen, with straight voting, each share of stock has one vote. The owner of 10,000 shares has 10,000 votes. Large companies have hundreds of thousands or even millions of shareholders. Shareholders can come to the annual meeting and vote in person, or they can transfer their right to vote to another party.

Obviously, management always tries to get as many proxies as possible transferred to it. However, if shareholders are not satisfied with management, an "outside" group of shareholders can try to obtain votes via proxy. They can vote by proxy in an attempt to replace management by electing enough directors. The resulting battle is called a *proxy fight*.

proxy
A grant of authority by a shareholder allowing another individual to vote his or her shares.

Classes of Stock   Some firms have more than one class of common stock. Often the classes are created with unequal voting rights. The Ford Motor Company, for example, has Class B common stock, which is not publicly traded (it is held by Ford family interests and trusts). This class has 40 percent of the voting power, even though it represents less than 10 percent of the total number of shares outstanding.

There are many other cases of corporations with different classes of stock. For example, at one time, General Motors had its "GM Classic" shares (the original) and two additional classes, Class E ("GME") and Class H ("GMH"). These classes were created to help pay for two large acquisitions, Electronic Data Systems and Hughes Aircraft. Another good example is Google, the Web search company, which only recently became publicly owned. Google has two classes of common stock, A and B. The Class A shares are held by the public, and each share has one vote. The Class B shares are held by company insiders, and each Class B share has 10 votes. As a result, Google's founders and managers control the company.

Historically, the New York Stock Exchange did not allow companies to create classes of publicly traded common stock with unequal voting rights. Exceptions (like Ford) appear to have been made. In addition, many non-NYSE companies have dual classes of common stock.

A primary reason for creating dual or multiple classes of stock has to do with control of the firm. If such stock exists, management of a firm can raise equity capital by issuing nonvoting or limited-voting stock while maintaining control.

The subject of unequal voting rights is controversial in the United States, and the idea of one share, one vote has a strong following and a long history. Interestingly, however, shares with unequal voting rights are quite common in the United Kingdom and elsewhere around the world.

Other Rights   The value of a share of common stock in a corporation is directly related to the general rights of shareholders. In addition to the right to vote for directors, shareholders usually have the following rights:

1. The right to share proportionally in dividends paid.
2. The right to share proportionally in assets remaining after liabilities have been paid in a liquidation.
3. The right to vote on stockholder matters of great importance, such as a merger. Voting is usually done at the annual meeting or a special meeting.

In addition, stockholders sometimes have the right to share proportionally in any new stock sold. This is called the *preemptive right*.

Essentially, a preemptive right means that a company that wishes to sell stock must first offer it to the existing stockholders before offering it to the general public. The purpose is to give stockholders the opportunity to protect their proportionate ownership in the corporation.

Dividends   A distinctive feature of corporations is that they have shares of stock on which they are authorized by law to pay dividends to their shareholders. **Dividends** paid to shareholders represent a return on the capital directly or indirectly contributed to the corporation by the shareholders. The payment of dividends is at the discretion of the board of directors.

dividends
Payments by a corporation to shareholders, made in either cash or stock.

Some important characteristics of dividends include the following:

1. Unless a dividend is declared by the board of directors of a corporation, it is not a liability of the corporation. A corporation cannot default on an undeclared dividend.

As a consequence, corporations cannot become bankrupt because of nonpayment of dividends. The amount of the dividend and even whether it is paid are decisions based on the business judgment of the board of directors.

2. The payment of dividends by the corporation is not a business expense. Dividends are not deductible for corporate tax purposes. In short, dividends are paid out of the corporation's aftertax profits.

3. Dividends received by individual shareholders are taxable. In 2008, the tax rate was 15 percent, but this favorable rate may change. However, corporations that own stock in other corporations are permitted to exclude 70 percent of the dividend amounts they receive and are taxed on only the remaining 30 percent.[5]

PREFERRED STOCK FEATURES

Preferred stock differs from common stock because it has preference over common stock in the payment of dividends and in the distribution of corporation assets in the event of liquidation. *Preference* means only that the holders of the preferred shares must receive a dividend (in the case of an ongoing firm) before holders of common shares are entitled to anything.

Preferred stock is a form of equity from a legal and tax standpoint. It is important to note, however, that holders of preferred stock sometimes have no voting privileges.

preferred stock
Stock with dividend priority over common stock, normally with a fixed dividend rate, sometimes without voting rights.

Stated Value Preferred shares have a stated liquidating value, usually $100 per share. The cash dividend is described in terms of dollars per share. For example, General Motors "$5 preferred" easily translates into a dividend yield of 5 percent of stated value.

Cumulative and Noncumulative Dividends A preferred dividend is *not* like interest on a bond. The board of directors may decide not to pay the dividends on preferred shares, and their decision may have nothing to do with the current net income of the corporation.

Dividends payable on preferred stock are either *cumulative* or *noncumulative;* most are cumulative. If preferred dividends are cumulative and are not paid in a particular year, they will be carried forward as an *arrearage*. Usually, both the accumulated (past) preferred dividends and the current preferred dividends must be paid before the common shareholders can receive anything.

Unpaid preferred dividends are *not* debts of the firm. Directors elected by the common shareholders can defer preferred dividends indefinitely. However, in such cases, common shareholders must also forgo dividends. In addition, holders of preferred shares are often granted voting and other rights if preferred dividends have not been paid for some time. For example, as of summer 1996, USAir had failed to pay dividends on one of its preferred stock issues for six quarters. As a consequence, the holders of the shares were allowed to nominate two people to represent their interests on the airline's board. Because preferred stockholders receive no interest on the accumulated dividends, some have argued that firms have an incentive to delay paying preferred dividends; but, as we have seen, this may mean sharing control with preferred stockholders.

Is Preferred Stock Really Debt? A good case can be made that preferred stock is really debt in disguise, a kind of equity bond. Preferred shareholders receive a stated dividend

---

[5]For the record, the 70 percent exclusion applies when the recipient owns less than 20 percent of the outstanding stock in a corporation. If a corporation owns more than 20 percent but less than 80 percent, the exclusion is 80 percent. If more than 80 percent is owned, the corporation can file a single "consolidated" return and the exclusion is effectively 100 percent.

only; and if the corporation is liquidated, preferred shareholders get a stated value. Often, preferred stocks carry credit ratings much like those of bonds. Furthermore, preferred stock is sometimes convertible into common stock, and preferred stocks are often callable.

In addition, many issues of preferred stock have obligatory sinking funds. The existence of such a sinking fund effectively creates a final maturity because it means that the entire issue will ultimately be retired. For these reasons, preferred stock seems to be a lot like debt. However, for tax purposes, preferred dividends are treated like common stock dividends.

In the 1990s, firms began to sell securities that looked a lot like preferred stocks but are treated as debt for tax purposes. The new securities were given interesting acronyms like TOPrS (trust-originated preferred securities, or toppers), MIPS (monthly income preferred securities), and QUIPS (quarterly income preferred securities), among others. Because of various specific features, these instruments can be counted as debt for tax purposes, making the interest payments tax deductible. Payments made to investors in these instruments are treated as interest for personal income taxes. Until 2003, interest payments and dividends were taxed at the same marginal tax rate. When the tax rate on dividend payments was reduced, these instruments were not included, so individuals must still pay their higher income tax rate on dividend payments received from these instruments.

Concept Questions

8.2a What is a proxy?

8.2b What rights do stockholders have?

8.2c Why is preferred stock called *preferred*?

8.3 The Stock Markets

Back in Chapter 1, we briefly mentioned that shares of stock are bought and sold on various stock exchanges, the two most important of which are the New York Stock Exchange and the NASDAQ. From our earlier discussion, recall that the stock market consists of a **primary market** and a **secondary market**. In the primary, or new issue, market, shares of stock are first brought to the market and sold to investors. In the secondary market, existing shares are traded among investors.

In the primary market, companies sell securities to raise money. We will discuss this process in detail in a later chapter. We therefore focus mainly on secondary market activity in this section. We conclude with a discussion of how stock prices are quoted in the financial press.

primary market
The market in which new securities are originally sold to investors.

secondary market
The market in which previously issued securities are traded among investors.

dealer
An agent who buys and sells securities from inventory.

broker
An agent who arranges security transactions among investors.

DEALERS AND BROKERS

Because most securities transactions involve dealers and brokers, it is important to understand exactly what is meant by the terms *dealer* and *broker*. A **dealer** maintains an inventory and stands ready to buy and sell at any time. In contrast, a **broker** brings buyers and sellers together but does not maintain an inventory. Thus, when we speak of used car dealers and real estate brokers, we recognize that the used car dealer maintains an inventory, whereas the real estate broker does not.

In the securities markets, a dealer stands ready to buy securities from investors wishing to sell them and sell securities to investors wishing to buy them. Recall from our previous chapter that the price the dealer is willing to pay is called the *bid price*. The price at which the dealer will sell is called the *ask price* (sometimes called the asked, offered, or offering price). The difference between the bid and ask prices is called the *spread*, and it is the basic source of dealer profits.

Dealers exist in all areas of the economy, not just the stock markets. For example, your local college bookstore is probably both a primary and a secondary market textbook dealer. If you buy a new book, this is a primary market transaction. If you buy a used book, this is a secondary market transaction, and you pay the store's ask price. If you sell the book back, you receive the store's bid price (often half of the ask price). The bookstore's spread is the difference between the two prices.

In contrast, a securities broker arranges transactions between investors, matching investors wishing to buy securities with investors wishing to sell securities. The distinctive characteristic of security brokers is that they do not buy or sell securities for their own accounts. Facilitating trades by others is their business.

How big is the bid–ask spread on your favorite stock? Check out the latest quotes at www.bloomberg.com.

ORGANIZATION OF THE NYSE

The New York Stock Exchange, or NYSE, popularly known as the Big Board, celebrated its bicentennial a few years ago. It has occupied its current location on Wall Street since the turn of the twentieth century. Measured in terms of dollar volume of activity and the total value of shares listed, it is the largest stock market in the world.

Members The NYSE has 1,366 exchange **members**. Prior to 2006, the exchange members were said to own "seats" on the exchange, and collectively the members of the exchange were also the owners. For this and other reasons, seats were valuable and were bought and sold fairly regularly. Seat prices reached a record $4 million in 2005.

In 2006, all of this changed when the NYSE became a publicly owned corporation. Naturally, its stock is listed on the NYSE. Now, instead of purchasing seats, exchange members must purchase trading licenses, the number of which is still limited to 1,366. In 2008, a license would set you back a cool $40,000—per year. Having a license entitles you to buy and sell securities on the floor of the exchange. Different members play different roles in this regard.

The largest number of NYSE members are registered as **commission brokers**. The business of a commission broker is to execute customer orders to buy and sell stocks. A commission broker's primary responsibility to customers is to get the best possible prices for their orders. The exact number varies, but usually about 500 NYSE members are commission brokers. NYSE commission brokers typically are employees of brokerage companies such as Merrill Lynch.

Second in number of NYSE members are **specialists**, so named because each of them acts as an assigned dealer for a small set of securities. With a few exceptions, each security listed for trading on the NYSE is assigned to a single specialist. Specialists are also called *market makers* because they are obligated to maintain a fair, orderly market for the securities assigned to them.

Specialists post bid prices and ask prices for securities assigned to them. Specialists make a market by standing ready to buy at bid prices and sell at asked prices when there is a temporary disparity between the flow of buy orders and that of sell orders for a security. In this capacity, they act as dealers for their own accounts.

member
As of 2006, a member is the owner of a trading license on the NYSE.

commission brokers
NYSE members who execute customer orders to buy and sell stock transmitted to the exchange floor.

specialist
A NYSE member acting as a dealer in a small number of securities on the exchange floor; often called a *market maker*.

floor brokers
NYSE members who execute orders for commission brokers on a fee basis; sometimes called *$2 brokers*.

Third in number of exchange members are **floor brokers**. Floor brokers are used by commission brokers who are too busy to handle certain orders themselves. Such commission brokers will delegate some orders to floor brokers for execution. Floor brokers are sometimes called *$2 brokers,* a name earned when the standard fee for their service was only $2.

SuperDOT system
An electronic NYSE system allowing orders to be transmitted directly to the specialist.

In recent years, floor brokers have become less important on the exchange floor because of the efficient **SuperDOT system** (the *DOT* stands for Designated Order Turnaround), which allows orders to be transmitted electronically directly to the specialist. SuperDOT trading now accounts for a substantial percentage of all trading on the NYSE, particularly on smaller orders.

floor traders
NYSE members who trade for their own accounts, trying to anticipate temporary price fluctuations.

Finally, a small number of NYSE members are **floor traders** who independently trade for their own accounts. Floor traders try to anticipate temporary price fluctuations and profit from them by buying low and selling high. In recent decades, the number of floor traders has declined substantially, suggesting that it has become increasingly difficult to profit from short-term trading on the exchange floor.

Operations   Now that we have a basic idea of how the NYSE is organized and who the major players are, we turn to the question of how trading actually takes place. Fundamentally, the business of the NYSE is to attract and process **order flow**. The term *order flow* means the flow of customer orders to buy and sell stocks. The customers of the NYSE are the millions of individual investors and tens of thousands of institutional investors who place their orders to buy and sell shares in NYSE-listed companies. The NYSE has been quite successful in attracting order flow. Currently, it is not unusual for well over a billion shares to change hands in a single day.

order flow
The flow of customer orders to buy and sell securities.

Floor Activity   It is quite likely that you have seen footage of the NYSE trading floor on television, or you may have visited the NYSE and viewed exchange floor activity from the visitors' gallery (it's worth the trip). Either way, you would have seen a big room, about the size of a basketball gym. This big room is called, technically, "the Big Room." There are a few other, smaller rooms that you normally don't see, one of which is called "the Garage" because that is what it was before it was taken over for trading.

Take a virtual field trip to the New York Stock Exchange at www.nyse.com.

On the floor of the exchange are a number of stations, each with a roughly figure-eight shape. These stations have multiple counters with numerous terminal screens above and on the sides. People operate behind and in front of the counters in relatively stationary positions.

Other people move around on the exchange floor, frequently returning to the many telephones positioned along the exchange walls. In all, you may be reminded of worker ants moving around an ant colony. It is natural to wonder, "What are all those people doing down there (and why are so many wearing funny-looking coats)?"

specialist's post
A fixed place on the exchange floor where the specialist operates.

As an overview of exchange floor activity, here is a quick look at what goes on. Each of the counters at a figure-eight–shaped station is a **specialist's post**. Specialists normally operate in front of their posts to monitor and manage trading in the stocks assigned to them. Clerical employees working for the specialists operate behind the counter. Moving from the many telephones lining the walls of the exchange out to the exchange floor and back again are swarms of commission brokers, receiving telephoned customer orders, walking out to specialists' posts where the orders can be executed, and returning to confirm order executions and receive new customer orders.

To better understand activity on the NYSE trading floor, imagine yourself as a commission broker. Your phone clerk has just handed you an order to sell 20,000 shares of Wal-Mart for a customer of the brokerage company that employs you. The customer wants to sell the stock at the best possible price as soon as possible. You immediately walk (running violates exchange rules) to the specialist's post where Wal-Mart stock is traded.

As you approach the specialist's post where Wal-Mart is traded, you check the terminal screen for information on the current market price. The screen reveals that the last executed trade was at 60.10 and that the specialist is bidding 60 per share. You could immediately sell to the specialist at 60, but that would be too easy.

Instead, as the customer's representative, you are obligated to get the best possible price. It is your job to "work" the order, and your job depends on providing satisfactory order execution service. So, you look around for another broker who represents a customer who wants to buy Wal-Mart stock. Luckily, you quickly find another broker at the specialist's post with an order to buy 20,000 shares. Noticing that the specialist is asking 60.10 per share, you both agree to execute your orders with each other at a price of 60.05. This price is exactly halfway between the specialist's bid and ask prices, and it saves each of your customers $.05 \times 20,000 = \$1,000$ as compared to dealing at the posted prices.

For a very actively traded stock, there may be many buyers and sellers around the specialist's post, and most of the trading will be done directly between brokers. This is called trading in the "crowd." In such cases, the specialist's responsibility is to maintain order and to make sure that all buyers and sellers receive a fair price. In other words, the specialist essentially functions as a referee.

More often, however, there will be no crowd at the specialist's post. Going back to our Wal-Mart example, suppose you are unable to quickly find another broker with an order to buy 20,000 shares. Because you have an order to sell immediately, you may have no choice but to sell to the specialist at the bid price of 60. In this case, the need to execute an order quickly takes priority, and the specialist provides the liquidity necessary to allow immediate order execution.

Finally, note that colored coats are worn by many of the people on the floor of the exchange. The color of the coat indicates the person's job or position. Clerks, runners, visitors, exchange officials, and so on wear particular colors to identify themselves. Also, things can get a little hectic on a busy day, with the result that good clothing doesn't last long; the cheap coats offer some protection.

NASDAQ OPERATIONS

In terms of total dollar volume of trading, the second largest stock market in the United States is NASDAQ (say "Naz-dak"). The somewhat odd name originally was an acronym for the National Association of Securities Dealers Automated Quotations system, but NASDAQ is now a name in its own right.

Introduced in 1971, the NASDAQ market is a computer network of securities dealers and others that disseminates timely security price quotes to computer screens worldwide. NASDAQ dealers act as market makers for securities listed on NASDAQ. As market makers, NASDAQ dealers post bid and ask prices at which they accept sell and buy orders, respectively. With each price quote, they also post the number of stock shares that they obligate themselves to trade at their quoted prices.

Like NYSE specialists, NASDAQ market makers trade on an inventory basis—that is, using their inventory as a buffer to absorb buy and sell order imbalances. Unlike the NYSE specialist system, NASDAQ features multiple market makers for actively traded stocks. Thus, there are two key differences between the NYSE and NASDAQ:

1. NASDAQ is a computer network and has no physical location where trading takes place.
2. NASDAQ has a multiple market maker system rather than a specialist system.

over-the-counter (OTC) market
Securities market in which trading is almost exclusively done through dealers who buy and sell for their own inventories.

Traditionally, a securities market largely characterized by dealers who buy and sell securities for their own inventories is called an **over-the-counter (OTC) market**. Consequently, NASDAQ is often referred to as an OTC market. However, in their efforts to promote a distinct image, NASDAQ officials prefer that the term OTC not be used when referring to the NASDAQ market. Nevertheless, old habits die hard, and many people still refer to NASDAQ as an OTC market.

By 2008, the NASDAQ had grown to the point that it was, by some measures, bigger than the NYSE. For example, on May 7, 2008, 2.3 billion shares were traded on the NASDAQ versus 1.3 billion on the NYSE. In dollars, NASDAQ trading volume for the day was $68.6 billion compared to $48.8 billion for the NYSE.

NASDAQ
(www.nasdaq.com)
has a great Web site; check it out!

The NASDAQ is actually made up of three separate markets: the NASDAQ Global Select Market, the NASDAQ Global Market, and the NASDAQ Capital Market. As the market for NASDAQ's larger and more actively traded securities, the Global Select Market lists about 1,200 companies (as of early 2008), including some of the best-known companies in the world, such as Microsoft and Intel. Global Market companies are somewhat smaller in size, and NASDAQ lists about 1,450 of these. Finally, the smallest companies listed on NASDAQ are in the NASDAQ Capital Market; about 550 are currently listed. Of course, as Capital Market companies become more established, they may move up to the Global Market or Global Select Market.

electronic communications network (ECN)
A Web site that allows investors to trade directly with each other.

ECNs In a very important development in the late 1990s, the NASDAQ system was opened to so-called **electronic communications networks (ECNs)**. ECNs are basically Web sites that allow investors to trade directly with one another. Investor buy and sell orders placed on ECNs are transmitted to the NASDAQ and displayed along with market maker bid and ask prices. As a result, the ECNs open up the NASDAQ by essentially allowing individual investors, not just market makers, to enter orders. As a result, the ECNs act to increase liquidity and competition.

Of course, the NYSE and NASDAQ are not the only places stocks are traded. See our nearby *Work the Web* box for a discussion of somewhat wilder markets.

You can get real-time stock quotes on the Web. See finance.yahoo.com *for details.*

STOCK MARKET REPORTING

In recent years, the reporting of stock prices and related information has increasingly moved from traditional print media, such as *The Wall Street Journal,* to various Web sites. Yahoo! Finance (finance.yahoo.com) is a good example. We went there and requested a

WORK THE WEB

Where do companies go when they can't (or don't want to) meet the listing requirements of the larger stock exchanges? Two options are the Over-the-Counter Bulletin Board (OTCBB) and the Pink Sheets. These two electronic markets are part of the Wild, Wild West of stock trading. The somewhat odd names have simple explanations. The OTCBB began as an electronic bulletin board that was created to facilitate OTC trading in nonlisted stocks. The name "Pink Sheets" just reflects the fact that, at one time, prices for such stocks were quoted on pink sheets of paper.

The well-known markets such as NASDAQ and the NYSE have relatively strict listing requirements. If a company fails to meet these requirements, it can be delisted. The OTCBB and the Pink Sheets, on the other hand, have no listing requirements. The OTCBB does require that companies file financial statements with the SEC (or other relevant agency), but the Pink Sheets does not.

(continued)

Stocks traded on these markets often have very low prices and are frequently referred to as *penny stocks, microcaps,* or even *nanocaps*. Relatively few brokers do any research on these companies, so information is often spread through word of mouth or the Internet, not the most reliable of sources. In fact, for many stocks, these markets often look like big electronic rumor mills and gossip factories. To get a feel for what trading looks like, we captured a typical screen from the OTCBB Web site (www.otcbb.com):

Market Statistics

Data delayed 15-20 minutes

OTCBB ▾   Vol Actives ▾   GO

Name	Symbol	Last	Tick	Chg	% Chg	Open	High	Low	Volume
Earth Biofuels Inc.	EBOF	.016	△	.001	6.67%	.016	.02	.014	771.16 m
SmarTire Systems Inc.	SMTR	.0002	—	.00	.00%	.0001	.0002	.0001	211.87 m
Syndication Inc.	SYDI	.0002	▼	-.0001	-33.33%	.0002	.0003	.0002	118.12 m
iVoice Inc.	IVOI	.0002	—	.00	.00%	.0001	.0002	.0001	72.12 m
AmeriResource Technologies Inc.	ARRT	.0001	—	.00	.00%	.0001	.0001	.0001	36.97 m
Avitar Inc.	AVTI	.0006	▼	-.0002	-25.00%	.0008	.0009	.0006	21.8 m
Universal Detection Technology	UDTT	.0005	—	.00	.00%	.0004	.0005	.0004	20.9 m
Fonix Corp.	FNIX	.0002	△	.0001	100.00%	.0002	.0002	.0001	18.85 m
Spongetech Delivery Systems Inc.	SPNG	.0468	△	.0068	17.00%	.042	.048	.04	17.14 m
Gulf Coast Oil & Gas Inc.	GCOG	.0016	△	.0002	14.29%	.0014	.0016	.0012	16.56 m

First, take a look at the returns. Fonix Corp. had a return at this point in the day of 100 percent! That's not something you see very often. Of course, the big return was generated with a whopping price increase of $.0001 per share. A stock listed on the OTCBB is often the most actively traded stock on any particular day. For example, by the end of this particular day, Microsoft was the most active stock on NASDAQ, trading about 69.5 million shares. Four stocks on the OTCBB traded even more shares. Earth Biofuels, Inc., led the way with slightly over 771 million shares traded. But, at an average price of, say $.015 per share, the total dollar volume in Earth Biofuels was all of $11,565,000. In contrast, trades in Microsoft amounted to about $2 billion.

The Pink Sheets (www.pinksheets.com) is operated by a privately owned company. To be listed on the Pink Sheets, a company just has to find a market maker willing to trade in the company's stock. Companies list on the Pink Sheets for various reasons. Small companies that do not wish to meet listing requirements are one type. Foreign companies often list on the Pink Sheets because they do not prepare their financial statements according to GAAP, a requirement for listing on U.S. stock exchanges. There are many companies that were formerly listed on bigger stock markets that were either delisted involuntarily or chose to "go dark" for various reasons, including, as we discussed in Chapter 1, the costs associated with Sarbox compliance.

All in all, the OTCBB and Pink Sheets can be pretty wild places to trade. Low stock prices allow for huge percentage returns on small stock price movements. Be advised, however, that attempts at manipulation and fraud are commonplace. Also, stocks on these markets are often thinly traded, meaning there is little volume. It is not unusual for a stock listed on either market to have no trades on a given day. Even two or three days in a row without a trade in a particular stock is not uncommon.

Questions

1. *After the close of the markets (4 PM Eastern time), go to finance.yahoo.com and find the stocks on the major exchanges that were the most active during the day. Now go to www.otcbb.com and find the most active stocks traded on the OTCBB for the same day. How many stocks on the OTCBB were more active than the most active stock on the NYSE? The NASDAQ?*

2. *What were the biggest percentage winners and losers on the OTCBB during the current day? How much did the stock price increase or decrease to account for this change?*

stock quote on wholesale club Costco, which is listed on the NASDAQ. Here is a portion of what we found:

COSTCO WHOLESALE C (NasdaqGS: COST)			
NEW Real-time: 73.31 ↑.07(.10%) 2:28PM ET			
Last Trade:	**73.28**	Day's Range:	**70.67 - 74.75**
Trade Time:	**2:13PM ET**	52wk Range:	**54.85 - 75.23**
Change:	↑ .04 (.05%)	Volume:	**6,857,298**
Prev Close:	**73.24**	Avg Vol (3m):	**4,929,560**
Open:	**73.83**	Market Cap:	**31.75B**
Bid:	**73.27 x 100**	P/E (ttm):	**27.63**
Ask:	**73.28 x 100**	EPS (ttm):	**2.65**
1y Target Est:	**70.17**	Div & Yield:	**.64 (.90%)**

COST 29-May 2:07pm (C)Yahoo!

Add COST to Your Portfolio
Set Alert for COST
Download Data
Download Annual Report
Add Quotes to Your Web Site

Most of this information is self-explanatory. Two prices are reported, one in real time ($73.31) and one with a 15-minute delay ($73.28). Availability of real-time prices for free is a relatively new development. The reported change is from the previous day's closing price. The opening price is the first trade of the day. We see the bid and ask prices of $73.27 and $73.28, respectively, along with the market "depth," which is the number of shares sought at the bid price and offered at the ask price. The "1y Target Est" is the average estimated stock price one year ahead based on estimates from security analysts who follow the stock.

Moving to the second column, we have the range of prices for this day, followed by the range over the previous 52 weeks. Volume is the number of shares traded today, followed by average daily volume over the last three months. Market cap is number of shares outstanding (from the most recent quarterly financial statements) multiplied by the current price per share. P/E is the PE ratio we discussed in Chapter 3. The earnings per share (EPS) used in the calculation is "ttm," meaning "trailing twelve months." Finally, we have the dividend on the stock, which is actually the most recent quarterly dividend multiplied by 4, and the dividend yield. Notice that the yield is just the reported dividend divided by the stock price: $.64/$73.28 = .009 = .9%.

Concept Questions

8.3a What is the difference between a securities broker and a securities dealer?

8.3b Which is bigger, the bid price or the ask price? Why?

8.3c How does NASDAQ differ from the NYSE?

8.4 Summary and Conclusions

This chapter has covered the basics of stocks and stock valuation:

1. The cash flows from owning a share of stock come in the form of future dividends. We saw that in certain special cases it is possible to calculate the present value of all the future dividends and thus come up with a value for the stock.

2. As the owner of shares of common stock in a corporation, you have various rights, including the right to vote to elect corporate directors. Voting in corporate elections can be either cumulative or straight. Most voting is actually done by proxy, and a

Visit us at www.mhhe.com/rwj

proxy battle breaks out when competing sides try to gain enough votes to elect their candidates for the board.

3. In addition to common stock, some corporations have issued preferred stock. The name stems from the fact that preferred stockholders must be paid first, before common stockholders can receive anything. Preferred stock has a fixed dividend.

4. The two biggest stock markets in the United States are the NYSE and NASDAQ. We discussed the organization and operation of these two markets, and we saw how stock price information is reported in the financial press.

This chapter completes Part 3 of our book. By now, you should have a good grasp of what we mean by *present value*. You should also be familiar with how to calculate present values, loan payments, and so on. In Part 4, we cover capital budgeting decisions. As you will see, the techniques you learned in Chapters 5–8 form the basis for our approach to evaluating business investment decisions.

CHAPTER REVIEW AND SELF-TEST PROBLEMS

8.1 Dividend Growth and Stock Valuation The Brigapenski Co. has just paid a cash dividend of $2 per share. Investors require a 16 percent return from investments such as this. If the dividend is expected to grow at a steady 8 percent per year, what is the current value of the stock? What will the stock be worth in five years?

8.2 More Dividend Growth and Stock Valuation In Self-Test Problem 8.1, what would the stock sell for today if the dividend was expected to grow at 20 percent per year for the next three years and then settle down to 8 percent per year, indefinitely?

ANSWERS TO CHAPTER REVIEW AND SELF-TEST PROBLEMS

8.1 The last dividend, D_0, was $2. The dividend is expected to grow steadily at 8 percent. The required return is 16 percent. Based on the dividend growth model, we can say that the current price is:

$$P_0 = D_1/(R - g) = D_0 \times (1 + g)/(R - g)$$
$$= \$2 \times 1.08/(.16 - .08)$$
$$= \$2.16/.08$$
$$= \$27$$

We could calculate the price in five years by calculating the dividend in five years and then using the growth model again. Alternatively, we could recognize that the stock price will increase by 8 percent per year and calculate the future price directly. We'll do both. First, the dividend in five years will be:

$$D_5 = D_0 \times (1 + g)^5$$
$$= \$2 \times 1.08^5$$
$$= \$2.9387$$

The price in five years would therefore be:

$$P_5 = D_5 \times (1 + g)/(R - g)$$
$$= \$2.9387 \times 1.08/.08$$
$$= \$3.1738/.08$$
$$= \$39.67$$

Visit us at www.mhhe.com/rwj

Once we understand the dividend model, however, it's easier to notice that:

$$P_5 = P_0 \times (1 + g)^5$$
$$= \$27 \times 1.08^5$$
$$= \$27 \times 1.4693$$
$$= \$39.67$$

Notice that both approaches yield the same price in five years.

8.2   In this scenario, we have supernormal growth for the next three years. We'll need to calculate the dividends during the rapid growth period and the stock price in three years. The dividends are:

$$D_1 = \$2.00 \times 1.20 = \$2.400$$
$$D_2 = \$2.40 \times 1.20 = \$2.880$$
$$D_3 = \$2.88 \times 1.20 = \$3.456$$

After three years, the growth rate falls to 8 percent indefinitely. The price at that time, P_3, is thus:

$$P_3 = D_3 \times (1 + g)/(R - g)$$
$$= \$3.456 \times 1.08/(.16 - .08)$$
$$= \$3.7325/.08$$
$$= \$46.656$$

To complete the calculation of the stock's present value, we have to determine the present value of the three dividends and the future price:

$$P_0 = \frac{D_1}{(1 + R)^1} + \frac{D_2}{(1 + R)^2} + \frac{D_3}{(1 + R)^3} + \frac{P_3}{(1 + R)^3}$$
$$= \frac{\$2.40}{1.16} + \frac{2.88}{1.16^2} + \frac{3.456}{1.16^3} + \frac{46.656}{1.16^3}$$
$$= \$2.07 + 2.14 + 2.21 + 29.89$$
$$= \$36.31$$

CONCEPTS REVIEW AND CRITICAL THINKING QUESTIONS

1. **Stock Valuation [LO1]** Why does the value of a share of stock depend on dividends?

2. **Stock Valuation [LO1]** A substantial percentage of the companies listed on the NYSE and NASDAQ don't pay dividends, but investors are nonetheless willing to buy shares in them. How is this possible given your answer to the previous question?

3. **Dividend Policy [LO1]** Referring to the previous questions, under what circumstances might a company choose not to pay dividends?

4. **Dividend Growth Model [LO1]** Under what two assumptions can we use the dividend growth model presented in the chapter to determine the value of a share of stock? Comment on the reasonableness of these assumptions.

5. **Common versus Preferred Stock [LO1]** Suppose a company has a preferred stock issue and a common stock issue. Both have just paid a $2 dividend. Which do you think will have a higher price, a share of the preferred or a share of the common?

Visit us at www.mhhe.com/rwj

6. **Dividend Growth Model** [LO1] Based on the dividend growth model, what are the two components of the total return on a share of stock? Which do you think is typically larger?

7. **Growth Rate** [LO1] In the context of the dividend growth model, is it true that the growth rate in dividends and the growth rate in the price of the stock are identical?

8. **Voting Rights** [LO2] When it comes to voting in elections, what are the differences between U.S. political democracy and U.S. corporate democracy?

9. **Corporate Ethics** [LO2] Is it unfair or unethical for corporations to create classes of stock with unequal voting rights?

10. **Voting Rights** [LO2] Some companies, such as Reader's Digest, have created classes of stock with no voting rights at all. Why would investors buy such stock?

11. **Stock Valuation** [LO1] Evaluate the following statement: Managers should not focus on the current stock value because doing so will lead to an overemphasis on short-term profits at the expense of long-term profits.

12. **Two-Stage Dividend Growth Model** [LO1] One of the assumptions of the two-stage growth model is that the dividends drop immediately from the high growth rate to the perpetual growth rate. What do you think about this assumption? What happens if this assumption is violated?

QUESTIONS AND PROBLEMS

1. **Stock Values** [LO1] The Jackson–Timberlake Wardrobe Co. just paid a dividend of $1.95 per share on its stock. The dividends are expected to grow at a constant rate of 6 percent per year indefinitely. If investors require an 11 percent return on The Jackson–Timberlake Wardrobe Co. stock, what is the current price? What will the price be in three years? In 15 years?

2. **Stock Values** [LO1] The next dividend payment by Hot Wings, Inc., will be $2.10 per share. The dividends are anticipated to maintain a 5 percent growth rate forever. If the stock currently sells for $48 per share, what is the required return?

3. **Stock Values** [LO1] For the company in the previous problem, what is the dividend yield? What is the expected capital gains yield?

4. **Stock Values** [LO1] Metroplex Corporation will pay a $3.04 per share dividend next year. The company pledges to increase its dividend by 3.8 percent per year indefinitely. If you require an 11 percent return on your investment, how much will you pay for the company's stock today?

5. **Stock Valuation** [LO1] Keenan Co. is expected to maintain a constant 5.2 percent growth rate in its dividends indefinitely. If the company has a dividend yield of 6.3 percent, what is the required return on the company's stock?

6. **Stock Valuation** [LO1] Suppose you know that a company's stock currently sells for $47 per share and the required return on the stock is 11 percent. You also know that the total return on the stock is evenly divided between a capital gains yield and a dividend yield. If it's the company's policy to always maintain a constant growth rate in its dividends, what is the current dividend per share?

7. **Stock Valuation** [LO1] Apocalyptica Corp. pays a constant $9.75 dividend on its stock. The company will maintain this dividend for the next 11 years and will then cease paying dividends forever. If the required return on this stock is 10 percent, what is the current share price?

BASIC
(Questions 1–9)

8.   **Valuing Preferred Stock [LO1]**   Resnor, Inc., has an issue of preferred stock outstanding that pays a $5.50 dividend every year in perpetuity. If this issue currently sells for $108 per share, what is the required return?

9.   **Stock Valuation and Required Return [LO1]**   Red, Inc., Yellow Corp., and Blue Company each will pay a dividend of $2.35 next year. The growth rate in dividends for all three companies is 5 percent. The required return for each company's stock is 8 percent, 11 percent, and 14 percent, respectively. What is the stock price for each company? What do you conclude about the relationship between the required return and the stock price?

INTERMEDIATE
(Questions 10–21)
✗

10.   **Stock Valuation [LO1]**   Great Pumpkin Farms just paid a dividend of $3.50 on its stock. The growth rate in dividends is expected to be a constant 5 percent per year indefinitely. Investors require a 14 percent return on the stock for the first three years, a 12 percent return for the next three years, and a 10 percent return thereafter. What is the current share price?

11.   **Nonconstant Growth [LO1]**   Metallica Bearings, Inc., is a young start-up company. No dividends will be paid on the stock over the next nine years because the firm needs to plow back its earnings to fuel growth. The company will pay a $10 per share dividend in 10 years and will increase the dividend by 5 percent per year thereafter. If the required return on this stock is 14 percent, what is the current share price?

12.   **Nonconstant Dividends [LO1]**   Bread, Inc., has an odd dividend policy. The company has just paid a dividend of $6 per share and has announced that it will increase the dividend by $4 per share for each of the next five years, and then never pay another dividend. If you require an 11 percent return on the company's stock, how much will you pay for a share today?

✗ 13.   **Nonconstant Dividends [LO1]**   Far Side Corporation is expected to pay the following dividends over the next four years: $11, $8, $5, and $2. Afterward, the company pledges to maintain a constant 5 percent growth rate in dividends forever. If the required return on the stock is 12 percent, what is the current share price?

14.   **Supernormal Growth [LO1]**   Marcel Co. is growing quickly. Dividends are expected to grow at a 30 percent rate for the next three years, with the growth rate falling off to a constant 6 percent thereafter. If the required return is 13 percent and the company just paid a $1.80 dividend, what is the current share price?

15.   **Supernormal Growth [LO1]**   Eva Corp. is experiencing rapid growth. Dividends are expected to grow at 25 percent per year during the next three years, 15 percent over the following year, and then 8 percent per year indefinitely. The required return on this stock is 13 percent, and the stock currently sells for $76 per share. What is the projected dividend for the coming year?

16.   **Negative Growth [LO1]**   Antiques R Us is a mature manufacturing firm. The company just paid a $10.46 dividend, but management expects to reduce the payout by 4 percent per year indefinitely. If you require an 11.5 percent return on this stock, what will you pay for a share today?

17.   **Finding the Dividend [LO1]**   Teder Corporation stock currently sells for $64 per share. The market requires a 10 percent return on the firm's stock. If the company maintains a constant 4.5 percent growth rate in dividends, what was the most recent dividend per share paid on the stock?

18.   **Valuing Preferred Stock [LO1]**   E-Eyes.com Bank just issued some new preferred stock. The issue will pay a $20 annual dividend in perpetuity, beginning 20 years

from now. If the market requires a 6.4 percent return on this investment, how much does a share of preferred stock cost today?

19. **Using Stock Quotes** [LO3] You have found the following stock quote for RJW Enterprises, Inc., in the financial pages of today's newspaper. What was the closing price for this stock that appeared in *yesterday's* paper? If the company currently has 25 million shares of stock outstanding, what was net income for the most recent four quarters?

| 52-WEEK | | STOCK (DIV) | YLD % | PE | VOL 100s | CLOSE | NET CHG |
HI	LO						
72.18	53.17	RJW 1.48	2.1	19	17652	??	−.23

20. **Two-Stage Dividend Growth Model** [LO1] Thirsty Cactus Corp. just paid a dividend of $1.25 per share. The dividends are expected to grow at 28 percent for the next eight years and then level off to a 6 percent growth rate indefinitely. If the required return is 13 percent, what is the price of the stock today?

21. **Two-Stage Dividend Growth Model** [LO1] Chartreuse County Choppers Inc. is experiencing rapid growth. The company expects dividends to grow at 25 percent per year for the next 11 years before leveling off at 6 percent into perpetuity. The required return on the company's stock is 12 percent. If the dividend per share just paid was $1.74, what is the stock price?

22. **Capital Gains versus Income** [LO1] Consider four different stocks, all of which have a required return of 19 percent and a most recent dividend of $4.50 per share. Stocks W, X, and Y are expected to maintain constant growth rates in dividends for the foreseeable future of 10 percent, 0 percent, and −5 percent per year, respectively. Stock Z is a growth stock that will increase its dividend by 20 percent for the next two years and then maintain a constant 12 percent growth rate thereafter. What is the dividend yield for each of these four stocks? What is the expected capital gains yield? Discuss the relationship among the various returns that you find for each of these stocks.

CHALLENGE
(Questions 22–28)
Ⓩ

23. **Stock Valuation** [LO1] Most corporations pay quarterly dividends on their common stock rather than annual dividends. Barring any unusual circumstances during the year, the board raises, lowers, or maintains the current dividend once a year and then pays this dividend out in equal quarterly installments to its shareholders.

    a. Suppose a company currently pays a $3.20 annual dividend on its common stock in a single annual installment, and management plans on raising this dividend by 6 percent per year indefinitely. If the required return on this stock is 12 percent, what is the current share price?

    b. Now suppose the company in (a) actually pays its annual dividend in equal quarterly installments; thus, the company has just paid a $.80 dividend per share, as it has for the previous three quarters. What is your value for the current share price now? (*Hint:* Find the equivalent annual end-of-year dividend for each year.) Comment on whether you think this model of stock valuation is appropriate.

24. **Nonconstant Growth** [LO1] Storico Co. just paid a dividend of $2.45 per share. The company will increase its dividend by 20 percent next year and will then reduce its dividend growth rate by 5 percentage points per year until it reaches the industry average of 5 percent dividend growth, after which the company will keep a constant growth rate forever. If the required return on Storico stock is 11 percent, what will a share of stock sell for today?

Visit us at www.mhhe.com/rwj

25. **Nonconstant Growth [LO1]** This one's a little harder. Suppose the current share price for the firm in the previous problem is $63.82 and all the dividend information remains the same. What required return must investors be demanding on Storico stock? (*Hint:* Set up the valuation formula with all the relevant cash flows, and use trial and error to find the unknown rate of return.)

26. **Constant Dividend Growth Model [LO1]** Assume a stock has dividends that grow at a constant rate forever. If you value the stock using the constant dividend growth model, how many years worth of dividends constitute one-half of the stock's current price?

27. **Two-Stage Dividend Growth [LO1]** Regarding the two-stage dividend growth model in the chapter, show that the price of a share of stock today can be written as follows:

$$P_0 = \frac{D_0 \times (1 + g_1)}{R - g_1} \times \left[1 - \left(\frac{1 + g_1}{1 + R}\right)^t\right] + \left(\frac{1 + g_1}{1 + R}\right)^t \times \frac{D_0 \times (1 + g_2)}{R - g_2}$$

Can you provide an intuitive interpretation of this expression?

28. **Two-Stage Dividend Growth [LO1]** The chapter shows that in the two-stage dividend growth model, the growth rate in the first stage, g_1, can be greater than or less than the discount rate, R. Can they be exactly equal? (*Hint:* Yes, but what does the expression for the value of the stock look like?)

MINICASE

Stock Valuation at Ragan, Inc.

Ragan, Inc., was founded nine years ago by brother and sister Carrington and Genevieve Ragan. The company manufactures and installs commercial heating, ventilation, and cooling (HVAC) units. Ragan, Inc., has experienced rapid growth because of a proprietary technology that increases the energy efficiency of its units. The company is equally owned by Carrington and Genevieve. The original partnership agreement between the siblings gave each 50,000 shares of stock. In the event either wished to sell stock, the shares first had to be offered to the other at a discounted price.

Although neither sibling wants to sell, they have decided they should value their holdings in the company. To get started, they have gathered the following information about their main competitors:

Expert HVAC Corporation's negative earnings per share were the result of an accounting write-off last year. Without the write-off, earnings per share for the company would have been $1.06.

Last year, Ragan, Inc., had an EPS of $4.54 and paid a dividend to Carrington and Genevieve of $63,000 each. The company also had a return on equity of 25 percent. The siblings believe that 20 percent is an appropriate required return for the company.

QUESTIONS

1. Assuming the company continues its current growth rate, what is the value per share of the company's stock?

Ragan, Inc., Competitors					
	EPS	DPS	Stock Price	ROE	R
Arctic Cooling, Inc.	$ .79	$.20	$14.18	10.00%	10.00%
National Heating & Cooling	1.38	.62	11.87	13.00	13.00
Expert HVAC Corp.	−.48	.38	13.21	14.00	12.00
Industry Average	$ .56	$.40	$13.09	12.33%	11.67%

2. To verify their calculations, Carrington and Genevieve have hired Josh Schlessman as a consultant. Josh was previously an equity analyst and covered the HVAC industry. Josh has examined the company's financial statements, as well as examining its competitors. Although Ragan, Inc., currently has a technological advantage, his research indicates that other companies are investigating methods to improve efficiency. Given this, Josh believes that the company's technological advantage will last only for the next five years. After that period, the company's growth will likely slow to the industry growth average. Additionally, Josh believes that the required return used by the company is too high. He believes the industry average required return is more appropriate. Under this growth rate assumption, what is your estimate of the stock price?

3. What is the industry average price–earnings ratio? What is the price–earnings ratio for Ragan, Inc.? Is this the relationship you would expect between the two ratios? Why?

4. Carrington and Genevieve are unsure how to interpret the price–earnings ratio. After some head scratching, they've come up with the following expression for the price–earnings ratio:

$$\frac{P_0}{E_1} = \frac{1-b}{R - (\text{ROE} \times b)}$$

Beginning with the constant dividend growth model, verify this result. What does this expression imply about the relationship between the dividend payout ratio, the required return on the stock, and the company's ROE?

5. Assume the company's growth rate slows to the industry average in five years. What future return on equity does this imply, assuming a constant payout ratio?

6. After discussing the stock value with Josh, Carrington and Genevieve agree that they would like to increase the value of the company stock. Like many small business owners, they want to retain control of the company, but they do not want to sell stock to outside investors. They also feel that the company's debt is at a manageable level and do not want to borrow more money. How can they increase the price of the stock? Are there any conditions under which this strategy would not increase the stock price?

After studying this chapter, you should understand:

LO1 The reasons why the net present value criterion is the best way to evaluate proposed investments.
LO2 The payback rule and some of its shortcomings.
LO3 The discounted payback rule and some of its shortcomings.
LO4 Accounting rates of return and some of the problems with them.
LO5 The internal rate of return criterion and its strengths and weaknesses.
LO6 The modified internal rate of return.
LO7 The profitability index and its relation to net present value.

9

NET PRESENT VALUE AND OTHER INVESTMENT CRITERIA

PART 4

Capital Budgeting

IN 2008, THE AUTOMOBILE MANUFACTURING INDUSTRY in North America was faced with chronic overcapacity. By some estimates, General Motors may have had as many as 12 factories more than it needed. But not all automobile manufacturers faced this problem. Toyota announced plans for its eighth North American assembly plant in Tupelo, Mississippi, a $1.3 billion (projected) investment. About the same time, Honda announced plans to build a new plant in southern Indiana at a cost of $550 million, and BMW announced an expansion of its Spartanburg, South Carolina, plant to build the new X6 model.

Toyota's new plant is an example of a capital budgeting decision. Decisions such as this one, with a price tag of over $1 billion, are obviously major undertakings, and the risks and rewards must be carefully weighed. In this chapter, we discuss the basic tools used in making such decisions.

In Chapter 1, we saw that increasing the value of the stock in a company is the goal of financial management. Thus, what we need to know is how to tell whether a particular investment will achieve that or not. This chapter considers a variety of techniques that are used in practice for this purpose. More important, it shows how many of these techniques can be misleading, and it explains why the net present value approach is the right one.

Master the ability to solve problems in this chapter by using a spreadsheet. Access Excel Master on the student Web site www.mhhe.com/rwj.

In Chapter 1, we identified the three key areas of concern to the financial manager. The first of these involved the question: What fixed assets should we buy? We called this the *capital budgeting decision.* In this chapter, we begin to deal with the issues that arise in answering this question.

The process of allocating or budgeting capital is usually more involved than just deciding whether to buy a particular fixed asset. We frequently face broader issues like whether we should launch a new product or enter a new market. Decisions such as these determine the nature of a firm's operations and products for years to come, primarily because fixed asset investments are generally long-lived and not easily reversed once they are made.

The most fundamental decision a business must make concerns its product line. What services will we offer or what will we sell? In what markets will we compete? What new products will we introduce? The answer to any of these questions will require that the firm commit its scarce and valuable capital to certain types of assets. As a result, all of these strategic issues fall under the general heading of capital budgeting. The process of capital budgeting could thus be given a more descriptive (not to mention impressive) name: *strategic asset allocation.*

For the reasons we have discussed, the capital budgeting question is probably the most important issue in corporate finance. How a firm chooses to finance its operations (the capital structure question) and how a firm manages its short-term operating activities (the working capital question) are certainly issues of concern, but the fixed assets define the business of the firm. Airlines, for example, are airlines because they operate airplanes, regardless of how they finance them.

Any firm possesses a huge number of possible investments. Each possible investment is an option available to the firm. Some options are valuable and some are not. The essence of successful financial management, of course, is learning to identify which are which. With this in mind, our goal in this chapter is to introduce you to the techniques used to analyze potential business ventures to decide which are worth undertaking.

We present and compare a number of different procedures used in practice. Our primary goal is to acquaint you with the advantages and disadvantages of the various approaches. As we will see, the most important concept in this area is the idea of net present value. We consider this next.

Net Present Value

9.1

In Chapter 1, we argued that the goal of financial management is to create value for the stockholders. The financial manager must thus examine a potential investment in light of its likely effect on the price of the firm's shares. In this section, we describe a widely used procedure for doing this: The net present value approach.

THE BASIC IDEA

An investment is worth undertaking if it creates value for its owners. In the most general sense, we create value by identifying an investment worth more in the marketplace than it costs us to acquire. How can something be worth more than it costs? It's a case of the whole being worth more than the cost of the parts.

For example, suppose you buy a run-down house for $25,000 and spend another $25,000 on painters, plumbers, and so on to get it fixed up. Your total investment is $50,000. When the work is completed, you place the house back on the market and find that it's worth $60,000. The market value ($60,000) exceeds the cost ($50,000) by $10,000. What you have done here is to act as a manager and bring together some fixed assets (a house), some labor (plumbers, carpenters, and others), and some materials (carpeting, paint, and so on). The net result is that you have created $10,000 in value. Put another way, this $10,000 is the *value added* by management.

With our house example, it turned out *after the fact* that $10,000 in value had been created. Things thus worked out nicely. The real challenge, of course, would have been to somehow identify *ahead of time* whether investing the necessary $50,000 was a good idea in the first place. This is what capital budgeting is all about—namely, trying to determine whether a proposed investment or project will be worth more, once it is in place, than it costs.

For reasons that will be obvious in a moment, the difference between an investment's market value and its cost is called the **net present value** of the investment, abbreviated **NPV**. In other words, net present value is a measure of how much value is created or added today by undertaking an investment. Given our goal of creating value for the stockholders, the capital budgeting process can be viewed as a search for investments with positive net present values.

net present value (NPV)
The difference between an investment's market value and its cost.

With our run-down house, you can probably imagine how we would go about making the capital budgeting decision. We would first look at what comparable, fixed-up properties were selling for in the market. We would then get estimates of the cost of buying a particular property and bringing it to market. At this point, we would have an estimated total cost and an estimated market value. If the difference was positive, then this investment would be worth undertaking because it would have a positive estimated net present value. There is risk, of course, because there is no guarantee that our estimates will turn out to be correct.

As our example illustrates, investment decisions are greatly simplified when there is a market for assets similar to the investment we are considering. Capital budgeting becomes much more difficult when we cannot observe the market price for at least roughly comparable investments. The reason is that we then face the problem of estimating the value of an investment using only indirect market information. Unfortunately, this is precisely the situation the financial manager usually encounters. We examine this issue next.

ESTIMATING NET PRESENT VALUE

Imagine we are thinking of starting a business to produce and sell a new product—say organic fertilizer. We can estimate the start-up costs with reasonable accuracy because we know what we will need to buy to begin production. Would this be a good investment? Based on our discussion, you know that the answer depends on whether the value of the new business exceeds the cost of starting it. In other words, does this investment have a positive NPV?

This problem is much more difficult than our "fixer upper" house example because entire fertilizer companies are not routinely bought and sold in the marketplace, so it is essentially impossible to observe the market value of a similar investment. As a result, we must somehow estimate this value by other means.

Based on our work in Chapters 5 and 6, you may be able to guess how we will go about estimating the value of our fertilizer business. We will first try to estimate the future cash flows we expect the new business to produce. We will then apply our basic discounted cash flow procedure to estimate the present value of those cash flows. Once we have this estimate, we will then estimate NPV as the difference between the present value of the future cash flows and the cost of the investment. As we mentioned in Chapter 5, this procedure is often called **discounted cash flow (DCF) valuation**.

discounted cash flow (DCF) valuation
The process of valuing an investment by discounting its future cash flows.

To see how we might go about estimating NPV, suppose we believe the cash revenues from our fertilizer business will be $20,000 per year, assuming everything goes as expected. Cash costs (including taxes) will be $14,000 per year. We will wind down the business in eight years. The plant, property, and equipment will be worth $2,000 as salvage at that time. The project costs $30,000 to launch. We use a 15 percent discount rate on new projects such as this one. Is this a good investment? If there are 1,000 shares of stock outstanding, what will be the effect on the price per share of taking this investment?

Find out more about capital budgeting for small businesses at www.smallbusinesslearning.net.

From a purely mechanical perspective, we need to calculate the present value of the future cash flows at 15 percent. The net cash inflow will be $20,000 cash income less $14,000 in costs per year for eight years. These cash flows are illustrated in Figure 9.1. As Figure 9.1 suggests, we effectively have an eight-year annuity of $20,000 − 14,000 = $6,000 per year, along with a single lump sum inflow of $2,000 in eight years. Calculating the present value of the future cash flows thus comes down to the same type of problem we considered in Chapter 6. The total present value is:

$$\text{Present value} = \$6,000 \times [1 - (1/1.15^8)]/.15 + (2,000/1.15^8)$$
$$= (\$6,000 \times 4.4873) + (2,000/3.0590)$$
$$= \$26,924 + 654$$
$$= \$27,578$$

FIGURE 9.1

Project Cash Flows ($000)

Time (years)	0	1	2	3	4	5	6	7	8
Initial cost	−$30								
Inflows		$ 20	$ 20	$ 20	$ 20	$ 20	$ 20	$ 20	$ 20
Outflows		−14	−14	−14	−14	−14	−14	−14	−14
Net inflow		$ 6	$ 6	$ 6	$ 6	$ 6	$ 6	$ 6	$ 6
Salvage									2
Net cash flow	−$30	$ 6	$ 6	$ 6	$ 6	$ 6	$ 6	$ 6	$ 8

When we compare this to the $30,000 estimated cost, we see that the NPV is:

$$NPV = -\$30,000 + 27,578 = -\$2,422$$

Therefore, this is *not* a good investment. Based on our estimates, taking it would *decrease* the total value of the stock by $2,422. With 1,000 shares outstanding, our best estimate of the impact of taking this project is a loss of value of $2,422/1,000 = $2.42 per share.

Our fertilizer example illustrates how NPV estimates can be used to determine whether an investment is desirable. From our example, notice that if the NPV is negative, the effect on share value will be unfavorable. If the NPV were positive, the effect would be favorable. As a consequence, all we need to know about a particular proposal for the purpose of making an accept–reject decision is whether the NPV is positive or negative.

Given that the goal of financial management is to increase share value, our discussion in this section leads us to the *net present value rule:*

> **An investment should be accepted if the net present value is positive and rejected if it is negative.**

In the unlikely event that the net present value turned out to be exactly zero, we would be indifferent between taking the investment and not taking it.

Two comments about our example are in order. First and foremost, it is not the rather mechanical process of discounting the cash flows that is important. Once we have the cash flows and the appropriate discount rate, the required calculations are fairly straightforward. The task of coming up with the cash flows and the discount rate is much more challenging. We will have much more to say about this in the next several chapters. For the remainder of this chapter, we take it as a given that we have estimates of the cash revenues and costs and, where needed, an appropriate discount rate.

The second thing to keep in mind about our example is that the −$2,422 NPV is an estimate. Like any estimate, it can be high or low. The only way to find out the true NPV would be to place the investment up for sale and see what we could get for it. We generally won't be doing this, so it is important that our estimates be reliable. Once again, we will say more about this later. For the rest of this chapter, we will assume the estimates are accurate.

Using the NPV Rule

EXAMPLE 9.1

Suppose we are asked to decide whether a new consumer product should be launched. Based on projected sales and costs, we expect that the cash flows over the five-year life of the project will be $2,000 in the first two years, $4,000 in the next two, and $5,000 in the last year. It will cost about $10,000 to begin production. We use a 10 percent discount rate to evaluate new products. What should we do here?

(continued)

Given the cash flows and discount rate, we can calculate the total value of the product by discounting the cash flows back to the present:

$$\text{Present value} = (\$2{,}000/1.1) + (2{,}000/1.1^2) + (4{,}000/1.1^3)$$
$$+ (4{,}000/1.1^4) + (5{,}000/1.1^5)$$
$$= \$1{,}818 + 1{,}653 + 3{,}005 + 2{,}732 + 3{,}105$$
$$= \$12{,}313$$

The present value of the expected cash flows is $12,313, but the cost of getting those cash flows is only $10,000, so the NPV is $12,313 − 10,000 = $2,313. This is positive; so, based on the net present value rule, we should take on the project.

As we have seen in this section, estimating NPV is one way of assessing the profitability of a proposed investment. It is certainly not the only way profitability is assessed, and we now turn to some alternatives. As we will see, when compared to NPV, each of the alternative ways of assessing profitability that we will examine is flawed in some key way; so NPV is the preferred approach in principle, if not always in practice.

SPREADSHEET STRATEGIES

Calculating NPVs with a Spreadsheet

Spreadsheets are commonly used to calculate NPVs. Examining the use of spreadsheets in this context also allows us to issue an important warning. Let's rework Example 9.1:

	A	B	C	D	E	F	G	H
1								
2		Using a spreadsheet to calculate net present values						
3								
4	From Example 9.1, the project's cost is $10,000. The cash flows are $2,000 per year for the first							
5	two years, $4,000 per year for the next two, and $5,000 in the last year. The discount rate is							
6	10 percent; what's the NPV?							
7								
8		Year	Cash Flow					
9		0	-$10,000		Discount rate =	10%		
10		1	2,000					
11		2	2,000		NPV =	$2,102.72	(*wrong* answer)	
12		3	4,000		NPV =	$2,312.99	(*right* answer)	
13		4	4,000					
14		5	5,000					
15								
16	The formula entered in cell F11 is =NPV(F9, C9:C14). This gives the wrong answer because the							
17	NPV function actually calculates present values, not *net* present values.							
18								
19	The formula entered in cell F12 is =NPV(F9, C10:C14) + C9. This gives the right answer because the							
20	NPV function is used to calculate the present value of the cash flows and then the initial cost is							
21	subtracted to calculate the answer. Notice that we added cell C9 because it is already negative.							

You can get a freeware NPV calculator at www.wheatworks.com.

In our spreadsheet example, notice that we have provided two answers. By comparing the answers to that found in Example 9.1, we see that the first answer is wrong even though we used the spreadsheet's NPV formula. What happened is that the "NPV" function in our spreadsheet is actually a PV function; unfortunately, one of the original spreadsheet programs many years ago got the definition wrong, and subsequent spreadsheets have copied it! Our second answer shows how to use the formula properly.

The example here illustrates the danger of blindly using calculators or computers without understanding what is going on; we shudder to think of how many capital budgeting decisions in the real world are based on incorrect use of this particular function. We will see another example of something that can go wrong with a spreadsheet later in the chapter.

Concept Questions

9.1a What is the net present value rule?

9.1b If we say an investment has an NPV of $1,000, what exactly do we mean?

The Payback Rule

9.2

It is common in practice to talk of the payback on a proposed investment. Loosely, the *payback* is the length of time it takes to recover our initial investment or "get our bait back." Because this idea is widely understood and used, we will examine it in some detail.

DEFINING THE RULE

We can illustrate how to calculate a payback with an example. Figure 9.2 shows the cash flows from a proposed investment. How many years do we have to wait until the accumulated cash flows from this investment equal or exceed the cost of the investment? As Figure 9.2 indicates, the initial investment is $50,000. After the first year, the firm has recovered $30,000, leaving $20,000. The cash flow in the second year is exactly $20,000, so this investment "pays for itself" in exactly two years. Put another way, the **payback period** is two years. If we require a payback of, say, three years or less, then this investment is acceptable. This illustrates the *payback period rule:*

payback period
The amount of time required for an investment to generate cash flows sufficient to recover its initial cost.

> **Based on the payback rule, an investment is acceptable if its calculated payback period is less than some prespecified number of years.**

In our example, the payback works out to be exactly two years. This won't usually happen, of course. When the numbers don't work out exactly, it is customary to work with fractional years. For example, suppose the initial investment is $60,000, and the cash flows are $20,000 in the first year and $90,000 in the second. The cash flows over the first two years are $110,000, so the project obviously pays back sometime in the second year. After the first year, the project has paid back $20,000, leaving $40,000 to be recovered. To figure

---

| **Calculating Payback** | **EXAMPLE 9.2** |

Here are the projected cash flows from a proposed investment:

Year	Cash Flow
1	$100
2	200
3	500

This project costs $500. What is the payback period for this investment?

The initial cost is $500. After the first two years, the cash flows total $300. After the third year, the total cash flow is $800, so the project pays back sometime between the end of year 2 and the end of year 3. Because the accumulated cash flows for the first two years are $300, we need to recover $200 in the third year. The third-year cash flow is $500, so we will have to wait $200/500 = .4 year to do this. The payback period is thus 2.4 years, or about two years and five months.

FIGURE 9.2

Net Project Cash Flows

Year	0	1	2	3	4
	−$50,000	$30,000	$20,000	$10,000	$5,000

TABLE 9.1

Expected Cash Flows for Projects A through E

Year	A	B	C	D	E
0	−$100	−$200	−$200	−$200	−$ 50
1	30	40	40	100	100
2	40	20	20	100	−50,000,000
3	50	10	10	−200	
4	60		130	200	

out the fractional year, note that this $40,000 is $40,000/90,000 = 4/9 of the second year's cash flow. Assuming that the $90,000 cash flow is received uniformly throughout the year, the payback would be 1⁴⁄₉ years.

Now that we know how to calculate the payback period on an investment, using the payback period rule for making decisions is straightforward. A particular cutoff time is selected—say, two years—and all investment projects that have payback periods of two years or less are accepted, whereas any that pay off in more than two years are rejected.

Table 9.1 illustrates cash flows for five different projects. The figures shown as the Year 0 cash flows are the costs of the investments. We examine these to indicate some peculiarities that can, in principle, arise with payback periods.

The payback for the first project, A, is easily calculated. The sum of the cash flows for the first two years is $70, leaving us with $100 − 70 = $30 to go. Because the cash flow in the third year is $50, the payback occurs sometime in that year. When we compare the $30 we need to the $50 that will be coming in, we get $30/50 = .6; so, payback will occur 60 percent of the way into the year. The payback period is thus 2.6 years.

Project B's payback is also easy to calculate: It *never* pays back because the cash flows never total up to the original investment. Project C has a payback of exactly four years because it supplies the $130 that B is missing in year 4. Project D is a little strange. Because of the negative cash flow in year 3, you can easily verify that it has two different payback periods, two years and four years. Which of these is correct? Both of them; the way the payback period is calculated doesn't guarantee a single answer. Finally, Project E is obviously unrealistic, but it does pay back in six months, thereby illustrating the point that a rapid payback does not guarantee a good investment.

ANALYZING THE RULE

When compared to the NPV rule, the payback period rule has some rather severe shortcomings. First, we calculate the payback period by simply adding up the future cash flows. There is no discounting involved, so the time value of money is completely ignored. The payback rule also fails to consider any risk differences. The payback would be calculated the same way for both very risky and very safe projects.

Perhaps the biggest problem with the payback period rule is coming up with the right cutoff period: We don't really have an objective basis for choosing a particular number. Put another way, there is no economic rationale for looking at payback in the first place, so we have no guide for how to pick the cutoff. As a result, we end up using a number that is arbitrarily chosen.

Year	Long	Short
0	-$250	-$250
1	100	100
2	100	200
3	100	0
4	100	0

TABLE 9.2

Investment Projected Cash Flows

Suppose we have somehow decided on an appropriate payback period of two years or less. As we have seen, the payback period rule ignores the time value of money for the first two years. More seriously, cash flows after the second year are ignored entirely. To see this, consider the two investments, Long and Short, in Table 9.2. Both projects cost $250. Based on our discussion, the payback on Long is $2 + (\$50/100) = 2.5$ years, and the payback on Short is $1 + (\$150/200) = 1.75$ years. With a cutoff of two years, Short is acceptable and Long is not.

Is the payback period rule guiding us to the right decisions? Maybe not. Suppose we require a 15 percent return on this type of investment. We can calculate the NPV for these two investments as:

$$NPV(Short) = -\$250 + (100/1.15) + (200/1.15^2) = -\$11.81$$
$$NPV(Long) = -\$250 + (100 \times \{[1 - (1/1.15^4)]/.15\}) = \$35.50$$

Now we have a problem. The NPV of the shorter-term investment is actually negative, meaning that taking it diminishes the value of the shareholders' equity. The opposite is true for the longer-term investment—it increases share value.

Our example illustrates two primary shortcomings of the payback period rule. First, by ignoring time value, we may be led to take investments (like Short) that actually are worth less than they cost. Second, by ignoring cash flows beyond the cutoff, we may be led to reject profitable long-term investments (like Long). More generally, using a payback period rule will tend to bias us toward shorter-term investments.

REDEEMING QUALITIES OF THE RULE

Despite its shortcomings, the payback period rule is often used by large and sophisticated companies when they are making relatively minor decisions. There are several reasons for this. The primary reason is that many decisions simply do not warrant detailed analysis because the cost of the analysis would exceed the possible loss from a mistake. As a practical matter, it can be said that an investment that pays back rapidly and has benefits extending beyond the cutoff period probably has a positive NPV.

Small investment decisions are made by the hundreds every day in large organizations. Moreover, they are made at all levels. As a result, it would not be uncommon for a corporation to require, for example, a two-year payback on all investments of less than $10,000. Investments larger than this would be subjected to greater scrutiny. The requirement of a two-year payback is not perfect for reasons we have seen, but it does exercise some control over expenditures and thus limits possible losses.

In addition to its simplicity, the payback rule has two other positive features. First, because it is biased toward short-term projects, it is biased toward liquidity. In other words, a payback rule tends to favor investments that free up cash for other uses quickly. This could be important for a small business; it would be less so for a large corporation. Second, the cash flows that are expected to occur later in a project's life are probably more uncertain. Arguably, a payback period rule adjusts for the extra riskiness of later cash flows, but it does so in a rather draconian fashion—by ignoring them altogether.

We should note here that some of the apparent simplicity of the payback rule is an illusion. The reason is that we still must come up with the cash flows first, and, as we discussed earlier, this is not at all easy to do. Thus, it would probably be more accurate to say that the *concept* of a payback period is both intuitive and easy to understand.

SUMMARY OF THE RULE

To summarize, the payback period is a kind of "break-even" measure. Because time value is ignored, you can think of the payback period as the length of time it takes to break even in an accounting sense, but not in an economic sense. The biggest drawback to the payback period rule is that it doesn't ask the right question. The relevant issue is the impact an investment will have on the value of the stock, not how long it takes to recover the initial investment.

Nevertheless, because it is so simple, companies often use it as a screen for dealing with the myriad minor investment decisions they have to make. There is certainly nothing wrong with this practice. As with any simple rule of thumb, there will be some errors in using it; but it wouldn't have survived all this time if it weren't useful. Now that you understand the rule, you can be on the alert for circumstances under which it might lead to problems. To help you remember, the following table lists the pros and cons of the payback period rule:

Advantages and Disadvantages of the Payback Period Rule	
Advantages	**Disadvantages**
1. Easy to understand.	1. Ignores the time value of money.
2. Adjusts for uncertainty of later cash flows.	2. Requires an arbitrary cutoff point.
3. Biased toward liquidity.	3. Ignores cash flows beyond the cutoff date.
	4. Biased against long-term projects, such as research and development, and new projects.

Concept Questions

9.2a In words, what is the payback period? The payback period rule?

9.2b Why do we say that the payback period is, in a sense, an accounting break-even measure?

9.3 The Discounted Payback

We saw that one shortcoming of the payback period rule was that it ignored time value. A variation of the payback period, the discounted payback period, fixes this particular problem. The **discounted payback period** is the length of time until the sum of the discounted cash flows is equal to the initial investment. The *discounted payback rule* would be:

discounted payback period
The length of time required for an investment's discounted cash flows to equal its initial cost.

> Based on the discounted payback rule, an investment is acceptable if its discounted payback is less than some prespecified number of years.

To see how we might calculate the discounted payback period, suppose we require a 12.5 percent return on new investments. We have an investment that costs $300 and has

TABLE 9.3

Ordinary and Discounted
Payback

Year	Cash Flow		Accumulated Cash Flow	
	Undiscounted	Discounted	Undiscounted	Discounted
1	$100	$89	$100	$ 89
2	100	79	200	168
3	100	70	300	238
4	100	62	400	300
5	100	55	500	355

cash flows of $100 per year for five years. To get the discounted payback, we have to discount each cash flow at 12.5 percent and then start adding them. We do this in Table 9.3. In Table 9.3, we have both the discounted and the undiscounted cash flows. Looking at the accumulated cash flows, we see that the regular payback is exactly three years (look for the highlighted figure in year 3) The discounted cash flows total $300 only after four years, however, so the discounted payback is four years, as shown.[1]

How do we interpret the discounted payback? Recall that the ordinary payback is the time it takes to break even in an accounting sense. Because it includes the time value of money, the discounted payback is the time it takes to break even in an economic or financial sense. Loosely speaking, in our example, we get our money back, along with the interest we could have earned elsewhere, in four years.

Figure 9.3 illustrates this idea by comparing the *future* value at 12.5 percent of the $300 investment to the *future* value of the $100 annual cash flows at 12.5 percent. Notice that the two lines cross at exactly four years. This tells us that the value of the project's cash flows catches up and then passes the original investment in four years.

Table 9.3 and Figure 9.3 illustrate another interesting feature of the discounted payback period. If a project ever pays back on a discounted basis, then it must have a positive NPV.[2] This is true because, by definition, the NPV is zero when the sum of the discounted cash flows equals the initial investment. For example, the present value of all the cash flows in Table 9.3 is $355. The cost of the project was $300, so the NPV is obviously $55. This $55 is the value of the cash flow that occurs *after* the discounted payback (see the last line in Table 9.3). In general, if we use a discounted payback rule, we won't accidentally take any projects with a negative estimated NPV.

Based on our example, the discounted payback would seem to have much to recommend it. You may be surprised to find out that it is rarely used in practice. Why? Probably because it really isn't any simpler to use than NPV. To calculate a discounted payback, you have to discount cash flows, add them up, and compare them to the cost, just as you do with NPV. So, unlike an ordinary payback, the discounted payback is not especially simple to calculate.

A discounted payback period rule has a couple of other significant drawbacks. The biggest one is that the cutoff still has to be arbitrarily set, and cash flows beyond that point are ignored.[3] As a result, a project with a positive NPV may be found unacceptable because

---

[1]In this case, the discounted payback is an even number of years. This won't ordinarily happen, of course. However, calculating a fractional year for the discounted payback period is more involved than it is for the ordinary payback, and it is not commonly done.

[2]This argument assumes the cash flows, other than the first, are all positive. If they are not, then these statements are not necessarily correct. Also, there may be more than one discounted payback.

[3]If the cutoff were forever, then the discounted payback rule would be the same as the NPV rule. It would also be the same as the profitability index rule considered in a later section.

FIGURE 9.3

Future Value of Project
Cash Flows

Future Value at 12.5%		
Year	$100 Annuity (Projected Cash Flow)	$300 Lump Sum (Projected Investment)
0	$ 0	$300
1	100	338
2	213	380
3	339	427
4	481	481
5	642	541

the cutoff is too short. Also, just because one project has a shorter discounted payback than another does not mean it has a larger NPV.

All things considered, the discounted payback is a compromise between a regular payback and NPV that lacks the simplicity of the first and the conceptual rigor of the second. Nonetheless, if we need to assess the time it will take to recover the investment required by a project, then the discounted payback is better than the ordinary payback because it considers time value. In other words, the discounted payback recognizes that we could have invested the money elsewhere and earned a return on it. The ordinary payback does not take this into account. The advantages and disadvantages of the discounted payback rule are summarized in the following table:

Advantages and Disadvantages of the Discounted Payback Period Rule	
Advantages	**Disadvantages**
1. Includes time value of money.	1. May reject positive NPV investments.
2. Easy to understand.	2. Requires an arbitrary cutoff point.
3. Does not accept negative estimated NPV investments.	3. Ignores cash flows beyond the cutoff date.
4. Biased toward liquidity.	4. Biased against long-term projects, such as research and development, and new projects.

| Calculating Discounted Payback | EXAMPLE 9.3 |

Consider an investment that costs $400 and pays $100 per year forever. We use a 20 percent discount rate on this type of investment. What is the ordinary payback? What is the discounted payback? What is the NPV?

The NPV and ordinary payback are easy to calculate in this case because the investment is a perpetuity. The present value of the cash flows is $100/.2 = $500, so the NPV is $500 − 400 = $100. The ordinary payback is obviously four years.

To get the discounted payback, we need to find the number of years such that a $100 annuity has a present value of $400 at 20 percent. In other words, the present value annuity factor is $400/100 = 4, and the interest rate is 20 percent per period; so what's the number of periods? If we solve for the number of periods, we find that the answer is a little less than nine years, so this is the discounted payback.

Concept Questions

9.3a In words, what is the discounted payback period? Why do we say it is, in a sense, a financial or economic break-even measure?

9.3b What advantage(s) does the discounted payback have over the ordinary payback?

The Average Accounting Return

9.4

Another attractive, but flawed, approach to making capital budgeting decisions involves the **average accounting return (AAR)**. There are many different definitions of the AAR. However, in one form or another, the AAR is always defined as:

$$\frac{\text{Some measure of average accounting profit}}{\text{Some measure of average accounting value}}$$

average accounting return (AAR)
An investment's average net income divided by its average book value.

The specific definition we will use is:

$$\frac{\text{Average net income}}{\text{Average book value}}$$

To see how we might calculate this number, suppose we are deciding whether to open a store in a new shopping mall. The required investment in improvements is $500,000. The store would have a five-year life because everything reverts to the mall owners after that time. The required investment would be 100 percent depreciated (straight-line) over five years, so the depreciation would be $500,000/5 = $100,000 per year. The tax rate is 25 percent. Table 9.4 contains the projected revenues and expenses. Net income in each year, based on these figures, is also shown.

To calculate the average book value for this investment, we note that we started out with a book value of $500,000 (the initial cost) and ended up at $0. The average book value during the life of the investment is thus ($500,000 + 0)/2 = $250,000. As long as we use straight-line depreciation, the average investment will always be one-half of the initial investment.[4]

---

[4]We could, of course, calculate the average of the six book values directly. In thousands, we would have ($500 + 400 + 300 + 200 + 100 + 0)/6 = $250.

TABLE 9.4

Projected Yearly Revenue
and Costs for Average
Accounting Return

	Year 1	Year 2	Year 3	Year 4	Year 5
Revenue	$433,333	$450,000	$266,667	$200,000	$133,333
Expenses	$200,000	$150,000	$100,000	$100,000	$100,000
Earnings before Depreciation	$233,333	$300,000	$166,667	$100,000	$ 33,333
Depreciation	$100,000	$100,000	$100,000	$100,000	$100,000
Earnings before Taxes	$133,333	$200,000	$ 66,667	$ 0	−$ 66,667
Taxes (25%)	33,333	50,000	16,667	0	− 16,667
Net Income	$100,000	$150,000	$ 50,000	$ 0	−$ 50,000

$$\text{Average net income} = \frac{\$100,000 + 150,000 + 50,000 + 0 - 50,000}{5} = \$50,000$$

$$\text{Average book value} = \frac{\$500,000 + 0}{2} = \$250,000$$

Looking at Table 9.4, we see that net income is $100,000 in the first year, $150,000 in the second year, $50,000 in the third year, $0 in Year 4, and −$50,000 in Year 5. The average net income, then, is:

[$100,000 + 150,000 + 50,000 + 0 + (−50,000)]/5 = $50,000

The average accounting return is:

$$\text{AAR} = \frac{\text{Average net income}}{\text{Average book value}} = \frac{\$50,000}{\$250,000} = 20\%$$

If the firm has a target AAR of less than 20 percent, then this investment is acceptable; otherwise it is not. The *average accounting return rule* is thus:

> **Based on the average accounting return rule, a project is acceptable if its average accounting return exceeds a target average accounting return.**

As we will now see, the use of this rule has a number of problems.

You should recognize the chief drawback to the AAR immediately. Above all else, the AAR is not a rate of return in any meaningful economic sense. Instead, it is the ratio of two accounting numbers, and it is not comparable to the returns offered, for example, in financial markets.[5]

One of the reasons the AAR is not a true rate of return is that it ignores time value. When we average figures that occur at different times, we are treating the near future and the more distant future in the same way. There was no discounting involved when we computed the average net income, for example.

The second problem with the AAR is similar to the problem we had with the payback period rule concerning the lack of an objective cutoff period. Because a calculated AAR is really not comparable to a market return, the target AAR must somehow be specified. There is no generally agreed-upon way to do this. One way of doing it is to calculate the AAR for the firm as a whole and use this as a benchmark, but there are lots of other ways as well.

---

[5]The AAR is closely related to the return on assets (ROA) discussed in Chapter 3. In practice, the AAR is sometimes computed by first calculating the ROA for each year and then averaging the results. This produces a number that is similar, but not identical, to the one we computed.

The third, and perhaps worst, flaw in the AAR is that it doesn't even look at the right things. Instead of cash flow and market value, it uses net income and book value. These are both poor substitutes. As a result, an AAR doesn't tell us what the effect on share price will be of taking an investment, so it doesn't tell us what we really want to know.

Does the AAR have any redeeming features? About the only one is that it almost always can be computed. The reason is that accounting information will almost always be available, both for the project under consideration and for the firm as a whole. We hasten to add that once the accounting information is available, we can always convert it to cash flows, so even this is not a particularly important fact. The AAR is summarized in the following table:

Advantages and Disadvantages of the Average Accounting Return	
Advantages	**Disadvantages**
1. Easy to calculate.	1. Not a true rate of return; time value of money is ignored.
2. Needed information will usually be available.	2. Uses an arbitrary benchmark cutoff rate.
	3. Based on accounting (book) values, not cash flows and market values.

Concept Questions

9.4a What is an average accounting rate of return (AAR)?

9.4b What are the weaknesses of the AAR rule?

The Internal Rate of Return

9.5

We now come to the most important alternative to NPV, the **internal rate of return**, universally known as the **IRR**. As we will see, the IRR is closely related to NPV. With the IRR, we try to find a single rate of return that summarizes the merits of a project. Furthermore, we want this rate to be an "internal" rate in the sense that it depends only on the cash flows of a particular investment, not on rates offered elsewhere.

internal rate of return (IRR)
The discount rate that makes the NPV of an investment zero.

To illustrate the idea behind the IRR, consider a project that costs $100 today and pays $110 in one year. Suppose you were asked, "What is the return on this investment?" What would you say? It seems both natural and obvious to say that the return is 10 percent because, for every dollar we put in, we get $1.10 back. In fact, as we will see in a moment, 10 percent is the internal rate of return, or IRR, on this investment.

Is this project with its 10 percent IRR a good investment? Once again, it would seem apparent that this is a good investment only if our required return is less than 10 percent. This intuition is also correct and illustrates the *IRR rule:*

Based on the IRR rule, an investment is acceptable if the IRR exceeds the required return. It should be rejected otherwise.

Imagine that we want to calculate the NPV for our simple investment. At a discount rate of R, the NPV is:

$$NPV = -\$100 + [110/(1 + R)]$$

Now, suppose we don't know the discount rate. This presents a problem, but we can still ask how high the discount rate would have to be before this project was deemed unacceptable. We know that we are indifferent between taking and not taking this investment when its NPV is just equal to zero. In other words, this investment is *economically* a break-even proposition when the NPV is zero because value is neither created nor destroyed. To find the break-even discount rate, we set NPV equal to zero and solve for R:

$$NPV = 0 = -\$100 + [110/(1 + R)]$$
$$\$100 = \$110/(1 + R)$$
$$1 + R = \$110/100 = 1.1$$
$$R = 10\%$$

This 10 percent is what we already have called the return on this investment. What we have now illustrated is that the internal rate of return on an investment (or just "return" for short) is the discount rate that makes the NPV equal to zero. This is an important observation, so it bears repeating:

> **The IRR on an investment is the required return that results in a zero NPV when it is used as the discount rate.**

The fact that the IRR is simply the discount rate that makes the NPV equal to zero is important because it tells us how to calculate the returns on more complicated investments. As we have seen, finding the IRR turns out to be relatively easy for a single-period investment. However, suppose you were now looking at an investment with the cash flows shown in Figure 9.4. As illustrated, this investment costs $100 and has a cash flow of $60 per year for two years, so it's only slightly more complicated than our single-period example. However, if you were asked for the return on this investment, what would you say? There doesn't seem to be any obvious answer (at least not to us). However, based on what we now know, we can set the NPV equal to zero and solve for the discount rate:

$$NPV = 0 = -\$100 + [60/(1 + IRR)] + [60/(1 + IRR)^2]$$

Unfortunately, the only way to find the IRR in general is by trial and error, either by hand or by calculator. This is precisely the same problem that came up in Chapter 5 when we found the unknown rate for an annuity and in Chapter 7 when we found the yield to maturity on a bond. In fact, we now see that in both of those cases, we were finding an IRR.

In this particular case, the cash flows form a two-period, $60 annuity. To find the unknown rate, we can try some different rates until we get the answer. If we were to start with a 0 percent rate, the NPV would obviously be $120 − 100 = $20. At a 10 percent discount rate, we would have:

$$NPV = -\$100 + (60/1.1) + (60/1.1^2) = \$4.13$$

FIGURE 9.4

Project Cash Flows

Year	0	1	2
	−$100	+$60	+$60

Discount Rate	NPV
0%	$20.00
5%	11.56
10%	4.13
15%	− 2.46
20%	− 8.33

TABLE 9.5

NPV at Different Discount Rates

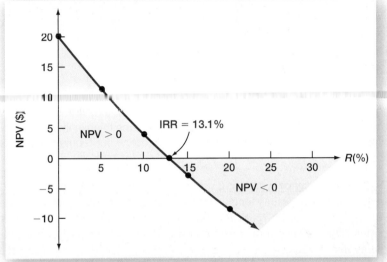

FIGURE 9.5

An NPV Profile

Now, we're getting close. We can summarize these and some other possibilities as shown in Table 9.5. From our calculations, the NPV appears to be zero with a discount rate between 10 percent and 15 percent, so the IRR is somewhere in that range. With a little more effort, we can find that the IRR is about 13.1 percent.[6] So, if our required return were less than 13.1 percent, we would take this investment. If our required return exceeded 13.1 percent, we would reject it.

By now, you have probably noticed that the IRR rule and the NPV rule appear to be quite similar. In fact, the IRR is sometimes simply called the *discounted cash flow,* or *DCF, return.* The easiest way to illustrate the relationship between NPV and IRR is to plot the numbers we calculated for Table 9.5. We put the different NPVs on the vertical axis, or *y*-axis, and the discount rates on the horizontal axis, or *x*-axis. If we had a very large number of points, the resulting picture would be a smooth curve called a **net present value profile.** Figure 9.5 illustrates the NPV profile for this project. Beginning with a 0 percent discount rate, we have $20 plotted directly on the *y*-axis. As the discount rate increases, the NPV declines smoothly. Where will the curve cut through the *x*-axis? This will occur where the NPV is just equal to zero, so it will happen right at the IRR of 13.1 percent.

In our example, the NPV rule and the IRR rule lead to identical accept–reject decisions. We will accept an investment using the IRR rule if the required return is less than 13.1 percent. As Figure 9.5 illustrates, however, the NPV is positive at any discount rate less than 13.1 percent, so we would accept the investment using the NPV rule as well. The two rules give equivalent results in this case.

net present value profile
A graphical representation of the relationship between an investment's NPVs and various discount rates.

---

[6]With a lot more effort (or a personal computer), we can find that the IRR is approximately (to 9 decimal places) 13.066238629 percent—not that anybody would ever want this many decimal places!

EXAMPLE 9.4   Calculating the IRR

A project has a total up-front cost of $435.44. The cash flows are $100 in the first year, $200 in the second year, and $300 in the third year. What's the IRR? If we require an 18 percent return, should we take this investment?

We'll describe the NPV profile and find the IRR by calculating some NPVs at different discount rates. You should check our answers for practice. Beginning with 0 percent, we have:

Discount Rate	NPV
0%	$164.56
5%	100.36
10%	46.15
15%	.00
20%	− 39.61

The NPV is zero at 15 percent, so 15 percent is the IRR. If we require an 18 percent return, then we should not take the investment. The reason is that the NPV is negative at 18 percent (verify that it is −$24.47). The IRR rule tells us the same thing in this case. We shouldn't take this investment because its 15 percent return is below our required 18 percent return.

At this point, you may be wondering if the IRR and NPV rules always lead to identical decisions. The answer is yes, as long as two very important conditions are met. First, the project's cash flows must be *conventional,* meaning that the first cash flow (the initial investment) is negative and all the rest are positive. Second, the project must be *independent,* meaning that the decision to accept or reject this project does not affect the decision to accept or reject any other. The first of these conditions is typically met, but the second often is not. In any case, when one or both of these conditions are not met, problems can arise. We discuss some of these next.

SPREADSHEET STRATEGIES

Calculating IRRs with a Spreadsheet

Because IRRs are so tedious to calculate by hand, financial calculators and especially spreadsheets are generally used. The procedures used by various financial calculators are too different for us to illustrate here, so we will focus on using a spreadsheet (financial calculators are covered in Appendix D). As the following example illustrates, using a spreadsheet is easy.

	A	B	C	D	E	F	G	H
1								
2			Using a spreadsheet to calculate internal rates of return					
3								
4	Suppose we have a four-year project that costs $500. The cash flows over the four-year life will be							
5	$100, $200, $300, and $400. What is the IRR?							
6								
7		Year	Cash Flow					
8		0	-$500					
9		1	100		IRR =	27.3%		
10		2	200					
11		3	300					
12		4	400					
13								
14								
15	The formula entered in cell F9 is =IRR(C8:C12). Notice that the year 0 cash flow has a negative							
16	sign representing the initial cost of the project.							
17								

PROBLEMS WITH THE IRR

The problems with the IRR come about when the cash flows are not conventional or when we are trying to compare two or more investments to see which is best. In the first case, surprisingly, the simple question: What's the return? can become difficult to answer. In the second case, the IRR can be a misleading guide.

Nonconventional Cash Flows   Suppose we have a strip-mining project that requires a $60 investment. Our cash flow in the first year will be $155. In the second year, the mine will be depleted, but we will have to spend $100 to restore the terrain. As Figure 9.6 illustrates, both the first and third cash flows are negative.

To find the IRR on this project, we can calculate the NPV at various rates:

Discount Rate	NPV
0%	−$5.00
10%	− 1.74
20%	− .28
30%	.06
40%	− .31

The NPV appears to be behaving in a peculiar fashion here. First, as the discount rate increases from 0 percent to 30 percent, the NPV starts out negative and becomes positive. This seems backward because the NPV is rising as the discount rate rises. It then starts getting smaller and becomes negative again. What's the IRR? To find out, we draw the NPV profile as shown in Figure 9.7.

In Figure 9.7, notice that the NPV is zero when the discount rate is 25 percent, so this is the IRR. Or is it? The NPV is also zero at $33\frac{1}{3}$ percent. Which of these is correct? The answer is both or neither; more precisely, there is no unambiguously correct answer. This is the **multiple rates of return** problem. Many financial computer packages (including a best-seller for personal computers) aren't aware of this problem and just report the first IRR that is found. Others report only the smallest positive IRR, even though this answer is no better than any other.

In our current example, the IRR rule breaks down completely. Suppose our required return is 10 percent. Should we take this investment? Both IRRs are greater than 10 percent, so, by the IRR rule, maybe we should. However, as Figure 9.7 shows, the NPV is negative at any discount rate less than 25 percent, so this is not a good investment. When should we take it? Looking at Figure 9.7 one last time, we see that the NPV is positive only if our required return is between 25 percent and $33\frac{1}{3}$ percent.

Nonconventional cash flows can occur in a variety of ways. For example, Northeast Utilities, owner of the Connecticut-located Millstone nuclear power plant, had to shut down the plant's three reactors in November 1995. The reactors were expected to be back online in January 1997. By some estimates, the cost of the shutdown would run about $334 million. In fact, all nuclear plants eventually have to be shut down forever, and the costs associated with decommissioning a plant are enormous, creating large negative cash flows at the end of the project's life.

multiple rates of return
The possibility that more than one discount rate will make the NPV of an investment zero.

FIGURE 9.6

Project Cash Flows

Year	0	1	2
	−$60	+$155	−$100

FIGURE 9.7

NPV Profile

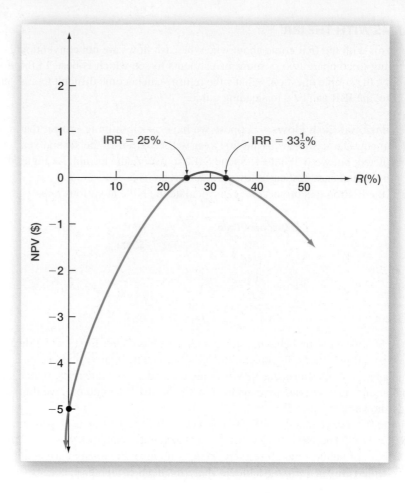

The moral of the story is that when the cash flows aren't conventional, strange things can start to happen to the IRR. This is not anything to get upset about, however, because the NPV rule, as always, works just fine. This illustrates the fact that, oddly enough, the obvious question—What's the rate of return?—may not always have a good answer.

EXAMPLE 9.5   **What's the IRR?**

You are looking at an investment that requires you to invest $51 today. You'll get $100 in one year, but you must pay out $50 in two years. What is the IRR on this investment?

You're on the alert now for the nonconventional cash flow problem, so you probably wouldn't be surprised to see more than one IRR. However, if you start looking for an IRR by trial and error, it will take you a long time. The reason is that there is no IRR. The NPV is negative at every discount rate, so we shouldn't take this investment under any circumstances. What's the return on this investment? Your guess is as good as ours.

| **"I Think; Therefore, I Know How Many IRRs There Can Be."** | **EXAMPLE 9.6** |

We've seen that it's possible to get more than one IRR. If you wanted to make sure that you had found all of the possible IRRs, how could you do it? The answer comes from the great mathematician, philosopher, and financial analyst Descartes (of "I think; therefore I am" fame). Descartes' Rule of Sign says that the maximum number of IRRs that there can be is equal to the number of times that the cash flows change sign from positive to negative and/or negative to positive.[7]

In our example with the 25 percent and 33⅓ percent IRRs, could there be yet another IRR? The cash flows flip from negative to positive, then back to negative, for a total of two sign changes. Therefore, according to Descartes' rule, the maximum number of IRRs is two and we don't need to look for any more. Note that the actual number of IRRs can be less than the maximum (see Example 9.5).

Mutually Exclusive Investments   Even if there is a single IRR, another problem can arise concerning mutually exclusive investment decisions. If two investments, X and Y, are mutually exclusive, then taking one of them means that we cannot take the other. Two projects that are not mutually exclusive are said to be independent. For example, if we own one corner lot, then we can build a gas station or an apartment building, but not both. These are mutually exclusive alternatives.

Thus far, we have asked whether a given investment is worth undertaking. However, a related question comes up often: Given two or more mutually exclusive investments, which one is the best? The answer is simple enough: The best one is the one with the largest NPV. Can we also say that the best one has the highest return? As we show, the answer is no.

To illustrate the problem with the IRR rule and mutually exclusive investments, consider the following cash flows from two mutually exclusive investments:

mutually exclusive investment decisions
A situation in which taking one investment prevents the taking of another.

Year	Investment A	Investment B
0	−$100	−$100
1	50	20
2	40	40
3	40	50
4	30	60

The IRR for A is 24 percent, and the IRR for B is 21 percent. Because these investments are mutually exclusive, we can take only one of them. Simple intuition suggests that investment A is better because of its higher return. Unfortunately, simple intuition is not always correct.

To see why investment A is not necessarily the better of the two investments, we've calculated the NPV of these investments for different required returns:

Discount Rate	NPV(A)	NPV(B)
0%	$60.00	$70.00
5	43.13	47.88
10	29.06	29.79
15	17.18	14.82
20	7.06	2.31
25	− 1.63	− 8.22

---

[7]To be more precise, the number of IRRs that are bigger than −100 percent is equal to the number of sign changes, or it differs from the number of sign changes by an even number. Thus, for example, if there are five sign changes, there are five IRRs, three IRRs, or one IRR. If there are two sign changes, there are either two IRRs or no IRRs.

FIGURE 9.8

NPV Profiles for Mutually Exclusive Investments

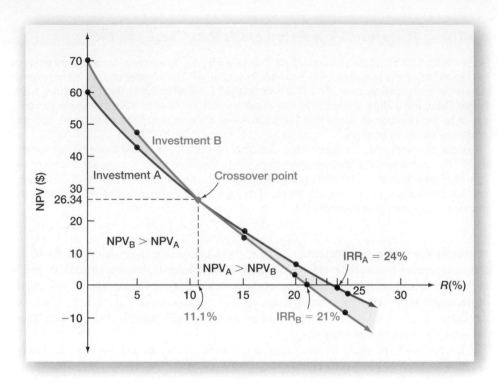

The IRR for A (24 percent) is larger than the IRR for B (21 percent). However, if you compare the NPVs, you'll see that which investment has the higher NPV depends on our required return. B has greater total cash flow, but it pays back more slowly than A. As a result, it has a higher NPV at lower discount rates.

In our example, the NPV and IRR rankings conflict for some discount rates. If our required return is 10 percent, for instance, then B has the higher NPV and is thus the better of the two even though A has the higher return. If our required return is 15 percent, then there is no ranking conflict: A is better.

The conflict between the IRR and NPV for mutually exclusive investments can be illustrated by plotting the investments' NPV profiles as we have done in Figure 9.8. In Figure 9.8, notice that the NPV profiles cross at about 11 percent. Notice also that at any discount rate less than 11 percent, the NPV for B is higher. In this range, taking B benefits us more than taking A, even though A's IRR is higher. At any rate greater than 11 percent, investment A has the greater NPV.

This example illustrates that when we have mutually exclusive projects, we shouldn't rank them based on their returns. More generally, anytime we are comparing investments to determine which is best, looking at IRRs can be misleading. Instead, we need to look at the relative NPVs to avoid the possibility of choosing incorrectly. Remember, we're ultimately interested in creating value for the shareholders, so the option with the higher NPV is preferred, regardless of the relative returns.

If this seems counterintuitive, think of it this way. Suppose you have two investments. One has a 10 percent return and makes you $100 richer immediately. The other has a 20 percent return and makes you $50 richer immediately. Which one do you like better? We would rather have $100 than $50, regardless of the returns, so we like the first one better.

Calculating the Crossover Rate

EXAMPLE 9.7

In Figure 9.8, the NPV profiles cross at about 11 percent. How can we determine just what this crossover point is? The *crossover rate,* by definition, is the discount rate that makes the NPVs of two projects equal. To illustrate, suppose we have the following two mutually exclusive investments:

Year	Investment A	Investment B
0	−$400	−$500
1	250	320
2	280	340

What's the crossover rate?

To find the crossover, first consider moving out of investment A and into investment B. If you make the move, you'll have to invest an extra $100 (= $500 − 400). For this $100 investment, you'll get an extra $70 (= $320 − 250) in the first year and an extra $60 (= $340 − 280) in the second year. Is this a good move? In other words, is it worth investing the extra $100?

Based on our discussion, the NPV of the switch, NPV(B − A), is:

$$NPV(B - A) = -\$100 + [70/(1 + R)] + [60/(1 + R)^2]$$

We can calculate the return on this investment by setting the NPV equal to zero and solving for the IRR:

$$NPV(B - A) = 0 = -\$100 + [70/(1 + R)] + [60/(1 + R)^2]$$

If you go through this calculation, you will find the IRR is exactly 20 percent. What this tells us is that at a 20 percent discount rate, we are indifferent between the two investments because the NPV of the difference in their cash flows is zero. As a consequence, the two investments have the same value, so this 20 percent is the crossover rate. Check to see that the NPV at 20 percent is $2.78 for both investments.

In general, you can find the crossover rate by taking the difference in the cash flows and calculating the IRR using the difference. It doesn't make any difference which one you subtract from which. To see this, find the IRR for (A − B); you'll see it's the same number. Also, for practice, you might want to find the exact crossover in Figure 9.8. (*Hint:* It's 11.0704 percent.)

Investing or Financing?   Consider the following two independent investments:

Year	Investment A	Investment B
0	−$100	$100
1	130	−130

The company initially pays out cash with investment A and initially receives cash for investment B. While most projects are more like investment A, projects like investment B also occur. For example, consider a corporation conducting a seminar where the participants pay in advance. Because large expenses are frequently incurred at the seminar date, cash inflows precede cash outflows.

For these two projects, suppose the required return for each investment project is 12 percent. According to the IRR decision rule, which, if either, project should we accept? If you calculate the IRRs, you will find that they are 30 percent for both projects.

According to the IRR decision rule, we should accept both projects. However, if we calculate the NPV of B at 12 percent, we get:

$$\$100 - \frac{\$130}{1.12} = -\$16.07$$

FIGURE 9.9   NPV Profile for Investing and Financing Investments

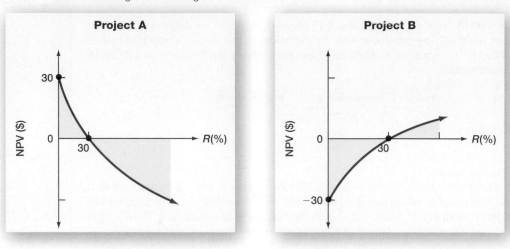

In this case, the NPV and IRR decision rules disagree. To see what's going on, Figure 9.9 shows the NPV profile for each project. As you can see, the NPV profile for B is upward sloping. Thus, the project should be accepted if the required return is *greater* than 30 percent.

When a project has cash flows like investment B's, the IRR is really a rate that you are paying, not receiving. For this reason, we say that the project has *financing type* cash flows, whereas investment A has *investing type* cash flows. You should take a project with financing-type cash flows only if it is an inexpensive source of financing, meaning that its IRR is *lower* than your required return.

REDEEMING QUALITIES OF THE IRR

Despite its flaws, the IRR is very popular in practice—more so than even the NPV. It probably survives because it fills a need that the NPV does not. In analyzing investments, people in general, and financial analysts in particular, seem to prefer talking about rates of return rather than dollar values.

In a similar vein, the IRR also appears to provide a simple way of communicating information about a proposal. One manager might say to another, "Remodeling the clerical wing has a 20 percent return." This may somehow seem simpler than saying, "At a 10 percent discount rate, the net present value is $4,000."

Finally, under certain circumstances, the IRR may have a practical advantage over the NPV. We can't estimate the NPV unless we know the appropriate discount rate, but we can still estimate the IRR. Suppose we didn't know the required return on an investment, but we found, for example, that it had a 40 percent return. We would probably be inclined to take it because it would be unlikely that the required return would be that high. The advantages and disadvantages of the IRR are summarized as follows:

Advantages and Disadvantages of the Internal Rate of Return	
Advantages	**Disadvantages**
1. Closely related to NPV, often leading to identical decisions.	1. May result in multiple answers or not deal with nonconventional cash flows.
2. Easy to understand and communicate.	2. May lead to incorrect decisions in comparisons of mutually exclusive investments.

THE MODIFIED INTERNAL RATE OF RETURN (MIRR)

To address some of the problems that can crop up with the standard IRR, it is often proposed that a modified version be used. As we will see, there are several different ways of calculating a modified IRR, or MIRR, but the basic idea is to modify the cash flows first and then calculate an IRR using the modified cash flows.

To illustrate, let's go back to the cash flows in Figure 9.6: $-\$60$, $+\$155$, and $-\$100$. As we saw, there are two IRRs, 25 percent and $33\frac{1}{3}$ percent. We next illustrate three different MIRRs, all of which have the property that only one answer will result, thereby eliminating the multiple IRR problem.

Method #1: The Discounting Approach   With the discounting approach, the idea is to discount all negative cash flows back to the present at the required return and add them to the initial cost. Then, calculate the IRR. Because only the first modified cash flow is negative, there will be only one IRR. The discount rate used might be the required return, or it might be some other externally supplied rate. We will use the project's required return.

If the required return on the project is 20 percent, then the modified cash flows look like this:

Time 0: $-\$60 + \dfrac{-\$100}{1.20^2} = -\$129.44$

Time 1: $+\$155$

Time 2: $+\$0$

If you calculate the MIRR now, you should get 19.74 percent.

Method #2: The Reinvestment Approach   With the reinvestment approach, we compound *all* cash flows (positive and negative) except the first out to the end of the project's life and then calculate the IRR. In a sense, we are "reinvesting" the cash flows and not taking them out of the project until the very end. The rate we use could be the required return on the project, or it could be a separately specified "reinvestment rate." We will use the project's required return. When we do, here are the modified cash flows:

Time 0: $-\$60$

Time 1: $+0$

Time 2: $-\$100 + (\$155 \times 1.2) = \$86$

The MIRR on this set of cash flows is 19.72 percent, or a little lower than we got using the discounting approach.

Method #3: The Combination Approach   As the name suggests, the combination approach blends our first two methods. Negative cash flows are discounted back to the present, and positive cash flows are compounded to the end of the project. In practice, different discount or compounding rates might be used, but we will again stick with the project's required return.

With the combination approach, the modified cash flows are as follows:

Time 0: $-\$60 + \dfrac{-\$100}{1.20^2} = -\$129.44$

Time 1: $+0$

Time 2: $\$155 \times 1.2 = \$186$

See if you don't agree that the MIRR is 19.87 percent, the highest of the three.

MIRR or IRR: Which Is Better?   MIRRs are controversial. At one extreme are those who claim that MIRRs are superior to IRRs, period. For example, by design, they clearly don't suffer from the multiple rate of return problem.

At the other end, detractors say that MIRR should stand for "meaningless internal rate of return." As our example makes clear, one problem with MIRRs is that there are different ways of calculating them, and there is no clear reason to say one of our three methods is better than any other. The differences are small with our simple cash flows, but they could be much larger for a more complex project. Further, it's not clear how to interpret an MIRR. It may look like a rate of return, but it's a rate of return on a modified set of cash flows, not the project's actual cash flows.

We're not going to take sides. However, notice that calculating an MIRR requires discounting, compounding, or both, which leads to two obvious observations. First, if we have the relevant discount rate, why not calculate the NPV and be done with it? Second, because an MIRR depends on an externally supplied discount (or compounding) rate, the answer you get is not truly an "internal" rate of return, which, by definition, depends on only the project's cash flows.

We *will* take a stand on one issue that frequently comes up in this context. The value of a project does not depend on what the firm does with the cash flows generated by that project. A firm might use a project's cash flows to fund other projects, to pay dividends, or to buy an executive jet. It doesn't matter: How the cash flows are spent in the future does not affect their value today. As a result, there is generally no need to consider reinvestment of interim cash flows.

Concept Questions

9.5a Under what circumstances will the IRR and NPV rules lead to the same accept–reject decisions? When might they conflict?

9.5b Is it generally true that an advantage of the IRR rule over the NPV rule is that we don't need to know the required return to use the IRR rule?

9.6 The Profitability Index

profitability index (PI)
The present value of an investment's future cash flows divided by its initial cost. Also called the *benefit–cost ratio*.

Another tool used to evaluate projects is called the **profitability index (PI)** or benefit–cost ratio. This index is defined as the present value of the future cash flows divided by the initial investment. So, if a project costs $200 and the present value of its future cash flows is $220, the profitability index value would be $220/200 = 1.1. Notice that the NPV for this investment is $20, so it is a desirable investment.

More generally, if a project has a positive NPV, then the present value of the future cash flows must be bigger than the initial investment. The profitability index would thus be bigger than 1 for a positive NPV investment and less than 1 for a negative NPV investment.

How do we interpret the profitability index? In our example, the PI was 1.1. This tells us that, per dollar invested, $1.10 in value or $.10 in NPV results. The profitability index thus measures "bang for the buck"—that is, the value created per dollar invested. For this reason, it is often proposed as a measure of performance for government or other not-for-profit investments. Also, when capital is scarce, it may make sense to allocate it to projects with the highest PIs. We will return to this issue in a later chapter.

The PI is obviously similar to the NPV. However, consider an investment that costs $5 and has a $10 present value and an investment that costs $100 with a $150 present value.

The first of these investments has an NPV of $5 and a PI of 2. The second has an NPV of $50 and a PI of 1.5. If these are mutually exclusive investments, then the second one is preferred even though it has a lower PI. This ranking problem is similar to the IRR ranking problem we saw in the previous section. In all, there seems to be little reason to rely on the PI instead of the NPV. Our discussion of the PI is summarized as follows:

Advantages and Disadvantages of the Profitability Index	
Advantages	**Disadvantages**
1. Closely related to NPV, generally leading to identical decisions.	1. May lead to incorrect decisions in comparisons of mutually exclusive investments.
2. Easy to understand and communicate.	
3. May be useful when available investment funds are limited.	

Concept Questions

9.6a What does the profitability index measure?

9.6b How would you state the profitability index rule?

The Practice of Capital Budgeting

9.7

Given that NPV seems to be telling us directly what we want to know, you might be wondering why there are so many other procedures and why alternative procedures are commonly used. Recall that we are trying to make an investment decision and that we are frequently operating under considerable uncertainty about the future. We can only *estimate* the NPV of an investment in this case. The resulting estimate can be very "soft," meaning that the true NPV might be quite different.

Because the true NPV is unknown, the astute financial manager seeks clues to help in assessing whether the estimated NPV is reliable. For this reason, firms would typically use multiple criteria for evaluating a proposal. For example, suppose we have an investment with a positive estimated NPV. Based on our experience with other projects, this one appears to have a short payback and a very high AAR. In this case, the different indicators seem to agree that it's "all systems go." Put another way, the payback and the AAR are consistent with the conclusion that the NPV is positive.

On the other hand, suppose we had a positive estimated NPV, a long payback, and a low AAR. This could still be a good investment, but it looks like we need to be much more careful in making the decision because we are getting conflicting signals. If the estimated NPV is based on projections in which we have little confidence, then further analysis is probably in order. We will consider how to evaluate NPV estimates in more detail in the next two chapters.

Large firms often have huge capital budgets. For example, in 2008, ExxonMobil announced that it expected to have about $25 billion in capital outlays during the year, up from $20 billion in 2007. About the same time, competitor ChevronTexaco announced that it would increase its capital budgeting for 2008 to $22.9 billion, up from $20 billion in 2007. Other companies with large capital spending budgets were General Motors, which projected capital spending of about $15 billion for 2008 and 2009 combined, and semiconductor company Intel, which projected capital spending of about $5.2 billion for 2008.

TABLE 9.6   Capital Budgeting Techniques in Practice

A. Historical Comparison of the Primary Use of Various Capital Budgeting Techniques							
	1959	**1964**	**1970**	**1975**	**1977**	**1979**	**1981**
Payback period	34%	24%	12%	15%	9%	10%	5.0%
Average accounting return (AAR)	34	30	26	10	25	14	10.7
Internal rate of return (IRR)	19	38	57	37	54	60	65.3
Net present value (NPV)	—	—	—	26	10	14	16.5
IRR or NPV	19	38	57	63	64	74	81.8

B. Percentage of CFOs Who Always or Almost Always Used a Given Technique in 1999				
Capital Budgeting Technique	**Percentage Always or Almost Always Using**	**Average Score [Scale is 4 (always) to 0 (never)]**		
		Overall	**Large Firms**	**Small Firms**
Internal rate of return	76%	3.09	3.41	2.87
Net present value	75	3.08	3.42	2.83
Payback period	57	2.53	2.25	2.72
Discounted payback period	29	1.56	1.55	1.58
Accounting rate of return	20	1.34	1.25	1.41
Profitability index	12	.83	.75	.88

SOURCES: J.R. Graham and C.R. Harvey, "The Theory and Practice of Corporate Finance: Evidence from the Field," *Journal of Financial Economics,* May–June 2001, pp. 187–244; J.S. Moore and A.K. Reichert, "An Analysis of the Financial Management Techniques Currently Employed by Large U.S. Corporations," *Journal of Business Finance and Accounting,* Winter 1983, pp. 623–45; M.T. Stanley and S.R. Block, "A Survey of Multinational Capital Budgeting," *The Financial Review,* March 1984, pp. 36–51.

Large-scale capital spending is often an industrywide occurrence. For example, in 2008, capital spending in the semiconductor industry was expected to be $51 billion. This tidy sum represented a 9 percent decrease over the industry capital spending in 2007, which was $56.04 billion. This decrease was in sharp contrast to the 18 percent increase from 2005 to 2006.

According to information released by the Census Bureau in 2008, capital investment for the economy as a whole was $1.31 trillion in 2006, $1.22 trillion in 2005, and $1.05 trillion in 2004. The totals for the three years therefore exceeded $3 trillion! Given the sums at stake, it is not too surprising that careful analysis of capital expenditures is something at which successful businesses seek to become adept.

There have been a number of surveys conducted asking firms what types of investment criteria they actually use. Table 9.6 summarizes the results of several of these. Panel A of the table is a historical comparison looking at the primary capital budgeting techniques used by large firms through time. In 1959, only 19 percent of the firms surveyed used either IRR or NPV, and 68 percent used either payback periods or accounting returns. It is clear that by the 1980s, IRR and NPV had become the dominant criteria.

Panel B of Table 9.6 summarizes the results of a 1999 survey of chief financial officers (CFOs) at both large and small firms in the United States. A total of 392 CFOs responded. What is shown is the percentage of CFOs who always or almost always used the various capital budgeting techniques we described in this chapter. Not surprisingly, IRR and NPV were the two most widely used techniques, particularly at larger firms. However, over half of the respondents always, or almost always, used the payback criterion as well. In fact, among smaller firms, payback was used just about as much as NPV and IRR. Less commonly used were discounted payback, accounting rates of return, and the profitability index. For future reference, the various criteria we have discussed are summarized in Table 9.7.

TABLE 9.7

Summary of Investment Criteria

I. Discounted Cash Flow Criteria

A. *Net present value (NPV):* The NPV of an investment is the difference between its market value and its cost. The NPV rule is to take a project if its NPV is positive. NPV is frequently estimated by calculating the present value of the future cash flows (to estimate market value) and then subtracting the cost. NPV has no serious flaws; it is the preferred decision criterion.

B. *Internal rate of return (IRR):* The IRR is the discount rate that makes the estimated NPV of an investment equal to zero; it is sometimes called the *discounted cash flow (DCF) return*. The IRR rule is to take a project when its IRR exceeds the required return. IRR is closely related to NPV, and it leads to exactly the same decisions as NPV for conventional, independent projects. When project cash flows are not conventional, there may be no IRR or there may be more than one. More seriously, the IRR cannot be used to rank mutually exclusive projects; the project with the highest IRR is not necessarily the preferred investment.

C. *Modified internal rate of return (MIRR):* The MIRR is a modification to the IRR. A project's cash flows are modified by (1) discounting the negative cash flows back to the present; (2) compounding cash flows to the end of the project's life; or (3) combining (1) and (2). An IRR is then computed on the modified cash flows. MIRRs are guaranteed to avoid the multiple rate of return problem, but it is unclear how to interpret them; and they are not truly "internal" because they depend on externally supplied discounting or compounding rates.

D. *Profitability index (PI):* The PI, also called the *benefit–cost ratio,* is the ratio of present value to cost. The PI rule is to take an investment if the index exceeds 1. The PI measures the present value of an investment per dollar invested. It is quite similar to NPV; but, like IRR, it cannot be used to rank mutually exclusive projects. However, it is sometimes used to rank projects when a firm has more positive NPV investments than it can currently finance.

II. Payback Criteria

A. *Payback period:* The payback period is the length of time until the sum of an investment's cash flows equals its cost. The payback period rule is to take a project if its payback is less than some cutoff. The payback period is a flawed criterion, primarily because it ignores risk, the time value of money, and cash flows beyond the cutoff point.

B. *Discounted payback period:* The discounted payback period is the length of time until the sum of an investment's discounted cash flows equals its cost. The discounted payback period rule is to take an investment if the discounted payback is less than some cutoff. The discounted payback rule is flawed, primarily because it ignores cash flows after the cutoff.

III. Accounting Criterion

A. *Average accounting return (AAR):* The AAR is a measure of accounting profit relative to book value. It is *not* related to the IRR, but it is similar to the accounting return on assets (ROA) measure in Chapter 3. The AAR rule is to take an investment if its AAR exceeds a benchmark AAR. The AAR is seriously flawed for a variety of reasons, and it has little to recommend it.

Concept Questions

9.7a What are the most commonly used capital budgeting procedures?

9.7b If NPV is conceptually the best procedure for capital budgeting, why do you think multiple measures are used in practice?

9.8 Summary and Conclusions

This chapter has covered the different criteria used to evaluate proposed investments. The seven criteria, in the order we discussed them, are these:

1. Net present value (NPV).
2. Payback period.
3. Discounted payback period.
4. Average accounting return (AAR).
5. Internal rate of return (IRR).
6. Modified internal rate of return (MIRR).
7. Profitability index (PI).

We illustrated how to calculate each of these and discussed the interpretation of the results. We also described the advantages and disadvantages of each of them. Ultimately a good capital budgeting criterion must tell us two things. First, is a particular project a good investment? Second, if we have more than one good project, but we can take only one of them, which one should we take? The main point of this chapter is that only the NPV criterion can always provide the correct answer to both questions.

For this reason, NPV is one of the two or three most important concepts in finance, and we will refer to it many times in the chapters ahead. When we do, keep two things in mind: (1) NPV is always just the difference between the market value of an asset or project and its cost, and (2) the financial manager acts in the shareholders' best interests by identifying and taking positive NPV projects.

Finally, we noted that NPVs can't normally be observed in the market; instead, they must be estimated. Because there is always the possibility of a poor estimate, financial managers use multiple criteria for examining projects. The other criteria provide additional information about whether a project truly has a positive NPV.

Visit us at www.mhhe.com/rwj

CHAPTER REVIEW AND SELF-TEST PROBLEMS

9.1   **Investment Criteria** This problem will give you some practice calculating NPVs and paybacks. A proposed overseas expansion has the following cash flows:

Year	Cash Flow
0	−$200
1	50
2	60
3	70
4	200

Calculate the payback, the discounted payback, and the NPV at a required return of 10 percent.

9.2   **Mutually Exclusive Investments** Consider the following two mutually exclusive investments. Calculate the IRR for each and the crossover rate. Under what circumstances will the IRR and NPV criteria rank the two projects differently?

Year	Investment A	Investment B
0	−$75	−$75
1	20	60
2	40	50
3	70	15

9.3   Average Accounting Return   You are looking at a three-year project with a projected net income of $2,000 in year 1, $4,000 in year 2, and $6,000 in year 3. The cost is $12,000, which will be depreciated straight-line to zero over the three-year life of the project. What is the average accounting return (AAR)?

ANSWERS TO CHAPTER REVIEW AND SELF-TEST PROBLEMS

9.1   In the following table, we have listed the cash flow, cumulative cash flow, discounted cash flow (at 10 percent), and cumulative discounted cash flow for the proposed project.

Year	Cash Flow Undiscounted	Cash Flow Discounted	Accumulated Cash Flow Undiscounted	Accumulated Cash Flow Discounted
1	$ 50	$ 45.45	$ 50	$ 45.45
2	60	49.59	110	95.04
3	70	52.59	180	147.63
4	200	136.60	380	284.23

Recall that the initial investment was $200. When we compare this to accumulated undiscounted cash flows, we see that payback occurs between years 3 and 4. The cash flows for the first three years are $180 total, so, going into the fourth year, we are short by $20. The total cash flow in year 4 is $200, so the payback is 3 + ($20/200) = 3.10 years.

Looking at the accumulated discounted cash flows, we see that the discounted payback occurs between years 3 and 4. The sum of the discounted cash flows is $284.23, so the NPV is $84.23. Notice that this is the present value of the cash flows that occur after the discounted payback.

9.2   To calculate the IRR, we might try some guesses, as in the following table:

Discount Rate	NPV(A)	NPV(B)
0%	$55.00	$50.00
10	28.83	32.14
20	9.95	18.40
30	− 4.09	7.57
40	−14.80	− 1.17

Several things are immediately apparent from our guesses. First, the IRR on A must be between 20 percent and 30 percent (why?). With some more effort, we find that it's 26.79 percent. For B, the IRR must be a little less than 40 percent (again, why?); it works out to be 38.54 percent. Also, notice that at rates between 0 percent and 10 percent, the NPVs are very close, indicating that the crossover is in that vicinity.

To find the crossover exactly, we can compute the IRR on the difference in the cash flows. If we take the cash flows from A minus the cash flows from B, the resulting cash flows are:

Year	A – B
0	$ 0
1	– 40
2	– 10
3	55

These cash flows look a little odd; but the sign changes only once, so we can find an IRR. With some trial and error, you'll see that the NPV is zero at a discount rate of 5.42 percent, so this is the crossover rate.

The IRR for B is higher. However, as we've seen, A has the larger NPV for any discount rate less than 5.42 percent, so the NPV and IRR rankings will conflict in that range. Remember, if there's a conflict, we will go with the higher NPV. Our decision rule is thus simple: Take A if the required return is less than 5.42 percent, take B if the required return is between 5.42 percent and 38.54 percent (the IRR on B), and take neither if the required return is more than 38.54 percent.

9.3   Here we need to calculate the ratio of average net income to average book value to get the AAR. Average net income is:

Average net income = ($2,000 + 4,000 + 6,000)/3 = $4,000

Average book value is:

Average book value = $12,000/2 = $6,000

So the average accounting return is:

AAR = $4,000/6,000 = 66.67%

This is an impressive return. Remember, however, that it isn't really a rate of return like an interest rate or an IRR, so the size doesn't tell us a lot. In particular, our money is probably not going to grow at a rate of 66.67 percent per year, sorry to say.

Visit us at www.mhhe.com/rwj

CONCEPTS REVIEW AND CRITICAL THINKING QUESTIONS

1. **Payback Period and Net Present Value [LO1, 2]** If a project with conventional cash flows has a payback period less than the project's life, can you definitively state the algebraic sign of the NPV? Why or why not? If you know that the discounted payback period is less than the project's life, what can you say about the NPV? Explain.

2. **Net Present Value [LO1]** Suppose a project has conventional cash flows and a positive NPV. What do you know about its payback? Its discounted payback? Its profitability index? Its IRR? Explain.

3. **Payback Period [LO2]** Concerning payback:

    a. Describe how the payback period is calculated, and describe the information this measure provides about a sequence of cash flows. What is the payback criterion decision rule?

    b. What are the problems associated with using the payback period to evaluate cash flows?

c. What are the advantages of using the payback period to evaluate cash flows? Are there any circumstances under which using payback might be appropriate? Explain.

4. **Discounted Payback** [LO3] Concerning discounted payback:

   a. Describe how the discounted payback period is calculated, and describe the information this measure provides about a sequence of cash flows. What is the discounted payback criterion decision rule?

   b. What are the problems associated with using the discounted payback period to evaluate cash flows?

   c. What conceptual advantage does the discounted payback method have over the regular payback method? Can the discounted payback ever be longer than the regular payback? Explain.

5. **Average Accounting Return** [LO4] Concerning AAR:

   a. Describe how the average accounting return is usually calculated, and describe the information this measure provides about a sequence of cash flows. What is the AAR criterion decision rule?

   b. What are the problems associated with using the AAR to evaluate a project's cash flows? What underlying feature of AAR is most troubling to you from a financial perspective? Does the AAR have any redeeming qualities?

6. **Net Present Value** [LO1] Concerning NPV:

   a. Describe how NPV is calculated, and describe the information this measure provides about a sequence of cash flows. What is the NPV criterion decision rule?

   b. Why is NPV considered a superior method of evaluating the cash flows from a project? Suppose the NPV for a project's cash flows is computed to be $2,500. What does this number represent with respect to the firm's shareholders?

7. **Internal Rate of Return** [LO5] Concerning IRR:

   a. Describe how the IRR is calculated, and describe the information this measure provides about a sequence of cash flows. What is the IRR criterion decision rule?

   b. What is the relationship between IRR and NPV? Are there any situations in which you might prefer one method over the other? Explain.

   c. Despite its shortcomings in some situations, why do most financial managers use IRR along with NPV when evaluating projects? Can you think of a situation in which IRR might be a more appropriate measure to use than NPV? Explain.

8. **Profitability Index** [LO7] Concerning the profitability index:

   a. Describe how the profitability index is calculated, and describe the information this measure provides about a sequence of cash flows. What is the profitability index decision rule?

   b. What is the relationship between the profitability index and NPV? Are there any situations in which you might prefer one method over the other? Explain.

9. **Payback and Internal Rate of Return** [LO2, 5] A project has perpetual cash flows of C per period, a cost of I, and a required return of R. What is the relationship between the project's payback and its IRR? What implications does your answer have for long-lived projects with relatively constant cash flows?

10. **International Investment Projects** [LO1] In January 2008, automobile manufacturer Volkswagen announced plans to build an automatic transmission and engine plant in South Carolina. Volkswagen apparently felt that it would be better able to compete and create value with U.S.-based facilities. Other companies such as Fuji

Film and Swiss chemical company Lonza have reached similar conclusions and taken similar actions. What are some of the reasons that foreign manufacturers of products as diverse as automobiles, film, and chemicals might arrive at this same conclusion?

11. **Capital Budgeting Problems** [LO1] What difficulties might come up in actual applications of the various criteria we discussed in this chapter? Which one would be the easiest to implement in actual applications? The most difficult?

12. **Capital Budgeting in Not-for-Profit Entities** [LO1] Are the capital budgeting criteria we discussed applicable to not-for-profit corporations? How should such entities make capital budgeting decisions? What about the U.S. government? Should it evaluate spending proposals using these techniques?

13. **Modified Internal Rate of Return** [LO6] One of the less flattering interpretations of the acronym MIRR is "meaningless internal rate of return." Why do you think this term is applied to MIRR?

14. **Net Present Value** [LO1] It is sometimes stated that "the net present value approach assumes reinvestment of the intermediate cash flows at the required return." Is this claim correct? To answer, suppose you calculate the NPV of a project in the usual way. Next, suppose you do the following:

   a. Calculate the future value (as of the end of the project) of all the cash flows other than the initial outlay assuming they are reinvested at the required return, producing a single future value figure for the project.

   b. Calculate the NPV of the project using the single future value calculated in the previous step and the initial outlay. It is easy to verify that you will get the same NPV as in your original calculation only if you use the required return as the reinvestment rate in the previous step.

15. **Internal Rate of Return** [LO5] It is sometimes stated that "the internal rate of return approach assumes reinvestment of the intermediate cash flows at the internal rate of return." Is this claim correct? To answer, suppose you calculate the IRR of a project in the usual way. Next, suppose you do the following:

   a. Calculate the future value (as of the end of the project) of all the cash flows other than the initial outlay assuming they are reinvested at the IRR, producing a single future value figure for the project.

   b. Calculate the IRR of the project using the single future value calculated in the previous step and the initial outlay. It is easy to verify that you will get the same IRR as in your original calculation only if you use the IRR as the reinvestment rate in the previous step.

QUESTIONS AND PROBLEMS

BASIC
(Questions 1–19)

1. **Calculating Payback** [LO2] What is the payback period for the following set of cash flows?

Year	Cash Flow
0	−$6,400
1	1,600
2	1,900
3	2,300
4	1,400

2. **Calculating Payback [LO2]** An investment project provides cash inflows of $765 per year for eight years. What is the project payback period if the initial cost is $2,400? What if the initial cost is $3,600? What if it is $6,500?

3. **Calculating Payback [LO2]** Buy Coastal, Inc., imposes a payback cutoff of three years for its international investment projects. If the company has the following two projects available, should it accept either of them?

Year	Cash Flow (A)	Cash Flow (B)
0	−$40,000	−$ 60,000
1	19,000	14,000
2	25,000	17,000
3	18,000	24,000
4	6,000	270,000

4. **Calculating Discounted Payback [LO3]** An investment project has annual cash inflows of $4,200, $5,300, $6,100, and $7,400, and a discount rate of 14 percent. What is the discounted payback period for these cash flows if the initial cost is $7,000? What if the initial cost is $10,000? What if it is $13,000?

5. **Calculating Discounted Payback [LO3]** An investment project costs $15,000 and has annual cash flows of $4,300 for six years. What is the discounted payback period if the discount rate is zero percent? What if the discount rate is 5 percent? If it is 19 percent?

6. **Calculating AAR [LO4]** You're trying to determine whether to expand your business by building a new manufacturing plant. The plant has an installation cost of $15 million, which will be depreciated straight-line to zero over its four-year life. If the plant has projected net income of $1,938,200, $2,201,600, $1,876,000, and $1,329,500 over these four years, what is the project's average accounting return (AAR)?

7. **Calculating IRR [LO5]** A firm evaluates all of its projects by applying the IRR rule. If the required return is 16 percent, should the firm accept the following project?

Year	Cash Flow
0	−$34,000
1	16,000
2	18,000
3	15,000

8. **Calculating NPV [LO1]** For the cash flows in the previous problem, suppose the firm uses the NPV decision rule. At a required return of 11 percent, should the firm accept this project? What if the required return was 30 percent?

9. **Calculating NPV and IRR [LO1, 5]** A project that provides annual cash flows of $28,500 for nine years costs $138,000 today. Is this a good project if the required return is 8 percent? What if it's 20 percent? At what discount rate would you be indifferent between accepting the project and rejecting it?

10. **Calculating IRR [LO5]** What is the IRR of the following set of cash flows?

Year	Cash Flow
0	−$19,500
1	9,800
2	10,300
3	8,600

Visit us at www.mhhe.com/rwj

11. Calculating NPV [LO1] For the cash flows in the previous problem, what is the NPV at a discount rate of zero percent? What if the discount rate is 10 percent? If it is 20 percent? If it is 30 percent?

12. NPV versus IRR [LO1, 5] Mahjong, Inc., has identified the following two mutually exclusive projects:

Year	Cash Flow (A)	Cash Flow (B)
0	−$43,000	−$43,000
1	23,000	7,000
2	17,900	13,800
3	12,400	24,000
4	9,400	26,000

a. What is the IRR for each of these projects? Using the IRR decision rule, which project should the company accept? Is this decision necessarily correct?

b. If the required return is 11 percent, what is the NPV for each of these projects? Which project will the company choose if it applies the NPV decision rule?

c. Over what range of discount rates would the company choose project A? Project B? At what discount rate would the company be indifferent between these two projects? Explain.

13. NPV versus IRR [LO1, 5] Consider the following two mutually exclusive projects:

Year	Cash Flow (X)	Cash Flow (Y)
0	−$15,000	−$15,000
1	8,150	7,700
2	5,050	5,150
3	6,800	7,250

Sketch the NPV profiles for X and Y over a range of discount rates from zero to 25 percent. What is the crossover rate for these two projects?

14. Problems with IRR [LO5] Light Sweet Petroleum, Inc., is trying to evaluate a generation project with the following cash flows:

Year	Cash Flow
0	−$45,000,000
1	78,000,000
2	−14,000,000

a. If the company requires a 12 percent return on its investments, should it accept this project? Why?

b. Compute the IRR for this project. How many IRRs are there? Using the IRR decision rule, should the company accept the project? What's going on here?

15. Calculating Profitability Index [LO7] What is the profitability index for the following set of cash flows if the relevant discount rate is 10 percent? What if the discount rate is 15 percent? If it is 22 percent?

Year	Cash Flow
0	−$14,000
1	7,300
2	6,900
3	5,700

16. **Problems with Profitability Index** [LO1, 7] The Weiland Computer Corporation is trying to choose between the following two mutually exclusive design projects:

Year	Cash Flow (I)	Cash Flow (II)
0	−$53,000	−$16,000
1	27,000	9,100
2	27,000	9,100
3	27,000	9,100

   a. If the required return is 10 percent and the company applies the profitability index decision rule, which project should the firm accept?

   b. If the company applies the NPV decision rule, which project should it take?

   c. Explain why your answers in (a) and (b) are different.

17. **Comparing Investment Criteria** [LO1, 2, 3, 5, 7] Consider the following two mutually exclusive projects:

Year	Cash Flow (A)	Cash Flow (B)
0	−$300,000	−$40,000
1	20,000	19,000
2	50,000	12,000
3	50,000	18,000
4	390,000	10,500

   Whichever project you choose, if any, you require a 15 percent return on your investment.

   a. If you apply the payback criterion, which investment will you choose? Why?

   b. If you apply the discounted payback criterion, which investment will you choose? Why?

   c. If you apply the NPV criterion, which investment will you choose? Why?

   d. If you apply the IRR criterion, which investment will you choose? Why?

   e. If you apply the profitability index criterion, which investment will you choose? Why?

   f. Based on your answers in (a) through (e), which project will you finally choose? Why?

18. **NPV and Discount Rates** [LO1] An investment has an installed cost of $684,680. The cash flows over the four-year life of the investment are projected to be $263,279, $294,060, $227,604, and $174,356. If the discount rate is zero, what is the NPV? If the discount rate is infinite, what is the NPV? At what discount rate is the NPV just equal to zero? Sketch the NPV profile for this investment based on these three points.

19. **MIRR** [LO6] Slow Ride Corp. is evaluating a project with the following cash flows:

Year	Cash Flow
0	−$16,000
1	6,100
2	7,800
3	8,400
4	6,500
5	−5,100

   The company uses a 10 percent interest rate on all of its projects. Calculate the MIRR of the project using all three methods.

Visit us at www.mhhe.com/rwj

Visit us at www.mhhe.com/rwj

INTERMEDIATE
(Questions 20–22)

20. MIRR [LO6] Suppose the company in the previous problem uses an 11 percent discount rate and an 8 percent reinvestment rate on all of its projects. Calculate the MIRR of the project using all three methods using these interest rates.

21. NPV and the Profitability Index [LO1, 7] If we define the NPV index as the ratio of NPV to cost, what is the relationship between this index and the profitability index?

22. Cash Flow Intuition [LO1, 2] A project has an initial cost of I, has a required return of R, and pays C annually for N years.

   a. Find C in terms of I and N such that the project has a payback period just equal to its life.

   b. Find C in terms of I, N, and R such that this is a profitable project according to the NPV decision rule.

   c. Find C in terms of I, N, and R such that the project has a benefit-cost ratio of 2.

CHALLENGE
(Questions 23–28)

23. Payback and NPV [LO1, 2] An investment under consideration has a payback of seven years and a cost of $724,000. If the required return is 12 percent, what is the worst-case NPV? The best-case NPV? Explain. Assume the cash flows are conventional.

24. Multiple IRRs [LO5] This problem is useful for testing the ability of financial calculators and computer software. Consider the following cash flows. How many different IRRs are there? (*Hint:* Search between 20 percent and 70 percent.) When should we take this project?

Year	Cash Flow
0	−$1,512
1	8,586
2	−18,210
3	17,100
4	−6,000

25. NPV Valuation [LO1] The Yurdone Corporation wants to set up a private cemetery business. According to the CFO, Barry M. Deep, business is "looking up." As a result, the cemetery project will provide a net cash inflow of $85,000 for the firm during the first year, and the cash flows are projected to grow at a rate of 6 percent per year forever. The project requires an initial investment of $1,400,000.

   a. If Yurdone requires a 13 percent return on such undertakings, should the cemetery business be started?

   b. The company is somewhat unsure about the assumption of a 6 percent growth rate in its cash flows. At what constant growth rate would the company just break even if it still required a 13 percent return on investment?

26. Problems with IRR [LO5] A project has the following cash flows:

Year	Cash Flow
0	$58,000
1	−34,000
2	−45,000

What is the IRR for this project? If the required return is 12 percent, should the firm accept the project? What is the NPV of this project? What is the NPV of the project if the required return is 0 percent? 24 percent? What is going on here? Sketch the NPV profile to help you with your answer.

27. **Problems with IRR** [LO5] McKeekin Corp. has a project with the following cash flows:

Year	Cash Flow
0	$20,000
1	−26,000
2	13,000

What is the IRR of the project? What is happening here?

28. **NPV and IRR** [LO1, 5] Anderson International Limited is evaluating a project in Erewhon. The project will create the following cash flows:

Year	Cash Flow
0	−$750,000
1	205,000
2	265,000
3	346,000
4	220,000

All cash flows will occur in Erewhon and are expressed in dollars. In an attempt to improve its economy, the Erewhonian government has declared that all cash flows created by a foreign company are "blocked" and must be reinvested with the government for one year. The reinvestment rate for these funds is 4 percent. If Anderson uses an 11 percent required return on this project, what are the NPV and IRR of the project? Is the IRR you calculated the MIRR of the project? Why or why not?

Bullock Gold Mining

Seth Bullock, the owner of Bullock Gold Mining, is evaluating a new gold mine in South Dakota. Dan Dority, the company's geologist, has just finished his analysis of the mine site. He has estimated that the mine would be productive for eight years, after which the gold would be completely mined. Dan has taken an estimate of the gold deposits to Alma Garrett, the company's financial officer. Alma has been asked by Seth to perform an analysis of the new mine and present her recommendation on whether the company should open the new mine.

Alma has used the estimates provided by Dan to determine the revenues that could be expected from the mine. She has also projected the expense of opening the mine and the annual operating expenses. If the company opens the mine, it will cost $600 million today, and it will have a cash outflow of $95 million nine years from today in costs associated with closing the mine and reclaiming the area surrounding it. The expected cash flows each year from the mine are shown in the table. Bullock Mining has a 12 percent required return on all of its gold mines.

Year	Cash Flow
0	−$600,000,000
1	75,000,000
2	120,000,000
3	160,000,000
4	210,000,000
5	240,000,000
6	160,000,000
7	130,000,000
8	90,000,000
9	−95,000,000

QUESTIONS

1. Construct a spreadsheet to calculate the payback period, internal rate of return, modified internal rate of return, and net present value of the proposed mine.

2. Based on your analysis, should the company open the mine?

3. Bonus question: Most spreadsheets do not have a built-in formula to calculate the payback period. Write a VBA script that calculates the payback period for a project.

Visit us at www.mhhe.com/rwj

10

MAKING CAPITAL INVESTMENT DECISIONS

LEARNING OBJECTIVES

After studying this chapter, you should understand:

LO1 How to determine the relevant cash flows for a proposed project.

LO2 How to determine if a project is acceptable.

LO3 How to set a bid price for a project.

LO4 How to evaluate the equivalent annual cost of a project.

IS THERE GREEN IN GREEN? General Electric (GE) thinks so. Through its "Ecomagination" program, the company planned to double research and development spending on green products, from $700 million in 2004 to $1.5 billion in 2010. With products such as a hybrid railroad locomotive (described as a 200-ton, 6,000-horsepower "Prius on rails"), GE's green initiative seems to be paying off. Revenue from green products was $14 billion in 2007, with a target of $25 billion in 2010. The company's internal commitment to reduced energy consumption saved it more than $100 million from 2004 to 2007, and the company was on target to reduce its water consumption by 20 percent by 2012, another considerable cost savings.

Master the ability to solve problems in this chapter by using a spreadsheet. Access Excel Master on the student Web site www.mhhe.com/rwj.

As you no doubt recognize from your study of the previous chapter, GE's decision to develop and market green technology represents a capital budgeting decision. In this chapter, we further investigate such decisions, how they are made, and how to look at them objectively.

This chapter follows up on our previous one by delving more deeply into capital budgeting. We have two main tasks. First, recall that in the last chapter, we saw that cash flow estimates are the critical input into a net present value analysis, but we didn't say much about where these cash flows come from; so we will now examine this question in some detail. Our second goal is to learn how to critically examine NPV estimates, and, in particular, how to evaluate the sensitivity of NPV estimates to assumptions made about the uncertain future.

So far, we've covered various parts of the capital budgeting decision. Our task in this chapter is to start bringing these pieces together. In particular, we will show you how to "spread the numbers" for a proposed investment or project and, based on those numbers, make an initial assessment about whether the project should be undertaken.

In the discussion that follows, we focus on the process of setting up a discounted cash flow analysis. From the last chapter, we know that the projected future cash flows are the key element in such an evaluation. Accordingly, we emphasize working with financial and accounting information to come up with these figures.

In evaluating a proposed investment, we pay special attention to deciding what information is relevant to the decision at hand and what information is not. As we will see, it is easy to overlook important pieces of the capital budgeting puzzle.

We will wait until the next chapter to describe in detail how to go about evaluating the results of our discounted cash flow analysis. Also, where needed, we will assume that we know the relevant required return, or discount rate. We continue to defer in-depth discussion of this subject to Part 5.

Project Cash Flows: A First Look

The effect of taking a project is to change the firm's overall cash flows today and in the future. To evaluate a proposed investment, we must consider these changes in the firm's cash flows and then decide whether they add value to the firm. The first (and most important) step, therefore, is to decide which cash flows are relevant.

RELEVANT CASH FLOWS

What is a relevant cash flow for a project? The general principle is simple enough: A relevant cash flow for a project is a change in the firm's overall future cash flow that comes about as a direct consequence of the decision to take that project. Because the relevant cash flows are defined in terms of changes in, or increments to, the firm's existing cash flow, they are called the **incremental cash flows** associated with the project.

The concept of incremental cash flow is central to our analysis, so we will state a general definition and refer back to it as needed:

> **The incremental cash flows for project evaluation consist of *any and all* changes in the firm's future cash flows that are a direct consequence of taking the project.**

This definition of incremental cash flows has an obvious and important corollary: Any cash flow that exists regardless of *whether or not* a project is undertaken is *not* relevant.

incremental cash flows
The difference between a firm's future cash flows with a project and those without the project.

THE STAND-ALONE PRINCIPLE

In practice, it would be cumbersome to actually calculate the future total cash flows to the firm with and without a project, especially for a large firm. Fortunately, it is not really necessary to do so. Once we identify the effect of undertaking the proposed project on the firm's cash flows, we need focus only on the project's resulting incremental cash flows. This is called the **stand-alone principle**.

What the stand-alone principle says is that once we have determined the incremental cash flows from undertaking a project, we can view that project as a kind of "minifirm" with its own future revenues and costs, its own assets, and, of course, its own cash flows. We will then be primarily interested in comparing the cash flows from this minifirm to the cost of acquiring it. An important consequence of this approach is that we will be evaluating the proposed project purely on its own merits, in isolation from any other activities or projects.

stand-alone principle
The assumption that evaluation of a project may be based on the project's incremental cash flows.

Concept Questions

10.1a What are the relevant incremental cash flows for project evaluation?

10.1b What is the stand-alone principle?

Incremental Cash Flows

We are concerned here with only cash flows that are incremental and that result from a project. Looking back at our general definition, we might think it would be easy enough to decide whether a cash flow is incremental. Even so, in a few situations it is easy to make mistakes. In this section, we describe some common pitfalls and how to avoid them.

SUNK COSTS

sunk cost
A cost that has already
been incurred and cannot
be removed and therefore
should not be considered in
an investment decision.

A **sunk cost,** by definition, is a cost we have already paid or have already incurred the liability to pay. Such a cost cannot be changed by the decision today to accept or reject a project. Put another way, the firm will have to pay this cost no matter what. Based on our general definition of incremental cash flow, such a cost is clearly not relevant to the decision at hand. So, we will always be careful to exclude sunk costs from our analysis.

That a sunk cost is not relevant seems obvious given our discussion. Nonetheless, it's easy to fall prey to the fallacy that a sunk cost should be associated with a project. For example, suppose General Milk Company hires a financial consultant to help evaluate whether a line of chocolate milk should be launched. When the consultant turns in the report, General Milk objects to the analysis because the consultant did not include the hefty consulting fee as a cost of the chocolate milk project.

Who is correct? By now, we know that the consulting fee is a sunk cost: It must be paid whether or not the chocolate milk line is actually launched (this is an attractive feature of the consulting business).

OPPORTUNITY COSTS

opportunity cost
The most valuable
alternative that is given up if
a particular investment is
undertaken.

When we think of costs, we normally think of out-of-pocket costs—namely those that require us to actually spend some amount of cash. An **opportunity cost** is slightly different; it requires us to give up a benefit. A common situation arises in which a firm already owns some of the assets a proposed project will be using. For example, we might be thinking of converting an old rustic cotton mill we bought years ago for $100,000 into upmarket condominiums.

If we undertake this project, there will be no direct cash outflow associated with buying the old mill because we already own it. For purposes of evaluating the condo project, should we then treat the mill as "free"? The answer is no. The mill is a valuable resource used by the project. If we didn't use it here, we could do something else with it. Like what? The obvious answer is that, at a minimum, we could sell it. Using the mill for the condo complex thus has an opportunity cost: We give up the valuable opportunity to do something else with the mill.[1]

There is another issue here. Once we agree that the use of the mill has an opportunity cost, how much should we charge the condo project for this use? Given that we paid $100,000, it might seem that we should charge this amount to the condo project. Is this correct? The answer is no, and the reason is based on our discussion concerning sunk costs.

The fact that we paid $100,000 some years ago is irrelevant. That cost is sunk. At a minimum, the opportunity cost that we charge the project is what the mill would sell for today (net of any selling costs) because this is the amount we give up by using the mill instead of selling it.[2]

SIDE EFFECTS

Remember that the incremental cash flows for a project include all the resulting changes in the *firm's* future cash flows. It would not be unusual for a project to have side, or spillover, effects, both good and bad. For example, in 2008, the time between the theatrical release of

---

[1]Economists sometimes use the acronym TANSTAAFL, which is short for "There ain't no such thing as a free lunch," to describe the fact that only very rarely is something truly free.

[2]If the asset in question is unique, then the opportunity cost might be higher because there might be other valuable projects we could undertake that would use it. However, if the asset in question is of a type that is routinely bought and sold (a used car, perhaps), then the opportunity cost is always the going price in the market because that is the cost of buying another similar asset.

a feature film and the release of the DVD had shrunk to 98 days compared to 200 days in 1998. This shortened release time was blamed for at least part of the decline in movie theater box office receipts. Of course, retailers cheered the move because it was credited with increasing DVD sales. A negative impact on the cash flows of an existing product from the introduction of a new product is called **erosion**.[3] In this case, the cash flows from the new line should be adjusted downward to reflect lost profits on other lines.

erosion
The cash flows of a new project that come at the expense of a firm's existing projects.

In accounting for erosion, it is important to recognize that any sales lost as a result of launching a new product might be lost anyway because of future competition. Erosion is relevant only when the sales would not otherwise be lost.

Side effects show up in a lot of different ways. For example, one of Walt Disney Company's concerns when it built Euro Disney was that the new park would drain visitors from the Florida park, a popular vacation destination for Europeans.

There are beneficial spillover effects, of course. For example, you might think that Hewlett-Packard would have been concerned when the price of a printer that sold for $500 to $600 in 1994 declined to below $100 by 2009, but such was not the case. HP realized that the big money is in the consumables that printer owners buy to keep their printers going, such as ink-jet cartridges, laser toner cartridges, and special paper. The profit margins for these products are substantial.

NET WORKING CAPITAL

Normally a project will require that the firm invest in net working capital in addition to long-term assets. For example, a project will generally need some amount of cash on hand to pay any expenses that arise. In addition, a project will need an initial investment in inventories and accounts receivable (to cover credit sales). Some of the financing for this will be in the form of amounts owed to suppliers (accounts payable), but the firm will have to supply the balance. This balance represents the investment in net working capital.

It's easy to overlook an important feature of net working capital in capital budgeting. As a project winds down, inventories are sold, receivables are collected, bills are paid, and cash balances can be drawn down. These activities free up the net working capital originally invested. So the firm's investment in project net working capital closely resembles a loan. The firm supplies working capital at the beginning and recovers it toward the end.

FINANCING COSTS

In analyzing a proposed investment, we will *not* include interest paid or any other financing costs such as dividends or principal repaid because we are interested in the cash flow generated by the assets of the project. As we mentioned in Chapter 2, interest paid, for example, is a component of cash flow to creditors, not cash flow from assets.

More generally, our goal in project evaluation is to compare the cash flow from a project to the cost of acquiring that project in order to estimate NPV. The particular mixture of debt and equity a firm actually chooses to use in financing a project is a managerial variable and primarily determines how project cash flow is divided between owners and creditors. This is not to say that financing arrangements are unimportant. They are just something to be analyzed separately. We will cover this in later chapters.

OTHER ISSUES

There are some other things to watch out for. First, we are interested only in measuring cash flow. Moreover, we are interested in measuring it when it actually occurs, not when it

---

[3]More colorfully, erosion is sometimes called *piracy* or *cannibalism*.

accrues in an accounting sense. Second, we are always interested in *aftertax* cash flow because taxes are definitely a cash outflow. In fact, whenever we write *incremental cash flows,* we mean aftertax incremental cash flows. Remember, however, that aftertax cash flow and accounting profit, or net income, are entirely different things.

> **Concept Questions**
>
> **10.2a** What is a sunk cost? An opportunity cost?
>
> **10.2b** Explain what erosion is and why it is relevant.
>
> **10.2c** Explain why interest paid is not a relevant cash flow for project evaluation.

10.3 Pro Forma Financial Statements and Project Cash Flows

The first thing we need when we begin evaluating a proposed investment is a set of pro forma, or projected, financial statements. Given these, we can develop the projected cash flows from the project. Once we have the cash flows, we can estimate the value of the project using the techniques we described in the previous chapter.

GETTING STARTED: PRO FORMA FINANCIAL STATEMENTS

pro forma financial statements
Financial statements projecting future years' operations.

Pro forma financial statements are a convenient and easily understood means of summarizing much of the relevant information for a project. To prepare these statements, we will need estimates of quantities such as unit sales, the selling price per unit, the variable cost per unit, and total fixed costs. We will also need to know the total investment required, including any investment in net working capital.

To illustrate, suppose we think we can sell 50,000 cans of shark attractant per year at a price of $4 per can. It costs us about $2.50 per can to make the attractant, and a new product such as this one typically has only a three-year life (perhaps because the customer base dwindles rapidly). We require a 20 percent return on new products.

Fixed costs for the project, including such things as rent on the production facility, will run $12,000 per year.[4] Further, we will need to invest a total of $90,000 in manufacturing equipment. For simplicity, we will assume that this $90,000 will be 100 percent depreciated over the three-year life of the project.[5] Furthermore, the cost of removing the equipment will roughly equal its actual value in three years, so it will be essentially worthless on a market value basis as well. Finally, the project will require an initial $20,000 investment in net working capital, and the tax rate is 34 percent.

In Table 10.1, we organize these initial projections by first preparing the pro forma income statement. Once again, notice that we have *not* deducted any interest expense. This will always be so. As we described earlier, interest paid is a financing expense, not a component of operating cash flow.

We can also prepare a series of abbreviated balance sheets that show the capital requirements for the project as we've done in Table 10.2. Here we have net working capital of

---

[4]By *fixed cost,* we literally mean a cash outflow that will occur regardless of the level of sales. This should not be confused with some sort of accounting period charge.

[5]We will also assume that a full year's depreciation can be taken in the first year.

Sales (50,000 units at $4/unit)	$200,000
Variable costs ($2.50/unit)	125,000
	$ 75,000
Fixed costs	12,000
Depreciation ($90,000/3)	30,000
EBIT	$ 33,000
Taxes (34%)	11,220
Net income	$ 21,780

TABLE 10.1

Projected Income Statement, Shark Attractant Project

	Year			
	0	1	2	3
Net working capital	$ 20,000	$20,000	$20,000	$20,000
Net fixed assets	90,000	60,000	30,000	0
Total investment	$110,000	$80,000	$50,000	$20,000

TABLE 10.2

Projected Capital Requirements, Shark Attractant Project

$20,000 in each year. Fixed assets are $90,000 at the start of the project's life (year 0), and they decline by the $30,000 in depreciation each year, ending up at zero. Notice that the total investment given here for future years is the total book, or accounting, value, not market value.

At this point, we need to start converting this accounting information into cash flows. We consider how to do this next.

PROJECT CASH FLOWS

To develop the cash flows from a project, we need to recall (from Chapter 2) that cash flow from assets has three components: operating cash flow, capital spending, and changes in net working capital. To evaluate a project, or minifirm, we need to estimate each of these.

Once we have estimates of the components of cash flow, we will calculate cash flow for our minifirm just as we did in Chapter 2 for an entire firm:

Project cash flow = Project operating cash flow

— Project change in net working capital

— Project capital spending

We consider these components next.

Project Operating Cash Flow   To determine the operating cash flow associated with a project, we first need to recall the definition of operating cash flow:

Operating cash flow = Earnings before interest and taxes

+ Depreciation

— Taxes

To illustrate the calculation of operating cash flow, we will use the projected information from the shark attractant project. For ease of reference, Table 10.3 repeats the income statement in more abbreviated form.

Given the income statement in Table 10.3, calculating the operating cash flow is straightforward. As we see in Table 10.4, projected operating cash flow for the shark attractant project is $51,780.

TABLE 10.3

Projected Income
Statement, Abbreviated,
Shark Attractant Project

Sales	$200,000
Variable costs	125,000
Fixed costs	12,000
Depreciation	30,000
EBIT	$ 33,000
Taxes (34%)	11,220
Net income	$ 21,780

TABLE 10.4

Projected Operating Cash
Flow, Shark Attractant
Project

EBIT	$ 33,000
Depreciation	+ 30,000
Taxes	− 11,220
Operating cash flow	$51,780

TABLE 10.5

Projected Total Cash
Flows, Shark Attractant
Project

	Year			
	0	1	2	3
Operating cash flow		$51,780	$51,780	$51,780
Changes in NWC	−$ 20,000			+ 20,000
Capital spending	− 90,000			
Total project cash flow	−$110,000	$51,780	$51,780	$71,780

Project Net Working Capital and Capital Spending   We next need to take care of the fixed asset and net working capital requirements. Based on our balance sheets, we know that the firm must spend $90,000 up front for fixed assets and invest an additional $20,000 in net working capital. The immediate outflow is thus $110,000. At the end of the project's life, the fixed assets will be worthless, but the firm will recover the $20,000 that was tied up in working capital.[6] This will lead to a $20,000 *inflow* in the last year.

On a purely mechanical level, notice that whenever we have an investment in net working capital, that same investment has to be recovered; in other words, the same number needs to appear at some time in the future with the opposite sign.

PROJECTED TOTAL CASH FLOW AND VALUE

Given the information we've accumulated, we can finish the preliminary cash flow analysis as illustrated in Table 10.5.

Now that we have cash flow projections, we are ready to apply the various criteria we discussed in the last chapter. First, the NPV at the 20 percent required return is:

$$\text{NPV} = -\$110,000 + 51,780/1.2 + 51,780/1.2^2 + 71,780/1.2^3$$
$$= \$10,648$$

---

[6]In reality, the firm would probably recover something less than 100 percent of this amount because of bad debts, inventory loss, and so on. If we wanted to, we could just assume that, for example, only 90 percent was recovered and proceed from there.

Based on these projections, the project creates over $10,000 in value and should be accepted. Also, the return on this investment obviously exceeds 20 percent (because the NPV is positive at 20 percent). After some trial and error, we find that the IRR works out to be about 25.8 percent.

In addition, if required, we could calculate the payback and the average accounting return, or AAR. Inspection of the cash flows shows that the payback on this project is just a little over two years (verify that it's about 2.1 years).[7]

From the last chapter, we know that the AAR is average net income divided by average book value. The net income each year is $21,780. The average (in thousands) of the four book values (from Table 10.2) for total investment is ($110 + 80 + 50 + 20)/4 = $65. So the AAR is $21,780/65,000 = 33.51 percent.[8] We've already seen that the return on this investment (the IRR) is about 26 percent. The fact that the AAR is larger illustrates again why the AAR cannot be meaningfully interpreted as the return on a project.

Concept Questions

10.3a What is the definition of project operating cash flow? How does this differ from net income?

10.3b For the shark attractant project, why did we add back the firm's net working capital investment in the final year?

More about Project Cash Flow   **10.4**

In this section, we take a closer look at some aspects of project cash flow. In particular, we discuss project net working capital in more detail. We then examine current tax laws regarding depreciation. Finally, we work through a more involved example of the capital investment decision.

A CLOSER LOOK AT NET WORKING CAPITAL

In calculating operating cash flow, we did not explicitly consider the fact that some of our sales might be on credit. Also, we may not have actually paid some of the costs shown. In either case, the cash flow in question would not yet have occurred. We show here that these possibilities are not a problem as long as we don't forget to include changes in net working capital in our analysis. This discussion thus emphasizes the importance and the effect of doing so.

Suppose that during a particular year of a project we have the following simplified income statement:

Sales	$500
Costs	310
Net income	$190

---

[7]We're guilty of a minor inconsistency here. When we calculated the NPV and the IRR, we assumed that all the cash flows occurred at end of year. When we calculated the payback, we assumed that the cash flows occurred uniformly throughout the year.

[8]Notice that the average total book value is not the initial total of $110,000 divided by 2. The reason is that the $20,000 in working capital doesn't "depreciate."

Depreciation and taxes are zero. No fixed assets are purchased during the year. Also, to illustrate a point, we assume that the only components of net working capital are accounts receivable and payable. The beginning and ending amounts for these accounts are as follows:

	Beginning of Year	End of Year	Change
Accounts receivable	$880	$910	+$30
Accounts payable	550	605	+ 55
Net working capital	$330	$305	−$25

Based on this information, what is total cash flow for the year? We can first just mechanically apply what we have been discussing to come up with the answer. Operating cash flow in this particular case is the same as EBIT because there are no taxes or depreciation; thus, it equals $190. Also, notice that net working capital actually *declined* by $25. This just means that $25 was freed up during the year. There was no capital spending, so the total cash flow for the year is:

$$\text{Total cash flow} = \text{Operating cash flow} - \text{Change in NWC} - \text{Capital spending}$$
$$= \$190 - (-25) - 0$$
$$= \$215$$

Now, we know that this $215 total cash flow has to be "dollars in" less "dollars out" for the year. We could therefore ask a different question: What were cash revenues for the year? Also, what were cash costs?

To determine cash revenues, we need to look more closely at net working capital. During the year, we had sales of $500. However, accounts receivable rose by $30 over the same time period. What does this mean? The $30 increase tells us that sales exceeded collections by $30. In other words, we haven't yet received the cash from $30 of the $500 in sales. As a result, our cash inflow is $500 − 30 = $470. In general, cash income is sales minus the increase in accounts receivable.

Cash outflows can be similarly determined. We show costs of $310 on the income statement, but accounts payable increased by $55 during the year. This means that we have not yet paid $55 of the $310, so cash costs for the period are just $310 − 55 = $255. In other words, in this case, cash costs equal costs less the increase in accounts payable.[9]

Putting this information together, we calculate that cash inflows less cash outflows are $470 − 255 = $215, just as we had before. Notice that:

$$\text{Cash flow} = \text{Cash inflow} - \text{Cash outflow}$$
$$= (\$500 - 30) - (310 - 55)$$
$$= (\$500 - 310) - (30 - 55)$$
$$= \text{Operating cash flow} - \text{Change in NWC}$$
$$= \$190 - (-25)$$
$$= \$215$$

More generally, this example illustrates that including net working capital changes in our calculations has the effect of adjusting for the discrepancy between accounting sales and costs and actual cash receipts and payments.

---

[9]If there were other accounts, we might have to make some further adjustments. For example, a net increase in inventory would be a cash outflow.

Samuel Weaver on Capital Budgeting at The Hershey Company

The capital program at The Hershey Company and most Fortune 500 or Fortune 1,000 companies involves a three-phase approach: planning or budgeting, evaluation, and postcompletion reviews.

The first phase involves identification of likely projects at strategic planning time. These are selected to support the strategic objectives of the corporation. This identification is generally broad in scope with minimal financial evaluation attached. Projects are classified as new product, cost savings, capacity expansion, etc. As the planning process focuses more closely on the short-term plans (or budgets), major capital expenditures are scrutinized more rigorously. Project costs are more closely honed, and specific projects may be reconsidered.

Each project is then individually reviewed and authorized. Planning, developing, and refining cash flows underlie capital analysis at Hershey. Once the cash flows have been determined, the application of capital evaluation techniques such as those using net present value, internal rate of return, and payback period is routine. Presentation of the results is enhanced using sensitivity analysis, which plays a major role for management in assessing the critical assumptions and resulting impact.

The final phase relates to postcompletion reviews in which the original forecasts of the project's performance are compared to actual results and/or revised expectations.

Capital expenditure analysis is only as good as the assumptions that underlie the project. The old cliché of GIGO (garbage in, garbage out) applies in this case. Incremental cash flows primarily result from incremental sales or margin improvements (cost savings). For the most part, a range of incremental cash flows can be identified from marketing research or engineering studies. However, for a number of projects, correctly discerning the implications and the relevant cash flows is analytically challenging. For example, when a new product is introduced and is expected to generate millions of dollars' worth of sales, the appropriate analysis focuses on the incremental sales after accounting for cannibalization of existing products.

One of the problems that we face at Hershey deals with the application of net present value, NPV, versus internal rate of return, IRR. NPV offers us the correct investment indication when dealing with mutually exclusive alternatives. However, decision makers at all levels sometimes find it difficult to comprehend the result. Specifically, an NPV of, say, $535,000 needs to be interpreted. It is not enough to know that the NPV is positive or even that it is more positive than an alternative. Decision makers seek to determine a level of "comfort" regarding how profitable the investment is by relating it to other standards.

Although the IRR may provide a misleading indication of which project to select, the result is provided in a way that can be interpreted by all parties. The resulting IRR can be mentally compared to expected inflation, current borrowing rates, the cost of capital, an equity portfolio's return, and so on. An IRR of, say, 18 percent is readily interpretable by management. Perhaps this ease of understanding is why surveys indicate that many Fortune 500 or Fortune 1,000 companies use the IRR method (in conjunction with NPV) as a primary evaluation technique.

In addition to the NPV versus IRR problem, there are a limited number of projects for which traditional capital expenditure analysis is difficult to apply because the cash flows can't be determined. When new computer equipment is purchased, an office building is renovated, or a parking lot is repaved, it is essentially impossible to identify the cash flows, so the use of traditional evaluation techniques is limited. These types of "capital expenditure" decisions are made using other techniques that hinge on management's judgment.

Samuel Weaver, Ph.D., is the former director, financial planning and analysis, for Hershey Chocolate North America. He is a certified management accountant and certified financial manager. His position combined the theoretical with the pragmatic and involved the analysis of many different facets of finance in addition to capital expenditure analysis.

Cash Collections and Costs	EXAMPLE 10.1

For the year just completed, the Combat Wombat Telestat Co. (CWT) reports sales of $998 and costs of $734. You have collected the following beginning and ending balance sheet information:

(continued)

	Beginning	Ending
Accounts receivable	$100	$110
Inventory	100	80
Accounts payable	100	70
Net working capital	$100	$120

Based on these figures, what are cash inflows? Cash outflows? What happened to each account? What is net cash flow?

Sales were $998, but receivables rose by $10. So cash collections were $10 less than sales, or $988. Costs were $734, but inventories fell by $20. This means that we didn't replace $20 worth of inventory, so costs are actually overstated by this amount. Also, payables fell by $30. This means that, on a net basis, we actually paid our suppliers $30 more than we received from them, resulting in a $30 understatement of costs. Adjusting for these events, we calculate that cash costs are $734 − 20 + 30 = $744. Net cash flow is $988 − 744 = $244.

Finally, notice that net working capital increased by $20 overall. We can check our answer by noting that the original accounting sales less costs (= $998 − 734) are $264. In addition, CWT spent $20 on net working capital, so the net result is a cash flow of $264 − 20 = $244, as we calculated.

DEPRECIATION

As we note elsewhere, accounting depreciation is a noncash deduction. As a result, depreciation has cash flow consequences only because it influences the tax bill. The way that depreciation is computed for tax purposes is thus the relevant method for capital investment decisions. Not surprisingly, the procedures are governed by tax law. We now discuss some specifics of the depreciation system enacted by the Tax Reform Act of 1986. This system is a modification of the **accelerated cost recovery system (ACRS)** instituted in 1981.

accelerated cost recovery system (ACRS)
A depreciation method under U.S. tax law allowing for the accelerated write-off of property under various classifications.

Modified ACRS Depreciation (MACRS)   Calculating depreciation is normally mechanical. Although there are a number of *ifs, ands,* and *buts* involved, the basic idea under MACRS is that every asset is assigned to a particular class. An asset's class establishes its life for tax purposes. Once an asset's tax life is determined, the depreciation for each year is computed by multiplying the cost of the asset by a fixed percentage.[10] The expected salvage value (what we think the asset will be worth when we dispose of it) and the expected economic life (how long we expect the asset to be in service) are not explicitly considered in the calculation of depreciation.

Some typical depreciation classes are given in Table 10.6, and associated percentages (as specified by the IRS) are shown in Table 10.7.[11]

A nonresidential real property, such as an office building, is depreciated over 31.5 years using straight-line depreciation. A residential real property, such as an apartment building, is depreciated straight-line over 27.5 years. Remember that land cannot be depreciated.[12]

---

[10]Under certain circumstances, the cost of the asset may be adjusted before computing depreciation. The result is called the *depreciable basis,* and depreciation is calculated using this number instead of the actual cost.

[11]For the curious, these depreciation percentages are derived from a double-declining balance scheme with a switch to straight-line when the latter becomes advantageous. Further, there is a half-year convention, meaning that all assets are assumed to be placed in service midway through the tax year. This convention is maintained unless more than 40 percent of an asset's cost is incurred in the final quarter. In this case, a midquarter convention is used. The odd-looking rounding is courtesy of the IRS.

[12]There are, however, depletion allowances for firms in extraction-type lines of business (such as mining). These are somewhat similar to depreciation allowances.

Class	Examples
Three-year	Equipment used in research
Five-year	Autos, computers
Seven-year	Most industrial equipment

TABLE 10.6

Modified ACRS Property Classes

	Property Class		
Year	Three-Year	Five-Year	Seven-Year
1	33.33%	20.00%	14.29%
2	44.45	32.00	24.49
3	14.81	19.20	17.49
4	7.41	11.52	12.49
5		11.52	8.93
6		5.76	8.92
7			8.93
8			4.46

TABLE 10.7

Modified ACRS Depreciation Allowances

To illustrate how depreciation is calculated, we consider an automobile costing $12,000. Autos are normally classified as five-year property. Looking at Table 10.7, we see that the relevant figure for the first year of a five-year asset is 20 percent.[13] The depreciation in the first year is thus $12,000 × .20 = $2,400. The relevant percentage in the second year is 32 percent, so the depreciation in the second year is $12,000 × .32 = $3,840, and so on. We can summarize these calculations as follows:

Year	MACRS Percentage	Depreciation	
1	20.00%	.2000 × $12,000 =	$ 2,400.00
2	32.00%	.3200 × 12,000 =	3,840.00
3	19.20%	.1920 × 12,000 =	2,304.00
4	11.52%	.1152 × 12,000 =	1,382.40
5	11.52%	.1152 × 12,000 =	1,382.40
6	5.76%	.0576 × 12,000 =	691.20
	100.00%		$12,000.00

Notice that the MACRS percentages sum up to 100 percent. As a result, we write off 100 percent of the cost of the asset, or $12,000 in this case.

Book Value versus Market Value   In calculating depreciation under current tax law, the economic life and future market value of the asset are not an issue. As a result, the book value of an asset can differ substantially from its actual market value. For example, with our $12,000 car, book value after the first year is $12,000 less the first year's depreciation of $2,400, or $9,600. The remaining book values are summarized in Table 10.8. After six years, the book value of the car is zero.

Suppose we wanted to sell the car after five years. Based on historical averages, it would be worth, say, 25 percent of the purchase price, or .25 × $12,000 = $3,000. If we actually

[13]It may appear odd that five-year property is depreciated over six years. The tax accounting reason is that it is assumed we have the asset for only six months in the first year and, consequently, six months in the last year. As a result, there are five 12 month periods, but we have some depreciation in each of six different tax years.

TABLE 10.8

MACRS Book Values

Year	Beginning Book Value	Depreciation	Ending Book Value
1	$12,000.00	$2,400.00	$9,600.00
2	9,600.00	3,840.00	5,760.00
3	5,760.00	2,304.00	3,456.00
4	3,456.00	1,382.40	2,073.60
5	2,073.60	1,382.40	691.20
6	691.20	691.20	.00

sold it for this, then we would have to pay taxes at the ordinary income tax rate on the difference between the sale price of $3,000 and the book value of $691.20. For a corporation in the 34 percent bracket, the tax liability would be .34 × $2,308.80 = $784.99.[14]

The reason taxes must be paid in this case is that the difference between market value and book value is "excess" depreciation, and it must be "recaptured" when the asset is sold. What this means is that, as it turns out, we overdepreciated the asset by $3,000 − 691.20 = $2,308.80. Because we deducted $2,308.80 too much in depreciation, we paid $784.99 too little in taxes, and we simply have to make up the difference.

Notice that this is *not* a tax on a capital gain. As a general (albeit rough) rule, a capital gain occurs only if the market price exceeds the original cost. However, what is and what is not a capital gain is ultimately up to taxing authorities, and the specific rules can be complex. We will ignore capital gains taxes for the most part.

Finally, if the book value exceeds the market value, then the difference is treated as a loss for tax purposes. For example, if we sell the car after two years for $4,000, then the book value exceeds the market value by $1,760. In this case, a tax saving of .34 × $1,760 = $598.40 occurs.

---

[14]The rules are different and more complicated with real property. Essentially, in this case, only the difference between the actual book value and the book value that would have existed if straight-line depreciation had been used is recaptured. Anything above the straight-line book value is considered a capital gain.

EXAMPLE 10.2   **MACRS Depreciation**

The Staple Supply Co. has just purchased a new computerized information system with an installed cost of $160,000. The computer is treated as five-year property. What are the yearly depreciation allowances? Based on historical experience, we think that the system will be worth only $10,000 when Staple gets rid of it in four years. What are the tax consequences of the sale? What is the total aftertax cash flow from the sale?

The yearly depreciation allowances are calculated by just multiplying $160,000 by the five-year percentages found in Table 10.7:

Year	MACRS Percentage	Depreciation		Ending Book Value
1	20.00%	.2000 × $160,000 =	$ 32,000	$128,000
2	32.00	.3200 × 160,000 =	51,200	76,800
3	19.20	.1920 × 160,000 =	30,720	46,080
4	11.52	.1152 × 160,000 =	18,432	27,648
5	11.52	.1152 × 160,000 =	18,432	9,216
6	5.76	.0576 × 160,000 =	9,216	0
	100.00%		$160,000	

(continued)

Notice that we have also computed the book value of the system as of the end of each year. The book value at the end of year 4 is $27,648. If Staple sells the system for $10,000 at that time, it will have a loss of $17,648 (the difference) for tax purposes. This loss, of course, is like depreciation because it isn't a cash expense.

What really happens? Two things. First, Staple gets $10,000 from the buyer. Second, it saves .34 × $17,648 = $6,000 in taxes. So, the total aftertax cash flow from the sale is a $16,000 cash inflow.

AN EXAMPLE: THE MAJESTIC MULCH AND COMPOST COMPANY (MMCC)

At this point, we want to go through a somewhat more involved capital budgeting analysis. Keep in mind as you read that the basic approach here is exactly the same as that in the shark attractant example used earlier. We have just added some real-world detail (and a lot more numbers).

MMCC is investigating the feasibility of a new line of power mulching tools aimed at the growing number of home composters. Based on exploratory conversations with buyers for large garden shops, MMCC projects unit sales as follows:

Year	Unit Sales
1	3,000
2	5,000
3	6,000
4	6,500
5	6,000
6	5,000
7	4,000
8	3,000

The new power mulcher will sell for $120 per unit to start. When the competition catches up after three years, however, MMCC anticipates that the price will drop to $110.

The power mulcher project will require $20,000 in net working capital at the start. Subsequently, total net working capital at the end of each year will be about 15 percent of sales for that year. The variable cost per unit is $60, and total fixed costs are $25,000 per year.

It will cost about $800,000 to buy the equipment necessary to begin production. This investment is primarily in industrial equipment, which qualifies as seven-year MACRS property. The equipment will actually be worth about 20 percent of its cost in eight years, or .20 × $800,000 = $160,000. The relevant tax rate is 34 percent, and the required return is 15 percent. Based on this information, should MMCC proceed?

Operating Cash Flows   There is a lot of information here that we need to organize. The first thing we can do is calculate projected sales. Sales in the first year are projected at 3,000 units at $120 apiece, or $360,000 total. The remaining figures are shown in Table 10.9.

Next, we compute the depreciation on the $800,000 investment in Table 10.10. With this information, we can prepare the pro forma income statements, as shown in Table 10.11. From here, computing the operating cash flows is straightforward. The results are illustrated in the first part of Table 10.13.

Change in NWC   Now that we have the operating cash flows, we need to determine the changes in NWC. By assumption, net working capital requirements change as sales change. In each year, MMCC will generally either add to or recover some of its project net working

TABLE 10.9

Projected Revenues,
Power Mulcher Project

Year	Unit Price	Unit Sales	Revenues
1	$120	3,000	$360,000
2	120	5,000	600,000
3	120	6,000	720,000
4	110	6,500	715,000
5	110	6,000	660,000
6	110	5,000	550,000
7	110	4,000	440,000
8	110	3,000	330,000

TABLE 10.10

Annual Depreciation,
Power Mulcher Project

Year	MACRS Percentage	Depreciation	Ending Book Value
1	14.29%	.1429 × $800,000 = $114,320	$685,680
2	24.49	.2449 × 800,000 = 195,920	489,760
3	17.49	.1749 × 800,000 = 139,920	349,840
4	12.49	.1249 × 800,000 = 99,920	249,920
5	8.93	.0893 × 800,000 = 71,440	178,480
6	8.92	.0892 × 800,000 = 71,360	107,120
7	8.93	.0893 × 800,000 = 71,440	35,680
8	4.46	.0446 × 800,000 = 35,680	0
	100.00%	$800,000	

TABLE 10.11 Projected Income Statements, Power Mulcher Project

	Year							
	1	2	3	4	5	6	7	8
Unit price	$ 120	$ 120	$ 120	$ 110	$ 110	$ 110	$ 110	$ 110
Unit sales	3,000	5,000	6,000	6,500	6,000	5,000	4,000	3,000
Revenues	$360,000	$600,000	$720,000	$715,000	$660,000	$550,000	$440,000	$330,000
Variable costs	180,000	300,000	360,000	390,000	360,000	300,000	240,000	180,000
Fixed costs	25,000	25,000	25,000	25,000	25,000	25,000	25,000	25,000
Depreciation	114,320	195,920	139,920	99,920	71,440	71,360	71,440	35,680
EBIT	$ 40,680	$ 79,080	$195,080	$200,080	$203,560	$153,640	$103,560	$ 89,320
Taxes (34%)	13,831	26,887	66,327	68,027	69,210	52,238	35,210	30,369
Net income	$ 26,849	$ 52,193	$128,753	$132,053	$134,350	$101,402	$ 68,350	$ 58,951

capital. Recalling that NWC starts out at $20,000 and then rises to 15 percent of sales, we can calculate the amount of NWC for each year as shown in Table 10.12.

As illustrated, during the first year, net working capital grows from $20,000 to .15 × $360,000 = $54,000. The increase in net working capital for the year is thus $54,000 − 20,000 = $34,000. The remaining figures are calculated in the same way.

TABLE 10.12

Changes in Net Working Capital, Power Mulcher Project

Year	Revenues	Net Working Capital	Cash Flow
0		$ 20,000	−$20,000
1	$360,000	54,000	− 34,000
2	600,000	90,000	− 36,000
3	720,000	108,000	− 18,000
4	715,000	107,250	750
5	660,000	99,000	8,250
6	550,000	82,500	16,500
7	440,000	66,000	16,500
8	330,000	49,500	16,500

TABLE 10.13   Projected Cash Flows, Power Mulcher Project

	Year								
	0	1	2	3	4	5	6	7	8
I. Operating Cash Flow									
EBIT		$ 40,680	$ 79,080	$195,080	$200,080	$203,560	$153,640	$103,560	$89,320
Depreciation		114,320	195,920	139,920	99,920	71,440	71,360	71,440	35,680
Taxes		− 13,831	− 26,887	− 66,327	− 68,027	− 69,210	− 52,238	− 35,210	− 30,369
Operating cash flow		$141,169	$248,113	$268,673	$231,973	$205,790	$172,762	$139,790	$94,631
II. Net Working Capital									
Initial NWC	−$ 20,000								
Change in NWC		−$34,000	−$ 36,000	−$18,000	$ 750	$ 8,250	$ 16,500	$ 16,500	$ 16,500
NWC recovery									49,500
Total change in NWC	−$ 20,000	−$34,000	−$ 36,000	−$18,000	$ 750	$ 8,250	$ 16,500	$ 16,500	$ 66,000
III. Capital Spending									
Initial outlay	−$800,000								
Aftertax salvage									$105,600
Capital spending	−$800,000								$105,600

Remember that an increase in net working capital is a cash outflow, so we use a negative sign in this table to indicate an additional investment that the firm makes in net working capital. A positive sign represents net working capital returning to the firm. Thus, for example, $16,500 in NWC flows back to the firm in year 6. Over the project's life, net working capital builds to a peak of $108,000 and declines from there as sales begin to drop off.

We show the result for changes in net working capital in the second part of Table 10.13. Notice that at the end of the project's life, there is $49,500 in net working capital still to be recovered. Therefore, in the last year, the project returns $16,500 of NWC during the year and then returns the remaining $49,500 at the end of the year for a total of $66,000.

TABLE 10.14   Projected Total Cash Flows, Power Mulcher Project

	Year								
	0	1	2	3	4	5	6	7	8
Operating cash flow		$141,169	$248,113	$268,673	$231,973	$205,790	$172,762	$139,790	$ 94,631
Change in NWC	−$ 20,000	− 34,000	− 36,000	− 18,000	750	8,250	16,500	16,500	66,000
Capital spending	− 800,000								105,600
Total project cash flow	−$820,000	$107,169	$212,113	$250,673	$232,723	$214,040	$189,262	$156,290	$266,231
Cumulative cash flow	−$820,000	−$712,831	−$500,718	−$250,045	−$ 17,322	$196,718	$385,980	$542,270	$808,501
Discounted cash flow @ 15%	− 820,000	93,190	160,388	164,822	133,060	106,416	81,823	58,755	87,031

Net present value (15%) = $65,485
Internal rate of return   = 17.24%
Payback   = 4.08 years

Capital Spending   Finally, we have to account for the long-term capital invested in the project. In this case, MMCC invests $800,000 at year 0. By assumption, this equipment will be worth $160,000 at the end of the project. It will have a book value of zero at that time. As we discussed earlier, this $160,000 excess of market value over book value is taxable, so the aftertax proceeds will be $160,000 × (1 − .34) = $105,600. These figures are shown in the third part of Table 10.13.

Total Cash Flow and Value   We now have all the cash flow pieces, and we put them together in Table 10.14. In addition to the total project cash flows, we have calculated the cumulative cash flows and the discounted cash flows. At this point, it's essentially plug-and-chug to calculate the net present value, internal rate of return, and payback.

If we sum the discounted flows and the initial investment, the net present value (at 15 percent) works out to be $65,485. This is positive, so, based on these preliminary projections, the power mulcher project is acceptable. The internal, or DCF, rate of return is greater than 15 percent because the NPV is positive. It works out to be 17.24 percent, again indicating that the project is acceptable.

Looking at the cumulative cash flows, we can see that the project has almost paid back after four years because the table shows that the cumulative cash flow is almost zero at that time. As indicated, the fractional year works out to be $17,322/214,040 = .08, so the payback is 4.08 years. We can't say whether or not this is good because we don't have a benchmark for MMCC. This is the usual problem with payback periods.

Conclusion   This completes our preliminary DCF analysis. Where do we go from here? If we have a great deal of confidence in our projections, there is no further analysis to be done. MMCC should begin production and marketing immediately. It is unlikely that this will be the case. It is important to remember that the result of our analysis is an estimate of NPV, and we will usually have less than complete confidence in our projections. This means we have more work to do. In particular, we will almost surely want to spend some time evaluating the quality of our estimates. We will take up this subject in the next chapter. For now, we look at some alternative definitions of operating cash flow, and we illustrate some different cases that arise in capital budgeting.

Concept Questions

10.4a Why is it important to consider changes in net working capital in developing cash flows? What is the effect of doing so?

10.4b How is depreciation calculated for fixed assets under current tax law? What effects do expected salvage value and estimated economic life have on the calculated depreciation deduction?

Alternative Definitions   10.5
of Operating Cash Flow

The analysis we went through in the previous section is quite general and can be adapted to just about any capital investment problem. In the next section, we illustrate some particularly useful variations. Before we do so, we need to discuss the fact that there are different definitions of project operating cash flow that are commonly used, both in practice and in finance texts.

As we will see, the different approaches to operating cash flow that exist all measure the same thing. If they are used correctly, they all produce the same answer, and one is not necessarily any better or more useful than another. Unfortunately, the fact that alternative definitions are used does sometimes lead to confusion. For this reason, we examine several of these variations next to see how they are related.

In the discussion that follows, keep in mind that when we speak of cash flow, we literally mean dollars in less dollars out. This is all we are concerned with. Different definitions of operating cash flow simply amount to different ways of manipulating basic information about sales, costs, depreciation, and taxes to get at cash flow.

For a particular project and year under consideration, suppose we have the following estimates:

Sales = $1,500

Costs = $700

Depreciation = $600

With these estimates, notice that EBIT is:

$$EBIT = Sales - Costs - Depreciation$$
$$= \$1,500 - 700 - 600$$
$$= \$200$$

Once again, we assume that no interest is paid, so the tax bill is:

$$Taxes = EBIT \times T$$
$$= \$200 \times .34 = \$68$$

where T, the corporate tax rate, is 34 percent.

When we put all of this together, we see that project operating cash flow, OCF, is:

$$OCF = EBIT + Depreciation - Taxes$$
$$= \$200 + 600 - 68 = \$732$$

There are some other ways to determine OCF that could be (and are) used. We consider these next.

THE BOTTOM-UP APPROACH

Because we are ignoring any financing expenses, such as interest, in our calculations of project OCF, we can write project net income as:

$$\text{Project net income} = \text{EBIT} - \text{Taxes}$$
$$= \$200 - 68$$
$$= \$132$$

If we simply add the depreciation to both sides, we arrive at a slightly different and very common expression for OCF:

$$\text{OCF} = \text{Net income} + \text{Depreciation}$$
$$= \$132 + 600 \qquad\qquad\qquad\qquad \textbf{[10.1]}$$
$$= \$732$$

This is the *bottom-up* approach. Here, we start with the accountant's bottom line (net income) and add back any noncash deductions such as depreciation. It is crucial to remember that this definition of operating cash flow as net income plus depreciation is correct only if there is no interest expense subtracted in the calculation of net income.

For the shark attractant project, net income was $21,780 and depreciation was $30,000, so the bottom-up calculation is:

$$\text{OCF} = \$21,780 + 30,000 = \$51,780$$

This is exactly the same OCF we had previously.

THE TOP-DOWN APPROACH

Perhaps the most obvious way to calculate OCF is:

$$\text{OCF} = \text{Sales} - \text{Costs} - \text{Taxes}$$
$$= \$1,500 - 700 - 68 = \$732 \qquad\qquad\qquad \textbf{[10.2]}$$

This is the *top-down* approach, the second variation on the basic OCF definition. Here, we start at the top of the income statement with sales and work our way down to net cash flow by subtracting costs, taxes, and other expenses. Along the way, we simply leave out any strictly noncash items such as depreciation.

For the shark attractant project, the operating cash flow can be readily calculated using the top-down approach. With sales of $200,000, total costs (fixed plus variable) of $137,000, and a tax bill of $11,220, the OCF is:

$$\text{OCF} = \$200,000 - 137,000 - 11,220 = \$51,780$$

This is just as we had before.

THE TAX SHIELD APPROACH

The third variation on our basic definition of OCF is the *tax shield* approach. This approach will be useful for some problems we consider in the next section. The tax shield definition of OCF is:

$$\text{OCF} = (\text{Sales} - \text{Costs}) \times (1 - T) + \text{Depreciation} \times T \qquad \textbf{[10.3]}$$

where T is again the corporate tax rate. Assuming that $T = 34\%$, the OCF works out to be:

$$\text{OCF} = (\$1,500 - 700) \times .66 + 600 \times .34$$
$$= \$528 + 204$$
$$= \$732$$

This is just as we had before.

This approach views OCF as having two components. The first part is what the project's cash flow would be if there were no depreciation expense. In this case, this would-have-been cash flow is $528.

The second part of OCF in this approach is the depreciation deduction multiplied by the tax rate. This is called the **depreciation tax shield**. We know that depreciation is a noncash expense. The only cash flow effect of deducting depreciation is to reduce our taxes, a benefit to us. At the current 34 percent corporate tax rate, every dollar in depreciation expense saves us 34 cents in taxes. So, in our example, the $600 depreciation deduction saves us $600 × .34 = $204 in taxes.

For the shark attractant project we considered earlier in the chapter, the depreciation tax-shield would be $30,000 × .34 = $10,200. The aftertax value for sales less costs would be ($200,000 − 137,000) × (1 − .34) = $41,580. Adding these together yields the value of OCF:

OCF = $41,580 + 10,200 = $51,780

depreciation tax shield
The tax saving that results from the depreciation deduction, calculated as depreciation multiplied by the corporate tax rate.

This calculation verifies that the tax shield approach is completely equivalent to the approach we used before.

CONCLUSION

Now that we've seen that all of these approaches are the same, you're probably wondering why everybody doesn't just agree on one of them. One reason, as we will see in the next section, is that different approaches are useful in different circumstances. The best one to use is whichever happens to be the most convenient for the problem at hand.

Concept Questions

10.5a What are the top-down and bottom-up definitions of operating cash flow?

10.5b What is meant by the term *depreciation tax shield*?

Some Special Cases of Discounted Cash Flow Analysis

10.6

To finish our chapter, we look at three common cases involving discounted cash flow analysis. The first case involves investments that are primarily aimed at improving efficiency and thereby cutting costs. The second case we consider comes up when a firm is involved in submitting competitive bids. The third and final case arises in choosing between equipment options with different economic lives.

We could consider many other special cases, but these three are particularly important because problems similar to these are so common. Also, they illustrate some diverse applications of cash flow analysis and DCF valuation.

EVALUATING COST-CUTTING PROPOSALS

One decision we frequently face is whether to upgrade existing facilities to make them more cost-effective. The issue is whether the cost savings are large enough to justify the necessary capital expenditure.

For example, suppose we are considering automating some part of an existing production process. The necessary equipment costs $80,000 to buy and install. The automation will save $22,000 per year (before taxes) by reducing labor and material costs. For simplicity, assume that the equipment has a five-year life and is depreciated to zero on a straight-line basis over that period. It will actually be worth $20,000 in five years. Should we automate? The tax rate is 34 percent, and the discount rate is 10 percent.

As always, the first step in making such a decision is to identify the relevant incremental cash flows. First, determining the relevant capital spending is easy enough. The initial cost is $80,000. The aftertax salvage value is $20,000 × (1 − .34) = $13,200 because the book value will be zero in five years. Second, there are no working capital consequences here, so we don't need to worry about changes in net working capital.

Operating cash flows are the third component to consider. Buying the new equipment affects our operating cash flows in two ways. First, we save $22,000 before taxes every year. In other words, the firm's operating income increases by $22,000, so this is the relevant incremental project operating income.

Second (and it's easy to overlook this), we have an additional depreciation deduction. In this case, the depreciation is $80,000/5 = $16,000 per year.

Because the project has an operating income of $22,000 (the annual pretax cost saving) and a depreciation deduction of $16,000, taking the project will increase the firm's EBIT by $22,000 − 16,000 = $6,000, so this is the project's EBIT.

Finally, because EBIT is rising for the firm, taxes will increase. This increase in taxes will be $6,000 × .34 = $2,040. With this information, we can compute operating cash flow in the usual way:

EBIT	$ 6,000
+ Depreciation	16,000
− Taxes	2,040
Operating cash flow	$19,960

So, our aftertax operating cash flow is $19,960.

It might be somewhat more enlightening to calculate operating cash flow using a different approach. What is actually going on here is very simple. First, the cost savings increase our pretax income by $22,000. We have to pay taxes on this amount, so our tax bill increases by .34 × $22,000 = $7,480. In other words, the $22,000 pretax saving amounts to $22,000 × (1 − .34) = $14,520 after taxes.

Second, the extra $16,000 in depreciation isn't really a cash outflow, but it does reduce our taxes by $16,000 × .34 = $5,440. The sum of these two components is $14,520 + 5,440 = $19,960, just as we had before. Notice that the $5,440 is the depreciation tax shield we discussed earlier, and we have effectively used the tax shield approach here.

We can now finish our analysis. Based on our discussion, here are the relevant cash flows:

	\multicolumn{6}{c}{Year}					
	0	**1**	**2**	**3**	**4**	**5**
Operating cash flow		$19,960	$19,960	$19,960	$19,960	$19,960
Capital spending	−$80,000					13,200
Total cash flow	−$80,000	$19,960	$19,960	$19,960	$19,960	$33,160

At 10 percent, it's straightforward to verify that the NPV here is $3,860, so we should go ahead and automate.

To Buy or Not to Buy

EXAMPLE 10.3

We are considering the purchase of a $200,000 computer-based inventory management system. It will be depreciated straight-line to zero over its four-year life. It will be worth $30,000 at the end of that time. The system will save us $60,000 before taxes in inventory-related costs. The relevant tax rate is 39 percent. Because the new setup is more efficient than our existing one, we will be able to carry less total inventory and thus free up $45,000 in net working capital. What is the NPV at 16 percent? What is the DCF return (the IRR) on this investment?

We can first calculate the operating cash flow. The aftertax cost savings are $60,000 × (1 − .39) = $36,600. The depreciation is $200,000/4 = $50,000 per year, so the depreciation tax shield is $50,000 × .39 = $19,500. Operating cash flow is thus $36,600 + 19,500 = $56,100 per year.

The capital spending involves $200,000 up front to buy the system. The aftertax salvage is $30,000 × (1 − .39) = $18,300. Finally, and this is the somewhat tricky part, the initial investment in net working capital is a $45,000 *inflow* because the system frees up working capital. Furthermore, we will have to put this back in at the end of the project's life. What this really means is simple: While the system is in operation, we have $45,000 to use elsewhere.

To finish our analysis, we can compute the total cash flows:

	Year				
	0	1	2	3	4
Operating cash flow		$56,100	$56,100	$56,100	$56,100
Change in NWC	$ 45,000				− 45,000
Capital spending	− 200,000				18,300
Total cash flow	−$155,000	$56,100	$56,100	$56,100	$29,400

At 16 percent, the NPV is −$12,768, so the investment is not attractive. After some trial and error, we find that the NPV is zero when the discount rate is 11.48 percent, so the IRR on this investment is about 11.5 percent.

SETTING THE BID PRICE

Early on, we used discounted cash flow analysis to evaluate a proposed new product. A somewhat different (and common) scenario arises when we must submit a competitive bid to win a job. Under such circumstances, the winner is whoever submits the lowest bid.

There is an old joke concerning this process: The low bidder is whoever makes the biggest mistake. This is called the winner's curse. In other words, if you win, there is a good chance you underbid. In this section, we look at how to go about setting the bid price to avoid the winner's curse. The procedure we describe is useful any time we have to set a price on a product or service.

As with any other capital budgeting project, we must be careful to account for all relevant cash flows. For example, industry analysts estimated that the materials in Microsoft's Xbox 360 cost $470 before assembly. Other items such as the power supply, cables, and controllers increased the materials cost by another $55. At a retail price of $399, Microsoft obviously loses a significant amount on each Xbox 360 it sells. Why would a manufacturer sell at a price well below breakeven? A Microsoft spokesperson stated that the company believed that sales of its game software would make the Xbox 360 a profitable project.

To illustrate how to go about setting a bid price, imagine we are in the business of buying stripped-down truck platforms and then modifying them to customer specifications for resale. A local distributor has requested bids for 5 specially modified trucks each year for the next four years, for a total of 20 trucks in all.

We need to decide what price per truck to bid. The goal of our analysis is to determine the lowest price we can profitably charge. This maximizes our chances of being awarded the contract while guarding against the winner's curse.

Suppose we can buy the truck platforms for $10,000 each. The facilities we need can be leased for $24,000 per year. The labor and material cost to do the modification works out to be about $4,000 per truck. Total cost per year will thus be $24,000 + 5 \times (10,000 + 4,000) = $94,000.

We will need to invest $60,000 in new equipment. This equipment will be depreciated straight-line to a zero salvage value over the four years. It will be worth about $5,000 at the end of that time. We will also need to invest $40,000 in raw materials inventory and other working capital items. The relevant tax rate is 39 percent. What price per truck should we bid if we require a 20 percent return on our investment?

We start by looking at the capital spending and net working capital investment. We have to spend $60,000 today for new equipment. The aftertax salvage value is $5,000 \times (1 - .39) = $3,050. Furthermore, we have to invest $40,000 today in working capital. We will get this back in four years.

We can't determine the operating cash flow just yet because we don't know the sales price. Thus, if we draw a time line, here is what we have so far:

	Year				
	0	**1**	**2**	**3**	**4**
Operating cash flow		+OCF	+OCF	+OCF	+OCF
Change in NWC	−$ 40,000				$40,000
Capital spending	− 60,000				3,050
Total cash flow	−$100,000	+OCF	+OCF	+OCF	+OCF + $43,050

With this in mind, note that the key observation is the following: The lowest possible price we can profitably charge will result in a zero NPV at 20 percent. At that price, we earn exactly 20 percent on our investment.

Given this observation, we first need to determine what the operating cash flow must be for the NPV to equal zero. To do this, we calculate the present value of the $43,050 nonoperating cash flow from the last year and subtract it from the $100,000 initial investment:

$100,000 - 43,050/1.20^4 = $100,000 - 20,761 = $79,239

Once we have done this, our time line is as follows:

	Year				
	0	**1**	**2**	**3**	**4**
Total cash flow	−$79,239	+OCF	+OCF	+OCF	+OCF

As the time line suggests, the operating cash flow is now an unknown ordinary annuity amount. The four-year annuity factor for 20 percent is 2.58873, so we have:

NPV = 0 = −$79,239 + OCF \times 2.58873

This implies that:

OCF = $79,239/2.58873 = $30,609

So the operating cash flow needs to be $30,609 each year.

We're not quite finished. The final problem is to find out what sales price results in an operating cash flow of $30,609. The easiest way to do this is to recall that operating cash flow can be written as net income plus depreciation (the bottom-up definition). The depreciation here is $60,000/4 = $15,000. Given this, we can determine what net income must be:

$$\text{Operating cash flow} = \text{Net income} + \text{Depreciation}$$
$$\$30,609 = \text{Net income} + \$15,000$$
$$\text{Net income} = \$15,609$$

From here, we work our way backward up the income statement. If net income is $15,609, then our income statement is as follows:

Sales	?
Costs	$94,000
Depreciation	15,000
Taxes (39%)	?
Net income	$15,609

We can solve for sales by noting that:

$$\text{Net income} = (\text{Sales} - \text{Costs} - \text{Depreciation}) \times (1 - T)$$
$$\$15,609 = (\text{Sales} - \$94,000 - \$15,000) \times (1 - .39)$$
$$\text{Sales} = \$15,609/.61 + 94,000 + 15,000$$
$$= \$134,589$$

Sales per year must be $134,589. Because the contract calls for five trucks per year, the sales price has to be $134,589/5 = $26,918. If we round this up a bit, it looks as though we need to bid about $27,000 per truck. At this price, were we to get the contract, our return would be just over 20 percent.

EVALUATING EQUIPMENT OPTIONS WITH DIFFERENT LIVES

The final problem we consider involves choosing among different possible systems, equipment setups, or procedures. Our goal is to choose the most cost-effective. The approach we consider here is necessary only when two special circumstances exist. First, the possibilities under evaluation have different economic lives. Second, and just as important, we will need whatever we buy more or less indefinitely. As a result, when it wears out, we will buy another one.

We can illustrate this problem with a simple example. Imagine we are in the business of manufacturing stamped metal subassemblies. Whenever a stamping mechanism wears out, we have to replace it with a new one to stay in business. We are considering which of two stamping mechanisms to buy.

Machine A costs $100 to buy and $10 per year to operate. It wears out and must be replaced every two years. Machine B costs $140 to buy and $8 per year to operate. It lasts for three years and must then be replaced. Ignoring taxes, which one should we choose if we use a 10 percent discount rate?

In comparing the two machines, we notice that the first is cheaper to buy, but it costs more to operate and it wears out more quickly. How can we evaluate these trade-offs? We can start by computing the present value of the costs for each:

Machine A: $PV = -\$100 + -10/1.1 + -10/1.1^2 = -\$117.36$

Machine B: $PV = -\$140 + -8/1.1 + -8/1.1^2 + -8/1.1^3 = -\$159.89$

equivalent annual cost (EAC)
The present value of a project's costs calculated on an annual basis.

Notice that *all* the numbers here are costs, so they all have negative signs. If we stopped here, it might appear that A is more attractive because the PV of the costs is less. However, all we have really discovered so far is that A effectively provides two years' worth of stamping service for $117.36, whereas B effectively provides three years' worth for $159.89. These costs are not directly comparable because of the difference in service periods.

We need to somehow work out a cost per year for these two alternatives. To do this, we ask: What amount, paid each year over the life of the machine, has the same PV of costs? This amount is called the **equivalent annual cost (EAC)**.

Calculating the EAC involves finding an unknown payment amount. For example, for machine A, we need to find a two-year ordinary annuity with a PV of $-$117.36 at 10 percent. Going back to Chapter 6, we know that the two-year annuity factor is:

$$\text{Annuity factor} = (1 - 1/1.10^2)/.10 = 1.7355$$

For machine A, then, we have:

$$\text{PV of costs} = -\$117.36 = \text{EAC} \times 1.7355$$
$$\text{EAC} = -\$117.36/1.7355$$
$$= -\$67.62$$

For machine B, the life is three years, so we first need the three-year annuity factor:

$$\text{Annuity factor} = (1 - 1/1.10^3)/.10 = 2.4869$$

We calculate the EAC for B just as we did for A:

$$\text{PV of costs} = -\$159.89 = \text{EAC} \times 2.4869$$
$$\text{EAC} = -\$159.89/2.4869$$
$$= -\$64.29$$

Based on this analysis, we should purchase B because it effectively costs $64.29 per year versus $67.62 for A. In other words, all things considered, B is cheaper. In this case, the longer life and lower operating cost are more than enough to offset the higher initial purchase price.

EXAMPLE 10.4   Equivalent Annual Costs

This extended example illustrates what happens to the EAC when we consider taxes. You are evaluating two different pollution control options. A filtration system will cost $1.1 million to install and $60,000 annually, before taxes, to operate. It will have to be completely replaced every five years. A precipitation system will cost $1.9 million to install but only $10,000 per year to operate. The precipitation equipment has an effective operating life of eight years. Straight-line depreciation is used throughout, and neither system has any salvage value. Which option should we select if we use a 12 percent discount rate? The tax rate is 34 percent.

We need to consider the EACs for the two systems because they have different service lives and will be replaced as they wear out. The relevant information can be summarized as follows:

	Filtration System	Precipitation System
Aftertax operating cost	$-$ 39,600	$-$ 6,600
Depreciation tax shield	74,800	80,750
Operating cash flow	$ 35,200	$ 74,150
Economic life	5 years	8 years
Annuity factor (12%)	3.6048	4.9676
Present value of operating cash flow	$ 126,888	$ 368,350
Capital spending	$-$ 1,100,000	$-$ 1,900,000
Total PV of costs	$-$ 973,112	$-$1,531,650

Notice that the operating cash flow is actually positive in both cases because of the large depreciation tax shields. This can occur whenever the operating cost is small relative to the purchase price.

To decide which system to purchase, we compute the EACs for both using the appropriate annuity factors:

Filtration system: $-\$973,112 = \text{EAC} \times 3.6048$

$$\text{EAC} = -\$269,951$$

Precipitation system: $-\$1,531,650 = \text{EAC} \times 4.9676$

$$\text{EAC} = -\$308,328$$

The filtration system is the cheaper of the two, so we select it. In this case, the longer life and smaller operating cost of the precipitation system are not sufficient to offset its higher initial cost.

Concept Questions

10.6a In setting a bid price, we used a zero NPV as our benchmark. Explain why this is appropriate.

10.6b Under what circumstances do we have to worry about unequal economic lives? How do you interpret the EAC?

Summary and Conclusions   10.7

This chapter has described how to put together a discounted cash flow analysis. In it, we covered:

1. The identification of relevant project cash flows: We discussed project cash flows and described how to handle some issues that often come up, including sunk costs, opportunity costs, financing costs, net working capital, and erosion.

2. Preparing and using pro forma, or projected, financial statements: We showed how information from such financial statements is useful in coming up with projected cash flows, and we also looked at some alternative definitions of operating cash flow.

3. The role of net working capital and depreciation in determining project cash flows: We saw that including the change in net working capital was important in cash flow analysis because it adjusted for the discrepancy between accounting revenues and costs and cash revenues and costs. We also went over the calculation of depreciation expense under current tax law.

4. Some special cases encountered in using discounted cash flow analysis: Here we looked at three special issues: evaluating cost-cutting investments, how to go about setting a bid price, and the unequal lives problem.

The discounted cash flow analysis we've covered here is a standard tool in the business world. It is a very powerful tool, so care should be taken in its use. The most important thing is to identify the cash flows in a way that makes economic sense. This chapter gives you a good start in learning to do this.

10.1 Capital Budgeting for Project X Based on the following information for project X, should we undertake the venture? To answer, first prepare a pro forma income statement for each year. Next calculate operating cash flow. Finish the problem by determining total cash flow and then calculating NPV assuming a 28 percent required return. Use a 34 percent tax rate throughout. For help, look back at our shark attractant and power mulcher examples.

Project X involves a new type of graphite composite in-line skate wheel. We think we can sell 6,000 units per year at a price of $1,000 each. Variable costs will run about $400 per unit, and the product should have a four-year life.

Fixed costs for the project will run $450,000 per year. Further, we will need to invest a total of $1,250,000 in manufacturing equipment. This equipment is seven-year MACRS property for tax purposes. In four years, the equipment will be worth about half of what we paid for it. We will have to invest $1,150,000 in net working capital at the start. After that, net working capital requirements will be 25 percent of sales.

10.2 Calculating Operating Cash Flow Mont Blanc Livestock Pens, Inc., has projected a sales volume of $1,650 for the second year of a proposed expansion project. Costs normally run 60 percent of sales, or about $990 in this case. The depreciation expense will be $100, and the tax rate is 35 percent. What is the operating cash flow? Calculate your answer using all of the approaches (including the top-down, bottom-up, and tax shield approaches) described in the chapter.

10.3 Spending Money to Save Money? For help on this one, refer back to the computerized inventory management system in Example 10.3. Here, we're contemplating a new automatic surveillance system to replace our current contract security system. It will cost $450,000 to get the new system. The cost will be depreciated straight-line to zero over the system's four-year expected life. The system is expected to be worth $250,000 at the end of four years after removal costs.

We think the new system will save us $125,000, before taxes, per year in contract security costs. The tax rate is 34 percent. What are the NPV and IRR for buying the new system? The required return is 17 percent.

10.1 To develop the pro forma income statements, we need to calculate the depreciation for each of the four years. The relevant MACRS percentages, depreciation allowances, and book values for the first four years are shown here:

Year	MACRS Percentage	Depreciation	Ending Book Value
1	14.29%	.1429 × $1,250,000 = $178,625	$1,071,375
2	24.49	.2449 × 1,250,000 = 306,125	765,250
3	17.49	.1749 × 1,250,000 = 218,625	546,625
4	12.49	.1249 × 1,250,000 = 156,125	390,500

Visit us at www.mhhe.com/rwj

The projected income statements, therefore, are as follows:

	Year			
	1	**2**	**3**	**4**
Sales	$6,000,000	$6,000,000	$6,000,000	$6,000,000
Variable costs	2,400,000	2,400,000	2,400,000	2,400,000
Fixed costs	450,000	450,000	450,000	450,000
Depreciation	178,625	306,125	218,625	156,125
EBIT	$2,971,375	$2,843,875	$2,931,375	$2,993,875
Taxes (34%)	− 1,010,268	− 966,918	− 996,668	1,017,918
Net income	$1,961,108	$1,876,958	$1,934,708	$1,975,958

Based on this information, here are the operating cash flows:

	Year			
	1	**2**	**3**	**4**
EBIT	$2,971,375	$2,843,875	$2,931,375	$2,993,875
Depreciation	178,625	306,125	218,625	156,125
Taxes	− 1,010,268	− 966,918	− 996,668	− 1,017,918
Operating cash flow	$2,139,732	$2,183,082	$2,153,332	$2,132,082

We now have to worry about the nonoperating cash flows. Net working capital starts out at $1,150,000 and then rises to 25 percent of sales, or $1,500,000. This is a $350,000 change in net working capital.

Finally, we have to invest $1,250,000 to get started. In four years, the book value of this investment will be $390,500, compared to an estimated market value of $625,000 (half of the cost). The aftertax salvage is thus $625,000 − .34 × ($625,000 − 390,500) = $545,270.

When we combine all this information, the projected cash flows for project X are as follows:

	Year				
	0	**1**	**2**	**3**	**4**
Operating cash flow		$2,139,732	$2,183,082	$2,153,332	$2,132,082
Change in NWC	−$1,150,000	− 350,000			1,500,000
Capital spending	− 1,250,000				545,270
Total cash flow	−$2,400,000	$1,789,732	$2,183,082	$2,153,332	$4,177,352

With these cash flows, the NPV at 28 percent is:

$$\text{NPV} = -\$2,400,000 + 1,789,732/1.28 + 2,183,082/1.28^2$$
$$+ 2,153,332/1.28^3 + 4,177,352/1.28^4$$
$$= \$2,913,649$$

So, this project appears quite profitable.

10.2 First, we can calculate the project's EBIT, its tax bill, and its net income:

$$\text{EBIT} = \text{Sales} - \text{Costs} - \text{Depreciation}$$
$$= \$1,650 - 990 - 100 = \$560$$
$$\text{Taxes} = \$560 \times .35 = \$196$$
$$\text{Net income} = \$560 - 196 = \$364$$

Visit us at www.mhhe.com/rwj

With these numbers, operating cash flow is:

$$OCF = EBIT + Depreciation - Taxes$$
$$= \$560 + 100 - 196$$
$$= \$464$$

Using the other OCF definitions, we have:

$$Bottom\text{-}up\ OCF = Net\ income + Depreciation$$
$$= \$364 + 100$$
$$= \$464$$
$$Top\text{-}down\ OCF = Sales - Costs - Taxes$$
$$= \$1,650 - 990 - 196$$
$$= \$464$$
$$Tax\ shield\ OCF = (Sales - Costs) \times (1 - .35) + Depreciation \times .35$$
$$= (\$1,650 - 990) \times .65 + 100 \times .35$$
$$= \$464$$

As expected, all of these definitions produce exactly the same answer.

10.3 The $125,000 pretax saving amounts to $(1 - .34) \times \$125,000 = \$82,500$ after taxes. The annual depreciation of $\$450,000/4 = \$112,500$ generates a tax shield of $.34 \times \$112,500 = \$38,250$ each year. Putting these together, we calculate that the operating cash flow is $\$82,500 + 38,250 = \$120,750$. Because the book value is zero in four years, the aftertax salvage value is $(1 - .34) \times \$250,000 = \$165,000$. There are no working capital consequences, so here are the cash flows:

	Year				
	0	**1**	**2**	**3**	**4**
Operating cash flow		$120,750	$120,750	$120,750	$120,750
Capital spending	−$450,000				165,000
Total cash flow	−$450,000	$120,750	$120,750	$120,750	$285,750

You can verify that the NPV at 17 percent is −$30,702, and the return on the new surveillance system is only about 13.96 percent. The project does not appear to be profitable.

CONCEPTS REVIEW AND CRITICAL THINKING QUESTIONS

1. **Opportunity Cost** [LO1] In the context of capital budgeting, what is an opportunity cost?

2. **Depreciation** [LO1] Given the choice, would a firm prefer to use MACRS depreciation or straight-line depreciation? Why?

3. **Net Working Capital** [LO1] In our capital budgeting examples, we assumed that a firm would recover all of the working capital it invested in a project. Is this a reasonable assumption? When might it not be valid?

4. **Stand-Alone Principle** [LO1] Suppose a financial manager is quoted as saying, "Our firm uses the stand-alone principle. Because we treat projects like minifirms in our evaluation process, we include financing costs because they are relevant at the firm level." Critically evaluate this statement.

Visit us at www.mhhe.com/rwj

5. **Equivalent Annual Cost** [LO4] When is EAC analysis appropriate for comparing two or more projects? Why is this method used? Are there any implicit assumptions required by this method that you find troubling? Explain.

6. **Cash Flow and Depreciation** [LO1] "When evaluating projects, we're concerned with only the relevant incremental aftertax cash flows. Therefore, because depreciation is a noncash expense, we should ignore its effects when evaluating projects." Critically evaluate this statement.

7. **Capital Budgeting Considerations** [LO1] A major college textbook publisher has an existing finance textbook. The publisher is debating whether to produce an "essentialized" version, meaning a shorter (and lower-priced) book. What are some of the considerations that should come into play?

To answer the next three questions, refer to the following example. In 2003, Porsche unveiled its new sports utility vehicle (SUV), the Cayenne. With a price tag of over $100,000, the Cayenne went from zero to 62 mph in 9.7 seconds. Porsche's decision to enter the SUV market was a response to the runaway success of other high-priced SUVs such as the Mercedes-Benz M-class. Vehicles in this class had generated years of high profits. The Cayenne certainly spiced up the market, and Porsche subsequently introduced the Cayenne Turbo, which goes from zero to 60 mph in 4.9 seconds and has a top speed of 171 mph. The price tag for the Cayenne Turbo in 2008? About $100,000!

Some analysts questioned Porsche's entry into the luxury SUV market. The analysts were concerned not only that Porsche was a late entry into the market, but also that the introduction of the Cayenne would damage Porsche's reputation as a maker of high-performance automobiles.

8. **Erosion** [LO1] In evaluating the Cayenne, would you consider the possible damage to Porsche's reputation erosion?

9. **Capital Budgeting** [LO1] Porsche was one of the last manufacturers to enter the sports utility vehicle market. Why would one company decide to proceed with a product when other companies, at least initially, decide not to enter the market?

10. **Capital Budgeting** [LO1] In evaluating the Cayenne, what do you think Porsche needs to assume regarding the substantial profit margins that exist in this market? Is it likely they will be maintained as the market becomes more competitive, or will Porsche be able to maintain the profit margin because of its image and the performance of the Cayenne?

QUESTIONS AND PROBLEMS

1. **Relevant Cash Flows** [LO1] Parker & Stone, Inc., is looking at setting up a new manufacturing plant in South Park to produce garden tools. The company bought some land six years ago for $6 million in anticipation of using it as a warehouse and distribution site, but the company has since decided to rent these facilities from a competitor instead. If the land were sold today, the company would net $6.4 million. The company wants to build its new manufacturing plant on this land; the plant will cost $14.2 million to build, and the site requires $890,000 worth of grading before it is suitable for construction. What is the proper cash flow amount to use as the initial investment in fixed assets when evaluating this project? Why?

BASIC
(Questions 1–18)

2. **Relevant Cash Flows** [LO1] Winnebagel Corp. currently sells 30,000 motor homes per year at $53,000 each, and 12,000 luxury motor coaches per year at

Visit us at www.mhhe.com/rwj

$91,000 each. The company wants to introduce a new portable camper to fill out its product line; it hopes to sell 19,000 of these campers per year at $13,000 each. An independent consultant has determined that if Winnebagel introduces the new campers, it should boost the sales of its existing motor homes by 4,500 units per year, and reduce the sales of its motor coaches by 900 units per year. What is the amount to use as the annual sales figure when evaluating this project? Why?

3. **Calculating Projected Net Income** [LO1] A proposed new investment has projected sales of $830,000. Variable costs are 60 percent of sales, and fixed costs are $181,000; depreciation is $77,000. Prepare a pro forma income statement assuming a tax rate of 35 percent. What is the projected net income?

4. **Calculating OCF** [LO1] Consider the following income statement:

Sales	$824,500
Costs	538,900
Depreciation	126,500
EBIT	?
Taxes (34%)	?
Net income	?

Fill in the missing numbers and then calculate the OCF. What is the depreciation tax shield?

5. **OCF from Several Approaches** [LO1] A proposed new project has projected sales of $108,000, costs of $51,000, and depreciation of $6,800. The tax rate is 35 percent. Calculate operating cash flow using the four different approaches described in the chapter and verify that the answer is the same in each case.

6. **Calculating Depreciation** [LO1] A piece of newly purchased industrial equipment costs $1,080,000 and is classified as seven-year property under MACRS. Calculate the annual depreciation allowances and end-of-the-year book values for this equipment.

7. **Calculating Salvage Value** [LO1] Consider an asset that costs $548,000 and is depreciated straight-line to zero over its eight-year tax life. The asset is to be used in a five-year project; at the end of the project, the asset can be sold for $105,000. If the relevant tax rate is 35 percent, what is the aftertax cash flow from the sale of this asset?

8. **Calculating Salvage Value** [LO1] An asset used in a four-year project falls in the five-year MACRS class for tax purposes. The asset has an acquisition cost of $7,900,000 and will be sold for $1,400,000 at the end of the project. If the tax rate is 35 percent, what is the aftertax salvage value of the asset?

9. **Calculating Project OCF** [LO1] Summer Tyme, Inc., is considering a new three-year expansion project that requires an initial fixed asset investment of $3.9 million. The fixed asset will be depreciated straight-line to zero over its three-year tax life, after which time it will be worthless. The project is estimated to generate $2,650,000 in annual sales, with costs of $840,000. If the tax rate is 35 percent, what is the OCF for this project?

10. **Calculating Project NPV** [LO1] In the previous problem, suppose the required return on the project is 12 percent. What is the project's NPV?

11. **Calculating Project Cash Flow from Assets** [LO1] In the previous problem, suppose the project requires an initial investment in net working capital of $300,000, and the fixed asset will have a market value of $210,000 at the end of the project. What is the project's year 0 net cash flow? Year 1? Year 2? Year 3? What is the new NPV?

12. **NPV and Modified ACRS** [LO1] In the previous problem, suppose the fixed asset actually falls into the three-year MACRS class. All the other facts are the same. What is the project's year 1 net cash flow now? Year 2? Year 3? What is the new NPV?

13. **Project Evaluation** [LO1] Dog Up! Franks is looking at a new sausage system with an installed cost of $560,000. This cost will be depreciated straight-line to zero over the project's five-year life, at the end of which the sausage system can be scrapped for $85,000. The sausage system will save the firm $165,000 per year in pretax operating costs, and the system requires an initial investment in net working capital of $29,000. If the tax rate is 34 percent and the discount rate is 10 percent, what is the NPV of this project?

14. **Project Evaluation** [LO1] Your firm is contemplating the purchase of a new $720,000 computer-based order entry system. The system will be depreciated straight line to zero over its five-year life. It will be worth $75,000 at the end of that time. You will save $260,000 before taxes per year in order processing costs, and you will be able to reduce working capital by $110,000 (this is a one-time reduction). If the tax rate is 35 percent, what is the IRR for this project?

15. **Project Evaluation** [LO1] In the previous problem, suppose your required return on the project is 20 percent and your pretax cost savings are $300,000 per year. Will you accept the project? What if the pretax cost savings are $240,000 per year? At what level of pretax cost savings would you be indifferent between accepting the project and not accepting it?

16. **Calculating EAC** [LO4] A five-year project has an initial fixed asset investment of $270,000, an initial NWC investment of $25,000, and an annual OCF of −$42,000. The fixed asset is fully depreciated over the life of the project and has no salvage value. If the required return is 11 percent, what is this project's equivalent annual cost, or EAC?

17. **Calculating EAC** [LO4] You are evaluating two different silicon wafer milling machines. The Techron I costs $290,000, has a three-year life, and has pretax operating costs of $67,000 per year. The Techron II costs $510,000, has a five-year life, and has pretax operating costs of $35,000 per year. For both milling machines, use straight-line depreciation to zero over the project's life and assume a salvage value of $40,000. If your tax rate is 35 percent and your discount rate is 10 percent, compute the EAC for both machines. Which do you prefer? Why?

18. **Calculating a Bid Price** [LO3] Alson Enterprises needs someone to supply it with 185,000 cartons of machine screws per year to support its manufacturing needs over the next five years, and you've decided to bid on the contract. It will cost you $940,000 to install the equipment necessary to start production; you'll depreciate this cost straight-line to zero over the project's life. You estimate that in five years, this equipment can be salvaged for $70,000. Your fixed production costs will be $305,000 per year, and your variable production costs should be $9.25 per carton. You also need an initial investment in net working capital of $75,000. If your tax rate is 35 percent and you require a 12 percent return on your investment, what bid price should you submit?

19. **Cost-Cutting Proposals** [LO2] Geary Machine Shop is considering a four-year project to improve its production efficiency. Buying a new machine press for $560,000 is estimated to result in $210,000 in annual pretax cost savings. The press falls in the MACRS five-year class, and it will have a salvage value at the end of the project of $80,000. The press also requires an initial investment in spare parts

INTERMEDIATE
(Questions 19–30)

inventory of $20,000, along with an additional $3,000 in inventory for each succeeding year of the project. If the shop's tax rate is 35 percent and its discount rate is 9 percent, should the company buy and install the machine press?

20. **Comparing Mutually Exclusive Projects** [LO1] Dangerfield Industrial Systems Company (DISC) is trying to decide between two different conveyor belt systems. System A costs $430,000, has a four-year life, and requires $110,000 in pretax annual operating costs. System B costs $570,000, has a six-year life, and requires $98,000 in pretax annual operating costs. Both systems are to be depreciated straight-line to zero over their lives and will have zero salvage value. Whichever project is chosen, it will *not* be replaced when it wears out. If the tax rate is 34 percent and the discount rate is 11 percent, which project should the firm choose?

21. **Comparing Mutually Exclusive Projects** [LO4] Suppose in the previous problem that DISC always needs a conveyor belt system; when one wears out, it must be replaced. Which project should the firm choose now?

22. **Calculating a Bid Price** [LO3] Consider a project to supply 100 million postage stamps per year to the U.S. Postal Service for the next five years. You have an idle parcel of land available that cost $2,400,000 five years ago; if the land were sold today, it would net you $2,700,000 aftertax. The land can be sold for $3,200,000 after taxes in five years. You will need to install $4.1 million in new manufacturing plant and equipment to actually produce the stamps; this plant and equipment will be depreciated straight-line to zero over the project's five-year life. The equipment can be sold for $540,000 at the end of the project. You will also need $600,000 in initial net working capital for the project, and an additional investment of $50,000 in every year thereafter. Your production costs are .5 cents per stamp, and you have fixed costs of $950,000 per year. If your tax rate is 34 percent and your required return on this project is 12 percent, what bid price should you submit on the contract?

23. **Interpreting a Bid Price** [LO3] In the previous problem, suppose you were going to use a three-year MACRS depreciation schedule for your manufacturing equipment, and you could keep working capital investments down to only $25,000 per year. How would this new information affect your calculated bid price?

24. **Comparing Mutually Exclusive Projects** [LO4] Vandalay Industries is considering the purchase of a new machine for the production of latex. Machine A costs $2,900,000 and will last for six years. Variable costs are 35 percent of sales, and fixed costs are $170,000 per year. Machine B costs $5,100,000 and will last for nine years. Variable costs for this machine are 30 percent of sales and fixed costs are $130,000 per year. The sales for each machine will be $10 million per year. The required return is 10 percent, and the tax rate is 35 percent. Both machines will be depreciated on a straight-line basis. If the company plans to replace the machine when it wears out on a perpetual basis, which machine should you choose?

25. **Equivalent Annual Cost** [LO4] Compact fluorescent lamps (CFLs) have become more popular in recent years, but do they make financial sense? Suppose a typical 60-watt incandescent light bulb costs $.50 and lasts 1,000 hours. A 15-watt CFL, which provides the same light, costs $3.50 and lasts for 12,000 hours. A kilowatt-hour of electricity costs $.101, which is about the national average. A kilowatt-hour is 1,000 watts for 1 hour. If you require a 10 percent return and use a light fixture 500 hours per year, what is the equivalent annual cost of each light bulb?

26. **Break-Even Cost** [LO2] The previous problem suggests that using CFLs instead of incandescent bulbs is a no-brainer. However, electricity costs actually vary quite

a bit depending on location and user type (you can get information on your rates from your local power company). An industrial user in West Virginia might pay $.04 per kilowatt-hour whereas a residential user in Hawaii might pay $.25. What's the break-even cost per kilowatt-hour in Problem 25?

27. **Break-Even Replacement** [LO2] The previous two problems suggest that using CFLs is a good idea from a purely financial perspective unless you live in an area where power is relatively inexpensive, but there is another wrinkle. Suppose you have a residence with a lot of incandescent bulbs that are used on average 500 hours a year. The average bulb will be about halfway through its life, so it will have 500 hours remaining (and you can't tell which bulbs are older or newer). At what cost per kilowatt-hour does it make sense to replace your incandescent bulbs today?

28. **Issues in Capital Budgeting** [LO1] The debate regarding CFLs versus incandescent bulbs (see Problems 25–27) has even more wrinkles. In no particular order:

    1. Incandescent bulbs generate a lot more heat than CFLs.

    2. CFL prices will probably decline relative to incandescent bulbs.

    3. CFLs unavoidably contain small amounts of mercury, a significant environmental hazard, and special precautions must be taken in disposing of burned-out units (and also in cleaning up a broken lamp). Currently, there is no agreed-upon way to recycle a CFL. Incandescent bulbs pose no disposal/breakage hazards.

    4. Depending on a light's location (or the number of lights), there can be a nontrivial cost to change bulbs (i.e., labor cost in a business).

    5. Coal-fired power generation accounts for a substantial portion of the mercury emissions in the U.S., though the emissions will drop sharply in the relatively near future.

    6. Power generation accounts for a substantial portion of CO_2 emissions in the U.S.

    7. CFLs are more energy and material intensive to manufacture. On-site mercury contamination and worker safety are issues.

    8. If you install a CFL in a permanent lighting fixture in a building, you will probably move long before the CFL burns out.

    9. Another lighting technology based on light emitting diodes (LEDs) exists and is improving. LEDs are currently much more expensive than CFLs, but costs are coming down. LEDs last much longer than CFLs and use even less power. Plus, LEDs don't contain mercury.

    10. GE announced in 2007 a new technology: high efficiency incandescent (HEI) bulbs. These new bulbs dramatically cut energy use and will, according to GE, ultimately be comparable to CFLs. They are targeted for 2010 release, though the initial product will not be as efficient as a CFL.

    Qualitatively, how do these issues affect your position in the CFL versus incandescent light bulb debate? Australia recently proposed banning the sale of incandescent bulbs altogether, as has at least one state legislator (from California, of course). Does your analysis suggest such a move is wise? Are there other regulations short of an outright ban that make sense to you?

29. **Replacement Decisions** [LO2] Your small remodeling business has two work vehicles. One is a small passenger car used for job-site visits and for other general business purposes. The other is a heavy truck used to haul equipment. The car gets

Visit us at www.mhhe.com/rwj

25 miles per gallon (mpg). The truck gets 10 mpg. You want to improve gas mileage to save money, and you have enough money to upgrade one vehicle. The upgrade cost will be the same for both vehicles. An upgraded car will get 40 mpg; an upgraded truck will get 12.5 mpg. The cost of gasoline is $3.70 per gallon. Assuming an upgrade is a good idea in the first place, which one should you upgrade? Both vehicles are driven 12,000 miles per year.

30. **Replacement Decisions** [LO2] In the previous problem, suppose you drive the truck x miles per year. How many miles would you have to drive the car before upgrading the car would be the better choice? *Hint:* Look at the relative gas savings.

CHALLENGE
(Questions 31–36)

31. **Calculating Project NPV** [LO1] You have been hired as a consultant for Pristine Urban-Tech Zither, Inc. (PUTZ), manufacturers of fine zithers. The market for zithers is growing quickly. The company bought some land three years ago for $1.4 million in anticipation of using it as a toxic waste dump site but has recently hired another company to handle all toxic materials. Based on a recent appraisal, the company believes it could sell the land for $1.5 million on an aftertax basis. In four years, the land could be sold for $1.6 million after taxes. The company also hired a marketing firm to analyze the zither market, at a cost of $125,000. An excerpt of the marketing report is as follows:

> The zither industry will have a rapid expansion in the next four years. With the brand name recognition that PUTZ brings to bear, we feel that the company will be able to sell 3,200, 4,300, 3,900, and 2,800 units each year for the next four years, respectively. Again, capitalizing on the name recognition of PUTZ, we feel that a premium price of $780 can be charged for each zither. Because zithers appear to be a fad, we feel at the end of the four-year period, sales should be discontinued.

PUTZ believes that fixed costs for the project will be $425,000 per year, and variable costs are 15 percent of sales. The equipment necessary for production will cost $4.2 million and will be depreciated according to a three-year MACRS schedule. At the end of the project, the equipment can be scrapped for $400,000. Net working capital of $125,000 will be required immediately. PUTZ has a 38 percent tax rate, and the required return on the project is 13 percent. What is the NPV of the project? Assume the company has other profitable projects.

32. **Project Evaluation** [LO1] Aguilera Acoustics, Inc. (AAI), projects unit sales for a new seven-octave voice emulation implant as follows:

Year	Unit Sales
1	93,000
2	105,000
3	128,000
4	134,000
5	87,000

Production of the implants will require $1,800,000 in net working capital to start and additional net working capital investments each year equal to 15 percent of the projected sales increase for the following year. Total fixed costs are $1,200,000 per year, variable production costs are $265 per unit, and the units are priced at $380 each. The equipment needed to begin production has an installed cost of $24,000,000. Because the implants are intended for professional singers, this equipment is considered industrial machinery and thus qualifies as seven-year MACRS property. In five years, this equipment can be sold for about 20 percent of its acquisition cost. AAI is in the 35 percent marginal tax bracket and has a required return on all its projects of 18 percent. Based on these preliminary project estimates, what is the NPV of the project? What is the IRR?

33. **Calculating Required Savings [LO2]** A proposed cost-saving device has an installed cost of $610,000. The device will be used in a five-year project but is classified as three-year MACRS property for tax purposes. The required initial net working capital investment is $55,000, the marginal tax rate is 35 percent, and the project discount rate is 12 percent. The device has an estimated year 5 salvage value of $40,000. What level of pretax cost savings do we require for this project to be profitable?

34. **Financial Break-Even Analysis [LO2]** To solve the bid price problem presented in the text, we set the project NPV equal to zero and found the required price using the definition of OCF. Thus the bid price represents a financial break-even level for the project. This type of analysis can be extended to many other types of problems.

    a. In Problem 18, assume that the price per carton is $13 and find the project NPV. What does your answer tell you about your bid price? What do you know about the number of cartons you can sell and still break even? How about your level of costs?

    b. Solve Problem 18 again with the price still at $13, but find the quantity of cartons per year that you can supply and still break even. *Hint:* It's less than 185,000.

    c. Repeat (b) with a price of $13 and a quantity of 185,000 cartons per year, and find the highest level of fixed costs you could afford and still break even. *Hint:* It's more than $305,000.

35. **Calculating a Bid Price [LO3]** Your company has been approached to bid on a contract to sell 17,500 voice recognition (VR) computer keyboards a year for four years. Due to technological improvements, beyond that time they will be outdated and no sales will be possible. The equipment necessary for the production will cost $3.4 million and will be depreciated on a straight-line basis to a zero salvage value. Production will require an investment in net working capital of $95,000 to be returned at the end of the project, and the equipment can be sold for $275,000 at the end of production. Fixed costs are $600,000 per year, and variable costs are $175 per unit. In addition to the contract, you feel your company can sell 3,000, 6,000, 8,000, and 5,000 additional units to companies in other countries over the next four years, respectively, at a price of $285. This price is fixed. The tax rate is 40 percent, and the required return is 13 percent. Additionally, the president of the company will undertake the project only if it has an NPV of $100,000. What bid price should you set for the contract?

36. **Replacement Decisions [LO2]** Suppose we are thinking about replacing an old computer with a new one. The old one cost us $650,000; the new one will cost $780,000. The new machine will be depreciated straight-line to zero over its five-year life. It will probably be worth about $150,000 after five years.

    The old computer is being depreciated at a rate of $130,000 per year. It will be completely written off in three years. If we don't replace it now, we will have to replace it in two years. We can sell it now for $210,000; in two years, it will probably be worth $60,000. The new machine will save us $145,000 per year in operating costs. The tax rate is 38 percent, and the discount rate is 12 percent.

a. Suppose we recognize that if we don't replace the computer now, we will be replacing it in two years. Should we replace now or should we wait? *Hint:* What we effectively have here is a decision either to "invest" in the old computer (by not selling it) or to invest in the new one. Notice that the two investments have unequal lives.

b. Suppose we consider only whether we should replace the old computer now without worrying about what's going to happen in two years. What are the relevant cash flows? Should we replace it or not? *Hint:* Consider the net change in the firm's aftertax cash flows if we do the replacement.

Visit us at www.mhhe.com/rwj

MINICASE

Conch Republic Electronics, Part 1

Conch Republic Electronics is a midsized electronics manufacturer located in Key West, Florida. The company president is Shelley Couts, who inherited the company. When it was founded over 70 years ago, the company originally repaired radios and other household appliances. Over the years, the company expanded into manufacturing and is now a reputable manufacturer of various electronic items. Jay McCanless, a recent MBA graduate, has been hired by the company's finance department.

One of the major revenue-producing items manufactured by Conch Republic is a personal digital assistant (PDA). Conch Republic currently has one PDA model on the market, and sales have been excellent. The PDA is a unique item in that it comes in a variety of tropical colors and is preprogrammed to play Jimmy Buffett music. However, as with any electronic item, technology changes rapidly, and the current PDA has limited features in comparison with newer models. Conch Republic spent $750,000 to develop a prototype for a new PDA that has all the features of the existing PDA but adds new features such as cell phone capability. The company has spent a further $200,000 for a marketing study to determine the expected sales figures for the new PDA.

Conch Republic can manufacture the new PDA for $155 each in variable costs. Fixed costs for the operation are estimated to run $4.7 million per year. The estimated sales volume is 74,000, 95,000, 125,000, 105,000, and 80,000 per each year for the next five years, respectively. The unit price of the new PDA will be $360. The necessary equipment can be purchased for $21.5 million and will be depreciated on a seven-year MACRS schedule. It is believed the value of the equipment in five years will be $4.1 million.

As previously stated, Conch Republic currently manufactures a PDA. Production of the existing model is expected to be terminated in two years. If Conch Republic does not introduce the new PDA, sales will be 80,000 units and 60,000 units for the next two years, respectively. The price of the existing PDA is $290 per unit, with variable costs of $120 each and fixed costs of $1,800,000 per year. If Conch Republic does introduce the new PDA, sales of the existing PDA will fall by 15,000 units per year, and the price of the existing units will have to be lowered to $255 each. Net working capital for the PDAs will be 20 percent of sales and will occur with the timing of the cash flows for the year; for example, there is no initial outlay for NWC, but changes in NWC will first occur in year 1 with the first year's sales. Conch Republic has a 35 percent corporate tax rate and a 12 percent required return.

Shelly has asked Jay to prepare a report that answers the following questions.

QUESTIONS

1. What is the payback period of the project?
2. What is the profitability index of the project?
3. What is the IRR of the project?
4. What is the NPV of the project?

LEARNING OBJECTIVES

After studying this chapter, you should understand:

LO1 How to calculate the return on an investment.

LO2 The historical returns on various important types of investments.

LO3 The historical risks on various important types of investments.

LO4 The implications of market efficiency.

SOME LESSONS FROM CAPITAL MARKET HISTORY

12

WITH THE S&P 500 INDEX UP about 3.5 percent and the NASDAQ stock market index up about 9.8 percent in 2007, stock market performance overall was mixed. However, investors in First Solar, maker of solar panels, had to feel sunny about the 796 percent gain in that stock, and investors in Onyx Pharmaceuticals had to feel pretty good about Onyx's 426 percent gain. Of course, not all stocks increased in value during the year. Stock in Novastar Financial, a mortgage lender, fell 97 percent during the year, and stock in Atherogenics, a pharmaceutical company, dropped 96 percent. These examples show that there were tremendous potential profits to be made during 2007, but there was also the risk of losing money—lots of it. So what should you, as a stock market investor, expect when you invest your own money? In this chapter, we study more than eight decades of market history to find out.

> Master the ability to solve problems in this chapter by using a spreadsheet. Access Excel Master on the student Web site www.mhhe.com/rwj.

Thus far, we haven't had much to say about what determines the required return on an investment. In one sense, the answer is simple: The required return depends on the risk of the investment. The greater the risk, the greater is the required return.

Having said this, we are left with a somewhat more difficult problem. How can we measure the amount of risk present in an investment? Put another way, what does it mean to say that one investment is riskier than another? Obviously, we need to define what we mean by *risk* if we are going to answer these questions. This is our task in the next two chapters.

From the last several chapters, we know that one of the responsibilities of the financial manager is to assess the value of proposed real asset investments. In doing this, it is important that we first look at what financial investments have to offer. At a minimum, the return we require from a proposed nonfinancial investment must be greater than what we can get by buying financial assets of similar risk.

Our goal in this chapter is to provide a perspective on what capital market history can tell us about risk and return. The most important thing to get out of this chapter is a feel for the numbers. What is a high return? What is a low one? More generally, what returns should we expect from financial assets, and what are the risks of such investments? This perspective is essential for understanding how to analyze and value risky investment projects.

We start our discussion of risk and return by describing the historical experience of investors in U.S. financial markets. In 1931, for example, the stock market lost 43 percent of its value. Just two years later, the stock market gained 54 percent. In more recent memory, the market lost about 25 percent of its value on October 19, 1987, alone. What lessons, if any, can financial managers learn from such shifts in the stock market? We will explore almost a century of market history to find out.

The number of Web sites devoted to financial markets and instruments is astounding— and increasing daily. Be sure to check out the RWJ Web page for links to finance-related sites! (www.mhhe.com/rwj)

Not everyone agrees on the value of studying history. On the one hand, there is philosopher George Santayana's famous comment: "Those who do not remember the past are condemned to repeat it." On the other hand, there is industrialist Henry Ford's equally famous comment: "History is more or less bunk." Nonetheless, perhaps everyone would agree with Mark Twain's observation: "October. This is one of the peculiarly dangerous months to speculate in stocks in. The others are July, January, September, April, November, May, March, June, December, August, and February."

Two central lessons emerge from our study of market history. First, there is a reward for bearing risk. Second, the greater the potential reward is, the greater is the risk. To illustrate these facts about market returns, we devote much of this chapter to reporting the statistics and numbers that make up the modern capital market history of the United States. In the next chapter, these facts provide the foundation for our study of how financial markets put a price on risk.

12.1 Returns

We wish to discuss historical returns on different types of financial assets. The first thing we need to do, then, is to briefly discuss how to calculate the return from investing.

DOLLAR RETURNS

If you buy an asset of any sort, your gain (or loss) from that investment is called the *return on your investment*. This return will usually have two components. First, you may receive some cash directly while you own the investment. This is called the *income component* of your return. Second, the value of the asset you purchase will often change. In this case, you have a capital gain or capital loss on your investment.[1]

How did the market do today? Find out at finance.yahoo.com.

To illustrate, suppose the Video Concept Company has several thousand shares of stock outstanding. You purchased some of these shares of stock in the company at the beginning of the year. It is now year-end, and you want to determine how well you have done on your investment.

First, over the year, a company may pay cash dividends to its shareholders. As a stockholder in Video Concept Company, you are a part owner of the company. If the company is profitable, it may choose to distribute some of its profits to shareholders (we discuss the details of dividend policy in a later chapter). So, as the owner of some stock, you will receive some cash. This cash is the income component from owning the stock.

In addition to the dividend, the other part of your return is the capital gain or capital loss on the stock. This part arises from changes in the value of your investment. For example, consider the cash flows illustrated in Figure 12.1. At the beginning of the year, the stock was selling for $37 per share. If you had bought 100 shares, you would have had a total outlay of $3,700. Suppose that, over the year, the stock paid a dividend of $1.85 per share. By the end of the year, then, you would have received income of:

Dividend = $1.85 × 100 = $185

Also, the value of the stock has risen to $40.33 per share by the end of the year. Your 100 shares are now worth $4,033, so you have a capital gain of:

Capital gain = ($40.33 − 37) × 100 = $333

---

[1]As we mentioned in an earlier chapter, strictly speaking, what is and what is not a capital gain (or loss) is determined by the IRS. We thus use the terms loosely.

FIGURE 12.1

Dollar Returns

On the other hand, if the price had dropped to, say, $34.78, you would have a capital loss of:

Capital loss = ($34.78 − 37) × 100 = −$222

Notice that a capital loss is the same thing as a negative capital gain.

The total dollar return on your investment is the sum of the dividend and the capital gain:

Total dollar return = Dividend income + Capital gain (or loss)   [12.1]

In our first example, the total dollar return is thus given by:

Total dollar return = $185 + 333 = $518

Notice that if you sold the stock at the end of the year, the total amount of cash you would have would equal your initial investment plus the total return. In the preceding example, then:

$$\begin{aligned} \text{Total cash if stock is sold} &= \text{Initial investment} + \text{Total return} \quad\quad\quad\text{[12.2]} \\ &= \$3,700 + 518 \\ &= \$4,218 \end{aligned}$$

As a check, notice that this is the same as the proceeds from the sale of the stock plus the dividends:

$$\begin{aligned} \text{Proceeds from stock sale} + \text{Dividends} &= \$40.33 \times 100 + 185 \\ &= \$4,033 + 185 \\ &= \$4,218 \end{aligned}$$

Suppose you hold on to your Video Concept stock and don't sell it at the end of the year. Should you still consider the capital gain as part of your return? Isn't this only a "paper" gain and not really a cash flow if you don't sell the stock?

The answer to the first question is a strong yes, and the answer to the second is an equally strong no. The capital gain is every bit as much a part of your return as the dividend, and you should certainly count it as part of your return. That you actually decided to keep the stock and not sell (you don't "realize" the gain) is irrelevant because you could have converted it to cash if you had wanted to. Whether you choose to do so or not is up to you.

After all, if you insisted on converting your gain to cash, you could always sell the stock at year-end and immediately reinvest by buying the stock back. There is no net difference between doing this and just not selling (assuming, of course, that there are no tax consequences from selling the stock). Again, the point is that whether you actually cash out and buy sodas (or whatever) or reinvest by not selling doesn't affect the return you earn.

PERCENTAGE RETURNS

It is usually more convenient to summarize information about returns in percentage terms, rather than dollar terms, because that way your return doesn't depend on how much you actually invest. The question we want to answer is this: How much do we get for each dollar we invest?

Go to www.
smartmoney.com/
marketmap *for a cool Java
applet that shows today's
returns by market sector.*

To answer this question, let P_t be the price of the stock at the beginning of the year and let D_{t+1} be the dividend paid on the stock during the year. Consider the cash flows in Figure 12.2. These are the same as those in Figure 12.1, except that we have now expressed everything on a per-share basis.

In our example, the price at the beginning of the year was $37 per share and the dividend paid during the year on each share was $1.85. As we discussed in Chapter 8, expressing the dividend as a percentage of the beginning stock price results in the dividend yield:

$$\text{Dividend yield} = D_{t+1}/P_t$$
$$= \$1.85/37 = .05 = 5\%$$

This says that for each dollar we invest, we get five cents in dividends.

The second component of our percentage return is the capital gains yield. Recall (from Chapter 8) that this is calculated as the change in the price during the year (the capital gain) divided by the beginning price:

$$\text{Capital gains yield} = (P_{t+1} - P_t)/P_t$$
$$= (\$40.33 - 37)/37$$
$$= \$3.33/37$$
$$= 9\%$$

FIGURE 12.2

Percentage Returns

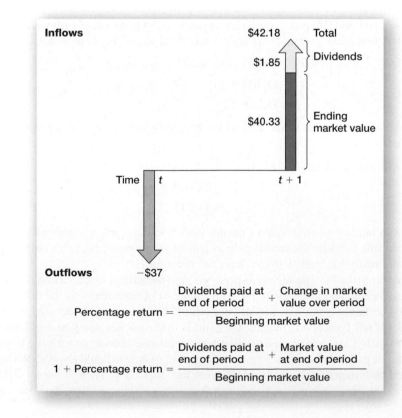

So, per dollar invested, we get nine cents in capital gains.

Putting it together, per dollar invested, we get 5 cents in dividends and 9 cents in capital gains; so we get a total of 14 cents. Our percentage return is 14 cents on the dollar, or 14 percent.

To check this, notice that we invested $3,700 and ended up with $4,218. By what percentage did our $3,700 increase? As we saw, we picked up $4,218 − 3,700 = $518. This is a $518/3,700 = 14% increase.

Calculating Returns

EXAMPLE 12.1

Suppose you bought some stock at the beginning of the year for $25 per share. At the end of the year, the price is $35 per share. During the year, you got a $2 dividend per share. This is the situation illustrated in Figure 12.3. What is the dividend yield? The capital gains yield? The percentage return? If your total investment was $1,000, how much do you have at the end of the year?

Your $2 dividend per share works out to a dividend yield of:

$$\text{Dividend yield} = D_{t+1}/P_t$$
$$= \$2/25 = .08 = 8\%$$

The per-share capital gain is $10, so the capital gains yield is:

$$\text{Capital gains yield} = (P_{t-1} - P_t)/P_t$$
$$= (\$35 - 25)/25$$
$$= \$10/25$$
$$= 40\%$$

The total percentage return is thus 48 percent.

If you had invested $1,000, you would have $1,480 at the end of the year, representing a 48 percent increase. To check this, note that your $1,000 would have bought you $1,000/25 = 40 shares. Your 40 shares would then have paid you a total of 40 × $2 = $80 in cash dividends. Your $10 per share gain would give you a total capital gain of $10 × 40 = $400. Add these together, and you get the $480 increase.

FIGURE 12.3

Cash Flow—An Investment Example

To give another example, stock in Goldman Sachs, the famous financial services company, began 2007 at $197.32 per share. Goldman paid dividends of $1.40 during 2007, and the stock price at the end of the year was $214.27. What was the return on Goldman for the year? For practice, see if you agree that the answer is 9.30 percent. Of course, negative returns occur as well. For example, again in 2007, JP Morgan Chase & Co.'s stock price at the beginning of the year was $46.09 per share, and dividends of $1.44 were paid. The stock ended the year at $42.92 per share. Verify that the loss was 3.75 percent for the year.

Concept Questions

12.1a What are the two parts of total return?

12.1b Why are unrealized capital gains or losses included in the calculation of returns?

12.1c What is the difference between a dollar return and a percentage return? Why are percentage returns more convenient?

12.2 The Historical Record

Roger Ibbotson and Rex Sinquefield conducted a famous set of studies dealing with rates of return in U.S. financial markets.[2] They presented year-to-year historical rates of return on five important types of financial investments. The returns can be interpreted as what you would have earned if you had held portfolios of the following:

For more about market history, visit www.globalfindata.com.

1. *Large-company stocks:* This common stock portfolio is based on the Standard & Poor's (S&P) 500 index, which contains 500 of the largest companies (in terms of total market value of outstanding stock) in the United States.

2. *Small-company stocks:* This is a portfolio composed of the stock corresponding to the smallest 20 percent of the companies listed on the New York Stock Exchange, again as measured by market value of outstanding stock.

3. *Long-term corporate bonds:* This is based on high-quality bonds with 20 years to maturity.

4. *Long-term U.S. government bonds:* This is based on U.S. government bonds with 20 years to maturity.

5. *U.S. Treasury bills:* This is based on Treasury bills (T-bills for short) with a one-month maturity.

These returns are not adjusted for inflation or taxes; thus, they are nominal, pretax returns.

In addition to the year-to-year returns on these financial instruments, the year-to-year percentage change in the consumer price index (CPI) is also computed. This is a commonly used measure of inflation, so we can calculate real returns using this as the inflation rate.

A FIRST LOOK

Before looking closely at the different portfolio returns, we take a look at the big picture. Figure 12.4 shows what happened to $1 invested in these different portfolios at the end of 1925. The growth in value for each of the different portfolios over the 82-year period ending in 2007 is given separately (the long-term corporate bonds are omitted). Notice that to get everything on a single graph, some modification in scaling is used. As is commonly

---

[2]R.G. Ibbotson and R.A. Sinquefield, *Stocks, Bonds, Bills, and Inflation* [SBBI] (Charlottesville, VA: Financial Analysis Research Foundation, 1982).

FIGURE 12.4   A $1 Investment in Different Types of Portfolios: 1925–2007 (Year-End 1925 = $1)

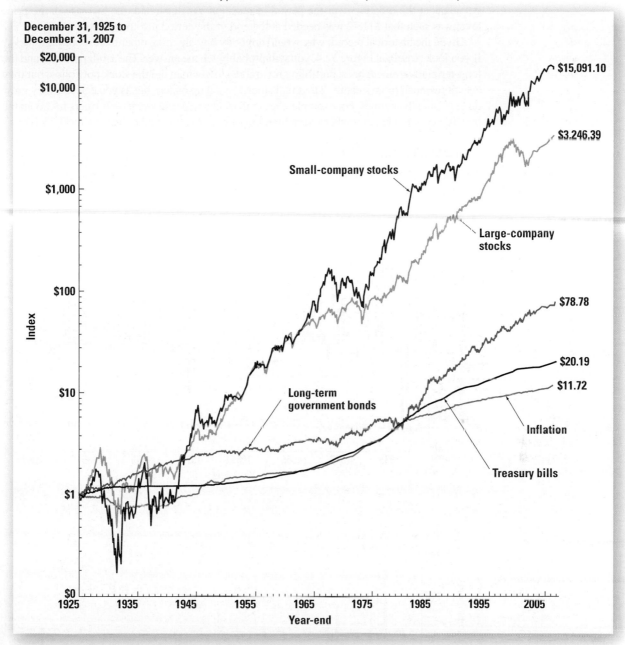

Redrawn from *Stocks, Bonds, Bills and Inflation: 2008 Yearbook,*™ annually updated work by Roger G. Ibbotson and Rex A. Sinquefield (Chicago: Morningstar). All rights reserved.

done with financial series, the vertical axis is scaled so that equal distances measure equal percentage (as opposed to dollar) changes in values.[3]

Looking at Figure 12.4, we see that the "small-cap" (short for small-capitalization) investment did the best overall. Every dollar invested grew to a remarkable $15,091.10 over the 82 years. The large-company common stock portfolio did less well; a dollar invested in it grew to $3,246.39.

Go to
bigcharts.marketwatch.com
*to see both intraday and
long-term charts.*

---

[3]In other words, the scale is logarithmic.

At the other end, the T-bill portfolio grew to only $20.19. This is even less impressive when we consider the inflation over the period in question. As illustrated, the increase in the price level was such that $11.72 was needed at the end of the period just to replace the original $1.

Given the historical record, why would anybody buy anything other than small-cap stocks? If you look closely at Figure 12.4, you will probably see the answer. The T-bill portfolio and the long-term government bond portfolio grew more slowly than did the stock portfolios, but they also grew much more steadily. The small stocks ended up on top; but as you can see, they grew quite erratically at times. For example, the small stocks were the worst performers for about the first 10 years and had a smaller return than long-term government bonds for almost 15 years.

A CLOSER LOOK

To illustrate the variability of the different investments, Figures 12.5 through 12.8 plot the year-to-year percentage returns in the form of vertical bars drawn from the horizontal axis.

FIGURE 12.5

Year-by-Year Total Returns on Large-Company Common Stocks

Redrawn from *Stocks, Bonds, Bills and Inflation: 2008 Yearbook,*™ annually updates work by Roger G. Ibbotson and Rex A. Sinquefield (Chicago: Morningstar). All rights reserved.

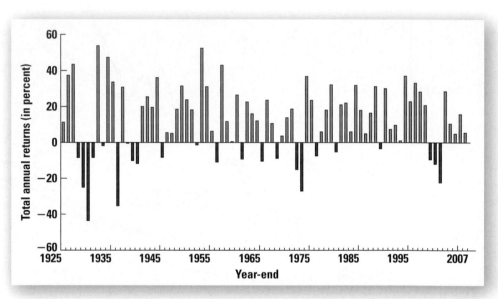

FIGURE 12.6

Year-by-Year Total Returns on Small-Company Stocks

Redrawn from *Stocks, Bonds, Bills and Inflation: 2008 Yearbook,*™ annually updates work by Roger G. Ibbotson and Rex A. Sinquefield (Chicago: Morningstar). All rights reserved.

FIGURE 12.7

Year-by-Year Total Returns on Bonds and Bills

Redrawn from *Stocks, Bonds, Bills and Inflation: 2008 Yearbook,*™ annually updates work by Roger G. Ibbotson and Rex A. Sinquefield (Chicago: Morningstar). All rights reserved.

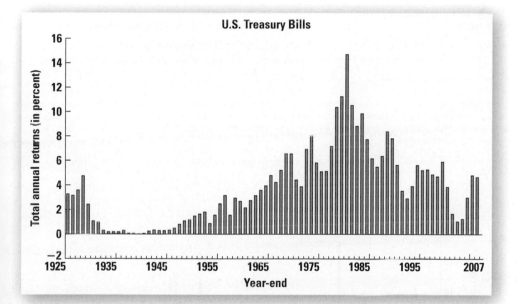

The height of the bar tells us the return for the particular year. For example, looking at the long-term government bonds (Figure 12.7), we see that the largest historical return (44.44 percent) occurred in 1982. This was a good year for bonds. In comparing these charts, notice the differences in the vertical axis scales. With these differences in mind, you can see how predictably the Treasury bills (Figure 12.7) behaved compared to the small stocks (Figure 12.6).

The returns shown in these bar graphs are sometimes very large. Looking at the graphs, for example, we see that the largest single-year return is a remarkable 142.87 percent for the small-cap stocks in 1933. In the same year, the large-company stocks returned "only" 52.94 percent. In contrast, the largest Treasury bill return was 15.21 percent in 1981. For future reference, the actual year-to-year returns for the S&P 500, long-term government bonds, Treasury bills, and the CPI are shown in Table 12.1.

The financial markets are the most carefully documented human phenomena in history. Every day, over 2,000 NYSE stocks are traded, and at least 6,000 more stocks are traded on other exchanges and ECNs. Bonds, commodities, futures, and options also provide a wealth of data. These data daily fill much of *The Wall Street Journal* (and numerous other newspapers), and are available as they happen on numerous financial websites. A record actually exists of almost every transaction, providing not only a real-time database but also a historical record extending back, in many cases, more than a century.

The global market adds another dimension to this wealth of data. The Japanese stock market trades over a billion shares a day, and the London exchange reports trades on over 10,000 domestic and foreign issues a day.

The data generated by these transactions are quantifiable, quickly analyzed and disseminated, and made easily accessible by computer. Because of this, finance has increasingly come to resemble one of the exact sciences. The use of financial market data ranges from the simple, such as using the S&P 500 to measure the performance of a portfolio, to the incredibly complex. For example, only a few decades ago, the bond market was the most staid province on Wall Street. Today, it attracts swarms of traders seeking to exploit arbitrage opportunities—small temporary mispricings—using real-time data and computers to analyze them.

Financial market data are the foundation for the extensive empirical understanding we now have of the financial markets. The following is a list of some of the principal findings of such research:

- Risky securities, such as stocks, have higher average returns than riskless securities such as Treasury bills.
- Stocks of small companies have higher average returns than those of larger companies.
- Long-term bonds have higher average yields and returns than short-term bonds.
- The cost of capital for a company, project, or division can be predicted using data from the markets.

Because phenomena in the financial markets are so well measured, finance is the most readily quantifiable branch of economics. Researchers are able to do more extensive empirical research than in any other economic field, and the research can be quickly translated into action in the marketplace.

Roger Ibbotson is professor in the practice of management at the Yale School of Management. He is founder of Ibbotson Associates, now a Morningstar, Inc. company and a major supplier of financial data and analysis. He is also chairman of Zebra Capital, an equity hedge fund manager. An outstanding scholar, he is best known for his original estimates of the historical rates of return realized by investors in different markets and for his research on new issues.

FIGURE 12.8

Year-by-Year Inflation

Redrawn from *Stocks, Bonds, Bills and Inflation: 2008 Yearbook,*™ annually updates work by Roger G. Ibbotson and Rex A. Sinquefield (Chicago: Morningstar). All rights reserved.

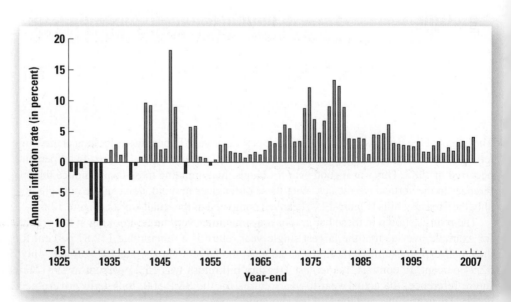

TABLE 12.1   Year-to-Year Total Returns: 1926–2007

Year	Large-Company Stocks	Long-Term Government Bonds	U.S. Treasury Bills	Consumer Price Index	Year	Large-Company Stocks	Long-Term Government Bonds	U.S. Treasury Bills	Consumer Price Index
1926	13.75%	5.69%	3.30%	−1.12%	1967	23.98	2.86	4.39	3.04
1927	35.70	6.58	3.15	−2.26	1968	11.03	2.25	5.49	4.72
1928	45.08	1.15	4.05	−1.16	1969	−8.43	−5.63	6.90	6.20
1929	−8.80	4.39	4.47	.58	1970	3.94	18.92	6.50	5.57
1930	−25.13	4.47	2.27	−6.40	1971	14.30	11.24	4.36	3.27
1931	−43.60	−2.15	1.15	−9.32	1972	18.99	2.39	4.23	3.41
1932	−8.75	8.51	.88	−10.27	1973	−14.69	3.30	7.29	8.71
1933	52.95	1.92	.52	.76	1974	−26.47	4.00	7.99	12.34
1934	−2.31	7.59	.27	1.52	1975	37.23	5.52	5.87	6.94
1935	46.79	4.20	.17	2.99	1976	23.93	15.56	5.07	4.86
1936	32.49	5.10	.17	1.45	1977	−7.16	.38	5.45	6.70
1937	−35.45	1.44	.27	2.86	1978	6.57	−1.26	7.64	9.02
1938	31.63	4.21	.06	−2.78	1979	18.61	1.26	10.56	13.29
1939	−1.43	3.84	.04	.00	1980	32.50	−2.48	12.10	12.52
1940	−10.36	5.70	.04	.71	1981	−4.92	4.04	14.60	8.92
1941	−12.02	.47	.14	9.93	1982	21.55	44.28	10.94	3.83
1942	20.75	1.80	.34	9.03	1983	22.56	1.29	8.99	3.79
1943	25.38	2.01	.38	2.96	1984	6.27	15.29	9.90	3.95
1944	19.49	2.27	.38	2.30	1985	31.73	32.27	7.71	3.80
1945	36.21	5.29	.38	2.25	1986	18.67	22.39	6.09	1.10
1946	−8.42	.54	.38	18.13	1987	5.25	−3.03	5.88	4.43
1947	5.05	−1.02	.62	8.84	1988	16.61	6.84	6.94	4.42
1948	4.99	2.66	1.00	2.99	1989	31.69	18.54	8.44	4.65
1949	17.81	4.58	1.12	−2.07	1990	−3.10	7.74	7.69	6.11
1950	30.05	−.98	1.22	5.93	1991	30.46	19.36	5.43	3.06
1951	23.79	−.20	1.56	6.00	1992	7.62	7.34	3.48	2.90
1952	18.39	2.43	1.75	.75	1993	10.08	13.06	3.03	2.75
1953	−1.07	2.28	1.87	.75	1994	1.32	−7.32	4.39	2.67
1954	52.23	3.08	.93	−.74	1995	37.58	25.94	5.61	2.54
1955	31.62	−.73	1.80	.37	1996	22.96	.13	5.14	3.32
1956	6.91	−1.72	2.66	2.99	1997	33.36	12.02	5.19	1.70
1957	−10.50	6.82	3.28	2.90	1998	28.58	14.45	4.86	1.61
1958	43.57	−1.72	1.71	1.76	1999	21.04	−7.51	4.80	2.68
1959	12.01	−2.02	3.48	1.73	2000	−9.10	17.22	5.98	3.39
1960	.47	11.21	2.81	1.36	2001	−11.89	5.51	3.33	1.55
1961	26.84	2.20	2.40	.67	2002	−22.10	15.15	1.61	2.4
1962	−8.75	5.72	2.82	1.33	2003	28.89	2.01	.94	1.9
1963	22.70	1.79	3.23	1.64	2004	10.88	8.12	1.14	3.3
1964	16.43	3.71	3.62	.97	2005	4.91	6.89	2.79	3.4
1965	12.38	.93	4.06	1.92	2006	15.79	.28	4.97	2.54
1966	−10.06%	5.12%	4.94%	3.46%	2007	5.40	10.85	4.52	4.08

SOURCES: Authors' calculation based on data obtained from *Global Financial Data* and other sources.

Concept Questions

12.2a With 20/20 hindsight, what do you say was the best investment for the period from 1926 through 1935?

12.2b Why doesn't everyone just buy small stocks as investments?

12.2c What was the smallest return observed over the 80 years for each of these investments? Approximately when did it occur?

12.2d About how many times did large-company stocks return more than 30 percent? How many times did they return less than −20 percent?

12.2e What was the longest "winning streak" (years without a negative return) for large-company stocks? For long-term government bonds?

12.2f How often did the T-bill portfolio have a negative return?

12.3   Average Returns: The First Lesson

As you've probably begun to notice, the history of capital market returns is too complicated to be of much use in its undigested form. We need to begin summarizing all these numbers. Accordingly, we discuss how to go about condensing the detailed data. We start out by calculating average returns.

CALCULATING AVERAGE RETURNS

The obvious way to calculate the average returns on the different investments in Table 12.1 is simply to add up the yearly returns and divide by 82. The result is the historical average of the individual values.

For example, if you add up the returns for the large-company stocks in Figure 12.5 for the 82 years, you will get about 10.09. The average annual return is thus 10.09/82 = 12.3%. You interpret this 12.3 percent just like any other average. If you were to pick a year at random from the 82-year history and you had to guess what the return in that year was, the best guess would be 12.3 percent.

AVERAGE RETURNS: THE HISTORICAL RECORD

Table 12.2 shows the average returns for the investments we have discussed. As shown, in a typical year, the small-company stocks increased in value by 17.1 percent. Notice also how much larger the stock returns are than the bond returns.

These averages are, of course, nominal because we haven't worried about inflation. Notice that the average inflation rate was 3.1 percent per year over this 82-year span. The nominal return on U.S. Treasury bills was 3.8 percent per year. The average real return on Treasury bills was thus approximately .7 percent per year; so the real return on T-bills has been quite low historically.

At the other extreme, small stocks had an average real return of about 17.1% − 3.1% = 14%, which is relatively large. If you remember the Rule of 72 (Chapter 5), then you know that a quick back-of-the-envelope calculation tells us that 14 percent real growth doubles your buying power about every five years. Notice also that the real value of the large-company stock portfolio increased by over 9 percent in a typical year.

Investment	Average Return
Large-company stocks	12.3%
Small-company stocks	17.1
Long-term corporate bonds	6.2
Long-term government bonds	5.8
U.S. Treasury bills	3.8
Inflation	3.1

TABLE 12.2

Average Annual Returns: 1926–2007

SOURCE: © *Stocks, Bonds, Bills, and Inflation 2008 Yearbook™*, annually updates work by Roger G. Ibbotson and Rex A. Sinquefield (Chicago: Morningstar). All rights reserved.

Investment	Average Return	Risk Premium
Large-company stocks	12.3%	8.5%
Small-company stocks	17.1	13.3
Long-term corporate bonds	6.2	2.4
Long-term government bonds	5.0	2.0
U.S. Treasury bills	3.8	.0

TABLE 12.3

Average Annual Returns and Risk Premiums: 1926–2007

SOURCE: © *Stocks, Bonds, Bills, and Inflation 2008 Yearbook™*, annually updates work by Roger G. Ibbotson and Rex A. Sinquefield (Chicago: Morningstar). All rights reserved.

RISK PREMIUMS

Now that we have computed some average returns, it seems logical to see how they compare with each other. One such comparison involves government-issued securities. These are free of much of the variability we see in, for example, the stock market.

The government borrows money by issuing bonds in different forms. The ones we will focus on are the Treasury bills. These have the shortest time to maturity of the different government bonds. Because the government can always raise taxes to pay its bills, the debt represented by T-bills is virtually free of any default risk over its short life. Thus, we will call the rate of return on such debt the *risk-free return,* and we will use it as a kind of benchmark.

A particularly interesting comparison involves the virtually risk-free return on T-bills and the very risky return on common stocks. The difference between these two returns can be interpreted as a measure of the *excess return* on the average risky asset (assuming that the stock of a large U.S. corporation has about average risk compared to all risky assets).

We call this the "excess" return because it is the additional return we earn by moving from a relatively risk-free investment to a risky one. Because it can be interpreted as a reward for bearing risk, we will call it a **risk premium**.

Using Table 12.2, we can calculate the risk premiums for the different investments; these are shown in Table 12.3. We report only the nominal risk premiums because there is only a slight difference between the historical nominal and real risk premiums.

The risk premium on T-bills is shown as zero in the table because we have assumed that they are riskless.

risk premium
The excess return required from an investment in a risky asset over that required from a risk-free investment.

THE FIRST LESSON

Looking at Table 12.3, we see that the average risk premium earned by a typical large-company stock is $12.3\% - 3.8\% = 8.5\%$. This is a significant reward. The fact that it exists historically is an important observation, and it is the basis for our first lesson: Risky assets, on average, earn a risk premium. Put another way, there is a reward for bearing risk.

Why is this so? Why, for example, is the risk premium for small stocks so much larger than the risk premium for large stocks? More generally, what determines the relative sizes of the risk premiums for the different assets? The answers to these questions are at the heart of modern finance, and the next chapter is devoted to them. For now, we can find part of the answer by looking at the historical variability of the returns on these different investments. So, to get started, we now turn our attention to measuring variability in returns.

Concept Questions

12.3a What do we mean by *excess return* and *risk premium*?

12.3b What was the real (as opposed to nominal) risk premium on the common stock portfolio?

12.3c What was the nominal risk premium on corporate bonds? The real risk premium?

12.3d What is the first lesson from capital market history?

12.4 The Variability of Returns: The Second Lesson

We have already seen that the year-to-year returns on common stocks tend to be more volatile than the returns on, say, long-term government bonds. We now discuss measuring this variability of stock returns so we can begin examining the subject of risk.

FREQUENCY DISTRIBUTIONS AND VARIABILITY

To get started, we can draw a *frequency distribution* for the common stock returns like the one in Figure 12.9. What we have done here is to count up the number of times the annual return on the common stock portfolio falls within each 10 percent range. For example, in Figure 12.9, the height of 13 in the range of 10 to 20 percent means that 13 of the 82 annual returns were in that range.

FIGURE 12.9   Frequency Distribution of Returns on Large-Company Stocks: 1926–2007

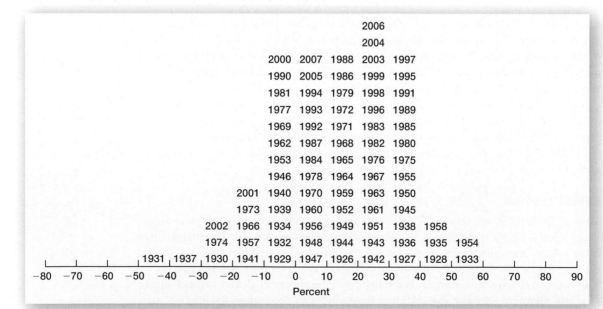

SOURCE: © *Stocks, Bonds, Bills, and Inflation 2008 Yearbook™*, annually updates work by Roger G. Ibbotson and Rex A. Sinquefield (Chicago: Morningstar). All rights reserved.

What we need to do now is to actually measure the spread in returns. We know, for example, that the return on small stocks in a typical year was 17.1 percent. We now want to know how much the actual return deviates from this average in a typical year. In other words, we need a measure of how volatile the return is. The **variance** and its square root, the **standard deviation**, are the most commonly used measures of volatility. We describe how to calculate them next.

variance
The average squared difference between the actual return and the average return.

THE HISTORICAL VARIANCE AND STANDARD DEVIATION

The variance essentially measures the average squared difference between the actual returns and the average return. The bigger this number is, the more the actual returns tend to differ from the average return. Also, the larger the variance or standard deviation is, the more spread out the returns will be.

standard deviation
The positive square root of the variance.

The way we will calculate the variance and standard deviation will depend on the specific situation. In this chapter, we are looking at historical returns; so the procedure we describe here is the correct one for calculating the *historical* variance and standard deviation. If we were examining projected future returns, then the procedure would be different. We describe this procedure in the next chapter.

To illustrate how we calculate the historical variance, suppose a particular investment had returns of 10 percent, 12 percent, 3 percent, and −9 percent over the last four years. The average return is (.10 + .12 + .03 − .09)/4 = 4%. Notice that the return is never actually equal to 4 percent. Instead, the first return deviates from the average by .10 − .04 = .06, the second return deviates from the average by .12 − .04 = .08, and so on. To compute the variance, we square each of these deviations, add them up, and divide the result by the number of returns less 1, or 3 in this case. Most of this information is summarized in the following table:

For an easy-to-read review of basic stats, check out www.robertniles.com.

	(1) Actual Return	(2) Average Return	(3) Deviation (1) − (2)	(4) Squared Deviation
	.10	.04	.06	.0036
	.12	.04	.08	.0064
	.03	.04	−.01	.0001
	−.09	.04	−.13	.0169
Totals	.16		.00	.0270

In the first column, we write the four actual returns. In the third column, we calculate the difference between the actual returns and the average by subtracting out 4 percent. Finally, in the fourth column, we square the numbers in the third column to get the squared deviations from the average.

The variance can now be calculated by dividing .0270, the sum of the squared deviations, by the number of returns less 1. Let Var(R), or σ^2 (read this as "sigma squared"), stand for the variance of the return:

$$\text{Var}(R) = \sigma^2 = .027/(4 - 1) = .009$$

The standard deviation is the square root of the variance. So, if SD(R), or σ, stands for the standard deviation of return:

$$\text{SD}(R) = \sigma = \sqrt{.009} = .09487$$

The square root of the variance is used because the variance is measured in "squared" percentages and thus is hard to interpret. The standard deviation is an ordinary percentage, so the answer here could be written as 9.487 percent.

In the preceding table, notice that the sum of the deviations is equal to zero. This will always be the case, and it provides a good way to check your work. In general, if we have T historical returns, where T is some number, we can write the historical variance as:

$$\text{Var}(R) = \frac{1}{T-1}[(R_1 - \overline{R})^2 + \cdots + (R_T - \overline{R})^2] \qquad [12.3]$$

This formula tells us to do what we just did: Take each of the T individual returns $(R_1, R_2, \ldots)$ and subtract the average return, $\overline{R}$; square the results, and add them all up; and finally, divide this total by the number of returns less 1, $(T - 1)$. The standard deviation is always the square root of $\text{Var}(R)$. Standard deviations are a widely used measure of volatility. Our nearby *Work the Web* box gives a real-world example.

EXAMPLE 12.2 | **Calculating the Variance and Standard Deviation**

Suppose the Supertech Company and the Hyperdrive Company have experienced the following returns in the last four years:

Year	Supertech Return	Hyperdrive Return
2005	−.20	.05
2006	.50	.09
2007	.30	−.12
2008	.10	.20

What are the average returns? The variances? The standard deviations? Which investment was more volatile?

To calculate the average returns, we add up the returns and divide by 4. The results are:

Supertech average return = $\overline{R}$ = .70/4 = .175
Hyperdrive average return = $\overline{R}$ = .22/4 = .055

To calculate the variance for Supertech, we can summarize the relevant calculations as follows:

Year	(1) Actual Return	(2) Average Return	(3) Deviation (1) − (2)	(4) Squared Deviation
2005	−.20	.175	−.375	.140625
2006	.50	.175	.325	.105625
2007	.30	.175	.125	.015625
2008	.10	.175	−.075	.005625
Totals	.70		.000	.267500

Because there are four years of returns, we calculate the variance by dividing .2675 by $(4 - 1) = 3$:

	Supertech	Hyperdrive
Variance (σ^2)	.2675/3 = .0892	.0529/3 = .0176
Standard deviation (σ)	$\sqrt{.0892}$ = .2987	$\sqrt{.0176}$ = .1327

For practice, verify that you get the same answer as we do for Hyperdrive. Notice that the standard deviation for Supertech, 29.87 percent, is a little more than twice Hyperdrive's 13.27 percent; Supertech is thus the more volatile investment.

THE HISTORICAL RECORD

Figure 12.10 summarizes much of our discussion of capital market history so far. It displays average returns, standard deviations, and frequency distributions of annual returns on a common scale. In Figure 12.10, for example, notice that the standard deviation for the small-stock portfolio (32.6 percent per year) is more than 10 times larger than the T-bill portfolio's standard deviation (3.1 percent per year). We will return to these figures momentarily.

NORMAL DISTRIBUTION

For many different random events in nature, a particular frequency distribution, the **normal distribution** (or *bell curve*), is useful for describing the probability of ending up in a given range. For example, the idea behind "grading on a curve" comes from the fact that exam score distributions often resemble a bell curve.

normal distribution
A symmetric, bell-shaped frequency distribution that is completely defined by its mean and standard deviation.

WORK THE WEB

Standard deviations are widely reported for mutual funds. For example, the Fidelity Magellan fund was one of the largest mutual funds in the United States at the time this was written. How volatile is it? To find out, we went to www.morningstar.com, entered the ticker symbol FMAGX, and clicked the "Risk Measures" link. Here is what we found:

Fidelity Magellan FMAGX   *Fidelity* INVESTMENTS

See Fund Family Data ▸▸

Volatility Measurements	Trailing 3-Yr through 04-30-08	*Trailing 5-Yr through 04-30-08
Standard Deviation	11.48	Sharpe Ratio	.52
Mean	10.56	Bear Market Decile Rank*	5

Modern Portfolio Theory Statistics		Trailing 3-Yr through 04-30-08
	Standard Index S&P 500 TR	Best Fit Index Morningstar US Gr TR
R-Squared	79	92
Beta	1.15	.91
Alpha	1.19	.74

The standard deviation for the Fidelity Magellan Fund is 11.48 percent. When you consider that the average stock has a standard deviation of about 50 percent, this seems like a low number. The reason for the low standard deviation has to do with the power of diversification, a topic we discuss in the next chapter. The mean is the average return, so over the last three years, investors in the Magellan Fund gained 10.56 percent per year. Also, under the Volatility Measurements section, you will see the Sharpe ratio. The Sharpe ratio is calculated as the risk premium of the asset divided by the standard deviation. As such, it is a measure of return relative to the level of risk taken (as measured by standard deviation). The "beta" for the Fidelity Magellan Fund is 1.15. We will have more to say about this number—lots more—in the next chapter.

Questions
1. Go to the Morningstar Web site at www.morningstar.com. What does the Sharpe ratio measure? What does the Bear Market Decile Rank measure?
2. Get a quote for the Fidelity Magellan fund at Morningstar. What are the five sectors that have the highest percentage investment for this fund? What are the five stocks with the highest percentage investment?

FIGURE 12.10   Historical Returns, Standard Deviations, and Frequency Distributions: 1926–2007

SERIES	AVERAGE RETURN	STANDARD DEVIATION	DISTRIBUTION
Large-company stocks	12.3%	20.0%	
Small-company stocks	17.1	32.6	*
Long-term corporate bonds	6.2	8.4	
Long-term government bonds	5.8	9.2	
Intermediate-term government bonds	5.5	5.7	
U.S. Treasury bills	3.8	3.1	
Inflation	3.1	4.2	

*The 1933 small-company stocks total return was 142.9 percent.

SOURCE: Modified from *Stocks, Bonds, Bills and Inflation 2008 Yearbook*,™ annually updates work by Roger G. Ibbotson and Rex A. Sinquefield (Chicago: Morningstar). All rights reserved.

Figure 12.11 illustrates a normal distribution and its distinctive bell shape. As you can see, this distribution has a much cleaner appearance than the actual return distributions illustrated in Figure 12.10. Even so, like the normal distribution, the actual distributions do appear to be at least roughly mound-shaped and symmetric. When this is true, the normal distribution is often a very good approximation.

Also, keep in mind that the distributions in Figure 12.10 are based on only 82 yearly observations, whereas Figure 12.11 is, in principle, based on an infinite number. So, if we had been able to observe returns for, say, 1,000 years, we might have filled in a lot of the irregularities and ended up with a much smoother picture in Figure 12.10. For our purposes, it is enough to observe that the returns are at least roughly normally distributed.

The usefulness of the normal distribution stems from the fact that it is completely described by the average and the standard deviation. If you have these two numbers, then there is nothing else to know. For example, with a normal distribution, the probability that we will end up within one standard deviation of the average is about 2/3. The probability

FIGURE 12.11

The Normal Distribution

NOTE: Illustrated returns are based on the historical return and standard deviation for a portfolio of large-firm common stocks.

Probability

68%

95%

99%

| -3σ | -2σ | -1σ | 0 | $+1\sigma$ | $+2\sigma$ | $+3\sigma$ |
| -47.7% | -27.7% | -7.7% | 12.3% | 32.3% | 52.3% | 72.3% |

Return on large-company stocks

that we will end up within two standard deviations is about 95 percent. Finally, the probability of being more than three standard deviations away from the average is less than 1 percent. These ranges and the probabilities are illustrated in Figure 12.11.

To see why this is useful, recall from Figure 12.10 that the standard deviation of returns on the large-company stocks is 20 percent. The average return is 12.3 percent. So, assuming that the frequency distribution is at least approximately normal, the probability that the return in a given year is in the range of −7.7 to 32.3 percent (12.3 percent plus or minus one standard deviation, 20 percent) is about 2/3. This range is illustrated in Figure 12.11. In other words, there is about one chance in three that the return will be *outside* this range. This literally tells you that, if you buy stocks in large companies, you should expect to be outside this range in one year out of every three. This reinforces our earlier observations about stock market volatility. However, there is only a 5 percent chance (approximately) that we would end up outside the range of −27.7 to 52.3 percent (12.3 percent plus or minus 2 × 20%). These points are also illustrated in Figure 12.11.

THE SECOND LESSON

Our observations concerning the year-to-year variability in returns are the basis for our second lesson from capital market history. On average, bearing risk is handsomely rewarded; but in a given year, there is a significant chance of a dramatic change in value. Thus our second lesson is this: The greater the potential reward, the greater is the risk.

USING CAPITAL MARKET HISTORY

Based on the discussion in this section, you should begin to have an idea of the risks and rewards from investing. For example, in mid-2008, Treasury bills were paying about 1.8 percent. Suppose we had an investment that we thought had about the same risk as a portfolio of large-firm common stocks. At a minimum, what return would this investment have to offer for us to be interested?

From Table 12.3, we see that the risk premium on large-company stocks has been 8.5 percent historically, so a reasonable estimate of our required return would be this premium plus the T-bill rate, 1.8% + 8.5% = 10.3%. This may strike you as being high; but if we were thinking of starting a new business, then the risks of doing so might resemble those of investing in small-company stocks. In this case, the historical risk premium is 13.3 percent, so we might require as much as 15.1 percent from such an investment at a minimum.

We will discuss the relationship between risk and required return in more detail in the next chapter. For now, you should notice that a projected internal rate of return, or IRR, on a risky investment in the 10 to 20 percent range isn't particularly outstanding. It depends on how much risk there is. This, too, is an important lesson from capital market history.

EXAMPLE 12.3   **Investing in Growth Stocks**

The term *growth stock* is frequently used as a euphemism for small-company stock. Are such investments suitable for "widows and orphans"? Before answering, you should consider the historical volatility. For example, from the historical record, what is the approximate probability that you will actually lose more than 16 percent of your money in a single year if you buy a portfolio of stocks of such companies?

Looking back at Figure 12.10, we see that the average return on small-company stocks is 17.1 percent and the standard deviation is 32.6 percent. Assuming the returns are approximately normal, there is about a 1/3 probability that you will experience a return outside the range of -15.5 to 49.7 percent ($17.1\% \pm 32.6\%$).

Because the normal distribution is symmetric, the odds of being above or below this range are equal. There is thus a 1/6 chance (half of 1/3) that you will lose more than 15.5 percent. So you should expect this to happen once in every six years, on average. Such investments can thus be *very* volatile, and they are not well suited for those who cannot afford the risk.

MORE ON THE STOCK MARKET RISK PREMIUM

As we have discussed, the historical stock market risk premium has been substantial. In fact, based on standard economic models, it has been argued that the historical risk premium is *too* big and is thus an overestimate of what is likely to happen in the future.

Of course, any time we use the past to predict the future, there is the danger that the past period we observe isn't representative of what the future will hold. For example, in this chapter, we studied the period 1925–2007. Perhaps investors got lucky over this period and earned particularly high returns. Data from earlier years is available, though it is not of the same quality. With that caveat in mind, researchers have traced returns back to 1802, and the risk premiums seen in the pre-1925 era are perhaps a little smaller, but not dramatically so.

Another possibility is that the U.S. stock market experience was unusually good. Investors in at least some other major countries did not do as well because their financial markets were nearly or completely wiped out because of revolution, war, and/or hyperinflation. A recent study addresses this issue by examining data from 1900–2005 for 17 countries.

Figure 12.12 shows the historical average stock market risk premium for all 17 countries over the 106-year period. Looking at the numbers, the U.S. risk premium is the 10th highest at 7.4 percent (which differs from our earlier estimate because of the differing time periods examined). The overall average risk premium is 7.1 percent. These numbers make it clear that U.S. investors did well, but not exceptionally so relative to investors in many other countries.

So, is the U.S. stock market risk premium estimated from 1925–2007 too high? The evidence seems to suggest that the answer is "maybe a little." One thing we haven't stressed so far is that even with 106 years of data, the average risk premium is still not measured with great precision. From a statistical standpoint, the standard error associated with the U.S. estimated risk premium of 7.4 percent is about 2 percent. So, even one standard error range covers 5.4 to 9.4 percent.

FIGURE 12.12

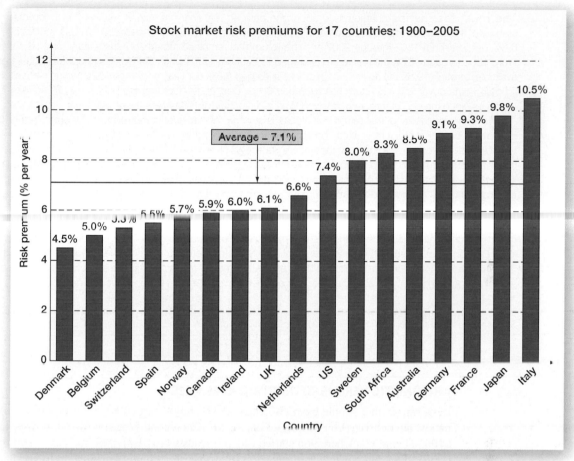

Stock market risk premiums for 17 countries: 1900–2005

SOURCE: Based on information in Elroy Dimson, Paul Marsh, and Michael Staunton, "The Worldwide Equity Premium: A Smaller Puzzle," in *Handbook of the Equity Risk Premium*, Rajnish Mehra, ed. (Elsevier: 2007).

Concept Questions

12.4a In words, how do we calculate a variance? A standard deviation?

12.4b With a normal distribution, what is the probability of ending up more than one standard deviation below the average?

12.4c Assuming that long-term corporate bonds have an approximately normal distribution, what is the approximate probability of earning 14.6 percent or more in a given year? With T-bills, roughly what is this probability?

12.4d What is the second lesson from capital market history?

More about Average Returns   12.5

Thus far in this chapter, we have looked closely at simple average returns. But there is another way of computing an average return. The fact that average returns are calculated two different ways leads to some confusion, so our goal in this section is to explain the two approaches and also the circumstances under which each is appropriate.

The most fascinating characteristic about the data on real financial market returns that I collected is the stability of the long-run real equity returns. The compound annual (geometric) real return on U.S. stocks averaged 6.8% per year from 1802 through 2007 and this return had remained remarkably stable over long-term periods. From 1802 through 1871, the real return averaged 7.0%, from 1871, when the Cowles Foundation data became available, through 1925, the real return on stocks averaged 6.6% per year, and since 1925, which the well-known Ibbotson data cover, the real return has averaged 6.7%. Despite the fact that the price level has increased over ten times since the end of the Second World War, real stock returns have still averaged 6.8%.

The long run stability of real returns on stocks is strongly indicative of *mean reversion of equity return*. Mean reversion means that stock returns can be very volatile in the short run, but show a remarkable stability in the long run. When my research was first published, there was much skepticism of the mean reversion properties of equity market returns, but now this concept is widely accepted for stocks. If mean reversion prevails, portfolios geared for the long-term should have a greater share of equities than short-term portfolios. This conclusion has long been the "conventional" wisdom on investing, but it does not follow if stock returns follow a random walk, a concept widely accepted by academics in the 1970s and 1980s.

When my data first appeared, there was also much discussion of "survivorship bias," the fact that the U.S. stock returns are unusually good because the U.S. was the most successful capitalist country. But three British researchers, Elroy Dimson, Paul Marsh, and Michael Staunton, surveyed stock returns in 16 countries since the beginning of the 20th century and wrote up their results in a book entitled *Triumph of the Optimists*. The authors concluded that U.S. stock returns do not give a distorted picture of the superiority of stocks over bonds worldwide.

Jeremy J. Siegel is the Russell E. Palmer Professor of Finance at The Wharton School of the University of Pennsylvania and author of Stocks for the Long Run *and* The Future Investors. *His research covers macroeconomics and monetary policy, financial market returns, and long-term economic trends.*

ARITHMETIC VERSUS GEOMETRIC AVERAGES

Let's start with a simple example. Suppose you buy a particular stock for $100. Unfortunately, the first year you own it, it falls to $50. The second year you own it, it rises back to $100, leaving you where you started (no dividends were paid).

What was your average return on this investment? Common sense seems to say that your average return must be exactly zero because you started with $100 and ended with $100. But if we calculate the returns year-by-year, we see that you lost 50 percent the first year (you lost half of your money). The second year, you made 100 percent (you doubled your money). Your average return over the two years was thus $(-50\% + 100\%)/2 = 25\%$!

geometric average return
The average compound return earned per year over a multiyear period.

arithmetic average return
The return earned in an average year over a multiyear period.

So which is correct, 0 percent or 25 percent? Both are correct: They just answer different questions. The 0 percent is called the **geometric average return**. The 25 percent is called the **arithmetic average return**. The geometric average return answers the question "What was your average compound return per year over a particular period?" The arithmetic average return answers the question "What was your return in an average year over a particular period?"

Notice that, in previous sections, the average returns we calculated were all arithmetic averages, so we already know how to calculate them. What we need to do now is (1) learn how to calculate geometric averages and (2) learn the circumstances under which one average is more meaningful than the other.

CALCULATING GEOMETRIC AVERAGE RETURNS

First, to illustrate how we calculate a geometric average return, suppose a particular investment had annual returns of 10 percent, 12 percent, 3 percent, and −9 percent over the last four years. The geometric average return over this four-year period is calculated as $(1.10 \times 1.12 \times 1.03 \times .91)^{1/4} - 1 = 3.66\%$. In contrast, the average arithmetic return we have been calculating is $(.10 + .12 + .03 - .09)/4 = 4.0\%$.

In general, if we have T years of returns, the geometric average return over these T years is calculated using this formula:

$$\text{Geometric average return} = [(1 + R_1) \times (1 + R_2) \times \cdots \times (1 + R_T)]^{1/T} - 1 \qquad \text{[12.4]}$$

This formula tells us that four steps are required:

1. Take each of the T annual returns $R_1, R_2, \ldots, R_T$ and add 1 to each (after converting them to decimals!).
2. Multiply all the numbers from step 1 together.
3. Take the result from step 2 and raise it to the power of $1/T$.
4. Finally, subtract 1 from the result of step 3. The result is the geometric average return.

Calculating the Geometric Average Return	EXAMPLE 12.4

Calculate the geometric average return for S&P 500 large-cap stocks for the first five years in Table 12.1, 1926–193

First, convert percentages to decimal returns, add 1, and then calculate their product:

S&P 500 Returns	Product
13.75	1.1375
35.70	×1.3570
45.08	×1.4508
−8.80	×.9120
−25.13	×.7487
	1.5291

Notice that the number 1.5291 is what our investment is worth after five years if we started with a $1 investment. The geometric average return is then calculated as follows:

$$\text{Geometric average return} = 1.5291^{1/5} - 1 = .0887, \text{ or } 8.87\%$$

Thus, the geometric average return is about 8.87 percent in this example. Here is a tip: If you are using a financial calculator, you can put $1 in as the present value, $1.5291 as the future value, and 5 as the number of periods. Then, solve for the unknown rate. You should get the same answer we did.

One thing you may have noticed in our examples thus far is that the geometric average returns seem to be smaller. This will always be true (as long as the returns are not all identical, in which case the two "averages" would be the same). To illustrate, Table 12.4 shows the arithmetic averages and standard deviations from Figure 12.10, along with the geometric average returns.

As shown in Table 12.4, the geometric averages are all smaller, but the magnitude of the difference varies quite a bit. The reason is that the difference is greater for more volatile investments. In fact, there is a useful approximation. Assuming all the numbers are expressed in decimals (as opposed to percentages), the geometric average return is approximately equal to the arithmetic average return minus half the variance. For example, looking at the large-company stocks, the arithmetic average is .123 and the standard deviation is .20, implying that the variance is .04. The approximate geometric average is thus .123 − .04/2 − .103, which is quite close to the actual value.

TABLE 12.4

Geometric versus
Arithmetic Average
Returns: 1926–2007

Series	Average Return		Standard Deviation
	Geometric	Arithmetic	
Large-company stocks	10.4%	12.3%	20.0%
Small-company stocks	12.5	17.1	32.6
Long-term corporate bonds	5.9	6.2	8.4
Long-term government bonds	5.5	5.8	9.2
Intermediate-term government bonds	5.3	5.5	5.7
U.S. Treasury bills	3.7	3.8	3.1
Inflation	3.0	3.1	4.2

EXAMPLE 12.5   **More Geometric Averages**

Take a look back at Figure 12.4. There, we showed the value of a $1 investment after 82 years. Use the value for the large-company stock investment to check the geometric average in Table 12.4.

In Figure 12.4, the large-company investment grew to $3,246.39 over 82 years. The geometric average return is thus

Geometric average return = $3{,}246.39^{1/82} - 1 = .1036$, or 10.4%

This 10.4% is the value shown in Table 12.4. For practice, check some of the other numbers in Table 12.4 the same way.

ARITHMETIC AVERAGE RETURN OR GEOMETRIC AVERAGE RETURN?

When we look at historical returns, the difference between the geometric and arithmetic average returns isn't too hard to understand. To put it slightly differently, the geometric average tells you what you actually earned per year on average, compounded annually. The arithmetic average tells you what you earned in a typical year. You should use whichever one answers the question you want answered.

A somewhat trickier question concerns which average return to use when forecasting future wealth levels, and there's a lot of confusion on this point among analysts and financial planners. First, let's get one thing straight: If you *know* the true arithmetic average return, then this is what you should use in your forecast. For example, if you know the arithmetic return is 10 percent, then your best guess of the value of a $1,000 investment in 10 years is the future value of $1,000 at 10 percent for 10 years, or $2,593.74.

The problem we face, however, is that we usually have only *estimates* of the arithmetic and geometric returns, and estimates have errors. In this case, the arithmetic average return is probably too high for longer periods and the geometric average is probably too low for shorter periods. So, you should regard long-run projected wealth levels calculated using arithmetic averages as optimistic. Short-run projected wealth levels calculated using geometric averages are probably pessimistic.

The good news is that there is a simple way of combining the two averages, which we will call *Blume's formula*.[4] Suppose we have calculated geometric and arithmetic return averages from *N* years of data, and we wish to use these averages to form a *T*-year average return forecast, $R(T)$, where *T* is less than *N*. Here's how we do it:

$$R(T) = \frac{T-1}{N-1} \times \text{Geometric average} + \frac{N-T}{N-1} \times \text{Arithmetic average} \qquad [12.5]$$

---

[4]This elegant result is due to Marshal Blume ("Unbiased Estimates of Long-Run Expected Rates of Return," *Journal of the American Statistical Association,* September 1974, pp. 634–638).

For example, suppose that, from 25 years of annual returns data, we calculate an arithmetic average return of 12 percent and a geometric average return of 9 percent. From these averages, we wish to make 1-year, 5-year, and 10-year average return forecasts. These three average return forecasts are calculated as follows:

$$R(1) = \frac{1-1}{24} \times 9\% + \frac{25-1}{24} \times 12\% = 12\%$$

$$R(5) = \frac{5-1}{24} \times 9\% + \frac{25-5}{24} \times 12\% = 11.5\%$$

$$R(10) = \frac{10-1}{24} \times 9\% + \frac{25-10}{24} \times 12\% = 10.875\%$$

Thus, we see that 1-year, 5-year, and 10-year forecasts are 12 percent, 11.5 percent, and 10.875 percent, respectively.

As a practical matter, Blume's formula says that if you are using averages calculated over a long period (such as the 82 years we use) to forecast up to a decade or so into the future, then you should use the arithmetic average. If you are forecasting a few decades into the future (as you might do for retirement planning), then you should just split the difference between the arithmetic and geometric average returns. Finally, if for some reason you are doing very long forecasts covering many decades, use the geometric average.

This concludes our discussion of geometric versus arithmetic averages. One last note: In the future, when we say "average return," we mean arithmetic unless we explicitly say otherwise.

Concept Questions

12.5a If you wanted to forecast what the stock market is going to do over the next year, should you use an arithmetic or geometric average?

12.5b If you wanted to forecast what the stock market is going to do over the next century, should you use an arithmetic or geometric average?

Capital Market Efficiency   12.6

Capital market history suggests that the market values of stocks and bonds can fluctuate widely from year to year. Why does this occur? At least part of the answer is that prices change because new information arrives, and investors reassess asset values based on that information.

The behavior of market prices has been extensively studied. A question that has received particular attention is whether prices adjust quickly and correctly when new information arrives. A market is said to be "efficient" if this is the case. To be more precise, in an **efficient capital market**, current market prices fully reflect available information. By this we simply mean that, based on available information, there is no reason to believe that the current price is too low or too high.

efficient capital market
A market in which security prices reflect available information.

The concept of market efficiency is a rich one, and much has been written about it. A full discussion of the subject goes beyond the scope of our study of corporate finance. However, because the concept figures so prominently in studies of market history, we briefly describe the key points here.

PRICE BEHAVIOR IN AN EFFICIENT MARKET

To illustrate how prices behave in an efficient market, suppose the F-Stop Camera Corporation (FCC) has, through years of secret research and development, developed a camera with an autofocusing system whose speed will double that of the autofocusing systems now available. FCC's capital budgeting analysis suggests that launching the new camera will be

FIGURE 12.13

Reaction of Stock Price to New Information in Efficient and Inefficient Markets

Efficient market reaction: The price instantaneously adjusts to and fully reflects new information; there is no tendency for subsequent increases and decreases to occur.
Delayed reaction: The price partially adjusts to the new information; eight days elapse before the price completely reflects the new information.
Overreaction: The price overadjusts to the new information; it overshoots the new price and subsequently corrects.

a highly profitable move; in other words, the NPV appears to be positive and substantial. The key assumption thus far is that FCC has not released any information about the new system; so, the fact of its existence is "inside" information only.

Now consider a share of stock in FCC. In an efficient market, its price reflects what is known about FCC's current operations and profitability, and it reflects market opinion about FCC's potential for future growth and profits. The value of the new autofocusing system is not reflected, however, because the market is unaware of the system's existence.

If the market agrees with FCC's assessment of the value of the new project, FCC's stock price will rise when the decision to launch is made public. For example, assume the announcement is made in a press release on Wednesday morning. In an efficient market, the price of shares in FCC will adjust quickly to this new information. Investors should not be able to buy the stock on Wednesday afternoon and make a profit on Thursday. This would imply that it took the stock market a full day to realize the implication of the FCC press release. If the market is efficient, the price of shares of FCC stock on Wednesday afternoon will already reflect the information contained in the Wednesday morning press release.

Figure 12.13 presents three possible stock price adjustments for FCC. In Figure 12.13, day 0 represents the announcement day. As illustrated, before the announcement, FCC's stock sells for $140 per share. The NPV per share of the new system is, say, $40, so the new price will be $180 once the value of the new project is fully reflected.

The solid line in Figure 12.13 represents the path taken by the stock price in an efficient market. In this case, the price adjusts immediately to the new information and no further changes in the price of the stock take place. The broken line in Figure 12.13 depicts a delayed reaction. Here it takes the market eight days or so to fully absorb the information. Finally, the dotted line illustrates an overreaction and subsequent adjustment to the correct price.

The broken line and the dotted line in Figure 12.13 illustrate paths that the stock price might take in an inefficient market. If, for example, stock prices don't adjust immediately to new information (the broken line), then buying stock immediately following the release of new information and then selling it several days later would be a positive NPV activity because the price is too low for several days after the announcement.

THE EFFICIENT MARKETS HYPOTHESIS

The **efficient markets hypothesis (EMH)** asserts that well-organized capital markets, such as the NYSE, are efficient markets, at least as a practical matter. In other words, an advocate of the EMH might argue that although inefficiencies may exist, they are relatively small and not common.

If a market is efficient, then there is a very important implication for market participants: All investments in that market are *zero* NPV investments. The reason is not complicated. If prices are neither too low nor too high, then the difference between the market value of an investment and its cost is zero; hence, the NPV is zero. As a result, in an efficient market, investors get exactly what they pay for when they buy securities, and firms receive exactly what their stocks and bonds are worth when they sell them.

What makes a market efficient is competition among investors. Many individuals spend their entire lives trying to find mispriced stocks. For any given stock, they study what has happened in the past to the stock price and the stock's dividends. They learn, to the extent possible, what a company's earnings have been, how much the company owes to creditors, what taxes it pays, what businesses it is in, what new investments are planned, how sensitive it is to changes in the economy, and so on.

Not only is there a great deal to know about any particular company, but there is also a powerful incentive for knowing it—namely, the profit motive. If you know more about some company than other investors in the marketplace, you can profit from that knowledge by investing in the company's stock if you have good news and by selling it if you have bad news.

The logical consequence of all this information gathering and analysis is that mispriced stocks will become fewer and fewer. In other words, because of competition among investors, the market will become increasingly efficient. A kind of equilibrium comes into being with which there is just enough mispricing around for those who are best at identifying it to make a living at it. For most other investors, the activity of information gathering and analysis will not pay.[5]

SOME COMMON MISCONCEPTIONS ABOUT THE EMH

No other idea in finance has attracted as much attention as that of efficient markets, and not all of the attention has been flattering. Rather than rehash the arguments here, we will be content to observe that some markets are more efficient than others. For example, financial markets on the whole are probably much more efficient than real asset markets.

Having said this, however, we can also say that much of the criticism of the EMH is misguided because it is based on a misunderstanding of what the hypothesis says and what it doesn't say. For example, when the notion of market efficiency was first publicized and debated in the popular financial press, it was often characterized by words to the effect that

efficient markets hypothesis (EMH)
The hypothesis that actual capital markets, such as the NYSE, are efficient.

 Look under the "Contents" link at www.investorhome.com *for more info on the EMH.*

---

[5]The idea behind the EMH can be illustrated by the following short story: A student was walking down the hall with her finance professor when they both saw a $20 bill on the ground. As the student bent down to pick it up, the professor shook his head slowly and, with a look of disappointment on his face, said patiently to the student, "Don't bother. If it were really there, someone else would have picked it up already." The moral of the story reflects the logic of the efficient markets hypothesis: If you think you have found a pattern in stock prices or a simple device for picking winners, you probably have not.

The concept of an efficient market is a special application of the "no free lunch" principle. In an efficient financial market, costless trading policies will not generate "excess" returns. After adjusting for the riskiness of the policy, the trader's return will be no larger than the return of a randomly selected portfolio, at least on average.

This is often thought to imply something about the amount of "information" reflected in asset prices. However, it really doesn't mean that prices reflect all information nor even that they reflect publicly available information. Instead it means that the connection between unreflected information and prices is too subtle and tenuous to be easily or costlessly detected.

Relevant information is difficult and expensive to uncover and evaluate. Thus, if costless trading policies are ineffective, there must exist some traders who make a living by "beating the market." They cover their costs (including the opportunity cost of their time) by trading. The existence of such traders is actually a necessary precondition for markets to become efficient. Without such professional traders, prices would fail to reflect everything that is cheap and easy to evaluate.

Efficient market prices should approximate a random walk, meaning that they will appear to fluctuate more or less randomly. Prices can fluctuate nonrandomly to the extent that their departure from randomness is expensive to discern. Also, observed price series can depart from apparent randomness due to changes in preferences and expectations, but this is really a technicality and does not imply a free lunch relative to current investor sentiments.

Richard Roll is Allstate Professor of Finance at UCLA. He is a preeminent financial researcher, and he has written extensively in almost every area of modern finance. He is particularly well known for his insightful analyses and great creativity in understanding empirical phenomena.

"throwing darts at the financial page will produce a portfolio that can be expected to do as well as any managed by professional security analysts."[6]

Confusion over statements of this sort has often led to a failure to understand the implications of market efficiency. For example, sometimes it is wrongly argued that market efficiency means that it doesn't matter how you invest your money because the efficiency of the market will protect you from making a mistake. However, a random dart thrower might wind up with all of the darts sticking into one or two high-risk stocks that deal in genetic engineering. Would you really want all of your money in two such stocks?

A contest run by *The Wall Street Journal* provides a good example of the controversy surrounding market efficiency. Each month, the *Journal* asked four professional money managers to pick one stock each. At the same time, it threw four darts at the stock page to select a comparison group. In the 147 five-and one-half month contests from July 1990 to September 2002, the pros won 90 times.

The fact that the pros are ahead of the darts by 90 to 57 suggests that markets are not efficient. Or does it? One problem is that the darts naturally tend to select stocks of average risk. The pros, however, are playing to win and naturally select riskier stocks, or so it is argued. If this is true, then, on average, we *expect* the pros to win. Furthermore, the pros' picks are announced to the public at the start. This publicity may boost the prices of the shares involved somewhat, leading to a partially self-fulfilling prophecy. Unfortunately, the *Journal* discontinued the contest in 2002, so this test of market efficiency is no longer ongoing.

More than anything else, what efficiency implies is that the price a firm will obtain when it sells a share of its stock is a "fair" price in the sense that it reflects the value of that stock given the information available about the firm. Shareholders do not have to worry that they are paying too much for a stock with a low dividend or some other sort of characteristic

---

[6]B. G. Malkiel, *A Random Walk Down Wall Street,* (revised and updated ed.) (New York: Norton, 2003).

because the market has already incorporated that characteristic into the price. We sometimes say that the information has been "priced out."

The concept of efficient markets can be explained further by replying to a frequent objection. It is sometimes argued that the market cannot be efficient because stock prices fluctuate from day to day. If the prices are right, the argument goes, then why do they change so much and so often? From our discussion of the market, we can see that these price movements are in no way inconsistent with efficiency. Investors are bombarded with information every day. The fact that prices fluctuate is, at least in part, a reflection of that information flow. In fact, the absence of price movements in a world that changes as rapidly as ours would suggest inefficiency.

THE FORMS OF MARKET EFFICIENCY

It is common to distinguish between three forms of market efficiency. Depending on the degree of efficiency, we say that markets are either *weak form efficient, semistrong form efficient,* or *strong form efficient.* The difference between these forms relates to what information is reflected in prices.

We start with the extreme case. If the market is strong form efficient, then *all* information of *every* kind is reflected in stock prices. In such a market, there is no such thing as inside information. Therefore, in our FCC example, we apparently were assuming that the market was not strong form efficient.

Casual observation, particularly in recent years, suggests that inside information does exist, and it can be valuable to possess. Whether it is lawful or ethical to use that information is another issue. In any event, we conclude that private information about a particular stock may exist that is not currently reflected in the price of the stock. For example, prior knowledge of a takeover attempt could be very valuable.

The second form of efficiency, semistrong form efficiency, is the most controversial. If a market is semistrong form efficient, then all *public* information is reflected in the stock price. The reason this form is controversial is that it implies that a security analyst who tries to identify mispriced stocks using, for example, financial statement information, is wasting time because that information is already reflected in the current price.

The third form of efficiency, weak form efficiency, suggests that, at a minimum, the current price of a stock reflects the stock's own past prices. In other words, studying past prices in an attempt to identify mispriced securities is futile if the market is weak form efficient. Although this form of efficiency might seem rather mild, it implies that searching for patterns in historical prices that will be useful in identifying mispriced stocks will not work (this practice is quite common).

What does capital market history say about market efficiency? Here again, there is great controversy. At the risk of going out on a limb, we can say that the evidence seems to tell us three things. First, prices appear to respond rapidly to new information, and the response is at least not grossly different from what we would expect in an efficient market. Second, the future of market prices, particularly in the short run, is difficult to predict based on publicly available information. Third, if mispriced stocks exist, then there is no obvious means of identifying them. Put another way, simpleminded schemes based on public information will probably not be successful.

Concept Questions

12.6a What is an efficient market?

12.6b What are the forms of market efficiency?

Visit us at www.mhhe.com/rwj

12.7 Summary and Conclusions

This chapter has explored the subject of capital market history. Such history is useful because it tells us what to expect in the way of returns from risky assets. We summed up our study of market history with two key lessons:

1. Risky assets, on average, earn a risk premium. There is a reward for bearing risk.
2. The greater the potential reward from a risky investment, the greater is the risk.

These lessons have significant implications for the financial manager. We will consider these implications in the chapters ahead.

   We also discussed the concept of market efficiency. In an efficient market, prices adjust quickly and correctly to new information. Consequently, asset prices in efficient markets are rarely too high or too low. How efficient capital markets (such as the NYSE) are is a matter of debate; but, at a minimum, they are probably much more efficient than most real asset markets.

CHAPTER REVIEW AND SELF-TEST PROBLEMS

12.1 Recent Return History Use Table 12.1 to calculate the average return over the years 1996 through 2000 for large-company stocks, long-term government bonds, and Treasury bills.

12.2 More Recent Return History Calculate the standard deviation for each security type using information from Problem 12.1. Which of the investments was the most volatile over this period?

ANSWERS TO CHAPTER REVIEW AND SELF-TEST PROBLEMS

12.1 We calculate the averages as follows:

	Actual Returns		
Year	Large-Company Stocks	Long-Term Government Bonds	Treasury Bills
1996	.2296	.0013	.0514
1997	.3336	.1202	.0519
1998	.2858	.1445	.0486
1999	.2104	−.0751	.0480
2000	−.0901	.1722	.0598
Average	.19386	.0726	.0519

12.2 We first need to calculate the deviations from the average returns. Using the averages from Problem 12.1, we get the following values:

Deviations from Average Returns			
Year	Large-Company Stocks	Long-Term Government Bonds	Treasury Bills
1996	.0357	−.0713	−.0005
1997	.1397	.0476	.0000
1998	.0919	.0719	−.0033
1999	.0165	−.1477	−.0039
2000	−.2840	.0996	.0079
Total	.0000	.0000	.0000

We square these deviations and calculate the variances and standard deviations:

Squared Deviations from Average Returns			
Year	Large-Company Stocks	Long-Term Government Bonds	Treasury Bills
1996	.0012773	.0050865	.0000003
1997	.0195273	.0022639	.0000000
1998	.0084530	.0051667	.0000112
1999	.0002736	.0218212	.0000155
2000	.0806333	.0099162	.0000618
Variance	.0275411	.0110636	.0000222
Std dev	.1659551	.1051838	.0047104

To calculate the variances, we added up the squared deviations and divided by 4, the number of returns less 1. Notice that the stocks had much more volatility than the bonds with a much larger average return. For large-company stocks, this was a particularly good period: The average return was 19.39 percent.

CONCEPTS REVIEW AND CRITICAL THINKING QUESTIONS

1. **Investment Selection** [LO4] Given that First Solar was up by over 796 percent for 2007, why didn't all investors hold this stock?

2. **Investment Selection** [LO4] Given that Novastar Financial was down by almost 97 percent for 2007, why did some investors hold the stock? Why didn't they sell out before the price declined so sharply?

3. **Risk and Return** [LO2, 3] We have seen that over long periods, stock investments have tended to substantially outperform bond investments. However, it is common to observe investors with long horizons holding entirely bonds. Are such investors irrational?

4. **Market Efficiency Implications** [LO4] Explain why a characteristic of an efficient market is that investments in that market have zero NPVs.

5. **Efficient Markets Hypothesis** [LO4] A stock market analyst is able to identify mispriced stocks by comparing the average price for the last 10 days to the average price for the last 60 days. If this is true, what do you know about the market?

Visit us at www.mhhe.com/rwj

6. **Semistrong Efficiency** [LO4] If a market is semistrong form efficient, is it also weak form efficient? Explain.

7. **Efficient Markets Hypothesis** [LO4] What are the implications of the efficient markets hypothesis for investors who buy and sell stocks in an attempt to "beat the market"?

8. **Stocks versus Gambling** [LO4] Critically evaluate the following statement: Playing the stock market is like gambling. Such speculative investing has no social value other than the pleasure people get from this form of gambling.

9. **Efficient Markets Hypothesis** [LO4] Several celebrated investors and stock pickers frequently mentioned in the financial press have recorded huge returns on their investments over the past two decades. Is the success of these particular investors an invalidation of the EMH? Explain.

10. **Efficient Markets Hypothesis** [LO4] For each of the following scenarios, discuss whether profit opportunities exist from trading in the stock of the firm under the conditions that (1) the market is not weak form efficient, (2) the market is weak form but not semistrong form efficient, (3) the market is semistrong form but not strong form efficient, and (4) the market is strong form efficient.

    a. The stock price has risen steadily each day for the past 30 days.

    b. The financial statements for a company were released three days ago, and you believe you've uncovered some anomalies in the company's inventory and cost control reporting techniques that are causing the firm's true liquidity strength to be understated.

    c. You observe that the senior managers of a company have been buying a lot of the company's stock on the open market over the past week.

QUESTIONS AND PROBLEMS ᕼᕱᴹ

BASIC
(Questions 1–12)

1. **Calculating Returns** [LO1] Suppose a stock had an initial price of $91 per share, paid a dividend of $2.40 per share during the year, and had an ending share price of $102. Compute the percentage total return.

2. **Calculating Yields** [LO1] In Problem 1, what was the dividend yield? The capital gains yield?

3. **Return Calculations** [LO1] Rework Problems 1 and 2 assuming the ending share price is $83.

4. **Calculating Returns** [LO1] Suppose you bought a 7 percent coupon bond one year ago for $1,040. The bond sells for $1,070 today.

    a. Assuming a $1,000 face value, what was your total dollar return on this investment over the past year?

    b. What was your total nominal rate of return on this investment over the past year?

    c. If the inflation rate last year was 4 percent, what was your total real rate of return on this investment?

5. **Nominal versus Real Returns** [LO2] What was the average annual return on large-company stock from 1926 through 2007:

    a. In nominal terms?

    b. In real terms?

6. **Bond Returns** [LO2] What is the historical real return on long-term government bonds? On long-term corporate bonds?

7. **Calculating Returns and Variability** [LO1] Using the following returns, calculate the arithmetic average returns, the variances, and the standard deviations for X and Y.

	Returns	
Year	X	Y
1	8%	16%
2	21	38
3	17	14
4	−16	−21
5	9	26

8. **Risk Premiums** [LO2, 3] Refer to Table 12.1 in the text and look at the period from 1970 through 1975.

   a. Calculate the arithmetic average returns for large-company stocks and T-bills over this period.

   b. Calculate the standard deviation of the returns for large-company stocks and T-bills over this period.

   c. Calculate the observed risk premium in each year for the large-company stocks versus the T-bills. What was the average risk premium over this period? What was the standard deviation of the risk premium over this period?

   d. Is it possible for the risk premium to be negative before an investment is undertaken? Can the risk premium be negative after the fact? Explain.

9. **Calculating Returns and Variability** [LO1] You've observed the following returns on Crash-n-Burn Computer's stock over the past five years: 7 percent, −12 percent, 11 percent, 38 percent, and 14 percent.

   a. What was the arithmetic average return on Crash-n-Burn's stock over this five-year period?

   b. What was the variance of Crash-n-Burn's returns over this period? The standard deviation?

10. **Calculating Real Returns and Risk Premiums** [LO1] For Problem 9, suppose the average inflation rate over this period was 3.5 percent and the average T-bill rate over the period was 4.2 percent.

   a. What was the average real return on Crash-n-Burn's stock?

   b. What was the average nominal risk premium on Crash-n-Burn's stock?

11. **Calculating Real Rates** [LO1] Given the information in Problem 10, what was the average real risk-free rate over this time period? What was the average real risk premium?

12. **Effects of Inflation** [LO2] Look at Table 12.1 and Figure 12.7 in the text. When were T-bill rates at their highest over the period from 1926 through 2007? Why do you think they were so high during this period? What relationship underlies your answer?

13. **Calculating Investment Returns** [LO1] You bought one of Great White Shark Repellant Co.'s 8 percent coupon bonds one year ago for $1,030. These bonds make annual payments and mature six years from now. Suppose you decide to sell your

INTERMEDIATE
(Questions 13–22)

bonds today, when the required return on the bonds is 7 percent. If the inflation rate was 4.2 percent over the past year, what was your total real return on investment?

14. **Calculating Returns and Variability** [LO1] You find a certain stock that had returns of 7 percent, −12 percent, 18 percent, and 19 percent for four of the last five years. If the average return of the stock over this period was 10.5 percent, what was the stock's return for the missing year? What is the standard deviation of the stock's return?

15. **Arithmetic and Geometric Returns** [LO1] A stock has had returns of 3 percent, 38 percent, 21 percent, −15 percent, 29 percent, and −13 percent over the last six years. What are the arithmetic and geometric returns for the stock?

16. **Arithmetic and Geometric Returns** [LO1] A stock has had the following year-end prices and dividends:

Year	Price	Dividend
1	$60.18	–
2	73.66	$ .60
3	94.18	.64
4	89.35	.72
5	78.49	.80
6	95.05	1.20

What are the arithmetic and geometric returns for the stock?

17. **Using Return Distributions** [LO3] Suppose the returns on long-term corporate bonds are normally distributed. Based on the historical record, what is the approximate probability that your return on these bonds will be less than −2.2 percent in a given year? What range of returns would you expect to see 95 percent of the time? What range would you expect to see 99 percent of the time?

18. **Using Return Distributions** [LO3] Assuming that the returns from holding small-company stocks are normally distributed, what is the approximate probability that your money will double in value in a single year? What about triple in value?

19. **Distributions** [LO3] In Problem 18, what is the probability that the return is less than −100 percent (think)? What are the implications for the distribution of returns?

20. **Blume's Formula** [LO1] Over a 40-year period an asset had an arithmetic return of 15.3 percent and a geometric return of 11.9 percent. Using Blume's formula, what is your best estimate of the future annual returns over 5 years? 10 years? 20 years?

21. **Blume's Formula** [LO1, 2] Assume that the historical return on large-company stocks is a predictor of the future returns. What return would you estimate for large-company stocks over the next year? The next 5 years? 20 years? 30 years?

22. **Calculating Returns** [LO2, 3] Refer to Table 12.1 in the text and look at the period from 1973 through 1980:

   a. Calculate the average return for Treasury bills and the average annual inflation rate (consumer price index) for this period.

   b. Calculate the standard deviation of Treasury bill returns and inflation over this period.

   c. Calculate the real return for each year. What is the average real return for Treasury bills?

   d. Many people consider Treasury bills risk-free. What do these calculations tell you about the potential risks of Treasury bills?

23. **Using Probability Distributions** [LO3] Suppose the returns on large-company stocks are normally distributed. Based on the historical record, use the cumulative normal probability table (rounded to the nearest table value) in the appendix of the text to determine the probability that in any given year you will lose money by investing in common stock.

CHALLENGE
(Questions 23–24)

24. **Using Probability Distributions** [LO3] Suppose the returns on long-term corporate bonds and T-bills are normally distributed. Based on the historical record, use the cumulative normal probability table (rounded to the nearest table value) in the appendix of the text to answer the following questions:

    a. What is the probability that in any given year, the return on long-term corporate bonds will be greater than 10 percent? Less than 0 percent?

    b. What is the probability that in any given year, the return on T-bills will be greater than 10 percent? Less than 0 percent?

    c. In 1979, the return on long-term corporate bonds was −4.18 percent. How likely is it that such a low return will recur at some point in the future? T-bills had a return of 10.56 percent in this same year. How likely is it that such a high return on T-bills will recur at some point in the future?

MINICASE

A Job at S&S Air

You recently graduated from college, and your job search led you to S&S Air. Because you felt the company's business was taking off, you accepted a job offer. The first day on the job, while you are finishing your employment paperwork, Chris Guthrie, who works in Finance, stops by to inform you about the company's 401(k) plan.

A 401(k) plan is a retirement plan offered by many companies. Such plans are tax-deferred savings vehicles, meaning that any deposits you make into the plan are deducted from your current pretax income, so no current taxes are paid on the money. For example, assume your salary will be $50,000 per year. If you contribute $3,000 to the 401(k) plan, you will pay taxes on only $47,000 in income. There are also no taxes paid on any capital gains or income while you are invested in the plan, but you do pay taxes when you withdraw money at retirement. As is fairly common, the company also has a 5 percent match. This means that the company will match your contribution up to 5 percent of your salary, but you must contribute to get the match.

The 401(k) plan has several options for investments, most of which are mutual funds. A mutual fund is a portfolio of assets. When you purchase shares in a mutual fund, you are actually purchasing partial ownership of the fund's assets. The return of the fund is the weighted average of the return of the assets owned by the fund, minus any expenses. The largest expense is typically the management fee, paid to the fund manager. The management fee is compensation for the manager, who makes all of the investment decisions for the fund.

S&S Air uses Bledsoe Financial Services as its 401(k) plan administrator. Here are the investment options offered for employees:

Company Stock One option in the 401(k) plan is stock in S&S Air. The company is currently privately held. However, when you interviewed with the owners, Mark Sexton and Todd Story, they informed you the company stock was expected to go public in the next three to four years. Until then, a company stock price is simply set each year by the board of directors.

Bledsoe S&P 500 Index Fund This mutual fund tracks the S&P 500. Stocks in the fund are weighted exactly the same as the S&P 500. This means the fund return is approximately the return on the S&P 500, minus expenses. Because an index fund purchases assets based on the composition of the index it is following, the fund manager is not required to research stocks and make investment decisions. The result is that the fund expenses are usually low. The Bledsoe S&P 500 Index Fund charges expenses of .15 percent of assets per year.

Bledsoe Small-Cap Fund This fund primarily invests in small-capitalization stocks. As such, the returns of the fund are more volatile. The fund can also invest 10 percent of its assets in companies based outside the United States. This fund charges 1.70 percent in expenses.

Visit us at www.mhhe.com/rwj

Bledsoe Large-Company Stock Fund This fund invests primarily in large-capitalization stocks of companies based in the United States. The fund is managed by Evan Bledsoe and has outperformed the market in six of the last eight years. The fund charges 1.50 percent in expenses.

Bledsoe Bond Fund This fund invests in long-term corporate bonds issued by U.S-domiciled companies. The fund is restricted to investments in bonds with an investment-grade credit rating. This fund charges 1.40 percent in expenses.

Bledsoe Money Market Fund This fund invests in short-term, high credit-quality debt instruments, which include Treasury bills. As such, the return on the money market fund is only slightly higher than the return on Treasury bills. Because of the credit quality and short-term nature of the investments, there is only a very slight risk of negative return. The fund charges .60 percent in expenses.

QUESTIONS

1. What advantages do the mutual funds offer compared to the company stock?

2. Assume that you invest 5 percent of your salary and receive the full 5 percent match from S&S Air. What EAR do you earn from the match? What conclusions do you draw about matching plans?

3. Assume you decide you should invest at least part of your money in large-capitalization stocks of companies based in the United States. What are the advantages and disadvantages of choosing the Bledsoe Large-Company Stock Fund compared to the Bledsoe S&P 500 Index Fund?

4. The returns on the Bledsoe Small-Cap Fund are the most volatile of all the mutual funds offered in the 401(k) plan. Why would you ever want to invest in this fund? When you examine the expenses of the mutual funds, you will notice that this fund also has the highest expenses. Does this affect your decision to invest in this fund?

5. A measure of risk-adjusted performance that is often used is the Sharpe ratio. The Sharpe ratio is calculated as the risk premium of an asset divided by its standard deviation. The standard deviation and return of the funds over the past 10 years are listed in the following table. Calculate the Sharpe ratio for each of these funds. Assume that the expected return and standard deviation of the company stock will be 18 percent and 70 percent, respectively. Calculate the Sharpe ratio for the company stock. How appropriate is the Sharpe ratio for these assets? When would you use the Sharpe ratio?

	10-Year Annual Return	Standard Deviation
Bledsoe S&P 500 Index Fund	11.48%	15.82%
Bledsoe Small-Cap Fund	16.68	19.64
Bledsoe Large-Company Stock Fund	11.85	15.41
Bledsoe Bond Fund	9.67	10.83

6. What portfolio allocation would you choose? Why? Explain your thinking carefully.

Visit us at www.mhhe.com/rwj

LEARNING OBJECTIVES

After studying this chapter, you should understand:

LO1 How to calculate expected returns.
LO2 The impact of diversification.
LO3 The systematic risk principle.
LO4 The security market line and the risk-return trade-off.

RETURN, RISK, AND THE SECURITY MARKET LINE

13

IN MAY OF 2008, ExxonMobil, Hormel Foods (maker of authentic Spam), and BJ's Wholesale Club joined a host of other companies in announcing earnings. ExxonMobil announced a record first quarter profit of $10.9 billion, while Hormel and BJ's announced earnings increases of 14 percent and 26 percent, respectively. You would expect earnings increases to be good news, and they usually are. Even so, ExxonMobil's stock price dropped 3.6 percent. A similar fate awaited Hormel and BJ's. Their stock prices fell by 3.9 percent and 2.1 percent, respectively.

The news for these companies seems positive, but the stock prices fell for all three. So when is good news really good news? The answer is fundamental to understanding risk and return, and—the good news is—this chapter explores it in some detail.

Master the ability to solve problems in this chapter by using a spreadsheet. Access Excel Master on the student Web site www.mhhe.com/rwj.

In our last chapter, we learned some important lessons from capital market history. Most important, we learned that there is a reward, on average, for bearing risk. We called this reward a *risk premium*. The second lesson is that this risk premium is larger for riskier investments. This chapter explores the economic and managerial implications of this basic idea.

Thus far, we have concentrated mainly on the return behavior of a few large portfolios. We need to expand our consideration to include individual assets. Specifically, we have two tasks to accomplish. First, we have to define risk and discuss how to measure it. We then must quantify the relationship between an asset's risk and its required return.

When we examine the risks associated with individual assets, we find there are two types of risk: systematic and unsystematic. This distinction is crucial because, as we will see, systematic risk affects almost all assets in the economy, at least to some degree, whereas unsystematic risk affects at most a small number of assets. We then develop the principle of diversification, which shows that highly diversified portfolios will tend to have almost no unsystematic risk.

The principle of diversification has an important implication: To a diversified investor, only systematic risk matters. It follows that in deciding whether to buy a particular individual asset, a diversified investor will only be concerned with that asset's systematic risk. This is a key observation, and it allows us to say a great deal about the risks and returns on individual assets. In particular, it is the basis for a famous relationship between risk and return called the *security market line,* or SML. To develop the SML, we introduce the equally famous "beta" coefficient, one of the centerpieces of modern finance. Beta and the

SML are key concepts because they supply us with at least part of the answer to the question of how to determine the required return on an investment.

13.1 Expected Returns and Variances

In our previous chapter, we discussed how to calculate average returns and variances using historical data. We now begin to discuss how to analyze returns and variances when the information we have concerns future possible returns and their probabilities.

EXPECTED RETURN

We start with a straightforward case. Consider a single period of time—say a year. We have two stocks, L and U, which have the following characteristics: Stock L is expected to have a return of 25 percent in the coming year. Stock U is expected to have a return of 20 percent for the same period.

In a situation like this, if all investors agreed on the expected returns, why would anyone want to hold Stock U? After all, why invest in one stock when the expectation is that another will do better? Clearly, the answer must depend on the risk of the two investments. The return on Stock L, although it is *expected* to be 25 percent, could actually turn out to be higher or lower.

For example, suppose the economy booms. In this case, we think Stock L will have a 70 percent return. If the economy enters a recession, we think the return will be -20 percent. In this case, we say that there are two *states of the economy,* which means that these are the only two possible situations. This setup is oversimplified, of course, but it allows us to illustrate some key ideas without a lot of computation.

Suppose we think a boom and a recession are equally likely to happen, for a 50–50 chance of each. Table 13.1 illustrates the basic information we have described and some additional information about Stock U. Notice that Stock U earns 30 percent if there is a recession and 10 percent if there is a boom.

Obviously, if you buy one of these stocks, say Stock U, what you earn in any particular year depends on what the economy does during that year. However, suppose the probabilities stay the same through time. If you hold Stock U for a number of years, you'll earn 30 percent about half the time and 10 percent the other half. In this case, we say that your **expected return** on Stock U, $E(R_U)$, is 20 percent:

expected return
The return on a risky asset expected in the future.

$$E(R_U) = .50 \times 30\% + .50 \times 10\% = 20\%$$

In other words, you should expect to earn 20 percent from this stock, on average.

For Stock L, the probabilities are the same, but the possible returns are different. Here, we lose 20 percent half the time, and we gain 70 percent the other half. The expected return on L, $E(R_L)$, is thus 25 percent:

$$E(R_L) = .50 \times -20\% + .50 \times 70\% = 25\%$$

Table 13.2 illustrates these calculations.

TABLE 13.1

States of the Economy and Stock Returns

State of Economy	Probability of State of Economy	Rate of Return if State Occurs	
		Stock L	Stock U
Recession	.50	−20%	30%
Boom	.50	70	10
	1.00		

(1) State of Economy	(2) Probability of State of Economy	Stock L		Stock U	
		(3) Rate of Return If State Occurs	(4) Product (2) × (3)	(5) Rate of Return If State Occurs	(6) Product (2) × (5)
Recession	.50	−.20	−.10	.30	.15
Boom	.50	.70	.35	.10	.05
	1.00		$E(R_L) = .25 = 25\%$		$E(R_U) = .20 = 20\%$

TABLE 13.2

Calculation of Expected Return

In our previous chapter, we defined the risk premium as the difference between the return on a risky investment and that on a risk-free investment, and we calculated the historical risk premiums on some different investments. Using our projected returns, we can calculate the *projected*, or *expected*, *risk premium* as the difference between the expected return on a risky investment and the certain return on a risk-free investment.

For example, suppose risk-free investments are currently offering 8 percent. We will say that the risk-free rate, which we label as R_f, is 8 percent. Given this, what is the projected risk premium on Stock U? On Stock L? Because the expected return on Stock U, $E(R_U)$, is 20 percent, the projected risk premium is:

$$\text{Risk premium} = \text{Expected return} - \text{Risk-free rate} \qquad [13.1]$$
$$= E(R_U) - R_f$$
$$= 20\% - 8\%$$
$$= 12\%$$

Similarly, the risk premium on Stock L is $25\% - 8\% = 17\%$.

In general, the expected return on a security or other asset is simply equal to the sum of the possible returns multiplied by their probabilities. So, if we had 100 possible returns, we would multiply each one by its probability and add up the results. The result would be the expected return. The risk premium would then be the difference between this expected return and the risk-free rate.

Unequal Probabilities

EXAMPLE 13.1

Look again at Tables 13.1 and 13.2. Suppose you think a boom will occur only 20 percent of the time instead of 50 percent. What are the expected returns on Stocks U and L in this case? If the risk-free rate is 10 percent, what are the risk premiums?

The first thing to notice is that a recession must occur 80 percent of the time (1 − .20 = .80) because there are only two possibilities. With this in mind, we see that Stock U has a 30 percent return in 80 percent of the years and a 10 percent return in 20 percent of the years. To calculate the expected return, we again just multiply the possibilities by the probabilities and add up the results:

$E(R_U) = .80 \times 30\% + .20 \times 10\% = 26\%$

Table 13.3 summarizes the calculations for both stocks. Notice that the expected return on L is −2 percent.

The risk premium for Stock U is $26\% - 10\% = 16\%$ in this case. The risk premium for Stock L is negative: $-2\% - 10\% = -12\%$. This is a little odd; but, for reasons we discuss later, it is not impossible.

(continued)

TABLE 13.3

Calculation of Expected
Return

(1) State of Economy	(2) Probability of State of Economy	Stock L		Stock U	
		(3) Rate of Return if State Occurs	(4) Product (2) × (3)	(5) Rate of Return if State Occurs	(6) Product (2) × (5)
Recession	.80	−.20	−.16	.30	.24
Boom	.20	.70	.14	.10	.02
			$E(R_L) = -.2\%$		$E(R_U) = .26\%$

CALCULATING THE VARIANCE

To calculate the variances of the returns on our two stocks, we first determine the squared deviations from the expected return. We then multiply each possible squared deviation by its probability. We add these up, and the result is the variance. The standard deviation, as always, is the square root of the variance.

To illustrate, let us return to the Stock U we originally discussed, which has an expected return of $E(R_U) = 20\%$. In a given year, it will actually return either 30 percent or 10 percent. The possible deviations are thus $30\% - 20\% = 10\%$ and $10\% - 20\% = -10\%$. In this case, the variance is:

$$\text{Variance} = \sigma^2 = .50 \times (10\%)^2 + .50 \times (-10\%)^2 = .01$$

The standard deviation is the square root of this:

$$\text{Standard deviation} = \sigma = \sqrt{.01} = .10 = 10\%$$

Table 13.4 summarizes these calculations for both stocks. Notice that Stock L has a much larger variance.

When we put the expected return and variability information for our two stocks together, we have the following:

	Stock L	Stock U
Expected return, $E(R)$	25%	20%
Variance, σ^2	.2025	.0100
Standard deviation, σ	45%	10%

Stock L has a higher expected return, but U has less risk. You could get a 70 percent return on your investment in L, but you could also lose 20 percent. Notice that an investment in U will always pay at least 10 percent.

Which of these two stocks should you buy? We can't really say; it depends on your personal preferences. We can be reasonably sure that some investors would prefer L to U and some would prefer U to L.

You've probably noticed that the way we have calculated expected returns and variances here is somewhat different from the way we did it in the last chapter. The reason is that in Chapter 12, we were examining actual historical returns, so we estimated the average return and the variance based on some actual events. Here, we have projected *future* returns and their associated probabilities, so this is the information with which we must work.

TABLE 13.4

Calculation of Variance

(1) State of Economy	(2) Probability of State of Economy	(3) Return Deviation from Expected Return	(4) Squared Return Deviation from Expected Return	(5) Product (2) × (4)
Stock L				
Recession	.50	$-.20 - .25 = -.45$	$-.45^2 = .2025$	.10125
Boom	.50	$.70 - .25 = .45$	$.45^2 = .2025$	.10125
				$\sigma_L^2 = .20250$
Stock U				
Recession	.50	$.30 - .20 = .10$	$.10^2 = .01$	.005
Boom	.50	$.10 - .20 = -.10$	$-.10^2 = .01$	.005
				$\sigma_U^2 = .010$

EXAMPLE 13.2

More Unequal Probabilities

Going back to Example 13.1, what are the variances on the two stocks once we have unequal probabilities? The standard deviations?

We can summarize the needed calculations as follows:

(1) State of Economy	(2) Probability of State of Economy	(3) Return Deviation from Expected Return	(4) Squared Return Deviation from Expected Return	(5) Product (2) × (4)
Stock L				
Recession	.80	$-.20 - (-.02) = -.18$	.0324	.02592
Boom	.20	$.70 - (-.02) = .72$	.5184	.10368
				$\sigma_L^2 = .12960$
Stock U				
Recession	.80	$.30 - .26 = .04$	.0016	.00128
Boom	.20	$.10 - .26 = -.16$	.0256	.00512
				$\sigma_U^2 = .00640$

Based on these calculations, the standard deviation for L is $\sigma_L = \sqrt{.1296} = .36 = 36\%$. The standard deviation for U is much smaller: $\sigma_U = \sqrt{.0064} = .08$ or 8%.

Concept Questions

13.1a How do we calculate the expected return on a security?

13.1b In words, how do we calculate the variance of the expected return?

Portfolios

13.2

Thus far in this chapter, we have concentrated on individual assets considered separately. However, most investors actually hold a **portfolio** of assets. All we mean by this is that investors tend to own more than just a single stock, bond, or other asset. Given that this is so, portfolio return and portfolio risk are of obvious relevance. Accordingly, we now discuss portfolio expected returns and variances.

portfolio
A group of assets such as stocks and bonds held by an investor.

TABLE 13.5

Expected Return on an Equally Weighted Portfolio of Stock L and Stock U

(1) State of Economy	(2) Probability of State of Economy	(3) Portfolio Return if State Occurs	(4) Product (2) × (3)
Recession	.50	$.50 \times -20\% + .50 \times 30\% = 5\%$	.025
Boom	.50	$.50 \times 70\% + .50 \times 10\% = 40\%$	.200
			$E(R_p) = 22.5\%$

PORTFOLIO WEIGHTS

portfolio weight
The percentage of a portfolio's total value that is in a particular asset.

There are many equivalent ways of describing a portfolio. The most convenient approach is to list the percentage of the total portfolio's value that is invested in each portfolio asset. We call these percentages the **portfolio weights**.

For example, if we have $50 in one asset and $150 in another, our total portfolio is worth $200. The percentage of our portfolio in the first asset is $50/$200 = .25. The percentage of our portfolio in the second asset is $150/$200, or .75. Our portfolio weights are thus .25 and .75. Notice that the weights have to add up to 1.00 because all of our money is invested somewhere.[1]

PORTFOLIO EXPECTED RETURNS

Let's go back to Stocks L and U. You put half your money in each. The portfolio weights are obviously .50 and .50. What is the pattern of returns on this portfolio? The expected return?

To answer these questions, suppose the economy actually enters a recession. In this case, half your money (the half in L) loses 20 percent. The other half (the half in U) gains 30 percent. Your portfolio return, R_p, in a recession is thus:

$$R_p = .50 \times -20\% + .50 \times 30\% = 5\%$$

Table 13.5 summarizes the remaining calculations. Notice that when a boom occurs, your portfolio will return 40 percent:

$$R_p = .50 \times 70\% + .50 \times 10\% = 40\%$$

As indicated in Table 13.5, the expected return on your portfolio, $E(R_p)$, is 22.5 percent.

We can save ourselves some work by calculating the expected return more directly. Given these portfolio weights, we could have reasoned that we expect half of our money to earn 25 percent (the half in L) and half of our money to earn 20 percent (the half in U). Our portfolio expected return is thus:

$$E(R_p) = .50 \times E(R_L) + .50 \times E(R_U)$$
$$= .50 \times 25\% + .50 \times 20\%$$
$$= 22.5\%$$

Want more information about investing? Visit www.thestreet.com.

This is the same portfolio expected return we calculated previously.

This method of calculating the expected return on a portfolio works no matter how many assets there are in the portfolio. Suppose we had n assets in our portfolio, where n is any number. If we let x_i stand for the percentage of our money in Asset i, then the expected return would be:

$$E(R_p) = x_1 \times E(R_1) + x_2 \times E(R_2) + \cdots + x_n \times E(R_n) \qquad [13.2]$$

---

[1] Some of it could be in cash, of course, but we would then just consider the cash to be one of the portfolio assets.

This says that the expected return on a portfolio is a straightforward combination of the expected returns on the assets in that portfolio. This seems somewhat obvious; but, as we will examine next, the obvious approach is not always the right one.

| | | EXAMPLE 13.3 |

Portfolio Expected Return

Suppose we have the following projections for three stocks:

State of Economy	Probability of State of Economy	Returns if State Occurs		
		Stock A	Stock B	Stock C
Boom	.40	10%	15%	20%
Bust	.60	8	4	0

We want to calculate portfolio expected returns in two cases. First, what would be the expected return on a portfolio with equal amounts invested in each of the three stocks? Second, what would be the expected return if half of the portfolio were in A, with the remainder equally divided between B and C?

Based on what we've learned from our earlier discussions, we can determine that the expected returns on the individual stocks are (check these for practice):

$E(R_A) = 8.8\%$

$E(R_B) = 8.4\%$

$E(R_C) = 8.0\%$

If a portfolio has equal investments in each asset, the portfolio weights are all the same. Such a portfolio is said to be *equally weighted.* Because there are three stocks in this case, the weights are all equal to ⅓. The portfolio expected return is thus:

$E(R_P) = (1/3) \times 8.8\% + (1/3) \times 8.4\% + (1/3) \times 8\% = 8.4\%$

In the second case, verify that the portfolio expected return is 8.5 percent.

PORTFOLIO VARIANCE

From our earlier discussion, the expected return on a portfolio that contains equal investments in Stocks U and L is 22.5 percent. What is the standard deviation of return on this portfolio? Simple intuition might suggest that because half of the money has a standard deviation of 45 percent and the other half has a standard deviation of 10 percent, the portfolio's standard deviation might be calculated as:

$\sigma_P = .50 \times 45\% + .50 \times 10\% = 27.5\%$

Unfortunately, this approach is completely incorrect!

Let's see what the standard deviation really is. Table 13.6 summarizes the relevant calculations. As we see, the portfolio's variance is about .031, and its standard deviation is less than we thought—it's only 17.5 percent. What is illustrated here is that the variance on a portfolio is not generally a simple combination of the variances of the assets in the portfolio.

We can illustrate this point a little more dramatically by considering a slightly different set of portfolio weights. Suppose we put 2/11 (about 18 percent) in L and the other 9/11 (about 82 percent) in U. If a recession occurs, this portfolio will have a return of:

$R_P = (2/11) \times -20\% + (9/11) \times 30\% = 20.91\%$

TABLE 13.6

Variance on an Equally Weighted Portfolio of Stock L and Stock U

(1) State of Economy	(2) Probability of State of Economy	(3) Portfolio Return if State Occurs	(4) Squared Deviation from Expected Return	(5) Product (2) × (4)
Recession	.50	5%	$(.05 - .225)^2 = .030625$	.0153125
Boom	.50	40	$(.40 - .225)^2 = .030625$	.0153125
			$\sigma_P^2 = .030625$	
			$\sigma_P = \sqrt{.030625} = 17.5\%$	

If a boom occurs, this portfolio will have a return of:

$$R_p = (2/11) \times 70\% + (9/11) \times 10\% = 20.91\%$$

Notice that the return is the same no matter what happens. No further calculations are needed: This portfolio has a zero variance. Apparently, combining assets into portfolios can substantially alter the risks faced by the investor. This is a crucial observation, and we will begin to explore its implications in the next section.

EXAMPLE 13.4 | **Portfolio Variance and Standard Deviation**

In Example 13.3, what are the standard deviations on the two portfolios? To answer, we first have to calculate the portfolio returns in the two states. We will work with the second portfolio, which has 50 percent in Stock A and 25 percent in each of Stocks B and C. The relevant calculations can be summarized as follows:

State of Economy	Probability of State of Economy	Rate of Return if State Occurs			
		Stock A	Stock B	Stock C	Portfolio
Boom	.40	10%	15%	20%	13.75%
Bust	.60	8	4	0	5.00

The portfolio return when the economy booms is calculated as:

$$E(R_p) = .50 \times 10\% + .25 \times 15\% + .25 \times 20\% = 13.75\%$$

The return when the economy goes bust is calculated the same way. The expected return on the portfolio is 8.5 percent. The variance is thus:

$$\sigma_P^2 = .40 \times (.1375 - .085)^2 + .60 \times (.05 - .085)^2$$
$$= .0018375$$

The standard deviation is thus about 4.3 percent. For our equally weighted portfolio, check to see that the standard deviation is about 5.4 percent.

Concept Questions

13.2a What is a portfolio weight?

13.2b How do we calculate the expected return on a portfolio?

13.2c Is there a simple relationship between the standard deviation on a portfolio and the standard deviations of the assets in the portfolio?

Announcements, Surprises, and Expected Returns

Now that we know how to construct portfolios and evaluate their returns, we begin to describe more carefully the risks and returns associated with individual securities. Thus far, we have measured volatility by looking at the difference between the actual return on an asset or portfolio, R, and the expected return, $E(R)$. We now look at why those deviations exist.

EXPECTED AND UNEXPECTED RETURNS

To begin, for concreteness, we consider the return on the stock of a company called Flyers. What will determine this stock's return in, say, the coming year?

The return on any stock traded in a financial market is composed of two parts. First, the normal, or expected, return from the stock is the part of the return that shareholders in the market predict or expect. This return depends on the information shareholders have that bears on the stock, and it is based on the market's understanding today of the important factors that will influence the stock in the coming year.

The second part of the return on the stock is the uncertain, or risky, part. This is the portion that comes from unexpected information revealed within the year. A list of all possible sources of such information would be endless, but here are a few examples:

News about Flyers research

Government figures released on gross domestic product (GDP)

The results from the latest arms control talks

The news that Flyers sales figures are higher than expected

A sudden, unexpected drop in interest rates

Based on this discussion, one way to express the return on Flyers stock in the coming year would be:

$$\text{Total return} = \text{Expected return} + \text{Unexpected return}$$
$$R = E(R) + U \qquad \text{[13.3]}$$

where R stands for the actual total return in the year, $E(R)$ stands for the expected part of the return, and U stands for the unexpected part of the return. What this says is that the actual return, R, differs from the expected return, $E(R)$, because of surprises that occur during the year. In any given year, the unexpected return will be positive or negative; but, through time, the average value of U will be zero. This simply means that on average, the actual return equals the expected return.

ANNOUNCEMENTS AND NEWS

We need to be careful when we talk about the effect of news items on the return. For example, suppose Flyers's business is such that the company prospers when GDP grows at a relatively high rate and suffers when GDP is relatively stagnant. In this case, in deciding what return to expect this year from owning stock in Flyers, shareholders either implicitly or explicitly must think about what GDP is likely to be for the year.

When the government actually announces GDP figures for the year, what will happen to the value of Flyers's stock? Obviously, the answer depends on what figure is released. More to the point, however, the impact depends on how much of that figure is *new* information.

At the beginning of the year, market participants will have some idea or forecast of what the yearly GDP will be. To the extent that shareholders have predicted GDP, that prediction will already be factored into the expected part of the return on the stock, E(R). On the other hand, if the announced GDP is a surprise, the effect will be part of U, the unanticipated portion of the return. As an example, suppose shareholders in the market had forecast that the GDP increase this year would be .5 percent. If the actual announcement this year is exactly .5 percent, the same as the forecast, then the shareholders don't really learn anything, and the announcement isn't news. There will be no impact on the stock price as a result. This is like receiving confirmation of something you suspected all along; it doesn't reveal anything new.

A common way of saying that an announcement isn't news is to say that the market has already "discounted" the announcement. The use of the word *discount* here is different from the use of the term in computing present values, but the spirit is the same. When we discount a dollar in the future, we say it is worth less to us because of the time value of money. When we discount an announcement or a news item, we say that it has less of an impact on the price because the market already knew much of it.

Going back to Flyers, suppose the government announces that the actual GDP increase during the year has been 1.5 percent. Now shareholders have learned something—namely, that the increase is one percentage point higher than they had forecast. This difference between the actual result and the forecast, one percentage point in this example, is sometimes called the *innovation* or the *surprise*.

This distinction explains why what seems to be good news can actually be bad news (and vice versa). Going back to the companies we discussed in our chapter opener, even though ExxonMobil's earnings were a quarterly record, the company was facing increased refinery costs, which it was not passing along to consumers. As a result, profits from the refinery division fell by about 50 percent. Additionally, the company's production of crude oil had fallen.

A key idea to keep in mind about news and price changes is that news about the future is what matters. For Hormel, analysts welcomed the good news about earnings, but also noted that those numbers were, in a very real sense, yesterday's news. Looking to the future, the company's CEO announced that he expected grain and energy prices to rise for the rest of the year, dampening future profitability. For BJ's Wholesale Club, the earnings announcement came on a day when the market turned sour in general. Keep this in mind as you read our next section.

To summarize, an announcement can be broken into two parts: the anticipated, or expected, part and the surprise, or innovation:

$$\text{Announcement} = \text{Expected part} + \text{Surprise} \qquad [13.4]$$

The expected part of any announcement is the part of the information that the market uses to form the expectation, E(R), of the return on the stock. The surprise is the news that influences the unanticipated return on the stock, U.

Our discussion of market efficiency in the previous chapter bears on this discussion. We are assuming that relevant information known today is already reflected in the expected return. This is identical to saying that the current price reflects relevant publicly available information. We are thus implicitly assuming that markets are at least reasonably efficient in the semistrong form.

Henceforth, when we speak of news, we will mean the surprise part of an announcement and not the portion that the market has expected and therefore already discounted.

Concept Questions

13.3a What are the two basic parts of a return?

13.3b Under what conditions will a company's announcement have no effect on common stock prices?

Risk: Systematic and Unsystematic

13.4

The unanticipated part of the return, that portion resulting from surprises, is the true risk of any investment. After all, if we always receive exactly what we expect, then the investment is perfectly predictable and, by definition, risk-free. In other words, the risk of owning an asset comes from surprises—unanticipated events.

There are important differences, though, among various sources of risk. Look back at our previous list of news stories. Some of these stories are directed specifically at Flyers, and some are more general. Which of the news items are of specific importance to Flyers?

Announcements about interest rates or GDP are clearly important for nearly all companies, whereas news about Flyers's president, its research, or its sales is of specific interest to Flyers. We will distinguish between these two types of events because, as we will see, they have different implications.

SYSTEMATIC AND UNSYSTEMATIC RISK

The first type of surprise—the one that affects many assets—we will label **systematic risk**. A systematic risk is one that influences a large number of assets, each to a greater or lesser extent. Because systematic risks have marketwide effects, they are sometimes called *market risks*.

The second type of surprise we will call **unsystematic risk**. An unsystematic risk is one that affects a single asset or a small group of assets. Because these risks are unique to individual companies or assets, they are sometimes called *unique* or *asset-specific risks*. We will use these terms interchangeably.

As we have seen, uncertainties about general economic conditions (such as GDP, interest rates, or inflation) are examples of systematic risks. These conditions affect nearly all companies to some degree. An unanticipated increase, or surprise, in inflation, for example, affects wages and the costs of the supplies that companies buy; it affects the value of the assets that companies own; and it affects the prices at which companies sell their products. Forces such as these, to which all companies are susceptible, are the essence of systematic risk.

In contrast, the announcement of an oil strike by a company will primarily affect that company and, perhaps, a few others (such as primary competitors and suppliers). It is unlikely to have much of an effect on the world oil market, however, or on the affairs of companies not in the oil business, so this is an unsystematic event.

SYSTEMATIC AND UNSYSTEMATIC COMPONENTS OF RETURN

The distinction between a systematic risk and an unsystematic risk is never really as exact as we make it out to be. Even the most narrow and peculiar bit of news about a company ripples through the economy. This is true because every enterprise, no matter how tiny, is a part of the economy. It's like the tale of a kingdom that was lost because one horse lost a

systematic risk
A risk that influences a large number of assets. Also, market risk.

unsystematic risk
A risk that affects at most a small number of assets. Also, unique or asset-specific risk.

shoe. This is mostly hairsplitting, however. Some risks are clearly much more general than others. We'll see some evidence on this point in just a moment.

The distinction between the types of risk allows us to break down the surprise portion, U, of the return on the Flyers stock into two parts. Earlier, we had the actual return broken down into its expected and surprise components:

$$R = E(R) + U$$

We now recognize that the total surprise component for Flyers, U, has a systematic and an unsystematic component, so:

$$R = E(R) + \text{Systematic portion} + \text{Unsystematic portion} \qquad [13.5]$$

Because it is traditional, we will use the Greek letter epsilon, ϵ, to stand for the unsystematic portion. Because systematic risks are often called market risks, we will use the letter m to stand for the systematic part of the surprise. With these symbols, we can rewrite the formula for the total return:

$$R = E(R) + U$$
$$= E(R) + m + \epsilon$$

The important thing about the way we have broken down the total surprise, U, is that the unsystematic portion, ϵ, is more or less unique to Flyers. For this reason, it is unrelated to the unsystematic portion of return on most other assets. To see why this is important, we need to return to the subject of portfolio risk.

Concept Questions

13.4a What are the two basic types of risk?

13.4b What is the distinction between the two types of risk?

13.5 Diversification and Portfolio Risk

For more about risk and diversification, visit www.investopedia.com/university.

We've seen earlier that portfolio risks can, in principle, be quite different from the risks of the assets that make up the portfolio. We now look more closely at the riskiness of an individual asset versus the risk of a portfolio of many different assets. We will once again examine some market history to get an idea of what happens with actual investments in U.S. capital markets.

THE EFFECT OF DIVERSIFICATION: ANOTHER LESSON FROM MARKET HISTORY

In our previous chapter, we saw that the standard deviation of the annual return on a portfolio of 500 large common stocks has historically been about 20 percent per year. Does this mean that the standard deviation of the annual return on a typical stock in that group of 500 is about 20 percent? As you might suspect by now, the answer is *no*. This is an extremely important observation.

To illustrate the relationship between portfolio size and portfolio risk, Table 13.7 illustrates typical average annual standard deviations for equally weighted portfolios that contain different numbers of randomly selected NYSE securities.

In Column 2 of Table 13.7, we see that the standard deviation for a "portfolio" of one security is about 49 percent. What this means is that if you randomly selected a single NYSE

(1) Number of Stocks in Portfolio	(2) Average Standard Deviation of Annual Portfolio Returns	(3) Ratio of Portfolio Standard Deviation to Standard Deviation of a Single Stock
1	49.24%	1.00
2	37.36	.76
4	29.69	.60
6	26.64	.54
8	24.98	.51
10	23.93	.49
20	21.68	.44
30	20.87	.42
40	20.46	.42
50	20.20	.41
100	19.69	.40
200	19.42	.39
300	19.34	.39
400	19.29	.39
500	19.27	.39
1,000	19.21	.39

TABLE 13.7

Standard Deviations of Annual Portfolio Returns

These figures are from Table 1 in M. Statman, "How Many Stocks Make a Diversified Portfolio?" *Journal of Financial and Quantitative Analysis* 22 (September 1987), pp. 353–64. They were derived from E.J. Elton and M.J. Gruber, "Risk Reduction and Portfolio Size: An Analytic Solution," *Journal of Business* 50 (October 1977), pp. 415–37.

stock and put all your money into it, your standard deviation of return would typically be a substantial 49 percent per year. If you were to randomly select two stocks and invest half your money in each, your standard deviation would be about 37 percent on average, and so on.

The important thing to notice in Table 13.7 is that the standard deviation declines as the number of securities is increased. By the time we have 100 randomly chosen stocks, the portfolio's standard deviation has declined by about 60 percent, from 49 percent to about 20 percent. With 500 securities, the standard deviation is 19.27 percent, similar to the 20 percent we saw in our previous chapter for the large common stock portfolio. The small difference exists because the portfolio securities and time periods examined are not identical.

THE PRINCIPLE OF DIVERSIFICATION

Figure 13.1 illustrates the point we've been discussing. What we have plotted is the standard deviation of return versus the number of stocks in the portfolio. Notice in Figure 13.1 that the benefit in terms of risk reduction from adding securities drops off as we add more and more. By the time we have 10 securities, most of the effect is already realized; and by the time we get to 30 or so, there is little remaining benefit.

Figure 13.1 illustrates two key points. First, some of the riskiness associated with individual assets can be eliminated by forming portfolios. The process of spreading an investment across assets (and thereby forming a portfolio) is called *diversification*. The **principle of diversification** tells us that spreading an investment across many assets will eliminate some of the risk. The blue shaded area in Figure 13.1, labeled "diversifiable risk," is the part that can be eliminated by diversification.

principle of diversification
Spreading an investment across a number of assets will eliminate some, but not all, of the risk.

FIGURE 13.1

Portfolio Diversification

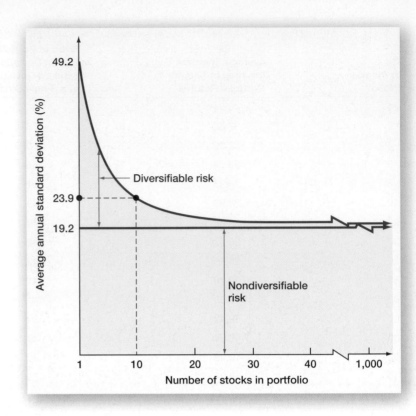

The second point is equally important. There is a minimum level of risk that cannot be eliminated simply by diversifying. This minimum level is labeled "nondiversifiable risk" in Figure 13.1. Taken together, these two points are another important lesson from capital market history: Diversification reduces risk, but only up to a point. Put another way, some risk is diversifiable and some is not.

To give a recent example of the impact of diversification, the Dow Jones Industrial Average (DJIA), which is a widely followed stock market index of 30 large, well-known U.S. stocks, was up about 9 percent in 2007. As we saw in our previous chapter, this gain represents a slightly below-average year for a portfolio of large-cap stocks. The biggest individual winners for the year were Honeywell (up 36 percent), Merck (up 33 percent), and McDonald's (up 33 percent). But not all 30 stocks were up: The losers included Citigroup (down a whopping 47 percent), Home Depot (down 33 percent), and General Motors (down 19 percent). Again, the lesson is clear: Diversification reduces exposure to extreme outcomes, both good and bad.

DIVERSIFICATION AND UNSYSTEMATIC RISK

From our discussion of portfolio risk, we know that some of the risk associated with individual assets can be diversified away and some cannot. We are left with an obvious question: Why is this so? It turns out that the answer hinges on the distinction we made earlier between systematic and unsystematic risk.

By definition, an unsystematic risk is one that is particular to a single asset or, at most, a small group. For example, if the asset under consideration is stock in a single company, the discovery of positive NPV projects such as successful new products and innovative cost savings will tend to increase the value of the stock. Unanticipated lawsuits, industrial accidents, strikes, and similar events will tend to decrease future cash flows and thereby reduce share values.

Here is the important observation: If we held only a single stock, the value of our investment would fluctuate because of company-specific events. If we hold a large portfolio, on the other hand, some of the stocks in the portfolio will go up in value because of positive company-specific events and some will go down in value because of negative events. The net effect on the overall value of the portfolio will be relatively small, however, because these effects will tend to cancel each other out.

Now we see why some of the variability associated with individual assets is eliminated by diversification. When we combine assets into portfolios, the unique, or unsystematic, events—both positive and negative—tend to "wash out" once we have more than just a few assets.

This is an important point that bears repeating:

> Unsystematic risk is essentially eliminated by diversification, so a portfolio with many assets has almost no unsystematic risk.

In fact, the terms *diversifiable risk* and *unsystematic risk* are often used interchangeably.

DIVERSIFICATION AND SYSTEMATIC RISK

We've seen that unsystematic risk can be eliminated by diversifying. What about systematic risk? Can it also be eliminated by diversification? The answer is no because, by definition, a systematic risk affects almost all assets to some degree. As a result, no matter how many assets we put into a portfolio, the systematic risk doesn't go away. Thus, for obvious reasons, the terms *systematic risk* and *nondiversifiable risk* are used interchangeably.

Because we have introduced so many different terms, it is useful to summarize our discussion before moving on. What we have seen is that the total risk of an investment, as measured by the standard deviation of its return, can be written as:

$$\text{Total risk} = \text{Systematic risk} + \text{Unsystematic risk} \qquad [13.6]$$

Systematic risk is also called *nondiversifiable risk* or *market risk.* Unsystematic risk is also called *diversifiable risk, unique risk,* or *asset-specific risk.* For a well-diversified portfolio, the unsystematic risk is negligible. For such a portfolio, essentially all of the risk is systematic.

Concept Questions

13.5a What happens to the standard deviation of return for a portfolio if we increase the number of securities in the portfolio?

13.5b What is the principle of diversification?

13.5c Why is some risk diversifiable? Why is some risk not diversifiable?

13.5d Why can't systematic risk be diversified away?

Systematic Risk and Beta   13.6

The question that we now begin to address is this: What determines the size of the risk premium on a risky asset? Put another way, why do some assets have a larger risk premium than other assets? The answer to these questions, as we discuss next, is also based on the distinction between systematic and unsystematic risk.

THE SYSTEMATIC RISK PRINCIPLE

Thus far, we've seen that the total risk associated with an asset can be decomposed into two components: systematic and unsystematic risk. We have also seen that unsystematic risk can be essentially eliminated by diversification. The systematic risk present in an asset, on the other hand, cannot be eliminated by diversification.

systematic risk principle
The expected return on a risky asset depends only on that asset's systematic risk.

Based on our study of capital market history, we know that there is a reward, on average, for bearing risk. However, we now need to be more precise about what we mean by risk. The **systematic risk principle** states that the reward for bearing risk depends only on the systematic risk of an investment. The underlying rationale for this principle is straightforward: Because unsystematic risk can be eliminated at virtually no cost (by diversifying), there is no reward for bearing it. Put another way, the market does not reward risks that are borne unnecessarily.

The systematic risk principle has a remarkable and very important implication:

> **The expected return on an asset depends only on that asset's systematic risk.**

For more about beta, see www.investools.com *and* moneycentral.msn.com.

There is an obvious corollary to this principle: No matter how much total risk an asset has, only the systematic portion is relevant in determining the expected return (and the risk premium) on that asset.

MEASURING SYSTEMATIC RISK

beta coefficient
The amount of systematic risk present in a particular risky asset relative to that in an average risky asset.

Because systematic risk is the crucial determinant of an asset's expected return, we need some way of measuring the level of systematic risk for different investments. The specific measure we will use is called the **beta coefficient**, for which we will use the Greek symbol β. A beta coefficient, or beta for short, tells us how much systematic risk a particular asset has relative to an average asset. By definition, an average asset has a beta of 1.0 relative to itself. An asset with a beta of .50, therefore, has half as much systematic risk as an average asset; an asset with a beta of 2.0 has twice as much.

Table 13.8 contains the estimated beta coefficients for the stocks of some well-known companies. The range of betas in Table 13.8 is typical for stocks of large U.S. corporations. Betas outside this range occur, but they are less common.

The important thing to remember is that the expected return, and thus the risk premium, of an asset depends only on its systematic risk. Because assets with larger betas have greater systematic risks, they will have greater expected returns. Thus, from Table 13.8, an investor who buys stock in ExxonMobil, with a beta of 1.14, should expect to earn less, on average, than an investor who buys stock in eBay, with a beta of about 2.13.

TABLE 13.8

Beta Coefficients for Selected Companies

SOURCE: Yahoo! Finance 2008 (*finance.yahoo.com*).

	Beta Coefficient (β_i)
The Gap	.48
Coca-Cola	.52
3M	.64
ExxonMobil	1.14
Abercrombie & Fitch	1.28
eBay	2.13
Google	2.60

One cautionary note is in order: Not all betas are created equal. Different providers use somewhat different methods for estimating betas, and significant differences sometimes occur. As a result, it is a good idea to look at several sources. See our nearby *Work the Web* box for more about beta.

| **Total Risk versus Beta** | **EXAMPLE 13.5** |

Consider the following information about two securities. Which has greater total risk? Which has greater systematic risk? Greater unsystematic risk? Which asset will have a higher risk premium?

	Standard Deviation	Beta
Security A	40%	.50
Security B	20	1.50

From our discussion in this section, Security A has greater total risk, but it has substantially less systematic risk. Because total risk is the sum of systematic and unsystematic risk, Security A must have greater unsystematic risk. Finally, from the systematic risk principle, Security B will have a higher risk premium and a greater expected return, despite the fact that it has less total risk.

PORTFOLIO BETAS

Earlier, we saw that the riskiness of a portfolio has no simple relationship to the risks of the assets in the portfolio. A portfolio beta, however, can be calculated, just like a portfolio expected return. For example, looking again at Table 13.8, suppose you put half of your money in ExxonMobil and half in Coca-Cola. What would the beta of this combination be? Because ExxonMobil has a beta of 1.14 and Coca-Cola has a beta of .52, the portfolio's beta, β_p, would be:

$$\beta_P = .50 \times \beta_{ExxonMobil} + .50 \times \beta_{Coca\text{-}Cola}$$
$$= .50 \times 1.14 + .50 \times .52$$
$$= .83$$

WORK THE WEB

You can find beta estimates at many sites on the Web. One of the best is finance.yahoo.com. Here is a snapshot of the "Key Statistics" screen for Amazon.com (AMZN):

Stock Price History	
Beta:	3.18
52-Week Change[3]:	14.30%
S&P500 52-Week Change[3]:	-9.22%
52-Week High (23-Oct-07)[3]:	101.09
52-Week Low (03-Mar-08)[3]:	61.20
50-Day Moving Average[3]:	76.84
200-Day Moving Average[3]:	78.69

(continued)

Management Effectiveness	
Return on Assets (ttm):	9.27%
Return on Equity (ttm):	55.73%

Income Statement	
Revenue (ttm):	15.96B
Revenue Per Share (ttm):	38.515
Qtrly Revenue Growth (yoy):	37.10%
Gross Profit (ttm):	3.35B
EBITDA (ttm):	957.00M
Net Income Avl to Common (ttm):	508.00M
Diluted EPS (ttm):	1.19
Qtrly Earnings Growth (yoy):	28.80%

The reported beta for Amazon.com is 3.18, which means that Amazon has about three times the systematic risk of a typical stock. You would expect that the company is very risky; and, looking at the other numbers, we agree. Amazon's ROA is 9.27 percent, a relatively good number. The reported ROE is about 55.73 percent, an amazing number! Why is Amazon's ROE so high? Until recently, the company had consistently lost money, and its accumulated losses over the years had entirely wiped out its book equity. As the result of recent profits, the shareholders equity account has become positive; but it is small, which leads to the large ROE. Given this, Amazon appears to be a good candidate for a high beta.

Questions
1. As we mentioned, the book value per share of stock for Amazon.com is relatively low. What is the current book value per share reported on this Web site?
2. What growth rate are analysts projecting for Amazon.com? How does this growth rate compare to the industry?

In general, if we had many assets in a portfolio, we would multiply each asset's beta by its portfolio weight and then add the results to get the portfolio's beta.

EXAMPLE 13.6   Portfolio Betas

Suppose we had the following investments:

Security	Amount Invested	Expected Return	Beta
Stock A	$1,000	8%	.80
Stock B	2,000	12	.95
Stock C	3,000	15	1.10
Stock D	4,000	18	1.40

What is the expected return on this portfolio? What is the beta of this portfolio? Does this portfolio have more or less systematic risk than an average asset?

(continued)

To answer, we first have to calculate the portfolio weights. Notice that the total amount invested is $10,000. Of this, $1,000/10,000 = 10% is invested in Stock A. Similarly, 20 percent is invested in Stock B, 30 percent is invested in Stock C, and 40 percent is invested in Stock D. The expected return, $E(R_P)$, is thus:

$$E(R_P) = .10 \times E(R_A) + .20 \times E(R_B) + .30 \times E(R_C) + .40 \times E(R_D)$$
$$= .10 \times 8\% + .20 \times 12\% + .30 \times 15\% + .40 \times 18\%$$
$$= 14.9\%$$

Similarly, the portfolio beta, β_P, is:

$$\beta_P = .10 \times \beta_A + .20 \times \beta_B + .30 \times \beta_C + .40 \times \beta_D$$
$$= .10 \times .80 + .20 \times .95 + .30 \times 1.10 + .40 \times 1.40$$
$$= 1.16$$

This portfolio thus has an expected return of 14.9 percent and a beta of 1.16. Because the beta is larger than 1, this portfolio has greater systematic risk than an average asset.

Concept Questions

13.6a What is the systematic risk principle?

13.6b What does a beta coefficient measure?

13.6c True or false: The expected return on a risky asset depends on that asset's total risk. Explain.

13.6d How do you calculate a portfolio beta?

Betas are easy to find on the Web. Try finance.yahoo.com and money.cnn.com.

The Security Market Line

13.7

We're now in a position to see how risk is rewarded in the marketplace. To begin, suppose that Asset A has an expected return of $E(R_A) = 20\%$ and a beta of $\beta_A = 1.6$. Furthermore, suppose that the risk-free rate is $R_f = 8\%$. Notice that a risk-free asset, by definition, has no systematic risk (or unsystematic risk), so a risk-free asset has a beta of zero.

BETA AND THE RISK PREMIUM

Consider a portfolio made up of Asset A and a risk-free asset. We can calculate some different possible portfolio expected returns and betas by varying the percentages invested in these two assets. For example, if 25 percent of the portfolio is invested in Asset A, then the expected return is:

$$E(R_P) = .25 \times E(R_A) + (1 - .25) \times R_f$$
$$= .25 \times 20\% + .75 \times 8\%$$
$$= 11\%$$

Similarly, the beta on the portfolio, β_P, would be:

$$\beta_P = .25 \times \beta_A + (1 - .25) \times 0$$
$$= .25 \times 1.6$$
$$= .40$$

Notice that because the weights have to add up to 1, the percentage invested in the risk-free asset is equal to 1 minus the percentage invested in Asset A.

One thing that you might wonder about is whether it is possible for the percentage invested in Asset A to exceed 100 percent. The answer is yes. This can happen if the investor borrows at the risk-free rate. For example, suppose an investor has $100 and borrows an additional $50 at 8 percent, the risk-free rate. The total investment in Asset A would be $150, or 150 percent of the investor's wealth. The expected return in this case would be:

$$E(R_p) = 1.50 \times E(R_A) + (1 - 1.50) \times R_f$$
$$= 1.50 \times 20\% - .50 \times 8\%$$
$$= 26\%$$

The beta on the portfolio would be:

$$\beta_P = 1.50 \times \beta_A + (1 - 1.50) \times 0$$
$$= 1.50 \times 1.6$$
$$= 2.4$$

We can calculate some other possibilities, as follows:

Percentage of Portfolio in Asset A	Portfolio Expected Return	Portfolio Beta
0%	8%	.0
25	11	.4
50	14	.8
75	17	1.2
100	20	1.6
125	23	2.0
150	26	2.4

In Figure 13.2A, these portfolio expected returns are plotted against the portfolio betas. Notice that all the combinations fall on a straight line.

The Reward-to-Risk Ratio   What is the slope of the straight line in Figure 13.2A? As always, the slope of a straight line is equal to "the rise over the run." In this case, as we move out of the risk-free asset into Asset A, the beta increases from zero to 1.6 (a "run" of 1.6). At

FIGURE 13.2A

Portfolio Expected Returns and Betas for Asset A

the same time, the expected return goes from 8 percent to 20 percent, a "rise" of 12 percent. The slope of the line is thus $12\%/1.6 = 7.5\%$.

Notice that the slope of our line is just the risk premium on Asset A, $E(R_A) - R_f$, divided by Asset A's beta, β_A:

$$\text{Slope} = \frac{E(R_A) - R_f}{\beta_A}$$

$$= \frac{20\% - 8\%}{1.6} = 7.5\%$$

What this tells us is that Asset A offers a *reward-to-risk* ratio of 7.5 percent.[2] In other words, Asset A has a risk premium of 7.50 percent per "unit" of systematic risk.

The Basic Argument   Now suppose we consider a second asset, Asset B. This asset has a beta of 1.2 and an expected return of 16 percent. Which investment is better, Asset A or Asset B? You might think that, once again, we really cannot say—some investors might prefer A; some investors might prefer B. Actually, however, we can say: A is better because, as we will demonstrate, B offers inadequate compensation for its level of systematic risk, at least, relative to A.

To begin, we calculate different combinations of expected returns and betas for portfolios of Asset B and a risk-free asset, just as we did for Asset A. For example, if we put 25 percent in Asset B and the remaining 75 percent in the risk-free asset, the portfolio's expected return will be:

$$E(R_P) = .25 \times E(R_B) + (1 - .25) \times R_f$$

$$= .25 \times 16\% + .75 \times 8\%$$

$$= 10\%$$

Similarly, the beta on the portfolio, β_P, would be:

$$\beta_P = .25 \times \beta_B + (1 - .25) \times 0$$

$$= .25 \times 1.2$$

$$= .30$$

Some other possibilities are as follows:

Percentage of Portfolio in Asset B	Portfolio Expected Return	Portfolio Beta
0%	8%	.0
25	10	.3
50	12	.6
75	14	.9
100	16	1.2
125	18	1.5
150	20	1.8

When we plot these combinations of portfolio expected returns and portfolio betas in Figure 13.2B, we get a straight line just as we did for Asset A.

---

[2] This ratio is sometimes called the *Treynor index*, after one of its originators.

FIGURE 13.2B

Portfolio Expected
Returns and Betas for
Asset B

FIGURE 13.2C

Portfolio Expected
Returns and Betas for
Both Assets

The key thing to notice is that when we compare the results for Assets A and B, as in Figure 13.2C, the line describing the combinations of expected returns and betas for Asset A is higher than the one for Asset B. This tells us that for any given level of systematic risk (as measured by β), some combination of Asset A and the risk-free asset always offers a larger return. This is why we were able to state that Asset A is a better investment than Asset B.

Another way of seeing that A offers a superior return for its level of risk is to note that the slope of our line for Asset B is:

$$\text{Slope} = \frac{E(R_B) - R_f}{\beta_B}$$

$$= \frac{16\% - 8\%}{1.2} = 6.67\%$$

Thus, Asset B has a reward-to-risk ratio of 6.67 percent, which is less than the 7.5 percent offered by Asset A.

The Fundamental Result   The situation we have described for Assets A and B could not persist in a well-organized, active market, because investors would be attracted to Asset A and away from Asset B. As a result, Asset A's price would rise and Asset B's price would fall. Because prices and returns move in opposite directions, A's expected return would decline and B's would rise.

This buying and selling would continue until the two assets plotted on exactly the same line, which means they would offer the same reward for bearing risk. In other words, in an active, competitive market, we must have the situation that:

$$\frac{E(R_A) - R_f}{\beta_A} = \frac{E(R_B) - R_f}{\beta_B}$$

This is the fundamental relationship between risk and return.

Our basic argument can be extended to more than just two assets. In fact, no matter how many assets we had, we would always reach the same conclusion:

> **The reward-to-risk ratio must be the same for all the assets in the market.**

This result is really not so surprising. What it says is that, for example, if one asset has twice as much systematic risk as another asset, its risk premium will simply be twice as large.

Because all of the assets in the market must have the same reward-to-risk ratio, they all must plot on the same line. This argument is illustrated in Figure 13.3. As shown, Assets A and B plot directly on the line and thus have the same reward-to-risk ratio. If an asset plotted above the line, such as C in Figure 13.3, its price would rise and its expected return would fall until it plotted exactly on the line. Similarly, if an asset plotted below the line, such as D in Figure 13.3, its expected return would rise until it too plotted directly on the line.

The arguments we have presented apply to active, competitive, well-functioning markets. The financial markets, such as the NYSE, best meet these criteria. Other markets,

FIGURE 13.3

Expected Returns and Systematic Risk

The fundamental relationship between beta and expected return is that all assets must have the same reward-to-risk ratio, $[E(R_i) - R_f]/\beta_i$. This means that they would all plot on the same straight line. Assets A and B are examples of this behavior. Asset C's expected return is too high; asset D's is too low.

such as real asset markets, may or may not. For this reason, these concepts are most useful in examining financial markets. We will thus focus on such markets here. However, as we discuss in a later section, the information about risk and return gleaned from financial markets is crucial in evaluating the investments that a corporation makes in real assets.

EXAMPLE 13.7   Buy Low, Sell High

An asset is said to be *overvalued* if its price is too high given its expected return and risk. Suppose you observe the following situation:

Security	Beta	Expected Return
SWMS Co.	1.3	14%
Insec Co.	.8	10

The risk-free rate is currently 6 percent. Is one of the two securities overvalued relative to the other?

To answer, we compute the reward-to-risk ratio for both. For SWMS, this ratio is (14% − 6%)/1.3 = 6.15%. For Insec, this ratio is 5 percent. What we conclude is that Insec offers an insufficient expected return for its level of risk, at least relative to SWMS. Because its expected return is too low, its price is too high. In other words, Insec is overvalued relative to SWMS, and we would expect to see its price fall relative to SWMS's. Notice that we could also say SWMS is undervalued relative to Insec.

THE SECURITY MARKET LINE

The line that results when we plot expected returns and beta coefficients is obviously of some importance, so it's time we gave it a name. This line, which we use to describe the relationship between systematic risk and expected return in financial markets, is usually called the **security market line (SML)**. After NPV, the SML is arguably the most important concept in modern finance.

security market line (SML)
A positively sloped straight line displaying the relationship between expected return and beta.

Market Portfolios   It will be very useful to know the equation of the SML. There are many different ways we could write it, but one way is particularly common. Suppose we consider a portfolio made up of all of the assets in the market. Such a portfolio is called a market portfolio, and we will express the expected return on this market portfolio as $E(R_M)$.

Because all the assets in the market must plot on the SML, so must a market portfolio made up of those assets. To determine where it plots on the SML, we need to know the beta of the market portfolio, β_M. Because this portfolio is representative of all of the assets in the market, it must have average systematic risk. In other words, it has a beta of 1. We could therefore express the slope of the SML as:

$$\text{SML slope} = \frac{E(R_M) - R_f}{\beta_M} = \frac{E(R_M) - R_f}{1} = E(R_M) - R_f$$

market risk premium
The slope of the SML—the difference between the expected return on a market portfolio and the risk-free rate.

The term $E(R_M) - R_f$ is often called the **market risk premium** because it is the risk premium on a market portfolio.

The Capital Asset Pricing Model   To finish up, if we let $E(R_i)$ and β_i stand for the expected return and beta, respectively, on any asset in the market, then we know that asset must plot on the SML. As a result, we know that its reward-to-risk ratio is the same as the overall market's:

$$\frac{E(R_i) - R_f}{\beta_i} = E(R_M) - R_f$$

If we rearrange this, then we can write the equation for the SML as:

$$E(R_i) = R_f + [E(R_M) - R_f] \times \beta_i \qquad \text{[13.7]}$$

This result is the famous **capital asset pricing model (CAPM)**.

The CAPM shows that the expected return for a particular asset depends on three things:

1. *The pure time value of money:* As measured by the risk-free rate, R_f, this is the reward for merely waiting for your money, without taking any risk.

2. *The reward for bearing systematic risk:* As measured by the market risk premium, $E(R_M) - R_f$, this component is the reward the market offers for bearing an average amount of systematic risk in addition to waiting.

3. *The amount of systematic risk:* As measured by β_i, this is the amount of systematic risk present in a particular asset or portfolio, relative to that in an average asset.

By the way, the CAPM works for portfolios of assets just as it does for individual assets. In an earlier section, we saw how to calculate a portfolio's β. To find the expected return on a portfolio, we simply use this β in the CAPM equation.

Figure 13.4 summarizes our discussion of the SML and the CAPM. As before, we plot expected return against beta. Now we recognize that, based on the CAPM, the slope of the SML is equal to the market risk premium, $E(R_M) - R_f$.

This concludes our presentation of concepts related to the risk–return trade-off. For future reference, Table 13.9 summarizes the various concepts in the order in which we discussed them.

capital asset pricing model (CAPM)
The equation of the SML showing the relationship between expected return and beta.

FIGURE 13.4

The Security Market Line (SML)

The slope of the security market line is equal to the market risk premium—that is, the reward for bearing an average amount of systematic risk. The equation describing the SML can be written:

$$F(R_i) = R_f + [E(R_M) - R_f] \times \beta_i$$

which is the capital asset pricing model (CAPM).

EXAMPLE 13.8   Risk and Return

Suppose the risk-free rate is 4 percent, the market risk premium is 8.6 percent, and a particular stock has a beta of 1.3. Based on the CAPM, what is the expected return on this stock? What would the expected return be if the beta were to double?

With a beta of 1.3, the risk premium for the stock is $1.3 \times 8.6\%$, or 11.18 percent. The risk-free rate is 4 percent, so the expected return is 15.18 percent. If the beta were to double to 2.6, the risk premium would double to 22.36 percent, so the expected return would be 26.36 percent.

TABLE 13.9

Summary of Risk and Return

I.   Total Risk

The *total risk* of an investment is measured by the variance or, more commonly, the standard deviation of its return.

II.   Total Return

The *total return* on an investment has two components: the expected return and the unexpected return. The unexpected return comes about because of unanticipated events. The risk from investing stems from the possibility of an unanticipated event.

III.   Systematic and Unsystematic Risks

Systematic risks (also called *market risks*) are unanticipated events that affect almost all assets to some degree because the effects are economywide. *Unsystematic risks* are unanticipated events that affect single assets or small groups of assets. Unsystematic risks are also called *unique* or *asset-specific risks*.

IV.   The Effect of Diversification

Some, but not all, of the risk associated with a risky investment can be eliminated by diversification. The reason is that unsystematic risks, which are unique to individual assets, tend to wash out in a large portfolio, but systematic risks, which affect all of the assets in a portfolio to some extent, do not.

V.   The Systematic Risk Principle and Beta

Because unsystematic risk can be freely eliminated by diversification, the *systematic risk principle* states that the reward for bearing risk depends only on the level of systematic risk. The level of systematic risk in a particular asset, relative to the average, is given by the beta of that asset.

VI.   The Reward-to-Risk Ratio and the Security Market Line

The *reward-to-risk ratio* for Asset i is the ratio of its risk premium, $E(R_i) - R_f$, to its beta, β_i:

$$\frac{E(R_i) - R_f}{\beta_i}$$

In a well-functioning market, this ratio is the same for every asset. As a result, when asset expected returns are plotted against asset betas, all assets plot on the same straight line, called the *security market line* (SML).

VII.   The Capital Asset Pricing Model

From the SML, the expected return on Asset i can be written:

$$E(R_i) = R_f + [E(R_M) - R_f] \times \beta_i$$

This is the *capital asset pricing model* (CAPM). The expected return on a risky asset thus has three components. The first is the pure time value of money (R_f), the second is the market risk premium [$E(R_M) - R_f$], and the third is the beta for that asset, (β_i).

Concept Questions

13.7a What is the fundamental relationship between risk and return in well-functioning markets?

13.7b What is the security market line? Why must all assets plot directly on it in a well-functioning market?

13.7c What is the capital asset pricing model (CAPM)? What does it tell us about the required return on a risky investment?

The SML and the Cost of Capital: A Preview   13.8

Our goal in studying risk and return is twofold. First, risk is an extremely important consideration in almost all business decisions, so we want to discuss just what risk is and how it is rewarded in the market. Our second purpose is to learn what determines the appropriate discount rate for future cash flows. We briefly discuss this second subject now; we will discuss it in more detail in a subsequent chapter.

THE BASIC IDEA

The security market line tells us the reward for bearing risk in financial markets. At an absolute minimum, any new investment our firm undertakes must offer an expected return that is no worse than what the financial markets offer for the same risk. The reason for this is simply that our shareholders can always invest for themselves in the financial markets.

The only way we benefit our shareholders is by finding investments with expected returns that are superior to what the financial markets offer for the same risk. Such an investment will have a positive NPV. So, if we ask, "What is the appropriate discount rate?" the answer is that we should use the expected return offered in financial markets on investments with the same systematic risk.

In other words, to determine whether an investment has a positive NPV, we essentially compare the expected return on that new investment to what the financial market offers on an investment with the same beta. This is why the SML is so important: It tells us the "going rate" for bearing risk in the economy.

THE COST OF CAPITAL

The appropriate discount rate on a new project is the minimum expected rate of return an investment must offer to be attractive. This minimum required return is often called the **cost of capital** associated with the investment. It is called this because the required return is what the firm must earn on its capital investment in a project just to break even. It can thus be interpreted as the opportunity cost associated with the firm's capital investment.

cost of capital
The minimum required return on a new investment.

Notice that when we say an investment is attractive if its expected return exceeds what is offered in financial markets for investments of the same risk, we are effectively using the internal rate of return (IRR) criterion that we developed and discussed in Chapter 9. The only difference is that now we have a much better idea of what determines the required return on an investment. This understanding will be critical when we discuss cost of capital and capital structure in Part 6 of our book.

Concept Questions

13.8a If an investment has a positive NPV, would it plot above or below the SML? Why?

13.8b What is meant by the term *cost of capital*?

13.9 Summary and Conclusions

This chapter has covered the essentials of risk. Along the way, we have introduced a number of definitions and concepts. The most important of these is the security market line, or SML. The SML is important because it tells us the reward offered in financial markets for bearing risk. Once we know this, we have a benchmark against which we can compare the returns expected from real asset investments to determine if they are desirable.

Because we have covered quite a bit of ground, it's useful to summarize the basic economic logic underlying the SML as follows:

1. Based on capital market history, there is a reward for bearing risk. This reward is the risk premium on an asset.

2. The total risk associated with an asset has two parts: systematic risk and unsystematic risk. Unsystematic risk can be freely eliminated by diversification (this is the principle of diversification), so only systematic risk is rewarded. As a result, the risk premium on an asset is determined by its systematic risk. This is the systematic risk principle.

3. An asset's systematic risk, relative to the average, can be measured by its beta coefficient, β_i. The risk premium on an asset is then given by its beta coefficient multiplied by the market risk premium, $[E(R_M) - R_f] \times \beta_i$.

4. The expected return on an asset, $E(R_i)$, is equal to the risk-free rate, R_f, plus the risk premium:

    $$E(R_i) = R_f + [E(R_M) - R_f] \times \beta_i$$

    This is the equation of the SML, and it is often called the capital asset pricing model (CAPM).

This chapter completes our discussion of risk and return. Now that we have a better understanding of what determines a firm's cost of capital for an investment, the next several chapters will examine more closely how firms raise the long-term capital needed for investment.

CHAPTER REVIEW AND SELF-TEST PROBLEMS

13.1 Expected Return and Standard Deviation This problem will give you some practice calculating measures of prospective portfolio performance. There are two assets and three states of the economy:

State of Economy	Probability of State of Economy	Rate of Return if State Occurs	
		Stock A	Stock B
Recession	.20	−.15	.20
Normal	.50	.20	.30
Boom	.30	.60	.40

What are the expected returns and standard deviations for these two stocks?

13.2 Portfolio Risk and Return Using the information in the previous problem, suppose you have $20,000 total. If you put $15,000 in Stock A and the remainder in Stock B, what will be the expected return and standard deviation of your portfolio?

13.3 Risk and Return Suppose you observe the following situation:

Security	Beta	Expected Return
Cooley, Inc.	1.8	22.00%
Moyer Co.	1.6	20.44%

If the risk-free rate is 7 percent, are these securities correctly priced? What would the risk-free rate have to be if they are correctly priced?

13.4 CAPM Suppose the risk-free rate is 8 percent. The expected return on the market is 16 percent. If a particular stock has a beta of .7, what is its expected return based on the CAPM? If another stock has an expected return of 24 percent, what must its beta be?

ANSWERS TO CHAPTER REVIEW AND SELF-TEST PROBLEMS

13.1 The expected returns are just the possible returns multiplied by the associated probabilities:

$$E(R_A) = (.20 \times -.15) + (.50 \times .20) + (.30 \times .60) = 25\%$$
$$E(R_B) = (.20 \times .20) + (.50 \times .30) + (.30 \times .40) = 31\%$$

The variances are given by the sums of the squared deviations from the expected returns multiplied by their probabilities:

$$\sigma_A^2 = .20 \times (-.15 - .25)^2 + .50 \times (.20 - .25)^2 + .30 \times (.60 - .25)^2$$
$$= (.20 \times -.40^2) + (.50 \times -.05^2) + (.30 \times .35^2)$$
$$= (.20 \times .16) + (.50 \times .0025) + (.30 \times .1225)$$
$$= .0700$$

$$\sigma_B^2 = .20 \times (.20 - .31)^2 + .50 \times (.30 - .31)^2 + .30 \times (.40 - .31)^2$$
$$= (.20 \times -.11^2) + (.50 \times -.01^2) + (.30 \times .09^2)$$
$$= (.20 \times .0121) + (.50 \times .0001) + (.30 \times .0081)$$
$$= .0049$$

The standard deviations are thus:

$$\sigma_A = \sqrt{.0700} = 26.46\%$$
$$\sigma_B = \sqrt{.0049} = 7\%$$

13.2 The portfolio weights are $15,000/20,000 = .75 and $5,000/20,000 = .25. The expected return is thus:

$$E(R_P) = .75 \times E(R_A) + .25 \times E(R_B)$$
$$= (.75 \times 25\%) + (.25 \times 31\%)$$
$$= 26.5\%$$

Alternatively, we could calculate the portfolio's return in each of the states:

State of Economy	Probability of State of Economy	Portfolio Return if State Occurs
Recession	.20	(.75 × −.15) + (.25 × .20) = −.0625
Normal	.50	(.75 × .20) + (.25 × .30) = .2250
Boom	.30	(.75 × .60) + (.25 × .40) = .5500

Visit us at www.mhhe.com/rwj

Visit us at www.mhhe.com/rwj

The portfolio's expected return is:

$$E(R_p) = (.20 \times -.0625) + (.50 \times .2250) + (.30 \times .5500) = 26.5\%$$

This is the same as we had before.

The portfolio's variance is:

$$\sigma_P^2 = .20 \times (-.0625 - .265)^2 + .50 \times (.225 - .265)^2$$
$$+ .30 \times (.55 - .265)^2$$
$$= .0466$$

So the standard deviation is $\sqrt{.0466} = 21.59\%$.

13.3 If we compute the reward-to-risk ratios, we get $(22\% - 7\%)/1.8 = 8.33\%$ for Cooley versus 8.4% for Moyer. Relative to that of Cooley, Moyer's expected return is too high, so its price is too low.

If they are correctly priced, then they must offer the same reward-to-risk ratio. The risk-free rate would have to be such that:

$$(22\% - R_f)/1.8 = (20.44\% - R_f)/1.6$$

With a little algebra, we find that the risk-free rate must be 8 percent:

$$22\% - R_f = (20.44\% - R_f)(1.8/1.6)$$
$$22\% - 20.44\% \times 1.125 = R_f - R_f \times 1.125$$
$$R_f = 8\%$$

13.4 Because the expected return on the market is 16 percent, the market risk premium is $16\% - 8\% = 8\%$. The first stock has a beta of .7, so its expected return is $8\% + .7 \times 8\% = 13.6\%$.

For the second stock, notice that the risk premium is $24\% - 8\% = 16\%$. Because this is twice as large as the market risk premium, the beta must be exactly equal to 2. We can verify this using the CAPM:

$$E(R_i) = R_f + [E(R_M) - R_f] \times \beta_i$$
$$24\% = 8\% + (16\% - 8\%) \times \beta_i$$
$$\beta_i = 16\%/8\%$$
$$= 2.0$$

CONCEPTS REVIEW AND CRITICAL THINKING QUESTIONS

1. **Diversifiable and Nondiversifiable Risks [LO3]** In broad terms, why is some risk diversifiable? Why are some risks nondiversifiable? Does it follow that an investor can control the level of unsystematic risk in a portfolio, but not the level of systematic risk?

2. **Information and Market Returns [LO3]** Suppose the government announces that, based on a just-completed survey, the growth rate in the economy is likely to be 2 percent in the coming year, as compared to 5 percent for the past year. Will security prices increase, decrease, or stay the same following this announcement? Does it make any difference whether the 2 percent figure was anticipated by the market? Explain.

3. **Systematic versus Unsystematic Risk [LO3]** Classify the following events as mostly systematic or mostly unsystematic. Is the distinction clear in every case?

   a. Short-term interest rates increase unexpectedly.

   b. The interest rate a company pays on its short-term debt borrowing is increased by its bank.

c. Oil prices unexpectedly decline.

d. An oil tanker ruptures, creating a large oil spill.

e. A manufacturer loses a multimillion-dollar product liability suit.

f. A Supreme Court decision substantially broadens producer liability for injuries suffered by product users.

4. **Systematic versus Unsystematic Risk [LO3]** Indicate whether the following events might cause stocks in general to change price, and whether they might cause Big Widget Corp.'s stock to change price:

a. The government announces that inflation unexpectedly jumped by 2 percent last month.

b. Big Widget's quarterly earnings report, just issued, generally fell in line with analysts' expectations.

c. The government reports that economic growth last year was at 3 percent, which generally agreed with most economists' forecasts.

d. The directors of Big Widget die in a plane crash.

e. Congress approves changes to the tax code that will increase the top marginal corporate tax rate. The legislation had been debated for the previous six months.

5. **Expected Portfolio Returns [LO1]** If a portfolio has a positive investment in every asset, can the expected return on the portfolio be greater than that on every asset in the portfolio? Can it be less than that on every asset in the portfolio? If you answer yes to one or both of these questions, give an example to support your answer.

6. **Diversification [LO2]** True or false: The most important characteristic in determining the expected return of a well-diversified portfolio is the variance of the individual assets in the portfolio. Explain.

7. **Portfolio Risk [LO2]** If a portfolio has a positive investment in every asset, can the standard deviation on the portfolio be less than that on every asset in the portfolio? What about the portfolio beta?

8. **Beta and CAPM [LO4]** Is it possible that a risky asset could have a beta of zero? Explain. Based on the CAPM, what is the expected return on such an asset? Is it possible that a risky asset could have a negative beta? What does the CAPM predict about the expected return on such an asset? Can you give an explanation for your answer?

9. **Corporate Downsizing [LO1]** In recent years, it has been common for companies to experience significant stock price changes in reaction to announcements of massive layoffs. Critics charge that such events encourage companies to fire longtime employees and that Wall Street is cheering them on. Do you agree or disagree?

10. **Earnings and Stock Returns [LO1]** As indicated by a number of examples in this chapter, earnings announcements by companies are closely followed by, and frequently result in, share price revisions. Two issues should come to mind. First, earnings announcements concern past periods. If the market values stocks based on expectations of the future, why are numbers summarizing past performance relevant? Second, these announcements concern accounting earnings. Going back to Chapter 2, such earnings may have little to do with cash flow—so, again, why are they relevant?

BASIC
(Questions 1–20)

1. **Determining Portfolio Weights** [LO1] What are the portfolio weights for a portfolio that has 180 shares of Stock A that sell for $45 per share and 140 shares of Stock B that sell for $27 per share?

2. **Portfolio Expected Return** [LO1] You own a portfolio that has $2,950 invested in Stock A and $3,700 invested in Stock B. If the expected returns on these stocks are 11 percent and 15 percent, respectively, what is the expected return on the portfolio?

3. **Portfolio Expected Return** [LO1] You own a portfolio that is 60 percent invested in Stock X, 25 percent in Stock Y, and 15 percent in Stock Z. The expected returns on these three stocks are 9 percent, 17 percent, and 13 percent, respectively. What is the expected return on the portfolio?

4. **Portfolio Expected Return** [LO1] You have $10,000 to invest in a stock portfolio. Your choices are Stock X with an expected return of 14 percent and Stock Y with an expected return of 10.5 percent. If your goal is to create a portfolio with an expected return of 12.4 percent, how much money will you invest in Stock X? In Stock Y?

5. **Calculating Expected Return** [LO1] Based on the following information, calculate the expected return:

State of Economy	Probability of State of Economy	Portfolio Return if State Occurs
Recession	.25	−.08
Boom	.75	.21

6. **Calculating Expected Return** [LO1] Based on the following information, calculate the expected return:

State of Economy	Probability of State of Economy	Portfolio Return if State Occurs
Recession	.20	−.05
Normal	.50	.12
Boom	.30	.25

7. **Calculating Returns and Standard Deviations** [LO1] Based on the following information, calculate the expected return and standard deviation for the two stocks:

State of Economy	Probability of State of Economy	Rate of Return if State Occurs	
		Stock A	Stock B
Recession	.15	.05	−.17
Normal	.65	.08	.12
Boom	.20	.13	.29

8. **Calculating Expected Returns** [LO1] A portfolio is invested 25 percent in Stock G, 55 percent in Stock J, and 20 percent in Stock K. The expected returns on these stocks are 8 percent, 15 percent, and 24 percent, respectively. What is the portfolio's expected return? How do you interpret your answer?

9. **Returns and Variances** [LO1] Consider the following information:

State of Economy	Probability of State of Economy	Rate of Return if State Occurs		
		Stock A	Stock B	Stock C
Boom	.35	.07	.15	.33
Bust	.65	.13	.03	−.06

a. What is the expected return on an equally weighted portfolio of these three stocks?

b. What is the variance of a portfolio invested 20 percent each in A and B and 60 percent in C?

10. **Returns and Standard Deviations** [LO1] Consider the following information:

State of Economy	Probability of State of Economy	Rate of Return if State Occurs		
		Stock A	Stock B	Stock C
Boom	.15	.30	.45	.33
Good	.45	.12	.10	.15
Poor	.35	.01	−.15	−.05
Bust	.05	−.06	−.30	−.09

a. Your portfolio is invested 30 percent each in A and C, and 40 percent in B. What is the expected return of the portfolio?

b. What is the variance of this portfolio? The standard deviation?

11. **Calculating Portfolio Betas** [LO4] You own a stock portfolio invested 25 percent in Stock Q, 20 percent in Stock R, 15 percent in Stock S, and 40 percent in Stock T. The betas for these four stocks are .84, 1.17, 1.11, and 1.36, respectively. What is the portfolio beta?

12. **Calculating Portfolio Betas** [LO4] You own a portfolio equally invested in a risk-free asset and two stocks. If one of the stocks has a beta of 1.38 and the total portfolio is equally as risky as the market, what must the beta be for the other stock in your portfolio?

13. **Using CAPM** [LO4] A stock has a beta of 1.05, the expected return on the market is 11 percent, and the risk-free rate is 5.2 percent. What must the expected return on this stock be?

14. **Using CAPM** [LO4] A stock has an expected return of 10.2 percent, the risk-free rate is 4.5 percent, and the market risk premium is 8.5 percent. What must the beta of this stock be?

15. **Using CAPM** [LO4] A stock has an expected return of 13.5 percent, its beta is 1.17, and the risk-free rate is 5.5 percent. What must the expected return on the market be?

16. **Using CAPM** [LO4] A stock has an expected return of 14 percent, its beta is 1.45, and the expected return on the market is 11.5 percent. What must the risk-free rate be?

17. **Using CAPM** [LO4] A stock has a beta of 1.35 and an expected return of 16 percent. A risk-free asset currently earns 4.8 percent.

a. What is the expected return on a portfolio that is equally invested in the two assets?

b. If a portfolio of the two assets has a beta of .95, what are the portfolio weights?

c. If a portfolio of the two assets has an expected return of 8 percent, what is its beta?

d. If a portfolio of the two assets has a beta of 2.70, what are the portfolio weights? How do you interpret the weights for the two assets in this case? Explain.

18. **Using the SML** [LO4] Asset W has an expected return of 15.2 percent and a beta of 1.25. If the risk-free rate is 5.3 percent, complete the following table for portfolios of Asset W and a risk-free asset. Illustrate the relationship between portfolio expected return and portfolio beta by plotting the expected returns against the betas. What is the slope of the line that results?

Percentage of Portfolio in Asset W	Portfolio Expected Return	Portfolio Beta
0%		
25		
50		
75		
100		
125		
150		

19. **Reward-to-Risk Ratios** [LO4] Stock Y has a beta of 1.3 and an expected return of 18.5 percent. Stock Z has a beta of .70 and an expected return of 12.1 percent. If the risk-free rate is 8 percent and the market risk premium is 7.5 percent, are these stocks correctly priced?

20. **Reward-to-Risk Ratios** [LO4] In the previous problem, what would the risk-free rate have to be for the two stocks to be correctly priced?

INTERMEDIATE
(Questions 21–24)

21. **Portfolio Returns** [LO2] Using information from the previous chapter on capital market history, determine the return on a portfolio that is equally invested in large-company stocks and long-term government bonds. What is the return on a portfolio that is equally invested in small-company stocks and Treasury bills?

22. **CAPM** [LO4] Using the CAPM, show that the ratio of the risk premiums on two assets is equal to the ratio of their betas.

23. **Portfolio Returns and Deviations** [LO2] Consider the following information about three stocks:

State of Economy	Probability of State of Economy	Rate of Return if State Occurs		
		Stock A	Stock B	Stock C
Boom	.35	.24	.36	.55
Normal	.50	.17	.13	.09
Bust	.15	.00	−.28	−.45

a. If your portfolio is invested 40 percent each in A and B and 20 percent in C, what is the portfolio expected return? The variance? The standard deviation?

b. If the expected T-bill rate is 3.80 percent, what is the expected risk premium on the portfolio?

c. If the expected inflation rate is 3.50 percent, what are the approximate and exact expected real returns on the portfolio? What are the approximate and exact expected real risk premiums on the portfolio?

Visit us at www.mhhe.com/rwj

24. **Analyzing a Portfolio** [LO2] You want to create a portfolio equally as risky as the market, and you have $1,000,000 to invest. Given this information, fill in the rest of the following table:

Asset	Investment	Beta
Stock A	$210,000	.85
Stock B	$320,000	1.20
Stock C		1.35
Risk-free asset		

CHALLENGE
(Questions 25–28)

25. **Analyzing a Portfolio** [LO2, 4] You have $100,000 to invest in a portfolio containing Stock X and Stock Y. Your goal is to create a portfolio that has an expected return of 18.5 percent. If Stock X has an expected return of 17.2 percent and a beta of 1.4, and Stock Y has an expected return of 13.6 percent and a beta of .95, how much money will you invest in stock Y? How do you interpret your answer? What is the beta of your portfolio?

26. **Systematic versus Unsystematic Risk** [LO3] Consider the following information about Stocks I and II:

State of Economy	Probability of State of Economy	Rate of Return if State Occurs	
		Stock I	Stock II
Recession	.25	.11	−.40
Normal	.50	.29	.10
Irrational exuberance	.25	.13	.56

The market risk premium is 8 percent, and the risk-free rate is 4 percent. Which stock has the most systematic risk? Which one has the most unsystematic risk? Which stock is "riskier"? Explain.

27. **SML** [LO4] Suppose you observe the following situation:

Security	Beta	Expected Return
Pete Corp.	1.35	.132
Repete Co.	.80	.101

Assume these securities are correctly priced. Based on the CAPM, what is the expected return on the market? What is the risk-free rate?

28. **SML** [LO4] Suppose you observe the following situation:

State of Economy	Probability of State	Return if State Occurs	
		Stock A	Stock B
Bust	.15	−.08	−.05
Normal	.70	.13	.14
Boom	.15	.48	.29

a. Calculate the expected return on each stock.

b. Assuming the capital asset pricing model holds and stock A's beta is greater than stock B's beta by .25, what is the expected market risk premium?

The Beta for Colgate-Palmolive

Joey Moss, a recent finance graduate, has just begun his job with the investment firm of Covili and Wyatt. Paul Covili, one of the firm's founders, has been talking to Joey about the firm's investment portfolio.

As with any investment, Paul is concerned about the risk of the investment as well as the potential return. More specifically, because the company holds a diversified portfolio, Paul is concerned about the systematic risk of current and potential investments. One such position the company currently holds is stock in Colgate-Palmolive (CL). Colgate-Palmolive is the well-known manufacturer of consumer products under brand names such as Colgate, Palmolive, Softsoap, Irish Spring, Ajax, and others.

Covili and Wyatt currently uses a commercial data vendor for information about its positions. Because of this, Paul is unsure exactly how the numbers provided are calculated. The data provider considers its methods proprietary, and it will not disclose how stock betas and other information are calculated. Paul is uncomfortable with not knowing exactly how these numbers are being computed and also believes that it could be less expensive to calculate the necessary statistics in-house. To explore this question, Paul has asked Joey to do the following assignments.

QUESTIONS

1. Go to finance.yahoo.com and download the ending monthly stock prices for Colgate-Palmolive for the last 60 months. Use the adjusted closing price, which adjusts for dividend payments and stock splits. Next, download the ending value of the S&P 500 index over the same period. For the historical risk-free rate, go to the St. Louis Federal Reserve Web site (www.stlouisfed.org) and find the three-month Treasury bill secondary market rate. Download this file. What are the monthly returns, average monthly returns, and standard deviations for

Colgate-Palmolive stock, the three-month Treasury bill, and the S&P 500 for this period?

2. Beta is often estimated by linear regression. A model often used is called the *market model,* which is:

$$R_t - R_{ft} = \alpha_i + \beta_i [R_{Mt} - R_{ft}] + \varepsilon_t$$

In this regression, R_t is the return on the stock and R_{ft} is the risk-free rate for the same period. R_{Mt} is the return on a stock market index such as the S&P 500 index. α_i is the regression intercept, and β_i is the slope (and the stock's estimated beta). ε_t represents the residuals for the regression. What do you think is the motivation for this particular regression? The intercept, α_i, is often called *Jensen's alpha.* What does it measure? If an asset has a positive Jensen's alpha, where would it plot with respect to the SML? What is the financial interpretation of the residuals in the regression?

3. Use the market model to estimate the beta for Colgate-Palmolive using the last 36 months of returns (the regression procedure in Excel is one easy way to do this). Plot the monthly returns on Colgate-Palmolive against the index and also show the fitted line.

4. When the beta of a stock is calculated using monthly returns, there is a debate over the number of months that should be used in the calculation. Rework the previous questions using the last 60 months of returns. How does this answer compare to what you calculated previously? What are some arguments for and against using shorter versus longer periods? Also, you've used monthly data, which are a common choice. You could have used daily, weekly, quarterly, or even annual data. What do you think are the issues here?

5. Compare your beta for Colgate-Palmolive to the beta you find on finance.yahoo.com. How similar are they? Why might they be different?

Visit us at www.mhhe.com/rwj

MATHEMATICAL TABLES

TABLE A.1
Future value of $1 at the end of t periods $= (1 + r)^t$

TABLE A.2
Present value of $1 to be received after t periods $= 1/(1 + r)^t$

TABLE A.3
Present value of an annuity of $1 per period for t periods $= [1 - 1/(1 + r)^t]/r$

TABLE A.4
Future value of an annuity of $1 per period for t periods $= [(1 + r)^t - 1]/r$

TABLE A.5
Cumulative normal distribution

APPENDIX A Mathematical Tables

TABLE A.1   Future value of \$1 at the end of t periods $= (1 + r)^t$

Period	Interest Rate								
	1%	2%	3%	4%	5%	6%	7%	8%	9%
1	1.0100	1.0200	1.0300	1.0400	1.0500	1.0600	1.0700	1.0800	1.0900
2	1.0201	1.0404	1.0609	1.0816	1.1025	1.1236	1.1449	1.1664	1.1881
3	1.0303	1.0612	1.0927	1.1249	1.1576	1.1910	1.2250	1.2597	1.2950
4	1.0406	1.0824	1.1255	1.1699	1.2155	1.2625	1.3108	1.3605	1.4116
5	1.0510	1.1041	1.1593	1.2167	1.2763	1.3382	1.4026	1.4693	1.5386
6	1.0615	1.1262	1.1941	1.2653	1.3401	1.4185	1.5007	1.5869	1.6771
7	1.0721	1.1487	1.2299	1.3159	1.4071	1.5036	1.6058	1.7138	1.8280
8	1.0829	1.1717	1.2668	1.3686	1.4775	1.5938	1.7182	1.8509	1.9926
9	1.0937	1.1951	1.3048	1.4233	1.5513	1.6895	1.8385	1.9990	2.1719
10	1.1046	1.2190	1.3439	1.4802	1.6289	1.7908	1.9672	2.1589	2.3674
11	1.1157	1.2434	1.3842	1.5395	1.7103	1.8983	2.1049	2.3316	2.5804
12	1.1268	1.2682	1.4258	1.6010	1.7959	2.0122	2.2522	2.5182	2.8127
13	1.1381	1.2936	1.4685	1.6651	1.8856	2.1329	2.4098	2.7196	3.0658
14	1.1495	1.3195	1.5126	1.7317	1.9799	2.2609	2.5785	2.9372	3.3417
15	1.1610	1.3459	1.5580	1.8009	2.0789	2.3966	2.7590	3.1722	3.6425
16	1.1726	1.3728	1.6047	1.8730	2.1829	2.5404	2.9522	3.4259	3.9703
17	1.1843	1.4002	1.6528	1.9479	2.2920	2.6928	3.1588	3.7000	4.3276
18	1.1961	1.4282	1.7024	2.0258	2.4066	2.8543	3.3799	3.9960	4.7171
19	1.2081	1.4568	1.7535	2.1068	2.5270	3.0256	3.6165	4.3157	5.1417
20	1.2202	1.4859	1.8061	2.1911	2.6533	3.2071	3.8697	4.6610	5.6044
21	1.2324	1.5157	1.8603	2.2788	2.7860	3.3996	4.1406	5.0338	6.1088
22	1.2447	1.5460	1.9161	2.3699	2.9253	3.6035	4.4304	5.4365	6.6586
23	1.2572	1.5769	1.9736	2.4647	3.0715	3.8197	4.7405	5.8715	7.2579
24	1.2697	1.6084	2.0328	2.5633	3.2251	4.0489	5.0724	6.3412	7.9111
25	1.2824	1.6406	2.0938	2.6658	3.3864	4.2919	5.4274	6.8485	8.6231
30	1.3478	1.8114	2.4273	3.2434	4.3219	5.7435	7.6123	10.063	13.268
40	1.4889	2.2080	3.2620	4.8010	7.0400	10.286	14.974	21.725	31.409
50	1.6446	2.6916	4.3839	7.1067	11.467	18.420	29.457	46.902	74.358
60	1.8167	3.2810	5.8916	10.520	18.679	32.988	57.946	101.26	176.03

continued on next page

10%	12%	14%	15%	16%	18%	20%	24%	28%	32%	36%
1.1000	1.1200	1.1400	1.1500	1.1600	1.1800	1.2000	1.2400	1.2800	1.3200	1.3600
1.2100	1.2544	1.2996	1.3225	1.3456	1.3924	1.4400	1.5376	1.6384	1.7424	1.8496
1.3310	1.4049	1.4815	1.5209	1.5609	1.6430	1.7280	1.9066	2.0972	2.3000	2.5155
1.4641	1.5735	1.6890	1.7490	1.8106	1.9388	2.0736	2.3642	2.6844	3.0360	3.4210
1.6105	1.7623	1.9254	2.0114	2.1003	2.2878	2.4883	2.9316	3.4360	4.0075	4.6526
1.7716	1.9738	2.1950	2.3131	2.4364	2.6996	2.9860	3.6352	4.3980	5.2899	6.3275
1.9487	2.2107	2.5023	2.6600	2.8262	3.1855	3.5832	4.5077	5.6295	6.9826	8.6054
2.1436	2.4760	2.8526	3.0590	3.2784	3.7589	4.2998	5.5895	7.2058	9.2170	11.703
2.3579	2.7731	3.2519	3.5179	3.8030	4.4355	5.1598	6.9310	9.2234	12.166	15.917
0.5007	0.1050	9.7070	1.0150	1.1111	0.2000	0.1011	0.0044	11.000	10.000	21.047
2.8531	3.4785	4.2262	4.6524	5.1173	6.1759	7.4301	10.657	15.112	21.199	29.439
3.1384	3.8960	4.8179	5.3503	5.9360	7.2876	8.9161	13.215	19.343	27.983	40.037
3.4523	4.3635	5.4924	6.1528	6.8858	8.5994	10.699	16.386	24.759	36.937	54.451
3.7975	4.8871	6.2613	7.0757	7.9875	10.147	12.839	20.319	31.691	48.757	74.053
4.1772	5.4736	7.1379	8.1371	9.2655	11.974	15.407	25.196	40.565	64.359	100.71
4.5950	6.1304	8.1372	9.3576	10.748	14.129	18.488	31.243	51.923	84.954	136.97
5.0545	6.8660	9.2765	10.761	12.468	16.672	22.186	38.741	66.461	112.14	186.28
5.5599	7.6900	10.575	12.375	14.463	19.673	26.623	48.039	85.071	148.02	253.34
6.1159	8.6128	12.056	14.232	16.777	23.214	31.948	59.568	108.89	195.39	344.54
6.7275	9.6463	13.743	16.367	19.461	27.393	38.338	73.864	139.38	257.92	468.57
7.4002	10.804	15.668	18.822	22.574	32.324	46.005	91.592	178.41	340.45	637.26
8.1403	12.100	17.861	21.645	26.186	38.142	55.206	113.57	228.36	449.39	866.67
8.9543	13.552	20.362	24.891	30.376	45.008	66.247	140.83	292.30	593.20	1178.7
9.8497	15.179	23.212	28.625	35.236	53.109	79.497	174.63	374.14	783.02	1603.0
10.835	17.000	26.462	32.919	40.874	62.669	95.396	216.54	478.90	1033.6	2180.1
17.449	29.960	50.950	66.212	85.850	143.37	237.38	634.82	1645.5	4142.1	10143.
45.259	93.051	188.88	267.86	378.72	750.38	1469.8	5455.9	19427.	66521.	*
117.39	289.00	700.23	1083.7	1670.7	3927.4	9100.4	46890.	*	*	*
304.48	897.60	2595.9	4384.0	7370.2	20555.	56348.	*	*	*	*

*The factor is greater than 99,999.

TABLE A.2   Present value of $1 to be received after t periods $= 1/(1 + r)^t$

Period	\multicolumn{9}{c}{Interest Rate}
	1%	2%	3%	4%	5%	6%	7%	8%	9%
1	.9901	.9804	.9709	.9615	.9524	.9434	.9346	.9259	.9174
2	.9803	.9612	.9426	.9246	.9070	.8900	.8734	.8573	.8417
3	.9706	.9423	.9151	.8890	.8638	.8396	.8163	.7938	.7722
4	.9610	.9238	.8885	.8548	.8227	.7921	.7629	.7350	.7084
5	.9515	.9057	.8626	.8219	.7835	.7473	.7130	.6806	.6499
6	.9420	.8880	.8375	.7903	.7462	.7050	.6663	.6302	.5963
7	.9327	.8706	.8131	.7599	.7107	.6651	.6227	.5835	.5470
8	.9235	.8535	.7894	.7307	.6768	.6274	.5820	.5403	.5019
9	.9143	.8368	.7664	.7026	.6446	.5919	.5439	.5002	.4604
10	.9053	.8203	.7441	.6756	.6139	.5584	.5083	.4632	.4224
11	.8963	.8043	.7224	.6496	.5847	.5268	.4751	.4289	.3875
12	.8874	.7885	.7014	.6246	.5568	.4970	.4440	.3971	.3555
13	.8787	.7730	.6810	.6006	.5303	.4688	.4150	.3677	.3262
14	.8700	.7579	.6611	.5775	.5051	.4423	.3878	.3405	.2992
15	.8613	.7430	.6419	.5553	.4810	.4173	.3624	.3152	.2745
16	.8528	.7284	.6232	.5339	.4581	.3936	.3387	.2919	.2519
17	.8444	.7142	.6050	.5134	.4363	.3714	.3166	.2703	.2311
18	.8360	.7002	.5874	.4936	.4155	.3503	.2959	.2502	.2120
19	.8277	.6864	.5703	.4746	.3957	.3305	.2765	.2317	.1945
20	.8195	.6730	.5537	.4564	.3769	.3118	.2584	.2145	.1784
21	.8114	.6598	.5375	.4388	.3589	.2942	.2415	.1987	.1637
22	.8034	.6468	.5219	.4220	.3418	.2775	.2257	.1839	.1502
23	.7954	.6342	.5067	.4057	.3256	.2618	.2109	.1703	.1378
24	.7876	.6217	.4919	.3901	.3101	.2470	.1971	.1577	.1264
25	.7798	.6095	.4776	.3751	.2953	.2330	.1842	.1460	.1160
30	.7419	.5521	.4120	.3083	.2314	.1741	.1314	.0994	.0754
40	.6717	.4529	.3066	.2083	.1420	.0972	.0668	.0460	.0318
50	.6080	.3715	.2281	.1407	.0872	.0543	.0339	.0213	.0134

continued on next page

10%	12%	14%	15%	16%	18%	20%	24%	28%	32%	36%
.9091	.8929	.8772	.8696	.8621	.8475	.8333	.8065	.7813	.7576	.7353
.8264	.7972	.7695	.7561	.7432	.7182	.6944	.6504	.6104	.5739	.5407
.7513	.7118	.6750	.6575	.6407	.6086	.5787	.5245	.4768	.4348	.3975
.6830	.6355	.5921	.5718	.5523	.5158	.4823	.4230	.3725	.3294	.2923
.6209	.5674	.5194	.4972	.4761	.4371	.4019	.3411	.2910	.2495	.2149
.5645	.5066	.4556	.4323	.4104	.3704	.3349	.2751	.2274	.1890	.1580
.5132	.4523	.3996	.3759	.3538	.3139	.2791	.2218	.1776	.1432	.1162
.4665	.4039	.3506	.3269	.3050	.2660	.2326	.1789	.1388	.1085	.0854
.4241	.3606	.3075	.2843	.2630	.2255	.1938	.1443	.1084	.0822	.0628
.3855	.3220	.2697	.2472	.2267	.1911	.1615	.1164	.0847	.0623	.0462
.3505	.2875	.2366	.2149	.1954	.1619	.1346	.0938	.0662	.0472	.0340
.3186	.2567	.2076	.1869	.1685	.1372	.1122	.0757	.0517	.0357	.0250
.2897	.2292	.1821	.1625	.1452	.1163	.0935	.0610	.0404	.0271	.0184
.2633	.2046	.1597	.1413	.1252	.0985	.0779	.0492	.0316	.0205	.0135
.2394	.1827	.1401	.1229	.1079	.0835	.0649	.0397	.0247	.0155	.0099
.2176	.1631	.1229	.1069	.0930	.0708	.0541	.0320	.0193	.0118	.0073
.1978	.1456	.1078	.0929	.0802	.0600	.0451	.0258	.0150	.0089	.0054
.1799	.1300	.0946	.0808	.0691	.0508	.0376	.0208	.0118	.0068	.0039
.1635	.1161	.0829	.0703	.0596	.0431	.0313	.0168	.0092	.0051	.0029
.1486	.1037	.0728	.0611	.0514	.0365	.0261	.0135	.0072	.0039	.0021
.1351	.0926	.0638	.0531	.0443	.0309	.0217	.0109	.0056	.0029	.0016
.1228	.0826	.0560	.0462	.0382	.0262	.0181	.0088	.0044	.0022	.0012
.1117	.0738	.0491	.0402	.0329	.0222	.0151	.0071	.0034	.0017	.0008
.1015	.0659	.0431	.0349	.0284	.0188	.0126	.0057	.0027	.0013	.0006
.0923	.0588	.0378	.0304	.0245	.0160	.0105	.0046	.0021	.0010	.0005
.0573	.0334	.0196	.0151	.0116	.0070	.0042	.0016	.0006	.0002	.0001
.0221	.0107	.0053	.0037	.0026	.0013	.0007	.0002	.0001	*	*
.0085	.0035	.0014	.0009	.0006	.0003	.0001	*	*	*	*

*The factor is zero to four decimal places.

TABLE A.3   Present value of an annuity of $1 per period for t periods $= [1 - 1/(1 + r)^t]/r$

Number of Periods	Interest Rate								
	1%	2%	3%	4%	5%	6%	7%	8%	9%
1	.9901	.9804	.9709	.9615	.9524	.9434	.9346	.9259	.9174
2	1.9704	1.9416	1.9135	1.8861	1.8594	1.8334	1.8080	1.7833	1.7591
3	2.9410	2.8839	2.8286	2.7751	2.7232	2.6730	2.6243	2.5771	2.5313
4	3.9020	3.8077	3.7171	3.6299	3.5460	3.4651	3.3872	3.3121	3.2397
5	4.8534	4.7135	4.5797	4.4518	4.3295	4.2124	4.1002	3.9927	3.8897
6	5.7955	5.6014	5.4172	5.2421	5.0757	4.9173	4.7665	4.6229	4.4859
7	6.7282	6.4720	6.2303	6.0021	5.7864	5.5824	5.3893	5.2064	5.0330
8	7.6517	7.3255	7.0197	6.7327	6.4632	6.2098	5.9713	5.7466	5.5348
9	8.5660	8.1622	7.7861	7.4353	7.1078	6.8017	6.5152	6.2469	5.9952
10	9.4713	8.9826	8.5302	8.1109	7.7217	7.3601	7.0236	6.7101	6.4177
11	10.3676	9.7868	9.2526	8.7605	8.3064	7.8869	7.4987	7.1390	6.8052
12	11.2551	10.5753	9.9540	9.3851	8.8633	8.3838	7.9427	7.5361	7.1607
13	12.1337	11.3484	10.6350	9.9856	9.3936	8.8527	8.3577	7.9038	7.4869
14	13.0037	12.1062	11.2961	10.5631	9.8986	9.2950	8.7455	8.2442	7.7862
15	13.8651	12.8493	11.9379	11.1184	10.3797	9.7122	9.1079	8.5595	8.0607
16	14.7179	13.5777	12.5611	11.6523	10.8378	10.1059	9.4466	8.8514	8.3126
17	15.5623	14.2919	13.1661	12.1657	11.2741	10.4773	9.7632	9.1216	8.5436
18	16.3983	14.9920	13.7535	12.6593	11.6896	10.8276	10.0591	9.3719	8.7556
19	17.2260	15.6785	14.3238	13.1339	12.0853	11.1581	10.3356	9.6036	8.9501
20	18.0456	16.3514	14.8775	13.5903	12.4622	11.4699	10.5940	9.8181	9.1285
21	18.8570	17.0112	15.4150	14.0292	12.8212	11.7641	10.8355	10.0168	9.2922
22	19.6604	17.6580	15.9369	14.4511	13.1630	12.0416	11.0612	10.2007	9.4424
23	20.4558	18.2922	16.4436	14.8568	13.4886	12.3034	11.2722	10.3741	9.5802
24	21.2434	18.9139	16.9355	15.2470	13.7986	12.5504	11.4693	10.5288	9.7066
25	22.0232	19.5235	17.4131	15.6221	14.0939	12.7834	11.6536	10.6748	9.8226
30	25.8077	22.3965	19.6004	17.2920	15.3725	13.7648	12.4090	11.2578	10.2737
40	32.8347	27.3555	23.1148	19.7928	17.1591	15.0463	13.3317	11.9246	10.7574
50	39.1961	31.4236	25.7298	21.4822	18.2559	15.7619	13.8007	12.2335	10.9617

continued on next page

10%	12%	14%	15%	16%	18%	20%	24%	28%	32%	36%
.9091	.8929	.8772	.8696	.8621	.8475	.8333	.8065	.7813	.7576	.7353
1.7355	1.6901	1.6467	1.6257	1.6052	1.5656	1.5278	1.4568	1.3916	1.3315	1.2760
2.4869	2.4018	2.3216	2.2832	2.2459	2.1743	2.1065	1.9813	1.8684	1.7663	1.6735
3.1699	3.0373	2.9137	2.8550	2.7982	2.6901	2.5887	2.4043	2.2410	2.0957	1.9658
3.7908	3.6048	3.4331	3.3522	3.2743	3.1272	2.9906	2.7454	2.5320	2.3452	2.1807
4.3550	4.1114	3.8887	3.7845	3.6847	3.4976	3.3255	3.0205	2.7594	2.5342	2.3388
4.8684	4.5638	4.2883	4.1604	4.0386	3.8115	3.6046	3.2423	2.9370	2.6775	2.4550
5.3349	4.9676	4.6389	4.4873	4.3436	4.0776	3.8372	3.4212	3.0758	2.7860	2.5404
5.7590	5.3282	4.9464	4.7716	4.6065	4.3030	4.0310	3.5655	3.1842	2.8681	2.6033
6.1446	5.6502	5.2161	5.0188	4.8332	4.4941	4.1925	3.6819	3.2689	2.9304	2.6495
6.4951	5.9377	5.4527	5.2337	5.0286	4.6560	4.3271	3.7757	3.3351	2.9776	2.6834
6.8137	6.1944	5.6603	5.4206	5.1971	4.7932	4.4392	3.8514	3.3868	3.0133	2.7084
7.1034	6.4235	5.8424	5.5831	5.3423	4.9095	4.5327	3.9124	3.4272	3.0404	2.7268
7.3667	6.6282	6.0021	5.7245	5.4675	5.0081	4.6106	3.9616	3.4587	3.0609	2.7403
7.6061	6.8109	6.1422	5.8474	5.5755	5.0916	4.6755	4.0013	3.4834	3.0764	2.7502
7.8237	6.9740	6.2651	5.9542	5.6685	5.1624	4.7296	4.0333	3.5026	3.0882	2.7575
8.0216	7.1196	6.3729	6.0472	5.7487	5.2223	4.7746	4.0591	3.5177	3.0971	2.7629
8.2014	7.2497	6.4674	6.1280	5.8178	5.2732	4.8122	4.0799	3.5294	3.1039	2.7668
8.3649	7.3658	6.5504	6.1982	5.8775	5.3162	4.8435	4.0967	3.5386	3.1090	2.7697
8.5136	7.4694	6.6231	6.2593	5.9288	5.3527	4.8696	4.1103	3.5458	3.1129	2.7718
8.6487	7.5620	6.6870	6.3125	5.9731	5.3837	4.8913	4.1212	3.5514	3.1158	2.7734
8.7715	7.6446	6.7429	6.3587	6.0113	5.4099	4.9094	4.1300	3.5558	3.1180	2.7746
8.8832	7.7184	6.7921	6.3988	6.0442	5.4321	4.9245	4.1371	3.5592	3.1197	2.7754
8.9847	7.7843	6.8351	6.4338	6.0726	5.4509	4.9371	4.1428	3.5619	3.1210	2.7760
9.0770	7.8431	6.8729	6.4641	6.0971	5.4669	4.9476	4.1474	3.5640	3.1220	2.7765
9.4269	8.0552	7.0027	6.5660	6.1772	5.5168	4.9789	4.1601	3.5693	3.1242	2.7775
9.7791	8.2438	7.1050	6.6418	6.2335	5.5482	4.9966	4.1659	3.5712	3.1250	2.7778
9.9148	8.3045	7.1327	6.6605	6.2463	5.5541	4.9995	4.1666	3.5714	3.1250	2.7778

TABLE A.4   Future value of an annuity of $1 per period for t periods $= [(1 + r)^t - 1]/r$

Number of Periods	Interest Rate								
	1%	2%	3%	4%	5%	6%	7%	8%	9%
1	1.0000	1.0000	1.0000	1.0000	1.0000	1.0000	1.0000	1.0000	1.0000
2	2.0100	2.0200	2.0300	2.0400	2.0500	2.0600	2.0700	2.0800	2.0900
3	3.0301	3.0604	3.0909	3.1216	3.1525	3.1836	3.2149	3.2464	3.2781
4	4.0604	4.1216	4.1836	4.2465	4.3101	4.3746	4.4399	4.5061	4.5731
5	5.1010	5.2040	5.3091	5.4163	5.5256	5.6371	5.7507	5.8666	5.9847
6	6.1520	6.3081	6.4684	6.6330	6.8019	6.9753	7.1533	7.3359	7.5233
7	7.2135	7.4343	7.6625	7.8983	8.1420	8.3938	8.6540	8.9228	9.2004
8	8.2857	8.5830	8.8932	9.2142	9.5491	9.8975	10.260	10.637	11.028
9	9.3685	9.7546	10.159	10.583	11.027	11.491	11.978	12.488	13.021
10	10.462	10.950	11.464	12.006	12.578	13.181	13.816	14.487	15.193
11	11.567	12.169	12.808	13.486	14.207	14.972	15.784	16.645	17.560
12	12.683	13.412	14.192	15.026	15.917	16.870	17.888	18.977	20.141
13	13.809	14.680	15.618	16.627	17.713	18.882	20.141	21.495	22.953
14	14.947	15.974	17.086	18.292	19.599	21.015	22.550	24.215	26.019
15	16.097	17.293	18.599	20.024	21.579	23.276	25.129	27.152	29.361
16	17.258	18.639	20.157	21.825	23.657	25.673	27.888	30.324	33.003
17	18.430	20.012	21.762	23.698	25.840	28.213	30.840	33.750	36.974
18	19.615	21.412	23.414	25.645	28.132	30.906	33.999	37.450	41.301
19	20.811	22.841	25.117	27.671	30.539	33.760	37.379	41.446	46.018
20	22.019	24.297	26.870	29.778	33.066	36.786	40.995	45.762	51.160
21	23.239	25.783	28.676	31.969	35.719	39.993	44.865	50.423	56.765
22	24.472	27.299	30.537	34.248	38.505	43.392	49.006	55.457	62.873
23	25.716	28.845	32.453	36.618	41.430	46.996	53.436	60.893	69.532
24	26.973	30.422	34.426	39.083	44.502	50.816	58.177	66.765	76.790
25	28.243	32.030	36.459	41.646	47.727	54.865	63.249	73.106	84.701
30	34.785	40.568	47.575	56.085	66.439	79.058	94.461	113.28	136.31
40	48.886	60.402	75.401	95.026	120.80	154.76	199.64	259.06	337.88
50	64.463	84.579	112.80	152.67	209.35	290.34	406.53	573.77	815.08
60	81.670	114.05	163.05	237.99	353.58	533.13	813.52	1253.2	1944.8

continued on next page

10%	12%	14%	15%	16%	18%	20%	24%	28%	32%	36%
1.0000	1.0000	1.0000	1.0000	1.0000	1.0000	1.0000	1.0000	1.0000	1.0000	1.0000
2.1000	2.1200	2.1400	2.1500	2.1600	2.1800	2.2000	2.2400	2.2800	2.3200	2.3600
3.3100	3.3744	3.4396	3.4725	3.5056	3.5724	3.6400	3.7776	3.9184	4.0624	4.2096
4.6410	4.7793	4.9211	4.9934	5.0665	5.2154	5.3680	5.6842	6.0156	6.3624	6.7251
6.1051	6.3528	6.6101	6.7424	6.8771	7.1542	7.4416	8.0484	8.6999	9.3983	10.146
7.7156	8.1152	8.5355	8.7537	8.9775	9.4420	9.9299	10.980	12.136	13.406	14.799
9.4872	10.089	10.730	11.067	11.414	12.142	12.916	14.615	16.534	18.696	21.126
11.436	12.300	13.233	13.727	14.240	15.327	16.499	19.123	22.163	25.678	29.732
13.579	14.776	16.085	16.786	17.519	19.086	20.799	24.712	29.369	34.895	41.435
15.937	17.549	19.337	20.304	21.321	23.521	25.959	31.643	38.593	47.062	57.352
18.531	20.655	23.045	24.349	25.733	28.755	32.150	40.238	50.398	63.122	78.998
21.384	24.133	27.271	29.002	30.850	34.931	39.581	50.895	65.510	84.320	108.44
24.523	28.029	32.089	34.352	36.786	42.219	48.497	64.110	84.853	112.30	148.47
27.975	32.393	37.581	40.505	43.672	50.818	59.196	80.496	109.61	149.24	202.93
31.772	37.280	43.842	47.580	51.660	60.965	72.035	100.82	141.30	198.00	276.98
35.950	42.753	50.980	55.717	60.925	72.939	87.442	126.01	181.87	262.36	377.69
40.545	48.884	59.118	65.075	71.673	87.068	105.93	157.25	233.79	347.31	514.66
45.599	55.750	68.394	75.836	84.141	103.74	128.12	195.99	300.25	459.45	700.94
51.159	63.440	78.969	88.212	98.603	123.41	154.74	244.03	385.32	607.47	954.28
57.275	72.052	91.025	102.44	115.38	146.63	186.69	303.60	494.21	802.86	1298.8
64.002	81.699	104.77	118.81	134.84	174.02	225.03	377.46	633.59	1060.8	1767.4
71.403	92.503	120.44	137.63	157.41	206.34	271.03	469.06	812.00	1401.2	2404.7
79.543	104.60	138.30	159.28	183.60	244.49	326.24	582.63	1040.4	1850.6	3271.3
88.497	118.16	158.66	184.17	213.98	289.49	392.48	723.46	1332.7	2443.8	4450.0
98.347	133.33	181.87	212.79	249.21	342.60	471.98	898.09	1706.8	3226.8	6053.0
164.49	241.33	356.79	434.75	530.31	790.95	1181.9	2640.9	5873.2	12941.	28172.
442.59	767.09	1342.0	1779.1	2360.8	4163.2	7343.9	22729.	69377.	*	*
1163.9	2400.0	4994.5	7217.7	10436.	21813.	45497.	*	*	*	*
3043.8	7471.6	18535.	29220.	46058.	*	*	*	*	*	*

*The factor is greater than 99,999.

TABLE A.5 Cumulative normal distribution

d	N(d)	d	N(d)	d	N(d)	d	N(d)	d	N(d)	d	N(d)
−3.00	.0013	−1.58	.0571	−.76	.2236	.06	.5239	.86	.8051	1.66	.9515
−2.95	.0016	−1.56	.0594	−.74	.2297	.08	.5319	.88	.8106	1.68	.9535
−2.90	.0019	−1.54	.0618	−.72	.2358	.10	.5398	.90	.8159	1.70	.9554
−2.85	.0022	−1.52	.0643	−.70	.2420	.12	.5478	.92	.8212	1.72	.9573
−2.80	.0026	−1.50	.0668	−.68	.2483	.14	.5557	.94	.8264	1.74	.9591
−2.75	.0030	−1.48	.0694	−.66	.2546	.16	.5636	.96	.8315	1.76	.9608
−2.70	.0035	−1.46	.0721	−.64	.2611	.18	.5714	.98	.8365	1.78	.9625
−2.65	.0040	−1.44	.0749	−.62	.2676	.20	.5793	1.00	.8413	1.80	.9641
−2.60	.0047	−1.42	.0778	−.60	.2743	.22	.5871	1.02	.8461	1.82	.9656
−2.55	.0054	−1.40	.0808	−.58	.2810	.24	.5948	1.04	.8508	1.84	.9671
−2.50	.0062	−1.38	.0838	−.56	.2877	.26	.6026	1.06	.8554	1.86	.9686
−2.45	.0071	−1.36	.0869	−.54	.2946	.28	.6103	1.08	.8599	1.88	.9699
−2.40	.0082	−1.34	.0901	−.52	.3015	.30	.6179	1.10	.8643	1.90	.9713
−2.35	.0094	−1.32	.0934	−.50	.3085	.32	.6255	1.12	.8686	1.92	.9726
−2.30	.0107	−1.30	.0968	−.48	.3156	.34	.6331	1.14	.8729	1.94	.9738
−2.25	.0122	−1.28	.1003	−.46	.3228	.36	.6406	1.16	.8770	1.96	.9750
−2.20	.0139	−1.26	.1038	−.44	.3300	.38	.6480	1.18	.8810	1.98	.9761
−2.15	.0158	−1.24	.1075	−.42	.3372	.40	.6554	1.20	.8849	2.00	.9772
−2.10	.0179	−1.22	.1112	−.40	.3446	.42	.6628	1.22	.8888	2.05	.9798
−2.05	.0202	−1.20	.1151	−.38	.3520	.44	.6700	1.24	.8925	2.10	.9821
−2.00	.0228	−1.18	.1190	−.36	.3594	.46	.6772	1.26	.8962	2.15	.9842
−1.98	.0239	−1.16	.1230	−.34	.3669	.48	.6844	1.28	.8997	2.20	.9861
−1.96	.0250	−1.14	.1271	−.32	.3745	.50	.6915	1.30	.9032	2.25	.9878
−1.94	.0262	−1.12	.1314	−.30	.3821	.52	.6985	1.32	.9066	2.30	.9893
−1.92	.0274	−1.10	.1357	−.28	.3897	.54	.7054	1.34	.9099	2.35	.9906
−1.90	.0287	−1.08	.1401	−.26	.3974	.56	.7123	1.36	.9131	2.40	.9918
−1.88	.0301	−1.06	.1446	−.24	.4052	.58	.7190	1.38	.9162	2.45	.9929
−1.86	.0314	−1.04	.1492	−.22	.4129	.60	.7257	1.40	.9192	2.50	.9938
−1.84	.0329	−1.02	.1539	−.20	.4207	.62	.7324	1.42	.9222	2.55	.9946
−1.82	.0344	−1.00	.1587	−.18	.4286	.64	.7389	1.44	.9251	2.60	.9953
−1.80	.0359	−.98	.1635	−.16	.4364	.66	.7454	1.46	.9279	2.65	.9960
−1.78	.0375	−.96	.1685	−.14	.4443	.68	.7518	1.48	.9306	2.70	.9965
−1.76	.0392	−.94	.1736	−.12	.4522	.70	.7580	1.50	.9332	2.75	.9970
−1.74	.0409	−.92	.1788	−.10	.4602	.72	.7642	1.52	.9357	2.80	.9974
−1.72	.0427	−.90	.1841	−.08	.4681	.74	.7704	1.54	.9382	2.85	.9978
−1.70	.0446	−.88	.1894	−.06	.4761	.76	.7764	1.56	.9406	2.90	.9981
−1.68	.0465	−.86	.1949	−.04	.4840	.78	.7823	1.58	.9429	2.95	.9984
−1.66	.0485	−.84	.2005	−.02	.4920	.80	.7881	1.60	.9452	3.00	.9987
−1.64	.0505	−.82	.2061	.00	.5000	.82	.7939	1.62	.9474	3.05	.9989
−1.62	.0526	−.80	.2119	.02	.5080	.84	.7995	1.64	.9495		
−1.60	.0548	−.78	.2177	.04	.5160						

This table shows the probability [N(d)] of observing a value less than or equal to d. For example, as illustrated, if d is −.24, then N(d) is .4052.

KEY EQUATIONS

$$B$$

CHAPTER 2

1. The balance sheet identity or equation:

   Assets = Liabilities
   + Shareholders' equity   [2.1]

2. The income statement equation:

   Revenues − Expenses = Income   [2.2]

3. The cash flow identity:

   Cash flow from assets =
   Cash flow to creditors +   [2.3]
   Cash flow to stockholders

   where

   a. Cash flow from assets = Operating cash
      flow (OCF) − Net capital spending −
      Change in net working capital (NWC)
      (1) Operating cash flow = Earnings
          before interest and taxes (EBIT) +
          Depreciation − Taxes
      (2) Net capital spending = Ending net
          fixed assets − Beginning net fixed
          assets + Depreciation
      (3) Change in net working capital =
          Ending NWC − Beginning NWC
   b. Cash flow to creditors = Interest paid −
      Net new borrowing
   c. Cash flow to stockholders = Dividends
      paid − Net new equity raised

CHAPTER 3

1. The current ratio:

   $$\text{Current ratio} = \frac{\text{Current assets}}{\text{Current liabilities}} \quad [3.1]$$

2. The quick or acid-test ratio:

   $$\text{Quick ratio} = \frac{\text{Current assets} - \text{Inventory}}{\text{Current liabilities}} \quad [3.2]$$

3. The cash ratio:

   $$\text{Cash ratio} = \frac{\text{Cash}}{\text{Current liabilities}} \quad [3.3]$$

4. The ratio of net working capital to total assets:

   Net working capital to total assets
   $$= \frac{\text{Net working capital}}{\text{Total assets}} \quad [3.4]$$

5. The interval measure:

   Interval measure
   $$= \frac{\text{Current assets}}{\text{Average daily operating costs}} \quad [3.5]$$

6. The total debt ratio:

   Total debt ratio
   $$= \frac{\text{Total assets} - \text{Total equity}}{\text{Total assets}} \quad [3.6]$$

7. The debt-equity ratio:

   Debt-equity ratio
   = Total debt/Total equity   [3.7]

8. The equity multiplier:

   Equity multiplier
   = Total assets/Total equity   [3.8]

9. The long-term debt ratio:

   Long-term debt ratio
   $$= \frac{\text{Long-term debt}}{\text{Long-term debt} + \text{Total equity}} \quad [3.9]$$

10. The times interest earned (TIE) ratio:

    $$\text{Times interest earned ratio} = \frac{\text{EBIT}}{\text{Interest}} \quad [3.10]$$

11. The cash coverage ratio:

    Cash coverage ratio
    $$= \frac{\text{EBIT} + \text{Depreciation}}{\text{Interest}} \quad [3.11]$$

12. The inventory turnover ratio:

    Inventory turnover
    $$= \frac{\text{Cost of goods sold}}{\text{Inventory}} \quad [3.12]$$

13. The average days' sales in inventory:

    Days' sales in inventory
    $$= \frac{365 \text{ days}}{\text{Inventory turnover}} \quad [3.13]$$

14. The receivables turnover ratio:

$$\text{Receivables turnover} = \frac{\text{Sales}}{\text{Accounts receivable}} \qquad [3.14]$$

15. The days' sales in receivables:

$$\text{Days' sales in receivables} = \frac{365 \text{ days}}{\text{Receivables turnover}} \qquad [3.15]$$

16. The net working capital (NWC) turnover ratio:

$$\text{NWC turnover} = \frac{\text{Sales}}{\text{NWC}} \qquad [3.16]$$

17. The fixed asset turnover ratio:

$$\text{Fixed asset turnover} = \frac{\text{Sales}}{\text{Net fixed assets}} \qquad [3.17]$$

18. The total asset turnover ratio:

$$\text{Total asset turnover} = \frac{\text{Sales}}{\text{Total assets}} \qquad [3.18]$$

19. Profit margin:

$$\text{Profit margin} = \frac{\text{Net income}}{\text{Sales}} \qquad [3.19]$$

20. Return on assets (ROA):

$$\text{Return on assets} = \frac{\text{Net income}}{\text{Total assets}} \qquad [3.20]$$

21. Return on equity (ROE):

$$\text{Return on equity} = \frac{\text{Net income}}{\text{Total equity}} \qquad [3.21]$$

22. The price-earnings (PE) ratio:

$$\text{PE ratio} = \frac{\text{Price per share}}{\text{Earnings per share}} \qquad [3.22]$$

23. The market-to-book ratio:

$$\text{Market-to-book ratio} = \frac{\text{Market value per share}}{\text{Book value per share}} \qquad [3.23]$$

24. The Du Pont identity:

$$\text{ROE} = \underbrace{\frac{\text{Net income}}{\text{Sales}} \times \frac{\text{Sales}}{\text{Assets}}}_{\text{Return on assets}} \times \frac{\text{Assets}}{\text{Equity}} \qquad [3.24]$$

ROE = Profit margin
× Total asset turnover
× Equity multiplier

CHAPTER 4

1. The dividend payout ratio:

$$\text{Dividend payout ratio} = \text{Cash dividends/Net income} \qquad [4.1]$$

2. The internal growth rate:

$$\text{Internal growth rate} = \frac{\text{ROA} \times b}{1 - \text{ROA} \times b} \qquad [4.2]$$

3. The sustainable growth rate:

$$\text{Sustainable growth rate} = \frac{\text{ROE} \times b}{1 - \text{ROE} \times b} \qquad [4.3]$$

4. The capital intensity ratio:

$$\text{Capital intensity ratio} = \frac{\text{Total assets}}{\text{Sales}}$$
$$= \frac{1}{\text{Total asset turnover}}$$

CHAPTER 5

1. The future value of $1 invested for t periods at rate of r per period:

$$\text{Future value} = \$1 \times (1 + r)^t \qquad [5.1]$$

2. The present value of $1 to be received t periods in the future at a discount rate of r:

$$\text{PV} = \$1 \times [1/(1 + r)^t] = \$1/(1 + r)^t \qquad [5.2]$$

3. The relationship between future value and present value (the basic present value equation):

$$\text{PV} \times (1 + r)^t = \text{FV}_t$$
$$\text{PV} = \text{FV}_t/(1 + r)^t = \text{FV}_t \times [1/(1 + r)^t] \qquad [5.3]$$

CHAPTER 6

1. The present value of an annuity of C dollars per period for t periods when the rate of return or interest rate is r:

$$\text{Annuity present value} = C \times \left(\frac{1 - \text{Present value factor}}{r} \right)$$
$$= C \times \left\{ \frac{1 - [1/(1 + r)^t]}{r} \right\} \qquad [6.1]$$

2. The future value factor for an annuity:

$$\text{Annuity FV factor} = (\text{Future value factor} - 1)/r \qquad [6.2]$$
$$= [(1 + r)^t - 1]/r$$

3. Annuity due value = Ordinary annuity value
$$\times (1 + r) \qquad [6.3]$$

4. Present value for a perpetuity:

$$\text{PV for a perpetuity} = C/r = C \times (1/r) \qquad [6.4]$$

5. Growing annuity present value

$$= C \left[\frac{1 - \left(\frac{1 + g}{1 + r} \right)^t}{r - g} \right] \qquad [6.5]$$

6. Growing perpetuity present value

$$= \frac{C}{r - g} \qquad [6.6]$$

7. Effective annual rate (EAR), where m is the number of times the interest is compounded during the year:

$$EAR = [1 + (\text{Quoted rate}/m)]^m - 1$$

8. Effective annual rate (EAR), where q stands for the continuously compounded quoted rate:

$$EAR = e^q - 1$$

CHAPTER 7

1. Bond value if bond has (1) a face value of F paid at maturity, (2) a coupon of C paid per period, (3) t periods to maturity, and (4) a yield of r per period:

$$\text{Bond value} = C \times [1 - 1/(1 + r)^t]/r + F/(1 + r)^t \qquad [7.1]$$

$$\text{Bond value} = \begin{array}{c} \text{Present value} \\ \text{of the coupons} \end{array} + \begin{array}{c} \text{Present value} \\ \text{of the face amount} \end{array}$$

2. The Fisher effect:

$$1 + R = (1 + r) \times (1 + h) \qquad [7.2]$$
$$R = r + h + r \times h \qquad [7.3]$$
$$R \approx r + h \qquad [7.4]$$

CHAPTER 8

1. The dividend growth model:

$$P_0 = \frac{D_0 \times (1 + g)}{R - g} = \frac{D_1}{R - g} \qquad [8.3]$$

2. Required return:

$$R = D_1/P_0 + g \qquad [8.7]$$

CHAPTER 9

1. Net present value (NPV):

$$NPV = \text{Present value of future cash flows} - \text{Investment cost}$$

2. Payback period:

Payback period = Number of years that pass before the sum of an investment's cash flows equals the cost of the investment

3. Discounted payback period:

Discounted payback period = Number of years that pass before the sum of an investment's *discounted* cash flows equals the cost of the investment

4. The average accounting return (AAR):

$$AAR = \frac{\text{Average net income}}{\text{Average book value}}$$

5. Internal rate of return (IRR):

IRR = Discount rate of required return such that the net present value of an investment is zero

6. Profitability index:

$$\text{Profitability index} = \frac{\text{PV of cash flows}}{\text{Cost of investment}}$$

CHAPTER 10

1. Bottom-up approach to operating cash flow (OCF):

$$OCF = \text{Net income} + \text{Depreciation} \qquad [10.1]$$

2. Top-down approach to operating cash flow (OCF):

$$OCF = \text{Sales} - \text{Costs} - \text{Taxes} \qquad [10.2]$$

3. Tax shield approach to operating cash flow (OCF):

$$OCF = (\text{Sales} - \text{Costs}) \times (1 - T) + \text{Depreciation} \times T \qquad [10.3]$$

CHAPTER 11

1. Accounting break-even level:

$$Q = (FC + D)/(P - v) \qquad [11.1]$$

2. Relationship between operating cash flow (OCF) and sales volume:

$$Q = (FC + OCF)/(P - v) \qquad [11.3]$$

3. Cash break-even level:

$$Q = FC/(P - v)$$

4. Financial break-even level:

$$Q = (FC + OCF^*)/(P - v)$$

where

$$OCF^* = \text{Zero NPV cash flow}$$

5. Degree of operating leverage (DOL):

$$DOL = 1 + FC/OCF \qquad [11.4]$$

CHAPTER 12

1. Variance of returns, Var(R) or σ^2:

$$\text{Var}(R) = \frac{1}{T - 1}[(R_1 - \overline{R})^2 + \cdots + (R_T - \overline{R})^2] \qquad [12.3]$$

2. Standard deviation of returns, SD(R) or σ:

$$SD(R) = \sqrt{\text{Var}(R)}$$

CHAPTER 13

1. Risk premium:

Risk premium = Expected return − Risk-free rate $\qquad [13.1]$

2. Expected return on a portfolio:

$$E(R_p) = x_1 \times E(R_1) + x_2 \times E(R_2) + \cdots + x_n \times E(R_n) \qquad [13.2]$$

3. The reward-to-risk ratio:

$$\text{Reward-to-risk ratio} = \frac{E[R_i] - R_f}{\beta_i}$$

4. The capital asset pricing model (CAPM):

$$E(R_i) = R_f + [E(R_M) - R_f] \times \beta_i \qquad [13.7]$$

CHAPTER 14

1. Required return on equity, R_E (dividend growth model):

$$R_E = D_1/P_0 + g \qquad [14.1]$$

2. Required return on equity, R_E (CAPM):

$$R_E = R_f + \beta_E \times (R_M - R_f) \qquad [14.2]$$

3. Required return on preferred stock, R_P:

$$R_P = D/P_0 \qquad [14.3]$$

4. The weighted average cost of capital (WACC):

$$\text{WACC} = (E/V) \times R_E + (D/V) \times R_D \times (1 - T_C) \qquad [14.6]$$

5. Weighted average flotation cost, f_A:

$$f_A = \frac{E}{V} \times f_E + \frac{D}{V} \times f_D \qquad [14.8]$$

CHAPTER 15

1. Rights offerings:

a. Number of new shares:

$$\text{Number of new shares} = \frac{\text{Funds to be raised}}{\text{Subscription price}} \qquad [15.1]$$

b. Number of rights needed:

$$\text{Number of rights needed to buy a share of stock} = \frac{\text{Old shares}}{\text{New shares}} \qquad [15.2]$$

c. Value of a right:

$$\text{Value of a right} = \text{Rights-on price} - \text{Ex-rights price}$$

CHAPTER 16

1. Modigliani-Miller propositions (no taxes):

a. Proposition I:

$$V_L = V_U$$

b. Proposition II:

$$R_E = R_A + (R_A - R_D) \times (D/E) \qquad [16.1]$$

2. Modigliani-Miller propositions (with taxes):

a. Value of the interest tax shield:

$$\begin{aligned}\text{Present value of the interest tax shield} &= (T_C \times D \times R_D)/R_D \qquad [16.2]\\ &= T_C \times D\end{aligned}$$

b. Proposition I:

$$V_L = V_U + T_C \times D \qquad [16.3]$$

c. Proposition II:

$$R_E = R_U + (R_U - R_D) \times (D/E) \times (1 - T_C) \qquad [16.4]$$

CHAPTER 18

1. The operating cycle:

$$\begin{aligned}\text{Operating cycle} &= \text{Inventory period} \\ &+ \text{Accounts receivable period} \qquad [18.4]\end{aligned}$$

2. The cash cycle:

$$\begin{aligned}\text{Cash cycle} &= \text{Operating cycle} \\ &- \text{Accounts payable period} \qquad [18.5]\end{aligned}$$

CHAPTER 19

1. Float measurement:

a. Average daily float:

$$\text{Average daily float} = \frac{\text{Total float}}{\text{Total days}} \qquad [19.1]$$

b. Average daily float:

$$\begin{aligned}\text{Average daily float} &= \text{Average daily receipts} \\ &\times \text{Weighted average delay} \qquad [19.2]\end{aligned}$$

2. The Baumol-Allais-Tobin (BAT) model:

a. Opportunity costs:

$$\text{Opportunity costs} = (C/2) \times R \qquad [19A.1]$$

b. Trading costs:

$$\text{Trading costs} = (T/C) \times F \qquad [19A.2]$$

c. Total cost:

$$\begin{aligned}\text{Total cost} &= \text{Opportunity costs} \\ &+ \text{Trading costs} \qquad [19A.3]\end{aligned}$$

d. The optimal initial cash balance:

$$C^* = \sqrt{(2T \times F)/R} \qquad [19A.4]$$

3. The Miller-Orr model:

a. The optimal cash balance:

$$C^* = L + (3/4 \times F \times \sigma^2/R)^{1/3} \qquad [19A.5]$$

b. The upper limit:

$$U^* = 3 \times C^* - 2 \times L \qquad [19A.6]$$

CHAPTER 20

1. The size of receivables:

$$\begin{aligned}\text{Accounts receivable} &= \text{Average daily sales} \times \text{ACP} \qquad [20.1]\end{aligned}$$

2. NPV of switching credit terms:

   a. Present value of switching:

   $$PV = [(P - v)(Q' - Q)]/R \qquad [20.4]$$

   b. Cost of switching:

   $$\text{Cost of switching} = PQ + v(Q' - Q) \qquad [20.5]$$

   c. NPV of switching:

   $$\begin{aligned}\text{NPV of switching} = &-[PQ + v(Q' - Q)]\\ &+ [(P - v)\\ &\times (Q' - Q)]/R\end{aligned} \qquad [20.6]$$

3. NPV of granting credit:

   a. With no repeat business:

   $$\text{NPV} = -v + (1 - \pi)P/(1 + R) \qquad [20.8]$$

   b. With repeat business:

   $$\text{NPV} = -v + (1 - \pi)(P - v)/R \qquad [20.9]$$

4. The economic order quantity (EOQ) model:

   a. Total carrying costs:

   $$\begin{aligned}\text{Total carrying costs}\\ = \text{Average inventory}\\ \times \text{Carrying costs per unit}\\ = (Q/2) \times CC\end{aligned} \qquad [20.10]$$

   b. Total restocking costs:

   $$\begin{aligned}\text{Total restocking costs}\\ = \text{Fixed cost per order}\\ \times \text{Number of orders} = F \times (T/Q)\end{aligned} \qquad [20.11]$$

   c. Total costs:

   $$\begin{aligned}\text{Total costs} = &\text{ Carrying costs}\\ &+ \text{Restocking costs}\\ = &(Q/2) \times CC\\ &+ F \times (T/Q)\end{aligned} \qquad [20.12]$$

   d. The optimal order size Q^*:

   $$Q^* = \sqrt{\frac{2T \times F}{CC}} \qquad [20.15]$$

CHAPTER 21

1. Purchasing power parity (PPP):

   $$E(S_t) = S_0 \times [1 + (h_{FC} - h_{US})]^t \qquad [21.3]$$

2. Interest rate parity (IRP):

   a. Exact, single period:

   $$F_1/S_0 = (1 + R_{FC})/(1 + R_{US}) \qquad [21.4]$$

   b. Approximate, multiperiod:

   $$F_t = S_0 \times [1 + (R_{FC} - R_{US})]^t \qquad [21.7]$$

3. Uncovered interest parity (UIP):

   $$E(S_t) = S_0 \times [1 + (R_{FC} - R_{US})]^t \qquad [21.9]$$

4. International Fisher effect (IFE):

   $$R_{US} - h_{US} = R_{FC} - h_{FC} \qquad [21.10]$$

ANSWERS TO SELECTED END-OF-CHAPTER PROBLEMS

CHAPTER 2

2. $171,600

7. Average rate = 31.90%
Marginal rate = 39%

10. −$180

14. a. $63,745
b. $22,100
c. $4,700
d. $845

18. a. $\text{Tax}_{\text{Growth}}$ = $19,870
$\text{Tax}_{\text{Income}}$ = $2,992,000
b. $3,400

22. a. 2008 = $1,661
2009 = $2,142
b. $22
c. Fixed assets sold = $63
Cash flow from assets = $1,896
d. Debt retired = $180
Cash flow to creditors = $121

26. Cash flow from assets = −$1,302.76
Cash flow to creditors = −$2,156.00
Cash flow to stockholders = $853.24

CHAPTER 3

2. Net income = $2.32 million
ROA = 13.26%
ROE = 20.71%

6. EPS = $2.88
DPS = $.83
BVPS = $25.24
Market-to-book ratio = 2.50 times
PE ratio = 21.87 times
P/S ratio = 2.94 times

10. 78.51 days

18. $194.06

22. Firm A: 18.46%
Firm B: 15.71%

26. a. 1.44 times; 1.40 times
b. .85 times; .83 times
c. .56 times; .51 times

d. .95 times
e. 8.56 times
f. 22.08 times
g. .39; .40
h. .65; .66
i. 1.65; 1.66
j. 5.70 times
k. 7.95 times
l. 11.93%
m. 11.36%
n. 18.91%

CHAPTER 4

2. −$1,252.50

5. $1,000.14

12. 6.84%

16. 5.26%

20. 1.74 times

22. Sustainable growth rate = 16.47%
New borrowing = $14,160.64
Internal growth rate = 6.04%

28. 16.16%

CHAPTER 5

2. $6,419.51
$14,999.39
$687,764.17
$315,795.75

6. 9.68%

10. $155,893,400

14. 9.90%

18. $438,120.97; $154,299.40

CHAPTER 6

2. @ 5%: PV_X = $42,646.93
PV_Y = $40,605.54
@ 15%: PV_X = $28,629.50
PV_Y = $30,275.86

6. $411,660.36

10. $347,222.22

14. First National EAR = 15.16%
First United EAR = 15.03%

18. $28,804.71

22. APR = 1,733.33%
EAR = 313,916,515.69%

26. $34,843.71

30. 8.17% semiannual
4.00% quarterly
1.32% monthly

38. $2,235,994

42. $368,936.54

46. Profit = $7,197.59
Breakeven = 15.10%

50. $37,051.41

54. $1,364.99

58. PV of lease payments = $14,672.91
PV of purchase = $13,345.18
Breakeven resale price = $21,363.01

60. EAR = 17.65%

64. Refundable fee:
APR = 6.89%
EAR = 7.12%
Nonrefundable fee:
APR = 6.80%
EAR = 7.02%

70. 8.07%

74. 6.48%

CHAPTER 7

4. 10.15%

8. 5.97%

12. 6.30%

26. a. 30,000 coupon bonds; 315,589 zeroes
b. $32,400,000; $315,588,822

28. $7,367.76

CHAPTER 8

2. 9.38%

6. $2.45

10. $63.47

14. $48.70

18. $96.15

20. $69.55

CHAPTER 9

4. 1.81 years; 2.54 years; 3.26 years

8. @ 11%: NPV = $5,991.49
@30%: NPV = −$4,213.93

12. a. $IRR_A = 20.44\%$
$IRR_B = 18.84\%$
b. $NPV_A = \$7,507.61$
$NPV_B = \$9,182.29$
c. Crossover rate = 15.30%

16. a. $PI_I = 1.267$
$PI_I = 1.414$
b. $NPV_I = \$14,145.00$
$NPV_{II} = \$6,630.35$

22. a. $C = I / N$
b. $C > I / PVIFA_{R\%,N}$
c. $C > 2.0 * I / PVIFA_{R\%,N}$

CHAPTER 10

2. $403,600,000

8. $1,387,792

12. $CF_0 = -\$4,200,000$
$CF_1 = \$1,631,455$
$CF_2 = \$1,738,243$
$CF_3 = \$1,916,303$
NPV = $42,232.43

16. −$117,803.98

22. $.03163

CHAPTER 11

2. Total costs = $6,222,800
Marginal cost = $38.94
Average cost = $51.86
Minimum revenue = $194,700

8. $D = 420,800$
$P = \$69.36$
VC = $37.57

12. OCF = $34,333
DOL = 4.786

18. DOL = 1.2480
$DOL_A = 2.7143$

22. $\Delta NPV/\Delta P = \$148,973.62$
$DNPV/\Delta Q = \$1,226.84$

30. DOL = 1.0381
$\Delta OCF = +2.97\%$

CHAPTER 12

2. $R_d = 2.64\%$
$R_c = 12.09\%$

6. 2.62%; 3.01%

16. $R_A = 11.83\%$
$R_G = 10.58\%$

20. 14.95%; 14.52%; 13.64%

CHAPTER 13

2. 13.23%

6. 12.50%

10. a. 7.64%
   b. $\sigma^2_P = .02436$
      $\sigma_P = 15.61\%$

14. .67

18. .0792

24. $C = \$324,074.07$
   $R_F = \$145,925.93$

26. $\beta_I = 2.06$
   $\sigma_I = 8.53\%$
   $\beta_{II} = .63$
   $\sigma_{II} = 33.96\%$

CHAPTER 14

2. 12.34%

4. $R_A = 11.47\%$; $R_G = 11.46\%$

8. Book value = $115,000,000
   Market value = $97,350,000
   Aftertax cost = 5.34%

12. a. $E/V = .3455$
      $D/V = .6545$
   b. $E/V = .8595$
      $D/V = .1405$

16. a. $D/V = .2290$
      $P/V = .0534$
      $E/V = .7176$
   b. 12.80%

20. Breakeven cost = $37,943,787

CHAPTER 15

2. a. $53; anything greater than $0
   b. 833,333, 4.92
   c. $52.16; $.84

6. 3,186,813

8. No change;
   declines by $.69;
   declines by $1.55

14. $38,467.41

CHAPTER 16

2. a. $1.82; $3.64; $4.73
   b. $1.56; $4.41; $6.11
6. a. $3.29; $3.00; $3.55
   b. $44,000
   c. $44,000
   d. $44,000
10. $2,070,000

12. a. 18.18%
   b. 12.66%
   c. 20.01%; 16.34%; 12.66%

16. $310,583.33

CHAPTER 17

2. a. 3,000 new shares
   b. 7,500 new shares

4. a. $54.00
   b. $78.26
   c. $63.16
   d. $157.50
   e. 583,333; 402,500; 498,750; 200,000

8. Shares outstanding = 466,900
   Capital surplus = $3,410,600

10. $P_0 = \$42.08$
   $D = \$25.88$

CHAPTER 18

2. Cash = $2,035
   Current assets = $5,590

4. a. I,I
   b. I,N
   c. D,D
   d. D,D
   e. D, N
   f. I,I

6. Operating cycle = 86.87 days
   Cash cycle = 36.50 days

8. a. $258.00; $279.00; $297.00; $282.90
   b. $246.00; $258.00; $279.00; $297.00
   c. $250.00; $265.00; $285.00; $292.30

10. a. $246,666.67
   b. $388,571.43
   c. $267,464.29
      $274,285.71
      $279,000.00

14. a. 4.89%
   b. 9.63%
   c. 9.52%

18. 11.76%

CHAPTER 19

2. a. $56,000
      −$52,000
      $4,000
   b. $56,000
      −$26,000
      $30,000

6. a. $28,620
   b. 2.49 days

  c. $28,620
  d. $5.31
  e. $17,225

10. NPV = $3,900,000
     Net savings = $195,000

APPENDIX 19A

19A.2 $2,661.45

19A.4 a. Opportunity cost = $37.50
       Trading cost = $266.67
     b. $4,000.00

19A.10 7.68%

CHAPTER 20

  2. $4,635,616

  6. Sales = $444,551.28
     Accounts receivable turnover = 9.359 times

10. NPV = $148,275

12. Carrying cost = $6,150
     Order cost = $4,940
     EOQ = 268.87
     Orders = 58.02 per year

16. Net savings = $6,850

APPENDIX 20A

20A.2 a. 2/15, net 30
      b. $297,000
      d. NPV = −$3,023,592
         Break-even price = $102.13
         Break-even discount = 11.88%

20A.4 b. $77.32
      c. NPV = −$74,622.27

CHAPTER 21

  6. Great Britain: 3.54%
     Japan: 1.04%
     Switzerland: 2.07%

10. b. Krone 5.1987

12. b. 6.12%

NAME INDEX

Page numbers followed by n refer to notes.

EQUATION INDEX

SUBJECT INDEX

Note: Key terms are in **boldface**; page numbers followed by n refer to notes.

Pedagogical Use of Color

Throughout the Ninth Edition of **Fundamentals of Corporate Finance**, we make color a functional dimension of the discussion. In almost every chapter, color plays an extensive and largely self-evident role. Color in these chapters alerts students to the relationship between numbers in a discussion and an accompanying table or figure

Chapter 2
Section 2.4
Blue: Identifies net captial spending and change in net working capital
Green: Identifies cash flow numbers

Chapters 3 and 4
Throughout the chapter
Blue: Identifies income statements
Green: Identifies balance sheets
(Also see all 23 ratios in Chapter 3)

Chapter 7
Section 7.1
Blue: Identifies key numbers that combine to determine the value of a bond
Green: Identifies the bond value
Section 7.4
Blue: Identifies the implicit interest expense
Green: Identifies the straight interest expense

Chapter 9
Section 9.5
Blue: Identifies Project A
Green: Identifies Project B

Chapter 12
Section 12.5 (See Figure 12.11)
Blue, Green and Bold Black: Identify the three normal distribution ranges and use them to illustrate from which range each number has been derived

Chapter 13
Sections 13.1 and 13.2
Blue: Identifies Stock L
Green: Identifies Stock U
Section 13.7
Blue: Identifies Asset B
Green: Identifies Asset A

Chapter 14
Section 14.2
Blue: Identifies dollar and percentage changes in dividends
Green: Identifies dividends

Chapter 15
Section 15.9
Blue: Identifies values of shares with and without dilution
Green: Identifies original values of shares

Chapter 16
Section 16.2
Blue: Identifies the propsed capital structure
Green: Identifies the original capital structure
Sections 16.4 and 16.6
Blue: Identifies Firm L
Green: Identifies Firm U

Chapter 17
Section 17.6 (See Table 17.2 and Figure 17.3)
Blue: Identifies large dividend payouts
Green: Identifies small dividend payouts

Chapter 18
Throughout the chapter
Blue: Identifies income statements
Green: Identifies balance sheets
Section 18.4
Blue: Identifies total cash collections
Green: Identifies total cash disbursements
Bold Black: Identifies the net cash inflows

Chapter 19
End-of-chapter Appendix
Blue: Identifies contributing costs
Green: Identifies the opportunity trading and total costs

Chapter 20
Throughout the chapter
Blue: Identifies numbers exceeding the cost-minimizing restock quantity
Green: Identifies numbers falling below the cost-minimizing restock quantity
Bold Black: Identifies cost-minimizing quantity

Chapter 21
Section 21.5
Blue: Identifies cash flows
Green: Identifies expected exchange rates

Alternate Edition – Additional Chapters

Chapter 23
Sections 23.2, 23.3, and 23.6
Blue: Identifies the payoff profile
Green: Identifies the risk profile
Bold Black: Identifies the hedge position

Chapter 24
Section 24.1
Blue: Identifies puts
Green: Identifies calls
Section 24.2
Blue: Identifies stock value
Green: Identifies portfolio value
Section 24.5
Blue: Identifies calls
Green: Identifies warrants

Chapter 26
Section 26.1 (See Tables 26.1, 26.2, and 26.3)
Blue: Identifies Firm A and Global Resources
Green: Identifies Firm B and Regional Enterprises
Bold Black: Identifies the merged firm, Firm AB, and the merged identity of Global Resources

Chapter 27
Tables 27.2 and 27.3
Blue: Identifies cash flow components
Green: Identifies total cash flow